Lecture Notes in Computer Science

Lecture Notes in Artificial Intelligence 16022
Founding Editor

Jörg Siekmann

Series Editors

Randy Goebel, *University of Alberta, Edmonton, Canada*
Wolfgang Wahlster, *DFKI, Berlin, Germany*
Zhi-Hua Zhou, *Nanjing University, Nanjing, China*

The series Lecture Notes in Artificial Intelligence (LNAI) was established in 1988 as a topical subseries of LNCS devoted to artificial intelligence.

The series publishes state-of-the-art research results at a high level. As with the LNCS mother series, the mission of the series is to serve the international R & D community by providing an invaluable service, mainly focused on the publication of conference and workshop proceedings and postproceedings.

Inês Dutra · Mykola Pechenizkiy · Paulo Cortez ·
Sepideh Pashami · Arian Pasquali · Nuno Moniz ·
Alípio M. Jorge · Carlos Soares ·
Pedro H. Abreu · João Gama
Editors

Machine Learning and Knowledge Discovery in Databases

Applied Data Science Track and Demo Track

European Conference, ECML PKDD 2025
Porto, Portugal, September 15–19, 2025
Proceedings, Part X

Editors
Inês Dutra
University of Porto
Porto, Portugal

Paulo Cortez
University of Minho
Guimarães, Portugal

Arian Pasquali
Faktion
Antwerpen, The Netherlands

Alípio M. Jorge
University of Porto
Porto, Portugal

Pedro H. Abreu
University of Coimbra
Coimbra, Portugal

Mykola Pechenizkiy
Eindhoven University of Technology
Eindhoven, The Netherlands

Sepideh Pashami
Halmstad University
Halmstad, Sweden

Nuno Moniz
University of Notre Dame
Notre Dame, IN, USA

Carlos Soares
University of Porto
Porto, Portugal

João Gama
University of Porto
Porto, Portugal

ISSN 0302-9743   ISSN 1611-3349 (electronic)
Lecture Notes in Artificial Intelligence
ISBN 978-3-032-06128-7   ISBN 978-3-032-06129-4 (eBook)
https://doi.org/10.1007/978-3-032-06129-4

LNCS Sublibrary: SL7 – Artificial Intelligence

© The Editor(s) (if applicable) and The Author(s), under exclusive license to Springer Nature Switzerland AG 2026
Chapter "Go with the Flow: Leveraging Physics-Informed Gradients to Solve Real-World Problems in Water Distribution Systems" is licensed under the terms of the Creative Commons Attribution 4.0 International License (http://creativecommons.org/licenses/by/4.0/). For further details see license information in the chapter.

This work is subject to copyright. All rights are solely and exclusively licensed by the Publisher, whether the whole or part of the material is concerned, specifically the rights of translation, reprinting, reuse of illustrations, recitation, broadcasting, reproduction on microfilms or in any other physical way, and transmission or information storage and retrieval, electronic adaptation, computer software, or by similar or dissimilar methodology now known or hereafter developed.
The use of general descriptive names, registered names, trademarks, service marks, etc. in this publication does not imply, even in the absence of a specific statement, that such names are exempt from the relevant protective laws and regulations and therefore free for general use.
The publisher, the authors and the editors are safe to assume that the advice and information in this book are believed to be true and accurate at the date of publication. Neither the publisher nor the authors or the editors give a warranty, expressed or implied, with respect to the material contained herein or for any errors or omissions that may have been made. The publisher remains neutral with regard to jurisdictional claims in published maps and institutional affiliations.

This Springer imprint is published by the registered company Springer Nature Switzerland AG
The registered company address is: Gewerbestrasse 11, 6330 Cham, Switzerland

If disposing of this product, please recycle the paper.

Preface

The 2025 edition of the European Conference on Machine Learning and Principles and Practice of Knowledge Discovery in Databases (ECML PKDD 2025) was held in the vibrant city of Porto, Portugal on September 15–19, 2025. This marks a significant return of the conference to Porto, following successful editions in 2005 and 2015, underscoring the city's enduring appeal as a hub for scientific exchange.

The annual ECML PKDD conference stands as a premier worldwide platform dedicated to showcasing the latest advancements and fostering insightful discussions in the fields of machine learning and knowledge discovery in databases. Held jointly since 2001, ECML PKDD has firmly established its reputation as the leading European conference in these disciplines. It provides researchers and practitioners with an unparalleled opportunity to exchange knowledge, share innovative ideas, and explore the latest technical advancements. Furthermore, the conference deeply values the synergy between foundational theoretical advances and groundbreaking practical data science applications, actively encouraging contributions that demonstrate how Machine Learning and Data Mining are being effectively employed to address complex real-world challenges.

A Hub for Responsible AI and Cutting-Edge Research

As the technological landscape continues to evolve and societal needs shift, the conference remains committed to adapting to and reflecting these dynamic changes. This year's event saw a robust engagement from the global research community with a substantial increase in the number of submissions.

The three main conference days were organised into five distinct tracks:

- The Research Track received an impressive number of 924 submissions, with 226 papers ultimately accepted, reflecting a highly competitive acceptance rate of 24.5%.
- The Applied Data Science Track received a total of 299 submissions, accepting 74 papers, resulting in an acceptance rate of 24.7%.
- The Journal Track continued to bridge the gap between conference and journal publications, accepting 43 papers (27 for the Machine Learning journal and 16 for the Data Mining and Knowledge Discovery journal) out of 297 submissions.
- The Nectar Track, focusing on recent scientific advances at the frontier of machine learning and data mining, received 30 submissions.
- The Demo Track showcased practical applications and prototypes, accepting 15 papers from a total of 30 submissions.

These proceedings cover the papers accepted in the Research and Applied Data Science tracks.

The high quality and diversity of the accepted papers across all tracks underscore the continued vitality and intellectual breadth of the machine learning and data mining communities. We extend our sincere gratitude to all authors for their valuable contributions, to the program committee members and reviewers for their diligent efforts in ensuring the rigorous double-blind review process, and to the organising committee for their tireless work in making ECML PKDD 2025 a resounding success. We believe these proceedings will serve as a valuable resource, inspiring future research and innovation in these rapidly advancing fields.

This year's conference featured seven insightful keynote talks that focused on crucial and emerging areas within Responsible AI, including trustworthy AI, interpretability, and explainability. The keynotes also explored fundamental theoretical issues, covering causality, neural-symbolic systems, large language models (LLMs), and AI for science. We were honoured to host leading experts who shared their valuable perspectives:

- Cynthia Rudin (Duke University) presented on "Many Good Models Lead to ...";
- Elias Bareinboim (Columbia University) discussed "Towards Causal Artificial Intelligence";
- Francisco Herrera (University of Granada) addressed "Not Just a Trend: Institutionalizing XAI for Responsible and Compliant AI Systems";
- Mirella Lapata (University of Edinburgh) explored "Compositional Intelligence: Coordinating Multiple LLMs for Complex Tasks";
- Nuria Oliver (ELLIS Alicante Foundation, Spain) spoke on "Towards a Fairer World: Uncovering and Addressing Human and Algorithmic Biases";
- Pedro Domingos (University of Washington) shared insights on "A Simple Unification of Neural and Symbolic AI"; and
- Sašo Džeroski (Jožef Stefan Institute, Slovenia) presented on "Artificial Intelligence for Science".

Fostering Diversity and Inclusion

Our Diversity and Inclusion initiative proudly awarded 10 scholarship grants of €500 to early-career researchers. These grants enabled individuals from developing countries and communities underrepresented in science and technology to attend the conference, present their work, and become integral members of the ECML PKDD community.

Acknowledging Our Contributors and Supporters

We extend our sincere gratitude to everyone who contributed to making ECML PKDD 2025 such a success. Our heartfelt thanks go to the authors, workshop and tutorial organisers, and all participants for their valuable scientific contributions.

An outstanding conference program would not be possible without the immense dedication and substantial time investment from our area chairs, program committee, and organising committee. The smooth execution of the event was also largely due to the hard work of our many volunteers and session chairs. A special acknowledgement goes to the local organisers for meticulously handling every detail, making the conference a truly memorable experience.

Finally, we are incredibly grateful for the generous financial support from our wonderful sponsors. We also appreciate Springer's ongoing support and Microsoft's provision of their CMT software for conference management, as well as their continued assistance. Our sincere thanks also go to the ECML PKDD Steering Committee for their invaluable advice and guidance over the past two years.

September 2025

João Gama
Pedro H. Abreu
Alípio M. Jorge
Carlos Soares
Rita P. Ribeiro
Pedro Larrañaga
Nathalie Japkowicz
Bernhard Pfahringer
Inês Dutra
Mykola Pechenizkiy
Sepideh Pashami
Paulo Cortez

Organization

Honorary Chair

Pavel Brazdil — University of Porto, Portugal

General Chairs

João Gama — University of Porto, Portugal
Pedro H. Abreu — University of Coimbra, Portugal
Alípio M. Jorge — University of Porto, Portugal
Carlos Soares — University of Porto, Portugal

Research Track Program Chairs

Bernhard Pfahringer — University of Waikato, New Zealand
Nathalie Japkowicz — American University, USA
Pedro Larrañaga — Technical University of Madrid, Spain
Rita P. Ribeiro — University of Porto, Portugal

Applied Data Science Track Program Chairs

Inês Dutra — University of Porto, Portugal
Mykola Pechenisky — TU Eindhoven, The Netherlands
Paulo Cortez — University of Minho, Portugal
Sepideh Pashami — Halmstad University, Sweden

Journal Track Chairs

Ana Carolina Lorena — Instituto Tecnológico de Aeronáutica, Brazil
Arlindo Oliveira — Instituto Superior Técnico, Portugal
Concha Bielza — Technical University of Madrid, Spain
Longbing Cao — Macquarie University, Australia
Tiago Almeida — Federal University of São Carlos, Brazil

Nectar Track Chairs

Ricard Gavaldà   Amalfi Analytics, Spain
Riccardo Guidotti   University of Pisa, Italy

Demo Track Chairs

Arian Pasquali   Faktion, Belgium
Nuno Moniz   University of Notre Dame, USA

Local Chairs

Bruno Veloso   University of Porto, Portugal
Rita Nogueira   INESC TEC, Portugal
Shazia Tabassum   INESC TEC, Portugal

Workshop Chairs

Irena Koprinska   University of Sydney, Australia
João Mendes Moreira   University of Porto, Portugal
Paula Branco   University of Ottawa, Canada

Tutorial Chairs

Alicia Troncoso   Universidad Pablo de Olavide, Spain
Nikolaj Tatti   University of Helsinki, Finland

PhD Forum Chairs

Raquel Sebastião   Polytechnic Institute of Viseu, Portugal
Yun Sing Koh   University of Auckland, New Zealand

Awards Committee Chairs

André Carvalho   University of São Paulo, Brazil
Amparo Alonso-Betanzos   University of A Coruña, Spain
Katharina Morik   TU Dortmund, Germany
Vítor Santos Costa   University of Porto, Portugal

Proceedings Chairs

João Vinagre   European Commission (JRC), Spain
Miriam Santos   University of Porto, Portugal
Shazia Tabassum   INESC TEC, Portugal

Diversity and Inclusion Chairs

Inês Sousa   Fraunhofer, Portugal
Zahraa Abdallah   University of Bristol, UK

Discovery Challenge Chairs

Carlos Ferreira   Polytechnic Institute of Porto, Portugal
Peter van der Putten Leiden University, The Netherlands
Rui Camacho   University of Porto, Portugal

Panel Chairs

Pedro H. Abreu   University of Coimbra, Portugal
Paula Brito   University of Porto, Portugal

Publicity Chair

Carlos Ferreira   Polytechnic Institute of Porto, Portugal

Sponsorship Chairs

Mariam Berry BNP Paribas, France
Nuno Moutinho University of Porto, Portugal
Rui Teles Accenture, Portugal

Social Media Chairs

Luis Roque ZAAI.ai, Portugal
Ricardo Pereira University of Coimbra, Portugal
Dalila Teixeira Creative Matter, USA

Web Chair

Thiago Andrade University of Porto, Portugal

Senior Program Committee – Research Track

Adam Jatowt University of Innsbruck, Austria
Andrea Passerini University of Trento, Italy
Anthony Bagnall University of Southampton, UK
Arno Knobbe Leiden University, Netherlands
Arno Siebes Universiteit Utrecht, Netherlands
Arto Klami University of Helsinki, Finland
Bernhard Pfahringer University of Waikato, New Zealand
Bettina Berendt TU Berlin, Germany
Celine Robardet INSA Lyon, France
Celine Vens KU Leuven, Belgium
Cesar Ferri Universitat Politècnica Valencia, Spain
Charalampos Tsourakakis Boston University, USA
Chedy Raissi Inria, France
Chen Gong Nanjing University of Science and Technology, China
Danai Koutra University of Michigan, USA
Dimitrios Gunopulos University of Athens, Greece
Donato Malerba Università degli Studi di Bari Aldo Moro, Italy
Dragi Kocev Jožef Stefan Institute, Slovenia
Dunja Mladenic Jožef Stefan Institute, Slovenia
Eirini Ntoutsi Universität der Bundeswehr München, Germany

Emmanuel Müller	TU Dortmund, Germany
Ernestina Menasalvas	Universidad Politécnica de Madrid, Spain
Esther Galbrun	University of Eastern Finland, Finland
Evaggelia Pitoura	University of Ioannina, Greece
Evangelos Papalexakis	University of California, Riverside, USA
Fabio A. Stella	University of Milano-Bicocca, Italy
Fabrizio Costa	Exeter University, UK
Fragkiskos Malliaros	CentraleSupélec, France
Georg Krempl	Utrecht University, Netherlands
Georgiana Ifrim	University College Dublin, Ireland
Gustavo Batista	University of New South Wales, Australia
Heikki Mannila	Aalto University, Finland
Hendrik Blockeel	KU Leuven, Belgium
Henrik Bostrom	KTH Royal Institute of Technology, Sweden
Henry Gouk	University of Edinburgh, UK
Ioannis Katakis	University of Nicosia, Cyprus
Jan N. Van Rijn	LIACS, Leiden University, Netherlands
Jefrey Lijffijt	Ghent University, Belgium
Jerzy Stefanowski	Poznań University of Technology, Poland
Jesse Davis	KU Leuven, Belgium
Jesse Read	Ecole Polytechnique, France
Jessica Lin	George Mason University, USA
Jesus Cerquides	IIIA-CSIC, Spain
Jilles Vreeken	CISPA Helmholtz Center for Information Security, Germany
João Gama	INESC TEC - LIAAD, Portugal
Jörg Wicker	University of Auckland, New Zealand
José Hernández-Orallo	Universitat Politècnica de Valencia, Spain
Junming Shao	University of Electronic Science and Technology of China, China
Kai Puolamaki	University of Helsinki, Finland
Manfred Jaeger	Aalborg University, Denmark
Marius Kloft	TU Kaiserslautern, Germany
Marius Lindauer	Leibniz University Hannover, Germany
Mark Last	Ben-Gurion University of the Negev, Israel
Matthias Renz	University of Kiel, Germany
Matthias Schubert	Ludwig-Maximilians-Universität München, Germany
Michele Lombardi	University of Bologna, Italy
Michèle Sebag	LISN CNRS, France
Nathalie Japkowicz	American University, USA
Paolo Frasconi	Università degli Studi di Firenze, Italy

Parisa Kordjamshidi	Michigan State University, USA
Pasquale Minervini	University of Edinburgh, UK
Pauli Miettinen	University of Eastern Finland, Finland
Pedro Larrañaga	Technical University of Madrid, Spain
Peer Kroger	Christian-Albrechts-Universität Kiel, Germany
Peter Flach	University of Bristol, UK
Ricardo B. Prudencio	Universidade Federal de Pernambuco, Brazil
Rita P. Ribeiro	University of Porto and INESC TEC, Portugal
Salvatore Ruggieri	University of Pisa, Italy
Sebastijan Dumancic	TU Delft, Netherlands
Sibylle Hess	TU Eindhoven, Netherlands
Sicco Verwer	Delft University of Technology, Netherlands
Siegfried Nijssen	Université catholique de Louvain, Belgium
Sophie Fellenz	RPTU Kaiserslautern-Landau, Germany
Stefano Ferilli	University of Bari, Italy
Stratis Ioannidis	Northeastern University, USA
Szymon Jaroszewicz	Polish Academy of Sciences, Poland
Tijl De Bie	Ghent University, Belgium
Ulf Brefeld	Leuphana University of Lüneburg, Germany
Varvara Vetrova	University of Canterbury, New Zealand
Wannes Meert	KU Leuven, Belgium
Wei Ye	Tongji University, China
Wenbin Zhang	Florida International University, USA
Willem Waegeman	Universiteit Gent, Belgium
Wouter Duivesteijn	Technische Universiteit Eindhoven, Netherlands
Xiao Luo	University of California, Los Angeles, USA
Yun Sing Koh	University of Auckland, New Zealand
Zied Bouraoui	CRIL CNRS and Université d'Artois, France

Senior Program Committee – Applied Data Science Track

Albrecht Zimmermann	Université de Caen Normandie, France
Andreas Hotho	University of Würzburg, Germany
Anirban Dasgupta	IIT Gandhinagar, India
Anna Monreale	University of Pisa, Italy
Annalisa Appice	University of Bari Aldo Moro, Italy
Bruno Cremilleux	Université de Caen Normandie, France
Carlotta Domeniconi	George Mason University, USA
Dejing Dou	BCG, USA
Fabio Pinelli	IMT Lucca, Italy
Fuzhen Zhuang	Beihang University, China

Gabor Melli	PredictionWorks, USA
Giuseppe Manco	ICAR-CNR, Italy
Glenn Fung	Independent Researcher, USA
Grzegorz Nalepa	Jagiellonian University, Poland
Hui Xiong	Hong Kong University of Science and Technology (Guangzhou), China
Inês Dutra	University of Porto, Portugal
Ioanna Miliou	Stockholm University, Sweden
Ira Assent	Aarhus University, Denmark
Jiayu Zhou	Michigan State University, USA
Jiliang Tang	Michigan State University, USA
Jingrui He	University of Illinois at Urbana-Champaign, USA
João Gama	INESC TEC - LIAAD, Portugal
Jose A. Gamez	Universidad de Castilla-La Mancha, Spain
Ke Liang	National University of Defense Technology, China
Kurt Driessens	Maastricht University, Netherlands
Lars Kotthoff	University of Wyoming, USA
Liang Sun	Alibaba Group, China
Martin Atzmueller	Osnabrück University and DFKI, Germany
Michael R. Berthold	KNIME, Germany
Michelangelo Ceci	University of Bari, Italy
Min-Ling Zhang	Southeast University, China
Mykola Pechenizkiy	TU Eindhoven, Netherlands
Myra Spiliopoulou	Otto-von-Guericke-Universität Magdeburg, Germany
Niklas Lavesson	Blekinge Institute of Technology, Sweden
Nikolaj Tatti	Helsinki University, Finland
Panagiotis Papapetrou	Stockholm University, Sweden
Paolo Frasconi	Università degli Studi di Firenze, Italy
Paulo Cortez	University of Minho, Portugal
Peggy Cellier	INSA Rennes, IRISA, France
Rayid Ghani	Carnegie Mellon University, USA
Sahar Asadi	King (Microsoft), UK
Sandeep Tata	Google, USA
Sepideh Pashami	Halmstad University, Sweden
Slawomir Nowaczyk	Halmstad University, Sweden
Sriparna Saha	IIT Patna, India
Thomas Liebig	TU Dortmund, Germany
Thomas Seidl	LMU Munich, Germany
Tom Diethe	AstraZeneca, UK
Tony Lindgren	Stockholm University, Sweden

Vincent S. Tseng — National Yang Ming Chiao Tung University, Taiwan
Vítor Santos Costa — Universidade do Porto, Portugal
Xingquan Zhu — Florida Atlantic University, USA
Yi Chang — Jilin University, China
Yinglong Xia — Meta, USA
Yongxin Tong — Beihang University, China
Yun Sing Koh — University of Auckland, New Zealand
Zhaochun Ren — Shandong University, China
Zheng Wang — Alibaba DAMO Academy, China
Zhiwei (Tony) Qin — Lyft, USA

Program Committee – Research Track

Christoph Bergmeir — Monash University, Australia
A. K. M. Mahbubur Rahman — Independent University, Bangladesh
Abdulhakim Qahtan — Utrecht University, Netherlands
Abhishek A. — Fujitsu Research, India
Acar Tamersoy — Microsoft, USA
Ad Feelders — Universiteit Utrecht, Netherlands
Adam Goodge — I2R, A*STAR, Singapore
Adele Jia — China Agricultural University, China
Adem Kikaj — KU Leuven, Belgium
Aditya Mohan — Leibniz Universität Hannover, Germany
Ajay A. Mahimkar — AT&T, USA
Akka Zemmari — Université de Bordeaux, France
Akshay Sethi — MasterCard, USA
Alborz Geramifard — Meta, USA
Alessandro Antonucci — IDSIA, Switzerland
Alessandro Melchiorre — Johannes Kepler University Linz, Austria
Alexander Dockhorn — Leibniz University Hannover, Germany
Alexander Schiendorfer — Technische Hochschule Ingolstadt, Germany
Alexander Schulz — CITEC, Bielefeld University, Germany
Alexandre Termier — Université de Rennes 1, France
Alexandre Verine — Ecole Normale Supérieure - PSL, France
Alexandru C. Mara — Ghent University, Belgium
Ali Ayadi — University of Strasbourg, France
Ali Ismail-Fawaz — IRIMAS, Université de Haute-Alsace, France
Alicja Wieczorkowska — Polish-Japanese Academy of Information Technology, Poland
Alipio M. G. Jorge — INESC TEC/University of Porto, Portugal

Alireza Gharahighehi	KU Leuven, Belgium
Alistair Shilton	Deakin University, Australia
Alneu A. Lopes	University of São Paulo, Brazil
Alper Demir	Izmir University of Economics, Turkey
Alvaro Figueira	CRACS and Universidade do Porto, Portugal
Amal Saadallah	TU Dortmund, Germany
Aman Chadha	Stanford University and Amazon, USA
Amer Krivosija	TU Dortmund, Germany
Amir H. Payberah	KTH Royal Institute of Technology, Sweden
Ammar Shaker	NEC Laboratories Europe, Europe
Ana Rita Nogueira	INESC TEC, Portugal
Anand Paul	Louisiana State University HSC, USA
Anastasios Gounaris	Aristotle University of Thessaloniki, Greece
Andre V. Carreiro	Fraunhofer Portugal AICOS, Portugal
André C. P. L. F. de Carvalho	University of São Paulo, Brazil
Andrea Cossu	University of Pisa, Italy
Andrea Mastropietro	University of Bonn, Germany
Andrea Pugnana	University of Trento, Italy
Andrea Tagarelli	DIMES - UNICAL, Italy
Andreas Bender	LMU Munich, Germany
Andreas Nürnberger	Otto-von-Guericke-Universität Magdeburg, Germany
Andreas Schwung	Fachhochschule Südwestfalen, Germany
Andrei Paleyes	University of Cambridge, UK
Andrzej Skowron	University of Warsaw, Poland
Andy Song	RMIT University, Australia
Angelica Liguori	ICAR-CNR, Italy
Anirban Dasgupta	IIT Gandhinagar, India
Anke Meyer-Baese	Florida State University, USA
Anna Beer	University of Vienna, Austria
Anna Krause	Universität Wurzburg and Chair X Data Science, Germany
Anna Monreale	University of Pisa, Italy
Annelot W. Bosman	Universiteit Leiden, Netherlands
Antoine Caradot	Hubert Curien Laboratory, France
Antonio Bahamonde	University of Oviedo, Spain
Antonio Mastropietro	Università di Pisa, Italy
Antonio Pellicani	Università degli Studi di Bari, Aldo Moro, Italy
Antonis Matakos	Aalto University, Finland
Antti Laaksonen	University of Helsinki, Finland
Aomar Osmani	LIPN-UMR CNRS, France
Aonghus Lawlor	University College Dublin, Ireland

Aparna S. Varde	Montclair State University, USA
Apostolos N. Papadopoulos	Aristotle University of Thessaloniki, Greece
Aritra Konar	KU Leuven, Belgium
Arjun Roy	Freie Universität Berlin, Germany
Arthur Charpentier	UQAM, Canada
Arunas Lipnickas	Kaunas University of Technology, Lithuania
Atsuhiro Takasu	National Institute of Informatics, Japan
Aurora Esteban	University of Cordoba, Spain
Baosheng Zhang	Tsinghua University, China
Barbara Toniella Corradini	University of Florence and University of Siena, Italy
Bardh Prenkaj	Technical University of Munich, Germany
Barry O'Sullivan	University College Cork, Ireland
Beilun Wang	Southeast University, China
Benjamin Halstead	University of Auckland, New Zealand
Benjamin Paassen	Bielefeld University, Germany
Benjamin Quost	Université de Technologie de Compiègne, France
Benoit Frenay	University of Namur, Belgium
Bernardo Moreno Sanchez	University of Helsinki, Finland
Bernhard Pfahringer	University of Waikato, New Zealand
Bertrand Cuissart	University of Caen, France
Bin Liu	Chongqing University of Posts and Telecommunications, China
Bin Shi	Xi'an Jiaotong University, China
Bin Wu	Zhengzhou University, China
Bin Zhou	National University of Defense Technology, China
Bitao Peng	Guangdong University of Foreign Studies, China
Bo Kang	Ghent University, Belgium
Bogdan Cautis	Université Paris-Saclay, France
Bojan Evkoski	Central European University, Hungary
Boshen Shi	Institute of Computing Technology, Chinese Academy of Sciences, China
Boualem Benatallah	Dublin City University, Ireland
Brandon Gower-Winter	Utrecht University, Netherlands
Bunil K. Balabantaray	NIT Meghalaya, India
Carlos Ferreira	INESC TEC, Portugal
Carlos Monserrat-Aranda	Universitat Politècnica de Valencia, Spain
Carson K. Leung	University of Manitoba, Canada
Catarina Silva	University of Coimbra, Portugal
Cecile Capponi	Aix-Marseille University, France
Celine Rouveirol	LIPN Université de Sorbonne Paris Nord, France

Cesar H. G. Andrade	Porto University, Portugal
Chandrajit Bajaj	University of Texas, Austin, USA
Chang Rajani	University of Helsinki, Finland
Charlotte Laclau	Polytechnique Institute, Télécom Paris, France
Charlotte Pelletier	Université de Bretagne du Sud, France
Chen Wang	DATA61, CSIRO, Australia
Cheng Cheng	Carnegie Mellon University, USA
Cheng Xie	Yunnan University, China
Chenglin Wang	East China Normal University, China
Chenwang Wu	University of Science and Technology of China, China
Chiara Pugliese	IIT Institute of National Research Council, Italy
Chien-Liang Liu	National Chiao Tung University, Taiwan
Chihiro Maru	Chuo University, Japan
Chongsheng Zhang	Henan University, China
Christian Beecks	FernUniversität in Hagen, Germany
Christian M. M. Frey	University of Technology Nuremberg, Germany
Christian Hakert	TU Dortmund, Germany
Christine Largeron	LabHC Lyon University, France
Christophe Rigotti	INSA Lyon, France
Christophe Rodrigues	DVRC Pôle universitaire Léonard de Vinci, France
Christos Anagnostopoulos	University of Glasgow, UK
Christos Diou Harokopio	University of Athens, Greece
Chuan Qin	Chinese Academy of Sciences, China
Chunchun Chen	Tongji University, China
Chunyao Song	Nankai University, China
Claire Nedellec	INRAE, MaIAGE, France
Claudio Borile	CENTAI Institute, Italy
Claudio Gallicchio	University of Pisa, Italy
Claudius Zelenka	Kiel University, Germany
Colin Bellinger	NRC and Dalhousie University, Canada
Collin Leiber	Aalto University, Finland
Cong Qi	New Jersey Institute of Technology, USA
Congfeng Cao	University of Amsterdam, Netherlands
Corrado Loglisci	Università degli Studi di Bari, Aldo Moro, Italy
Cuicui Luo	University of Chinese Academy of Sciences, China
Cuneyt G. Akcora	University of Central Florida, USA
Cynthia C. S. Liem	Delft University of Technology, Netherlands
Dalius Matuzevicius	Vilnius Gediminas Technical University, Lithuania

Dan Li	Sun Yat-sen University, China
Danai Koutra	University of Michigan, USA
Dang Nguyen	Deakin University, Australia
Daniel Neider	TU Dortmund, Germany
Daniel Schlor	Universität Würzburg, Germany
Danil Provodin	TU Eindhoven, Netherlands
Danyang Xiao	Sun Yat-sen University, China
Dario Garcia-Gasulla	Barcelona Supercomputing Center (BSC), Spain
Dario Garigliotti	University of Bergen, Norway
Darius Plonis	Vilnius Gediminas Technical University, Lithuania
Dariusz Brzezinski	Poznań University of Technology, Poland
David Gomez	Universidad Politecnica de Madrid, Spain
David Holzmüller	University of Stuttgart, Germany
David Q. Sun	Apple, USA
Davide Evangelista	University of Bologna, Italy
Debo Cheng	University of South Australia, Australia
Deepayan Chakrabarti	University of Texas at Austin, USA
Deng-Bao Wang	Southeast University, China
Denilson Barbosa	University of Alberta, Canada
Denis Huseljic	University of Kassel, Germany
Denis Lukovnikov	Ruhr-Universität Bochum, Germany
Destercke Sebastien	UTC, France
Di Jin	TikTok, USA
Di Wu	Chongqing Institute of Green and Intelligent Technology, Chinese Academy of Sciences, China
Diana Benavides Prado	University of Auckland, New Zealand
Dianhui Wang	Independent Researcher, Australia
Diego Carrera	STMicroelectronics, Switzerland
Diletta Chiaro	Università degli Studi di Napoli Federico II, Italy
Dimitri Staufer	TU Berlin, Germany
Dimitrios Katsaros	University of Thessaly, Greece
Dimitrios Rafailidis	University of Thessaly, France
Dino Ienco	INRAE, France
Dmitry Kobak	University of Tübingen, Germany
Domenico Redavid	University of Bari, Italy
Dominik M. Endres	Philipps-Universität Marburg, Germany
Dominique Gay	Université de La Réunion, France
Dong Li	Baylor University, USA
Duarte Folgado	Fraunhofer Portugal AICOS, Portugal
Duo Xu	Georgia Institute of Technology, USA

Edoardo Serra	Boise State University, USA
Edouard Fouche	Karlsruhe Institute of Technology (KIT), Germany
Eduardo F. Montesuma	Université Paris-Saclay, France
Edward Apeh	Bournemouth University, UK
Edwin Simpson	University of Bristol, UK
Ehsan Aminian	INESC TEC, Portugal
Ekaterina Antonenko	Mines Paris - PSL, France
Eliana Pastor	Politecnico di Torino, Italy
Emanuela Marasco	George Mason University, USA
Emilio Dorigatti	LMU Munich, Germany
Emilio Parrado-Hernandez	Universidad Carlos III de Madrid, Spain
Emmanouil Krasanakis	CERTH, Greece
Emmanouil Panagiotou	Freie Universität Berlin, Germany
Emre Gursoy	Koc University, Turkey
Engelbert Mephu Nguifo	Université Clermont Auvergne, CNRS, LIMOS, France
Eran Treister	Ben-Gurion University of the Negev, Israel
Erasmo Purificato	Otto-von-Guericke Universität Magdeburg, Germany
Erik Novak	Jožef Stefan Institute, Slovenia
Erwan Le Merrer	Inria, France
Esra Akbas	Georgia State University, USA
Esther-Lydia Silva-Ramirez	Universidad de Cadiz, Spain
Evaldas Vaičiukynas	Kaunas University of Technology, Lithuania
Evangelos Kanoulas	University of Amsterdam, Netherlands
Evelin Amorim	INESC TEC, Portugal
Fabian C. Spaeh	Boston University, USA
Fabio Fassetti	Università della Calabria, Italy
Fabio Fumarola	Prometeia, Italy
Fabio Mercorio	University of Milan-Bicocca, Italy
Fabio Vandin	University of Padova, Italy
Fandel Lin	University of Southern California, USA
Federica Granese	Inria, Université Côte d'Azur, France
Federico Baldo	University of Bologna, Italy
Federico Sabbatini	National Institute for Nuclear Physics (INFN), Italy
Feifan Zhang	China Agricultural University, China
Felipe Kenji Nakano	KU Leuven, Belgium
Fernando Martinez-Plumed	Universitat Politècnica de Valencia, Spain
Filipe Rodrigues	Technical University of Denmark (DTU), Denmark

Flavio Giobergia	Politecnico di Torino, Italy
Florent Masseglia	Inria, France
Florian Beck	JKU Linz, Austria
Florian Lemmerich	University of Passau, Germany
Francesca Naretto	University of Pisa, Italy
Francesco Piccialli	University of Naples Federico II, Italy
Francesco Renna	Universidade do Porto, Portugal
Francisco Pereira	DTU, Denmark
Franco Raimondi	Gran Sasso Science Institute, Italy
Frederic Koriche	Université d'Artois, CRIL CNRS, France
Frederic Pennerath	CentraleSupélec - LORIA, France
Furong Peng	Shanxi University, China
Gabriel Marques Tavares	LMU Munich, Germany
Gabriele Sartor	University of Turin, Italy
Gabriele Venturato	KU Leuven, Belgium
Gaetan De Waele	Ghent University, Belgium
Gaia Saveri	University of Trieste, Italy
Gang Li	Deakin University, Australia
Gaoyuan Du	Amazon, USA
Gavin Smith	University of Nottingham, UK
Geming Xia	National University of Defense Technology, China
Geng Zhao	Heidelberg University, Germany
Gennaro Vessio	University of Bari Aldo Moro, Italy
Geoffrey I. Webb	Monash, Australia
Georgia Baltsou	Centre for Research & Technology, Greece
Geraldin Nanfack	Concordia University, Canada
Germain Forestier	University of Haute Alsace, France
Gerrit Grossmann	DFKI, Germany
Gerrit J. J. van den Burg	Alan Turing Institute, UK
Gherardo Varando	Universitat de Valencia, Spain
Giacomo Medda	University of Cagliari, Italy
Gilberto Bernardes	INESC TEC and University of Porto, Portugal
Giorgio Venturin	University of Padova, Italy
Giovanna Castellano	University of Bari Aldo Moro, Italy
Giovanni Ponti	ENEA, Italy
Giovanni Stilo	Università degli Studi dell'Aquila, Italy
Gisele Pappa	UFMG, Brazil
Giuseppe Manco	ICAR-CNR, IT, Italy
Gizem Gezici	Scuola Normale Superiore, Italy
Gjergji Kasneci	TU Munich, Germany
Goreti Marreiros	ISEP/GECAD, Portugal

Graziella De Martino	University of Bari, Aldo Moro, Italy
Grazina Korvel	Vilnius University, Lithuania
Grigorios Tsoumakas	Aristotle University of Thessaloniki, Greece
Guangyin Jin	National University of Defense Technology, China
Guangzhong Sun	University of Science and Technology of China, China
Guanjin Wang	Murdoch University, Australia
Guilherme Weigert Cassales	University of Waikato, New Zealand
Guillaume Derval	UC Louvain - ICTEAM, Belgium
Guorui Quan	University of Manchester, UK
Guoxi Zhang	Beijing Institute of General Artificial Intelligence, China
Gustau Camps-Valls	Universitat de Valencia, Spain
Gustav Sir	Czech Technical University, Czech Republic
Gustavo Batista	University of New South Wales, Australia
Hachem Kadri	Aix-Marseille University, France
Hadi Asghari	Humboldt Institute for Internet and Society, Germany
Haifeng Sun	University of Science and Technology of China, China
Haihui Fan	Institute of Information Engineering, Chinese Academy of Sciences, China
Haizhou Du	Shanghai University of Electric Power, China
Hajer Salem	AUDENSIEL, France
Hakim Hacid	TII, United Arab Emirates
Hamid Bouchachia	Bournemouth University, UK
Han Wang	Xidian University, China
Hang Yu	Shanghai University, China
Hanna Sumita	Institute of Science Tokyo, Japan
Hao Niu	KDDI Research, Japan
Hao Xue	University of New South Wales, Australia
Hao Yan	Carleton University, Canada
Haowen Zhang	Zhejiang Sci-Tech University, China
Harsh Borse	IIT Kharagpur, India
Heitor M. Gomes	Victoria University of Wellington, New Zealand
Helder Oliveira	FCUP and INESC TEC, Portugal
Helge Langseth	Norwegian University of Science and Technology, Norway
Hendrik Blockeel	KU Leuven, Belgium
Henrique O. Marques	University of Southern Denmark, Denmark
Henryk Maciejewski	Wroclaw University of Science and Technology, Poland

Hideaki Ishibashi	Kyushu Institute of Technology, Japan
Hilde J. P. Weerts	Eindhoven University of Technology, Netherlands
Holger Froening	University of Heidelberg, Germany
Holger Karl	HPI, Germany
Hongbo Bo	University of Bristol, UK
Hongyang Chen	Zhejiang Lab, China
Hua Chu	Xidian University, China
Huaiyu Wan	Beijing Jiaotong University, China
Huaming Chen	University of Sydney, Australia
Huandong Wang	Tsinghua University, China
Huanlai Xing	Southwest Jiaotong University, China
Hui Ji	University of Pittsburgh, USA
Hui (Wendy) Wang	Stevens Institute of Technology, USA
Huiping Chen	University of Birmingham, UK
Humberto Bustince	Universidad Publica de Navarra, Spain
Huong Ha	RMIT University, Australia
Idir Benouaret	Epita Research Laboratory, France
Ines Sousa	Fraunhofer AICOS, Portugal
Ingo Thon	Siemens AG, Germany
Inigo Jauregi Unanue	University of Technology Sydney, Australia
Ioannis Sarridis	Centre for Research & Technology, Greece
Issam Falih	Université Clermont Auvergne, CNRS, LIMOS, France
Ivan Vankov	iris.ai, Norway
Ivor Cribben	University of Alberta, Canada
Jaemin Yoo	KAIST, South Korea
Jakir Hossain	University at Buffalo, USA
Jakub Klikowski	Wroclaw University of Science and Technology, Poland
Jalaj Bhandari	Columbia University, USA
Jaleed Khan	University of Oxford, UK
James Goulding	University of Nottingham, UK
Jan Kalina	Czech Academy of Sciences, Czech Republic
Jan P. Mielniczuk	Polish Academy of Sciences, Poland
Jan Ramon	Inria, France
Jan Verwaeren	Ghent University, Belgium
Jannis Brugger	TU Darmstadt, Germany
Jean-Marc Andreoli	Naverlabs Europe, Netherlands
Jedrzej Potoniec	Poznań University of Technology, Poland
Jeronimo Arenas-Garcia	Universidad Carlos III de Madrid, Spain
Jhony H. Giraldo	Télécom Paris, Institut Polytechnique de Paris, France

Jia Cai	Guangdong University of Finance and Economics, China
Jiahui Jin	Southeast University, China
Jiang Zhong	Independent Researcher, China
Jianwu Wang	University of Maryland, Baltimore County, USA
Jiawei Chen	Tianjin University, China
Jiaxin Ding	Shanghai Jiao Tong University, China
Jidong Yuan	Beijing Jiaotong University, China
Jie Song	Zhejiang University, China
Jie Wu	Fudan University, China
Jie Yang	University of Wollongong, China
Jimeng Shi	Florida International University, USA
Jin Chen	Hong Kong University of Science and Technology, China
Jin Liang	South China Normal University, China
Jing Ren	NUDT, China
Jing Wang	Amazon, USA
Jinghui Zhong	South China University of Technology, China
Jingtao Ding	Tsinghua University, China
Jinli Zhang	Beijing University of Technology, China
Jiri Sima	Czech Academy of Sciences, Czech Republic
João Gama	University of Porto, Portugal
Joao Mendes-Moreira	University of Porto, Portugal
Joao Vinagre	European Commission (JRC), Spain
Joaquim Silva	NOVA LINCS, Universidade Nova de Lisboa, Portugal
Jochen De Weerdt	KU Leuven, Belgium
Joe Mellor	University of Edinburgh, UK
Johanne Cohen	LISN-CNRS, France
Johannes Jakubik	IBM Research, USA
John W. Sheppard	Montana State University, USA
Jonata Tyska Carvalho	Federal University of Santa Catarina, Brazil
Jordi Guitart	Barcelona Supercomputing Center (BSC), Spain
Joris Mattheijssens	Ghent University, Belgium
Jose M. Costa Pereira	University of Porto, Portugal
Jose Oramas	University of Antwerp, sqIRL/IDLab, imec, Belgium
Jose Tomas Palma	University of Murcia, Spain
Joydeep Chandra	Indian Institute of Technology, Patna, India
Juan A. Botia	University of Murcia, Spain
Juan Rodriguez	Universidad de Burgos, Spain
Jukka Heikkonen	University of Turku, Finland

Julien Delaunay	Inria, France
Julien Ferry	Polytechnique Montreal, Canada
Julien Perez	EPITA, France
Jun Zhuang	Boise State University, USA
Jun Yu Hou	Nanjing University, China
Junbo Zhang	JD Intelligent Cities Research, USA
Junze Liu	University of California, Irvine, USA
Jurgita Kapočiūtė-Dzikienė	Tilde SIA, University of Latvia and Tilde IT, Vytautas Magnus University, Lithuania
Justina Mandravickaitė	Vytautas Magnus University, Lithuania
Kamil Adamczewski	Max Planck Institute for Intelligent Systems, Germany
Kamil Michal Ksiazek	Jagiellonian University, Poland
Karim Radouane	Université Sorbonne Paris Nord, France
Kary Framing	Umeå University, Sweden
Katerina Taskova	University of Auckland, New Zealand
Katharina Dost	Jožef Stefan Institute, Slovenia
Kaushik Roy	University of South Carolina, USA
Kejia Chen	Nanjing University of Posts and Telecommunications, China
Ken Kobayashi	Tokyo Institute of Technology, Japan
Khaled Mohammed Saifuddin	Northeastern University, USA
Khalid Benabdeslem	Université de Lyon 1, France
Kim Thang Nguyen	LIG, University Grenoble-Alpes, France
Kira Maag	Heinrich-Heine-Universität Düsseldorf, Germany
Koji Maruhashi	Fujitsu Research, Japan
Koyel Mukherjee	Adobe Research, USA
Kristen M. Scott	KU Leuven, Belgium
Krzysztof Ruda	Polish Academy of Sciences, Poland
Krzysztof Slot	Lodz University of Technology, Poland
Kuldeep Singh	Cerence, Germany
Kushankur Ghosh	University of Alberta, Canada
Lamine Diop	EPITA, France
Latifa Oukhellou	IFSTTAR, France
Laurence Park	Western Sydney University, Australia
Laurens Devos	KU Leuven, Belgium
Len Feremans	Universiteit Antwerpen, Belgium
Lena Wiese	Goethe University Frankfurt, Germany
Lenaig Cornanguer	CISPA Helmholtz Center for Information Security, Germany
Lennert De Smet	KU Leuven, Belgium
Lev Reyzin	University of Illinois at Chicago, USA

Li Wang	National University of Defense Technology, China
Liang Du	Shanxi University, China
Lianyong Qi	China University of Petroleum (East China), China
Lijie Hu	King Abdullah University of Science and Technology, Saudi Arabia
Lijing Zhu	Bowling Green State University, USA
Lingling Zhang	Capital Normal University, China
Lingyue Fu	Shanghai Jiao Tong University, China
Linh Le Pham Van	Deakin University, Australia
Livio Bioglio	University of Turin, Italy
Lixing Yu	Yunnan University, China
Liyan Song	Harbin Institute of Technology, China
Longlong Sun	Chang'an University, China
Luca Corbucci	University of Pisa, Italy
Luca Ferragina	University of Calabria, Italy
Luca Romeo	University of Macerata, Italy
Lucas Pereira	LARSyS, Tecnico Lisboa, Portugal
Luciano Caroprese	ICAR-CNR, Italy
Ludovico Boratto	University of Cagliari, Italy
Luis Rei	Jožef Stefan Institute, Slovenia
Mahardhika Pratama	University of South Australia, Australia
Maiju Karjalainen	University of Eastern Finland, Finland
Makoto Onizuka	Osaka University, Japan
Manali Sharma	Samsung, South Korea
Maneet Singh	MasterCard, India
Manuel M. Garcia-Piqueras	Universidad de Castilla La Mancha, Spain
Manuele Bicego	University of Verona, Italy
Mao A. Cheng	University of California, Berkeley, USA
Marc Plantevit	EPITA, France
Marc Tommasi	Lille University, France
Marcel Wever	Leibniz University Hannover, Germany
Marcilio de Souto	LIFO/Université d'Orleans, France
Marco Lippi	University of Florence, Italy
Marco Loog	Radboud University, Netherlands
Marco Mellia	Politecnico di Torino, Italy
Marco Podda	University of Pisa, Italy
Marco Polignano	Università di Bari, Italy
Marco Viviani	Università degli Studi di Milano Bicocca, Italy
Maria Vasconcelos	Fraunhofer Portugal AICOS, Portugal
Maria Sofia Bucarelli	Sapienza University of Rome, Italy

Mariana Oliveira	Universidade do Porto, Portugal
Mariana Vargas Vieyra	MostlyAI, Austria
Marielle Malfante	CEA, France
Marina Litvak	Shamoon College of Engineering, Israel
Mario Antunes	Universidade de Aveiro, Portugal
Mario Andres Munoz	University of Melbourne, Australia
Marius Koppel	Johannes Gutenberg University Mainz, Germany
Mark Junjie Li	Shenzhen University, China
Marko Robnik-Sikonja	University of Ljubljana, Slovenia
Marta Soare	Université d'Orleans, France
Martin Holena	Czech Academy of Sciences, Czech Republic
Martin Pilat	Charles University, Czech Republic
Martino Ciaperoni	Aalto University, Finland
Marwan Hassani	TU Eindhoven, Netherlands
Masahiro Suzuki	University of Tokyo, Japan
Massimo Guarascio	ICAR-CNR, Italy
Matej Mihelcic	University of Zagreb, Croatia
Mathias Verbeke	KU Leuven, Belgium
Mathieu Lefort	Université de Lyon, France
Matteo Francobaldi	University of Bologna, Italy
Matteo Riondato	Amherst College, USA
Matteo Salis	University of Turin, Italy
Matthew B. Middlehurst	University of Southampton, UK
Matthia Sabatelli	University of Groningen, Netherlands
Mattia Cerrato	JGU Mainz, Germany
Mattia Setzu	University of Pisa, Italy
Mattis Hartwig	German Research Center for Artificial Intelligence, Germany
Matyas Bohacek	Stanford University, USA
Maximilian T. Fischer	University of Konstanz, Germany
Maximilian Münch	University of Applied Sciences, Würzburg-Schweinfurt, Germany
Maximilian Stubbemann	University of Hildesheim, Germany
Maximilian Thiessen	TU Wien, Austria
Maximilian von Zastrow	Southern Denmark University, Denmark
Megha Khosla	TU Delft, Netherlands
Meiyun Zuo	Renmin University of China, China
Meng Liu	National University of Defense Technology, China
Mengying Zhu	Zhejiang University, China
Michael Granitzer	University of Passau, Germany
Michael B. Ito	University of Michigan, USA

Michael G. Madden	National University of Ireland, Galway, Ireland
Michal Wozniak	Wroclaw University of Science and Technology, Poland
Michele Fontana	Università di Pisa, Italy
Michiel Stock	Ghent University, Belgium
Miguel Rocha	University of Minho, Portugal
Miguel Silva	INESC TEC, Portugal
Mike Holenderski	Eindhoven University of Technology, Netherlands
Milos Savic	University of Novi Sad, Serbia
Mina Rezaei	LMU Munich, Germany
Minh P. Nguyen	University of Texas, Austin, USA
Minyoung Choe	Korea Advanced Institute of Science and Technology, South Korea
Minyu Chen	Shanghai Jiaotong University, China
Miquel Perello-Nieto	University of Bristol, UK
Mira Kristin Jurgens	Ghent University, Belgium
Miriam Santos	University of Porto, Portugal
Mirko Bunse	TU Dortmund, Germany
Mirko Polato	University of Turin, Italy
Mitra Baratchi	LIACS, University of Leiden, Netherlands
Mohammed Elbamby	Telefonica Scientific Research, Spain
Moises Rocha dos Santos	University of Porto, Portugal
Monowar Bhuyan	Umeå University, Sweden
Morteza Rakhshaninejad	Ghent University, Belgium
Mounim A. El Yacoubi	Télécom SudParis, France
Muhammad Rajabinasab	University of Southern Denmark, Denmark
Muhao Guo	Arizona State University, USA
Mustapha Lebbah	Paris Saclay University-Versailles, France
Nabeel Hussain Syed	Rheinland-Pfälzische Technische Universität, Kaiserslautern-Landau, Germany
Nandyala Hemachandra	Indian Institute of Technology Bombay, India
Nannan Wu	Tianjin University, China
Nanqing Dong	Shanghai Artificial Intelligence Laboratory, China
Naresh Manwani	International Institute of Information Technology, Hyderabad, India
Natan Tourne	Ghent University, Belgium
Nate Veldt	Texas A&M, USA
Nathalie Japkowicz	American University, USA
Natthawut Kertkeidkachorn	Japan Advanced Institute of Science and Technology (JAIST), Japan
Ngoc-Son Vu	ENSEA, France
Nhat-Tan Bui	University of Arkansas, USA

Nian Li	Tsinghua University, China
Nick Lim	University of Waikato, New Zealand
Nico Piatkowski	Fraunhofer IAIS, Germany
Nicolas Roque dos Santos	University of São Paulo, Brazil
Niklas A. Strauss	LMU Munich, Germany
Nikolaj Tatti	Helsinki University, Finland
Nikolaos Nikolaou	University College London, UK
Nikolaos Stylianou	Information Technologies Institute, Greece
Nikos Kanakaris	University of Southern California, USA
Ning Xu	Southeast University, China
Nripsuta Saxena	University of Southern California, USA
Nuwan Gunasekara	Halmstad University, Sweden
Olga Kurasova	Vilnius University, Lithuania
Olga Slizovskaia	AstraZeneca, UK
Olivier Teste	IRIT, University of Toulouse, France
Oswald C.	NIT Trichy, India
Oswaldo Solarte-Pabon	Universidad del Valle, Colombia
Ozge Alacam	University of Bielefeld, Germany
P. S. Sastry	Indian Institute of Science, India
Pablo Olmos	Universidad Carlos III de Madrid, Spain
Panagiotis Karras	University of Copenhagen, Denmark
Panagiotis Symeonidis	University of the Aegean, Greece
Pance Panov	Jožef Stefan Institute, Slovenia
Paolo Bonetti	Politecnico di Milano, Italy
Paolo Merialdo	Università degli Studi Roma Tre, Italy
Paolo Mignone	University of Bari Aldo Moro, Italy
Pascal Welke	TU Wien, Austria
Patrick Y. Wu	American University, USA
Paul Caillon	LAMSADE Université Paris Dauphine - PSL, France
Paul Davidsson	Malmo University, Sweden
Paul Prasse	University of Potsdam, Germany
Paulo J. Azevedo	Universidade do Minho, Portugal
Pawel Teisseyre	Warsaw University of Technology, Poland
Pawel Zyblewski	Wroclaw University of Science and Technology, Poland
Pedro G. Ferreira	University of Porto, Portugal
Pedro Larrañaga	Technical University of Madrid, Spain
Pedro Ribeiro	University of Porto, Portugal
Pedro H. Abreu	CISUC, Portugal
Peijie Sun	Tsinghua University, China
Peng Wu	Shanghai Jiao Tong University, China

Pengpeng Qiao	Institute of Science Tokyo, Japan
Peter Karsmakers	KU Leuven, Belgium
Peter Schneider-Kamp	SDU, Denmark
Peter van der Putten	Leiden University, Netherlands
Petia Georgieva	University of Aveiro, Portugal
Philipp Vaeth	Technical University of Applied Sciences Würzburg-Schweinfurt and Universität Bielefeld, Germany
Philippe Preux	Inria, France
Phung Lai	SUNY-Albany, USA
Pierre Geurts	Montefiore Institute, University of Liège, Belgium
Pierre Monnin	Université Côte d'Azur, Inria, CNRS, I3S, France
Pierre Schaus	UC Louvain, Belgium
Pierre Wolinski	Paris Dauphine University - PSL, France
Pieter Robberechts	KU Leuven, Belgium
Pietro Sabatino	ICAR-CNR, Italy
Pingchuan Ma	HKUST, China
Piotr Habas	Amazon, USA
Piotr Lipinski	University of Wroclaw, Poland
Piotr Porwik	University of Silesia, Katowice, Poland
Prithwish Chakraborty	IBM Corporation, USA
Lucie Flek	Marburg University, Germany
Przemyslaw Biecek	Warsaw University of Technology, Poland
Qiang Sheng	Institute of Computing Technology, Chinese Academy of Sciences, China
Qiang Zhou	Nanjing University of Aeronautics and Astronautics, China
Rafet Sifa	Fraunhofer IAIS, Germany
Raha Moraffah	Arizona State University, USA
Raivydas Simanas	Vilnius University, Lithuania
Rajeev Rastogi	Amazon, USA
Ranya Almohsen	Baylor College of Medicine, USA
Raphael Romero	Ghent University, Belgium
Raquel Sebastiao	ESTGV-IPV & IEETA-UA, Portugal
Ravi Kolla	Sony Research India, India
Raza Ul Mustafa	Loyola University, USA
Remy Cazabet	Université de Lyon 1, France
Renhe Jiang	University of Tokyo, Japan
Reza Akbarinia	Inria, France
Ricardo P. M. Cruz	University of Porto (FEUP), Portugal
Ricardo B. Prudencio	Universidade Federal de Pernambuco, Brazil
Ricardo Rios	Federal University of Bahia, Brazil

Ricardo Santos	Fraunhofer Portugal AICOS, Portugal
Riccardo Guidotti	University of Pisa, Italy
Robertas Damasevicius	Vytautas Magnus University, Lithuania
Roberto Corizzo	American University, USA
Roberto Interdonato	CIRAD, France
Rocio Chongtay	University of Southern Denmark, Denmark
Rohit Babbar	University of Bath, UK and Aalto University, Finland
Romain Tavenard	Université de Rennes, LETG/IRISA, France
Rosana Veroneze	LBiC, Italy
Ruggero G. Pensa	University of Turin, Italy
Rui Meng	BNU-HKBU United International College, USA
Rui Yu	University of Louisville, USA
Ruixuan Liu	Emory University, USA
Runqun Xiong	Southeast University, China
Runxue Bao	University of Pittsburgh, USA
Ruochun Jin	National University of Defense Technology, China
Ruta Juozaitiene	Vytautas Magnus University, Lithuania
Rytis Maskeliunas	Polsl, Poland
Salvatore Ruggieri	University of Pisa, Italy
Sam Verboven	Vrije Universiteit Brussel, Belgium
Sangkyun Lee	Korea University, South Korea
Sara Abdali	University of California, Riverside, USA
Sarah Masud	LCS2, IIIT-D, India
Sarwan Ali	Georgia State University, USA
Satoru Koda	Fujitsu Limited, Japan
Sebastian Buschjager	Lamarr Institute for ML and AI, Germany
Sebastian Jimenez	Ghent University, Belgium
Sebastian Meznar	Jožef Stefan Institute, Ljubljana, Slovenia
Sebastian Ventura Soto	University of Cordoba, Spain
Sebastien Razakarivony	Safran, France
Selpi Selpi	Chalmers University of Technology, Sweden
Sergio Greco	University of Calabria, Italy
Sergio Jesus	Feedzai, Portugal
Sha Lu	University of South Australia, Australia
Shalini Priya	Indian Institute of Technology Patna, India
Shanqing Guo	Shandong University, China
Shaofu Yang	Southeast University, China
Shazia Tabassum	INESCTEC, Portugal
Shengxiang Gao	Kunming University of Science and Technology, China

Shichao Pei	University of Massachusetts, Boston, USA
Shin Matsushima	University of Tokyo, Japan
Shin-ichi Maeda	Preferred Networks, Japan
Shiwen Ni	Chinese Academy of Sciences, China
Shiyou Qian	Shanghai Jiao Tong University, China
Shu Zhao	Anhui University, China
Shuai Li	University of Cambridge, UK and University of Tokyo, Japan, Tsinghua University, China
Shuang Cheng	Institute of Computing Technology, Chinese Academy of Sciences, China
Shubhranshu Shekhar	Brandeis University, USA
Shurui Cao	Carnegie Mellon University, USA
Shuteng Niu	Mayo Clinic, USA
Siamak Ghodsi	Leibniz University of Hannover, Germany
Sihai Zhang	University of Science and Technology of China, China
Silvia Chiusano	Politecnico di Torino, Italy
Silviu Maniu	Université de Grenoble Alpes, France
Simon Gottschalk	L3S Research Center, Leibniz Universität Hannover, Germany
Simona Nistico	University of Calabria, Italy
Simone Angarano	Politecnico di Torino, Italy
Sinong Zhao	Nankai University, China
Siwei Wang	Intelligent Game and Decision Lab, China
Sofoklis Kitharidis	LIACS, Netherlands
Songlin Du	University of Melbourne, Australia
Songlin Du	Southeast University, China
Soumyajit Chatterjee	Nokia Bell Labs, USA
Sourav Dutta	Huawei Research Centre, China
Stefan Duffner	University of Lyon, France
Stefan Heindorf	Paderborn University, Germany
Stefan Kesselheim	Forschungszentrum Jülich, Germany
Stefano Bortoli	Huawei Research Center, China
Stefanos Vrochidis	Information Technologies Institute, CERTH, Greece
Steffen Thoma	FZI Research Center for Information Technology, Germany
Stephan Doerfel	Kiel University of Applied Sciences, Germany
Steven D. Prestwich	University College Cork, Ireland
Suman Banerjee	IIT Jammu, India
Sunil Aryal	Deakin University, Australia
Surabhi Adhikari	Columbia University, USA

Susan McKeever	TU Dublin, Ireland
Swati Swati	Universität der Bundeswehr München, Germany
Szymon Wojciechowski	Wroclaw University of Science and Technology, Poland
Talip Ucar	AstraZeneca, UK
Taro Tezuka	University of Tsukuba, Japan
Tatiana Passali	Aristotle University of Thessaloniki, Greece
Tatiane Nogueira Rios	UFBA, Brazil
Telmo M. Silva Filho	University of Bristol, UK
Teng Lin	Hong Kong University of Technology (Guangzhou), China
Teng Zhang	Huazhong University of Science and Technology, China
Thach Le Nguyen	Insight Centre, Ireland
Thang Duy Dang	Fujitsu Limited, Japan
Thanh-Son Nguyen	A*STAR, Singapore
Theresa Eimer	Leibniz University Hannover, Germany
Thiago Andrade	INESC TEC & University of Porto, Portugal
Thomas Bonald	Telecom Paris, France
Thomas Guyet	Inria, Centre de Lyon, France
Thomas Lampert	University of Strasbourg, France
Thomas L. Lee	University of Edinburgh, UK
Thomas Mortier	Ghent University, Belgium
Tianyi Chen	Boston University, USA
Tie Luo	University of Kentucky, USA
Tiehang Duan	Mayo Clinic, USA
Tijl De Bie	Ghent University, Belgium
Timilehin B. Aderinola	University College Dublin, Ireland
Timo Bertram	Johannes-Kepler Universität, Germany
Timo Ropinski	Ulm University, Germany
Tobias A. Hille	University of Kassel, Germany
Tom Hanika	University of Hildesheim, Germany
Tomas Kliegr	University of Economics, Prague, Czech Republic
Tomasz Michalak	University of Warsaw and Ideas NCBiR, Poland
Tomasz Walkowiak	Wroclaw University of Science and Technology, Poland
Tommaso Zoppi	University of Florence, Italy
Tong Li	Hong Kong University of Technology, China
Tong Mo	Peking University, China
Tongya Zheng	Hangzhou City University, China
Tonio Weidler	Maastricht University, Netherlands
Tony Lindgren	Stockholm University, Sweden

Tsunenori Mine	Kyushu University, Japan
Tuan Le	New Mexico State University, USA
Tuwe Lofstrom	Jönköping University, Sweden
Ulf Johansson	Jönköping University, Sweden
Vadim Ermolayev	Ukrainian Catholic University, Ukraine
Vahan Martirosyan	CentraleSupélec, Belgium
Vana Kalogeraki	Athens University of Economics and Business, Greece
Vanessa Gomez-Verdejo	Universidad Carlos III de Madrid, Spain
Vasileios Iosifidis	SCHUFA Holding, Germany
Vasilis Gkolemis	ATHENA RC, Greece
Victor Charpenay	Mines Saint-Etienne, France
Vincent Derkinderen	KU Leuven, Belgium
Vincent Lemaire	Orange Research, France
Vincenzo Pasquadibisceglie	University of Bari, Aldo Moro, Italy
Virginijus Marcinkevicius	Vilnius University, Lithuania
Vitor Cerqueira	University of Porto, Portugal
Vivek Kumar	Universität der Bundeswehr München, Germany
Vivek Srikumar	University of Utah, USA
Wagner Meira Jr.	UFMG, Brazil
Wei Wu	Ben Gurion University of the Negev, Israel
Weichen Li	RPTU Kaiserslautern-Landau, Germany
Weifeng Xu	Independent Researcher, China
Weike Pan	Shenzhen University, China
Weiwei Jiang	Beijing University of Posts and Telecommunications, China
Weiwei Sun	Carnegie Mellon University, USA
Weiwei Yuan	Nanjing University of Aeronautics and Astronautics, China
Weixiong Rao	Tongji University, China
Wen-Bo Xie	Southwest Petroleum University, China
Wenhao Li	Tongji University, China
Wenhao Zheng	Shopee, Singapore
Wenjie Feng	National University of Singapore, Singapore
Wenjie Xi	George Mason University, USA
Wenshui Luo	Nanjing University of Science and Technology, China
Wentao Yu	Nanjing University of Science and Technology, China
Wenzhe Yi	Wuhan University, China
Wenzhong Li	Nanjing University, China
Wojciech Rejchel	Nicolaus Copernicus University, Torun, Poland

Xi Jiang	Southern University of Science and Technology, China
Xiang Li	East China Normal University, China
Xiang Lian	Kent State University, USA
Xiao Ma	Beijing University of Posts and Telecommunications, China
Xiao Zhang	Shandong University, China
Xiaobing Zhou	Yunnan University, China
Xiaofeng Cao	University of Technology Sydney, Australia
Xiaofeng Gao	Shanghai Jiaotong University, China
Xiaojun Chen	Institute of Information Engineering, Chinese Academy of Sciences, China
Xiao-Jun Zeng	University of Manchester, UK
Xiaoming Zhang	Beihang University, China
Xiaoting Zhao	Etsy, USA
Xiaowei Mao	Beijing Jiaotong University, China
Xiaoyu Shi	Chinese Academy of Sciences, China
Xin Du	University of Edinburgh, UK
Xin Qin	California State University, Long Beach, USA
Xing Tang	Tencent, China
Xing Xing	Tongji University, China
Xinning Zhu	Beijing University of Posts and Telecommunications, China
Xinpeng Lv	National University of Defense Technology, China
Xintao Wu	University of Arkansas, USA
Xinyang Zhang	University of Illinois at Urbana-Champaign, USA
Xinyu Guan	Xi'an Jiaotong University, China
Xixun Lin	Chinese Academy of Sciences, China
Xiyue Zhang	University of Bristol, UK
Xuan-Hong Dang	IBM T.J. Watson Research Center, USA
Xue Li	University of Queensland, Australia
Xue Yan	Institute of Automation, Chinese Academy of Sciences, China
Xuefeng Chen	Chongqing University, China
Xuemin Wang	Guilin University of Electronic Technology, China
Yachuan Zhang	East China University of Science and Technology, China
Yan Zhang	Peking University, China
Yang Li	University of North Carolina at Chapel Hill, USA
Yang Shu	East China Normal University, China
Yang Wei	Nanjing University of Science and Technology, China

Yanhao Wang	East China Normal University, China
Yanmin Zhu	Shanghai Jiao Tong University, China
Yansong Y. L. Li	University of Ottawa, Canada
Yao-Xiang Ding	Nanjing University, China
Yaqi Xie	Carnegie Mellon University, USA
Yasutoshi Ida	NTT, Japan
Yaying Zhang	Tongji University, China
Ye Zhu	Deakin University, Australia
Yeon-Chang Lee	Ulsan National Institute of Science and Technology, South Korea
Yexiang Xue	Purdue University, USA
Yi Wang	Xinjiang Technical Institute of Physics and Chemistry, Chinese Academy of Sciences, China
Yifeng Gao	University of Texas, Rio Grande Valley, USA
Yilun Jin	Hong Kong University of Science and Technology, China
Yin Zhang	University of Electronic Science and Technology of China, China
Ying Chen	RMIT University, Australia
Yinsheng Li	Fudan University, China
Yong Li	Huawei European Research Center, China
Yongyu Wang	JD Logistics, China
Youhei Akimoto	University of Tsukuba/RIKEN AIP, Japan
You-Wei Luo	Sun Yat-sen University and Jiaying University, China
Yuchen Li	Baidu, China
Yuchen Yang	Harbin Institute of Technology, China
Yudi Zhang	Eindhoven University of Technology, Netherlands
Yuhao Li	University of Melbourne, Australia
Yuheng Jia	Southeast University, China
Yujia Zheng	CMU, USA
Yulong Pei	TU Eindhoven, Netherlands
Yuncheng Jiang	South China Normal University, China
Yuntao Shou	Xi'an Jiaotong University, China
Yunyun Wang	Nanjing University of Posts and Telecommunications, China
Yutong Ye	East China Normal University, China
Yuzhou Chen	University of California, Riverside, USA
Zahraa Abdallah	University of Bristol, UK
Zaineb Chelly Dagdia	UVSQ, Paris-Saclay, France
Zehua Cheng	University of Oxford, UK
Zeyu Chen	University of Auckland, New Zealand

Zhaocheng Ge	Huazhong University of Science and Technology, China
Zhe Yang	Soochow University, China
Zhen Liu	Guangdong University of Foreign Studies, China
Zheng Chen	Osaka University, Japan
Zhenghao Liu	Northeastern University, China
Zhenyu Yang	Macquarie University, Australia
Zhi Li	Tsinghua University, China
Zhichao Han	ETHZ, Switzerland
Zhihui Wang	Fudan University, China
Zhilong Shan	South China Normal University, China
Zhipeng Yin	Florida International University, USA
Zhipeng Zou	Nanjing University of Science and Technology, China
Zhiwen Xiao	Southwest Jiaotong University, China
Zhiwen Zhang	LocationMind, Japan
Zhixin Li	Guangxi Normal University, China
Zhiyong Cheng	Shandong Academy of Sciences, China
Zhong Chen	Southern Illinois University, USA
Zhong Li	Leiden University, Netherlands
Zhong Zhang	Tsinghua University, China
Zhongjing Yu	Peking University, China
Zhuang Liu	Dongbei University of Finance and Economics, China
Zhuo Cao	Forschungszentrum Jülich, Germany
Zhuoming Xie	Guangdong University of Technology, China
Zhuoqun Li	Louisiana State University, USA
Zicheng Zhao	Nanjing University of Science and Technology, China
Zichong Wang	Florida International University, USA
Zifeng Ding	University of Cambridge, UK
Ziheng Chen	Walmart, USA
Zijie J. Wang	Georgia Tech, USA
Zirui Zhuang	Beijing University of Posts and Telecommunications, China
Zixing Song	Chinese University of Hong Kong, China
Ziyu Wang	University of Tokyo, Japan
Ziyue Li	University of Cologne, Germany
Zongxia Xie	Tianjin University, China
Zongyue Li	LMU Munich, Germany
Zuojin Tang	Zhejiang University, China

List of Editors

Inês Dutra	University of Porto, Portugal
Mykola Pechenisky	TU Eindhoven, The Netherlands
Paulo Cortez	University of Minho, Portugal
Sepideh Pashami	Halmstad University, Sweden
Arian Pasquali Faktion	Belgium
Nuno Moniz	University of Notre Dame, USA
Alípio Jorge	University of Porto, Portugal
Carlos Soares	University of Porto, Portugal
João Gama	University of Porto, Portugal
Pedro H. Abreu	University of Coimbra, Portugal

Program Committee – Applied Data Science Track

Nasrullah Sheikh	IBM Research, USA
Aakarsh Malhotra	MasterCard, USA
Aakash Goel	Amazon, USA
Abdoulaye Sakho	Artefact, France
Abhijeet Pendyala	Ruhr-Universität Bochum, Germany
Abu Shad Ahammed	University of Siegen, Germany
Adi Lin	Didi, China
Aditya Gautam	Meta, USA
Ahmed K. Mohamed	Meta, USA
Akihiro Yoshida	Kyushu University, Japan
Akshay Sethi	MasterCard, USA
Alejandro Kuratomi	Stockholm University, Sweden
Alessandro Gambetti	Nova School of Business and Economics, Portugal
Alessandro Leite	INSA Rouen, Inria, France
Alessio Russo	Politecnico di Milano, Italy
Alex Beeson	University of Warwick, UK
Alexander Galozy	Halmstad University, Sweden
Alexander Karlsson	University of Skovde, Sweden
Alexander Kovalenko	Czech Technical University in Prague, Czech Republic
Alexey Zaytsev	Skoltech, Russia
Alina Bazarova	Forschungszentrum Jülich, Germany
Alix Lheritier	Amadeus SAS, France
Allan Tucker	Brunel University London, UK
Alvaro Figueira	CRACS and Universidade do Porto, Portugal

Aman Gulati	Amazon, USA
Amira Soliman	Halmstad University, Sweden
Ana Gjorgjevikj	Jožef Stefan Institute, Slovenia
Anders Holst	RISE SICS, Sweden
André C. P. L. F. de Carvalho	University of São Paulo, Brazil
Andrea Seveso	University of Milan-Bicocca, Italy
Andreas Bender	LMU Munich, Germany
Andreas Henelius	Independent Researcher, Finland
Andreas Holzinger	University of Natural Resources and Life Sciences, Vienna, Austria
Andrei Shelopugin	Independent Researcher, Brazil
Angelo Impedovo	Niuma, Italy
Aniket Chakrabarti	Amazon, USA
Animesh Prasad	Roku, USA
Anisio Lacerda	UFMG, Brazil
Anli Ji	Georgia State University, USA
Antoine Doucet	La Rochelle Université, France
Anton Borg	Blekinge Institute of Technology, Sweden
Antonio Bevilacqua	Meetecho, Italy
Antonis Klironomos	University of Mannheim, Germany
Aron Henriksson	Stockholm University, Sweden
Artur Chudzik	Polish-Japanese Academy of Information Technology, Poland
Arun Venkitaraman	EPFL, Switzerland
Arunabha Choudhury	ASML, Netherlands
Asem Omari	Higher Colleges of Technology, UAE
Ashman Mehra	Birla Institute of Technology and Science, India
Ashwani Rao	Amazon, USA
Asier Rodriguez	BBVA, Spain
Asma Atamna	Ruhr-Universität Bochum, Germany
Atiye Sadat Hashemi	Halmstad University, Sweden
Atul Anand Gopalakrishnan	SUNY Buffalo, USA
Avani Wildani	Emory University, USA
Aviv Rovshitz	Ben-Gurion University of the Negev, Israel
Axel Brando	Barcelona Supercomputing Center (BSC) and Universitat de Barcelona (UB), Spain
Azadeh Alavi	RMIT University, Australia
Beihong Jin	Institute of Software, China
Benoit Frenay	University of Namur, Belgium
Berkay Aydin	Georgia State University, USA
Bijaya Adhikari	University of Iowa, USA
Bin Li	Alibaba Group, China

Bo Pang	University of Auckland, New Zealand
Bogdan Ruszczak	Opole University of Technology, Poland
Bohao Qu	Agency for Science, China
Bruno Veloso	INESC TEC, FEP-UP, Portugal
Buyue Qian	Xi'an Jiaotong University, China
Camille Kurtz	Université Paris Cité, France
Cangbai Li	Guangdong University of Technology, China
Carlo Metta	ISTI CNR, Italy
Carlos N. Silla	Pontifical Catholic University of Paraná (PUCPR), Brazil
Cecile Bothorel	IMT Atlantique, France
Cesar Ferri	Universitat Politècnica Valencia, Spain
Chang Li	Apple, USA
Chang-Dong Wang	Sun Yat-sen University, China
Chaofan Li	Karlsruhe Institute of Technology, Germany
Chaoyuan Zuo	Nankai University, China
Chen Gao	Tsinghua University, China
Chen Li	Computer Network Information Center, China
Chen Zhao	Baylor University, USA
Chen-Wei Chang	Virginia Tech, USA
Chenxi Xue	Nanjing Normal University, China
Chongke Bi	Tianjin University, China
Christian M. Adriano	Hasso-Plattner Institute, Germany
Christophe Rodrigues	DVRC Pôle universitaire Léonard de Vinci, France
Chuan Li	Sorbonne University, LIPADE, France
Chunhui Zhang	Dartmouth College, USA
Cristina Soguero Ruiz	Rey Juan Carlos University, Spain
Daheng Wang	Amazon, USA
Daifeng Li	Sun Yat-sen University, China
Damien Fay	HPE Labs, Ireland
Dania Herzalla	Technology Innovation Institute, UAE
Daniel Lemire	University of Quebec (TELUQ), Canada
Daniel Trejo Banos	SDSC, USA
Daochen Zha	Rice University, USA
Dawei Cheng	Tongji University, China
Dayne Freitag	SRI International, USA
Di Yao	Institute of Computing Technology, China
Dimitris Nick Dimitriadis	Aristotle University of Thessaloniki, Greece
Diogo F. Soares	Universidade de Lisboa, Portugal
Dirk Pflueger	University of Stuttgart, Germany
Doheon Han	University of Notre Dame, USA

Dongxiang Zhang	Zhejiang University, China
Dongxiao Yu	Shandong University, China
Dugang Liu	Guangdong Laboratory of Artificial Intelligence and Digital Economy (Shenzen), China
Ece Calikus	Uppsala University, Sweden
Edwyn Brient	Thales LAS/Mines Paris PSL, France
Efstathios Stamatatos	University of the Aegean, Greece
Elaine Faria	UFU, Brazil
Elio Masciari	University of Naples, Italy
Emilie Devijver	Université Grenoble Alpes, Inria, CNRS, Grenoble INP, LIG, France
Emmanuelle Claeys	IRIT, France
Enayat Rajabi	Halmstad University, Sweden
Enda Barrett	University of Galway, Ireland
Enyan Dai	Hong Kong University of Science and Technology (Guangzhou), China
Eric Peukert	ScaDS.AI, Germany
Eric Sanjuan	Avignon University, France
Erik Frisk	Linköping University, Sweden
Eui-Hong (Sam) Han	The Washington Post, USA
Eunil Park	Sungkyunkwan University, South Korea
Fabio Carrara	CNR-ISTI, Italy
Fabiola Pereira	Federal University of Uberlandia, Brazil
Fan Yang	Rice University, USA
Fangzhao Wu	MSRA, China
Fangzhou Shi	Didi Chuxing, China
Fathima Nuzla Ismail	State University of New York, USA
Flavio Bertini	University of Parma, Italy
Francesco Dente	EURECOM, France
Francesco Guerra	University of Modena e Reggio Emilia, Italy
Francesco Scala	CNR-ICAR, Italy
Francesco Spinnato	University of Pisa, Italy
Francesco Paolo Nerini	Sapienza University of Rome, Italy
Francisco P. Romero	UCLM, Spain
Franco Maria Nardini	ISTI-CNR, Italy
Francois Schwarzentruber	ENS Lyon, France
Fudong Lin	University of Delaware, USA
Gabriel Augusto Pinheiro	UNIFESP, Brazil
Gan Sun	South China University of Technology, China
Gargi Srivastava	Rajiv Gandhi Institute of Petroleum Technology Jais, India
Giacomo Boracchi	Politecnico di Milano, Italy

Giuseppe Garofalo	DistriNet, KU Leuven, Belgium
Giuseppina Andresini	University of Bari Aldo Moro, Italy
Goran Falkman	University of Skovde, Sweden
Grzegorz Nalepa	Jagiellonian University, Poland
Guanggang Geng	Jinan University, China
Guojun Liang	Halmstad University, Sweden
Haifang Li	Baidu, China
Haina Tang	University of Chinese Academy of Sciences, China
Hancheng Ge	Amazon, USA
Hao Li	National University of Defense Technology, China
Haohui Chen	CSIRO, Australia
Haomin Yu	Aalborg University, Denmark
Haoyi Xiong	Baidu, China
Hiba Najjar	DFKI, Germany
Hillol Kargupta	Agnik, USA
Hong Zhou	Meta, USA
Hongbin Pei	Xi'an Jiao Tong University, China
Hou-Wan Long	Chinese University of Hong Kong, China
Hua Wei	Arizona State University, USA
Huaiyuan Yao	Xi'an Jiaotong University, China
Huan Song	Amazon, USA
Hubert Baniecki	University of Warsaw, Poland
Hyunsung Kim	KAIST, Fitogether, South Korea
Ibtihal El Mimouni	Inria, France
Ildar Baimuratov	L3S Research Center, Germany
Ilir Jusufi	Blekinge Institute of Technology, Sweden
Inaam Ashraf	Bielefeld University, Germany
Ines Sousa	Fraunhofer AICOS, Portugal
Iris Heerlien	Saxion, Netherlands
Isak Samsten	Stockholm University, Sweden
Ishan Verma	TCS Research, India
Ismail Hakki Toroslu	METU, Turkey
Ivan Carrera	EPN, Ecuador
Jaakko Hollmen	Stockholm University, Sweden
Jairo Cugliari	Laboratoire ERIC, France
Jakub Nalepa	Silesian University of Technology, Poland
Jelica Vasiljeivić	Hoffmann-La Roche, Switzerland
Jens Lundstrom	Halmstad University, Sweden
Jesse Davis	KU Leuven, Belgium
Jiahui Bai	Meta, USA

Jiajun Gu	Carnegie Mellon University, USA
Jiali Pan	Department of Information Management, USA
Jian Yu	Auckland University of Technology, New Zealand
Jiangbin Zheng	Westlake University, China
Jianhua Yin	Shandong University, China
Jingbo Zhou	Baidu, China
Jingjing Liu	MD Anderson Cancer Center, USA
Jingwen Shi	Michigan State University, USA
Jingxuan Wei	University of Chinese Academy of Sciences, China
Jinyoung Han	Sungkyunkwan University, South Korea
Jiue-An Yang	City of Hope Beckman Research Institute, USA
Joao R. Campos	University of Coimbra, Portugal
Jochen De Weerdt	KU Leuven, Belgium
Joe Tekli	Lebanese American University, Lebanon
Joel Ky	University of Lorraine, CNRS, Inria, France
John McCall	Robert Gordon University, UK
John Mitros	University College Dublin, Ireland
Jonas Fischer	Ruhr-Universität Bochum, Germany
Jonas Nordqvist	Linnaeus University, Sweden
Joydeep Chandra	Indian Institute of Technology Patna, India
Julian Martin Rodemann	LMU Munich, Germany
Jun Shen	University of Wollongong, Australia
Junichi Tatemura	Google, USA
Junxuan Li	Microsoft, USA
Jyun-Yu Jiang	Amazon Science, USA
Kai Wang	Shanghai Jiao Tong University, China
Kaiping Zheng	National University of Singapore, Singapore
Kaiwen Dong	University of Notre Dame, USA
Katarzyna Bozek	University of Cologne, Germany
Katerina Schindlerova	UniVie, Austria
Katharina Dost	Jožef Stefan Institute, Slovenia
Katsiaryna Mirylenka	Zalando SE, Germany
Keith Burghardt	ISI, Germany
Klaus Brinker	Hamm-Lippstadt University of Applied Sciences, Germany
Koki Kawabata	Osaka University, Japan
Korbinian Randl	Stockholm University, Sweden
Krzysztof Krawiec	Poznań University of Technology, Poland
Krzysztof Kutt	Jagiellonian University, Poland
Kwan Hui Lim	Singapore University of Technology and Design, Singapore

Lamija Lemes	University of Zenica, Bosnia & Herzegovina
Le Nguyen	University of Oulu, Finland
Lei Li	Hong Kong University of Science and Technology (Guangzhou), China
Lei Liu	York University, Canada
Li Liu	Chongqing University, China
Li Zhang	University College London, UK
Liang Tang	Google, USA
Liang Tong	NEC Labs America, USA
Liang Wang	Alibaba Group, China
Lina Yao	University of New South Wales, Australia
Lingxiao Li	Michigan State University, USA
Lingyang Chu	McMaster University, Canada
Lixin Zou	Wuhan University, China
Lluis Garcia-Pueyo	Meta, USA
Lou Salaun	Nokia Bell Labs, USA
Luca Corbucci	University of Pisa, Italy
Luca Pappalardo	ISTI, Italy
Luca Romeo	University of Macerata, Italy
Luis Ferreira	Olympus Medical Products Portugal, Portugal
Luis Miguel Matos	ALGORITMI Centre, Portugal
Lukas Grasmann	TU Wien, Austria
Lukas Pensel	Johannes Gutenberg University Mainz, Germany
Maciej Grzenda	Warsaw University of Technology, Poland
Maciej Piernik	Poznań University of Technology, Poland
Madiraju Srilakshmi	Dream Sports, India
Mads C. Hansen	A.P. Moller-Maersk, Denmark
Mahardhika Pratama	University of South Australia, Australia
Mahmoud Rahat	Halmstad University, Sweden
Man Tianxing	Jilin University, China
Manish Gupta	Microsoft, USA
Manos Papagelis	York University, Canada
Manuel Lopes	Instituto Tecnico Superior, Portugal
Manuel Portela	Universitat Pompeu Fabra, Spain
Marc Tommasi	Lille University, France
Marco Fisichella	Leibniz Universität, Hannover, Germany
Maria Riveiro	Jonkoping University, Sweden
Maria Ulan	RISE Research Institutes of Sweden, Sweden
Marian Scuturici	LIRIS, France
Marianne Clausel	IECL, France
Mario Doller	University of Applied Sciences, Kufstein, Austria
Marius Schwammle	DLR/BT, Germany

Markus Gotz	Karlsruhe Institute of Technology (KIT), Germany
Markus Leyser	Technische Universität Dresden, Germany
Martin Boldt	Blekinge Institute of Technology, Sweden
Martin Mladenov	Google, USA
Martin Vita	Institute of Physics, Czech Academy of Sciences, Czech Republic
Matthias Demant	Fraunhofer ISE, Germany
Matthias Galipaud	SDSC, Switzerland
Matthias Petri	Amazon, USA
Matthieu Latapy	CNRS, France
Maurice Van Keulen	University of Twente, Netherlands
Maxime Cordy	University of Luxembourg, Luxembourg
Maxwell J. Jacobson	Purdue University, USA
Md Nahid Hasan	Miami University, USA
Md Zia Ullah	Edinburgh Napier University, UK
Mehtab Alam Syed	CIRAD, France
Melanie Neubauer	University of Leoben, Austria
Meng Chen	Shandong University, China
Mengxuan Zhang	Australian National University, Australia
Miao Fan	NavInfo, China
Michael Bain	University of New South Wales, Australia
Michele Bernardini	Uni eCampus.It, Italy
Michiel Dhont	EluciDATA Lab of Sirris, Belgium
Mickael Coustaty	L3i Laboratory, France
Miguel Couceiro	LORIA, France
Mihaela Mitici	Utrecht University, Netherlands
Min Lee	Singapore Management University, Singapore
Min Hun Lee	Singapore Management University, Singapore
Mina Rezaei	LMU Munich, Germany
Ming Ma	Inner Mongolia University, China
Minghao Chen	Tencent, China
Mirco Nanni	CNR-ISTI Pisa, Italy
Mirjam Wattenhofer	Google, USA
Mirko Marras	University of Cagliari, Italy
Mitra Heidari	University of Melbourne, Australia
Modesto Castrillon-Santana	Universidad de Las Palmas de Gran Canaria, Spain
Mohammadmehdi Saberioon	German Research Centre for Geosciences, Germany
Mohammed Amer	Fujitsu Research of Europe, Germany
Mohammed Ghaith Altarabichi	Halmstad University, Sweden

Mojgan Kouhounestani	University of Melbourne, Australia
Moonki Hong	Sogang University, South Korea
Munira Syed	Procter & Gamble, USA
Nan Li	Microsoft, USA
Narendhar Gugulothu	TCS Research, India
Nedra Mellouli	LIASD, Portugal
Ngoc Son Le	University of Hildesheim, Germany
Niklas Lavesson	Blekinge Institute of Technology, Sweden
Niraj Kumar	Fujitsu, Japan
Nitish Kumar	MasterCard, USA
Nuno Cruz Garcia	FCUL, Portugal
Nuno R. P. S. Guimaraes	INESC TEC, University of Porto, Portugal
Nuwan Gunasekara	Halmstad University, Sweden
Pablo Picazo-Sanchez	Halmstad University, Sweden
Pablo Torrijos Arenas	Universidad de Castilla-La Mancha, Spain
Pablo Jose Del Moral Pastor	Ekkono.ai, Finland
Pan He	Auburn University, USA
Panagiotis Kanellopoulos	University of Essex, UK
Panagiotis Papadakos	FORTH-ICS, Greece
Pandey Shourya Prasad	International Institute of Information Technology, Bangalore, India
Panpan Xu	Amazon AWS, USA
Paola Velardi	Sapienza University of Rome, Italy
Paolo Cintia	Kode, Italy
Pascal Plettenberg	Intelligent Embedded Systems, Italy
Paul Boniol	Inria, France
Pavel Blinov	Sber AI Lab, Russia
Pawel Parczyk	Wroclaw University of Science and Technology, Poland
Pedro M. Ferreira	University of Lisbon, Portugal
Pedro Seber	MIT, USA
Peng Qiao	NUDT, China
Pengyuan Wang	University of Georgia, USA
Petr Olegovich Sokerin	Skoltech, Russia
Philipp Bach	University of Hamburg, Germany
Philipp Froehlich	TU Darmstadt, Germany
Philipp Schmidt	Amazon Research, USA
Philipp Zech	University of Innsbruck, Austria
Pinar Karagoz	Middle East Technical University (METU), Turkey
Ping Luo	Chinese Academy of Sciences, China
Po Yang	University of Sheffield, UK

Pop Petrica	Technical University of Cluj-Napoca, Romania
Prathap Manohar Joshi R	Zoho Corporation, India
Praveen Borra	Florida Atlantic University, USA
Praveen Paruchuri	IIIT Hyderabad, India
Qian Li	Curtin University, Australia
Qihang Yao	Georgia Institute of Technology, USA
Qiwei Han	Nova School of Business and Economics, Portugal
Quentin Duchemin	Université Gustave Eiffel, France
Radu Tudor Ionescu	University of Bucharest, Romania
Rafal Kucharski	Jagiellonian University, Poland
Rafet Sifa	Fraunhofer IAIS & University of Bonn, Germany
Ramasamy Savitha	I2R A*STAR, Singapore
Ran Yu	DSIS Research Group, Singapore
Ranga Raju Vatsavai	North Carolina State University, USA
Raphael Couturier	University of Bourgogne Franche-Comte (UBFC), France
Renato M. Assuncao	ESRI, USA
Renaud Lambiotte	University of Oxford, UK
Reuben Kshitiz Borrison	ABB, Switzerland
Reza Shirvany	Zalando SE, Germany
Ricardo R. Pereira	Feedzai, Portugal
Riccardo Rosati	Università Politecnica delle Marche, Ancona, Italy
Richard Allmendinger	University of Manchester, UK
Richard Nordsieck	XITASO GmbH IT and Software Solutions, Germany
Richi Nayak	Queensland University of Technology, Australia
Roberto Trasarti	CNR, Italy
Rogerio Luis de C. Costa	Polytechnic of Leiria, Portugal
Romain Ilbert	Huawei Paris Research Center, France
Roy Ka-Wei Lee	Singapore University of Technology and Design, Singapore
Ruilin Wang	University of Aberdeen, UK
Sabrina Gaito	Università degli Studi di Milano, Italy
Sai Karthikeya Vemuri	Computer Vision Group Jena, Italy
Saisubramaniam Gopalakrishnan	Quantiphi, USA
Sajjad Shumaly	Max-Planck-Institut for Polymer Research, Germany
Salvatore Rinzivillo	KDD Lab, ISTI, CNR, Italy
Samaneh Shafee	LASIGE, Portugal
Sandra Wissing	Fachhochschule Münster, Germany

Sarwan Ali	Georgia State University, USA
Sebastian Becker	Fraunhofer ISST, Germany
Sebastian Honel	Linnaeus University, Sweden
Selin Colakhasanoglu	Saxion University of Applied Sciences, Netherlands
Senzhang Wang	Central South University, China
Sepideh Nahali	York University, Canada
Shahrooz Abghari	Blekinge Institute of Technology, Sweden
Shahroz Tariq	CSIRO, Australia
Shang Yanlei	BUPT, China
Shen Liang	Paris Cité University, France
Shengheng Liu	Southeast University, China
Shereen Elsayed	University of Hildesheim, Germany
Shi-ting Wen	NingboTech University, China
Shiv Krishna Jaiswal	Walmart Global Tech, USA
Shoujin Wang	Macquarie University, Australia
Shuai Li	University of Cambridge, UK and University of Tokyo, UK
Shuchu Han	Capital One Financial Group, Japan
Simon F. Weinberger	EssilorLuxottica, France
Siyuan Chen	Guangzhou University, China
Snehanshu Saha	BITS Pilani Goa Campus, India
Souhaib Ben Taieb	University of Mons, Abu Dhabi
Sriparna Saha	IIT Patna, India
Stefan Rueping	Fraunhofer IAIS, Germany
Stephane Chretien	Université Lyon 2, France
Sunil Aryal	Deakin University, Australia
Susana Ladra	University of A Coruña, Spain
Szymon Bobek	Jagiellonian University, Poland
Szymon Jaroszewicz	Institute of Computer Science, Poland
Szymon Wilk	Poznań University of Technology, Poland
Tanel Tammet	Tallinn University of Technology, Estonia
Thanh Thi Nguyen	Monash University, Australia
Thiago Zangato	Université Sorbonne Paris Nord, France
Theodora Tsikrika	Information Technologies Institute, Greece
Thibault Girardin	Université Jean Monnet, France
Thomas Czernichow	Darwinlabs, Portugal
Thorsteinn Rognvaldsson	Halmstad University, Sweden
Tiago Mendes-Neves	FEUP/INESC TEC, Portugal
Tianshu Yu	Chinese University of Hong Kong (Shenzhen), China
Ting Su	Imperial College London, UK

Tingrui Qiao — University of Auckland, New Zealand
Tobias Glasmachers — Ruhr-Universität Bochum, Germany
Tomas Olsson — RISE SICS, Sweden
Tome Eftimov — Jožef Stefan Institute, Slovenia
Topon Paul — Toshiba Corporation, Japan
Tsuyoshi Okita — Kyushu Institute of Technology, Japan
Unmesh Padalkar — Dream Sports, India
Vahid Shahrivari Joghan — Utrecht University, Netherlands
Valerio Bonsignori — Unipisa, Italy
Vanessa Borst — University of Würzburg, Germany
Venkata Sai Prakash Mukkamala — Quantiphi Analytics, USA
Veselka Boeva — Blekinge Institute of Technology, Sweden
Viacheslav Komisarenko — University of Tartu, Estonia
Vikas Gupta — HPCL, India
Vinayak Gupta — University of Washington, Seattle, USA
Vincent Auriau — Artefact Research Center, France
Vincenzo Pasquadibisceglie — University of Bari, Aldo Moro, Italy
Vincenzo Scotti — KASTEL, Germany
Vinothkumar Kolluru — Stevens Institute of Technology, USA
Vladimir Mic — Aarhus University, Denmark
Wang-Zhou Dai — Nanjing University, China
Wee Siong Ng — Institute for Infocomm Research, Singapore
Wei Cheng — NEC Laboratories America, USA
Wei Li — Harbin Engineering University, China
Wei Wang — Tsinghua University, China
Wei-Peng Chen — Fujitsu Research of America, USA
Wentao Wang — Michigan State University, USA
Wentao Wu — Microsoft Research, USA
Wray Buntine — VinUniversity, Vietnam
Xianchao Wu — Nvidia, USA
Xiang Lian — Kent State University, USA
Xianli Zhang — Xi'an Jiaotong University, China
Xiaobo Jin — Xi'an Jiaotong-Liverpool University, China
Xiaofei Zhou — University of Chinese Academy of Sciences, China
Xiaofeng Gao — Shanghai Jiaotong University, China
Xiaolin Han — Northwestern Polytechnical University, China
Xin Huang — Hong Kong Baptist University, China
Xin Liu — East China Normal University, China
Xing Tang — Tencent, China
Xiuqiang He — Tencent, China
Xiuyuan Hu — Tsinghua University, China

Xueping Peng	University of Technology Sydney, Australia
Yanchang Zhao	CSIRO, Australia
Yang Guo	Xidian University Hangzhou Institute of Technology, China
Yang Song	Apple, USA
Yijun Zhao	Fordham University, USA
Yinghui Wu	Case Western Reserve University, USA
Yingzhen Lin	Harbin Institute of Technology (Shenzhen), China
Yintao Yu	University of Illinois at Urbana-Champaign, USA
Yixiang Fang	Chinese University of Hong Kong, China
Yixuan Cao	Institute of Computing Technology, China
Yizheng Huang	York University, Canada
Yongchao Liu	Ant Group, China
Yu Huang	Indiana University, USA
Yu Wang	University of Oregon, USA
Yuantao Fan	Halmstad University, Sweden
Yucheng Zhou	University of Macau, China
Yue Shi	Meta, USA
Yueyuan Zheng	Beihang University, China
Yunchuan Shi	University of Sydney, Australia
Yunjun Gao	Zhejiang University, China
Yuting Ding	Southeast University, China
Yuzhuo Li	University of Auckland, New Zealand
Zahra Kharazian	Stockholm University, Sweden
Zahra Taghiyarrenani	Halmstad University, Sweden
Zahraa Abdallah	University of Bristol, UK
Zeyi Wen	Hong Kong University of Science and Technology (Guangzhou), China
Zeyu Zhu	National University of Defense Technology, China
Zhanyu Liu	Shanghai Jiao Tong University, China
Zhaogeng Liu	Jilin University, China
Zhaohui Liang	National Library of Medicine, USA
Zhen Zhang	Shandong University, China
Zhendong Chu	Squirrel Ai Learning, China
Zheng Zhang	University of California, USA
Zhengze Li	University of Göttingen, Germany
Zhibin Gu	Hebei Normal University, China
Zhuang Liu	Dongbei University of Finance and Economics, China
Ziyu Guan	Xidian University, China
Zoltan Miklos	Université de Rennes, France

Zunlei Feng   Zhejiang University, China

Program Committee – Demo Track

Andrzej Wójtowicz	Adam Mickiewicz University, Poznań, Poland
Anna Sokol	University of Notre Dame, USA
Arian Pasquali	Faktion AI, Belgium
Bruno Veloso	INESC TEC - FEP-UP, Portugal
Chongsheng Zhang	Henan University, China
Christos Doulkeridis	University of Piraeus, Greece
Danqing Zhang	PathOnAI.org, USA
Fátima Rodrigues	INESC TEC, Portugal
Grigorii Khvatskii	University of Notre Dame, USA
Joe Germino	University of Notre Dame, USA
Jungwon Seo	University of Stavanger, Norway
Ke Li	University of Exeter, England
Manfred Jaeger	Aalborg University, Denmark
Marcin Luckner	Warsaw University of Technology, Poland
Mehwish Alam	Institut Polytechnique de Paris, France
Nuno Moniz	University of Notre Dame, USA
Tânia Carvalho	FCUP, Portugal
Vitor Cerqueira	FEUP, Portugal
Wei-Wei Du	National Yang Ming Chiao Tung University, Taiwan

Additional Reviewers

Andrea D'Angelo
Patrick Altmeyer
Guiseppina Adresini
Vedangi Bengali
Michele Bernardini
Zhi Cao
Louis Carpentier
Alessio Cascione
Lilia Chebbah
Meng Ding
Roberto Esposito
Alina Fastowski
Roger Ferrod
Michele Fontana

Chang Gong
Michal Grzejdziak-Zdziarski
Paul Hahn
Antonia Hain
Md Athikul Islam
Michael Ito
Philipp Jahn
Rahul Kumar
Bishal Lakha
Yuwen Liu
Jerry Lonlac
Shijie Luo
Francesca Naretto
Navid Nobani

Diego Coello de Portugal
Joana Santos
Francesco Scala
Richard Serrano
Nuno Silva
Francesco Spinnato
Pedro C. Vieira
Xiao Wang

Yunyun Wang
Qi Wen
Jianye Xie
Huaiyuan Yao
Yutong Ye
Obaidullah Zaland
Efstratios Zaradoukas
Nan Zhang

Sponsors

Diamond

Platinum

Organization

Gold

Silver

NEC
\Orchestrating a brighter world

Bronze

Sponsored by AstraZeneca

Other Sponsors

Partners

Keynotes

Many Good Models Leads to ...

Cynthia Rudin

Duke University, USA

Abstract. As it turns out, many good models leads to amazing things! The Rashomon Effect, coined by Leo Breiman, describes the phenomenon that there exist many equally good predictive models for the same dataset.

This phenomenon happens for many real datasets, and when it does it sparks both magic and consternation, but mostly magic. In light of the Rashomon Effect, my collaborators and I propose to reshape the way we think about machine learning, particularly for tabular data problems in the nondeterministic (noisy) setting. I'll address how the Rashomon Effect impacts (1) the existence of simple-yet-accurate models, (2) flexibility to address user preferences, such as fairness and monotonicity, without losing performance, (3) uncertainty in predictions, fairness, and explanations, (4) reliable variable importance, (5) algorithm choice, specifically, providing advanced knowledge of which algorithms might be suitable for a given problem, and (6) public policy. I'll also discuss a theory of when the Rashomon Effect occurs and why: interestingly, noise in data leads to a large Rashomon Effect. My goal is to illustrate how the Rashomon Effect can have a massive impact on the use of machine learning for complex problems in society.

Towards Causal Artificial Intelligence

Elias Bareinboim

Columbia University, USA

Abstract. While a significant portion of AI scientists and engineers believe we are on the verge of achieving highly general forms of AI, I offer a critical appraisal of this view through a causal lens. In particular, building on foundational developments in the field, I will present my perspective on the relationship between intelligence and causality – and the central role of the latter in building intelligent systems and advancing credible data science.

I frame this discussion in terms of five core capabilities that we should expect from an intelligent AI system: performing causal reasoning and articulating explanations; making precise, surgical, and sample-efficient decisions; generalizing across changing conditions and environments; generating and simulating in a causally consistent manner; and learning causal structures and variables.

In this talk, I will elaborate on this perspective and share current progress toward building causally intelligent AI systems. A more detailed discussion of this thesis is provided in my forthcoming textbook, a draft of which is available here: https://causalai-book.net/.

Not Just a Trend: Institutionalizing XAI for Responsible and Compliant AI Systems

Francisco Herrera

Granada University, Spain

Abstract. As artificial intelligence (AI) systems increasingly mediate decisions in high-stakes domains – from healthcare and finance to public policy – the demand for explainable AI (XAI) has grown rapidly. Yet many current XAI approaches remain disconnected from the practical needs of stakeholders and the requirements of emerging regulatory frameworks. This talk argues that XAI must not be treated as a passing trend or optional technical add-on, but as a foundational principle in the design and deployment of AI systems. We critically examine the state of the field, exposing the gap between model-centric explainability and stakeholder-centric accountability. In response, we propose a framework that aligns explainability with legal, ethical, and social responsibilities, emphasizing co-design with affected users, sensitivity to institutional contexts, and governance over opacity. Our goal is to advance XAI from superficial compliance toward deeply integrated transparency that fosters trust, accountability, and responsible innovation.

Compositional Intelligence: Coordinating Multiple LLMs for Complex Tasks

Mirella Lapata

University of Edinburgh, UK

Abstract. Recent years have witnessed the rise of increasingly larger and more sophisticated language models (LMs) capable of performing every task imaginable, sometimes at (super)human level. In this talk, I will argue that in many realistic scenarios, solely relying on a single general-purpose LLM is suboptimal. A single LLM is likely to underrepresent real-world data distributions, heterogeneous skills, and task-specific requirements. Instead, I will discuss multi-LLM collaboration as an alternative to monolithic generative modeling. By orchestrating multiple LLMs, each with distinct roles, perspectives, or competencies, we can achieve more effective problem-solving while being more inclusive and explainable. I will illustrate this approach through two case studies: narrative story generation and visual question answering, showing how a society of agents can collectively tackle complex tasks while pursuing complementary subgoals. Additionally, I will explore how these agent societies leverage reasoning to improve performance.

Towards a Fairer World: Uncovering and Addressing Human and Algorithmic Biases

Nuria Oliver

ELLIS Alicante Foundation, Spain

Abstract. In my talk, I will first briefly present ELLIS Alicante1, the only ELLIS unit that has been created from scratch as a non-profit research foundation devoted to responsible AI for Social Good. Next, I will provide an overview of AI with a focus on the ethical implications and limitations of today's AI systems, including algorithmic discrimination and bias. On this topic, I will present a few examples of our work on uncovering and mitigating both human and algorithmic biases with AI.

On the human front, I will present the body of work that we have carried out in the context of AI-based beauty filters that are so popular on social media. On the algorithmic front, I will explain the main approaches to address algorithmic discrimination and I will present three novel methods to achieve fairer decisions.

Tensor Logic: A Simple Unification of Neural and Symbolic AI

Pedro Domingos

University of Washington, USA

Abstract. Deep learning has achieved remarkable successes in language generation and other tasks, but is extremely opaque and notoriously unreliable. Both of these problems can be overcome by combining it with the sound reasoning and transparent knowledge representation capabilities of symbolic AI. Tensor logic accomplishes this by unifying tensor algebra and logic programming, the formal languages underlying respectively deep learning and symbolic AI. Tensor logic is based on the observation that predicates are compactly represented Boolean tensors, and can be straightforwardly extended to compactly represent numeric ones. The two key constructs in tensor logic are tensor join and project, numeric operations that generalize database join and project. A tensor logic program is a set of tensor equations, each expressing a tensor as a series of tensor joins, a tensor project, and a univariate nonlinearity applied elementwise. Tensor logic programs can succinctly encode most deep architectures and symbolic AI systems, and many new combinations.

In this talk I will describe the foundations and main features of tensor logic, and present efficient inference and learning algorithms for it. A system based on tensor logic achieves state-of-the-art results on a suite of language and reasoning tasks. How tensor logic will fare on trillion-token corpora and associated tasks remains an open question.

Artificial Intelligence for Science

Sašo Džeroski

Jožef Stefan Institute, Slovenia

Abstract. Artificial intelligence is already transforming science, with its future impact expected to be even greater. Realizing this potential requires addressing key scientific challenges, such as ensuring explainability (of models and their predictions), learning effectively from limited data, and integrating data with prior domain knowledge. It also requires the provision of support for open and reproducible science through formalizing and sharing scientific knowledge.

I will present an overview of my research on the development of AI methods suitable for use in science. These include methods for explainable machine learning – including multi-target prediction and relational learning – that deliver accurate yet interpretable models suitable for complex scientific domains. These methods have been applied in environmental science, life science and materials science. Learning from limited data is critical in science. I will discuss two complementary approaches: semi-supervised learning, which leverages unlabeled data directly, together with labeled data, and foundation models, which use representations learned from vast unlabeled data to support downstream tasks with minimal supervision, i.e., limited amounts of labeled data. Both paradigms expand AI's reach into data-scarce scientific problems.

I will then present our work on automated scientific modeling, where we learn interpretable models of dynamical systems – such as process-based models and differential equations – from time series data and domain knowledge. Finally, I will highlight the role of ontologies and semantic technologies in experimental computer science, including machine learning and optimization. In these areas, we have developed ontologies for the representation and annotation of both data and other artefacts produced by science, such as algorithms, models, and results of experiments.

Contents – Part X

Industry (4.0, 5.0, Manufacturing, ...)

Physics-Based Region Clustering to Boost Inference on Computational Fluid Dynamics Flow Fields 3
   Riccardo Margheritti, Onofrio Semeraro, Maurizio Quadrio, and Giacomo Boracchi

Sparsifying Instance Segmentation Models for Efficient Vision-Based Industrial Recycling 21
   Melanie Neubauer, Ozan Özdenizci, Justus Piater, and Elmar Rueckert

Smart Cities, Transportation and Utilities (e.g., Energy)

Go with the Flow: Leveraging Physics-Informed Gradients to Solve Real-World Problems in Water Distribution Systems 41
   Inaam Ashraf, Janine Strotherm, Luca Hermes, and Barbara Hammer

Leveraging External Factors in Household-Level Electrical Consumption Forecasting Using Hypernetworks 60
   Fabien Bernier, Maxime Cordy, and Yves Le Traon

Enhancing Dynamic Control of Inertial District Energy Networks Through a Physics-Informed State-Space Model 76
   Taha Boussaid, François Rousset, Marc Clausse, and Vasile-Marian Scuturici

KCLNet: Physics-Informed Power Flow Prediction via Constraints Projections 95
   Pantelis Dogoulis, Karim Tit, and Maxime Cordy

Risk-Based Thresholding for Reliable Anomaly Detection in Concentrated Solar Power Plants 111
   Yorick Estievenart, Sukanya Patra, and Souhaib Ben Taieb

Learning Topology Actions for Power Grid Control: A Graph-Based Soft-Label Imitation Learning Approach 129
   Mohamed Hassouna, Clara Holzhüter, Malte Lehna, Matthijs de Jong, Jan Viebahn, Bernhard Sick, and Christoph Scholz

Progressive Decomposition-Enhanced Time-Varying Graph Neural
Network for Traffic Forecasting 147
Jianuo Ji, Hongbin Dong, and Xiaoping Zhang

CESI: Sparse Input Spatial Interpolation for Heterogeneous and Noisy
Hybrid Wireless Sensor Networks 164
Chaofan Li, Till Riedel, and Michael Beigl

Enhancing Traffic Accident Classifications: Application of NLP Methods
for City Safety 180
Enes Özeren, Alexander Ulbrich, Sascha Filimon, David Rügamer, and Andreas Bender

Low Visibility Forecasting Using Numerical Weather Prediction Data 196
Topon Paul, Vidhisha Reddy, Sai Prem Kumar Ayyagari, Ryusei Shingaki, Kaneharu Nishino, and Yoshiaki Shiga

Curriculum RL Meets Monte Carlo Planning: Optimization of a Real
World Container Management Problem 213
Abhijeet Pendyala and Tobias Glasmachers

Urban Verticalization and Water Consumption: A Data-Driven Approach
for São Paulo 229
Arthur Hiratsuka Rezende and André P. de L. F. de Carvalho

Order Acquisition Under Competitive Pressure: A Rapidly Adaptive
Reinforcement Learning Approach for Ride-Hailing Subsidy Strategies 246
Fangzhou Shi, Xiaopeng Ke, Xinye Xiong, Kexin Meng, Chang Men, and Zhengdan Zhu

Ordinal Aligned Domain Generalization for Sensor-Based Time Series
Regression 263
Yunchuan Shi, Wei Li, and Albert Y. Zomaya

Social Sciences (Social Good, Psycology, History, ...)

Density-Aware Walks for Coordinated Campaign Detection 283
Atul Anand Gopalakrishnan, Jakir Hossain, Tuğrulcan Elmas, and Ahmet Erdem Sarıyüce

Fairness is in the Details : Face Dataset Auditing 299
Valentin Lafargue, Emmanuelle Claeys, and Jean-Michel Loubes

Sports

On Identifying Fast Road Races: Decomposing Race Conditions
and Individual Performance Level 319
   Klaus Brinker

Trajectory Imputation in Multi-agent Sports with Derivative-Accumulating
Self-ensemble 336
   *Han-Jun Choi, Hyunsung Kim, Minho Lee, Minchul Jeong,
Changjo Kim, Jinsung Yoon, and Sang-Ki Ko*

A Scalable Approach for Unified Large Events Models in Soccer 354
   Tiago Mendes-Neves, Luís Meireles, and João Mendes-Moreira

Web and Social Networks

Who is at Risk? Analyzing the Risk of Radicalization Among Reddit Users 375
   Ece Calikus, Gianmarco De Francisci Morales, and Aristides Gionis

Knowledge Distillation for Job Title Prediction and Project
Recommendation in Open Source Communities 393
   Xin Liu, Hang Su, and Xuesong Lu

Collaborative Interest-Aware Graph Learning for Group Identification 410
   Rui Zhao, Beihong Jin, Beibei Li, and Yiyuan Zheng

MASTFM: Meta-learning and Data Augmentation to Stress Test
Forecasting Models 427
   Ricardo Inácio, Vítor Cerqueira, Marília Barandas, and Carlos Soares

Time Series Machine Learning with Aeon: Classification and Regression 432
   *Matthew Middlehurst, Anthony Bagnall, Germain Forestier,
Ali Ismail-Fawaz, and Antoine Guillaume*

Machine Learning for Data Streams with CapyMOA 438
   *Yibin Sun, Heitor Murilo Gomes, Anton Lee, Nuwan Gunasekara,
Guilherme Weigert Cassales, Jia Justin Liu, Marco Heyden,
Vitor Cerqueira, Maroua Bahri, Yun Sing Koh, Bernhard Pfahringer,
and Albert Bifet*

ProxyLLM : LLM-Driven Framework for Customer Support Through
Text-Style Transfer 444
   Sehyeong Jo and Jungwon Seo

Introducing PYRA: A High-Level Linter for Data Science Software 449
  Greta Dolcetti, Vincenzo Arceri, Antonella Mensi, Enea Zaffanella,
  Caterina Urban, and Agostino Cortesi

SustainaML: Enhancing Transparency, Control, and Green Sustainability
in AutoML 454
  Mehak Mushtaq Malik and Radwa El Shawi

An LLM-Based Decision Support System for Strategic Decision-Making 460
  Majd Alkayyal, Simon Malberg, and Georg Groh

BellatrExplorer: An Interactive Random Forest Local Explainability
Dashboard 465
  Robbe D'hondt and Celine Vens

T-REX: Table – Refute or Entail eXplainer 470
  Tim Luka Horstmann, Baptiste Geisenberger, and Mehwish Alam

Fairbeat: Assessing and Mitigating Bias with the Composite Balance Score 475
  Pierre-Antoine Lequeu, Sofiane Lagraa, Geoffroy Robin,
  and Moussa Ouedraogo

PRIMULA- 3for Probabilistic Modeling and Reasoning on Graph Data 481
  Raffaele Pojer and Manfred Jaeger

LLM GameLab: An Interactive Platform for Testing Large Language
Models in Board Games 486
  Paulina Morillo, Alex Terreros, Cèsar Ferri, and José Hernández-Orallo

EXTREMUM: A Web-Based Tool to Generate and Explore Counterfactual
Explanations on Tabular and Time-Series Data 491
  Athanasios Lakes, Luis Quintero, and Panagiotis Papapetrou

VisualTreeSearch: Understanding Web Agent Test-Time Scaling 497
  Danqing Zhang, Yaoyao Qian, Shiying He, Yuanli Wang, Jingyi Ni,
  and Junyu Cao

DetoxAI: A Python Toolkit for Debiasing Deep Learning Models
in Computer Vision 502
  Ignacy Stępka, Lukasz Sztukiewicz, Michał Wiliński,
  and Jerzy Stefanowski

Obfuscation of Sensitive Text in Audiovisual Content Using AI 506
  Kexin Jiang-Chen and Cèsar Ferri

WildInsight: a Chatbot for Wildlife Conservation Research 511
  Anna Sokol, Xiangliang Zhang, and Nitesh V. Chawla

Future Designer - Generative AI Meets Interior Design 516
  Filip Nowicki, Arkadiusz Charliński, and Andrzej Wójtowicz

Author Index 521

Industry (4.0, 5.0, Manufacturing, ...)

Physics-Based Region Clustering to Boost Inference on Computational Fluid Dynamics Flow Fields

Riccardo Margheritti[1]([✉]), Onofrio Semeraro[2], Maurizio Quadrio[3], and Giacomo Boracchi[1]

[1] DEIB, Politecnico di Milano, 20133 Milano, Italy
{riccardo.margheritti,giacomo.boracchi}@polimi.it
[2] Lab. Interdisciplinaire des Sciences du Numérique (LISN), CNRS, Univ. Paris-Saclay, 91400 Orsay, France
onofrio.semeraro@universite-paris-saclay.fr
[3] DAER, Politecnico di Milano, 20133 Milano, Italy
maurizio.quadrio@polimi.it

Abstract. The high dimensionality and variability of Computational Fluid Dynamics (CFD) data pose a significant challenge for Machine Learning (ML) models. The only solutions in the literature addressing inference from CFD flow fields are based on expert-driven features, which consist of fluid dynamic quantities averaged on specific regions of the entire computational domain. However, using handcrafted features can limit the scalability and portability of existing methods, and result in the loss of critical flow field information that might be essential for capturing non-linear patterns inherent in the CFD data. We propose a method to replace handcrafted features with features defined on regions obtained by clustering. Our approach combines: i) physics-based clustering, to identify meaningful regions within the flow field, ii) cluster-based feature extraction, to capture localized fluid dynamics properties, and iii) set-learning models to process the extracted information. Our solution allows integrating physics-based modeling with ML, and provides a portable and flexible pipeline capable of effectively dealing with the variability and dimensionality of CFD flow fields. We validate our method on publicly available CFD datasets (from the aerospace domain) and apply it to a realistic scenario, that is, the classification of pathologies in real 3D human upper airways extracted from CT scans, acquired in collaboration with a medical hospital. Experimental results demonstrate the accuracy and scalability of our method, and highlight its potential for leveraging CFD data in ML frameworks for other scientific and engineering applications.

Keywords: Computational Fluid Dynamics · Machine Learning · Physics-Based Clustering · Set Learning · Features Extraction

1 Introduction

Computational Fluid Dynamics (CFD), i.e., solving the numerical version of differential equations of the fluid motion, plays a crucial role in a large number of applications [1]. By solving the Navier–Stokes equations over a discretized domain, CFD provides detailed information on velocity, pressure, and several other flow variables, simulating real-world problems in a wide spectrum of fields, from aerodynamics [2] and weather prediction [3] to biomedical engineering (e.g., airflow analysis in respiratory diseases), and energy applications (e.g., wind farms and turbomachinery). From CFD, experts can evaluate performance, optimize designs, and gain a deeper understanding of fluid behavior in complex systems. The high dimensionality of CFD outputs and the computational cost of simulations, however, pose significant challenges for data analysis through Machine Learning (ML). Gathering annotated CFD datasets, in fact, is particularly difficult, as generating labeled data often requires running expensive simulations and relying on expert domain knowledge. Moreover, the size and complexity of CFD flow fields, which often involve millions of spatial points and tens of flow variables per point, make it impractical to directly train ML models on raw CFD data. This underscores the need for compact and informative data representations. Yet, ML represents a natural approach to CFD, as it can reduce computational burden, provide valuable insights, and extract meaningful patterns from fluid dynamics.

The classical approach for feeding CFD data to a ML model consists of a handcrafted feature extraction, where domain experts or CFD specialists design features to capture specific flow properties within selected regions. These regions are spatial subdomains of the flow field, defined based on prior knowledge, whose selection process acts as an information filtering step that substantially reduces the dimensionality of the CFD data. Despite being intuitive, this procedure introduces a critical limitation: the same selected regions must be consistently identified and propagated to all the samples in the training and test sets, which may not always be straightforward. As an example, in the context of airflow analysis within the human upper airways, Schillaci et al. [4] proposed a CFD classifier that serves as a precursor to our work. In particular, they define cross-sectional planes a priori within simplified human geometries (visible in the middle of Fig. 1) to extract averaged flow features. While this approach reduces data dimensionality, it also imposes rigid constraints that may limit generalization to new samples with different anatomical variations or airflow conditions. To the best of our knowledge, this is also the only method currently addressing the inference of non-computable quantities from CFD data, and therefore constitutes the current state of the art for this task. Although effective, handcrafted features can limit portability, lead to information loss, and require intensive domain expertise. Recent advances in ML, particularly in unsupervised learning and deep learning models, offer new opportunities to address these limitations [2,3].

In this work, we propose a method to overcome the drawbacks of handcrafted feature extraction by making a step towards data-driven methods. Our idea is to identify adaptive regions inside the flow field through clustering and extract features from these, without relying on any a priori engineered region selection. We ground our approach on three main components: i) a physics-based clustering, inspired by [3], that identifies meaningful regions in the flow field by leveraging

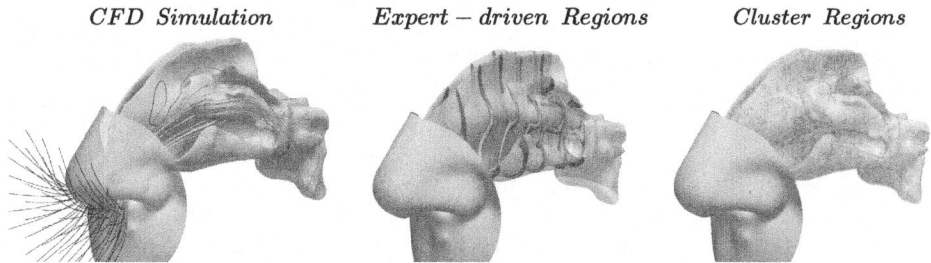

Fig. 1. On the left, the figure shows the flow streamlines in the upper airways. The middle highlights Schillaci et al.'s [4] cross-sections for CFD feature extraction, while the right shows regions from our clustering algorithm.

the physical principles inherent in the governing equations; ii) in-cluster features extraction, which captures localized fluid dynamic properties along with geometrical and statistical quantities; and iii) set learning models [5] to process the information extracted from clusters.

Unlike traditional expert-driven region selection, our clustering algorithm adopts a data-driven approach grounded on the governing equations of fluid dynamics to define the regions on which we compute features. An example of this can be seen on the right-hand side of Fig. 1, which illustrates the application of such clustering to human upper airways. By defining these regions using physical principles rather than heuristic choices, we ensure greater generalizability and adaptability across different scenarios, making our method inherently more portable than expert-driven approaches. However, replacing predefined regions with clusters introduces new challenges: since the number and order of clusters are not fixed a priori, directly comparing clusters across different samples becomes challenging. To address this, we adopt two complementary strategies: one directly processes the unordered clusters using set-learning models, which operate on unordered sets of features and do not require a predefined cluster order, while the other restores cluster comparability through a propagation mechanism, mapping clusters from a reference sample onto new samples to preserve consistency in cluster definition. These strategies enable our method to effectively handle variability in cluster structures while retaining the advantages of a physics-based, data-driven approach. Another key advantage of our method is that we can extrapolate information from the whole CFD data without relying on sub-portions of the computational domain, which inevitably leads to a loss of information.

We conduct our experiments on different scenarios of increasing complexity. First, we validate our method on two large datasets of 2D flow fields from the aerospace domain, including both publicly available data [6] and an extended version we generated. In this setting, where a large amount of data is available, we focus on two regression tasks: i) predicting the 4-digit NACA (National Advisory Committee for Aeronautics) airfoil code as in [4], and ii) estimating parametrized geometric defects (e.g., bumps, cavities, or cut trailing edges) on the surface of NACA airfoils. To further assess the robustness of our approach in a more challenging real-world scenario with limited data, we apply it to iii) the classification of pathologies in 3D human upper airways extracted from patients' CT scans. Despite the reduced number of samples in this setting, our method maintains consistent performance, demonstrating its ability to generalize across different flow domains and data availability conditions.

The main contributions of our work are: i) We extract informative features from CFD data by identifying physics-based regions in the flow field; ii) We take a step toward end-to-end processing of CFD data for ML models, moving beyond existing expert-driven methods; iii) We validate our approach on datasets of varying complexity, showing improved performance over the state-of-the-art method by Schillaci et al. [4].

2 Related Work

Over the past 5–10 years, the application of ML in the field of fluid mechanics has experienced significant growth. This is evident from the increasing quantity and quality of published material [1,7,8]. The dominant use of ML for CFD focuses on bypassing the solution of differential equations that govern fluid motion, e.g., by physics-informed neural networks (PINNs) [9,10]. Another prominent research direction addresses turbulence modeling, where for instance, Ling et al. [11] used deep neural networks to refine the Spalart-Allmaras turbulence model [12]. Fukami et al. [13] explored ML for regression tasks, such as flow field reconstruction and estimation, and applied convolutional neural networks for super-resolution tasks, training models to extract key flow features. However, these studies primarily aim to improve or accelerate existing CFD capabilities by using fluid dynamic quantities as both input and output of their ML models. In contrast, our work focuses on a less-explored area: extracting meaningful information from CFD data to predict quantities that CFD alone cannot compute (e.g., pathologies). This problem is particularly challenging because of the dimensionality of CFD data and the difficulty in finding public datasets of annotated CFD simulations.

Given the large amount of data returned from CFD, feeding a ML model directly with flow fields is computationally prohibitive, whereby feature extraction methods are crucial to reduce complexity and focus on the most relevant information. A classical approach to feature extraction relies on expert-driven, handcrafted features designed to capture specific flow properties in predefined regions. For instance, Schillaci et al. [4] extracted predefined spatial regions from the flow field, and averaged fluid dynamic quantities within each region. This method was used to infer geometric properties in two different scenarios: i) predicting the NACA code from CFD data around airfoils, and ii) identifying pathologies from the internal flow in a simplified human nose. While effective, this approach relies heavily on domain expertise, is restricted to small sub-portions of the flow field, which may lead to the loss of critical information, and lacks portability across different scenarios.

Recent advances in ML, particularly in unsupervised learning and deep learning models, offer new opportunities to overcome the limitations of expert-driven approaches and highlight a growing trend toward end-to-end methods. For instance, Callaham et al. [3] employ Gaussian mixture models (GMM) and sparse principal component analysis (SPCA) to identify dominant physical processes in CFD flow fields. Their method segments flow regions based on local balance relationships in the governing equations, enabling the discovery of physically meaningful subspaces where certain terms in the Navier–Stokes equations can be neglected. Similarly, Saetta et al. [2] employ GMMs to segment homogeneous flow regions in CFD solutions, identifying boundary layers, shock waves, and external inviscid flow. Their approach eliminates the need for case-dependent thresholds and human intervention, achieving results comparable to reference methods in aerodynamics. These works exemplify the increasing adoption of ML for structuring CFD data and enhancing analysis beyond traditional heuristic techniques. However, while [2] and [3] focus on data exploration and unsupervised structure identification, our approach leverages physics-based clustering explicitly for feature extraction and supervised inference. To the best of our knowledge, end-to-end trainable solutions have not yet been adopted in high-fidelity flow fields, and the method proposed by Schillaci et al. [4] remains the only published approach that uses CFD data to predict quantities that cannot be directly computed from the flow variables themselves. Inspired by [2] and [3], we target the prediction of such non-computable quantities (e.g., airfoil defects, pathologies), integrating flow segmentation into a trainable pipeline for regression and classification tasks. By grounding clustering on the governing equations rather than heuristics, we enhance portability and mark a significant step toward end-to-end ML methods for CFD analysis.

3 Problem Formulation

The flow field returned by a CFD simulation consists of a set of scalar and vector fields defined over a spatial domain $\Omega \subset \mathbb{R}^3$, discretized into n cells. These fields are derived by solving the discretized Navier–Stokes equations with boundary conditions applied to the geometrical boundary $\Gamma \subset \mathbb{R}^3$. CFD simulations typically produce several output flow variables, which are usually time-dependent. To simplify the analysis, we remove the dependency on time by considering steady-state solutions or time-averaged quantities, whereby a generic vectorial flow quantity $\boldsymbol{\phi}$ can be written in Cartesian coordinates as:

$$\boldsymbol{\phi}(\mathbf{x}) = \left[\phi_x(\mathbf{x}), \phi_y(\mathbf{x}), \phi_z(\mathbf{x})\right]^T,$$

where $\mathbf{x} = (x, y, z) \in \Omega$.

Each cell i in the discretized domain Ω is associated with a vector $\mathbf{Q}_i \in \mathbb{R}^D$ of D flow variables, such that $\mathbf{Q}_i = \left[q_1, q_2, \ldots, q_D\right]^T$, where each q_i represents either a spatial coordinate, a scalar flow variable $\phi(\boldsymbol{x})$ (e.g., pressure), or a component of a vectorial flow quantity $\boldsymbol{\phi}(\boldsymbol{x})$ (e.g., velocity components u_x, u_y, u_z).

The complete CFD output can be represented as a matrix $\mathbf{F} \in \mathbb{R}^{n \times D}$, containing all flow quantities across the discretized domain:

$$\mathbf{F} = \begin{bmatrix} \mathbf{Q}_1, \mathbf{Q}_2, \cdots, \mathbf{Q}_n \end{bmatrix}^T.$$

In some applications (e.g., human upper airways), n can easily range in the order of $n \approx 10^7$, while the dimensionality of each cell, D, typically spans tens of flow variables.

Our objective is to train a model $\mathcal{K}$ that predicts a target variable Y from the CFD data $\mathbf{F}$, $\mathcal{K} : \mathbf{F} \mapsto Y$, where Y may represent categorical (e.g., pathology classification) or continuous values (e.g., defects parameters). This requires a labeled training dataset $\{(\mathbf{F}_j, Y_j)\}$, where $\mathbf{F}_j$ represents the input features extracted from the j-th simulation, and Y_j denotes the corresponding target variable.

4 Method

Our method starts with the construction of the matrix $\mathbf{C} \in \mathbb{R}^{n \times N}$ from the CFD data matrix $\mathbf{F} \in \mathbb{R}^{n \times D}$. We do that by inserting the raw flow variables from $\mathbf{F}$ into the governing equations of the CFD solver, computing N derived quantities corresponding to the N terms that appear in the equations (top-right corner of Fig. 2). A clustering algorithm is then applied to the rows of $\mathbf{C}$, where each row is associated with a single CFD cell represented by its N derived quantities. The clustering step groups the flow field into meaningful regions based on this physics-based representation (bottom-right corner of Fig. 2), capturing the underlying dynamics of the flow. Thus, within each cluster, characterized by a specific physical phenomenon (illustrated at the bottom of Fig. 2), we compute fluid dynamic and geometric features, such as average flow quantities, cluster areas, and centroids. Clustering reduces the dimensionality of each simulation by condensing the data into a compact set of vectors $\mathbf{P}$, where each vector represents a cluster and contains features extracted from it, associated with the cluster's centroid. This set of feature vectors is then used as input to an ML model trained to predict different target quantities (bottom-left of Fig. 2).

4.1 Physics-Based Clustering

To reduce the dimensionality of $\mathbf{F}$ and extract meaningful structures, we apply clustering to the CFD data. The clustering step is based on the physics of the problem, as it leverages terms derived from the momentum equations of motion of the model we use to perform CFD simulations, such as the Reynolds-averaged Navier–Stokes (RANS) equations [14], or Large Eddy simulations (LES) equations, as inputs of the clustering algorithm.

Clustering Inputs. Inspired by [3], we apply clustering not directly to the CFD matrix $\mathbf{F} \in \mathbb{R}^{n \times D}$, but to a transformed matrix $\mathbf{C} \in \mathbb{R}^{n \times N}$, obtained by a

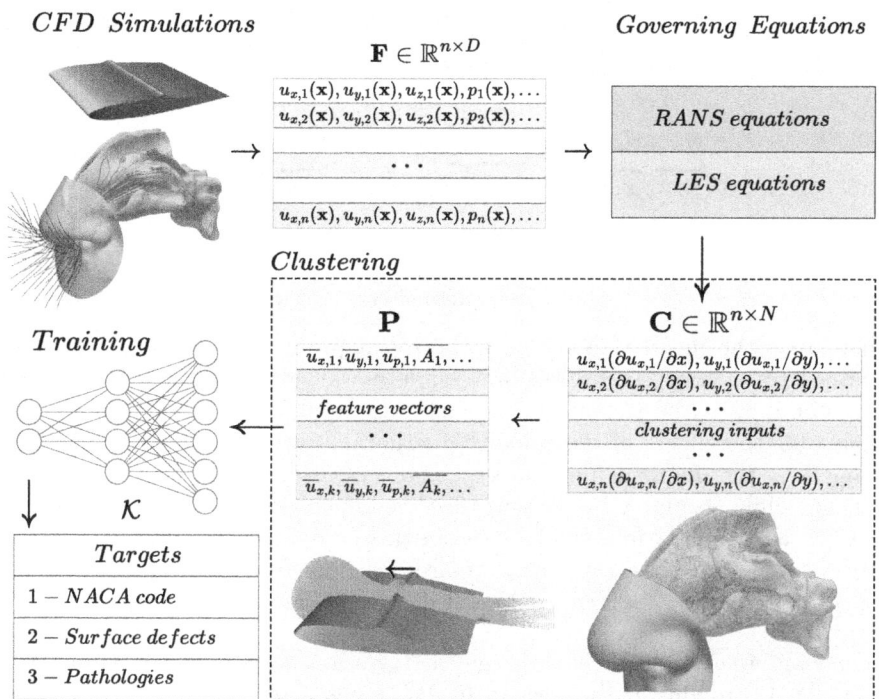

Fig. 2. Overview of our method. Starting from CFD simulations, we collect the flow field data in the matrix $\mathbf{F} \in \mathbb{R}^{n \times D}$ (top-left). We derive the matrix $\mathbf{C}$ by processing $\mathbf{F}$ through the governing equations (top-right), and use it as input for the physics-based clustering of the flow domain. The clustering step groups the flow field into meaningful regions, capturing the underlying physical properties. From each cluster, we extract statistical, geometric, and physical features, building a set of feature vectors $\mathbf{P}$ (bottom-right). These are then fed into a machine learning model $\mathcal{K}$ for training (bottom-left), with the goal of predicting target quantities.

mapping of $\mathbf{F}$ through the governing equations. In CFD, each cell in the computational domain is represented by a vector of flow variables $\mathbf{Q}_i \in \mathbb{R}^D$ (as mentioned in Sect. 3), containing raw CFD quantities such as velocity, pressure, and turbulence-related terms. Similarly, each column of $\mathbf{C}$ is defined cell-by-cell by a new vector of CFD quantities $\mathbf{C}_i \in \mathbb{R}^N$ which contains the terms of the equations used by the CFD solver. This transformation maps the CFD data $\mathbf{F} \in \mathbb{R}^{n \times D}$ to the matrix $\mathbf{C} \in \mathbb{R}^{n \times N}$, where in general $N < D$. By applying clustering directly to the rows of $\mathbf{C}$, which include the terms derived from the governing equations, we ensure that the process captures the underlying physics, allowing the model to identify meaningful regions guided by the flow dynamics.

We report in (1) the RANS equations, an analytical model for turbulent flows that decomposes flow variables into a mean component, which represents the averaged flow behavior in time, and a fluctuating component, which captures turbulence effects. For RANS equations, $\mathbf{C}_i$ includes the Cartesian components of the advection term, pressure gradient, turbulent and laminar diffusion, and turbulent kinetic energy (TKE) terms, namely:

$$\underbrace{\nabla \cdot (\mathbf{u} \otimes \mathbf{u})}_{\text{Advection}} = \underbrace{\nu \nabla^2 \mathbf{u}}_{\text{Laminar diffusion}} + \underbrace{\nabla \cdot (\nu_t \nabla \mathbf{u})}_{\text{Turbulent diffusion}} - \underbrace{\frac{1}{\rho} \nabla p}_{\text{Pressure gradient}} - \underbrace{\nabla \left(\frac{2}{3} k\right)}_{\text{TKE}}, \quad (1)$$

where $\mathbf{u}$ is the mean velocity, p is the mean pressure, ρ is the fluid density (assumed to be constant for incompressible flows), ν is the kinematic viscosity of the fluid, ν_t is the turbulent viscosity computed via a turbulence model to account for the effects of the velocity fluctuations u'_i and pressure fluctuations p', and k is the TKE, defined as $k = \frac{1}{2}(\mathbf{u}' \cdot \mathbf{u}')$. The operator ∇ denotes the gradient, while $\nabla \cdot$ and ∇^2 represent the divergence and Laplacian, respectively. For LES, we define $\mathbf{C}$ in a similar way: in this case, a spatial filtering operation replaces time averaging, separating the resolved large-scale structures from the subgrid-scale motions, which are modeled through turbulence closures.

Clustering Algorithm. We leverage a Bayesian Gaussian Mixture Model (BGMM) [15] to cluster the rows of $\mathbf{C}$. By doing that, we identify flow regions based on the underlying physical properties of the flow (at the bottom of Fig. 2), which we then use to extract features in $\mathbf{P}$. The key characteristic of the BGMM is the use of covariance matrices to model the statistical distribution of each cluster extracted from $\mathbf{C}$, effectively capturing correlations between the terms in (1). This allows the BGMM to distinguish regions governed by different flow phenomena, such as boundary layer development, shear layers, separation zones, and wake structures. Moreover, the variational Bayesian inference framework autonomously determines the optimal number of clusters k, eliminating manual tuning and allowing each simulation to return a different number of clusters. By doing that, the clustering adapts to the physics of each simulation, making our method as general as possible. To improve numerical stability and convergence, we initialize the Gaussian components using the centroids obtained from k-means clustering.

4.2 Feature Extraction

We associate each cluster with its centroid and compute a set of in-cluster quantities to be used as a feature vector. The idea is to generalize the regional averaging approach used in [4], replacing predefined spatial regions with clusters while incorporating a broader set of features. These include the averages of flow variables, turbulence quantities, and clustering inputs defined in Sect. 4.1 as columns of $\mathbf{C}$, weighted by the cell area or volume, along with the cluster area or volume. This process reduces the dimensionality of the clustering input $\mathbf{C} \in \mathbb{R}^{n \times N}$ to a compact set of feature vectors $\mathbf{P} = \{\mathbf{P}_i \in \mathbb{R}^l, \ i = 1, ..., k\}$, where $k \ll n$ is the number of clusters returned by the BGMM, and $l = \mathcal{O}(N)$ represents the number of extracted features per cluster. Notably, $\mathbf{P}_i$ also includes the coordinates of the centroids to preserve spatial information, which is fundamental for a Point Transformer, the architecture we employ for set learning. We further highlight that $\mathbf{P}$ is not directly comparable across different flow fields, as both k and the ordering of clusters in $\mathbf{P}$ can vary from case to case.

4.3 Clustering Strategies

The clustering process condenses the CFD data from the matrix $\mathbf{C} \in \mathbb{R}^{n \times N}$ to a more compact set representation $\mathbf{P}$. In this process, however, we cannot directly control the ordering of the clusters returned by the BGMM, that is, the order in which the clusters appear in set $\mathbf{P}$. Therefore, using a non-permutation invariant ML model $\mathcal{K}$ can lead to mutually inconsistent training samples and misclassification. We thus adopt two different strategies to build the set $\mathbf{P}$:

– *Free clustering (C-FREE)*: We let the order and the number of the clusters vary in each simulation by applying a BGMM independently to each CFD flow field. By adopting this approach, the order of the k clusters in $\mathbf{P}$ is uncontrolled and needs to be accounted for in the choice of model $\mathcal{K}$. Nevertheless, we do not impose any fixed clustering structure, and the method is more flexible and adaptive to different flow conditions and scenarios. Here, we treat $\mathbf{P}$ as an ensemble of feature vectors where the ordering is not relevant. We use a set-learning model [5] for $\mathcal{K}$ trained on $\mathbf{P}$, providing a straightforward solution that naturally handles unordered data sets.
– *Clustering propagation (C-PROP)*: Set-learning models are less effective than classical MLPs on ordered data. Therefore, we provide a method to consistently define clusters across different simulations. In particular, we first select a reference CFD simulation where clusters have been computed as described in Sect. 4.1. We then propagate these clusters to all other CFD flow fields by matching the clustered data in $\mathbf{C}$ to those of the reference simulation. Specifically, given $\mathbf{C}^{\mathrm{ref}}$ from the reference clusters and $\mathbf{C}^s$ from a new simulation s, we assign each cell in $\mathbf{C}^s_j$ to the closest cells $\mathbf{C}^{\mathrm{ref}}_i$ based on a Euclidean distance metric $d(\mathbf{C}^{\mathrm{ref}}_i, \mathbf{C}^s_j)$. This matching process is implemented using a *k-d tree* [16], and the core rationale relies on preserving similarity in the space of the columns of $\mathbf{C}$.

As the clustering inputs are derived directly from the terms of the governing equations, we ensure that the cluster propagation inherently captures the physics of the problem. With this approach, on the one hand, we preserve the number and the order of the clusters in $\mathbf{P}$ across simulations, maintaining consistency in the representation of the flow field and enabling direct comparisons between simulations. On the other hand, we constrain simulations to only capture the physical phenomena that characterize the reference simulations, reducing generality.

4.4 Inference Models

Depending on the clustering strategy we adopt, we employ different ML models: in *C-PROP*, where the clustering is propagated from the reference $\mathbf{C}^{\text{ref}}$, we train a simple MLP. However, in the case of *C-FREE*, we require a model capable of handling sets as input, i.e., unordered inputs of varying dimensions. To achieve this, in the *C-FREE* setting, we use for $\mathcal{K}$ a Point Transformer model (PT) [5] which provides a dual advantage: along with the invariance to input order, it also extracts spatial information from the clusters by leveraging self-attention mechanisms specifically designed for point clouds, modeling interactions between features extracted from clusters based on their geometric proximity and feature similarity. This ability to learn spatially-aware representations can be a fundamental aspect in a CFD context as spatial information is crucial for understanding the physics of the problem. Furthermore, as we work with relatively small yet inherently highly complex datasets, it is essential to extract as much meaningful information as possible to enhance the learning process and improve inference performance.

5 Experiments

We test our method on three distinct tasks of increasing complexity, each addressing a different application of CFD analysis: airfoil shape identification, surface defect detection on airfoils, and pathology classification in real human upper airways extracted from patients' CT scans. In each scenario, we conduct four parallel experiments in which we extract features in set $\mathbf{P}$ using different methods, as described in the following section. We directly compare our pipeline against the handcrafted-feature-based approach proposed by Schillaci et al. [4], which represents the current state of the art for the inference of non-computable quantities from CFD data, and use it as a baseline across all tasks. We first validate our approach on a publicly available dataset [6] and an extended version that we produced. These datasets consist of 2D flow fields with a large number of samples, allowing for extensive evaluation. Then, we apply our method to a more realistic real-world problem, that is, pathology identification in human upper airways directly extracted from CT scans, where data availability is significantly more limited and expensive. Additionally, this dataset consists of 3D flow fields, increasing the complexity of the problem by introducing an additional spatial dimension and geometric variability. This transition from a controlled, data-rich 2D setting to a real-world, data-scarce 3D scenario enables a comprehensive assessment of the method's adaptability and robustness.

5.1 Considered Methods

In this section, we describe the experiments we performed to evaluate our method. We consider 4 parallel approaches to extract $\mathbf{P}$, each differing in the clustering and feature selection strategy. The first approach, *HC* (Hand-Crafted features), serves as a baseline method. It relies on expert-driven feature selection proposed in [4], where CFD quantities are manually extracted based on prior domain knowledge, without leveraging clustering. In *CR+HC* (Clustering Regions with Hand-Crafted features), we introduce our clustering method to identify regions, while retaining the same feature as in *HC*. This allows us to assess how clustering influences performance without altering the feature set with respect to *HC*. A more data-driven approach is adopted in *FREE-CR+FC* (Free Cluster Regions with Full Clustering features), where both clustering regions and feature selection are determined without constraints using the *C-FREE* strategy, described in Sect. 4.3. In this case, we employ a PT for training and testing, as detailed in Sect. 4.4. Finally, in *PROP-CR+FC* (Propagated Cluster Regions with Full Clustering features), we enforce cluster consistency across simulations by propagating clusters from a reference case using the *C-PROP* strategy. Unlike *FREE-CR+FC*, this approach aligns clusters across different flow fields, allowing for direct comparisons of their feature representations. Similarly to *HC* and *CR+HC*, in this method we employ an MLP for training and testing. In the following paragraphs, we provide details on the dataset structure and the process used to generate features for each experiment.

5.2 Datasets and Tasks

Airfoil Shape Identification (AirNACA). We consider the family of NACA (National Advisory Committee for Aeronautics) four-digit airfoils. We aim to train a regressor $\mathcal{K}$ that predicts the NACA code, thus the airfoil shape, directly from the CFD solution. The shape of a NACA airfoil is defined by a four-digit code, which parametrizes the maximum camber as a percentage of the chord c (I digit, ranging from 0 to 9, where c is the straight-line distance from the airfoil leading to the trailing edge), its position along the chord in tenths of c (II digits, also from 0 to 9)), and the maximum thickness as a percentage of c (last two digits together, ranging from 05 to 50). Therefore, the identification task reduces to a regression over 3 integer numbers.

The 2D computational domain Ω is centered on the airfoil and extends over a radius of $500c$, with unitary chord c, comprising an order of $\mathcal{O}(10^5)$ discretized cells. The angle of attack is set to $\alpha = 10°$, with a freestream velocity of $30\,\text{m/s}$, and the RANS equations are used for turbulence modeling. The dataset comprises 3025 different flow fields, generated by varying the NACA digits and solving the corresponding CFD problems. The complete dataset of RANS simulations is publicly available on Zenodo (10.5281/zenodo.4638071 [6]; the source code of the proposed framework for the *AirNACA* task is provided at 10.5281/zenodo.15637850.

Surface Defect Detection (AirDEF). The second dataset extends the NACA airfoil dataset by introducing controlled geometric deformations to simulate manufacturing defects, structural damage, or ice accretion. The simulation setup remains identical to the previous case, maintaining the same computational domain, boundary conditions, and freestream parameters. We consider bumps, cavities, and cut trailing edges, which are parameterized and encoded in a 3-digit code. Each airfoil undergoes controlled deformations by introducing a set of 18 different surface defects applied individually or in combination, for a total of 3600 CFD flow fields. Bumps and cavities, as shown in Fig. 4, are modeled with Gaussian functions at the chord midpoint: a bump raises a section of the airfoil, while a cavity creates a small indentation. The first two digits ([−2:2]) define the orientation (bump or cavity) and the intensity of the deformation, which can reach up to the 4% of the chord c. The last digit ([0:2]) controls the intensity of the cut at the trailing edge, which can raise up to the 5% of c.

Pathology Identification in Real Upper Airways (NosePAT). The third dataset consists of LES simulations of airflows in human upper airways, focusing on the identification of septal deviations and turbinate hypertrophies on real 3D patient geometries obtained from CT scan segmentation. A septal deviation is a condition where the nasal septum is deviated to one side, potentially obstructing airflow and causing breathing difficulties. Turbinate hypertrophy refers to the excessive enlargement of the nasal turbinates, leading to nasal congestion.

The dataset is derived from 7 CT scans of healthy patients provided by *ASST Santi Paolo e Carlo*, a medical institution we are collaborating with. ENT (Ear, Nose, and Throat) specialists manually introduced geometric deformations to synthetically simulate nasal pathologies, varying their locations and severities to create a diverse set of pathological cases. This process resulted in 309 synthetic pathological geometries, on which we performed LES simulations of a steady-state inspiration. The CFD simulations were performed using Open-FOAM, employing the LES technique under incompressible flow assumptions. By using real CT scans for dataset generation, this approach captures anatomical variability while preserving realism. In addition to the 309 synthetic geometries, we extracted 10 real pathological cases (5 septal deviations, 5 hypertrophies) from CT scans to evaluate whether a model trained on synthetic data can accurately detect real conditions (we refer to this experiment as **_NoseREAL_**).

The computational domain discretizes the upper airways' internal volume, enclosing the nostrils within a spherical boundary to simulate an open environment. Each mesh consists of $\mathcal{O}(10^7)$ cells, each storing tens of fluid dynamic quantities. Simulations run on 96 cores on a high-performance computing system, requiring 160 GB of RAM and tens of thousands of core-hours, producing around 40 GB of data each. Generating real human upper airway data demands specialized expertise and substantial computational resources.

Figure 3 shows the cumulative distribution of mesh cells and total volume by cell size. Most cells' volume range between 2×10^{-13} m^3 and 5×10^{-13} m^3, but they contribute minimally to the total volume, which is largely concentrated (80%) in cells around 3×10^{-10} m^3. To reduce computational costs, after LES simulations, we filter out cells with $V < 3 \times 10^{-12}$ m^3 (violet dashed line in Fig. 3), reducing data by 91% while retaining 95% of the total volume. The removed cells, located near walls (on a millimeter scale), are essential for CFD accuracy but contain little information related to pathology effects, which manifest on larger

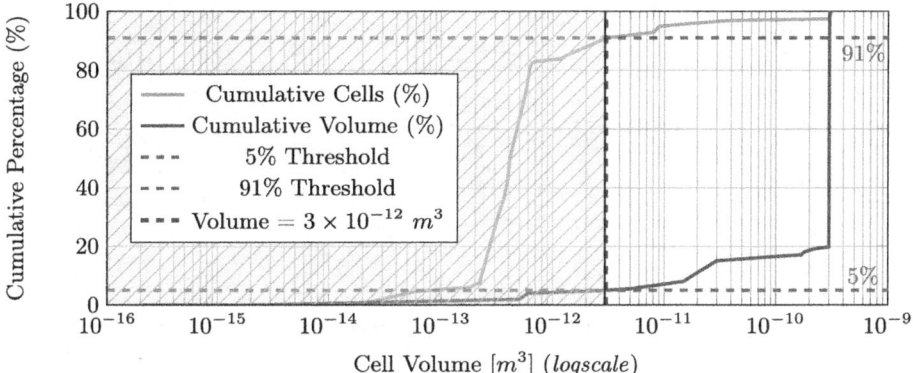

Fig. 3. Cumulative percentage distribution of Cell Volume and Number of Cells with respect to the size of the cells. The dashed lines represent the percentage of volume we lose with the filtering (red line), the percentage of memory we save (light blue line), and the volume threshold (violet line). (Color figure online)

scales. This filtering is purely for computational efficiency, and including these cells would only add information, potentially improving performance.

5.3 Feature Extraction

For the **HC** experiment, we compute the same features from the CFD flow fields as in [4]. In *AirNACA* and *AirDEF*, this involves computing region-averaged velocity magnitude and pressure on expert-defined regions along three vertical lines perpendicular to the airfoil chord (left-hand side of Fig. 4) at $x = -c$, $x = 1c$, and $x = 10c$. Each segment contains 8 regions symmetrically distributed around $y = 0$, with boundaries defined by the y-coordinates at $[-500, -10, -1, -0.1, 0, 0.1, 1, 10, 500]c$. Each regional average is weighted over the cells' area to account for their uneven dimension. In *NosePAT* and *NoseREAL*, we define 6 sections with the first and last one marking the start and end of the olfactory region (right-hand side of Fig. 4), while the remaining 4 are evenly spaced between them. On these, we compute the regional average of the velocity magnitude $|u|$ separately for the left and right semi-sections. By doing that, each LES simulation is compressed to 12 features that are used as inputs of $\mathcal{K}$.

For **CR+HC**, we apply C-PROP clustering as described in Sect. 4.3 using as reference a NACA0012 in *AirNACA* and *AirDEF*, and one of the 7 healthy patients used to generate the training set as reference for propagating clusters in *NosePAT* and *NoseREAL*. Within clusters, we compute the same regional averages as for HC, mentioned in the previous paragraph.

For **FREE-CR+FC** and **PROP-CR+FC**, we fully apply our clustering method as described in Sect. 4, using for PROP-CR+FC the same references as for CR+HC.

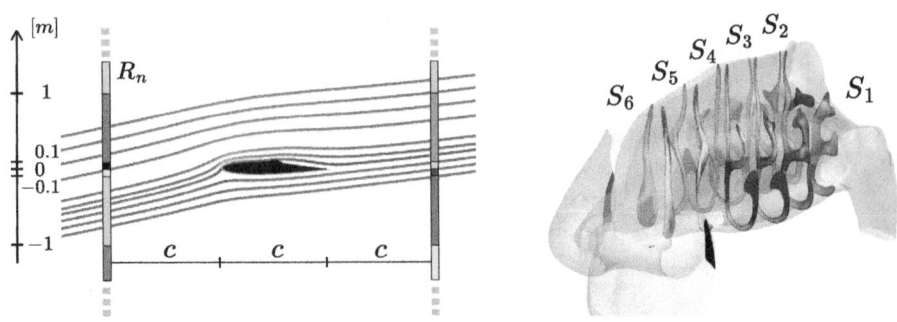

Fig. 4. Handcrafted regions in *AirNACA* and *AirDEF* (left) and *NosePAT* (right).

5.4 Models Training and Evaluation

As in [4], we stick to training simple MLPs for *HC*, *CR+HC* and for *PROP-CR+FC*, while we adopt a Point Transformer model for *FREE-CR+FC*. We define models with a comparable number of parameters (around $50K$ parameters in *AirNACA* and *AirDEF*, and $30K$ for *NosePAT*) to evaluate the performance when considering architectures having similar learning capacities. In *AirNACA* and *AirDEF*, the dataset is standardized and shuffled before being split into five folds for cross-validation. In each fold, one subset is used for testing, while the rest is split into training and validation (80% and 20%). We train our models using the mean squared error (MSE) as loss function. As these are regression tasks and the predicted values are not necessarily integers, they are rounded to obtain the final output code. We report the averaged results across the five folds, considering the mean absolute error (MAE) over each estimated code and the classification accuracy, which represents the percentage of correctly predicted codes when rounding predictions to the nearest integer.

In *NosePAT*, we evaluate the performance of our models with a Leave-One-Patient-Out Cross-Validation (*LOPOCV*): in this approach, all the synthetic samples derived from each of the 7 healthy patients are iteratively excluded from the training set and used as test cases, ensuring that models are evaluated on anatomies that were never seen during training. For each iteration, the remaining patients' data are split into 85% for training and 15% for validation. Eventually we average the results of the test over all the excluded patients. Unlike the previous regression tasks, this problem is now framed as a binary classification task, and models are trained using categorical cross-entropy as the loss function. The primary evaluation metric is classification accuracy. In the *NoseREAL* experiment, we train our models on the complete synthetic dataset and then test on the set of real pathological samples, assessing the performance on never-seen-before anatomies and pathological forms.

5.5 Experimental Results

The results of our experiments are reported in Table 1 and 2. Table 1 shows the test accuracy of the inference models trained using features extracted with

Table 1. Test accuracy of *HC*, *CR+HC*, *PROP-CR+FC* and *FREE-CR+FC*. On the right-hand side of the table, we report the score on the set of real pathological patients.

	Test Accuracy			Score
	AirNACA	*AirDEF*	*NosePAT*	*NoseREAL*
HC	84.6%	65.6%	**88.8%**	**8/10**
CR+HC	85.0%	83.2%	71.5%	6/10
PROP-CR+FC	**86.5%**	**88.7%**	86.8%	**8/10**
FREE-CR+FC	85.1%	84.3%	77.5%	7/10

Table 2. Mean Absolute Error (MAE) and standard deviation (std) for each digit of the regression code in *AirNACA* and *AirDEF* tasks.

	Mean Absolute Error (MAE) and Standard Deviation (std)										
	AirNACA						*AirDEF*				
	I digit		II digit		III digit		I digit		II digit		III digit	
	MAE	±std	MAE	±std	MAE	±std	MAE	±std	MAE	±std	MAE	±std
HC	0.17	0.23	0.30	0.24	0.17	0.26	0.35	0.25	0.33	0.18	0.11	0.15
CR+HC	0.16	0.20	0.28	0.21	0.16	0.23	0.22	0.21	0.21	0.17	0.03	0.12
PROP-CR+FC	**0.14**	0.19	**0.24**	0.21	**0.15**	0.24	**0.18**	0.19	**0.19**	0.18	**0.01**	0.11
FREE-CR+FC	**0.14**	0.21	0.26	0.20	0.16	0.19	0.21	0.22	0.21	0.18	0.02	0.09
Range	[0:9]		[0:9]		[05:50]		[-2:2]		[-2:2]		[0:2]	

methods described in Sect. 5.1. We stress that in regression tasks (*AirNACA* and *AirDEF*) we round the results to the nearest integer and evaluate the accuracy. Alongside the accuracy of the *LOPOCV* for the *NosePAT* task, we also report the scores of the classifier on the set of real pathological patients (*NoseREAL*). Table 2 contains the MAEs and the standard deviations over the test set predictions for each individual digit that composes the regression code.

Table 1, shows that the clustering is overall beneficial in almost every task. For both *AirNACA* and *AirDEF*, the clustering progressively improves the classification accuracy of *HC*, both when considering clustering regions in *CR+HC*, and when using all the in-cluster features (*PROP-CR+FC*). We argue this improvement is due to the use of physics-based identified cluster regions and the more informative features we extract from those regions, which also contain geometric information that is crucial for identifying defects. This is particularly evident in the case of *AirDEF*, where *HC* alone achieves the lowest performance. In *HC*, indeed, we extract information from regions that are distant from the airfoil, making it less effective in capturing the local aerodynamic effects of defects. Although *FREE-CR+FC* outperforms *HC* in both *AirNACA* and *AirDEF*, its accuracy remains lower than that of *PROP-CR+FC*. This result is consistent with the increased difficulty of the inference problem in *FREE-CR+FC*, where cluster ordering is not constrained.

In *NosePAT*, we report the test accuracy of the *LOPOCV* described in Sect. 5.4. The trend in *CR+HC*, *PROP-CR+FC* and *FREE-CR+FC* is confirmed, demonstrating that including in the training set more in-cluster features enhances the classification performance. Also, in the case *FREE-CR+FC*, the accuracy reduces with respect to *PROP-CR+FC*, reflecting the higher complexity of the problem. However, in *NosePAT*, *HC* achieves the best test performance, which is not surprising as the 6 transversal sections we use in *HC* to extract features are designed ad-hoc for this particular task, and two of these align with pathological deformations, directly capturing critical information.

Table 1 shows also the scores of the classifier on the set of real pathological patients, which represent a significant real-world application. In this experiment, we train a classifier on CFD data from synthetically pathological geometries and then test it on actual pathological conditions. Despite the relatively small dimension of the dataset, the results demonstrate that we can effectively identify real pathologies on unseen patients using solely CFD data. *PROP-CR+FC*, in fact, achieves an 8/10 score with a trend between *CR+HC*, *FC+PROP-C*, and *FREE-CR+FC* similar to *AirNACA* and *AirDEF*.

From Table 2, we observe that the II digit in *AirNACA* consistently exhibits the highest MAE across all experiments, indicating it is the most challenging parameter to predict. Conversely, the third digit, representing airfoil thickness, is well predicted, showing the lowest MAE relative to its range. Similarly, in *AirDEF*, the third digit also achieves the lowest MAE, while the first two digits yield comparable errors. Here, the last digit corresponds to a trailing-edge cut, whose high predictability is likely due to its distinct aerodynamic impact, as it generates a structured wake effectively captured by physics-based clustering.

Overall, results from *AirNACA* and *AirDEF* confirm that our method improves inference performance on aerospace datasets while maintaining consistency across experiments. *NosePAT* demonstrates that our method can be applied to a complex real-world task such as pathology identification, even when relying on limited CFD data.

5.6 Computational Considerations

Our method introduces additional computational overhead due to the clustering step and the use of more advanced learning architectures with respect to the baseline approach proposed in [4]. Clustering was performed on the Leonardo Data Centric General Purpose (DCGP) partition of the CINECA HPC system, using 3 compute nodes each equipped with 2× Intel Xeon Platinum 8480+ CPUs, with 56 cores per CPU. In our implementation, we run one clustering process per core in parallel. We apply BGMM to the matrix $\mathbf{C} \in \mathbb{R}^{n \times N}$, where n is the number of CFD cells. For the 2D airfoil simulations (*AirNACA* and *AirDEF* tasks), where $n \approx 300K$, the BGMM requires around 10âĂŞ12 min per sample. In the *NosePAT* dataset, we filtered out the smallest cells, removing 91% of the data but retaining 95% of the total volume as described in Sect. 5.2, resulting in roughly 1.5–1.7 million cells per sample. Clustering on this reduced set takes about 1.5 h per sample (consistent with the linear scaling of the BGMM with n), and this cost remains manageable and predictable. This overhead is absent in the *HC* baseline, which uses manually defined regions. However, in practice, defining such regions, especially in anatomically complex domains like human upper airways, requires expert input and manual inspection, introducing a non-negligible human effort. Our method removes this dependency by automatically identifying meaningful flow regions in a data-driven manner.

In terms of inference time, the Point Transformer model used in the *FREE-CR+FC* setting is more computationally demanding than the MLPs we employed in *HC*, *HC+FC*, and *PROP-CR+FC*. While all architectures are constrained to have a similar number of parameters within the same task, the Point Transformer involves more complex operations, such as attention over sets of clusters, which lead to longer training times (tens of minutes on an NVIDIA A6000 Ada GPU), whereas the MLPs typically converge in a matter of minutes. We consider this additional training overhead acceptable, given the improved flexibility and generalization achieved by the set-learning architecture.

In summary, although our method introduces additional computational costs with respect to the handcrafted baseline, it provides a scalable and general solution that eliminates manual feature engineering and enables consistent application across diverse CFD domains.

6 Conclusion

In this work, we proposed a physics-based clustering framework to extract meaningful flow structures from CFD data, enhancing the inference of non-computable quantities in aerodynamic and biomedical applications. By replacing expert-driven feature selection with a clustering strategy based on governing equations, our method takes a step toward end-to-end approaches. We validated our method on aerospace datasets for airfoil shape and defect identification and extended its application to pathology classification in human upper airways. The results demonstrated improved inference performance over traditional handcrafted features. Moreover, our approach proved robust across different datasets, highlighting its portability and scalability in diverse CFD scenarios. In future works, we will explore more end-to-end methods to directly extract relevant information and gain deeper insights into CFD data, minimizing expert-driven processing.

Reproducibility. We provide the implementation of the *AirNACA* task presented in this work, based on the public dataset available at 10.5281/zenodo.4638071. The repository includes scripts for feature extraction, clustering, and model training, and is publicly available at 10.5281/zenodo.15637850.

Acknowledgements. The Authors are grateful to A. Bulfamante and C. Pipolo for the time spent as ENT experts. Computing time has been provided by the Italian CINECA HPC Center in Bologna under the *IscrB_StocLung* grant. The Authors also acknowledge NVIDIA Corporation for the donation of the A6000 Ada GPUs donated within the NVIDIA Academic Grant Program awarded to Giacomo Boracchi for the proposal entitled "*Leveraging ML for CFD Flow Field Classification*". This publication is part of the project PNRR-NGEU which has received funding from MUR-DM 351/2022.

Disclosure of Interests. The authors have no competing interests to declare that are relevant to the content of this article.

References

1. Brunton, S., Noack, B., Koumoutsakos, P.: Machine learning for fluid mechanics. Annu. Rev. Fluid Mech. **52**, 477–508 (2020)
2. Saetta, E., Tognaccini, R.: Identification of flow field regions by machine learning. In: AIAA SCITECH 2022 Forum, pages 1503–1518. American Institute of Aeronautics and Astronautics, San Diego, CA (2022)
3. Callaham, J.L., Koch, J.V., Brunton, B.W., Kutz, J.N., Brunton, S.L.: Learning dominant physical processes with data-driven balance models. Nat. Commun. **12**(1), 1016 (2021)
4. Schillaci, A., Quadrio, M., Pipolo, C., Restelli, M., Boracchi, G.: Inferring functional properties from fluid dynamics features. In: 2020 25th International Conference on Pattern Recognition (ICPR), pp. 4091–4098 (2021)
5. Zhao, H., Jiang, L., Jia, J., Torr, P., Koltun, V.: Point Transformer. In: 2021 IEEE/CVF International Conference on Computer Vision (ICCV), pp. 16239–16248 (2021). ISSN: 2380-7504
6. Schillaci, A., Quadrio, M., Boracchi, G.: A database of CFD-computed flow fields around airfoils for machine-learning applications (2021)
7. Brenner, M.P., Eldredge, J.D., Freund, J.B.: Perspective on machine learning for advancing fluid mechanics. Phys. Rev. Fluids **4**(10), 100501 (2019)
8. Ashton, N., et al.: WindsorML: high-fidelity computational fluid dynamics dataset for automotive aerodynamics. In: Advances in Neural Information Processing Systems (NeurIPS), vol. 37, pp. 37823–37835 (2024)
9. Raissi, M., Yazdani, A., Karniadakis, G.E.: Hidden fluid mechanics: learning velocity and pressure fields from flow visualizations. Science **367**(6481), 1026–1030 (2020)
10. Pin, W., Pan, K., Ji, L., Gong, S., Feng, W., Yuan, W., Pain, C.: Navier–stokes generative adversarial network: a physics-informed deep learning model for fluid flow generation. Neural Comput. Appl. **34**(14), 11539–11552 (2022)
11. Ling, J., Kurzawski, A., Templeton, J.: Reynolds averaged turbulence modelling using deep neural networks with embedded invariance. J. Fluid Mech. **807**, 155–166 (2016)
12. Spalart, P., Allmaras, S.: A one-equation turbulence model for aerodynamic flows. In: 30th Aerospace Sciences Meeting and Exhibit, Reno, NV, pp. 439–445. American Institute of Aeronautics and Astronautics (1992)
13. Fukami, K., Fukagata, K., Taira, K.: Assessment of supervised machine learning methods for fluid flows. Theoret. Comput. Fluid Dyn. **34**(4), 497–519 (2020). https://doi.org/10.1007/s00162-020-00518-y
14. Sohr, H.: The Navier–Stokes Equations. Birkhäuser (2001)
15. Escobar, M.D., West, M.: Bayesian density estimation and inference using mixtures. J. Am. Stat. Assoc. **90**(430), 577–588 (1995)
16. Jon Louis Bentley: Multidimensional binary search trees used for associative searching. Commun. ACM **18**(9), 509–517 (1975)

Sparsifying Instance Segmentation Models for Efficient Vision-Based Industrial Recycling

Melanie Neubauer[1(✉)], Ozan Özdenizci[2], Justus Piater[3], and Elmar Rueckert[1]

[1] Chair of Cyber-Physical-Systems, Technical University of Leoben, Leoben, Austria
{melanie.neubauer,rueckert}@unileoben.ac.at
[2] Institute of Machine Learning and Neural Computation, Graz University of Technology, Graz, Austria
oezdenizci@tugraz.at
[3] Department of Computer Science, University of Innsbruck, Innsbruck, Austria
justus.piater@uibk.ac.at

Abstract. Recycling is essential to the circular economy. However, efficient material sorting, particularly in steel scrap recycling, remains challenging due to material diversity and contamination. Visual computing via deep learning offers a significant promise in automation, with models such as YOLO and Mask R-CNN excelling in object detection and segmentation. However, high computational requirements often limit industrial deployment, which necessitates more efficient algorithmic solutions targeted for such applied machine learning problems. We introduce a novel approach to prune large image segmentation models based on *instance-based importance scores (IBIS)*, specifically tailored to the problem of instance segmentation for automated steel scrap recycling. Our method identifies and prunes low priority parameters by leveraging parameter importance scores estimated by considering the presence of recyclable instances to be segmented in the frames. Moreover, we utilize a novel custom dataset constructed for the instance segmentation task during copper and steel scrap recycling, which involves recyclable objects of different sizes with various levels of difficulty. Our evaluations demonstrate promising computational efficiency gains without significant performance drops, while also enabling powerful out-of-distribution generalization, a game-changing capability. Finally, we discuss the potential of our work for real-world industrial applications, enabling resource-efficient deep learning deployment in large-scale automated sorting systems.

Keywords: instance segmentation · steel scrap recycling · neural network pruning · sparsity · out-of-distribution generalization

1 Introduction

As the European Union (EU) advances toward its goal of becoming a sustainable, climate-neutral economy by 2050 under the European Green Deal [5], pressure is mounting on energy-intensive industries like steel manufacturing to adopt more environment friendly practices. Steel production remains one of the most carbon-intensive industrial processes globally, contributing to 5.7% of total EU emissions [33]. Recycling plays a pivotal role in reducing the environmental impact of such industries, yet effective material sorting especially in complex environments like steel scrap recycling remains a challenge. Traditional sorting relies heavily on manual labor, which is slow, costly, and error-prone, making it unsuitable for large-scale, real-time operations. To address these challenges, automated solutions based on machine learning and computer vision have become increasingly important [6,32]. These technologies offer significant improvements in sorting efficiency and scalability, especially for the diverse and often contaminated materials found in recycling streams. Real-time image segmentation and object detection models are at the core of these systems, enabling faster and more accurate classification of materials. However, effective deployment of these models in real-world industrial settings often require significant computational efficiency improvements in terms of memory and energy requirements.

In the field of recycling, deep learning based models, particularly in image segmentation and object detection, have proven effective in automating material classification [7]. Deep neural network architectures such as YOLO (You Only Look Once) [29] and Mask R-CNN [13] are commonly used for real-time detection due to their inference speed and accuracy, making them suitable for various recycling applications, including waste sorting and steel scrap classification. These models have shown promise in differentiating between different types of materials, such as plastics, metals, and paper [3], thereby enabling automated separation. Among these, YOLO variants are often regarded as state-of-the-art for real-time applications in recycling, due to their strong downstream task performances. However, these models also pose significant computational challenges, particularly in industrial settings where real-time processing often requires handling 50–100 frames per second, each involving 100–10.000 objects. Furthermore, high memory consumption and increased inference times limits their deployment on edge devices or in resource-constrained environments. To address these issues, efficient solutions must balance high performance with reduced computational and memory demands for large-scale automated recycling.

Model sparsification based on weight pruning is a widely-studied approach for reducing the memory usage and computational load of deep neural networks [15]. Pruning involves removing less important parameters from a pre-trained model, leading to smaller, more efficient networks with minimal sacrifice in accuracy [11]. Particularly in semantic segmentation tasks, pruning techniques have been successfully applied to U-Net type models to reduce model size, computational complexity, and memory requirements while maintaining high performance [21]. We present a novel neural network pruning criterion that utilizes **instance-based importance scores (IBIS)**, to prune YOLO-based steel scrap industrial recycling segmentation models. Our method harnesses parameter gradients from an instance-based strategy, allowing us to identify and remove less critical parameters while preserving essential features needed for accurate scrap classification. We conduct extensive experiments on a novel dataset specifically designed for industrial copper and steel scrap recycling applications, evaluating feasibility of our method in real-world industrial settings. Our contributions are as follows:

- We present a model pruning criterion that utilizes *instance-based importance scores (IBIS)* to prune YOLO-based steel scrap segmentation models, and significantly reduce model size while maintaining high performance.
- We introduce a novel dataset constructed for instance segmentation during copper and steel scrap recycling in a real-world industrial setting, which involves recyclable objects of different sizes with hierarchical task difficulty.
- We empirically show that our approach enhances computational efficiency with up to 95% reduction in model size, while maintaining high performance. Moreover, we demonstrate strong out-of-distribution generalization capabilities of our approach, with enhanced robustness to different scrap material sizes observed for the first time during inference.

2 Related Work

We present an overview of key advancements in real-time image segmentation, object detection, and neural network pruning, with a specific emphasis on their applications in the recycling industry and steel scrap classification.

2.1 Real-Time Image Segmentation and Object Detection

Real-time image segmentation and object detection are crucial tasks in computer vision, with applications ranging from autonomous driving to medical imaging and industrial automation like in the recycling industry. In the context of recycling, these techniques enable efficient material classification and sorting. Traditional object detection methods, such as R-CNN [9] and Fast R-CNN [8], achieved strong accuracy but were computationally expensive, limiting their real-time applicability. The introduction of Mask R-CNN [13] improved instance segmentation by generating precise pixel-wise object masks. However, these models remained slow and required significant computational resources.

To address the speed limitations of these models, the YOLO (You Only Look Once) [29] series was developed, significantly improving detection efficiency while maintaining high accuracy. Recent versions, such as YOLOv11 [16], further enhance performance by integrating object segmentation, detection, and classification into a single framework, making it suitable for recycling applications. Despite these advancements, deploying these models in industrial settings remains challenging due to resource constraints and real-time processing demands.

2.2 Visual Computing in Steel Scrap Recycling

The use of deep learning for scrap material classification has gained traction in recent years. Previous studies [34] have demonstrated the effectiveness of convolutional neural networks (CNNs) in intelligent waste recognition, leading to improvements in classification, sorting, and recycling efficiency. Some approaches, such as the system introduced in [35], leverage machine vision for steel scrap quality inspection, while others, like ConvoWaste [26], apply image processing techniques to classify various waste types. However, several challenges hinder the development of robust machine learning solutions for steel scrap classification. Unlike well-researched categories such as vehicles or human faces, steel scrap remains an underexplored domain with limited publicly available datasets [30]. Existing datasets focus on landfill waste or non-shredded scrap [2], making them less suitable for training deep learning models tailored to shredded steel scrap [27].

Additionally, variations in shredded scrap output across different industrial shredders introduce further complexities [1]. The configuration, blade design, and operational parameters of each shredder influence the final output, making it difficult to create standardized datasets that generalize across different recycling plants. These factors highlight the need for adaptable and efficient machine learning models capable of handling diverse scrap materials.

2.3 Neural Network Pruning

Pruning neural networks is a widely explored technique for reducing model complexity while preserving performance [11]. Seminal works, such as Optimal Brain Damage [19] and Optimal Brain Surgeon [12], introduced structured pruning strategies by identifying and removing less critical weights. State-of-the-art methods, such as global magnitude-based pruning (GMP) [11], single-shot network pruning (SNIP) [20], pruning considering pre-training (PCPT) [18] and Taylor expansion criterion based pruning [24], refine this concept by estimating the *importance* of individual weights or filters and eliminating redundant components in a single-shot. Recent works extended these with novel criteria on how importance scores are derived [4,10,28,31].

In segmentation tasks, pruning has been successfully applied to models like U-Net [21] to achieve significant reductions in model size and floating point operations (FLOPs) while maintaining accuracy. Filter pruning techniques in CNN-based segmentation models have shown promising results in reducing computational complexity without degrading segmentation performance. In [22] they focus on dynamic pruning in region-merging-based segmentation, significantly reducing computational complexity while maintaining segmentation accuracy, enabling large-scale applications in remote sensing. Another work [14] introduces context-aware pruning for deep neural networks, leveraging inter-channel dependencies to sparsify models while preserving performance, demonstrating effectiveness across various segmentation architectures. Despite these advancements, existing pruning methods often overlook task-specific importance measures, particularly in industrial recycling applications. We introduce a novel pruning concept based on instance-based importance scores, tailored to instance segmentation models (e.g., YOLO [16]) for steel scrap classification.

Table 1. Detailed breakdown of the steel and copper scrap material allocation in the prepared datasets, including the material sizes, weights and quantities.

	Material Size	Weight [kg]	Quantity	Material Allocation		
				Dataset 1	Dataset 2	Dataset 3
Steel Scrap	Large	9	45	✓	✓	✓
	Medium-Large	20	95	✓	✓	✓
	Medium	9	72		✓	✓
	Small-Medium	6	80			✓
	Small	2.5	104			✓
Copper Scrap	Large	15	17	✓	✓	✓
	Medium	8.5	47		✓	✓
	Small	1	37			✓
	Total	**46.5**	**497**			

3 Industrial Steel Scrap Recycling Dataset

We focus on the recycling process of steel scrap derived from end-of-life vehicles and electrical appliances, which are shredded to produce the E40 scrap fraction [25]. Despite initial pre-sorting using magnetic separators, the resulting material still contains a significant proportion of unwanted contaminants, like copper objects. We address real time detection and segmentation of these undesirable particles with deep learning based instance segmentation models.

Due to the absence of publicly available labeled segmentation datasets for steel scrap, we developed a custom dataset tailored to our application. Specifically, our dataset encompasses a diverse range of objects varying in size, with a particular focus on components containing copper, such as cables and embedded wiring. The collected material is classified into two primary categories: steel scrap (considered acceptable) and copper scrap (considered contaminants). Steel scrap consists of particles that are entirely free from copper inclusions, while copper scrap includes both visibly contaminated pieces and those with concealed copper elements. The dataset composition and material quantities used in our simulations are detailed in Table 1. To maintain a hierarchically structured dataset and facilitate effective model training, the scrap particles were carefully sorted by size, ensuring balanced representation and manageable data complexity.

3.1 Data Recording

We collected three datasets by parsing video recordings of a conveyor belt from top view, where materials were manually positioned to ensure controlled conditions. Each dataset was recorded over five iterations, with slight adjustments to the positioning of the particles in each run. To enhance variability and generalization, we maintained a consistent distance between particles, while capturing

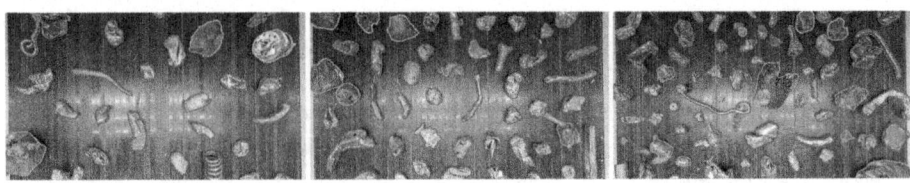

(a) Sample from Dataset 1   (b) Sample from Dataset 2   (c) Sample from Dataset 3

Fig. 1. Materials represented in the datasets vary in terms of object size, quantity, and the spacing between them. Objects segmented in red belong to the steel scrap objects category, while those segmented in green represent copper scrap objects. (Color figure online)

them from different angles using a GoPro Hero 11 camera configured with optimized settings. The camera recorded at 100 frames per second, ensuring smooth and detailed footage. The conveyor belt operated at a speed of approximately 0.4 to 0.5 m/sec during recordings. A shutter speed of 1/100 was selected to balance exposure and motion clarity, while the sharpness setting was adjusted to high to enhance the visibility of fine details. These settings were chosen to maximize image quality and facilitate accurate segmentation and classification.

We extracted individual frames from these videos to create our datasets. To ensure sufficient variation between frames while avoiding excessive redundancy, we selected every second frame from the recordings. The full dataset was then labeled by human experts using an automated segmentation tool [27] to ensure accuracy and reliability. The complexity of the datasets varies based on factors such as the number, size, and spatial distribution of the particles. Our datasets (shown in Fig. 1) were designed to support both model training and evaluation. Dataset 1 comprises 5,694 images, which were split into three subsets: 67% (3,831 images) for training, 16% (907 images) for validation, and 17% (956 images) for testing. In contrast, Dataset 2 (1,187 images) and Dataset 3 (1,599 images) were exclusively designated as test sets to assess generalization capabilities. This partitioning strategy ensures rigorous evaluations, with Dataset 1 serving as both training/validation and testing, while Datasets 2 and 3 provide insights into the model's performance on unseen data.

Table 1 provides an overview of the dataset composition and material distribution. Dataset 1 primarily features larger steel and copper scrap particles, with additional variations introduced in subsequent datasets. The datasets also differ in object density per frame, reflecting increasing complexity. Dataset 1 contains approximately 30–40 objects per frame, ensuring a structured yet moderately challenging environment for initial training and validation. Dataset 2 increases the density to 40–50 objects per frame, introducing greater variation in object positioning while maintaining a manageable level of overlap. Dataset 3 presents the highest complexity, with up to 70 objects per frame, better representing real-world industrial scenarios with a diverse mix of particle sizes and spacing.

 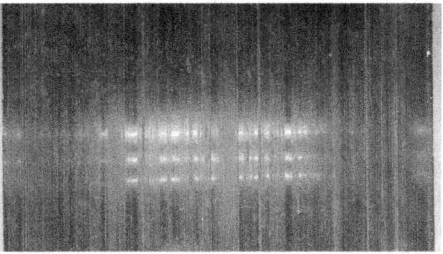

(a) Example input frame x with various instances to be segmented, used to compute $\nabla_{w_j}\mathcal{L}(f(x,w),y)$ for each parameter.

(b) Example image $\tilde{x}$ without instances to be segmented, used to compute $\nabla_{w_j}\mathcal{L}(f(\tilde{x},w),\mathbf{0})$ for each parameter.

Fig. 2. Example image frames from our training set $\mathcal{D}_{\text{train}}$, which is used to estimate the importance scores necessary to prune our neural network models.

4 Pruning Segmentation Models via Instance-Based Importance Scores (IBIS)

We propose a novel pruning method, instance-based importance scores (IBIS), that leverages gradient information from multiple sources to evaluate the significance of model weights. We calculate averaged gradients across standard training images (as in Fig. 2a), while also incorporating gradients obtained from images without any objects or labels (Fig. 2b). By analyzing the difference between these two gradient distributions, we derive an importance score that effectively identifies less critical weights. This strategy offers a more refined assessment of weight importance, leading to an efficient and effective pruning process.

Importance Score Calculation: Given a model $f(x;\boldsymbol{w})$ and a training set $\mathcal{D}_{\text{train}}$, we denote the training set as consisting of pairs $\{(x_i, y_i)\}_{i=1}^{N}$, where x_i is the input image, y_i is the corresponding label, and N is the total number of training samples. In neural network pruning, we aim to optimize a global binary pruning mask $\boldsymbol{m} \in \{0,1\}^n$, with n being the number of parameters. We obtain a new model $f(x; \boldsymbol{m} \odot \boldsymbol{w}')$ with $\|\boldsymbol{m} \odot \boldsymbol{w}'\|_0 \leq (1-\mathcal{R}) \cdot n$, where the symbol $\odot$ denotes element-wise multiplication and $\mathcal{R} \in [0,1)$ represents the pruning ratio (e.g., when $\mathcal{R} = 0.85$, our model sparsity is 85%). The finetuning process updates the model parameters from $\boldsymbol{w}$ to $\boldsymbol{w}'$. We define a non-binary, continuous-valued parameter importance vector s and determine the binary mask values as: $m_j = \mathbb{1}\left[s_j - \tilde{s}_\gamma\right]$, $\forall j \in \{1,...n\}$, where $\gamma = (1-\mathcal{R}) \cdot n$ and $\tilde{s} = \text{SortDescending}(s)$, so that $\tilde{s}_\gamma$ is the γ-largest element in s, and $\mathbb{1}[.]$ denotes the indicator function. For a selected model instance j, an importance score s_j^{IBIS} is computed as follows,

$$s_j^{\text{IBIS}} = |w_j| \cdot [1 - \exp(-c)], \quad \text{where} \qquad (1)$$

$$c = \left|\mathbb{E}_{(x,y) \sim \mathcal{D}_{\text{train}}}\left[\nabla_{w_j}\mathcal{L}(f(x;\boldsymbol{w}),y)\right] - \nabla_{w_j}\mathcal{L}(f(\tilde{x};\boldsymbol{w}),\mathbf{0})\right|. \qquad (2)$$

is the variable which denotes the absolute difference between the two gradients. Here, $\tilde{x}$ represents a background image (shown in Fig. 2b), and the absence of segmentation labels is denoted by **0**.

Design Intuition: Here, the term $1-\exp(-c)$ controls how much of the weight magnitude $|w_j|$ contributes to the parameter importance score, with $c \in [0, \infty)$ acting as a tuning parameter that determines the degree of attenuation. This tuning parameter enforces the importance scores to be bounded within $[0, |w_j|)$, where larger values of c (indicating greater differences between the two gradients) result in a stronger influence of parameter magnitudes on the score s_j^{IBIS}. To the contrary, for small values of c (i.e., very little difference between the gradient terms regardless of the presence of instance to be segmented), the parameter importance score would approach zero. This formulation differs from Global Magnitude Pruning (GMP), which ranks weights solely by their absolute magnitudes, pruning the smallest ones without considering gradient-based significance. Unlike SNIP, which multiplies weights by their gradients without distinguishing whether the gradients are influenced by objects in the image, our approach leverages c, capturing the difference between the standard gradient and the gradient from an image without objects (i.e., without labels). This results in a more refined pruning criterion that prioritizes weights based on their relevance to object regions rather than treating all gradients uniformly.

In our implementation of IBIS, we apply the pruning ratio $\mathcal{R}$ globally to the model, thus the per-layer unstructured sparsity rates can vary. It is important to note that our pruning method has only a single hyperparameter, the pruning ratio $\mathcal{R}$, which simplifies the utility of the method.

5 Experimental Setup

We evaluate the effectiveness of our pruning criterion by comparing it to state-of-the-art importance score estimation techniques. For each method, we prune the same pre-trained baseline YOLO11n-seg model [16] and finetune for the same duration, then assess performance on an unseen test set.

5.1 Baseline Pruning Methods

Global Magnitude Pruning (GMP). [11] is a common pruning technique. Its main goal is to shrink the model by eliminating less critical parameters, like weights, while maintaining its performance. MP calculates the importance of each parameter by evaluating its magnitude, and it prunes the parameters with the smallest values, which are considered less influential to the model's overall performance. The importance score for GMP pruning is computed as:

$$s_j^{\text{GMP}} = |w_j|, \tag{3}$$

where, in contrast to IBIS, only the absolute magnitudes of the weights are considered, ignoring the gradient information.

Single-Shot Network Pruning (SNIP). [20] is a technique that simplifies the process by identifying and eliminating less important connections in a single step. SNIP assesses the significance of each weight by calculating the gradient of the loss with respect to the weight. This score assesses the importance of each weight by computing the product of its magnitude and the expected gradient of the loss and prunes those that have the least impact on the overall network performance, via the score:

$$s_j^{\text{SNIP}} = \left| w_j \cdot \mathbb{E}_{(x,y) \sim \mathcal{D}_{\text{train}}} \left[\nabla_{w_j} \mathcal{L}(f(x; \boldsymbol{w}), y) \right] \right|. \tag{4}$$

Here, differently than the GMP importance score, both the weights and the gradients are utilized for calculating the score.

Pruning Considering Pre-Training (PCPT). [18] is a pruning method that distinguishes between two types of parameters: (a) stable, large-value parameters that change little during fine-tuning, and (b) unstable, small-value parameters that change chaotically. Parameters of type (a) are pruned based on their magnitude, while type (b) parameters are pruned using the SNIP method, which captures changes due to downstream task optimization. The score defined as:

$$s_j^{\text{PCPT}} = \left| w_j \cdot \mathbb{E}_{(x,y) \sim \mathcal{D}_{\text{train}}} \left[\nabla_{w_j} \mathcal{L}(f(x; \boldsymbol{w}), y) \right] \right| + \alpha \cdot w_j^2, \tag{5}$$

depicts that PCPT extends the original SNIP importance score by introducing a parameter α, which is multiplied by the square of the weights.

5.2 Model Training Configurations

For the initial training, we used the following key configurations. The model architecture was based on the *yolo11n-seg.yaml* file from the Ultralytics [17] library. The training process was set to run for 20 epochs with a batch size of 32 and an image size of 640 × 640 pixels. A single NVIDIA GeForce RTX 4090 GPU was utilized for simulations. The optimizer used was Adam, with a learning rate of 0.01, and weight decay applied at 0.0005 to reduce the risk of overfitting. The training included a warmup period of 3 epochs, where the learning rate increased gradually, and the momentum started at 0.8. To optimize training efficiency, automatic mixed precision [23] was enabled, allowing for faster computations while maintaining model accuracy. The training also involved validation, using a separate validation set from our dataset. These configurations were selected to balance model performance and training efficiency. For the pruning baseline method PCPT, we selected $\alpha = 0.001$ through cross-validation.

Fine-tuning the model weights was conducted over 10 epochs, with early stopping was activated 2 epochs of no improvement. During this phase, we used a learning rate of 0.001 as opposed to the initial training configuration. Both the training and validation sets were utilized for fine-tuning, while the test set was reserved for evaluation at the end of the process to assess the final model performance. In our experiments, the sparsity ratio for $\mathcal{R}$ concerns the convolutional layers. The total network sparsity can slightly vary in our simulations.

Table 2. Comparison of object segmentation performance mAP50-95 (%) across different sparsity levels with various pruning criteria. Accuracies are averaged over 3 random seeds. Values in parentheses indicate standard deviations.

	#params	GFLOPs	Segmentation mAP50-95 (%)				
			Random	GMP [11]	SNIP [20]	PCPT [18]	IBIS (Ours)
Dense	2 835 153	10.36	76.80 (0.0)				
Sparse (25%)	2 104 061	9.68	13.87 (14.3)	74.50 (0.6)	74.57 (0.4)	74.60 (0.4)	**74.60** (0.7)
Sparse (50%)	1 402 138	9.08	15.60 (14.3)	**74.77** (0.4)	74.23 (1.4)	74.50 (0.4)	74.43 (0.5)
Sparse (75%)	699 097	6.65	0.43 (0.4)	75.03 (0.9)	74.97 (0.6)	75.37 (1.0)	**76.10** (1.0)
Sparse (85%)	421 458	4.76	11.83 (20.2)	74.9 (1.4)	76.07 (2.0)	76.63 (1.7)	**76.73** (1.9)
Sparse (90%)	281 036	3.62	0.47 (0.4)	75.13 (1.5)	74.50 (1.5)	74.07 (1.2)	**77.43** (1.4)
Sparse (95%)	140 457	2.37	0.03 (0.1)	75.97 (0.7)	73.63 (0.8)	73.77 (1.0)	**76.23** (1.4)

5.3 Evaluation Metrics

We assess performance and efficiency in the context of segmentation and bounding box tasks mainly based on the mAP50-95 (Mean Average Precision at Intersection over Union (IoU) thresholds from 50% to 90%) metrics [17].

Segmentation mAP50-95: This metric evaluates segmentation quality across IoU thresholds (50–95%). The model optimizes segmentation performance using multiple losses, including Mask Loss for mask alignment, binary cross-entropy loss for pixel-wise classification, and dice loss for improved mask overlap. Additional consistency losses may enhance smoothness in predictions [16].

Bounding Box mAP50-95: This metric evaluates object detection performance across IoU thresholds from 50% to 95%. The model optimizes detection using multiple losses, including classification loss, Bounding Box Loss, IoU Loss and objectness loss, which collectively enhance detection accuracy [16].

Efficiency Metrics: In addition to accuracy, the number of non-zero parameters (#params) is tracked to assess the model's size and complexity. This metric provides insight into storage and computational requirements, which is crucial for deploying the model on resource-constrained devices. We also estimate the number of FLOPs (floating point operations) to evaluate the computational complexity of the model during forward pass operations at inference time.

6 Experimental Results

In this section, we present the results of applying our pruning method. After pruning, all models undergo the same fine-tuning phase, during which they are trained on a combined training and validation set to recover any performance

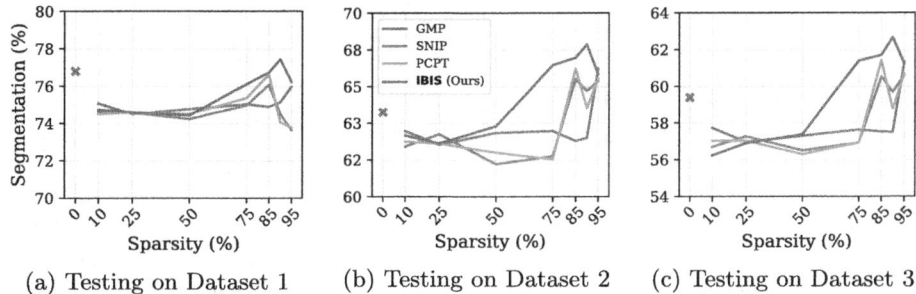

(a) Testing on Dataset 1 (b) Testing on Dataset 2 (c) Testing on Dataset 3

Fig. 3. Segmentation mAP50-95 (%) across different sparsity levels and pruning methods. Average over three seeds with increasing complexity of the validation set. The red cross marks the evaluation result of the dense model. (Color figure online)

loss introduced by the pruning process. Subsequently, we evaluated the models on the test set to assess their generalization performance.

We compare our method to existing approaches, followed by an evaluation of its performance on out-of-distribution segmentation tasks. Next, we investigate the trade-off between model performance and size. Finally, we conduct an ablation study to evaluate the effectiveness of different instance-based methods.

6.1 Comparisons with Existing Methods

Table 2 presents a comparison of segmentation performance (mAP50-90) across various sparsity levels and pruning methods, including GMP, SNIP, and our proposed approach, IBIS. The table illustrates the reduction in model parameters and computational cost (GFLOPs) as the sparsity level increases, with results are averaged over three random seeds. At 0% sparsity (dense model), the model achieves a high mAP50-90 of 76.80% (first row in Table 2). As the sparsity increases from 25% to 95%, the parameter count decreases significantly, and the performance varies across different pruning methods. Notably, our method, IBIS, consistently outperforms the other methods for sparsity levels greater than or equal to 75%, albeit by a small margin. While no clear second-best method emerges, IBIS remains the top choice overall. Furthermore, the table compares the GFLOPs for each configuration, showing the reduction in computational cost as the model sparsity increases. Despite the decrease in parameters, IBIS maintains high accuracy, demonstrating superior performance under high sparsity.

6.2 Impact of Pruning on Out-of-Distribution Segmentation

Figure 3 illustrates the impact of different pruning methods on segmentation performance across varying sparsity levels. The results, averaged over three seeds (denoted by the standard deviation in Table 2), are evaluated on three increasingly complex test sets. The x-axis represents the sparsity percentage, while the

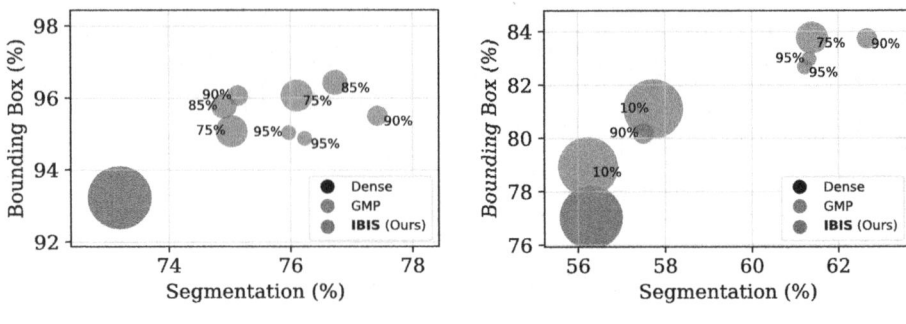

(a) Results of testing on Dataset 1 (b) Results of testing on Dataset 3

Fig. 4. Trade-off comparison of different models' performance and size, averaged over three seeds. The marker sizes indicate the number of non-zero parameters, providing a visual representation of model complexity. (Color figure online)

y-axis denotes segmentation mAP50-90. The comparison includes global magnitude pruning (GMP), SNIP, and our proposed IBIS method. The findings demonstrate that our approach (red lines) consistently outperforms other pruning techniques at higher sparsity levels, even on more complex datasets. Notably, while other methods experience a decline in segmentation accuracy as sparsity increases, our IBIS-based pruning retains or even enhances performance, indicating better robustness to out-of-distribution variations in the dataset.

The red cross ('x') in each plot marks the dense model's result, serving as a reference for evaluating pruning strategies. While pruning typically reduces accuracy; however, our IBIS method maintains—or even surpasses—the performance of the dense model at certain sparsity levels. As shown in Fig. 3, performance improves in some cases, likely due to the effects of fine-tuning.

6.3 Trade-Off Between Model Performance and Size

Figure 4 presents a comparative analysis of segmentation and bounding box mAP50-95 metrics for different pruning strategies. Mainly, our results on the bounding box metrics follow a similar trend as in the segmentation metric results from our previous discussions (see red circles appearing towards the top right of the plots in Fig. 4). Additionally, we test out-of-distribution generalization capabilities on Dataset 3, since it has the highest task difficulty. The x-axis represents segmentation accuracy, while the y-axis denotes bounding box accuracy. We compare the performance of the dense YOLOv11 model (black) against pruned variants using GMP (blue) and our IBIS method (red).

Figure 4(a) shows that on Dataset 1, IBIS-pruned models achieve a favorable balance between accuracy and sparsity. On Dataset 3, see Fig. 4(b), it is shown that features a more challenging distribution of objects, the advantage of IBIS pruning becomes even more apparent. While GMP pruning significantly reduces segmentation accuracy at higher sparsity levels, it shows an accuracy

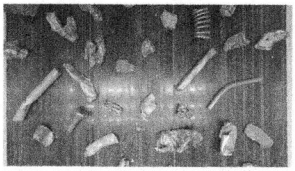 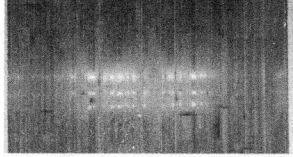 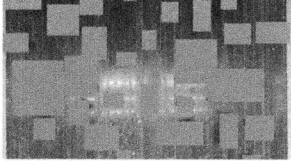

(a) Example input x (b) Patterned Masking   (c) Gray Box Masking

Fig. 5. Comparison of masking strategies used in gradient estimation ablations.

Table 3. Results for segmentation and bounding-box performance under different masking scenarios. Accuracies are averaged over 3 random seeds.

	Segmentation mAP50-95 (%)			Bounding-Box mAP50-95 (%)		
	IBIS	Patterned Masking	Gray Box Masking	IBIS	Patterned Masking	Gray Box Masking
Sparse (25%)	**74.60**	74.17	74.50	95.80	95.77	**95.83**
Sparse (50%)	74.43	74.23	**74.77**	95.70	**96.00**	95.93
Sparse (75%)	**76.10**	75.03	75.03	**96.07**	95.27	95.37
Sparse (85%)	**76.73**	75.30	75.13	**96.43**	96.07	95.93
Sparse (90%)	**77.43**	75.37	75.33	95.50	**96.00**	95.67
Sparse (95%)	**76.23**	75.97	76.00	94.87	**95.13**	95.10

increase again at 95% sparsity. In contrast, our approach maintains competitive performance with a significantly reduced parameter count. These results highlight IBIS's in optimizing neural networks for real-world recycling applications while ensuring a favorable trade-off between model size and predictive accuracy.

6.4 Ablation Study with Masking-Based Score Estimates

We analyze the impact of different masking strategies during pruning on segmentation and bounding-box performance across various sparsity levels. Table 3 presents the results for segmentation (mAP50-95) and bounding-box (mAP50-95) under three scenarios: **IBIS** (Fig. 2), **Patterned Masking** (Fig. 5b), and **Gray Box Masking** (Fig. 5c). IBIS computes importance scores using full-background frames, a lightweight and effective approach requiring only a background-only image. If such a frame is unavailable, alternative masking strategies like Patterned and Gray Box Masking could also be considered.

In the Patterned Masking strategy, objects in the images are masked using background patches. Instead of masking objects with a uniform color, we mask them with patches extracted from the background of the original frame. This technique preserves natural scene structure, helping the model learn in a more contextually realistic manner, but introduces inconsistencies at object boundaries. In contrast, Gray Box Masking fully masks objects with solid gray boxes,

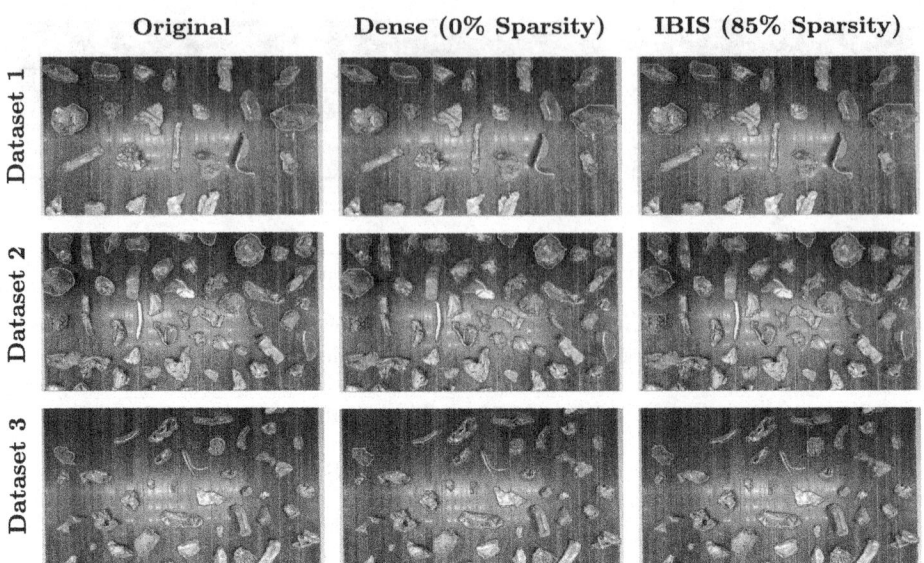

Fig. 6. Comparison of segmentation results on three different test sets (Dataset 1, Dataset 2, and Dataset 3). Each column corresponds to a different model: (1) Original, (2) Dense, and (3) IBIS. The leftmost images in each row show the original ground truth labels, while the middle and right images show the segmentation results from the Dense model and IBIS method, respectively.

forcing the model to rely solely on the surrounding context for importance estimation. Importance scores in these settings are computed as:

$$\bar{s}_j^{\text{OCC}} = |w_j| \cdot [1 - \exp(-\bar{c})], \quad \text{where} \tag{6}$$

$$\bar{c} = \left| \mathbb{E}_{(x,y) \sim \mathcal{D}_{\text{train}}} [\nabla_{w_j} \mathcal{L}(f(x; \boldsymbol{w}), y)] - \mathbb{E}_{(x,y) \sim \mathcal{D}_{\text{train}}} [\nabla_{w_j} \mathcal{L}(f(\bar{x}; \boldsymbol{w}), \bar{y})] \right|. \tag{7}$$

In IBIS, c (Eq. 2) uses the gradient from a single background image $\tilde{x}$, while this method uses $\bar{c}$, the averaged gradient from masked images $\bar{x}$. Table 3 shows that all masking strategies perform similarly at lower sparsity levels. However, as sparsity increases, differences emerge. For segmentation, Patterned Masking tends to underperform at higher sparsity levels (90–95%), suggesting that inconsistencies in background patch placement negatively impact model generalization. Meanwhile, Gray Box Masking remains competitive across all sparsity levels, achieving comparable or superior results to IBIS in some cases. For bounding-box detection, all methods perform closely at moderate sparsity levels, but at extreme sparsity (90–95%), Patterned Masking shows a slight advantage over IBIS, while Gray Box Masking remains stable. These findings highlight the importance of masking strategy selection in pruning. When full-background frames are unavailable, Patterned and Gray Box Masking are viable alternatives, with the latter offering more consistent performance under extreme sparsity.

7 Conclusion

We introduce IBIS, an instance-based importance scoring method for pruning segmentation models used in an industrial recycling setting. Unlike traditional pruning approaches like GMP and SNIP, IBIS leverages gradient-based importance scores, prioritizing weights based on their relevance to object regions rather than treating all gradients uniformly. This approach preserves critical features and maintains high segmentation accuracy, particularly at high sparsity levels.

Our results demonstrate that IBIS not only reduces model size and inference costs but also enhances generalization, even in out-of-distribution scenarios. This makes it a viable solution for resource-constrained applications such as real-time recycling systems. Furthermore, we show that masking strategy selection influences pruning effectiveness. When full-background frames are unavailable, Gray Box Masking offers a slight advantage at extreme sparsity, providing a robust alternative. As shown in Fig. 6, IBIS, with 85% sparsity, achieves better performance than the dense model (0% sparsity), demonstrating its practical effectiveness and robustness in real-world applications. To support future research and industrial deployment, we plan to publicly release the full annotated dataset used in this study. Overall, IBIS balances efficiency and accuracy, making it a promising approach for scalable industrial deep learning applications with lightweight neural network models.

Acknowledgements. The project "KIRAMET KI based Recycling Metalcompound-Waste" (Project number FO999899661) is funded by the Austrian Research Promotion Agency (FFG) and the Federal Ministry for Climate Action, Environment, Energy, Mobility, Innovation, and Technology. Video and photo material of steel waste were recorded at the Digital Waste Research Lab of the Chair of Waste Processing Technology and Waste Management, TU Leoben. Scholz Austria GmbH contributed as a partner for scrap test specimens and a research collaborator.

References

1. Aboussouan, L., et al.: Steel scrap fragmentation by shredders. Powder Technol. **105**(1–3), 288–294 (1999)
2. Bashkirova, D., et al.: Zerowaste dataset: towards deformable object segmentation in cluttered scenes. In: Proceedings of the IEEE/CVF Conference on Computer Vision and Pattern Recognition, pp. 21147–21157 (2022)
3. Bircanoğlu, C., et al.: Recyclenet: intelligent waste sorting using deep neural networks. In: Innovations in intelligent systems and applications (INISTA), pp. 1–7. IEEE (2018)
4. Chen, T., et al.: Only train once: a one-shot neural network training and pruning framework. Adv. Neural. Inf. Process. Syst. **34**, 19637–19651 (2021)
5. European Commission: Communication from the commission to the European parliament, the European council, the council, the European economic and social committee, and the committee of the regions: The European green deal (2019)

6. Fournier-Viger, P., et al.: Machine learning for intelligent industrial design. In: Joint European Conference on Machine Learning and Knowledge Discovery in Databases, pp. 158–172 (2021)
7. Gedam, P.B., et al.: A systematic review: development of AI based computer vision scrap sorting system for metal scrap. In: International Conference on Multi-Agent Systems for Collaborative Intelligence (ICMSCI), pp. 876–881. IEEE (2025)
8. Girshick, R.: Fast R-CNN. In: Proceedings of the IEEE International Conference on Computer Vision, pp. 1440–1448 (2015)
9. Girshick, R., et al.: Rich feature hierarchies for accurate object detection and semantic segmentation. In: Proceedings of the IEEE Conference on Computer Vision and Pattern Recognition, pp. 580–587 (2014)
10. Gritsch, J.V., et al.: Preserving real-world robustness of neural networks under sparsity constraints. In: Joint European Conference on Machine Learning and Knowledge Discovery in Databases, pp. 337–354 (2024)
11. Han, S., et al.: Learning both weights and connections for efficient neural network. In: Advances in Neural Information Processing Systems, vol. 28 (2015)
12. Hassibi, B., et al.: Optimal brain surgeon and general network pruning. In: IEEE International Conference on Neural Networks, pp. 293–299 (1993)
13. He, K., et al.: Mask R-CNN. In: Proceedings of the IEEE International Conference on Computer Vision, pp. 2961–2969 (2017)
14. He, W., et al.: Cap: context-aware pruning for semantic segmentation. In: Proceedings of the IEEE/CVF Winter Conference on Applications of Computer Vision, pp. 960–969 (2021)
15. He, Y., Xiao, L.: Structured pruning for deep convolutional neural networks: a survey. IEEE Trans. Pattern Anal. Mach. Intell. **46**(5), 2900–2919 (2023)
16. Jocher, G., Qiu, J.: Ultralytics yolo11 (2024). https://github.com/ultralytics/ultralytics
17. Jocher, G., et al.: Ultralytics YOLO (2023). https://ultralytics.com
18. Kohama, H., et al.: Single-shot pruning for pre-trained models: rethinking the importance of magnitude pruning. In: Proceedings of the IEEE/CVF International Conference on Computer Vision, pp. 1433–1442 (2023)
19. LeCun, Y., et al.: Optimal brain damage. In: Advances in Neural Information Processing Systems, vol. 2 (1989)
20. Lee, N., et al.: Snip: single-shot network pruning based on connection sensitivity. arXiv preprint arXiv:1810.02340 (2018)
21. López-González, C.I., et al.: Filter pruning for convolutional neural networks in semantic image segmentation. Neural Netw. **169**, 713–732 (2024)
22. Lv, X., et al.: Pruning for image segmentation: improving computational efficiency for large-scale remote sensing applications. ISPRS J. Photogramm. Remote. Sens. **202**, 13–29 (2023)
23. Micikevicius, P., et al.: Mixed precision training. arXiv preprint arXiv:1710.03740 (2017)
24. Molchanov, P., et al.: Pruning convolutional neural networks for resource efficient inference. arXiv preprint arXiv:1611.06440 (2016)
25. Muchová, L., et al.: End-of-waste criteria for iron and steel scrap: technical proposals. Joint Research Centre-Institute for Prospective Technological Studies. Luxembourg Publications Office of the European Union (2010)
26. Nafiz, M.S., et al.: ConvoWaste: an automatic waste segregation machine using deep learning. In: 3rd International Conference on Robotics, Electrical and Signal Processing Techniques (ICREST), pp. 181–186. IEEE (2023)

27. Neubauer, M., Rückert, E.: Semi-autonomous fast object segmentation and tracking tool for industrial applications. In: 21st International Conference on Ubiquitous Robots (UR), pp. 77–83. IEEE (2024)
28. Quétu, V., et al.: The simpler the better: an entropy-based importance metric to reduce neural networks' depth. In: Joint European Conference on Machine Learning and Knowledge Discovery in Databases, pp. 92–108 (2024)
29. Redmon, J., et al.: You only look once: unified, real-time object detection. In: Proceedings of the IEEE Conference on Computer Vision and Pattern Recognition, pp. 779–788 (2016)
30. Schäfer, M., et al.: DOES-A multimodal dataset for supervised and unsupervised analysis of steel scrap. Sci. Data **10**(1), 780 (2023)
31. Tanaka, H., et al.: Pruning neural networks without any data by iteratively conserving synaptic flow. Adv. Neural. Inf. Process. Syst. **33**, 6377–6389 (2020)
32. Teixeira, S., et al.: Improving smart waste collection using AutoML. In: Joint European Conference on Machine Learning and Knowledge Discovery in Databases, pp. 283–298 (2021)
33. Watch, C.M.: Decarbonising steel: a guide to the steel sector's decarbonisation (2022). https://carbonmarketwatch.org/wp-content/uploads/2022/03/CMW_Decarbonising-Steel_v02.pdf
34. Wu, T.W., et al.: Applications of convolutional neural networks for intelligent waste identification and recycling: a review. Resour. Conserv. Recycl. **190**, 106813 (2023)
35. Xu, W., et al.: Classification and rating of steel scrap using deep learning. Eng. Appl. Artif. Intell. **123**, 106241 (2023)

Smart Cities, Transportation and Utilities (e.g., Energy)

Go with the Flow: Leveraging Physics-Informed Gradients to Solve Real-World Problems in Water Distribution Systems

Inaam Ashraf, Janine Strotherm[(✉)], Luca Hermes, and Barbara Hammer

Faculty of Technology, Bielefeld University, Inspiration 1, 33619 Bielefeld, Germany
{mashraf,jstrotherm,lhermes,bhammer}@techfak.uni-bielefeld.de

Abstract. Clean drinking water is essential for a sustainable society as emphasized by UN's sustainable developmental goal 6. Efficient management of water distribution systems (WDSs) is vital to ensure this goal. Conventional approaches rely on computationally expensive hydraulic simulations. Instead, using a pre-trained physics-informed graph neural network as a surrogate model, we solve such real-world problems with gradient methods. This does not only enable end-to-end optimization of WDS attributes but demonstrates the more general concept of leveraging the differentiability of a deep surrogate model to solve downstream tasks related to the underlying complex system. In this work, we demonstrate this novel principle by focusing on three tasks: First, we estimate hydraulic states from sparse sensory information, achieving SOTA performance. Second, we use the surrogate model combined with information theory to solve the task of optimal sensor placement. We use the sparse-to-dense pressure estimation task to gauge the quality of our sensor placements, which itself is non-trivial. Finally, we plan the rehabilitation of WDSs by optimizing pipe diameters in response to changing demands. To the best of our knowledge, we are the first to use the concept of end-to-end differentiability of complex systems via deep surrogate models to solve real-world tasks in WDSs.

Keywords: Physics-informed Machine Learning · Graph neural networks · Surrogate models · Digital twins · Water distribution networks

1 Introduction

The increasing availability of physics-informed machine learning (ML) methodologies allows the development of efficient and reliable surrogate models, i.e.,

---

I. Ashraf, J. Strotherm and L. Hermes—Authors contributed equally.

Supplementary Information The online version contains supplementary material available at https://doi.org/10.1007/978-3-032-06129-4_3.

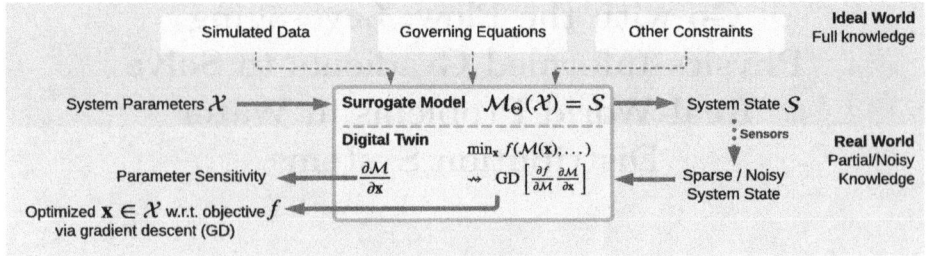

Fig. 1. The main concept of leveraging gradients of a surrogate model $\mathcal{M}$ with parameters Θ. Given a surrogate model (top) that predicts system states $\mathcal{S}$ from system parameters $\mathcal{X}$, its derivative can be used to solve real-world problems as a digital twin (bottom) like sensitivity analysis, inferring the system state, or optimizing system parameters $\mathbf{x} \in \mathcal{X}$ given an objective f. This only requires noisy/sparse state information.

ML models that mimic the physics of the real world [16]. Integration of such surrogate models into real-world scenarios makes them *digital twins* [13]. Critical infrastructure, such as energy and transportation systems as well as water distribution systems (WDSs), is one example where these models are of high relevance [4]. Here, important functionality ranges from reliable state estimation, predictive control, up to improved resilience.

We focus on one specific example, namely WDSs, where both data and models are available. In this context, states such as demands, pressures and flows are of high importance, but are also subject to high uncertainty. A state of the art (SOTA) surrogate model for WDSs has been proposed recently in the form of a physics-informed graph convolutional network (PI-GCN), which is trained based on realistic demands and underlying hydraulic principles [2].

However, while surrogate models typically aim to learn a physically well-defined dynamic directly, tasks in real-world settings often depend on partially unknown quantities. This results in optimization targets that are ill-posed or require architectures which are narrowly tailored to the problem at hand. We want to leverage the property of surrogate models to intrinsically represent the underlying physical structure. Figure 1 highlights our general idea that the backward pass of surrogates can be used to align any combination of known and unknown variables in a physically meaningful way and hence leverage this information to an efficient solution of downstream tasks which occur in this context. Specifically, due to fast computation and the differentiability that comes with a deep learning (DL) approach, such surrogate models enable us to solve important water-related downstream tasks in an end-to-end manner.

In this work, we will formalize the general principle and demonstrate its potential on three relevant tasks: Sparse-to-dense pressure estimation, sensor placement, and network rehabilitation. Although applied in a domain-specific context, this work targets a broader picture, as differentiability allows us to optimize any variable associated with the system that is an input to the surrogate model. This opens the floor to further downstream tasks in real-world scenarios, yielding flexible digital twins based on the backward pass of the surrogate model.

Contributions. Our contributions are threefold:

1. We model the general principle of using the backward pass of a physics-informed surrogate model as a digital twin, which allows to efficiently solve downstream tasks related to the underlying system.
2. We showcase the practicality of this concept in the context of WDSs:
    (a) We propose a new approach for the sparse-to-dense pressure estimation task with high generalizability. As this problem is ill-posed, our method generates a distribution of physically plausible hydraulic states.
    (b) We propose an improved approach to sensor placement by using the gradients of a PI-GCN surrogate model as a measure of sensitivity in combination with information theory.
    (c) We propose a new approach for the network rehabilitation task by gradient-based optimization of the diameters of the pipes that are inputs to the PI-GCN surrogate model.
3. We compare all methods to the SOTA baselines and thoroughly justify our evaluation methods.

Social and Domain Impact. Since WDSs belong to critical infrastructure, every methodology that improves the SOTA, for example in terms of accuracy or computational complexity, has a high social impact as it improves urban monitoring, planning and rehabilitation. Our proposed methods do not only satisfy this criterion but are also immediately applicable and extendable to other systems of critical infrastructure, given the availability of a differentiable surrogate model of the system.

2 Related Work

State Estimation in WDSs. A WDS consists of nodes such as junctions, reservoirs, and tanks connected via links such as pipes, pumps, and valves. Its physical states are characterized by pressure heads and demands at the nodes and flows through links. State estimation describes the task of mapping nodal demands and reservoir pressure heads to flows and pressure heads in the whole WDS. This task can be solved with hydraulic simulators such as EPANET [17]. ML surrogate models have been proposed to solve the state estimation task as a replacement for EPANET [2,12,23]. The most recent SOTA in DL is a PI-GCN [2]. This model is the only one that is regularized by the physical properties of the underlying system; it is less prone to overfit the training distribution.

Sparse-to-Dense Pressure Estimation. For downstream tasks, the pressure heads at every node in a WDS are of interest. In the real world, however, pressure is only known at locations where sensors are installed. Simulators such as EPANET could be used to generate the dense pressure state from demands, but the demands themselves are fully or partially unknown. Hence, simulators or surrogates alone cannot solve this problem. Estimating the full state from sparse sensor readings – sparse-to-dense state estimation – constitutes an ill-posed problem since multiple states can correspond to the same sensor readings; no analytic solutions have been proposed for this task. Recent DL approaches tackle this problem based on intrinsic regularization [1,10,20]. All of these works employ different types of graph convolutional networks (GCNs) with good results, but limited generalization to unseen WDS attributes.

Sensor Placement. WDS operations depend on information from sensors. As providing each node with a sensor is infeasible, sensor placement at selected junctions is a well-known optimization task [5,9,11,14,18]. Some existing algorithms come from the water domain directly [9,18]; recently, ML methods were leveraged [5,14]. Our work combines and improves concepts from [9] and [18] to solve the task of sensor placement. [9] solve a multi-objective optimization problem (OP) based on pressure sensitivity, estimated from hand-crafted gradients, and entropy, derived from these gradients as a measure of network coverage. We access the actual gradients of the differentiable PI-GCN surrogate model instead and use mutual information that assures potential sensors with high pressure sensitivity not to be redundant. [18] also use mutual information, but depend on the downstream task of leakage detection.

Network Rehabilitation. WDS planning and rehabilitation is a complicated and multi-objective task [15,21]. Given constraints and uncertainties in the future, planning and rehabilitation tasks are usually formulated as a multi-objective OP [3,6]. In the water community, genetic algorithms such as NSGA-II [7] are used to solve the latter, which are computationally expensive.

3 Background: Tasks in Water Distribution Systems

A WDS can be modeled as a graph, consisting of nodes $V = \{v_1, \ldots, v_{n_n}\}$ (consumer junctions, reservoirs and tanks) and edges $E = \{e_1, \ldots, e_{n_e}\} = \{e_{vu} \mid \forall v \in V, u \in \mathcal{N}(v)\}$ (pipes, pumps and valves). Among all nodes, we consider the set of reservoir nodes V_r, the consumer nodes $V_c = V \setminus V_r$ and the sensor nodes $V_s \subset V_c$, which are equipped with a sensor that measures the pressure head $h_v \in \mathbb{R}_+$ at the corresponding node $v \in V_s$. The state of a WDS is characterized by pressure heads $\mathbf{h} = (h_v)_{v \in V} \in \mathbb{R}_+^{n_n}$ at every node and water demands $\mathbf{d} = (d_v)_{v \in V_c} \in \mathbb{R}_+^{n_c}$ at every consumer node along with the water flows $\mathbf{q} = (q_e)_{e \in E} \in \mathbb{R}^{n_e}$ through every pipe. The relationships between these variables are governed by hydraulic principles, summarized in appendix A.1. A triplet $(\mathbf{h}, \mathbf{d}, \mathbf{q})$ that satisfies these hydraulics is called *physically correct*.

State Estimation. An important task in WDS is to estimate physically correct states $(\mathbf{h}, \mathbf{d}, \mathbf{q})$ of a WDS given initial conditions, like pressure heads $\mathbf{h}_{V_r} := (h_v)_{v \in V_r}$ at the reservoirs and the demands $\mathbf{d} = (d_v)_{v \in V_c}$ at the consumer nodes.

We will stick to the convention of subscripting a set to a vector if the vector is limited to that set. Especially, $\mathbf{h}_V = \mathbf{h}, \mathbf{d}_{V_c} = \mathbf{d}$ and $\mathbf{q}_E = \mathbf{q}$ holds. The first DL approach [2] for state estimation based on reservoir heads and consumer demands only is fully differentiable, unlike the SOTA hydraulic simulator EPANET [17]. This enables us to propose novel solutions for typical challenges in WDSs, which we present in the next subsections.

3.1 Sparse to Dense Pressure Estimation

Definition 1 (Sparse-to-dense pressure estimation). *Given a set of reservoir and sensor nodes V_r and V_s in a WDS, and observed pressure heads $\mathbf{h}_{V_r \cup V_s}$, sparse-to-dense pressure estimation aims at estimating the pressure heads $\mathbf{h}$ in the whole network.*

Baselines. This task was first approached by [1,10]. [10] train a spectral GCN that requires sparse heads $\mathbf{h}_{V_r \cup V_s}$ as inputs to obtain the heads $\mathbf{h}$ as an output. The more recent work of [1] presents an improved but less generalizable GCN that also requires pipe attributes in addition to the sparse pressures $\mathbf{h}_{V_r \cup V_s}$.

3.2 Sensor Placement

Definition 2 (Sensor placement). *Given a set of consumer nodes $V_c \subset V$ in a WDS and a budget $n_s \in \mathbb{N}$, sensor placement aims at finding an optimal subset of sensors $V_s \subset V_c$ of cardinality $|V_s| = n_s$.*

Optimality hereby depends on the task at hand and usually is related to the idea of deriving the behavior of the unobserved nodes $V_c \setminus V_s$ from the observable heads $\mathbf{h}_{V_s}$ at the sensor nodes. A common approach is to find the sensor nodes $V_s \subset V_c$ that optimize subsequent detection algorithms such as reducing the amount of undetected leakages in a WDS [18]. However, a disadvantage of such supervised modeling is the necessity of the labels, which might be difficult to observe, and specificity to the task.

Baselines. As a remedy, [9] propose a sensor placement methodology that solely relies on heads $\mathbf{h}$ based on different demands $\mathbf{d}$. They use hand-crafted and discretized derivatives to estimate the sensitivity of a node $v \in V$, measured by its change in head h_v depending on the change in roughness and pipe burst, and integrate it into an OP. They solve the latter by applying the popular multicriterial genetic algorithm NSGA-II [3,6,7]. In addition, we implement two other baselines: For the first, we choose sensors randomly. The second is motivated by the spatial structure: We apply spectral graph clustering [8] based on the WDS structure and pipe attributes and choose one sensor node per cluster randomly.

3.3 Network Rehabilitation

In general, network rehabilitation aims at modifying an already existing WDS as a consequence of changing demands in the future. In close cooperation with water-domain experts, we define the task of adapting diameters to changing demands. The expected new demands cannot be satisfied by the WDS due to too small pipe diameters. Therefore, some pipes need to be replaced by pipes with larger diameters while minimizing the changes and thus the required costs. Moreover, new diameters lead to new pressure heads that need to satisfy lower and upper pressure bounds for operational reasons.

Definition 3 (Diameter rehabilitation). *Given a set of consumer nodes $V_c \subset V$ in a WDS, expected new demands $\overline{\mathbf{d}}_i$ for $i = 1, ..., n$, which are higher than previous ones, current pipe diameters $\overline{\boldsymbol{\delta}} = (\overline{\delta}_e)_{e \in E} \in \mathbb{R}_+^{n_e}$, and lower and upper pressure bounds $\mathbf{h}_{V_c}^-, \mathbf{h}_{V_c}^+ \in \mathbb{R}_+^{n_c}$ on consumer nodes; diameter rehabilitation aims at finding new pipe diameters $\boldsymbol{\delta} = (\delta_e)_{e \in E} \in \mathbb{R}_+^{n_e}$ that obey the new demands and cause new pressure heads $\overline{\mathbf{h}}_i$ that obey the pressure bounds, i.e., $h_v^- \leq \overline{h}_{iv} \leq h_v^+$ for all $i = 1, ..., n$ and $v \in V_c$.*

Baselines. Currently, stochastic optimization algorithms are used to solve network rehabilitation tasks [15]. We will compare our approach with the popular multi-objective optimization scheme NSGA-II [3,6,7] mentioned before.

4 Background: PI-GCN Surrogate Model

Our work builds upon [2] that introduces a PI-GCN that is able to estimate physically correct states $(\tilde{\mathbf{h}}, \tilde{\mathbf{q}}, \tilde{\mathbf{d}})$ of a WDS given its heads $\mathbf{h}_{V_r}$ at reservoir nodes and its demands $\mathbf{d} = \mathbf{d}_{V_c}$ at consumer nodes (cf. *State Estimation* in Sect. 3). It consists of a trainable part and an integrative part which corrects predicted values to obey hydraulic principles. It is trained based on the objective function $\mathcal{L}_{\text{PI-GCN}} = \mathcal{L}(\mathbf{d}, \hat{\mathbf{d}}) + \rho \mathcal{L}(\mathbf{d}, \tilde{\mathbf{d}}) + \delta \mathcal{L}(\hat{\mathbf{q}}, \tilde{\mathbf{q}})$, where $(\hat{\mathbf{d}}, \hat{\mathbf{q}})$ and $(\tilde{\mathbf{d}}, \tilde{\mathbf{q}})$ are the intermediate outputs from the GCN and the final outputs of the PI-GCN model, respectively. A detailed description is given in appendix A.2. Depending on the task to be solved, the inputs to the model are given or will be estimated.

5 Methodology

The main concept of this work is to leverage physics-informed gradients accessible through a fully differentiable surrogate model. This allows solving the downstream tasks introduced in Sect. 3 by using gradient information (or more general, Jacobians) with respect to different parameters of the WDS.

In this work, we use the state estimation surrogate from [2] introduced in Sect. 4. More precisely, after training the PI-GCN for its optimal parameters $\Theta_{\text{opt.}}$ as in [2], we fix these parameters $\Theta_{\text{opt.}}$ and introduce a new objective

$f : \mathbb{R}^{n_{\text{in}}} \to \mathbb{R}^{n_{\text{out}}}$, $\mathbf{x} \mapsto f(\mathbf{x})$, which formalizes the downstream task. Consecutively, we use the differentiability of the function f, which is induced by the differentiability of the PI-GCN, to optimize the task-dependent parameter $\mathbf{x} \in \mathbb{R}^{n_{\text{in}}}$. A summary of the task-dependent network parameter $\mathbf{x}$ and the function f per task is displayed in Table 1. Additionally, the general concept of leveraging gradients independent of WDSs is displayed in Fig. 1.

Table 1. Choices for the parameter $\mathbf{x} \in \mathbb{R}^{n_{\text{in}}}$ and function $f : \mathbb{R}^{n_{\text{in}}} \to \mathbb{R}^{n_{\text{out}}}$.

Task	Task-dep. parameter	Objective function
Sparse-to-dense pressure estimation	$\mathbf{d}$	Eq. (1)
Sensor placement	$\mathbf{d}$	$\tilde{\mathbf{h}} = \tilde{\mathbf{h}}(\mathbf{d})$
Network rehabilitation	$\boldsymbol{\delta}$	Eq. (9)

5.1 Sparse to Dense Pressure Estimation

Given the assumptions from Definition 1, we utilize the differentiability of a trained PI-GCN [2] to estimate the pressure heads $\mathbf{h}$ in the whole network.

Required Data. To leverage this model, we assume the availability of *prior or realistic* consumer demands $\mathbf{d}_i$ for $i = 1, ..., n$. Since the reservoir heads are given by definition of the sparse-to-dense pressure estimation task, we do not require further data to leverage this model.

Objective Function. For this task, we choose the input demands $\mathbf{d} \in \mathbb{R}^{n_c}_+$ as the task-dependent network parameter. In order to find optimized demands $\mathbf{d}$ that produce outputs $(\tilde{\mathbf{h}}, \tilde{\mathbf{q}}, \tilde{\mathbf{d}})$ such that the heads $\tilde{\mathbf{h}}$ suit the sparse heads $\mathbf{h}_{V_r \cup V_s}$ on reservoir and sensor nodes, we choose $f(\mathbf{x}) = f(\mathbf{d})$ to be a suitable loss function with respect to which the demands $\mathbf{d}$ are optimized:

$$f(\mathbf{x}) = f(\mathbf{d}) = \mathcal{L}_{\text{S2D}}(\mathbf{d}) = \sum_{v \in V_r \cup V_s} |\tilde{h}_v(\mathbf{d}) - h_v|^2. \qquad (1)$$

Minimizing this loss through back-propagation yields WDS states $\mathbf{d} \mapsto (\tilde{\mathbf{h}}, \tilde{\mathbf{q}}, \tilde{\mathbf{d}})$ such that $\tilde{\mathbf{h}}_{V_r \cup V_s} \approx \mathbf{h}_{V_r \cup V_s}$ holds. The model's final output $\tilde{\mathbf{h}}$ is the solution to the sparse-to-dense pressure estimation task as defined in Definition 1.

Remark 1 (Availability of realistic demands). Our methodology is of high significance for other domain-related tasks: It does not only yield $\tilde{\mathbf{h}}$ as the solution to the sparse-to-dense pressure estimation task, but the whole WDS states $(\tilde{\mathbf{h}}, \tilde{\mathbf{q}}, \tilde{\mathbf{d}})$. Especially, we also obtain *realistic* demands $\tilde{\mathbf{d}}$ and flows $\tilde{\mathbf{q}}$, which are required for other downstream tasks, such as sensor placement (Subsect. 5.2).

Initial Parameters. In order to optimize the loss $\mathcal{L}_{\text{S2D}}(\mathbf{d})$ with respect to (w.r.t.) the demands $\mathbf{d}$ via back-propagation, we need to initialize a starting point $\mathbf{d}_0$ and choose a reservoir and sensor head observation $\mathbf{h}_{V_r \cup V_s}$ for a fixed set of sensors V_s. However, as the sparse-to-dense pressure estimation task is ill-posed, different initializations $\mathbf{d}_0$ can lead to different solutions $\hat{\mathbf{h}}$ still satisfying $\tilde{\mathbf{h}}_{V_r \cup V_s} = \mathbf{h}_{V_r \cup V_s}$.

Therefore, in order to obtain statistically significant results, we will consider different statistics over multiple solutions $\tilde{\mathbf{h}}_{li}$ via Monte Carlo sampling. The multiple solutions are obtained by different initializations $\mathbf{d}_{li}$ based on multiple sensor readings $\mathbf{h}_{lV_r \cup V_s}$ for $l = 1, ..., n_0$ and a suitably chosen subset $\{\mathbf{d}_i \mid i \in I_l\}$ of the demands $\mathbf{d}_i$ for $i = 1, ..., n$ (with I_l a subset of $\{1, ..., n\}$ such that $|I_l| = n_1 < n$ holds). We give detailed descriptions in appendix B.1.

Evaluation. We evaluate the solutions $\tilde{\mathbf{h}}_{li}$ of the sparse-to-dense pressure estimation task for $l = 1, ..., n_0$ and $i \in I_l$ by measuring the mean relative absolute error (MRAE) between these solutions and the true heads $\mathbf{h}_{lV_r \cup V_s}$ over the reservoir and sensor nodes, i.e.,

$$\text{MRAE}_{\text{S2D1}} = \frac{1}{n_0 n_1 (n_r + n_s)} \sum_{l=1}^{n_0} \sum_{i \in I_l} \sum_{v \in V_r \cup V_s} \frac{|\tilde{h}_{liv} - h_{lv}|}{h_{lv}}. \quad (2)$$

Additionally, we compare our solutions $\tilde{\mathbf{h}}_{li}$ over all nodes to the solutions $\hat{\mathbf{h}}_{li}$ of EPANET, representing the ground truth since real-world data is not available. We obtain the latter by inputting the demands $\tilde{\mathbf{d}}_{li}$ for $l = 1, ..., n_0$ and $i \in I_l$ that are also output of the model of [2] to EPANET. We record the MRAE between these two solutions:

$$\text{MRAE}_{\text{S2D2}} = \frac{1}{n_0 n_1 n_n} \sum_{l=1}^{n_0} \sum_{i \in I_l} \sum_{v \in V} \frac{|\tilde{h}_{liv} - \hat{h}_{liv}|}{\hat{h}_{liv}}. \quad (3)$$

5.2 Sensor Placement

Given the assumptions from Definition 2, we leverage information from the gradients of a trained PI-GCN of [2] together with information theory to find an optimal subset of sensors $V_s \subset V_c$.

Required Data. To leverage this model, we assume the availability of *realistic* reservoir heads and consumer demands $\mathbf{h}_{iV_r}$ and $\mathbf{d}_i$ for $i = 1, ..., n$, respectively.

Gradients. Intuitively, as sensors at nodes measure the heads, sensors are needed at places where heads are sensitive to a change in demands in the WDS. Therefore, for the sensor placement task, we again choose the task-dependent network parameter as the input demands $\mathbf{d} \in \mathbb{R}_+^{n_c}$. Choosing the function $f(\mathbf{x}) = (f_v(\mathbf{d}))_{v \in V_c} = \tilde{\mathbf{h}}_{V_c} \in \mathbb{R}_+^{n_c}$ as the heads on consumer nodes outputted by the PI-GCN, the sensor placement relates to the question for which node $v \in V_c$, the function f_v changes most w.r.t. any change of some demands $\mathbf{d}$.

This, in turn, translates to the question which function f_v has the largest gradient $\nabla_\mathbf{d} f_v(\mathbf{d}) = (\mathbf{J_d} f(\mathbf{d}))_v$. over all consumer nodes $v \in V_c$.

As PI-GCN is non-linear, the Jacobians $\mathbf{J_d} f(\mathbf{d})$ might differ for different input demands $\mathbf{d}$, we therefore seek the subset of sensor nodes V_s that optimizes the mean gradient norm over samples $\mathbf{d}_i$ for $i = 1, ..., n$ and sensor nodes $v \in V_s$:

$$\left\{\underset{V_s \subset V_c, |V_s|=n_s}{\operatorname{argmax}} \frac{1}{nn_s} \sum_{i=1}^{n} \sum_{v \in V_s} ||\nabla_\mathbf{d} f_v(\mathbf{d}_i)||_2. \right. \tag{4}$$

Limitations of Plain Gradients. OP (4) comes with two drawbacks: First, the optimization over subsets $V_s \subset V_c$ with budget n_s requires $\binom{n_c}{n_s}$ calls of the loss functions, which in most real-world scenarios makes it computationally expensive. Second, the head distributions of neighboring nodes or nodes in close proximity are often highly correlated. Therefore, neighboring nodes $v, u \in V_c$ usually have similar gradients $\nabla_\mathbf{d} f_v(\mathbf{d}_i)$ and $\nabla_\mathbf{d} f_u(\mathbf{d}_i)$ for any $i \in \{1, ..., n\}$. Due to their correlation, however, the information provided by the two nodes is redundant. In other words, the two nodes have high mutual information.

Mutual Information and Its Approximation. We solve the second problem by simultaneously decreasing the mutual information between the random variables H_v and H_u that are distributed according to the pressure heads at corresponding nodes $v, u \in V_c$. Since these heads are real-valued, the mutual information is formally defined by their continuous densities $\varphi_v, \varphi_u, \varphi_{vu}$ (definition 6 in appendix A.3). In practice, the densities $\varphi_v, \varphi_u, \varphi_{vu}$ are unknown. We solve this problem by approximating them by step functions. The approach is based on the idea of using normalized histograms with $n_b \in \mathbb{N}$ bins $A_j := [a_j, a_{j+1})$ for $j = 0, ..., n_b - 2$ and $A_{n_b-1} = [a_{n_b-1}, a_{n_b}]$. The histograms are created based on the Monte Carlo samples $f(\mathbf{d}_i) = \tilde{\mathbf{h}}_{iV_c} = (\tilde{h}_{iv})_{v \in V_c}$ for $i = 1, ..., n$.

As the focus of this work is not on the approximation of mutual information, the definition and a detailed derivation of the approximation of the mutual information of two continuously distributed random variables based on the approximated densities are given in appendix A.3. The main result of appendix A.3 is the following theorem, which we will make use of in the experiments.

Theorem 1 (Approximated mutual information). *In the setting of definition 5 and 7 (definition of density approximation and mutual information, respectively),*

$$\hat{I}(H_v, H_u) = \sum_{j_1=0}^{n_b-1} \sum_{j_2=0}^{n_b-1} p_{j_1,j_2}(v, u) \cdot \log \left(\frac{p_{j_1,j_2}(v, u)}{p_{j_1}(v) \cdot p_{j_2}(u)} \right) \quad \text{with}$$

$$p_{j_1,j_2}(v, u) = \frac{1}{n} \sum_{i=1}^{n} \mathbb{1}_{A_{j_1} \times A_{j_2}}(\tilde{h}_{iv}, \tilde{h}_{iu}),$$

$$p_j(v) = \frac{1}{n} \sum_{i=1}^{n} \mathbb{1}_{A_j}(\tilde{h}_{iv}) \quad \text{holds.}$$

Theorem 1 states that the approximated mutual information $\hat{I}(\mathrm{H}_v, \mathrm{H}_u)$ of two real-valued random variables with unknown densities equals the mutual information of the discrete probability distribution given by the relative amount of sampled observations $\tilde{\mathbf{h}}_{iV_c}$ for $i = 1, ..., n$ in the discretized bins A_j and $A_{j_1} \times A_{j_2}$ for $j, j_1, j_2 \in \{0, ..., n_b - 1\}$. The graph of these discretized densities corresponds to nothing more but the normalized histograms obtained by the Monte Carlo samples $\tilde{\mathbf{h}}_{iV_c}$. Visualizations of such approximated densities will be presented in Subsect. 6.2.

By theorem 3 in appendix A.3, the approximated mutual information converges towards the true mutual information when the number of observed samples are chosen as $n \geq n_b^2$ and the number of bins n_b goes to infinity.

Final Algorithm. A natural step is to extend OP (4) by the mean mutual information, i.e.,

$$\left\{ \underset{V_s \subset V_c, |V_s|=n_s}{\operatorname{argmax}} \frac{1}{nn_s} \sum_{i=1}^{n} \sum_{v \in V_s} \|\nabla_{\mathbf{d}} f_v(\mathbf{d}_i)\|_2 - \frac{1}{n_s} \sum_{v,u \in V_s} \hat{I}(\mathrm{H}_v, \mathrm{H}_u) \right. \tag{5}$$

between each two sensor nodes $v, u \in V_s$. However, testing this for each possible subset $V_s \subset V_c$ would also be computationally expensive. We solve this problem by using the algorithm of [18] in conjunction with our per-node objectives. More precisely, we define our objectives (cf. Eq. (5)) per node $v \in V_c$ as

$$\mathcal{L}_1(v) = \frac{1}{n} \sum_{i=1}^{n} \|\nabla_{\mathbf{d}} \tilde{h}_{iv}\|_2, \quad \mathcal{L}_2(v) = \frac{1}{n_s} \sum_{u \in V_s} \hat{I}(\mathrm{H}_v, \mathrm{H}_u) \tag{6}$$

instead of considering objectives per subset $V_s \subset V$. Consequently, given a hyperparameter $\lambda \in [0, 1]$, Algorithm 1 iteratively optimizes OPs consisting of these two normalized losses to iteratively add a node to the sensor node set V_s.

Algorithm 1. Sensor placement algorithm

In: Consumer nodes V_c, budget n_s, sampled heads $\tilde{\mathbf{h}}_{iV_c}$, hyperparameter $\lambda \in [0, 1]$.
1: $V_s = \emptyset$
2: $V_s \longleftarrow \underset{v \in V_c}{\operatorname{argmax}} \; \mathcal{L}_1(v)$
3: **while** $|V_s| < n_s$ **do**
4:     **for** $v \in V_c \setminus V_s$ **do**
5:         Compute $\mathcal{L}_1(v), \mathcal{L}_2(v)$
6:     **end for**
7: $V_s \longleftarrow \underset{v \in V_c \setminus V_s}{\operatorname{argmax}} \; \lambda \frac{\mathcal{L}_1(v) - \min_{\mathcal{L}_1}}{\max_{\mathcal{L}_1} - \min_{\mathcal{L}_1}} - (1 - \lambda) \frac{\mathcal{L}_2(v) - \min_{\mathcal{L}_2}}{\max_{\mathcal{L}_2} - \min_{\mathcal{L}_2}}$
8: **end while**
Out: Sensor nodes V_s.

In short, our method combines the idea of using derivatives as a measure of sensitivity per node and mutual information as a measure of redundancy between sensor nodes. Unlike other approaches, we have direct access to the derivatives and do not depend on any downstream task. The algorithm's output V_s is the solution to the sensor placement task as defined in Definition 2.

Evaluation. The quality of sensor placement is usually evaluated based on different downstream tasks in the WDS, such as leakage detection [18]. However, as elaborated above, a strength of our approach is the independence on downstream tasks. This is relevant in cases where the labels of the corresponding downstream tasks are not reliable and might not correspond to the ground truth.

At the same time, without the availability of a downstream task, this makes the evaluation of sensor placement itself a non-trivial task. In general, we expect the sensors to observe as much information as possible within the system, or equivalently, not observing redundant information. Therefore, we propose the mean mutual information over sensor nodes

$$\hat{I}_{\text{SP}} = \frac{1}{n_s(n_s - 1)} \sum_{v \in V_s} \sum_{u \in V_s \setminus \{v\}} \hat{I}(\mathrm{H}_v, \mathrm{H}_u) \tag{7}$$

as a downstream-task-independent evaluation measure (cf. Theorem 1).

For a downstream-task-dependent evaluation measure, we observe that the task of sparse-to-dense pressure estimation is based on a fixed set of sensor nodes V_s. Therefore, we can use the solutions $\tilde{\mathbf{h}}_{li}$ from the sparse-to-dense pressure estimation task for $l = 1, ..., n_0$ and $i \in I_l$ (cf. Subsect. 5.1) to evaluate different sensor placements. For a fixed observation of reservoir and sensor heads $\mathbf{h}_{l V_r \cup V_s}$ for $l \in \{1, ..., n_0\}$ and for a fixed node $v \in V$, a better set of sensors V_s will lead to solutions $(\tilde{h}_{liv})_{i \in I_l}$ more similar to each other, or in other words, to a less surprising underlying distribution. In this case, we aim to minimize its entropy. We compute the entropy similar to how we approximate the mutual information in this subsection. For more details, we refer to appendix B.2. Up to a constant, the discrete entropy is given by

$$\hat{E}(\mathrm{H}_{lv}) = -\sum_{j=0}^{n_b - 1} p_j(v) \cdot \log(p_j(v))$$

with $p_j(v)$ as defined in Theorem 1 (or theorem 5 in appendix A.3), but using the new heads $\tilde{\mathbf{h}}_{li}$ for $i \in I_l \subset \{1, ..., n\}$ instead of the heads $\tilde{\mathbf{h}}_i$ for $i = 1, ..., n$.

Finally, to summarize the entropy, we report the mean $\hat{E}_{\text{SP1}}$ and $\hat{E}_{\text{SP2}}$ over all reservoir and sensor observations $l = 1, ..., n_0$ as well as reservoir and sensor nodes $V_r \cup V_s$, and all nodes V, respectively:

$$\hat{E}_{\text{SP1}} = \frac{1}{n_0 n_r} \sum_{l=1}^{n_0} \sum_{v \in V_r \cup V_s} \hat{E}(\mathrm{H}_{lv}), \quad \hat{E}_{\text{SP2}} = \frac{1}{n_0 n_n} \sum_{l=1}^{n_0} \sum_{v \in V} \hat{E}(\mathrm{H}_{lv}). \tag{8}$$

5.3 Network Rehabilitation

So far, we demonstrated how the gradients of a surrogate model can be used to optimize nodal parameters. In the context of network rehabilitation, we want to optimize diameters, i.e. edge parameters that we can optimize with our method as well. Given the assumptions from Definition 3, we utilize the differentiability of a trained PI-GCN of [2] to find new pipe diameters $\boldsymbol{\delta}$.

Required Data. To leverage this model, we assume the availability of *realistic* reservoir heads $\mathbf{h}_{iV_r}$ for $i = 1, ..., n$. Since the demands are given per definition of the network rehabilitation task, we do not require further data.

Objective Function. Using the future demands $\overline{\mathbf{d}}_i$ as inputs to the model, we obtain heads $\overline{\mathbf{h}}_i := \tilde{\mathbf{h}}_i$ for $i = 1, ..., n$ which should obey the given pressure constraints. The network rehabilitation task can then be formulated as the following OP:

$$\min_{\boldsymbol{\delta}=(\delta_e)_{e\in E}\in\mathbb{R}_+^{n_e}} \sum_{e\in E} |\delta_e - \overline{\delta}_e| \quad \text{s.t.} \quad \tilde{h}_{iv} \geq h_v^-, \ \tilde{h}_{iv} \leq h_v^+ \quad \forall v \in V_c, i = 1, ..., n.$$

This problem can be solved by the before-mentioned genetic algorithm NSGA-II [3,6,7], which will serve as a baseline.

A computationally less costly alternative can be obtained using our gradient-based concept: As the heads $\tilde{\mathbf{h}}_i$ are an output of the model, they depend on the WDS's diameters $\boldsymbol{\delta}$ which we want to optimize. Therefore, this time, we can choose the task-dependent network parameter to be these pipe diameters $\boldsymbol{\delta} = (\delta_e)_{e\in E} \in \mathbb{R}_+^{n_e}$. Consecutively, to make use of the differentiability of PI-GCN, we transform the OP into a single, (almost-everywhere) differentiable loss function which we optimize w.r.t. to the pipe diameters $\boldsymbol{\delta}$, where $\alpha, \beta, \gamma \in [0, 1]$ are hyperparameters:

$$f(\mathbf{x}) = f(\boldsymbol{\delta}) = \mathcal{L}_{\text{NR}}(\boldsymbol{\delta}) = \alpha \cdot \mathcal{L}_{\text{PI-GCN}}(\boldsymbol{\delta}) + \beta \cdot \sum_{e\in E} |\overline{\delta}_e - \delta_e|$$
$$- \gamma \cdot \frac{1}{n} \sum_{i=1}^n \sum_{v\in V} (\max\{h_v^+ - \tilde{h}_{iv}(\boldsymbol{\delta}), 0\} + \max\{\tilde{h}_{iv}(\boldsymbol{\delta}) - h_v^-, 0\}). \quad (9)$$

Finally, after having trained the diameters $\boldsymbol{\delta}$, the optimized diameters correspond to the solution of the network rehabilitation task, delivering optimal changes required for each pipe in the WDS in order to satisfy future demands and pressure constraints as defined in Definition 3.

Initial Parameters. In order to optimize the loss $\mathcal{L}_{\text{NR}}(\boldsymbol{\delta})$ w.r.t. the diameter $\boldsymbol{\delta}$ via back-propagation, we need to initialize a starting point $\boldsymbol{\delta}_0$. In this case, we simply choose the old diameters $\boldsymbol{\delta}_0 = \overline{\boldsymbol{\delta}}$. They will not satisfy the pressure head constraints, leading to a large loss $\mathcal{L}_{\text{NR}}(\boldsymbol{\delta})$ that will be optimized iteratively.

Evaluation. We evaluate the solutions $\boldsymbol{\delta}$ of the network rehabilitation task by measuring the absolute cost (AC) and the mean absolute cost (MAC) between these solutions and the initial diameters $\overline{\boldsymbol{\delta}}$ over the edges, approximated by

$$\text{AC}_{\text{NR}} = \sum_{e\in E} |\overline{\delta}_e - \delta_e|, \quad \text{MAC}_{\text{NR}} = \frac{1}{n_e} \sum_{e\in E} |\overline{\delta}_e - \delta_e|. \quad (10)$$

Table 2. MRAE$_{S2D1}$ (cf. Eq. (2)) and MRAE$_{S2D2}$ (cf. Eq. (3)) of the sparse-to-dense pressure estimation task on different WDSs.

Method	Hanoi	Fossolo	Pescara	Area-C	Zhi Jiang
			MRAE$_{S2D1}$		
mGCN	10.82 ± 2.33	0.62 ± 0.06	3.61 ± 0.83	1.82 ± 0.41	13.64 ± 0.49
ChebNet	1.75 ± 0.89	0.05 ± 0.03	0.28 ± 0.33	0.10 ± 0.09	0.21 ± 0.30
Ours	**0.10 ± 0.15**	**0.00 ± 0.00**	**0.16 ± 0.07**	**0.03 ± 0.04**	**0.17 ± 0.20**
			MRAE$_{S2D2}$		
mGCN	7.68 ± 1.97	0.42 ± 0.02	2.63 ± 0.88	1.63 ± 0.41	12.08 ± 1.26
ChebNet	1.38 ± 0.73	0.02 ± 0.01	0.66 ± 0.23	0.09 ± 0.08	0.25 ± 0.35
Ours	**0.14 ± 0.16**	**0.01 ± 0.00**	**0.23 ± 0.19**	**0.03 ± 0.04**	**0.17 ± 0.20**

6 Experiments

We conduct experiments on the same five WDS datasets as [2] do. Details of those can be found in appendix C.1. As we solve all tasks from Sect. 3 utilizing trained models from [2], details on the training can be found in appendix C.2.

6.1 Sparse to Dense Pressure Estimation

Per WDS, we sample $n_0 \cdot n_1 = 100 \cdot 48 = 480$ initialized demands $\mathbf{d}_0$ according to Subsect. 5.1. They correspond to $n_0 = 100$ different demands per $n_1 = 48$ different reservoir and sensor observations. Table 2 shows the MRAE$_{S2D1}$ (cf. Eq. (2)) and MRAE$_{S2D2}$ (cf. Eq. (3)) for different WDSs. The mGCN baseline model from [1] does not generalize well to unseen WDS attributes since it uses these pipe features as input. The ChebNet GCN model from [10] only uses sparse pressures as input and performs better than mGCN. We obtain significantly better results as compared to the baseline methods on all networks and both in comparison to the true sensor observations (MRAE$_{S2D1}$) and in comparison to the results of EPANET (MRAE$_{S2D2}$).

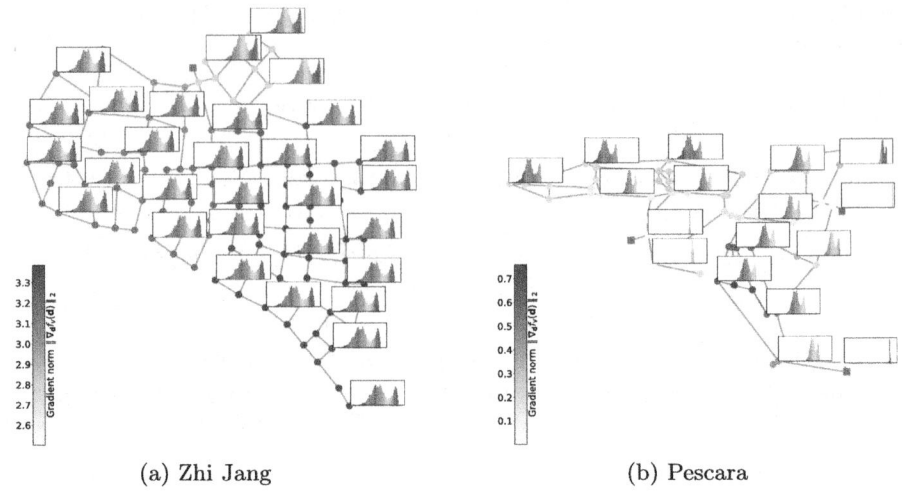

(a) Zhi Jang (b) Pescara

Fig. 2. Visualization of mean gradient norms in accordance with $\mathcal{L}_1$ and the approximated densities of head distributions that serve as a basis for $\mathcal{L}_2$.

6.2 Sensor Placement

We apply Algorithm 1 to all five WDSs and for different configurations of the hyperparameter $\lambda \in [0,1]$. A large λ puts more emphasis on $\mathcal{L}_1$, i.e. the gradients of the nodes, while a smaller λ puts more emphasis on $\mathcal{L}_2$, i.e., the mutual information between sensor nodes (cf. Eq. (6)). To get an intuition for the two loss functions, Fig. 2 displays the mean gradient norms in accordance with $\mathcal{L}_1$ and the approximated densities of head distributions that serve as a basis for $\mathcal{L}_2$ (cf. paragraph *Mutual information and its approximation* in Subsect. 5.2) for the Zhi Jiang and Pescara WDSs.

Consequently, Fig. 3 displays different sensor configurations based on different such hyperparameters in the WDS Zhi Jiang. As described in Subsect. 5.2, $\lambda = 1$ that results in focusing on the gradients only leads to a cluster of sensors, located in an area where the largest gradients appear. In contrast, $\lambda = 0$ causes sensor placement according to their mutual information only (except for the first sensor, which is picked according to its gradient, cf. Algorithm 1), which separates them all over the network. Typically, the mutual information between nodes close to a reservoir and nodes that are not close is low, hence some sensor nodes are placed close to a reservoir. Hyperparameters $\lambda \in (0,1)$ lead to a solution that distributes the sensors according to their mutual information while considering the gradient sizes.

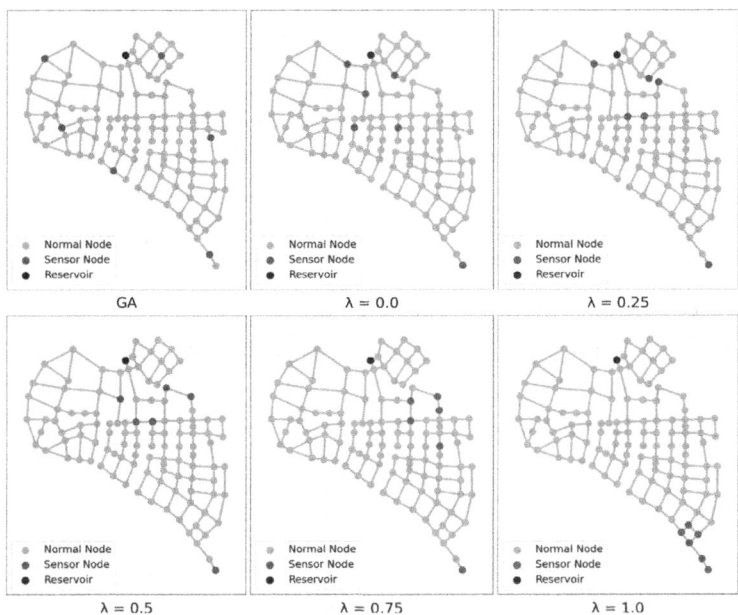

Fig. 3. Visualization of different sensor configurations based on different hyperparameters in the WDS Zhi Jiang.

Table 3 shows the downstream task-independent mean mutual information $\hat{I}_{\mathrm{SP}}$ (cf. Eq. (7)) per WDS and hyperparameter λ. It can be seen that the sensor configurations with a smaller λ cause smaller mutual information, meaning that

Table 3. Mean mutual information $\hat{I}_{\mathrm{SP}}$ (cf. Eq. (7)) for the sensor placement task for different sensor configurations in dependence of different hyperparameter λ and on different WDSs. Lowest values are highlighted in **bold** and second lowest in gray.

Method	Hanoi	Fossolo	Pescara	Area-C	Zhi Jiang
Random SP	1.99 ± 0.00	1.62 ± 0.00	1.64 ± 0.50	2.61 ± 0.10	2.76 ± 0.16
Clustering SP	2.59 ± 0.00	1.09 ± 0.00	1.73 ± 0.30	2.58 ± 0.10	2.74 ± 0.15
NSGA-II [9]	2.39 ± 0.00	1.97 ± 0.00	1.84 ± 0.24	2.56 ± 0.08	2.67 ± 0.10
Ours $\lambda = 0.00$	**0.00 ± 0.00**	**0.00 ± 0.00**	**0.24 ± 0.20**	**2.30 ± 0.12**	**2.61 ± 0.06**
Ours $\lambda = 0.125$	**0.00 ± 0.00**	**0.00 ± 0.00**	**0.24 ± 0.20**	2.36 ± 0.12	**2.61 ± 0.06**
Ours $\lambda = 0.25$	**0.00 ± 0.00**	**0.00 ± 0.00**	**0.24 ± 0.20**	2.36 ± 0.12	2.64 ± 0.07
Ours $\lambda = 0.50$	2.54 ± 0.00	1.97 ± 0.00	0.85 ± 0.93	2.65 ± 0.09	2.68 ± 0.07
Ours $\lambda = 0.75$	2.54 ± 0.00	1.97 ± 0.00	2.79 ± 0.17	2.67 ± 0.08	2.73 ± 0.13
Ours $\lambda = 1.00$	2.54 ± 0.00	2.14 ± 0.00	2.91 ± 0.08	3.24 ± 0.00	3.25 ± 0.02

they observe more information from the network. For smaller λ, we also obtain better results as compared to the baseline methods.

Additionally, table 10 in appendix C.3 shows the downstream task-dependent mean entropy $\hat{E}_{SP1}$ and $\hat{E}_{SP2}$ (cf. Eq. (8)) by WDS and per hyperparameter λ. Similar to the mutual information, the entropy $\hat{E}_{SP1}$ on reservoir and sensor nodes is lower for smaller λ as compared to larger λ, and smaller than the baselines in four out of five cases. The method with the lowest entropy $\hat{E}_{SP2}$ on all nodes differs among different WDSs and emphasizes that the evaluation of sensor placement on only one downstream task is not enough. Instead, future work should focus on the evaluation on several downstream tasks in order to investigate the average performance of sensor placement over all these tasks.

6.3 Network Rehabilitation

For each WDS, we consider multiple future demand collections and report the mean metrics as presented in Subsect. 5.3 over these collections. Table 4 shows the (mean) absolute cost AC_{NR} and MAC_{NR} (cf. Eq. (10)) per WDS, which demonstrates the potential benefits of our approach as compared to the baseline.

Additionally, Fig. 4 visualizes the percentage change of diameters in response to a change in demands in the WDS Pescara. At nodes close to the increased demands, the pipe diameters get increased the most, whereas the diameters close to the leftmost reservoir remain mostly unchanged. From the perspective of construction cost this is generally beneficial, although actual cost calculations include many more parameters and considerations. Extending our loss function by such a term can be an interesting avenue for future research.

Table 4. (Mean) absolute error AC_{NR} and MAC_{NR} (cf. Eq. 10) for the network rehabilitation task on different WDSs.

Method	Hanoi	Fossolo	Pescara	Area-C	Zhi Jiang
	AC_{NR}				
NSGA-II (NR)	365.6	801.8	1,596.0	233.6	121.3
Ours	**243.2**	**468.4**	**794.3**	**135.6**	**90.1**
	MAC_{NR}				
NSGA-II (NR)	10.8	13.8	16.1	2.1	0.7
Ours	**7.1**	**8.1**	**8.0**	**1.2**	**0.5**

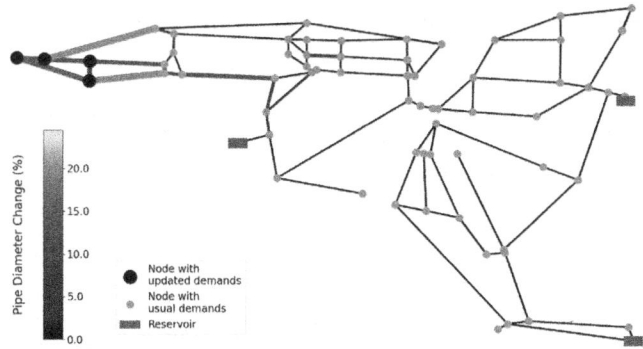

Fig. 4. Rehabilitation of the WDS Pescara. Black nodes experience a demand increase that leads to pressure dropping below the minimum pressure constraint (h_v^-). Our rehabilitation method increases the pipe diameters (colored lines) to allow for the additional flow required to satisfy h_v^-.

7 Conclusion and Future Work

In this work, we use the latest improvement in state estimation in WDSs using PI-GCN surrogate models as a starting point to solve several water-related downstream tasks such as sparse-to-dense pressure estimation, sensor placement, and network rehabilitation. This list is non-exhaustive and only demonstrates the possibilities that come with the differentiable state estimator presented by [2]. Moreover, this methodology extends to other differentiable surrogate models and is flexible w.r.t. available state information, allowing the backward pass of the surrogate model to be used as a digital twin. For example, sparse-to-dense pressure estimation requires the knowledge of prior consumer demands, which experts can usually provide. Meanwhile, sensor placement requires the knowledge of realistic reservoir heads and consumer demands, which can be obtained by the former method (cf. Remark 1). Lastly, network rehabilitation requires only knowledge of realistic reservoir heads, which is reasonable to assume for most situations. This allows immediate application of our solutions in practice, emphasizing the significance of our work to the water domain.

Limitations of this work are tightly coupled to the limitations of the PI-GCNs used for optimization. Scaling and the ability of our method to generalize are upper-bounded by the scaling of the surrogate model. However, our methods work with any differentiable physics-informed model and will benefit from further development of such. Moreover, all of our proposed methods are adaptable and can be improved given more information and data from the domain experts. For example, evaluating our sensor placement method on real-world data and different downstream tasks is an interesting avenue for future research. Incorporating an elaborate cost function into the task of network rehabilitation can lead to more structured results, as required by water experts.

Acknowledgments. We gratefully acknowledge funding from the European Research Council (ERC) under the ERC Synergy Grant Water-Futures (Grant agreement No. 951424).

Disclosure of Interests. The authors have no competing interests to declare that are relevant to the content of this article.

References

1. Ashraf, I., Hermes, L., Artelt, A., Hammer, B.: Spatial graph convolution neural networks for water distribution systems. In: Advances in Intelligent Data Analysis XXI. Springer (2023)
2. Ashraf, I., Strotherm, J., Hermes, L., Hammer, B.: Physics-informed graph neural networks for water distribution systems. In: Proceedings of the AAAI Conference on Artificial Intelligence, vol. 38 (2024)
3. Babayan, A.V., Savic, D.A., Walters, G.A.: Multi-objective optimization of water distribution system design under uncertain demand and pipe roughness. In: Topics on System Analysis and Integrated Water Resources Management. Elsevier (2007)
4. Brucherseifer, E., Winter, H., Mentges, A., Mühlhäuser, M., Hellmann, M.: Digital twin conceptual framework for improving critical infrastructure resilience. Automatisierungstechnik **69** (2021)
5. Candelieri, A., Ponti, A., Giordani, I., Archetti, F.: Lost in optimization of water distribution systems: better call bayes. Water **14** (2022)
6. Creaco, E., Franchini, M., Walski, T.M.: Taking account of uncertainty in demand growth when phasing the construction of a water distribution network. J. Water Resour. Plann. Manag. **141** (2015)
7. Deb, K., Pratap, A., Agarwal, S., Meyarivan, T.: A fast and elitist multiobjective genetic algorithm: NSGA-II. IEEE Trans. Evol. Comput. **6** (2002)
8. Donath, W., Hoffman, A.: Algorithms for partitioning graphs and computer logic based on eigenvectors of connection matrices. IBM Tech. Discl. Bull. **15**(3), 938–944 (1972)
9. Ferreira, B., Antunes, A., Carriço, N., Covas, D.: Multi-objective optimization of pressure sensor location for burst detection and network calibration. Comput. Chem. Eng. **162** (2022)
10. Hajgató, G., Gyires-Tóth, B., Paál, G.: Reconstructing nodal pressures in water distribution systems with graph neural networks. arXiv preprint arXiv:2104.13619 (2021)
11. Hu, C., Li, M., Zeng, D., Guo, S.: A survey on sensor placement for contamination detection in water distribution systems. Wirel. Netw. **24** (2018)
12. Kerimov, B., Taormina, R., Tscheikner-Gratl, F.: Towards transferable metamodels for water distribution systems with edge-based graph neural networks. Water Res. (2024)
13. Kreuzer, T., Papapetrou, P., Zdravkovic, J.: Artificial intelligence in digital twins–a systematic literature review. Data Knowl. Eng. **151** (2024)
14. Magini, R., Moretti, M., Boniforti, M.A., Guercio, R.: A machine-learning approach for monitoring water distribution networks (WDNs). Sustainability **15** (2023)
15. Mala-Jetmarova, H., Sultanova, N., Savic, D.: Lost in optimisation of water distribution systems? A literature review of system design. Water **10** (2018)

16. Nakka, R., Harursampath, D., Ponnusami, S.A.: A generalised deep learning-based surrogate model for homogenisation utilising material property encoding and physics-based bounds. Sci. Rep. **13** (2023)
17. Rossman, L., Woo, H., Tryby, M., Shang, F., Janke, R., Haxton, T.: Epanet 2.2 user's manual, water infrastructure division. CESER (2020)
18. Santos-Ruiz, I., López-Estrada, F.R., Puig, V., Valencia-Palomo, G., Hernández, H.R.: Pressure sensor placement for leak localization in water distribution networks using information theory. Sensors **22** (2022)
19. Scott, D.W.: Multivariate Density Estimation: Theory, Practice, and Visualization. Wiley (2015)
20. Truong, H., Tello, A., Lazovik, A., Degeler, V.: Graph neural networks for pressure estimation in water distribution systems. Water Resour. Res. **60** (2024)
21. Tsiami, L., Makropoulos, C., Savic, D.: Staged design of water distribution networks: a reinforcement learning approach. Eng. Proc. **69** (2024)
22. Vrachimis, S., Kyriakou, M., Eliades, D., Polycarpou, M.: Leakdb: a benchmark dataset for leakage diagnosis in water distribution networks description of benchmark. In: Proceedings of WDSA/CCWI Joint Conference, vol. 1 (2018)
23. Xing, L., Sela, L.: Graph neural networks for state estimation in water distribution systems: application of supervised and semisupervised learning. J. Water Resour. Plann. Manag. **148** (2022)

Open Access This chapter is licensed under the terms of the Creative Commons Attribution 4.0 International License (http://creativecommons.org/licenses/by/4.0/), which permits use, sharing, adaptation, distribution and reproduction in any medium or format, as long as you give appropriate credit to the original author(s) and the source, provide a link to the Creative Commons license and indicate if changes were made.

The images or other third party material in this chapter are included in the chapter's Creative Commons license, unless indicated otherwise in a credit line to the material. If material is not included in the chapter's Creative Commons license and your intended use is not permitted by statutory regulation or exceeds the permitted use, you will need to obtain permission directly from the copyright holder.

Leveraging External Factors in Household-Level Electrical Consumption Forecasting Using Hypernetworks

Fabien Bernier(✉), Maxime Cordy, and Yves Le Traon

SnT, University of Luxembourg, Esch-sur-Alzette, Luxembourg
{fabien.bernier,maxime.cordy,yves.letraon}@uni.lu

Abstract. Accurate electrical consumption forecasting is crucial for efficient energy management and resource allocation. While traditional time series forecasting relies on historical patterns and temporal dependencies, incorporating external factors—such as weather indicators—has shown significant potential for improving prediction accuracy in complex real-world applications. However, the inclusion of these additional features often degrades the performance of global predictive models trained on entire populations, despite improving individual household-level models. To address this challenge, we found that a hypernetwork architecture can effectively leverage external factors to enhance the accuracy of global electrical consumption forecasting models, by specifically adjusting the model weights to each consumer.

We collected a comprehensive dataset spanning two years, comprising consumption data from over 6000 luxembourgish households and corresponding external factors such as weather indicators, holidays, and major local events. By comparing various forecasting models, we demonstrate that a hypernetwork approach outperforms existing methods when associated to external factors, reducing forecasting errors and achieving the best accuracy while maintaining the benefits of a global model.

Keywords: Time series forecasting · Hypernetworks · Multivariate · Multiprofile

1 Introduction

Time series forecasting has traditionally relied on historical patterns and temporal dependencies to predict future values. However, in complex real-world applications such as electrical consumption prediction, the incorporation of external factors has proven crucial for improving forecast accuracy [19]. These exogenous variables provide additional context that can significantly influence consumption patterns beyond what historical data alone can reveal.

Supplementary Information The online version contains supplementary material available at https://doi.org/10.1007/978-3-032-06129-4_4.

In the specific case of electrical load forecasting, numerous studies have demonstrated that consumption patterns are heavily influenced by external factors such as weather conditions, calendar effects, and socio-economic indicators [8]. Temperature, in particular, has been shown to have a strong relationship with electricity demand, as heating and cooling needs vary significantly with ambient temperature [2]. Additionally, calendar variables including holidays, weekends, and seasonal patterns have been shown to capture regular variations in consumption behavior effectively [19,25]. These behaviors, however, are household-specific—e.g., a household using electric heating has a consumption more sensitive to cold temperatures than a household relying on gas. This represents a challenge to global forecasting models, which therefore have to capture specific behaviors when predicting the consumption.

In order to forecast consumption, two strategies can be distinguished:

- **Global model:** A unified model trained on aggregated data across the entire consumer population. This centralized approach facilitates comprehensive pattern recognition across diverse consumption behaviors, enhancing generalization capabilities while minimizing computational infrastructure requirements. Furthermore, recent architectural innovations specifically address multi-channel time series [11,23].
- **Individual models:** A dedicated model trained for each consumer entity. These specialized models capture household-specific consumption patterns with high fidelity. While traditionally resource-intensive in terms of computation and storage, recent advances in federated learning mitigate these constraints [17], though hardware limitations for on-device machine learning deployment remain significant.

To compare these two paradigms, we assess them on real-world data provided by an industrial partner, containing more than 6000 households consumptions over two years and corresponding external factors, ranging from weather data to football[1] events. As our results later demonstrate, although incorporating external factors as features theoretically enhances performance, these lead to overall performance degradation in global models. Conversely, individual models excel at mapping external factors to consumer-specific responses, but introduce substantial computational and storage overhead that scales linearly with the consumer population. In particular, this approach fails to capitalize on the substantial behavioral similarities across consumers. Since many households share comparable consumption patterns [20], training completely separate models results in significant parameter redundancy, as each individual model essentially learns the same forecasting task (electricity consumption) with variations to accommodate specific consumer profiles. This redundancy wastes computational resources and misses opportunities for knowledge sharing across similar consumer segments.

In order to bridge the gap between global models efficiency and individual models precision, hypernetworks offer a promising architectural paradigm, illustrated in Fig. 1. Hypernetworks [7] are meta-models designed to generate

---

[1] *Football* in this paper refers to *"soccer"*.

the weights of a primary task network conditioned on specific inputs. In our context, a hypernetwork can dynamically produce customized parameters for each consumer based on their unique embedding and current situation. This approach maintains the personalization advantages of individual models while dramatically reducing the parameter space, rather than maintaining thousands of separate forecasting models.

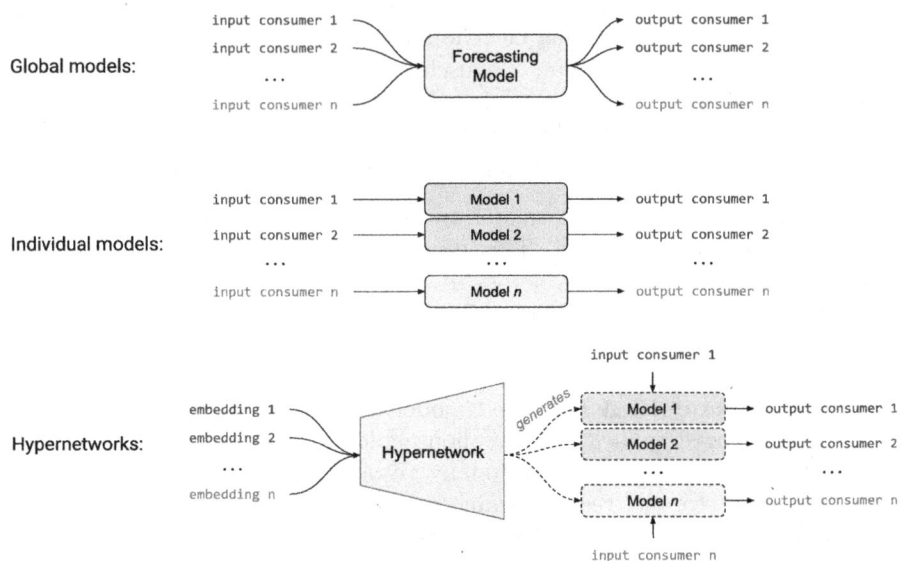

Fig. 1. Difference between global and individual models, and the proposed in-between solution using hypernetworks.

In this paper, we introduce a novel approach using hypernetworks and consumer-specific embeddings that enable global models to differentiate between individual households. These compact embeddings require minimal storage compared to full individual model parameters while preserving household-specific information. Our experimental results demonstrate that the hypernetwork architecture is the only one in the tested benchmark to leverage external factors to reduce forecasting error—and ultimately get the lowest error, beating state-of-the-art models by up to 16%—while conventional approaches result in performance degradation. This improvement enables more accurate, individualized forecasting within a computationally efficient framework.

2 Background

Time series forecasting has evolved from classical statistical methods to advanced deep learning architectures. Traditional approaches like ARIMA [16] rely on temporal dependencies within univariate series but struggle with incorporating exogenous variables effectively. More recently, neural network-based models have demonstrated significant improvements in handling complex time series tasks.

Transformer-based architectures [18] have been adapted for time series forecasting, with models like Informer [26] addressing the quadratic complexity limitations of vanilla transformers. N-HiTS [1] extends the interpretable N-BEATS framework [15] by introducing hierarchical interpolation and multi-rate data processing for improved performance across multiple horizons.

When it comes to electricity load forecasting, a critical challenge is to effectively incorporate multiple information channels, including historical consumption and various exogenous factors. Recent architectures specifically target this *multivariate* challenge: iTransformer [11] revolutionizes time series modeling by treating individual features as tokens and timestamps as channels, inverting the traditional approach. PatchTST [13] applies patching strategies to decompose time series into subseries, enabling more robust feature extraction. Lately, CARD [23] introduced channel attention mechanisms that dynamically weight the importance of different input variables.

These models however still have to process the input time series to figure out the consumer's profile, which can be highly different from one time series to another. Additionally, recognizing consumers profiles may also require longer input time series (e.g. in order to analyze their behaviors during vacations). Mixture of Experts (MoE) models [9] offer another approach to handling heterogeneous patterns in time series data. These architectures dynamically route inputs to specialized subnetworks, allowing the model to develop expertise given a specific embedding. Mixture of Linear Experts (MoLE) [12] extends this concept by creating embeddings that represent input characteristics in order to create this embedding, further improving adaptability to diverse time series behaviors.

Hypernetworks [7] represent a powerful paradigm where one network generates the weights for another. In the domain of time series, this approach has shown particular promise for addressing distribution shifts in time series [3] and has been applied to implicit neural representations as demonstrated in HyperTime [4]. Hypernetworks are especially relevant for our work as they can efficiently generate consumer-specific parameters from compact embeddings, potentially capturing individual household behaviors without requiring separate models for each consumer.

In the context of electricity load forecasting, these architectural innovations offer promising directions for improving prediction accuracy while maintaining computational efficiency. Our work builds upon these foundations to address the specific challenges of capturing consumer-specific responses to exogenous factors.

3 Hypernetworks for Time Series Forecasting

3.1 Problem Formulation

We address the task of forecasting electrical consumption time series for a diverse set of consumers while incorporating various external factors. Let $\mathcal{X} = \{x_1, x_2, \ldots, x_N\}$ represent the set of N consumer entities, each with its own hourly electrical consumption time series. For each consumer x_i, we denote its consumption at time t as $x_{i,t} \in \mathbb{R}$. Additionally, we have a set of numerical external factors $\Phi = \{\phi_1, \phi_2, \ldots, \phi_k\}$ (additional time series, such as temperature) and categorical external factors $\mathcal{C} = \{c_1, c_2, \ldots, c_m\}$.

Our objective is to predict future consumption values $y_{i,t:t+h} := x_{i,t+L:t+L+h}$ for a horizon h for every consumer i, given historical consumption $x_{i,t:t+L}$ for an input length L and external factors $\Phi_{t:t+L}$ and $\mathcal{C}_{t:t+L}$.

3.2 Model Architecture

Our proposed architecture consists of three main components: (1) an embedding layer for categorical variables, (2) a hypernetwork that generates consumer-specific weights, and (3) a linear forecasting model with these consumer-specific weights. The hypernetwork itself can be seen as a weights generator—that outputs matrices for the linear model—and essentially shares the same architecture than an image decoder [14]. An overview of the pipeline is illustrated in Fig. 2.

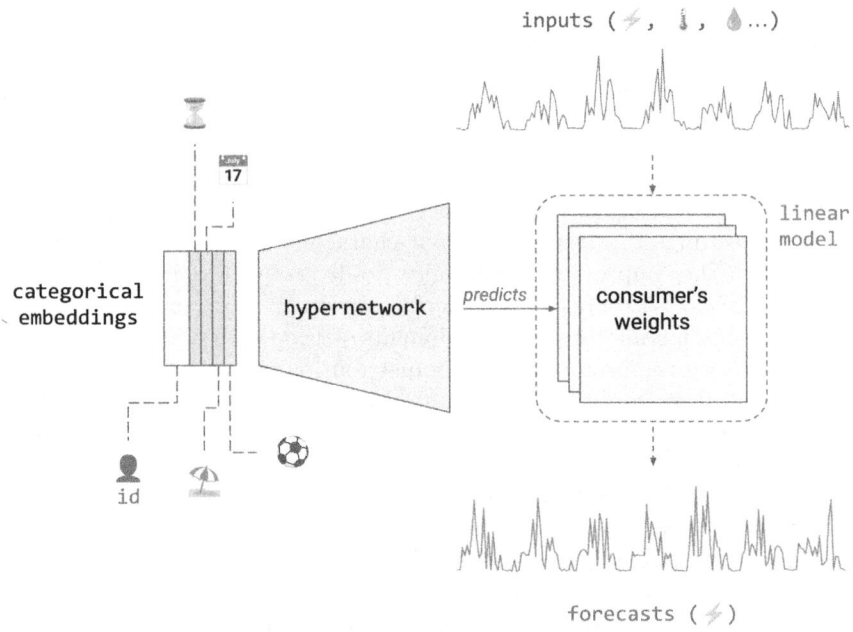

Fig. 2. Overview of the hypernetwork pipeline

Embedding Representation for Categorical Variables. For each categorical external factor $c_j \in \mathcal{C}$, we learn a dense embedding representation:

$$\mathbf{e}_j = \text{Embed}(c_j) \in \mathbb{R}^{d_j} \tag{1}$$

where d_j is the embedding dimension for factor j. Specifically, when categorical features are related and complementary, we sum their embeddings as follows:

$$\mathbf{e}_{\text{event}} = \begin{cases} \mathbf{e}_{\text{no event}}, & \text{if } c_{\text{event}_k} = 0 \text{ for all } k \\ \sum_{k \in \{k \mid c_{\text{event}_k} = 1\}} \mathbf{e}_{\text{event}_k}, & \text{otherwise} \end{cases} \tag{2}$$

All categorical embeddings are reshaped to matrices of size (p, q) and stacked together to form the hypernetwork input, as shown in Fig. 3. The resulting input tensor is denoted $\mathbf{z}_{i,t}$. The output matrices predicted by the hypernetwork have proportional dimensions from the inputs, and are of shape $(p \times u, q \times u)$, where u is the upscaling factor.

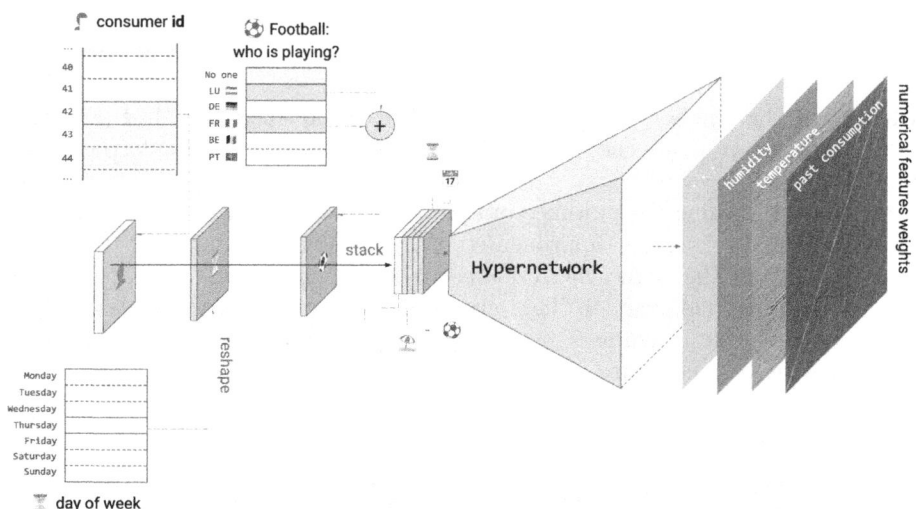

Fig. 3. Illustration of example embeddings. Each consumer ID and other known categorical features are transformed to embeddings, which are reshaped and stacked together to form the Hypernetwork input.

Forecasting Mechanism. The hypernetwork H_θ with parameters θ takes the concatenated features $\mathbf{z}_t$ and generates the weights for a consumer-specific linear forecasting model:

$$\mathbf{W}_{i,t} = H_\theta(\mathbf{z}_{i,t}) \in \mathbb{R}^{L \times h \times p} \tag{3}$$

where $p = k+1$ is the input dimension to the linear model, corresponding to the number of input time series; L is the input length, and h is the forecast horizon.

The consumer-specific weights $\mathbf{W}_{i,t}$ are then used in a linear model to produce the final forecasts. For each consumer i at time t, the input to the linear model includes both historical consumption values $x_{i,t:t+L} \in \mathbb{R}^L$ and the numerical external factors $\Phi_{t:t+L} \in \mathbb{R}^{k \times L}$.

The forecast for the next h time steps is then computed as:

$$\hat{\mathbf{y}}_{i,t:t+h} = \mathbf{W}_{i,t} \cdot \begin{pmatrix} x_{i,t:t+L} \\ \phi_{1,t:t+L} \\ \ldots \\ \phi_{k,t:t+L} \end{pmatrix} \tag{4}$$

Loss Function and Optimization. We jointly optimize the hypernetwork parameters θ along with all categorical feature embeddings e_i by minimizing the Mean Squared Error (MSE) between predictions and ground truth:

$$\min_{\theta, \{e_i\}} \sum_{i=1}^{N} \sum_{t \in \mathcal{T}} \|\hat{\mathbf{y}}_{i,t:t+h} - \mathbf{y}_{i,t:t+h}\|^2 \tag{5}$$

where N is the number of consumers, $\mathcal{T}$ is the set of time points in the training data, $\hat{\mathbf{y}}_{i,t:t+h}$ represents the predicted values, and $\mathbf{y}_{i,t:t+h}$ represents the ground truth values.

It is worth noting that unlike traditional neural networks where weights are directly optimized, in our approach, the hypernetwork parameters θ are optimized such that they can generate effective consumer-specific weights $\mathbf{W}_{i,t}$ for the linear forecasting model. This approach allows the model to dynamically adapt to different consumers' consumption patterns while leveraging shared knowledge across the entire consumer base.

3.3 Experimental Setup

Dataset. We collected a dataset comprising hourly data over a period of two years (2020 and 2021):

- **Numerical features:**
  - x: Consumption data (kWh) for $N = 6,010$ households and businesses in Luxembourg, provided by the national grid operator;
  - $\phi_{\text{temp}}, \phi_{\text{hum}}, \phi_{\text{wind}}, \phi_{\text{sun}}$: Weather indicators—temperature (°C), humidity (%), wind speed (km/h), sunlight (minutes of sun within one hour)[2];

---

[2] For simplicity purposes, these indicators are global for all consumers (weather in Luxembourg City), as the geographical area of study is small with few local variations.

– **Categorical features:**
  - i: Consumer ID, ranging from 0 to 6,009;
  - $c_{hour}, c_{dw}, c_{dm}, c_{month}$: Timestamps data—hour of day (24 values), day of week (7), day of month (31), month of year (12);
  - c_{sh}, c_{ph}: School holiday indicator (boolean), public holiday (boolean);
  - $c_{team_1}, \ldots, c_{team_5}$: 5 booleans, indicating wether Luxembourg, Germany, France, Belgium or Portugal will be playing in the current day or not—which are relevant teams for the studied region.

As it is usual for electric load forecasting [6], we set a forecast horizon of 1 week ($h = 168$), from an input length of 2 weeks ($L = 336$). We compare results with and without the inclusion of external factors, and run further experiments where only the consumer ID is provided in addition to electrical consumption. The dataset is partitioned chronologically into train/validation/test sets with standard 70%/10%/20% ratios following established time series forecasting protocols [22]. We preprocess the data by standardizing consumption values, temperature, and wind speed, while applying min-max normalization to humidity and sunlight variables as these represent naturally bounded quantities.

Hyperparameters. We set the upscaling factor u to 24, which fits with the daily seasonality characteristics of electricity consumption. Given this factor and the needed sizes of the output matrices (336×168), we have to make inputs of size 14×7. To achieve this, we concatenate two 7×7 matrices, leading to 49-dimensional vectors. One reason for this choice is the flexibility this concatenation offers: one could easily change the number of weeks in the input length or forecast horizon by getting shapes of $7a \times 7b$. For consumer IDs, we allocate twice the embedding capacity ($7 \times 7 \times 2$) to capture the more complex behavioral patterns associated with individual users. These embedding tensors are concatenated along the channel dimension before being processed by the model through four residual blocks, ultimately generating weight matrices of dimension 336×168 that map input sequences to forecast horizons. Experiments are repeated 10 times to reduce randomness effects.

Baseline Models. One natural additional solution to experiment with is Mixture of Linear Experts [12], as they demonstrate strong performance in general time series forecasting. Especially, each expert can specialize in specific groups of consumers, and embeddings can simply be used to attribute expert importance. We consider three MoLE variants, MoLE_DLinear, MoLE_RLinear and MoLE_RMLP, the latter consisting in two dense layers expert models. 16 experts are used, as this setting allowed the good performance shown in [12]. When using categorical features, we use the same embeddings as for hypernetworks, which are then linearly mapped to a probability distribution vector that assigns experts importance.

Baseline models also include state-of-the-art forecasting models with a focus on multiple channels processing: iTransformer (2024 [11]), CARD (2024 [23]),

NHits (2023 [1]), PatchTST (2022 [13]), RLinear (2022 [10]). For completeness, we include ARIMA as a classical statistical baseline which, despite its computational complexity, often provides competitive performance for structured time series forecasting tasks. Since the baseline models are designed for continuous multivariate time series, we adapt categorical features for fair comparison. For most categorical variables, we employ one-hot encoding to create additional binary channels. However, for the high-cardinality consumer ID feature, this approach would create an impractical number of channels. Instead, we learn low-dimensional embeddings for consumer IDs and repeat these embeddings across the temporal dimension, maintaining consistent representation while controlling dimensionality. The code is available on Github[3].

Finally, we compare these results with individual RLinear models being trained for every individual consumer—not predicted by the hypernetwork—in contrast with global models cited above.

Infrastructure. We use a Quadro RTX 8000 49GB GPU for all the experiments.

4 Results

Table 1. MSE and MAE values for different models and datasets. Models denoted with an asterisk * are not meant to handle categorical features: the consumer's ID embedding is provided in additional time series channels

Model	No external factor		Consumer ID only		+ External factors	
	MSE	MAE	MSE	MAE	MSE	MAE
Our method	-	-	0.1771	0.1872	<u>0.1734</u>	<u>0.1805</u>
MoLE_DLinear	0.1788	0.1899	0.1798	0.1891	0.1807	0.1904
MoLE_RLinear	0.1786	0.1836	0.1795	0.1844	0.1787	0.1839
MoLE_RMLP	0.1774	0.1820	0.1788	0.1832	0.1778	0.1826
Individual RLinears*	-	-	0.1741	0.1819	**0.1725**	**0.1792**
RLinear*	0.1806	0.1901	0.1874	0.1990	0.1888	0.2044
iTransformer*	0.1834	0.1867	0.1866	0.1894	0.1969	0.1966
CARD*	0.1759	0.1816	0.1760	0.1817	0.1765	0.1822
NHits*	0.1757	0.1849	0.1759	0.1851	0.1763	0.1854
PatchTST*	0.1759	0.1817	0.1762	0.1822	0.1768	0.1856
ARIMA	0.1780	0.1893	-	-	-	-

Our experimental results demonstrate several key findings regarding the performance of various time series forecasting models, as shown in Table 1. The

---

[3] https://github.com/serval-uni-lu/hypernetworks-time-series.

comparison across different input configurations yields important insights for model selection and deployment in real-world scenarios. The standard error is always $< 10^{-4}$ in the table, with two minor exceptions. More detail is provided in appendix.

4.1 Impact of External Factors

Perhaps the most surprising finding is that incorporating external factors generally degrades model performance across almost all architectures. This contradicts the common assumption that additional information should improve predictive accuracy. Only individual models and our hypernetwork approach exhibit improved performance when leveraging external factors, with decreases in both MSE and MAE compared to using consumer ID only or no external factors.

This exceptional behavior of hypernetworks suggests they possess a unique ability to effectively filter and use external information without introducing additional noise or complexity that harms prediction accuracy. The architecture's approach to handling multiple input channels appears fundamentally more effective than competing methods.

Consumer ID Embeddings. The performance when using only consumer ID embeddings as additional channels provides insights into how different models handle the introduction of this information. The MoLE models are the only global ones to improve the forecasting quality with the consumer ID provided— they are, however, with the hypernetworks, the only models designed to handle this specific input. Models not explicitly designed for this purpose always show a small degradation of performance. Despite not being optimized for categorical features, Transformer models still perform reasonably well in this scenario.

4.2 Performance Across Model Architectures

The Hypernetwork architecture exhibits superior performance compared to other models by successfully *imitating* the individual models approach and getting closer to its final performance, achieving the second lowest MSE (0.1734) and MAE (0.1805) when incorporating external factors. This represents a notable improvement over traditional approaches and even other deep learning models. CARD and NHits follow closely behind, with NHits demonstrating particularly strong performance (MSE: 0.1763, MAE: 0.1854), making it a viable alternative when no external factors are available.

Interestingly, the classical Arima model (MSE: 0.1780, MAE: 0.1893) remains competitive despite being significantly less complex than the deep learning approaches. This suggests that for certain forecasting tasks, traditional statistical methods should not be dismissed outright.

4.3 Cost

Training time. Our hypernetwork approach achieves a favorable trade-off between computational resources and prediction accuracy. While generating consumer-specific weights introduces additional computational overhead during training compared to global models, this cost is substantially lower than training individual models for each consumer. Specifically, our approach reduces training time by 7 h (approximately 70%) compared to individualized RLinear models.

Memory. The memory efficiency of our approach is particularly notable. The consumer embeddings require only 589K parameters (2.4MB), whereas individual linear models for all 6,010 consumers demand 3.392 billion parameters. This represents a parameter reduction factor of over 5,700×. Extrapolating to a real-world deployment with 1 million consumers, our approach would require only megabytes of storage compared to approximately 2.3TB for individual models. This dramatic reduction in model size not only decreases storage requirements but also eliminates the significant I/O overhead that would occur when loading individual models from disk during inference—a practical consideration not captured in our GPU-only-based timing experiments.

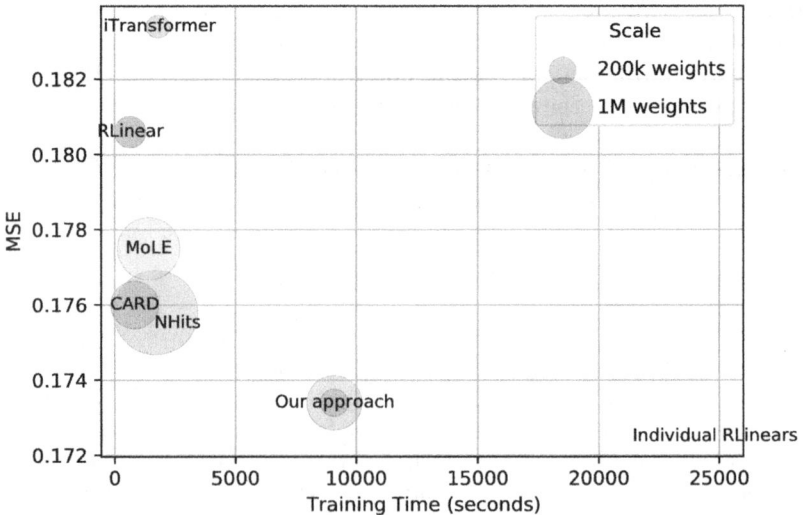

Fig. 4. Comparison of models training time vs. the best resulting MSE. Bubble sizes refer to the number of weights. For our approach, we distinguish the size of the hypernetwork itself, and the size including all 6010 consumers embeddings. The size for individual RLinear models (bottom right) is not shown as it would fill in all the figure.

4.4 Generalizing Consumers Embeddings

As consumers might evolve over time, with new ones arriving and others leaving, embeddings often need to be updated. This can be achieved by optimizing the embeddings in order to reduce the final forecasting error. One advantage of this method is that this task can be easily parallelized, and the hypernetwork model itself doesn't necessarily need to be retrained. Figure 5 reveals that our hypernetwork approach, when trained on merely 8% of the consumer base (500 out of 6010 consumers), outperforms competing models across the entire dataset, given consumers' embeddings after training. This adaptive capability presents a significant advantage in dynamic real-world settings where consumer populations continually evolve, as the model maintains strong predictive performance while requiring minimal retraining.

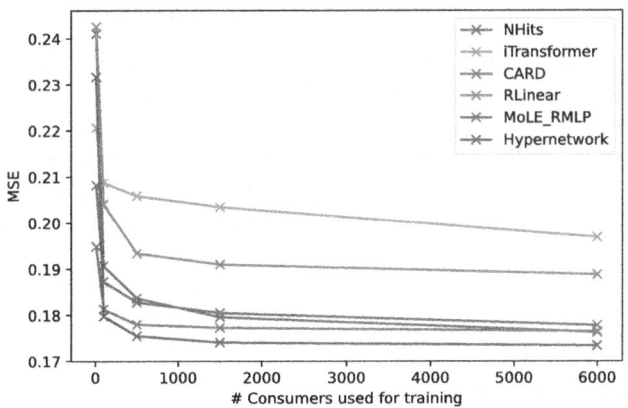

Fig. 5. Performance evaluated on the full dataset when only a portion of the 6010 consumers is used to train models

4.5 Ablation Studies

Inclusion of Categorical Features. As several models are not explicitly designed to handle categorical features, it is important to verify that these models are not penalized by such inclusions. Results in Table 2 show that categorical features have overall no significant impact on their performance, with MSE varying by at most 5×10^{-4} and MAE by at most 7×10^{-4}. Some models even show marginal improvements with categorical features (e.g., NHits exhibits lower MSE and MAE with categorical features included). This stability might suggest that the performance degradation observed in Table 1 is predominantly attributable to numerical features rather than categorical ones.

Table 2. Performance (± standard error) with and without categorical features, for models that only handle numerical time series as inputs (asterisked in Table 1)

Model	With categorical features		Without categorical features	
	MSE	MAE	MSE	MAE
iTransformer	0.1969 ± 0.0013	**0.1966** ± 0.0012	**0.1966** ± 0.0014	0.1971 ± 0.0012
CARD	0.1765 ± 0.0000	0.1822 ± 0.0001	**0.1764** ± 0.0000	0.1822 ± 0.0001
NHits	**0.1763** ± 0.0002	**0.1854** ± 0.0005	0.1768 ± 0.0002	0.1861 ± 0.0005
PatchTST	0.1768 ± 0.0001	**0.1856** ± 0.0001	**0.1767** ± 0.0001	0.1857 ± 0.0001
RLinear	**0.1888** ± 0.0000	**0.2044** ± 0.0001	0.1890 ± 0.0000	0.2048 ± 0.0001

Importance of Different External Factors. Table 3 demonstrates the significant contribution of each external factor to model performance. The experiment incorporating all external factors achieves the lowest error, while removing any category of factors leads to performance degradation. Temporal indicators emerge as the most critical component, with their removal causing the largest increase in error, followed by weather indicators and perhaps more interestingly football events. We also observe that including more external factors systematically decreases the standard error, thus making the performance less uncertain. Overall, these results quantitatively validate the hypernetwork's capacity to effectively integrate diverse external signals, capturing complex interdependencies between seemingly disparate factors and the target variable.

Table 3. MSE and MAE values (± standard error) for the hypernetwork model with and without groups of external factors

Removed data	MSE	MAE
Weather indicators	0.1768 ± 0.0008	0.1865 ± 0.0013
Date & time indicators	0.1777 ± 0.0010	0.1875 ± 0.0018
Football events	0.1761 ± 0.0004	0.1850 ± 0.0009
∅	**0.1734** ± 0.0002	**0.1808** ± 0.0004

5 Discussion

Mixed role of external factors. The findings from our study challenge the prevailing assumption that integrating more external factors naturally enhances forecasting accuracy. Our results indicate that, for most models, the inclusion of additional external factors often leads to performance degradation. This suggests that the signal-to-noise ratio introduced by these external factors may not always be beneficial, highlighting the complexity involved in effectively leveraging such data.

Linearity of the forecasting process. While the end forecast is inherently linear and may not capture complex patterns directly [24], the linear weights themselves are dynamically generated by the hypernetwork, which is nonlinear. This unique capability allows the linear model to adapt to more complex situations by tailoring weights to individual consumer behaviors, effectively making the final forecast nonlinear w.r.t. the input embeddings.

Adaptability. Hypernetworks present a notable exception by using external information without compromising performance, showcasing their capability in adapting to the varying significance of different input channels. New consumer embeddings can effectively be added over time to adapt to the demand evolution, which makes this solution suitable for real-world scenario. Encoders could be used in the future to be more effective than gradient descent in order to optimize these new embeddings.

Future work. Long time series embedding models [5, 21] could be used to create consumers embeddings optimized to serve as hypernetwork's input. This would allow even faster profile embedding without having to apply gradient descent. More complex models than simple linear models could also be considered as for the hypernetwork's output. As already suggest with MoLE models, adding simple layers to the output model could potentially increase the performance.

6 Conclusion

In conclusion, our investigation into leveraging hypernetworks for electrical consumption forecasting reveals their potential as a robust alternative to traditional methods. By successfully exploiting external factors without degrading model performance for a reasonable cost, hypernetworks offer a promising direction for future research, especially in applications requiring the integration of diverse data channels. The results highlight the need for continued exploration into models that effectively balance complexity and accuracy, with improvements yet to be made to optimize new consumers embeddings, overall encouraging advancements in time series forecasting, especially with real-world applications.

Acknowledgment. The authors would like to thank Creos Luxembourg S.A. for its support and valuable feedback.

References

1. Challu, C., Olivares, K.G., Oreshkin, B.N., Ramirez, F.G., Canseco, M.M., Dubrawski, A.: Nhits: neural hierarchical interpolation for time series forecasting. In: Proceedings of the AAAI Conference on Artificial Intelligence, vol. 37, pp. 6989–6997 (2023)

2. Chen, Y., et al.: Short-term electrical load forecasting using the support vector regression (svr) model to calculate the demand response baseline for office buildings. Appl. Energy **195**, 659–670 (2017). https://doi.org/10.1016/j.apenergy.2017.03.034, https://www.sciencedirect.com/science/article/pii/S0306261917302581
3. Duan, W., He, X., Zhou, L., Thiele, L., Rao, H.: Combating distribution shift for accurate time series forecasting via hypernetworks. In: 2022 IEEE 28th International Conference on Parallel and Distributed Systems (ICPADS), pp. 900–907. IEEE (2023)
4. Fons, E., Sztrajman, A., El-Laham, Y., Iosifidis, A., Vyetrenko, S.: Hypertime: Implicit neural representation for time series. arXiv preprint arXiv:2208.05836 (2022)
5. Fraikin, A., Bennetot, A., Allassonnière, S.: T-rep: Representation learning for time series using time-embeddings. arXiv preprint arXiv:2310.04486 (2023)
6. Gasparin, A., Lukovic, S., Alippi, C.: Deep learning for time series forecasting: the electric load case. CAAI Trans. Intell. Technol. **7**(1), 1–25 (2022)
7. Ha, D., Dai, A., Le, Q.V.: Hypernetworks. arXiv preprint arXiv:1609.09106 (2016)
8. Hong, T., Fan, S.: Probabilistic electric load forecasting: A tutorial review. Int. J. Forecast. **32**(3), 914–938 (2016). https://doi.org/10.1016/j.ijforecast.2015.11.011, https://www.sciencedirect.com/science/article/pii/S0169207015001508
9. Jacobs, R.A., Jordan, M.I., Nowlan, S.J., Hinton, G.E.: Adaptive mixtures of local experts. Neural Comput. **3**(1), 79–87 (1991)
10. Li, Z., Qi, S., Li, Y., Xu, Z.: Revisiting long-term time series forecasting: An investigation on linear mapping (2023), https://arxiv.org/abs/2305.10721
11. Liu, Y., et al.: itransformer: Inverted transformers are effective for time series forecasting (2024). https://arxiv.org/abs/2310.06625
12. Ni, R., Lin, Z., Wang, S., Fanti, G.: Mixture-of-linear-experts for long-term time series forecasting. In: International Conference on Artificial Intelligence and Statistic, pp. 4672–4680. PMLR (2024)
13. Nie, Y., Nguyen, N.H., Sinthong, P., Kalagnanam, J.: A time series is worth 64 words: Long-term forecasting with transformers. arXiv preprint arXiv:2211.14730 (2022)
14. van den Oord, A., Vinyals, O., Kavukcuoglu, K.: Neural discrete representation learning (2018). https://arxiv.org/abs/1711.00937
15. Oreshkin, B.N., Carpov, D., Chapados, N., Bengio, Y.: N-beats: Neural basis expansion analysis for interpretable time series forecasting. arXiv preprint arXiv:1905.10437 (2019)
16. Parzen, E.: Some recent advances in time series modeling. IEEE Trans. Autom. Control **19**(6), 723–730 (1974)
17. Savi, M., Olivadese, F.: Short-term energy consumption forecasting at the edge: a federated learning approach. IEEE Access **9**, 95949–95969 (2021). https://doi.org/10.1109/ACCESS.2021.3094089
18. Vaswani, A., et al.: Attention is all you need. Adv. Neural Inform. Process. Syst. **30** (2017)
19. Wang, Y., Chen, Q., Hong, T., Kang, C.: Review of smart meter data analytics: applications, methodologies, and challenges. IEEE Trans. Smart Grid **10**(3), 3125–3148 (May 2019). https://doi.org/10.1109/tsg.2018.2818167
20. Wang, Y., Chen, Q., Kang, C., Xia, Q.: Clustering of electricity consumption behavior dynamics toward big data applications. IEEE Trans. Smart Grid **7**(5), 2437–2447 (2016)
21. Wang, Y., et al.: Timexer: Empowering transformers for time series forecasting with exogenous variables. arXiv preprint arXiv:2402.19072 (2024)

22. Wu, H., Xu, J., Wang, J., Long, M.: Autoformer: decomposition transformers with auto-correlation for long-term series forecasting. Adv. Neural. Inf. Process. Syst. **34**, 22419–22430 (2021)
23. Xue, W., Zhou, T., Wen, Q., Gao, J., Ding, B., Jin, R.: Card: Channel aligned robust blend transformer for time series forecasting (2024). https://arxiv.org/abs/2305.12095
24. Zeng, A., Chen, M., Zhang, L., Xu, Q.: Are transformers effective for time series forecasting? In: Proceedings of the AAAI Conference on Artificial Intelligence, vol. 37, pp. 11121–11128 (2023)
25. Zhang, C., Zhou, J., Li, C., Fu, W., Peng, T.: A compound structure of elm based on feature selection and parameter optimization using hybrid backtracking search algorithm for wind speed forecasting. Energy Convers. Manage. **143**, 360–376 (2017). https://doi.org/10.1016/j.enconman.2017.04.007, https://www.sciencedirect.com/science/article/pii/S0196890417303126
26. Zhou, H., et al.: Informer: beyond efficient transformer for long sequence time-series forecasting. In: Proceedings of the AAAI Conference on Artificial Intelligence, vol. 35, pp. 11106–11115 (2021)

Enhancing Dynamic Control of Inertial District Energy Networks Through a Physics-Informed State-Space Model

Taha Boussaid[1,2(✉)], François Rousset[1], Marc Clausse[1], and Vasile-Marian Scuturici[2]

[1] INSA Lyon, CNRS, CETHIL, UMR 5008, 69100 Villeurbanne, France
taha.boussaid@insa-lyon.fr
[2] INSA Lyon, CNRS, LIRIS, UMR 5205, 69100 Villeurbanne, France

Abstract. Control optimization is essential to achieve high performance and cost efficiency in large-scale physical systems such as inertial district energy networks. These systems play a key role in mitigating climate change, particularly in heating and cooling. They integrate multiple energy sources and require intelligent control strategies to minimize costs while preserving high efficiency. However, the complexity of their underlying dynamics and the high computational load associated with their numerical simulation often make predictive control prohibitively slow or limited to short time horizons. In this work, we introduce a hybrid modeling framework where predictive control is accelerated using a physics-informed spatio-temporal graph neural network as a state-space surrogate model. Unlike existing models, our approach incorporates first-principle conservation laws to improve accuracy and generalization. This approach drastically reduces simulation time by four orders of magnitude, enabling faster decision-making. Using real-world data, we introduce a time-series augmentation technique combining Gaussian scaling and time slicing to improve model performance. Extensive experiments were conducted to evaluate the accuracy and generalization capacity of the learned model. Once validated, several optimization techniques were implemented, including evolutionary algorithms and reinforcement learning, which are assessed against rule-based control. Results show that this approach enables scalable predictions and efficient control, achieving up to 29% energy cost savings during mid-season while cutting optimization time from days to mere minutes.

Keywords: Predictive Control · Surrogate Modeling · Sustainable Energy Systems

1 Introduction

Mitigating climate change requires substantial reduction in greenhouse gas emissions [27]. To do so, the international energy agency (IEA) outlines the need to deploy large energy networks with multiple low-carbon-footprint energy sources to reach net-zero emissions by 2050 [21]. District heating networks are an example of such large inertial energy networks infrastructure [2]. The term 'inertial' refers to the system's thermal inertia, where the thermal mass of pipes and storage induces a time delay between heat production and demand. These networks use simultaneously various renewable energy sources such as biomass, geothermal, solar thermal in addition to thermal energy storage (TES). Incorporating an increasing number of energy sources requires rethinking smart control strategies to ensure efficient system deployment and achieve sustainable energy transition. Nevertheless, the different dynamics of energy sources (non-linearities, response time, intermittence etc.) bring new complexity to numerical simulation, which then makes the optimization of such systems prohibitively time-consuming, ranging from several hours [15] to days [13], using traditional approaches such as mixed integer non-linear programming (MINLP).

To address this limitation, recent works have used deep learning models, known for their fast inference and strong approximation capabilities in capturing complex dependencies and dynamics [10]. This technique was applied to diverse types of dynamical systems such as climate forecasting [33], thermal and electrical load forecasting [12,35], fluid dynamics and electromagnetics [8], among others.

However, applying deep learning to physical systems presents some challenges. Many studies rely on benchmark datasets with high-frequency sampling (e.g., 1 ms or 4 s) and simplified dynamics, often defined by few state variables or initial conditions [25,36]. In contrast, real-world systems are rarely monitored at such fine time steps and depend on numerous state variables and external inputs, such as weather disturbances. Moreover, while some real-world applications exist, no systematic methodology or design framework has been established for inertial district energy networks, in contrast to electric grids [40].

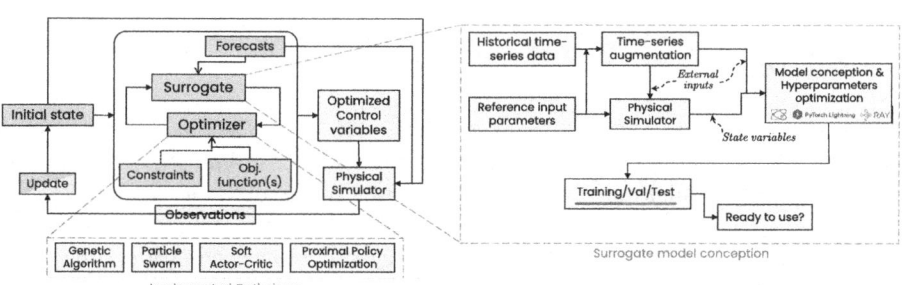

Fig. 1. Proposed methodology: Left block shows neural model predictive control using a validated surrogate model with evolutionary and RL optimizers. Right block schematizes surrogate model design, training, and validation pipeline.

In this work, we propose a hybrid strategy for control optimization of inertial district energy networks. The developed approach, schematized in Fig. 1, leverages the graph representation of such systems to develop an appropriate physics-informed spatio-temporal graph neural network (PI-STGCN). Unlike prior research, our proposition can handle various energy sources at different locations along with multiple consumer nodes to learn a state-space representation between these entities. The surrogate model development pipeline, shown in the right block of Fig. 1, relies on hyperparameters optimization and historical time-series augmentation during the learning phase. We demonstrate that, in addition to expanding the dataset size, the latter technique enables the incorporation of physically plausible scenarios into the training set. The effectiveness of our strategy is demonstrated through its application to a real-world system combining an inertial energy source (biomass) and an intermittent source (solar). The primary contributions can be summarized as follows:

- We introduce a system-agnostic methodology to accelerate optimal control of inertial district energy systems, leveraging their graph topology to model diverse producer and consumer types.
- We adapt Gaussian scaling and time warping to augment time-series data, exposing the model to plausible training scenarios. Furthermore, integrating a generic first-principle conservation equation enhances predictive confidence, resulting in a physics-informed model architecture.
- The proposed state-space surrogate is validated through extensive experiments and benchmarks. Scalability is demonstrated using a synthetic dataset, that is made publicly available. In addition, the optimization is carried out with several optimizers to assess their performance and the resulting control strategies.
- Applied to a real-world system with multiple energy sources and stringent constraints (e.g., power ramps, minimum time-on/off), our method achieves up to 29% energy cost reductions and reduces computational time by up to four orders of magnitude.

2 Related Work

Model predictive control (MPC), as schematized in Fig. 1 (left block), requires an accurate system model to perform predictive simulations. The control algorithm must accurately model and predict the system's behavior under various control scenarios. In control theory, this dynamical model is often expressed in a state-space, where the dynamics follow an ordinary differential equation (ODE) [7]. An optimal control problem is mathematically formulated for an optimization time-horizon $\mathcal{H}^{\text{opt}} = [0, \, t_f]$ as follows:

$$\frac{dx(t)}{dt} = f\left(x(t), \, u(t), \, d(t)\right), \quad \text{and} \quad x(0) = x_0,$$
$$C\left(t_f, \, u\right) = \int_0^{t_f} g\left(t, \, x_u(t), \, u(t)\right) dt + h(t_f, x_u(t_f)), \quad (1)$$
$$\text{s.t.} \quad x_u(t) = \arg\min \, C(t_f, u) \quad \text{and} \quad l\left(t, \, x(t), \, u(t)\right) \leq 0 \quad \forall t.$$

where f represents the non-linear system dynamics, $x \in \mathbb{R}^{n_x}$ is the vector of state variables, $u \in \mathbb{R}^{n_u}$ and $d \in \mathbb{R}^{n_d}$ are the vectors of control variables and external disturbances respectively. The cost function C is composed of a running cost g and a terminal cost h evaluated at $t = t_f$, the end of the optimization horizon $\mathcal{H}^{opt}$. In addition, state and control variables must satisfy a set of constraints l along the optimization horizon. State-space models can be learned in two distinct ways, discrete-time (DT) or continuous-time (CT) models [3,4]. DT models are more common and easier to construct as data is represented via discrete elements (arrays, vectors, etc.).

In the field of inertial district energy systems, a number of studies proposed surrogate DT models [9,19,20,29]. For example, the authors of [19] proposed to associate a recurrent neural network (RNN) to each consumer node in a district heating network (DHN). However, they only considered a single producer network, and the surrogate model conception relies on creating and connecting RNN cells. Graph neural networks (GNNs) encode topological features as inductive bias, as in [9], where a graph attention-based model was used to accelerate dynamic simulations by 1 to 2 orders of magnitude. However, no physical constraints were included, and only single-producer networks were studied. Other studies [20,29] proposed control strategies for district energy systems in which heat load forecasts are generated by GNN-based models, while the physical system still relied on a physical simulation which is computationally expensive. In terms of optimization techniques, evolutionary algorithms such as genetic algorithms (GA) are widely used to handle complex optimizations and have proven to be a reliable technique for inertial district energy systems optimization [34,39]. Another recent approach for control of energy systems employs deep reinforcement learning (RL) and showcased promising results [14,26]. For example, a soft actor-critic (SAC) agent achieved 5.79% reduction in fuel costs compared to rule-based control (RBC) over a two-days horizon in [14]. However, the study did not assess performance over longer horizons or across different periods of the year, limiting the results to the selected days.

Our work extends the previously reviewed research by introducing an application agnostic methodology to accelerate predictive control of multi-source district energy systems. The modularity of our framework is also demonstrated through its coupling with various optimizers, including both learning-based and evolutionary-based approaches. The surrogate model leverages spatio-temporal graph neural networks [22] and benefits from recent demonstrations showing that 'time-then-space' architectures offer superior expressivity compared to 'time-and-space' representations [17]. To further enhance generalizability, a physics-informed approach is used in training, where a mass conservation constraint, applicable to all inertial district energy systems, is added to the loss function.

3 Methodology

3.1 State-Space Surrogate Model

Inertial district energy networks consist of several producers delivering energy to consumers via a network of pipes and control valves as shown in Fig. 2a. These

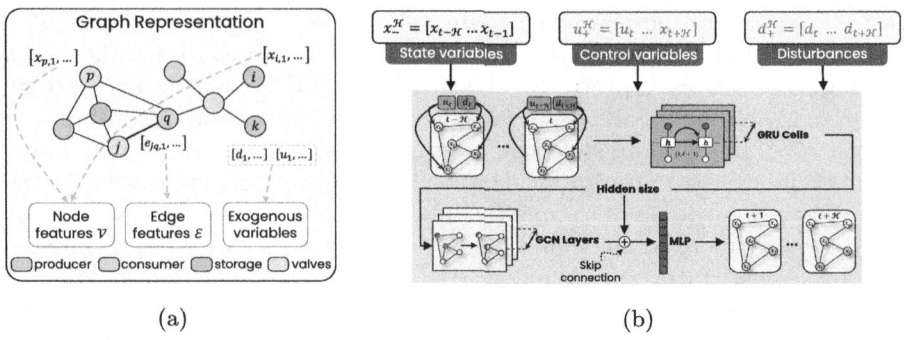

Fig. 2. Figure (a) illustrates a generic graph representation of the physical components of an inertial district energy system. Figure (b) depicts the surrogate model (PI-STGCN) architecture which integrates past state variables ($x_-^{\mathcal{H}}$), future control signals ($u_+^{\mathcal{H}}$) and disturbances ($d_+^{\mathcal{H}}$).

systems can be modeled as a graph $\mathcal{G} = (\mathcal{V}, \mathcal{E})$, where nodes $\mathcal{V}$ represent producers, consumers, storage or valves, and edges $\mathcal{E}$ correspond to pipes. Each graph entity holds multiple interconnected physical features, nodes are characterized by state variables (e.g. x = temperature) and the pipes by descriptive features such as their length and diameter. Moreover the entire system is influenced by exogenous variables, classified as disturbances (e.g. d = weather) or control variables (e.g. u = mass flowrate). Modern district energy networks incorporate diverse producer types at various locations [24]. Thermal energy storage further enhances flexibility by enabling asynchronous production and peak shaving.

The finite horizon optimal control problem in Eq. 1 seeks to optimize system trajectories while satisfying constraints. It minimizes a cost function C (e.g. fuel costs) over control variables u within the time horizon $\mathcal{H}^{\text{opt}}$. Here, the system dynamics (f in Eq. 1, computationally heavy) are replaced by a deep learning model f_θ (i.e., inference function), where θ represents model parameters. Due to system inertia and long-duration constraints on producers, predictive models require not only future control inputs and forecasted disturbances, but also historical state observations. This motivates the use of an autoregressive model formulation:

$$x_+^{\mathcal{H}^{\text{sm}}} = f_\theta \left(x_-^{\mathcal{H}^{\text{sm}}}, u_+^{\mathcal{H}^{\text{sm}}}, d_+^{\mathcal{H}^{\text{sm}}} \right). \tag{2}$$

where $\mathcal{H}^{\text{sm}}$ is the predictive range of the surrogate model, typically shorter than the optimization horizon $\mathcal{H}^{\text{opt}}$. The symbol + indicate predicted variables, meaning values from the current time t to $t + \mathcal{H}^{\text{sm}}$. Symbol − indicates past observations or measurements of state variables, meaning values from $t - \mathcal{H}^{\text{sm}}$ to t. The surrogate model parameters θ are optimized through supervised learning using a dataset generated from a high-fidelity physical simulator validated against real-world data. This dataset captures the system response (i.e. state variables) to various control inputs and disturbances. The inference function f_θ is a result of the surrogate model architecture shown in Fig. 2b. In addition to the past state variables, the future control variables u and disturbances d are diffused to each node so that the contained information is available to all network components. Next, these node inputs go through the encoder-processor-decoder where gated recurrent units (GRU) are used for encoding and graph convolution (GCN) for message passing. Figure 2b also introduces three hyperparameters that will be optimized: number of GRU layers, the hidden size (HS) and the number of GCN layers. The surrogate model is trained as the following optimization problem:

$$\begin{aligned}\underset{\theta}{\text{minimize}}\quad & \frac{1}{N_b}\sum_b \frac{1}{\mathcal{H}^{\text{sm}}}\sum_{t_b}^{t_b+\mathcal{H}^{\text{sm}}}\left[\frac{1}{|\mathcal{V}|}\sum_n \|\hat{x}_{b,n,t}-x_{b,n,t}\|_2^2 + \lambda \cdot \mathcal{F}_m^2(\hat{x})\right], \\ \text{s.t.}\quad & \mathcal{F}_m(\hat{x}) = \sum_{\text{producers}}\hat{x}_{b,n,t} - \sum_{\text{consumers}}\hat{x}_{b,n,t}, \\ & \hat{x}_+^{\mathcal{H}^{\text{sm}}} = f_\theta\left(x_-^{\mathcal{H}^{\text{sm}}}, u_+^{\mathcal{H}^{\text{sm}}}, d_+^{\mathcal{H}^{\text{sm}}}\right).\end{aligned} \quad (3)$$

In Eq. 3, the loss term is weighted (via $\lambda > 0$) with a physical constraint term represented by $\mathcal{F}_m$. This term is the mass flow rates conservation over the network: the sum of the mass flow rates sent to the consumers must be equal to the sum of mass flow rates sent by the producers. The loss is averaged and calculated over a batch of size N_b and across all the nodes in the network $\mathcal{V}$. This surrogate model (PI-STGCN) is compared to other approaches, namely vector-autoregressive (VARx), a multi-layer perceptron (MLP) and a recurrent neural network based on gated recurrent units (RNN).

3.2 Training and Validation Pipeline

The training and validation pipeline explained in this section is schematized in the right block of Fig. 1. To construct the training dataset, historical measurements are in general available for such systems, specially weather, heat demand and control variables. Therefore, data samples (i.e., $\{x_+^{\mathcal{H}^{\text{sm}}}, x_-^{\mathcal{H}^{\text{sm}}}, u_+^{\mathcal{H}^{\text{sm}}}, d_+^{\mathcal{H}^{\text{sm}}}\}$) are constructed by sliding over the training dataset as shown in Fig. 3a by a number of time steps called 'stride', its minimum value corresponds to the physical simulation time step, and the impact of choosing larger values is analyzed in Sect. 5.

The training dataset is constructed following the augmentation procedure schematized in Fig. 3b. In fact, the effectiveness of deep learning models depends on large training datasets. However, labeled data in many real-world time series applications are often scarce [37]. In model predictive control, the system response (i.e. state variables) are influenced by both the control variables and the external disturbances, via physical equations and constraints (recall Eq. 1). Therefore, the surrogate model must effectively capture the hidden dependencies between the state variables and the exogenous ones. This is the core idea schematized in Fig. 3b where the latter variables are augmented using the following procedure. We propose to augment time series by combining Gaussian

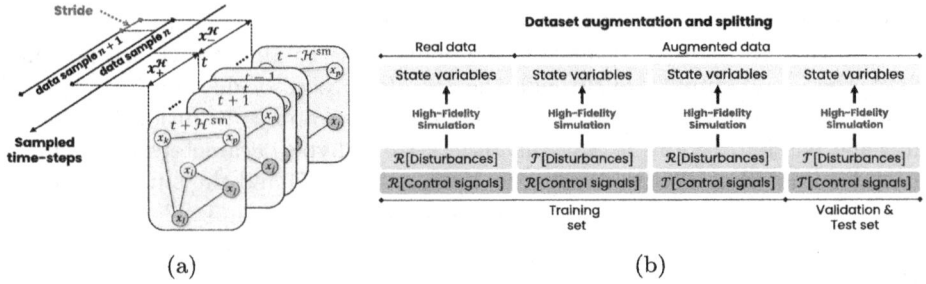

Fig. 3. Figure (a) illustrates dataset construction using a sliding window, with the 'stride' hyperparameter discussed later. Figure (b) presents the augmentation method based on state-space formulation. The original dataset, derived from real-world exogenous variables ($\mathcal{R}$), is used as a baseline. Each exogenous variable is then independently augmented ($\mathcal{T}$) and simulated using a high-fidelity physical digital twin.

scaling and window warping [32,37]. Let $z_{t|t+k} = [z_t, z_{t+1}, \ldots, z_{t+k}]$ denote a time series sample spanning k time steps, starting from t, the resulting augmented time series $z_{t|t+k}^{\text{aug}}$ is computed via:

$$\mathcal{T}\left[z_{t|t+k}\right] = [\underbrace{\gamma_0 \cdot z_t, \ldots, \gamma_1 \cdot z_{t+\Delta}}_{\Delta \ window}, \ldots, \underbrace{\gamma_j \cdot z_{t+j\Delta}, \ldots, \gamma_j \cdot z_{t+k}}_{\Delta \ window}], \tag{4}$$

where $\gamma \sim \mathcal{N}\left(1, \sigma_{aug}^2\right)$, $\mathcal{N}$ is the normal distribution, and $1 < \Delta < k$ is a fixed time window. Δ acts as the sampling frequency for scaling coefficients, meaning the data is scaled every Δ steps. State variables cannot be directly augmented, as their evolution is governed by physical laws. Instead, only control (u) and disturbance (d) inputs are augmented, thus, the resulting state trajectories are implicitly augmented through simulation of these inputs. The dataset is then scaled using min-max normalization and split to three distinct sets: training, validation and test (see Fig. 3b). The PI-STGCN model is trained using AdamW. Moreover, hyperparameters optimization is performed using the asynchronous successive halving algorithm (ASHA) from [23]. The considered hyperparameters and their corresponding range are given in Table 1 (a). The best model is then trained to reach its optimal performance, all experiments are performed on a 48 GB NVIDIA A40 GPU.

3.3 Optimization Techniques

As shown in Fig. 1, the model predictive control leverages the trained surrogate model to perform control optimization. The complexity of the studied system dynamics requires reliable and robust optimizers. In the literature, evolutionary algorithms such as genetic algorithms (GA) and particle swarm optimization (PSO) were widely adopted [5,28,39]. Recently, deep reinforcement learning has also demonstrated its ability to handle the complex optimization of such systems [14,26]. Therefore we implement four optimizers:

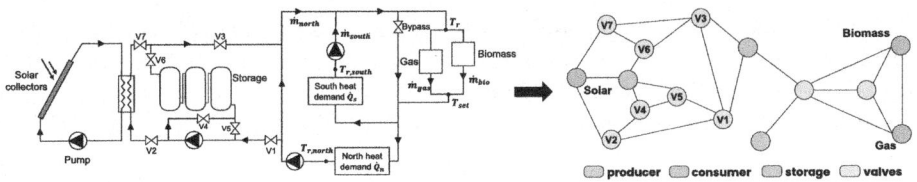

Fig. 4. Schematic of the real-world system and its graph representation, including biomass and gas boilers, solar field with thermal storage.

- **Evolutionary algorithms:** genetic algorithm (GA) and particle swarm optimization (PSO) are implemented using pymoo package [6]. The first is known for its robust exploration which avoids local optima, the second is used for its faster convergence rate [16].
- **Deep reinforcement learning:** the two on-policy and off-policy paradigms are tested by implementing proximal policy optimization (PPO) and soft actor-critic (SAC) respectively [31].

The optimal control problem in Eq. 1 can be directly solved using evolutionary algorithms, as they handle cost minimization and constraints separately. For RL, optimization constraints are added as penalty terms in the reward function.

4 Experiments

4.1 Study Case Description

The real-world system is illustrated in Fig. 4 and we have access to a physical simulator developed in Dymola, along with real consumption data and weather history. It incorporates three producers: biomass boiler, gas boiler, and a solar field connected to thermal storage. Several valves can be seen between the solar field and the storage, they allow different cycles: charging or discharging the storage, or direct injection from the solar field to the network. This system has several constraints, making it a representative case that requires complex control strategies: A) The biomass boiler must remain on for at least 72 h when started and off for at least 12 h when stopped. Besides, power variations are limited with ramp constraints. B) Solar energy must be used when available to avoid overheating and maximize renewable integration. C) Producers must supply sufficient heat to meet demand while maintaining temperature levels above a fixed threshold.

In the state-space formulation, mass flow rates are state variables for boilers and control valves. Boiler mass flow rates are proportional to power output, while valve flow rates indicate open or closed states. For consumers and storage, fluid temperature is considered as the state variable. In storage, temperature reflects stored heat, while consumer temperatures indicate the heat demand. The system also depends on external disturbances: solar irradiance G_{irr} and ambient temperature T_{amb}, which affect solar energy production, as well as heat demand in the northern $\dot{Q}_n$ and southern $\dot{Q}_s$ clusters. The predictive control optimizes energy source usage, determining when to activate sources, set power levels, and adjust flow rates. To do so, the network operators control the mass flow rates sent to each cluster, which updates Eq. 1 as follows:

$$u(t) = [\dot{m}_n(t), \dot{m}_s(t)], \text{ and } d(t) = \left[G_{irr}(t), T_{ext}(t), \dot{Q}_n(t), \dot{Q}_s(t)\right]. \quad (5)$$

The cost function C is set to the economic operational cost of the network and can be written as:

$$C(t_f, u) = \int_0^{t_f} c_{bio} \cdot \dot{Q}_{bio}(t) + c_{gas} \cdot \dot{Q}_{gas}(t) \, dt. \quad (6)$$

where c_{bio} and c_{gas} are fuel costs (in €/kWh) and $\dot{Q}$ the energy provided by biomass and gas respectively. Moreover, the optimal control must satisfy two constraints:

$$\left(\frac{u_{i,t} - u_{i,t-1}}{dt}\right)^2 \leq \delta_u, \text{ and } x_{i,t} \geq x_{min} \; \forall t \in \mathcal{H}^{opt}, \; i \in \{n, s\}. \quad (7)$$

The first constraint limits control variable variations to protect hydraulic pumps, while the second ensures outlet temperatures stay above a threshold for comfort and safety. As outlined in Sect. 3.3, constrained optimizations must be adapted to align with the reward-learning framework of RL agents. Accordingly, both PPO and SAC were trained using the following reward function:

$$r_t = -\frac{C_t}{C^*} - \frac{\lambda_u}{\mathcal{H}^{sm}} \sum_i \sum_t^{t+\mathcal{H}^{sm}} \left(\frac{u_{i,t} - u_{i,t-1}}{dt}\right)^2 - \frac{\lambda_x}{\mathcal{H}^{sm}} \sum_i \sum_t^{t+\mathcal{H}^{sm}} e^{x_{min} - x_{i,t}}. \quad (8)$$

This formulation balances three terms: minimizing economic costs (normalized by the RBC cost C^*), enforcing smooth control variations (weighted by λ_u), and ensuring temperature constraints (weighted by λ_x).

4.2 Scalability Test Cases

Confidentiality limits access to real-world district energy network data, especially for large, variable-sized networks. While the studied system (in Sect. 4.1) is representative in terms of energy sources and constraints, the lack of publicly available data makes synthetic testing essential. To address this, we introduce a synthetic dataset to evaluate scalability, focusing on the number of connected nodes[1].

---

[1] Link to dataset: https://doi.org/10.17605/OSF.IO/ZBJ5W.

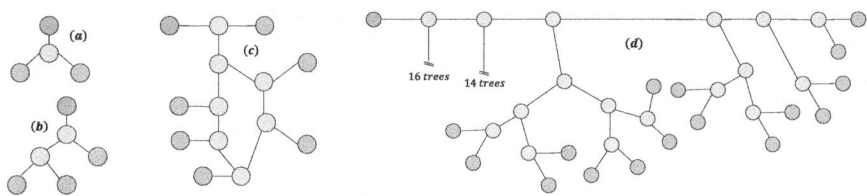

Fig. 5. Synthetic use cases for surrogate model scalability assessment. The number of nodes is 4 in (a), 6 in (b), 14 in (c) and 100 in (d).

A dynamic simulator was used to generate a one-year simulation for each network in Fig. 5 using a 10, 15 and 20-minute time step. The used open-source physical solver (TESPy [38]) has been validated on different use cases [11, 18]. The networks include consumers with different usage profiles -residential, commercial, administrative- generated using the demandlib package [30].

Each node has four state variables: inlet/outlet pressure and inlet/return temperatures. Disturbances include heat demand per consumer and ambient temperature, while control variables are supply temperature and mass flow rate of the producer node. Therefore, the scalability evaluates multiple aspects: adaptability to networks of varying sizes and the flexibility of the architecture in handling different numbers of state variables, control variables and disturbances.

5 Results

The prediction performance of the proposed surrogate model is evaluated using multiple regression metrics. All models are tested on the same dataset, consisting of the fully augmented year (recall Fig. 3b). Examples of augmented inputs are shown in Fig. 6a and 6b. To ensure realistic signals, augmentation is applied every $\Delta = 3$ hours, with σ_{aug} calibrated so that $\gamma_i \in [0.9, 1.1]$, keeping input variations within feasible bounds, especially for control variables like pumps flow rates. Two accuracy metrics are used: the mean squared error (MSE), which quantifies overall absolute prediction error on normalized data, and the symmetric mean absolute percentage error (sMAPE), which expresses the mean absolute error as a percentage. For precision, the coefficient of determination (R^2) is computed, and the percentage of mass balance compliance ($\mathcal{F}_m$) is reported.

5.1 Prediction Performance

In the following, results are shown for the best model configuration found through hyperparameters optimization. The ASHA samples 150 different configuration from the search space specified in Table 1(a). Unless pruned earlier by the optimizer, each configuration was trained for a maximum of 30 epochs. The top two configurations in Table 1(b) share the same architecture, differing only in l_r and λ, with 3.2M trainable parameters. Other surrogate models are set to the same parameter count for performance comparison, except for VARx, which has

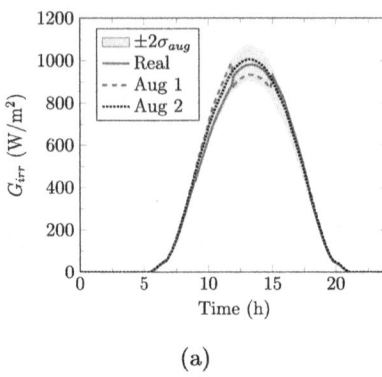 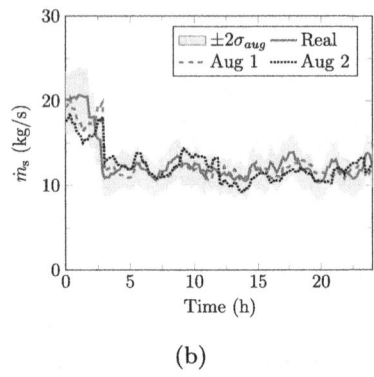

Fig. 6. Figures (a) and (b) show typical examples of solar irradiance and control variable augmentation over a one-day period.

Table 1. Hyperparameter search space and results. For (b): MSE is $\times 10^{-2}$, l_r is $\times 10^{-4}$ and $\mathcal{H}^{\mathrm{sm}} = 12$ h (i.e., same for all 5 configurations).

(a) ASHA search space

hyperparameter	search space
Batch size (N_b)	{64, 128}
Hidden size (HS)	{128, 256, 512}
GRU & GCN layers	{1, 2, 4}
Horizon ($\mathcal{H}^{\mathrm{sm}}$)	{6 h, 12 h, 24 h}
$l_r \in [10^{-4}, 10^{-1}]$	$\lambda \in [10^{-2}, 1]$

b) Top 5 configurations

rank	mse	gru/gcn	l_r	λ	HS	N_b
1	1.163	2/1	0.7	1	512	128
2	1.164	2/1	0.4	0.1	512	64
3	1.171	4/4	0.5	0.1	128	64
4	1.183	4/1	0.6	0.3	256	64
5	1.184	2/4	1.2	0.1	256	64

a fixed number of parameters. The stride hyperparameter is set to the smallest possible value (stride = 10 min).

In Fig. 7a–7c, the proposed surrogate model (PI-STGCN) outperforms all other models. Specifically, sMAPE is around 1.3%, and mass balance $\mathcal{F}_m$ is satisfied for 99% of tested samples. The impact of including $\mathcal{F}_m$ in the loss function (Eq. 3) is clear when comparing with STGCN, which shows degraded performance across all metrics. The MLP model performs significantly worse than the others, as it lacks both temporal dependencies (captured by all the others) and spatial dependencies (captured by STGCN and PI-STGCN).

The sensitivity analysis in Fig. 7b highlights the benefits of dataset augmentation. Training with 1 real year (RY) and 2 augmented years (AY) reduces sMAPE by 30%, MSE by 10%, and increases R^2 by 4% compared to using only 1 RY. Figure 7d examines the impact of the 'stride' hyperparameter from Fig. 3a. Three stride values were tested using the optimal model and 1RY+2AY dataset. The smallest stride (10 min) matches the real sampling frequency of weather data and numerical simulations. Results show a 42% lower sMAPE with s = 10 min vs. 1 h. In fact, a smaller stride increases training samples and enhances the model's

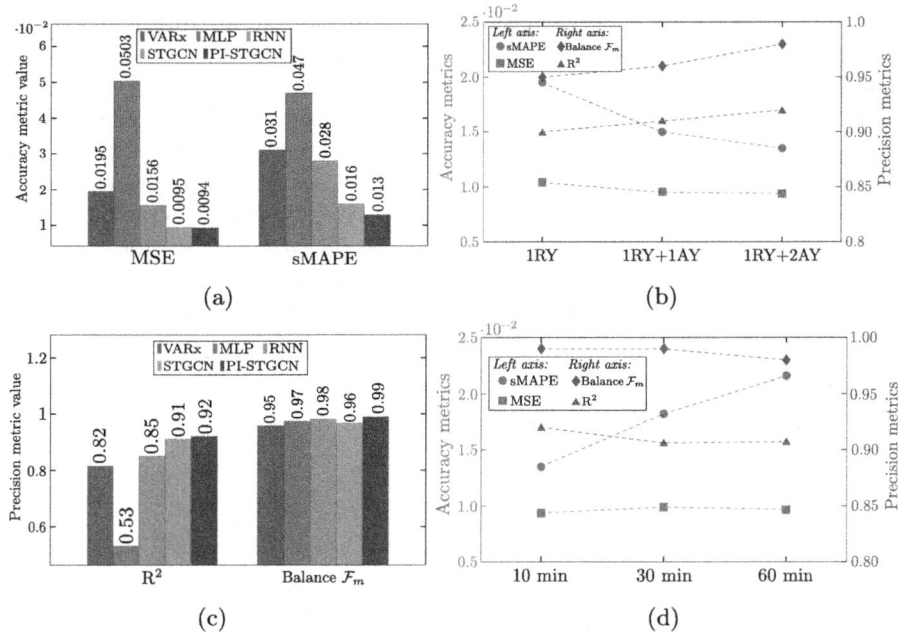

Fig. 7. Figures (a) and (c) compare the PI-STGCN model with other approaches using the real-world case from Fig. 4. Figures (b) and (d) analyze the model's sensitivity to the augmented dataset size (RY: real year, AY: augmented year) and the stride hyperparameter (10, 30 and 60 min) respectively.

ability to capture fast dynamics, particularly mass flow rates. However, high performance is still maintained across all tested strides, demonstrating robustness to different sampling rates. An example of PI-STGCN predictions on a test sample are shown in Fig. 8.

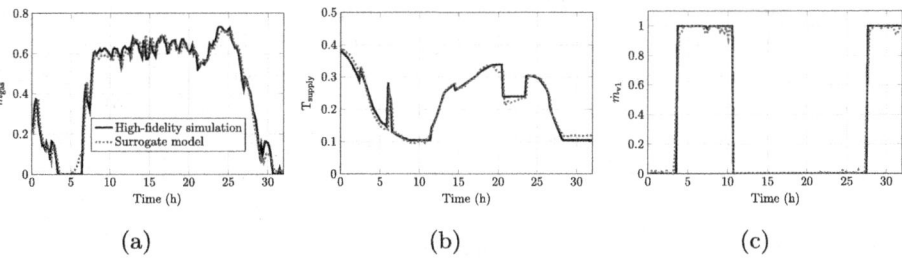

Fig. 8. An example of PI-STGCN predictions (red dotted curve) compared to high-fidelity simulation (black curve) over an illustrative period. The model accurately captures system dynamics, with prediction errors within an acceptable range for network operators. (Color figure online)

It can be seen that different dynamic patterns are well captured, both fast (8a) and relatively slow (8b) evolutions are learned. Moreover, the on/off behavior of control valves (8c) is precisely learned, this makes the model remarkably accurate. More quantitatively, the mean absolute errors (MAE) are in acceptable range for network operators: the supply temperature error remains below 1 K, the return temperatures below 1.5 K, and biomass/gas flow errors stay under 2 kg/s. Finally, the surrogate model achieves this high accuracy while reducing computational time by four orders of magnitude per data sample (speed-up factor $1.9 \cdot 10^4$) compared to Dymola physical simulator.

The results of the scalability assessment (using the networks of Fig. 5) are reported in Table 2.

Table 2. PI-STGCN scalability evaluation on the test cases from Fig 5.

Network	$\mathcal{V} = 4$	$\mathcal{V} = 6$	$\mathcal{V} = 14$	$\mathcal{V} = 100$
MSE	$1.2 \cdot 10^{-3}$	$1.2 \cdot 10^{-3}$	$1.9 \cdot 10^{-4}$	$8.1 \cdot 10^{-5}$
sMAPE	0.21	0.18	0.15	0.10
R^2	0.98	0.99	0.97	0.98
Simulation/sample	27 s	41 s	203 s	665 s
Inference/sample	20 ms	23 ms	52 ms	330 ms
Simulation/node	6.7 s	6.8 s	14.5 s	6.7 s
Inference/node	5 ms	3.8 ms	3.7 ms	3.3 ms

The surrogate model maintains high accuracy across all tested networks, with R^2 consistently above 0.97 and MSE decreasing as network size increases, indicating robustness in larger test cases. Physical simulations become increasingly expensive, with per-sample run-time rising from 27 s to 665 s, while surrogate inference remains efficient, increasing only from 20 ms to 330 ms. On average, this corresponds to a three order of magnitude reduction, which is lower than the $1.9 \cdot 10^4$ reduction observed when comparing inference to Dymola simulations. In fact, TESPy simulation used here includes certain physical simplifications, making it less computationally intensive than Dymola. On a per-node basis, inference time decreases with network size, from 5 ms to 3.3 ms, whereas simulation time remains stable around 6.7 s per node. This suggests that the surrogate model's inference time scales sub-linearly with the number of nodes.

5.2 Application to Control Optimization

After validating the learned state-space model, we demonstrate its use in optimal control. As shown in Fig. 1, the surrogate model estimates objective function values for control scenarios generated by the optimizers. To evaluate performance across seasons, optimal control is run over a full year using a sliding window with $\mathcal{H}^{opt} = 3$ days, illustrated in Fig. 9a. GA and PSO were executed until cost variations remained within a 5 euros tolerance for at least 10 generations or until the maximum number of iterations (200) was reached. PPO and SAC explored optimization periods until reaching a maximum cumulative reward, requiring 1.5 million (2 h 40 min) and 1 million (5 h 55 min) iterations, respectively. Prior to training, reward weights (λ_u, λ_x) in Eq. 8 were optimized using ASHA with Optuna's multi-objective framework [1]. The search space was $[10^{-3}, 1]$ for each weight, and the best pair was selected to maximize cost reduction while minimizing penalty terms (see details in Appendix A.1).

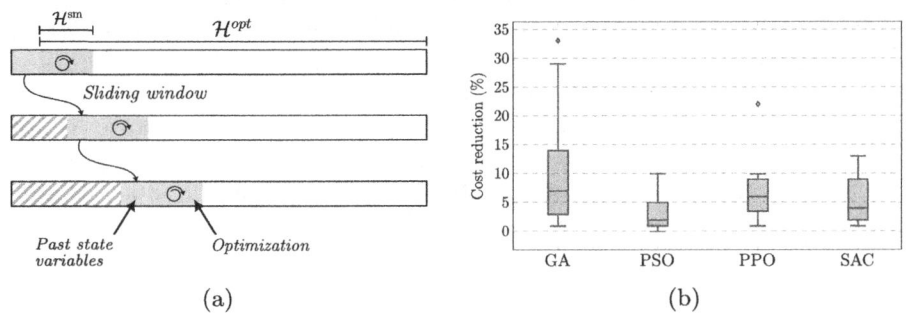

Fig. 9. Figure (a) illustrates the sliding window control deployed. Figure (b) summarizes the cost reductions results for the four implemented optimizers.

The optimization results are summarized in the box plot in Fig. 9b, showing cost reductions only for periods where optimizers were effective. During high-demand winter periods, when the boilers are at full capacities, cost reduction margins are smaller, with optimized costs just 0.1% lower than RBC, so they are not reported here. In contrast, mid-season periods showed greater savings due to the increased flexibility offered by solar energy and the variable heat demand. GA achieved the highest reductions, up to 33% with a median of 7%, followed by PPO (6%), SAC (4.5%), and PSO (3%). The two evolutionary-based methods show contrasting behavior: PSO had a faster convergence rate but tended to get stuck in local optima, explaining its lower performance. For RL agents, some periods with higher cost reductions were excluded due to violations of temperature constraints (Eq. 7), thus, the reward function needs further refinement. Another alternative is a hierarchical architecture with two agents: one enforcing constraints, the other optimizing cost.

A key feature of our methodology is the significant reduction in computation time. For instance, a single period optimization using GA or PSO takes about 10 min, while it would require more than 24 h if Dymola simulator was used. This improvement enables real-time optimal control and underscores the advantages of deep learning models in accelerating the optimization and deployment of inertial district energy systems.

6 Conclusion

In this work, we presented a deep learning-based methodology for optimal control of computationally intensive multi-source inertial district energy networks. We provide an system-agnostic framework for training and validating a physics-informed surrogate model, leveraging historical data augmentation and hyperparameters optimization. The dynamics were precisely learned, with sMAPE values lower than 1.3% and R^2 values over 0.97. Furthermore, the trained model modularity is demonstrated by leveraging it with both evolutionary-based optimizers and reinforcement learning agents. Our results demonstrate significant improvements, with cost reductions of up 30% in mid-season and a drastic decrease in computational time (up to four orders of magnitude). Future lines of work will address the current limitations: Improve the reward function to increase the effectiveness of RL strategies and include stochastic forecasts to better capture real-world noise and variability. Another perspective is considering cases with unusual disturbances (e.g. extreme weather) and/or equipment failures, followed by an analysis of the control strategies found by the optimizers.

Acknowledgments. This work was supported by the French Ministry of Higher Education and Research.

Disclosure of Interests. The authors have no competing interests to declare that are relevant to the content of this article.

A Appendix

A.1 RL Hyperparameters Optimization

For each agent, ASHA samples 25 configurations. SAC is trained for 150,000 steps, while PPO runs for 250,000 steps due to slower convergence. Each term in the reward function (Eq. 8) is evaluated as a separate metric: the negative cost reduction (%), the temperature penalty, and the flowrates penalty (both normalized). The optimization minimizes these three metrics, and the resulting Pareto fronts are shown in Fig. 10.

The optimal hyperparameters (λ_u, λ_x) are selected as the closest point (distance wise) to the "ideal" minimum for each objective individually. The other hyperparameters are taken from RL Zoo[2] and are reported below in Table 3.

---

[2] https://github.com/DLR-RM/rl-baselines3-zoo.

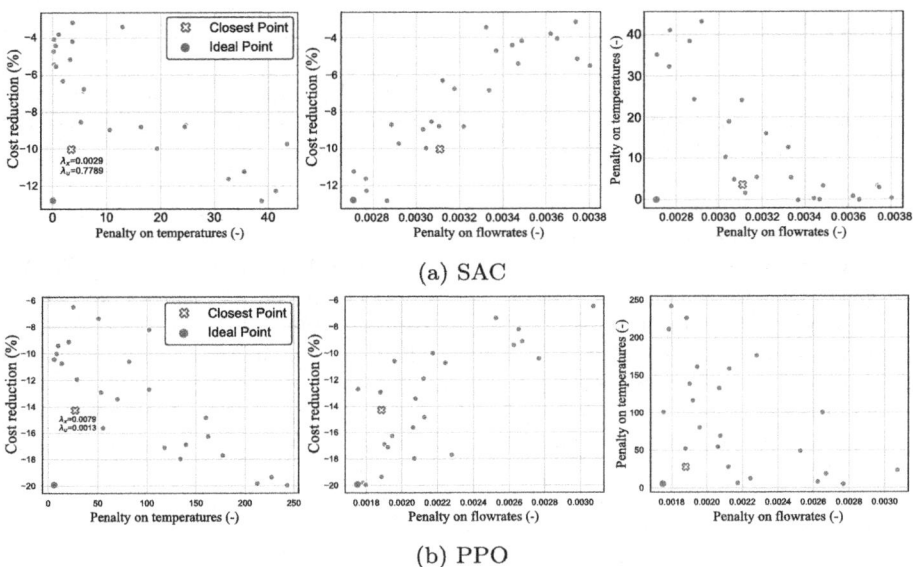

Fig. 10. Hyperparameter optimization results. Each subplot shows a projection of the 3-objective Pareto surface for SAC and PPO.

Table 3. Other hyperparameters for SAC and PPO.

Hyperparameter	SAC	PPO
Shared		
Batch size (N_b)	128	64
Discount factor (γ)	0.99	
Learning rate	$3 \cdot 10^{-4}$	
SAC-Specific		
Buffer size ($N_\mathcal{B}$)	10^4	–
Training frequency & Gradient cycle	1	–
Target smoothing coefficient	0.005	–
Target update interval	100	–
PPO-Specific		
Number of collected steps (N_{steps})	–	1920
Gradient cycle (N_{epochs})	–	10
Actor & Critic Networks		
Number of hidden layers	2	2
Number of hidden units	256	64
Non-linear activations	ReLU	Tanh

References

1. Akiba, T., Sano, S., Yanase, T., Ohta, T., Koyama, M.: Optuna: a next-generation hyperparameter optimization framework. In: Proceedings of the 25th ACM SIGKDD International Conference on Knowledge Discovery and Data Mining (2019)
2. Angelidis, O., Ioannou, A., Friedrich, D., Thomson, A., Falcone, G.: District heating and cooling networks with decentralized energy substations: opportunities and barriers for holistic energy system decarbonisation. Energy **269**, 126740 (2023)
3. Ayed, I., de Bézenac, E., Pajot, A., Brajard, J., Gallinari, P.: Learning dynamical systems from partial observations. arXiv preprint arXiv:1902.11136 (2019)
4. Beintema, G.I., Schoukens, M., Tóth, R.: Continuous-time identification of dynamic state-space models by deep subspace encoding. In: ICLR (2023)
5. Betancourt Schwarz, M., Veyron, M., Clausse, M.: Impact of flexibility implementation on the control of a solar district heating system. In: Solar, vol. 4, pp. 1–14. MDPI (2023)
6. Blank, J., Deb, K.: pymoo: multi-objective optimization in python. IEEE Access **8**, 89497–89509 (2020)
7. Blaud, P.C., Chevrel, P., Claveau, F., Haurant, P., Mouraud, A.: From multiphysics models to neural network for predictive control synthesis. Opt. Control Appl. Methods (2021)
8. Botache, D., et al.: Enhancing multi-objective optimisation through machine learning-supported multiphysics simulation. In: Bifet, A., Krilavičius, T., Miliou, I., Nowaczyk, S. (eds.) ECML PKDD 2024. LNCS, vol. 14950, pp. 297–312. Springer, Cham (2024). https://doi.org/10.1007/978-3-031-70381-2_19
9. Boussaid, T., Rousset, F., Scuturici, V.M., Clausse, M.: Enabling fast prediction of district heating networks transients via a physics-guided graph neural network. Appl. Energy **370**, 123634 (2024)
10. Bronstein, M.M., Bruna, J., Cohen, T., Veličković, P.: Geometric deep learning: grids, groups, graphs, geodesics, and gauges. arXiv preprint arXiv:2104.13478 (2021)
11. Chen, C., Witte, F., Tuschy, I., Kolditz, O., Shao, H.: Parametric optimization and comparative study of an organic rankine cycle power plant for two-phase geothermal sources. Energy **252**, 123910 (2022)
12. Chitalia, G., Pipattanasomporn, M., Garg, V., Rahman, S.: Robust short-term electrical load forecasting framework for commercial buildings using deep recurrent neural networks. Appl. Energy **278**, 115410 (2020)
13. Delubac, R., Serra, S., Sochard, S., Reneaume, J.M.: A dynamic optimization tool to size and operate solar thermal district heating networks production plants. Energies **14**(23), 8003 (2021)
14. Deng, J., et al.: Deep reinforcement learning for fuel cost optimization in district heating. Sustain. Cities Soc. **99**, 104955 (2023)
15. Dorotić, H., Pukšec, T., Duić, N.: Multi-objective optimization of district heating and cooling systems for a one-year time horizon. Energy **169**, 319–328 (2019)
16. Gad, A.G.: Particle swarm optimization algorithm and its applications: a systematic review. Arch. Comput. Methods Eng. **29**(5), 2531–2561 (2022)
17. Gao, J., Ribeiro, B.: On the equivalence between temporal and static graph representations for observational predictions. In: International Conference on Machine Learning. PMLR (2022)

18. Gasanzade, F., Witte, F., Tuschy, I., Bauer, S.: Integration of geological compressed air energy storage into future energy supply systems dominated by renewable power sources. Energy Convers. Manage. **277**, 116643 (2023)
19. de Giuli, L.B., La Bella, A., Scattolini, R.: Physics-informed neural network modeling and predictive control of district heating systems. IEEE Trans. Control Syst. Technol. (2024)
20. Huang, Y., Zhao, Y., Wang, Z., Liu, X., Liu, H., Fu, Y.: Explainable district heat load forecasting with active deep learning. Appl. Energy **350**, 121753 (2023)
21. IEA: Net zero roadmap: A global pathway to keep the 1.5 °C goal in reach (2023). licence: CC BY 4.0
22. Ji, J., et al.: Spatio-temporal self-supervised learning for traffic flow prediction. In: Proceedings of the AAAI Conference, vol. 37, pp. 4356–4364 (2023)
23. Li, L., et al.: Massively parallel hyperparameter tuning. arXiv preprint arXiv:1810.05934 (2018)
24. Pakere, I., Feofilovs, M., Lepiksaar, K., Vītoliņš, V., Blumberga, D.: Multi-source district heating system full decarbonization strategies: technical, economic, and environmental assessment. Energy **285**, 129296 (2023)
25. Pfaff, T., Fortunato, M., Sanchez-Gonzalez, A., Battaglia, P.W.: Learning mesh-based simulation with graph networks. arXiv preprint arXiv:2010.03409 (2020)
26. Pinto, G., Deltetto, D., Capozzoli, A.: Data-driven district energy management with surrogate models and deep reinforcement learning. Appl. Energy **304**, 117642 (2021)
27. Portner, H., et al.: Climate change 2022: impacts, adaptation and vulnerability. Technical report, IPCC (2022)
28. Qin, C., Yan, Q., He, G.: Integrated energy systems planning with electricity, heat and gas using particle swarm optimization. Energy **188**, 116044 (2019)
29. Saloux, E., Runge, J., Zhang, K.: Operation optimization of multi-boiler district heating systems using artificial intelligence-based model predictive control: Field demonstrations. Energy **285**, 129524 (2023)
30. Schachler B, M.C., et al.: demandlib: creating heat and power demand profiles from annual values (2021). https://oemof.org/libraries/demandlib
31. Sutton, R.S.: Reinforcement Learning: An Introduction. A Bradford Book (2018)
32. Tran, L., Choi, D.: Data augmentation for inertial sensor-based gait deep neural network. IEEE Access **8**, 12364–12378 (2020)
33. Verma, Y., Heinonen, M., Garg, V.: ClimODE: climate and weather forecasting with physics-informed neural ODEs. In: ICLR (2024)
34. Wang, X., Liu, Y., Zhao, J., Liu, C., Liu, J., Yan, J.: Surrogate model enabled deep reinforcement learning for hybrid energy community operation. Appl. Energy **289**, 116722 (2021)
35. Wang, Z., Liu, X., Huang, Y., Zhang, P., Fu, Y.: A multivariate time series graph neural network for district heat load forecasting. Energy **278**, 127911 (2023)
36. Weigand, J., Deflorian, M., Ruskowski, M.: Input-to-state stability for system identification with continuous-time Runge-Kutta neural networks. Int. J. Control **96**(1), 24–40 (2023)
37. Wen, Q., et al.: Time series data augmentation for deep learning: a survey. In: Proceedings of the Thirtieth International Joint Conference on Artificial Intelligence, IJCAI-21, pp. 4653–4660 (2021). https://doi.org/10.24963/ijcai.2021/631
38. Witte, F., Tuschy, I.: TESPy: Thermal Engineering Systems in Python. J. Open Sour. Softw. **5**(49), 2178 (2020). https://doi.org/10.21105/joss.02178 https://doi.org/10.21105/joss.02178

39. Wu, M., et al.: An integrated energy system optimization strategy based on particle swarm optimization algorithm. Energy Rep. **8**, 679–691 (2022)
40. Yu, Y., Jiang, X., Huang, D., Li, Y., Yue, M., Zhao, T.: PIDGeuN: graph neural network-enabled transient dynamics prediction of networked microgrids through full-field measurement. IEEE Access (2024)

KCLNet: Physics-Informed Power Flow Prediction via Constraints Projections

Pantelis Dogoulis(✉), Karim Tit, and Maxime Cordy

SerVal, SnT, University of Luxembourg, Kirchberg, Luxembourg City, Luxembourg
{panteleimon.dogoulis,karim.tit,maxime.cordy}@uni.lu

Abstract. In the modern context of power systems, rapid, scalable, and physically plausible power flow predictions are essential for ensuring the grid's safe and efficient operation. While traditional numerical methods have proven robust, they require extensive computation to maintain physical fidelity under dynamic or contingency conditions. In contrast, recent advancements in artificial intelligence (AI) have significantly improved computational speed; however, they often fail to enforce fundamental physical laws during real-world contingencies, resulting in physically implausible predictions. In this work, we introduce KCLNet, a physics-informed graph neural network that incorporates Kirchhoff's Current Law as a hard constraint via hyperplane projections. KCLNet attains competitive prediction accuracy while ensuring zero KCL violations, thereby delivering reliable and physically consistent power flow predictions critical to secure the operation of modern smart grids.

Keywords: physics-informed · graph learning · powerflow prediction

1 Introduction

The evolution of modern power systems has introduced novel challenges for reliable and efficient grid operation. At the heart of these challenges lies the power flow prediction problem, a fundamental task that involves computing the steady-state operating conditions of a power grid under varying load, generation, and contingency conditions. Traditionally, this problem has been solved using numerical methods that solve non-linear equations derived from Kirchhoff's laws [1,22,23]. However, the increasing complexity and scale of power systems, driven by the integration of renewable energy sources and distributed generation, have required the development of more scalable and adaptive techniques [14].

Recent advances in machine learning [7,13,15] offer a promising alternative by leveraging simulated and real-time data to predict power flow dynamics with speed and accuracy. However, the power flow prediction problem is inherently related to the physical laws that govern electrical networks. Inaccurate predictions can have severe consequences, particularly under contingency conditions, where the failure of a single component must not compromise system stability. This is known as the N-1 criterion and is a widely recognized reliability standard in power grid operations [4,24]. Consequently, there is a critical need for machine learning models that are capable of producing physically plausible solutions, even in real-world contingency scenarios.

Physics-Informed Machine Learning (PIML) [12,20] has emerged as a robust theoretical framework to address this challenge by integrating domain-specific physical principles directly into the learning process. Conventional PIML strategies typically fall into one of three categories: (a) incorporating soft constraints via the loss function to penalize deviations from physical laws; (b) leveraging simulation results or specialized weight initialization as a foundation for model training; or (c) embedding the relevant physical principles directly into the model architecture [9]. In the context of power flow prediction, most of the previous works have predominantly relied on the soft constraint approach.

In this work, we focus on the integration of Kirchhoff's Current Law, a cornerstone of electrical circuit theory, directly into the model, as a hard linear constraint. Even though, under some strong theoretical assumptions, the conventional approach of imposing soft constraints in the loss function can guide the learning process, it does not guarantee absolute adherence to physical laws. This limitation is increasingly prominent in extreme or unseen operating conditions like the N-1 scenario. By contrast, our approach enforces Kirchhoff's law as a strict equality constraint within the optimization problem, ensuring that every prediction generated by the model is physically plausible[1]. This is especially crucial for power flow prediction, where even minor deviations from established laws can propagate into significant operational risks under contingency scenarios.

Our contribution can be summarized as follows:

- We propose a novel physics-informed machine learning model that integrates Kirchhoff's law as a hard equality constraint, ensuring physically accurate predictions under normal operating conditions and contingency scenarios.
- We provide a critical assessment of the limitations inherent to conventional soft constraint approaches, particularly in the context of N-1 contingency scenarios.
- We validate our methodology using simulated data depicting real-world operating grid scenarios, demonstrating enhanced reliability and operational safety in modern power systems.

2 Definition of the Power Flow Prediction Problem

The power flow prediction problem is central to the analysis and operation of electrical power systems, as it involves determining the steady-state conditions of a grid based on prescribed inputs such as generation levels, load demands, and network topology. Conventionally, the problem is formulated as a set of nonlinear algebraic equations derived from Kirchhoff's Current Law (KCL), which are typically solved using iterative numerical methods like the Newton-Raphson

---

[1] Code Repo: https://github.com/dogoulis/ecml-pf-pred.

algorithm. In this section, we first review the classical formulation and solution methodologies for the power flow problem before discussing its reformulation within a machine learning framework. For clarity, we begin with a concise overview of the power grid terminology and we briefly describe one important security criterion for the operation of the power grids.

Power Grid Terminology: In power system analysis, a *bus* is a node where it represents elements such as generators, loads, or transformers and is generally characterized by four parameters: active power (P), reactive power (Q), voltage magnitude (V_m) and phase angle (V_a). Buses can be categorized into generators (PV buses), loads (PQ buses) or slack buses. The latest serves as the grid's reference point by absorbing active and reactive power, based on the discrepancies of the other nodes. A *transmission line* is a branch that links two buses, with its behavior described by electrical parameters such as resistance (r) and reactance (x).

N-1 Criterion: In power grids, the N-1 criterion is a reliability standard that mandates the grid must continue to operate securely even if any single component (such as a transmission line) fails. This criterion ensures that the network has sufficient redundancy and reserve capacity, so that the loss of one element does not lead to system instability or compromise the continuity of the power supply.

Kirchhoff's Current Law: At the core of power system analysis lie Kirchhoff's laws, which govern the conservation of energy and charge in electrical networks. KCL states that the algebraic sum of currents entering a node must equal the sum of currents leaving the node. In power grids which we are interested in, this principle can be expressed in terms of the active and the reactive power, under some operational hypotheses. At any bus i, the net active power injection P_i is equal to the sum of the active powers P_{ij} flowing through all the transmission lines connected to that bus:

$$\begin{cases} P_i = \sum_{j \in \mathcal{N}(i)} P_{ij} \\ Q_i = \sum_{j \in \mathcal{N}(i)} Q_{ij} \end{cases} \quad (1)$$

where P_i, Q_i are the active and reactive powers injected at bus i, P_{ij}, Q_{ij} represent the active and the reactive powers flowing from bus i to bus j, and $\mathcal{N}(i)$ denotes the set of buses connected to bus i. Using Kirchhoff's laws as a foundation, we can derive a set of nonlinear algebraic equations which describe the power balance at each bus. These equations incorporate other physical entities of the grid (voltage magnitudes and angles) as well as the transmission line's intrinsic characteristics. For an N-bus system, active (P_i) and reactive (Q_i) power injections at bus i are given by:

$$\begin{cases} P_i = V_i \sum_{j=1}^{N} V_j \left(G_{ij} \cos \theta_{ij} + B_{ij} \sin \theta_{ij} \right) \\ Q_i = V_i \sum_{j=1}^{N} V_j \left(G_{ij} \sin \theta_{ij} - B_{ij} \cos \theta_{ij} \right) \end{cases} \quad (2)$$

where V_i is the voltage magnitude at bus i, $\theta_{ij} = \theta_i - \theta_j$ is the phase angle difference between buses i and j, while G_{ij} and B_{ij} denote the conductance and susceptance of the transmission line connecting i and j. The resulting system of nonlinear equations is commonly solved using iterative numerical techniques. One of the most widely used methods is the *Newton-Raphson* method, which is favored for its quadratic convergence properties. The method iteratively refines an initial guess of the powers and the voltages by solving the following update equation:

$$\mathbf{x}^{(k+1)} = \mathbf{x}^{(k)} - \mathbf{J}^{-1}(\mathbf{x}^{(k)})\,\mathbf{f}(\mathbf{x}^{(k)}), \tag{3}$$

where: $\mathbf{x}$ is the vector of state variables, $\mathbf{f}(\mathbf{x})$ represents the mismatch between the calculated and specified power injections, $\mathbf{J}(\mathbf{x})$ is the Jacobian matrix of partial derivatives of $\mathbf{f}$ with respect to $\mathbf{x}$. Although the Newton-Raphson method and its variants provide reliable solutions under normal operating conditions, they can be computationally intensive for large-scale networks or in scenarios with rapidly changing system conditions (i.e. contingencies).

3 Related Work

Recent advances in applying artificial intelligence to power flow prediction can be broadly divided into methods that rely primarily on learning from data without explicit physical constraints, and methods that incorporate physics-based guidance or constraints during training. An example of the former is described in [5], where the authors propose a neural network to tackle the power flow prediction problem based on a guided-dropout technique, and they validate their approach in different contingency cases. Similarly, the authors in [7] propose LeapNet, a latent-space network that handles structural or parametric shifts by encoding inputs into a hidden representation, applying a conditional "leap" dependent on discrete topology changes, and decoding back to flow predictions. Furthermore, in [16], the authors introduce two modeling approaches: a partial least squares (PLS) regression model and a Bayesian linear regression model. Both models are derived from a linearized formulation of the underlying problem, which is obtained by adopting specific assumptions regarding grid operations.

In contrast, several *physics-informed* approaches add explicit power-flow constraints. The authors in [13] propose a method that enforces piecewise-linearity, combining a baseline linearization (derived from the Jacobian at a nominal operating point of the grid) with ReLU-based low-rank updates to compactly approximate the power flow equations, thus introducing a physics-based term into the network's architecture. PowerflowNet [15] employs a graph neural network architecture equipped with message passing layers, augmented by an additional loss term representing the squared mismatch between the neural network's predicted power injections and the injections computed from the power-flow equations, thus penalizing physical inconsistency. The authors in [10] propose a physics-informed geometric deep learning scheme that encodes the grid's topology via graph neural networks, with partial derivatives or power flow constraints contributing to the training loss and encouraging alignment with Kirchhoff's laws. Finally, the authors at [6] present a Graph Neural Solver for AC power flows that leverages message passing across nodes and edges while penalizing Kirchhoff's law violations. Most of these works can be broadly classified under the term of PIML, where physical constraints are included into the loss function as an additional term. Concretely, the total loss function can be formulated as follows:

$$\mathcal{L}(\theta) = \underbrace{\mathcal{L}_{\text{reg}}(\theta)}_{\text{MSE}} + \mathcal{L}_{\text{physics}}(\theta), \tag{4}$$

where $\mathcal{L}_{\text{reg}}(\theta)$ is a standard regression loss (commonly the mean squared error) that measures the discrepancy between the model's predictions and the ground-truth data, and $\mathcal{L}_{\text{physics}}(\theta)$ is a term enforcing physical consistency, most commonly by penalizing the mismatch in the power flow equations described in (2). Additionally, it is important to note that the formulation of power flow prediction is not universally standardized; some approaches focus on estimating transmission line flows while others predict nodal injections. However, by leveraging the governing physical equations, these formulations can often be interchanged, although the extent of this conversion is inherently dependent on the initial problem definition. In our approach, crucially, physical constraints are embedded *directly* into the model architecture, thereby ensuring that all predictions rigorously conform to the underlying physical laws (see Sect. 4 below).

4 Proposed Method

4.1 Grid Represented as a Graph

A power grid can be naturally modeled as a graph $\mathcal{G} = (\mathcal{V}, \mathcal{E})$, where the set of nodes $\mathcal{V}$ represents buses and the set of edges $\mathcal{E}$ corresponds to the transmission lines connecting them (see Fig. 1). Each node is endowed with three attributes: active (P_i) and reactive power injections (Q_i) and voltage magnitudes (V_i) (note that here we omit the V_a feature), while each edge is characterized by intrinsic electrical parameters which are the resistance (r_i) and the reactance (x_i). The principal objective is to compute the active and reactive power flows at both ends of each edge (transmission line).

4.2 Model Architecture

Figure 2 presents an overview of the complete architecture of the proposed GNN-based model for power flow prediction. The model takes as input the node features $\mathbf{x}_i$ and the edge attributes $\mathbf{e}_{ij}$, which together encode the electrical and topological characteristics of the network. Mathematically, the overall model implements a function

$$f : (\mathbf{X}, \mathbf{E}) \to \hat{\mathbf{Y}},$$

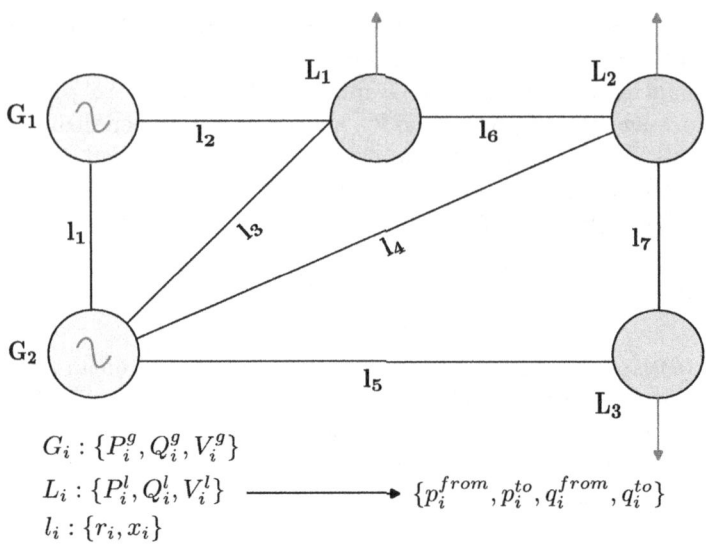

Fig. 1. Illustration of a power grid (IEEE5) represented as a graph. Two generator nodes (G_1 and G_2, shown in yellow) are connected to three load nodes (L_1, L_2, and L_3, shown in pink) through multiple transmission lines (labeled l_1, l_2, l_3, l_4, l_5, l_6, and l_7). Each generator node is associated with the node features $\{P_i^g, Q_i^g, V_i^g\}$, while each load node is associated with $\{P_i^l, Q_i^l, V_i^l\}$. The edge features are ($\{r_i, x_i\}$), which represent the intrinsic electrical characteristics of the transmission lines (as discussed in Sect. 2). The formulation of the problem is to predict the associated from- and to-bus vector: $(p_i^{from}, p_i^{to}, q_i^{from}, q_i^{to})$. (Color figure online)

where $\mathbf{X} \in \mathbb{R}^{N \times 3}$ is the node feature matrix, $\mathbf{E} \in \mathbb{R}^{|E| \times 2}$ is the edge attribute matrix, and $\hat{\mathbf{Y}} \in \mathbb{R}^{|E| \times 4}$ contains the predicted flow parameters for each edge. In the initial stage, an MLP-based message passing module inspired by [15] processes the concatenated vector

$$\mathbf{z}_{ij} = [\mathbf{x}_i, \mathbf{x}_j, \mathbf{e}_{ij}],$$

for each edge (i, j). This module computes the hidden state as:

$$\mathbf{h}_{ij} = W_2 \operatorname{LeakyReLU}(W_1 \mathbf{z}_{ij} + \mathbf{b}_1) + \mathbf{b}_2,$$

where W_1 and W_2 are weight matrices and $\mathbf{b}_1$ and $\mathbf{b}_2$ are bias vectors. The intermediate embedding for node i is then obtained by aggregating the messages from its neighbors:

$$\mathbf{x}_i' = \sum_{j \in \mathcal{N}(i)} \mathbf{h}_{ij}.$$

These intermediate embeddings are further refined by a **GATv2Conv** layer [2], which employs a multi-head attention mechanism. In this layer, both the updated

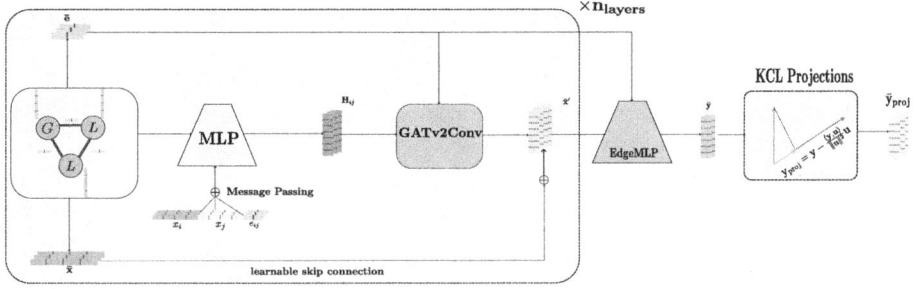

Fig. 2. Illustration of the proposed KCLNet.

node embeddings $\mathbf{x}'_i$ and the edge attributes $\mathbf{e}_{ij}$ contribute to the computation of attention coefficients a_{ij}, and the refined node embeddings are given by

$$\mathbf{x}''_i = \sum_{j \in \mathcal{N}(i)} a_{ij}\, \mathbf{x}'_j.$$

To preserve the original node information and facilitate effective gradient propagation, a learnable skip connection is incorporated. The original node features are first projected into the hidden space via

$$\tilde{\mathbf{x}}_i = W_{\text{skip}}\, \mathbf{x}_i,$$

and then combined with the refined embeddings:

$$\hat{\mathbf{x}}_i = \mathbf{x}''_i + \tilde{\mathbf{x}}_i.$$

Finally, edge-level predictions are derived by constructing representations for each edge. For a given edge (i,j), the final node embeddings corresponding to nodes i and j are concatenated with the edge attributes:

$$\mathbf{z}_{ij}^{\text{edge}} = [\hat{\mathbf{x}}_i,\, \hat{\mathbf{x}}_j,\, \mathbf{e}_{ij}],$$

and the resulting vector is passed through an additional MLP, referred to as **EdgeMLP**, to produce the predicted flow parameters:

$$\hat{\mathbf{y}}_{ij} = \text{EdgeMLP}\left(\mathbf{z}_{ij}^{\text{edge}}\right).$$

4.3 KCL Projections for Physical Constraints

Kirchhoff's Current Law (KCL) states that, at each bus, the total incoming power must equal the total outgoing power (see Eq. (1)). To impose this principle, we proceed with the following notations:

- For each bus $i \in \{1, \ldots, N\}$, let $P_{\text{net}}(i)$ and $Q_{\text{net}}(i)$ be the *measured* active and reactive power injections, respectively.
- For each line (edge) e, let $p_e^{\text{from}}, p_e^{\text{to}}$ denote the *predicted* active power flows, and $q_e^{\text{from}}, q_e^{\text{to}}$ the *predicted* reactive power flows.

Given a bus i, define its *calculated* active and reactive power injections as

$$P_{\text{calc}}(i) = \sum_{e \in \mathcal{E}^{\text{from}}(i)} p_e^{\text{from}} + \sum_{e \in \mathcal{E}^{\text{to}}(i)} p_e^{\text{to}}, \quad Q_{\text{calc}}(i) = \sum_{e \in \mathcal{E}^{\text{from}}(i)} q_e^{\text{from}} + \sum_{e \in \mathcal{E}^{\text{to}}(i)} q_e^{\text{to}},$$

where $\mathcal{E}^{\text{from}}(i)$ and $\mathcal{E}^{\text{to}}(i)$ denote the sets of edges for which bus i is respectively the source and the target.

KCL in Terms of Predicted Flows. From Eq. (1), the KCL requirement at each bus i can be expressed as

$$P_{\text{net}}(i) + P_{\text{calc}}(i) = P_{\text{net}}(i) + \sum_{e \in \mathcal{E}^{\text{from}}(i)} p_e^{\text{from}} + \sum_{e \in \mathcal{E}^{\text{to}}(i)} p_e^{\text{to}} = 0, \quad (5)$$

for active power, and

$$Q_{\text{net}}(i) + Q_{\text{calc}}(i) = Q_{\text{net}}(i) + \sum_{e \in \mathcal{E}^{\text{from}}(i)} q_e^{\text{from}} + \sum_{e \in \mathcal{E}^{\text{to}}(i)} q_e^{\text{to}} = 0, \quad (6)$$

for reactive power.

Projection Operators. We enforce these constraints by constructing hyperplane projections for each node. Specifically, for bus i, we define two projections: Π_i^P (for active power) and Π_i^Q (for reactive power). Both operators act on the prediction vector $\mathbf{y} \in \mathbb{R}^{|E| \times 4}$ to ensure that KCL holds at i.

Normal Vectors. First, define the vectors $\mathbf{a}^{P,i}, \mathbf{a}^{Q,i} \in \mathbb{R}^{|E| \times 4}$ that capture the contribution of each component of $\mathbf{y}$ to the net power injection at bus i. From Eqs. (5) and (6), the entries of $\mathbf{a}^{P,i}$ are

$$a_{e,l}^{P,i} = \begin{cases} 1, & \text{if } e \in \mathcal{E}^{\text{from}}(i) \text{ and } l = 1, \\ 1, & \text{if } e \in \mathcal{E}^{\text{to}}(i) \text{ and } l = 2, \\ 0, & \text{otherwise,} \end{cases}$$

and $\mathbf{a}^{Q,i}$ is defined similarly for reactive power.

Projection Formulas. Using these normal vectors, the orthogonal (affine) hyperplane projections that zero out the KCL violations at bus i are

$$\Pi_i^P(\mathbf{y}) \stackrel{\text{def}}{=} \mathbf{y} - \frac{\langle \mathbf{a}^{P,i}, \mathbf{y} \rangle + P_{\text{net}}(i)}{\|\mathbf{a}^{P,i}\|^2} \mathbf{a}^{P,i}, \quad \Pi_i^Q(\mathbf{y}) \stackrel{\text{def}}{=} \mathbf{y} - \frac{\langle \mathbf{a}^{Q,i}, \mathbf{y} \rangle + Q_{\text{net}}(i)}{\|\mathbf{a}^{Q,i}\|^2} \mathbf{a}^{Q,i}.$$

Applying Π_i^P removes the component of $\mathbf{y}$ collinear to $\mathbf{a}^{P,i}$ that violates Eq. (5), while Π_i^Q does the same for Eq. (6).

Sequential Node Projections. Combining these local projections for each of the N buses, and choosing some variable-ordering permutation $\sigma : \{1, \ldots, N\} \to \{1, \ldots, N\}$, we define

$$\Pi_\sigma^{\text{KCL}} \stackrel{\text{def}}{=} \Pi_{\sigma(1)}^P \circ \Pi_{\sigma(1)}^Q \circ \Pi_{\sigma(2)}^P \circ \Pi_{\sigma(2)}^Q \circ \cdots \circ \Pi_{\sigma(N)}^P \circ \Pi_{\sigma(N)}^Q.$$

Although applying Π_σ^{KCL} once may not fully enforce all KCL constraints (since projections generally do *not* commute), *repeated* application of Π_σ^{KCL} will asymptotically converge to a KCL-feasible solution, as in Kaczmarz's iterative hyperplane method [11]. In practice, however, finding a good ordering σ is non-trivial; one often resorts to random selection [3] and convergence can be slow.

Alternative Formulation. An alternative to applying node-by-node projections is to assemble all KCL constraints into a single linear system and *directly* project onto its solution space using the Moore-Penrose pseudoinverse [18].

Constructing the System $A\mathbf{y} + \mathbf{b} = 0$. Recall Eqs. (5)–(6), which describe KCL at each bus i. Each of these can be written as a dot-product constraint:

$$\langle \mathbf{a}^{P,i}, \mathbf{y} \rangle + P_{\text{net}}(i) = 0, \qquad \langle \mathbf{a}^{Q,i}, \mathbf{y} \rangle + Q_{\text{net}}(i) = 0,$$

where $\mathbf{a}^{P,i}$ and $\mathbf{a}^{Q,i}$ are the normal vectors defined earlier.

The main idea is now to stack all these constraints into a linear system

$$A\mathbf{y} + \mathbf{b} = \mathbf{0},$$

where $A \in \mathbb{R}^{m \times d}$ and $\mathbf{b} \in \mathbb{R}^m$, with $d = 4|E|, m = 2N$. Concretely,

$$A \stackrel{\text{def}}{=} \begin{pmatrix} (\mathbf{a}^{P,1})^\top \\ (\mathbf{a}^{P,2})^\top \\ \vdots \\ (\mathbf{a}^{P,N})^\top \\ (\mathbf{a}^{Q,1})^\top \\ (\mathbf{a}^{Q,2})^\top \\ \vdots \\ (\mathbf{a}^{Q,N})^\top \end{pmatrix} \quad \text{and} \quad \mathbf{b} \stackrel{\text{def}}{=} \begin{pmatrix} P_{\text{net}}(1) \\ P_{\text{net}}(2) \\ \vdots \\ P_{\text{net}}(N) \\ Q_{\text{net}}(1) \\ Q_{\text{net}}(2) \\ \vdots \\ Q_{\text{net}}(N) \end{pmatrix}.$$

So that, solving $A\mathbf{y} + \mathbf{b} = \mathbf{0}$ enforces *all* KCL equations at once.

Moore-Penrose Approach [19]. An *orthogonal* (least-squares) projection onto the affine space of admissible solutions $\{\mathbf{z} \in \mathbb{R}^d : A\mathbf{z} + \mathbf{b} = \mathbf{0}\}$ is given by

$$\tilde{\mathbf{y}} = \mathbf{y} - A^\dagger (A\mathbf{y} + \mathbf{b}),$$

where $A^\dagger \in \mathbb{R}^{d \times m}$ is the Moore–Penrose inverse of A. By definition, if we let

$$A = U \Sigma V^\top$$

be the singular-value decomposition (SVD) of A (where U and V are orthonormal, and Σ is diagonal in the nonzero singular values), then

$$A^\dagger \stackrel{\text{def}}{=} V \Sigma^\dagger U^\top,$$

with $\Sigma^\dagger$ being the reciprocal of all nonzero singular values (and zero in any null dimensions).

Optimization View. This global projection via pseudoinverse solves the problem

$$\min_{\widetilde{\mathbf{y}}} \|\widetilde{\mathbf{y}} - \mathbf{y}\|^2 \quad \text{subject to} \quad A\widetilde{\mathbf{y}} + \mathbf{b} = 0,$$

i.e. it is the *closest point in Euclidean distance* to the original prediction $\mathbf{y}$ that satisfies *all* KCL constraints. Therefore, the Moore–Penrose projection is the *optimal* way to solve the KCL equations system, in the least-squares sense, starting from prediction $\mathbf{y}$. This also spares the choice of the variable ordering σ above, whose optimization is a hard combinatorial problem.

Algorithmic Steps. One can thus enforce KCL as follows:

Require: $\mathbf{y} \in \mathbb{R}^d$ (*initial predicted flows*)
Require: $A \in \mathbb{R}^{m \times d}$, $\mathbf{b} \in \mathbb{R}^m$, $A^\dagger \in \mathbb{R}^{d \times m}$ (*KCL system*)
1: $\mathbf{r} \leftarrow A\mathbf{y} + \mathbf{b}$ // KCL residual
2: $\widetilde{\mathbf{y}} \leftarrow \mathbf{y} - A^\dagger \mathbf{r}$
3: **return** $\widetilde{\mathbf{y}}$

As above, because A and $A^\dagger$ only depend on the *topology* of the power grid, they can be assembled *once* for a fixed network structure. In addition, this projection can be implemented in practice as two fully connected linear layers, with a residual connection for the second one, which allows for full back-propagation and thus training of the full architecture, e.g. via stochastic gradient descent.

Physically Consistent Predictions. Integration of the global Moore-Penrose pseudoinverse projection step described above, into the model's architecture, as a last layer, ensures that the final predicted flows satisfy the power conservation principle. In contrast, as discussed in Sect. 3, most methods in the literature merely direct the model towards lower KCL violations by incorporating them into the loss function, thereby offering no assurances regarding physical consistency.

5 Experiments

In this section, we systematically evaluate our proposed approach with two primary objectives. First, we benchmark the model against state-of-the-art methods on standard IEEE test cases under both nominal and contingency (N-1) conditions, focusing on predictive accuracy and adherence to physical constraints. Second, we perform an ablation study to assess specifically the impact of the final projection layer on performance and physical feasibility.

5.1 Datasets

To conduct our experiments, we employ two widely used benchmark datasets from the power engineering community and have also become standard benchmarks in recent deep-learning research: the IEEE 14-bus and IEEE 118-bus test cases. Each dataset comprises a single grid instance with nominal values assigned to every bus, containing 14 and 118 buses, respectively. To adapt these datasets for a machine learning framework, we augment the available data by generating multiple independent and identically distributed (iid) instances by sampling near the nominal values. New data instances are generated for all buses by sampling from a normal distribution centered at their nominal values with a small variance. Specifically, the active power, voltage magnitude, and reactive power are sampled as follows: $P \sim \mathcal{N}(\bar{P}, 0.01)$, $V \sim \mathcal{N}(\bar{V}, 0.01)$, $Q \sim \mathcal{N}(\bar{Q}, 0.01)$, where the bar over the variable denotes the nominal value of the corresponding variable. After generating these perturbed grid parameters, we obtain the ground truth for the targeted variables using the Newton-Raphson method mentioned above.

5.2 Implementation Details

In this study, we simulated 20000 distinct operational scenarios for power grids, capturing a comprehensive range of realistic conditions representative of real-time grid operations. Additionally, to assess model robustness under contingency conditions, we generated N-1 contingency scenarios by removing a single transmission line at random, while excluding the one that is directly connected to the slack bus. In particular, these N-1 cases were excluded from the training set, ensuring an unbiased evaluation of the robustness of the models to realistic grid perturbations. We trained our models using the AdamW optimizer [17]. The learning rate was equal to 10^{-3}, while Xavier normal initialization [8] was applied to the linear layers of the proposed network. All training and evaluation processes were performed on a server with a single NVIDIA GeForce RTX 4080 SUPER GPU.

Metrics: To assess the accuracy of our models, we employ the Mean Squared Error (MSE) with respect to the ground-truth as a primary metric. Indeed, this method is the gold standard in the literature. Additionally, to ensure physical feasibility, we quantify the average KCL satisfaction for each grid. Mathematically, let N denote the total number of buses in the network and $P_{\text{net}}(i)$ and $P_{\text{calc}}(i)$ denote respectively the net injected and calculated power at bus i, as in 4.3. The global energy conservation loss for active power is then defined as the mean squared mismatch between the measured and calculated injections:

$$\mathcal{L}_P = \frac{1}{N} \sum_{i=1}^{N} \left(P_{\text{net}}(i) + P_{\text{calc}}(i) \right)^2,$$

and similarly for reactive power:

$$\mathcal{L}_Q = \frac{1}{N} \sum_{i=1}^{N} (Q_{\text{net}}(i) + Q_{\text{calc}}(i))^2.$$

Finally, the overall physics-informed loss, which quantifies the degree of Kirchhoff's Current Law (KCL) satisfaction, is given by:

$$\mathcal{L}_{\text{KCL}} = \frac{1}{2}(\mathcal{L}_P + \mathcal{L}_Q).$$

5.3 Comparison with Other Models

We compare our model against three well-established models from the literature [7,13,15]. Note, that since the classical Newton-Raphson solver already generates the ground-truth labels for our datasets, using it as a benchmark would be redundant, since by definition it will show *zero error*. However, graph-based approaches have showcased much faster performance in previous works [15], which also highlights the importance of these surrogate models. The selection of these models was motivated by their diverse approaches to integrating physics-informed knowledge: one model omits such integration entirely, another incorporates partial domain knowledge through its architectural design, and the third enforces a soft physics constraint via its loss function. Since the power flow prediction problem has not yet been uniformly defined, each architecture addresses the task within its own formal framework (as discussed in Sect. 3). Therefore, since PowerFlowNet predicts node features, we compute the average squared mismatch using the equations in 2.

5.4 N-Case Analysis

In the nominal operating scenario (N-case), we evaluated model performance on the IEEE 14-bus and IEEE 118-bus test cases. As shown in Table 1, the observed MSEs ranged from 0.169 to 0.746. Although KodyNet reported a lower MSE on the IEEE 14-bus case (0.169), it also exhibited a relatively higher mismatch in Kirchhoff's Current Law (KCL) (1.288). In contrast, KCLNet maintained zero KCL violation, with MSE values of 0.381 on IEEE14 and 0.273 on IEEE118. We observe that the predictions obtained using the larger IEEE118 network generally outperform those from smaller networks. This can be attributed to the inherently local nature of power flow prediction, whereby localized errors have a reduced impact on the overall grid performance in larger systems compared to more confined network models.

5.5 N-1 Case Analysis

Under N-1 contingency conditions, where a single transmission line is removed to simulate grid perturbations, the overall MSE increased across all models, as

Table 1. Performance results in N-case: We report the average of 10 runs of the MSE and KCL violation for each model on the IEEE 14-bus and IEEE 118-bus datasets under nominal operating conditions. For each metric, the corresponding standard deviation (std) is provided in parentheses. The model with the best (lowest) MSE is highlighted in bold. Values reported as 0.000 indicate numerical errors on the order of 1e-4, with all results rounded to three decimal places.

Dataset	Model	MSE	KCL Violation
IEEE118	LeapNet	0.591 (0.001)	1.169 (0.019)
	KodyNet	0.298 (0.004)	0.359 (0.002)
	PowerFlowNet	0.642 (0.003)	0.327 (0.001)
	KCLNet	**0.273** (0.002)	**0.000** (0.000)
IEEE14	LeapNet	0.439 (0.001)	1.664 (0.148)
	KodyNet	**0.169** (0.001)	1.288 (0.093)
	PowerFlowNet	0.746 (0.028)	1.933 (0.042)
	KCLNet	0.381 (0.005)	**0.000** (0.000)

detailed in Table 2. Notably, KCLNet continued to enforce complete compliance with KCL (zero violation), while recording MSE values of 0.533 on IEEE14 and 0.2768 on IEEE118. Furthermore, it is evident that within the larger IEEE118 dataset, the MSE of the proposed architecture is close to that observed in the complete network (N-case). A natural interpretation is that the removal of a single transmission line predominantly affects only a localized region of the grid, rather than inducing widespread, global changes in performance. The other models, despite achieving comparable MSEs, displayed non-negligible KCL violations. These observations suggest that embedding physical constraints into the modeling framework can contribute to maintaining feasibility under both nominal and perturbed grid conditions, although further analysis is required to fully elucidate the trade-offs involved.

5.6 Ablation Study

In this section, we assess the impact of the final projection layer of our KCLNet model. Specifically, we remove the KCL projection layer to relax the hard physical constraints during training, thereby expanding the loss space. We observe that removing the final projection layer generally allows the network to achieve a lower MSE, which is expected as the loss space becomes less constrained by the hard projection (Table 3). For example, under the N-case scenario on IEEE14, the MSE drops from 0.381 (with projection) to 0.353, and similarly, in the N-1 case the MSE reduces from 0.533 to 0.492. Although for IEEE118 under normal conditions the MSE shows a slight increase (from 0.273 to 0.296), the overall trend suggests that the relaxation permits better optimization of the primary objective. Notably, the corresponding KCL violations are relatively low (ranging from 0.039 to 0.047), slightly below those seen in the other models. This indicates

Table 2. Performance results in N-1 case: We report the average of 10 runs of the Mean Squared Error MSE and KCL violation for each model on the IEEE 14-bus and IEEE 118-bus datasets under nominal operating conditions. For each metric, the corresponding standard deviation (std) is provided in parentheses. The model with the best (lowest) MSE is highlighted in bold. Values reported as 0.000 indicate numerical errors on the order of 1e-4, with all results rounded to three decimal places.

Dataset	Model	MSE	KCL Violation
IEEE118	LeapNet	0.643 (0.002)	1.149 (0.061)
	KodyNet	0.591 (0.003)	0.361 (0.007)
	PowerFlowNet	0.981 (0.001)	0.845 (0.001)
	KCLNet	**0.2768** (0.000)	**0.000** (0.000)
IEEE14	LeapNet	0.452 (0.004)	1.632 (0.109)
	KodyNet	**0.199** (0.001)	1.292 (0.130)
	PowerFlowNet	0.845 (0.023)	1.629 (0.040)
	KCLNet	0.533 (0.003)	**0.000** (0.000)

that even without the final projection layer enforcing strict physical constraints, the model still achieves a reasonable level of physical feasibility while benefiting from a more flexible loss landscape.

Table 3. Performance of KCLNet without the final projection layer under nominal (N case) and contingency (N-1 case) conditions. We report the mean and standard deviation in parentheses, calculated over 10 runs.

Dataset	N Case		N-1 Case	
	MSE	KCL Violation	MSE	KCL Violation
IEEE118	0.296 (0.002)	0.039 (0.001)	0.272 (0.000)	0.047 (0.002)
IEEE14	0.353 (0.001)	0.043 (0.001)	0.492 (0.001)	0.046 (0.001)

6 Conclusion

In this work, we introduced a physics-informed machine learning approach for power flow prediction that integrates Kirchhoff's Current Law (KCL) as a hard constraint via hyperplane projections. Our proposed model, *KCLNet*, consists of a Graph Neural Network architecture followed by a physics-informed projection layer, ensuring every prediction remains physically plausible under both nominal and contingency ($N-1$) operating conditions. Experimental evaluations on the IEEE 14-bus and IEEE 118-bus test cases show that KCLNet, while maintaining competitive Mean Squared Error (MSE) values on smaller grids, achieves the lowest MSE on the larger IEEE 118-bus system. Meanwhile, it enforces KCL with zero numerical violation–an outcome contrasting with other state-of-the-art methods that, despite occasionally achieving lower MSEs on smaller test grids, exhibit non-negligible KCL deviations.

These results indicate that directly embedding physical constraints into the model architecture not only enhances reliability but also contributes to operational safety in real-world grid scenarios. Notably, the scalability and strong performance on the larger IEEE 118-bus system suggest that KCLNet is well-suited for more extensive networks in practice.

Future Extensions. Beyond our current scope, we next propose two directions that could further expand the applicability and impact of KCLNet,

- **Nonlinear Network Equations and Diffusion-Based Projections:** When the steady state of a physical system is governed by nonlinear equations, one could explore deterministic diffusion or similar iterative methods to approximate the projection on the nonlinear constraint manifold.

- **Application to Various Physical Networks Scenarios:** The analogy between electrical flows and other resource flows is especially relevant in contemporary *smart grid* and *smart city* applications, where Kirchhoff-like conservation principles arise naturally. For instance, [21] demonstrates a traffic management system guided by network "circuit" theorems akin to KCL. Extending KCLNet to such contexts promises physically consistent predictions in a wide range of complex, networked systems.

Acknowledgments. This research is supported by FNR Luxembourg INTER/FNRS/20/15077233/ Scaling Up and CREOS S.A. We would like to thank Yves Reckinger and Robert Graglia for their valuable feedback.

References

1. Akram, S., Ann, Q.U.: Newton raphson method. Int. J. Sci. Eng. Res. **6**(7), 1748–1752 (2015)
2. Brody, S., Alon, U., Yahav, E.: How attentive are graph attention networks? arXiv preprint arXiv:2105.14491 (2021)
3. Dai, L., Soltanalian, M., Pelckmans, K.: On the randomized Kaczmarz algorithm. IEEE Signal Process. Lett. **21**(3), 330–333 (2014)
4. Dogoulis, P., Jimenez, M., Ghamizi, S., Cordy, M., Traon, Y.L.: Robustness analysis of ai models in critical energy systems. arXiv preprint arXiv:2406.14361 (2024)
5. Donnot, B., Guyon, I., Schoenauer, M., Marot, A., Panciatici, P.: Fast power system security analysis with guided dropout. arXiv preprint arXiv:1801.09870 (2018)
6. Donon, B., Clément, R., Donnot, B., Marot, A., Guyon, I., Schoenauer, M.: Neural networks for power flow: graph neural solver. Electric Power Syst. Res. **189**, 106547 (2020)
7. Donon, B., et al.: Leap nets for system identification and application to power systems. Neurocomputing **416**, 316–327 (2020)

8. Glorot, X., Bengio, Y.: Understanding the difficulty of training deep feedforward neural networks. In: Proceedings of the Thirteenth International Conference on Artificial Intelligence and Statistics, pp. 249–256. JMLR Workshop and Conference Proceedings (2010)
9. Huang, B., Wang, J.: Applications of physics-informed neural networks in power systems-a review. IEEE Trans. Power Syst. **38**(1), 572–588 (2022)
10. Jongh, S., Gielnik, F., Mueller, F., Schmit, L., Suriyah, M., Leibfried, T.: Physics-informed geometric deep learning for inference tasks in power systems. Electric Power Syst. Res. **211**, 108362 (2022)
11. Kaczmarz, S.: Approximate solution of systems of linear equationsâĂă. Int. J. Control **57**(6), 1269–1271 (1993)
12. Karniadakis, G.E., Kevrekidis, I.G., Lu, L., Perdikaris, P., Wang, S., Yang, L.: Physics-informed machine learning. Nature Rev. Phys. **3**(6), 422–440 (2021)
13. Kody, A., Chevalier, S., Chatzivasileiadis, S., Molzahn, D.: Modeling the ac power flow equations with optimally compact neural networks: application to unit commitment. Electric Power Syst. Res. **213**, 108282 (2022)
14. Leyli Abadi, M., et al.: Lips-learning industrial physical simulation benchmark suite. Adv. Neural. Inf. Process. Syst. **35**, 28095–28109 (2022)
15. Lin, N., Orfanoudakis, S., Cardenas, N.O., Giraldo, J.S., Vergara, P.P.: Powerflownet: power flow approximation using message passing graph neural networks. Int. J. Electr. Power Energy Syst. **160**, 110112 (2024)
16. Liu, Y., Zhang, N., Wang, Y., Yang, J., Kang, C.: Data-driven power flow linearization: a regression approach. IEEE Trans. Smart Grid **10**(3), 2569–2580 (2018)
17. Loshchilov, I., Hutter, F.: Decoupled weight decay regularization. arXiv preprint arXiv:1711.05101 (2017)
18. Penrose, R.: A generalized inverse for matrices. Math. Proc. Cambridge Philos. Soc. **51**, 406–413 (1955)
19. Piziak, R., Odell, P.: Affine projections. Comput. Math. Appl. **48**(1), 177–190 (2004)
20. Qian, E., Kramer, B., Peherstorfer, B., Willcox, K.: Lift & learn: Physics-informed machine learning for large-scale nonlinear dynamical systems. Physica D **406**, 132401 (2020)
21. Raghavan, K., et al.: Smart traffic systems guided by principles of traffic circuit theorems. In: 2020 IEEE 8th R10 Humanitarian Technology Conference (R10-HTC), pp. 1–5 (2020)
22. Sereeter, B., Vuik, C., Witteveen, C.: On a comparison of newton-raphson solvers for power flow problems. J. Comput. Appl. Math. **360**, 157–169 (2019)
23. Wasley, R., Shlash, M.A.: Newton-raphson algorithm for 3-phase load flow. In: Proceedings of the Institution of Electrical Engineers, vol. 121, pp. 630–638. IET (1974)
24. Zima, M., Andersson, G.: On security criteria in power systems operation. In: IEEE Power Engineering Society General Meeting, 2005, pp. 3089–3093. IEEE (2005)

Risk-Based Thresholding for Reliable Anomaly Detection in Concentrated Solar Power Plants

Yorick Estievenart[1], Sukanya Patra[1], and Souhaib Ben Taieb[2(✉)]

[1] University of Mons, Mons, Belgium
yorick.estievenart@gmail.com, sukanya.patra@umons.ac.be
[2] Mohamed bin Zayed University of Artificial Intelligence,
Abu Dhabi, United Arab Emirates
souhaib.bentaieb@mbzuai.ac.ae

Abstract. Efficient and reliable operation of Concentrated Solar Power (CSP) plants is essential for meeting the growing demand for sustainable energy. However, high-temperature solar receivers face severe operational risks, such as freezing, deformation, and corrosion, resulting in costly downtime and maintenance. To monitor CSP plants, cameras mounted on solar receivers record infrared images at irregular intervals ranging from one to five minutes throughout the day. Anomalous images can be detected by thresholding an anomaly score, where the threshold is chosen to optimize metrics such as the F1-score on a validation set. This work proposes a framework, using risk control, for generating more reliable decision thresholds with finite-sample coverage guarantees on any chosen risk function. Our framework also incorporates an abstention mechanism, allowing high-risk predictions to be deferred to domain experts. Second, we propose a density forecasting method to estimate the likelihood of an observed image given a sequence of previously observed images, using this likelihood as its anomaly score. Third, we analyze the deployment results of our framework across multiple training scenarios over several months for two CSP plants. This analysis provides valuable insights to our industry partner for optimizing maintenance operations. Finally, given the confidential nature of our dataset, we provide an extended simulated dataset (https://tinyurl.com/macmnjyt), leveraging recent advancements in generative modeling to create diverse thermal images that simulate multiple CSP plants. Our code is publicly available (https://github.com/yoest/reliable-ad-csp).

Keywords: Deep Image Anomaly Detection · Risk Control · Irregular Time-series · Non-stationarity · Concentrated Solar Power Plants · Density Estimation · Reliable Decision Thresholds

---

Supplementary Information The online version contains supplementary material available at https://doi.org/10.1007/978-3-032-06129-4_7.

1 Introduction

The global transition toward greener and more sustainable renewable energy sources is hindered by two critical challenges: (i) on-demand generation and (ii) dispatchability. Concentrated Solar Power (CSP) plants offer a promising solution, leveraging thermal energy storage to provide electricity even when sunlight is unavailable. Among the various CSP configurations, central tower-based plants are the most prevalent, using an array of mirrors to concentrate sunlight onto a receiver, where a heat transfer medium absorbs and stores the energy. However, the extreme operating temperatures make these systems highly susceptible to failures such as metal fatigue and tube blockages, directly impacting their efficiency, reliability, and operational lifespan. To mitigate these risks, thermal imaging from infrared cameras is used to monitor CSP plants. Nonetheless, the sheer volume and complexity of thermal image data render manual monitoring impractical, necessitating the development of an automated, data-driven Predictive Maintenance (PdM) pipeline. This problem naturally aligns with anomaly detection (AD), where the goal is to identify abnormal behaviours.

Despite significant progress in both deep and shallow AD research [20,32], existing image- and video-based approaches fall short in addressing the problem of detecting anomalous behaviours of operational CSP plants due to three key challenges. First, the lack of interpretability of the anomaly scores hinders decision-making in high-stakes applications without an appropriate thresholding strategy [28]. Traditional approaches rely on performance metrics such as F1-score or GMean to determine thresholds depending on the available labelled samples. These methods do not guarantee that the results will remain consistent in a deployment setting. Moreover, they assume that all CSP plants define risk similarly and follow the same operational strategies. In reality, this often differs (e.g., deploying a maintenance team may be preferable to replacing a tower component). Second, deep learning-based AD models are often perceived as unreliable [28] due to the uncertainty in predictions stemming from their inability to properly estimate the decision boundary, particularly when training data is limited. Thus, practitioners are hesitant to use the predictions even when the associated uncertainty is minimal, severely limiting their adoption in real-world applications. Also, unlike classical image- and video-based AD data, CSP plant monitoring involves thermal images without semantic content, lacks a fixed frame rate, and exhibits significant non-stationarity and temporal dependencies due to pronounced daily seasonal patterns. As a result, conventional image- and video-based anomaly detection methods are inappropriate. A recent forecasting-based AD method, ForecastAD [24], attempts to address these challenges by measuring per-pixel errors between predicted and observed thermal images. However, reconstruction-based AD methods suffer a critical flaw: models trained on normal data can inadvertently reconstruct and misclassify anomalous images as normal [10,22], leading to unreliable detection.

To overcome these limitations, we propose a principled, robust AD framework tailored for CSP plant monitoring. First, we introduce a risk-controlling thresholding strategy for anomaly scores that satisfies finite-sample performance guarantees on any chosen risk function (e.g., false positive rate or F1-score)—a critical requirement for reliable predictive maintenance (PdM) in industrial settings. To enhance trust and adoption, we integrate a machine-learning-with-abstention framework [27] with adaptive thresholds that account for the overlap between normal and anomalous score distributions. This approach defers high-risk predictions to domain experts, ensuring human intervention when uncertainty is high. Furthermore, we propose an AD method based on density forecasting, DensityAD, which leverages conditional normalizing flows to model the likelihood of an observed sample being normal, given past thermal images and timestamps. This approach mitigates the limitations of reconstruction-based methods and enables likelihood-based thresholding for more effective anomaly detection. Our key contributions are:

- We propose a framework for computing reliable anomaly detection thresholds with finite-sample performance guarantees for any chosen risk function. The framework includes an abstention mechanism that defers decisions to domain experts under high uncertainty.
- We develop an unsupervised AD method that computes anomaly scores using density forecasting by estimating the conditional likelihood of an observed infrared image given a sequence of previously observed images.
- We conduct an extensive deployment analysis of our framework across multiple real-world scenarios over several months, using data from two CSP plants. This analysis provides valuable insights to our industry partner for maintenance operations.
- We release a simulated dataset by leveraging recent advancements in generative modelling to create diverse infrared images that emulate real-world data from CSP plants.

Our work not only advances the state of anomaly detection in renewable energy systems but also serves as an important milestone for future research in robust, data-driven PdM strategies for critical infrastructure monitoring.

2 Anomaly Detection in Thermal Images from CSP Plants

In the following, we describe our AD use case and the associated dataset.

Use-Case. Concentrated Solar Power (CSP) plants are designed to harness solar energy for large-scale electricity generation while addressing two major challenges commonly associated with renewable energy sources – on-demand generation and dispatchability. Among the four primary CSP technologies currently in use, namely, Solar Tower, Parabolic Trough, Linear Fresnel, and Dish-Stirling systems, this study specifically focuses on the operational aspects of Solar Tower-based CSP plants. These plants comprise two critical components:

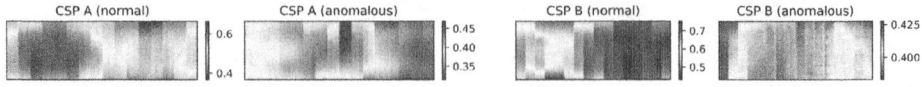

Fig. 1. Example of thermal images from CSP A and B.

the Thermal Solar Receiver and the Steam Generator. Positioned atop a central tower, the Solar Receiver functions as a solar furnace, absorbing concentrated sunlight reflected by an array of heliostats–movable mirrors strategically arranged on the ground around the tower. A high-capacity heat transfer medium, such as molten salts, circulates through vertical heat exchanger tubes configured as panels within the receiver, absorbing the thermal energy from the concentrated sunlight. This heated transfer medium is subsequently stored in a Thermal Energy Storage (TES) system. It is later used to generate superheated steam, which drives the Steam Generator to produce electricity. Thus, the incorporation of TES enables the on-demand power generation capability of CSP plants and positions them as viable alternatives to conventional fossil fuel-based power plants. Despite their advantages, CSP plants encounter significant operational challenges operating in extremely high temperatures. These challenges include blockage or deformation of heat exchanger tubes, metal fatigue, and corrosion, all of which can impact plant efficiency and reliability. Therefore, continuous monitoring and real-time failure detection are crucial to ensuring uninterrupted power generation and preventing costly system failures. In this study, we focus on detecting failures and anomalous behaviours in the Thermal Solar Receiver.

Dataset. As previously discussed, the receiver consists of vertical heat exchanger tubes arranged in panels through which the heat transfer medium flows. During normal operation, the temperature of this medium increases as it moves through the tubes, absorbing heat from concentrated sunlight. It results in a surface temperature gradient along the flow direction, which is captured by infrared (IR) cameras. In this study, our goal is to identify anomalous behaviours of the solar receiver by monitoring these temperature gradients. The *solar receiver dataset* used in this study consists of sequences of IR images taken at irregular intervals ranging from one to five minutes throughout the day, with each sequence corresponding to an operational day of the CSP plant. Notably, the dataset lacks ground truth labels, as domain experts do not have prior knowledge of all possible failure types, and anomalies are inherently unknown apriori. Each operational day at the CSP plant comprises three distinct phases: (i) *preheating*, to prevent molten salt from freezing, (ii) *filling/draining*, during which salt circulates at the start and is drained at the end of the operation, and (iii) the *power* phase, where the salt absorbs thermal energy for power generation. Each phase exhibits a distinct surface temperature profile, which must be accounted for in modelling to ensure reliable AD. For example, low surface temperatures are expected during *preheating*, but the same behaviour during the *power* phase may signal a failure.

Building on prior work [24], we expanded the *solar receiver dataset* to include data from two distinct CSP plants, referred to as A and B, for anonymity. Specifically, we have access to 16343 samples from CSP A and 15181 from CSP B. Although the dataset exhibits similar key characteristics—such as non-stationarity, irregular sampling, and temporal dependence—certain differences exist across the plants. Notably, the thermal image resolutions differ, with CSP A capturing images of size 184×608 pixels, while CSP B captures images of size 196×528 pixels. Furthermore, CSP B exhibits an inversion in the thermal flow direction (left to right), whereas CSP A follow a right-to-left flow pattern. Examples of thermal images for both CSP plants can be seen in Fig. 1. To maintain confidentiality, all thermal images have been normalized before analysis.

3 Background

Notations. We consider an unsupervised AD setting, where the training dataset, denoted as $\mathcal{D}_N = \{x_i\}_{i=1}^n$, consists of n *unlabeled* samples. Each sample $x_i = (y_i, t_i) \in \mathcal{X}$ is a tuple, where $\mathcal{X} = \mathbb{R}_+^d \times \mathbb{R}_+$. The first component, $y_i \in \mathcal{Y}$, represents a thermal image of dimension $d = H \times W$, where H and W denote the height and width, respectively, with $\mathcal{Y} = \mathbb{R}_+^d$. The second component, $t_i \in \mathbb{R}_+$, corresponds to the timestamp at which the thermal image y_i was captured. Following prior works [31], we assume that the training dataset $\mathcal{D}_N$ predominantly contains normal samples. Additionally, we introduce another *labelled* dataset, $\mathcal{D}_R = \{(x_i, z_i)\}_{i=1}^{n_R}$, consisting of n_R labeled pairs, where $n_R \ll n$. Each label $z_i \in \{0, 1\}$ indicates whether the corresponding sample is normal ($z_i = 0$) or anomalous ($z_i = 1$). Furthermore, the dataset $\mathcal{D}_R$ is partitioned into three disjoint subsets: validation ($\mathcal{D}_V$), calibration ($\mathcal{D}_C$), and test ($\mathcal{D}_T$).

Unsupervised AD. The goal of unsupervised AD is to estimate an anomaly score function $s(\cdot) : \mathcal{X} \to \mathbb{R}$ using $\mathcal{D}_N$, such that normal samples receive lower scores. A label (0 for normal or 1 for anomalous) is then assigned to a new test sample $x \in \mathcal{X}$ by thresholding its anomaly score:

$$\hat{z} = h(x) = \begin{cases} 0, & \text{if } s(x) \leq \lambda, \\ 1, & \text{if } s(x) > \lambda, \end{cases} \quad (1)$$

where $h : \mathcal{X} \to \{0, 1\}$ is the labelling function and $\lambda \in \mathbb{R}$ is a threshold to be determined, whose optimal value depends on the proportion of anomalies in the test set [26,29]. However, since the true proportion is unknown in practice, existing methods rely on test performance metrics to select a threshold $\lambda \in \Lambda$ from a set of feasible thresholds $\Lambda \subset \mathbb{R}$. Commonly adopted approaches include:

- **F1-score** [2]. The threshold λ_F yields the highest F1-score:

$$\lambda_F = \arg\max_{\lambda \in \Lambda} \text{F1-Score}(\mathcal{H}_V), \quad (2)$$

where $\mathcal{H}_V = \{(h(x), z) \mid (x, z) \in \mathcal{D}_V\}$ and F1-Score computes the harmonic mean of precision and recall.

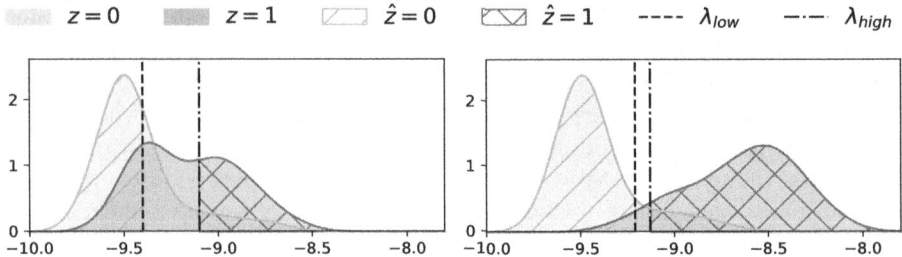

Fig. 2. Illustration of thresholds for AD with abstention under high (left) and low (right) overlap in anomaly score distributions of normal and anomalous samples.

- **G-Mean** [17]. The threshold λ_G maximizes the G-Mean:

$$\lambda_G = \arg\max_{\lambda \in \Lambda} \text{ G-Mean}(\mathcal{H}_V), \quad (3)$$

  where G-Mean computes the geometric mean of precision and recall.
- **Z-score.** Let $\mathcal{S}_V$ be the set of anomaly scores for normal samples in $\mathcal{D}_V$, defined as $\mathcal{S}_V = \{s(x) \mid (x, 0) \in \mathcal{D}_V\}$ with the corresponding mean and standard deviation denoted by $\mu_{\mathcal{S}_V}$ and $\sigma_{\mathcal{S}_V}$, respectively. The threshold λ_z is set k standard deviations above $\mu_{\mathcal{S}_V}$. Unlike Eq. 1, where the threshold is applied directly to $s(x)$, here it is applied to the z-scores, defined as $s_z(x) = \left| \frac{s(x) - \mu_{\mathcal{S}_V}}{\sigma_{\mathcal{S}_V}} \right|$.

For a comprehensive discussion on existing methods for selecting λ, we refer to [26]. A key limitation of these approaches is that they do not account for uncertainty when the anomaly score distributions of normal and anomalous samples overlap, as illustrated in Fig. 2. However, given the high-risk nature of AD applications, it is essential to abstain from assigning labels under high uncertainty. This allows domain experts to intervene, reducing the risk of incorrect classifications and ensuring more reliable decision-making.

Unsupervised AD with Abstention. To enable abstention from labeling under high uncertainty, we augment the labeling function with an abstention label (Ⓡ) and introduce two thresholds (λ^l and λ^h), reformulating $h(x)$ as follows:

$$\hat{z} = h(x) = \begin{cases} 0, & \text{if } x \in \hat{C}_{\text{nor}}, \quad \hat{C}_{\text{nor}} = \{x' \in \mathcal{X} \mid s(x') \leq \lambda^l\}, \\ 1, & \text{if } x \in \hat{C}_{\text{ano}}, \quad \hat{C}_{\text{ano}} = \{x' \in \mathcal{X} \mid s(x') \geq \lambda^h\}, \\ \text{Ⓡ}, & \text{if } x \in \hat{C}_{\text{abs}}, \quad \hat{C}_{\text{abs}} = \{x' \in \mathcal{X} \mid \lambda^l < s(x') < \lambda^h\}, \end{cases} \quad (4)$$

where $\hat{C}_{\text{nor}}$ is the *normal prediction region*, $\hat{C}_{\text{ano}}$ is the *anomalous prediction region*, and $\hat{C}_{\text{abs}}$ is the *abstention region*, where the model refrains from making a decision.

Figure 2 illustrates two examples of this decision-making process. The parameters λ^l and λ^h define the normal and anomalous prediction regions while also regulating the abstention region, thereby controlling the abstention rate.

Ideally, the pair of thresholds (λ^l, λ^h) should adapt to the anomaly score distribution, effectively capturing the overlap between normal and anomalous scores. A trivial yet uninformative approach is to set $\lambda^l = -\infty$ and $\lambda^h = +\infty$, which results in abstaining from prediction for all samples. We aim to propose a principled method for selecting a reliable pair of thresholds.

4 Reliable Decision Thresholds for AD

Let us define a Risk-Controlling Prediction Set (RCPS) $\widehat{C}_\lambda$ for a given threshold $\lambda \in \Lambda \subset \mathbb{R}$ as follows:

Definition 1 (RCPS [6]). *Let $\lambda \in \Lambda$ be a random variable and $R(\cdot): 2^\mathcal{X} \to \mathbb{R}$ a risk function. The set $\widehat{C}_\lambda$ is defined as an (α, δ)-risk-controlling prediction set if it satisfies the condition $\mathbb{P}(R(\widehat{C}_\lambda) \leq \alpha) \geq 1 - \delta$, where $\alpha \in [0, 1]$ is the risk tolerance and $\delta \in [0, 1]$ is the error level.*

One method for constructing an RCPS is *conformal risk control*, an extension of conformal prediction (CP) [3] designed to control the expected value of a risk function, assuming it is monotonically non-increasing with respect to a single threshold λ. However, this approach is limited to a single-parameter setting, as in (1), and relies on a restrictive assumption about the risk function.

To overcome these limitations, we propose leveraging the *Learn then Test* (LTT) procedure [4]. We consider the unsupervised AD problem with abstention, as defined in (4). Our objective is to determine a pair of reliable thresholds (λ^l, λ^h) that define a RCPS $\widehat{C}_{(\lambda^l, \lambda^h)} = \widehat{C}_{\text{nor}} \cup \widehat{C}_{\text{ano}}$ with finite-sample coverage guarantees for any given risk function $R(\cdot): 2^\mathcal{X} \to \mathbb{R}$ (e.g., the false positive rate). Additionally, we seek to adapt the abstention rate based on the complexity of the risk function.

Our LTT Procedure for Reliable Threshold Selection. We propose an extension of the LTT procedure, denoted as xLTT, which generalizes the framework to consider a pair of thresholds (λ^l, λ^h) instead of a single threshold λ. The procedure begins by defining a set of paired threshold values, $\Lambda = \{(\lambda^l_{(a)}, \lambda^h_{(b)}) \mid a, b \in \{1, \ldots, m\}, \lambda^l_{(a)} \leq \lambda^h_{(b)}\}$. Next, we define the null hypotheses $\mathcal{H}_j : \hat{R}_{n_C}(\widehat{C}_{(\lambda^l_j, \lambda^h_j)}) > \alpha$ for each $(\lambda^l_j, \lambda^h_j) \in \Lambda$, $j \in \{1, \ldots, |\Lambda|\}$ and $\alpha \in [0, 1]$, where $\hat{R}_{n_C}(\cdot): 2^\mathcal{X} \to \mathbb{R}$ is an empirical risk function computed on the calibration set $\mathcal{D}_C$. Accepting $\mathcal{H}_j$ indicates that $(\lambda^l_j, \lambda^h_j)$ does not control the risk. To decide whether to accept or reject $\mathcal{H}_j$ and thus verify whether the risk is controlled for a given pair $(\lambda^l_j, \lambda^h_j)$, we compute a valid p-value p_j for every $\mathcal{H}_j$ using α. This is achieved via a concentration inequality (e.g., the Hoeffding-Bentkus inequality [6]). Based on the set of p-values $P = \{p_j\}_{j \in \{1, \ldots, |\Lambda|\}}$, we then select the threshold pairs for which the risk is controlled. Since multiple comparisons increase the likelihood of false positives, a correction function $\mathcal{A}: P \to P'$ with $P' \subseteq P$ is required to maintain the desired risk control. For example, we define the set $\mathcal{O} = \mathcal{A}(P) \subset \Lambda$ using Bonferroni correction as

$\mathcal{A}(P) = \{(\lambda^l_j, \lambda^h_j) \mid p_j \leq \frac{\delta}{|\mathcal{A}|}, p_j \in P\}$. If $\mathcal{O} = \emptyset$, we set $\mathcal{O} = \{(-\infty, \infty)\}$. Finally, any pair $(\lambda^l, \lambda^h) \in \mathcal{O}$ ensures that $\hat{C}_{(\lambda^l, \lambda^h)}$ forms a risk-controlling prediction set. This method enables the use of any risk function in a post-hoc manner (i.e., without requiring retraining of a given anomaly detector), making it particularly valuable for AD in CSP plants with diverse and evolving requirements.

Optimal Threshold Selection for AD. Now that we have obtained the set $\mathcal{O}$ of threshold pairs that control the risk, our next objective is to (1) avoid trivial selections where $\lambda^l = -\infty$ and $\lambda^h = \infty$, and (2) minimize false positives and false negatives while keeping the abstention rate as low as possible. Let $\mathcal{I}_1 = \{i \mid z_i = 1\}$ and $\mathcal{I}_0 = \{i \mid z_i = 0\}$ be the set of indices for anomalous and normal points, respectively. $\hat{z}_i$ are the predicted labels computed using (4), with $i = 1, \ldots, |\mathcal{D}_V|$. We propose selecting the optimal thresholds λ^l_* and λ^h_* by computing:

$$\lambda^l_*, \lambda^h_* = \arg\min_{\lambda^l, \lambda^h \in \mathcal{O}} \underbrace{\frac{|\{i \in \mathcal{I}_1 \mid \hat{z}_i = 0\}|}{|\mathcal{I}_1|}}_{\text{False Negative Rate (FNR)}} + \underbrace{\frac{|\{i \in \mathcal{I}_0 \mid \hat{z}_i = 1\}|}{|\mathcal{I}_0|}}_{\text{False Positive Rate (FPR)}} + \underbrace{\frac{|\{i \mid \hat{z}_i = \varnothing\}|}{|\mathcal{D}_V|}}_{\text{Abstention Rate}}.$$

Density-Based Anomaly Score Functions. Recent work [23] examined the intrinsic connection between anomaly detection and conformal prediction, demonstrating how insights from each field can mutually enhance the other. Building on this perspective, we leverage recent advancements in CP [13] to develop novel anomaly score functions $s(\cdot)^1$ for the labeling function in (4). These score functions are further integrated with the reliable threshold selection procedure xLTT.

Our framework is based upon an invertible, conditional generative model (e.g., normalizing flows) $\hat{g} : \mathcal{V} \times \mathcal{C} \times \mathbb{R}_+ \to \mathcal{Y}$, where $\mathcal{V}$ is a latent variable with a known distribution and $\mathcal{C}$ is the space of the conditioning variable. We defer the discussion of the exact model used to Sect. 5. Formally, $\hat{g}(\hat{g}^{-1}(y; c, t); c, t) = y$ for any $c \in \mathcal{C}$, $y \in \mathcal{Y}$ and $t \in \mathbb{R}_+$. The invertibility allows us to compute the exact density $\hat{f}(y \mid c, t)$ via the change of variables formula. For a test observation $x = (y, t)$, and given $\hat{g}$, we consider the following two approaches:

– DR-xLTT. The negative log-likelihood is the score function:

$$s_{\text{DR}}(x; c) = -\log(\hat{f}(y \mid c, t)). \tag{5}$$

– L-xLTT. The second approach is based on an invertible model, following the L-CP method introduced in [13]. Unlike the output space $\mathcal{Y}$, we expect the latent space $\mathcal{V}$ to be more structured, where normal samples are ideally clustered near the origin. Consequently, in L-xLTT, we frame the decision-making process as a one-class classification problem in the latent space. Assuming the latent variable follows a standard normal distribution, we use the ℓ_2 distance

---

[1] Hereafter, the score function incorporates contextual information c.

of the latent representation from the origin as the anomaly score for a test point x:

$$s_L(x; c) = \|v\|, \quad \text{where } v = \hat{g}^{-1}(y; c, t). \tag{6}$$

5 Density-Based AD Model

The most recent AD model for CSP plants, `ForecastAD`, is a reconstruction-based AD methods. However, prior research has shown that anomalies, despite significantly different from normal data, can often be reconstructed in practice [10]. For instance, in a bimodal distribution, the distance between the two peaks is greater than the distance between a peak and the local minimum separating them. In such cases, when a prediction aligns with one of the peaks, observations near the local minimum exhibit lower reconstruction errors and thus are incorrectly deemed more likely [22]. Figure 3 presents examples of IR images that are well reconstructed but are anomalous and exhibit empirically low density.

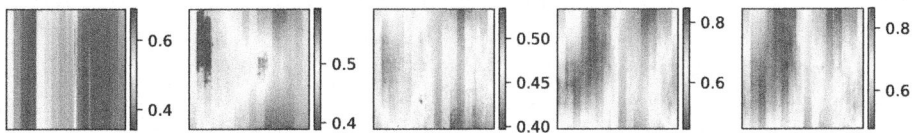

Fig. 3. Well-reconstructed anomalous thermal images with empirically low density.

To overcome such limitations of reconstruction-based approaches, we introduce `DensityAD`, an invertible generative model that directly estimates the density of thermal images given the contextual information from past images. `DensityAD` operates in two main steps: (i) concatenating the K preceding images and their timestamps as a context vector c, and (ii) leveraging this context to estimate the density of the current observation $x = (y, t)$, i.e. $f(y \mid c, t)$.

Context encoding. Building on [24], given a test observation $x_i = (y_i, t_i)$, we construct a rich contextual representation c_i for AD by encoding both spatial and temporal information from the preceding K images. First, at each time step t_{i-k}, where $k = 1, \cdots, K$, the corresponding image y_{i-k} is mapped into a lower-dimensional latent space. Specifically, we define an image encoder $\phi_e(\cdot; W_e) : \mathcal{Y} \to \mathcal{V}'$, which transforms images from the high-dimensional input space $\mathcal{Y}$ into a lower dimensional latent space $\mathcal{V}' = \mathbb{R}^{d'}$, where $d' \ll d$. Then, to capture temporal dependencies, we consider two temporal features: the inter-arrival time $\tau_{i-k} = t_{i-k} - t_{i-(k+1)}$, which represents the time elapsed since the previous observation, and the relative time since the start of operation $\gamma_{i-k} = t_{i-k} - t_0$, which situates the observation within the broader operational cycle. These temporal attributes are encoded using a sinusoidal function $\psi(\cdot)$. The final embedding for each data point (y_{i-k}, t_{i-k}) is then constructed by concatenating the temporal encodings with the image embedding as $\hat{c}_{i-k} = \phi_e(y_{i-k}; W_e) \oplus \psi_\tau(\tau_{i-k}) \oplus \psi_\gamma(\gamma_{i-k})$. Lastly, to generate the fixed-dimensional context vector c_i at time step t_i, the embeddings of the past K images are aggregated using a deep sequence model.

Conditional Normalizing Flow. The conditional PDF $f(y_i \mid c_i, t_i)$ of the current image y_i, given context c_i at timestep t_i, is estimated using a conditional normalizing flow, specifically GLOW [21]. The invertibility property of normalizing flows [16,30] enables exact likelihood computation, which is essential for the threshold selection methods discussed in Sect. 4. To model $f(y_i \mid c_i, t_i)$, we apply conditional invertible transformations g, mapping y_i to a latent variable v_i as $v_i = g(y_i; c_i, t_i)$. The conditional log-likelihood is then computed using the change-of-variables formula. For further details, we refer the reader to [21].

6 Experiments

Here, we compare the performance of DensityAD against existing baselines and assess the efficacy of our proposed decision thresholds for risk-controlled AD.

6.1 Experimental Setup

Dataset. We use data from two CSP plants, denoted as A and B. The validation set also serves as a calibration set. For the first data point of each day, both τ and γ are initialized to a small positive value, $\epsilon = $ 1e-5.

Baselines. In our evaluation, we compare the performance of DensityAD against deep image-based AD methods, specifically CFlow [14] and DRÆM [37]. To extend the comparison to AD approaches that incorporate historical sequences of observations, similar to DensityAD, we include a spatiotemporal autoencoder (STAE) architecture [12,15,34] and TimeSformer [9], a transformer-based video classification framework, as baselines, along with ForecastAD [24].

Experimental Details. To prevent numerical instability during training, images are resized to 64 × 64, and we employ 3 flows per block across 5 blocks. The model is trained using the Adam optimizer with a learning rate of 0.0001 and a weight decay of 0.00001. Early stopping is applied based on the validation AUPR[2], maintaining a fixed balance between normal and anomalous samples in the validation set during training to mitigate the impact of dataset imbalance. The baseline models are trained following their published training setups. We used TimeSformer as the encoder in an encoder-decoder architecture, using the decoder from ForecastAD, and trained with a mean squared error loss. For the decision thresholds, we use $\alpha = \delta = 0.1$. We conduct an ablation study in Section 2 of the supplementary material on the context length K and the importance of time embeddings τ and γ. Based on the analysis, we opt for the sequence length $K = 30$ and only consider τ in DensityAD for modelling the temporal dynamics.

---

[2] Area Under the Precision-Recall Curve (AUPR).

Table 1. AUROC and AUPR performances of `DensityAD` against baseline methods. Style: best in **bold**, and second best underlined.

CSP	Model	AUROC (%) ↑	AUPR (%) ↑
A	CFlow [14]	76.46 ± 0.92	70.32 ± 1.20
	DRÆM [37]	81.55 ± 1.9	74.8 ± 2.79
	STAE	<u>89.47 ± 1.59</u>	87.38 ± 2.4
	TimeSformer [9]	87.8 ± 2.46	83.36 ± 3.15
	ForecastAD [24]	86.28 ± 1.74	<u>87.57 ± 1.38</u>
	DensityAD	**94.25 ± 0.2**	**93.88 ± 0.48**
B	CFlow [14]	55.8 ± 5.47	57.56 ± 4.85
	DRÆM [37]	78.82 ± 5.72	71.75 ± 8.56
	STAE	<u>89.9 ± 1.18</u>	88.98 ± 1.68
	TimeSformer [9]	88.59 ± 2.14	<u>89.84 ± 1.29</u>
	ForecastAD [24]	81.76 ± 0.7	82.88 ± 1.39
	DensityAD	**91.93 ± 0.52**	**90.66 ± 0.46**

Evaluation Metrics. We evaluate `DensityAD` using two primary metrics: the AUROC[3] and the AUPR. Additionally, we assess the proposed thresholding methods by reporting the risk, along with the F1-score and the corresponding abstention rate for two controlled risk measures relevant to our context: the FPR and the F1-score. These choices are not fixed—any risk function can be selected to meet the specific requirements of a CSP plant. We also report these risk measures for existing threshold selection methods. For all experiments, we present the mean over three runs along with one standard error.

6.2 Results and Discussion

AD Models. Table 1 presents the performance of `DensityAD` for both CSP plants. The results indicate that `DensityAD` consistently outperforms all baseline methods on both datasets. While STAE, `ForecastAD`, and TimeSformer perform well, they still fall short of the performance achieved by our `DensityAD`.

Anomaly scores. Figure 4 shows the distributions of normal and anomalous scores for test samples on CSP A, using the proposed scores, introduced in Sect. 4 (i.e., s_{DR} and s_L) and the reconstruction score s_{REC} from `ForecastAD`. In this example, s_{DR} and s_{REC} scores effectively distinguish normal from anomalous samples, as shown by the overlapping area (OA) between both distributions.

Anomaly Threshold Selection. Fig. 5 provides an overview of the threshold selection approaches. The results clearly show that the proposed methods effectively control risk for both risk functions, whereas existing methods do not

---

[3] Area Under the Receiver Operating Characteristic Curve (AUROC).

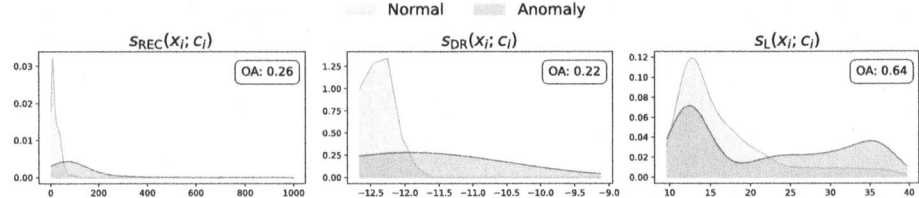

Fig. 4. Empirical score distributions of normal and anomalous test samples from CSP A for our proposed score functions and the one used by `ForecastAD`, with the overlapping area (OA) between both distributions in the top right corner.

Table 2. Total CPU time and memory used for training the models.

	ForecastAD		DensityAD	
	CSP A	CSP B	CSP A	CSP B
Training time (s)	4151 ± 327	2204 ± 334	3760 ± 836	3248 ± 411
Memory used (Gb)	1.63 ± 0.13	1.73 ± 0.05	1.73 ± 0.02	1.63 ± 0.02
Inference time (ms)	194 ± 6.73	177 ± 1.44	201.3 ± 17.41	178 ± 2.37

offer such guarantees. The `DR-xLTT` methods demonstrate strong performance, balancing risk control with a high F1-score while maintaining a low abstention rate. Notably, they outperform approaches that select the maximum validation set value. Furthermore, these methods adapt to the complexity of the risk function, recognizing that controlling the F1-score presents greater predictive challenges than the FPR. They also fully adjust to user requirements, increasing the abstention rate when constraints are too stringent (e.g., attempting to control the F1-score with a weak underlying model).

Computation Requirements. The models are trained using a single NVIDIA A100 GPU with 40 GB of memory, along with 8 CPU cores and 20 GB of RAM. Table 2 presents the training times (excluding the risk-control), memory usage and inference time for a single test point. As shown in Table 1, `DensityAD` performs better than `ForecastAD` while using similar resources.

7 Deployment

We deployed our threshold selection methods using `DensityAD` on 5 and 6 months of anonymized data from CSP plants A and B, respectively. Figure 6 presents the thresholding results, where the FPR is used as the controlled risk. The results demonstrate that risk is effectively controlled in deployment, with `DR-xLTT` emerging as the most consistent method across both CSP plants. All methods maintain a low abstention rate, making them well-suited for deployment. Additionally, the deployment results align closely with those observed during testing. Performance fluctuations across months can be attributed to variations

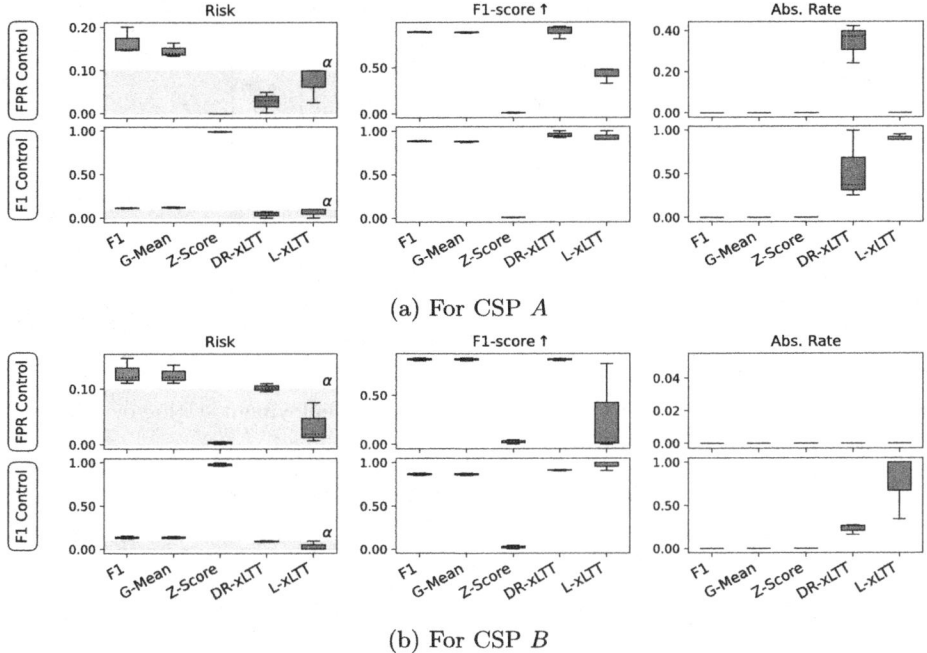

Fig. 5. Risk control over FPR (top row) and F1-score (bottom row) for existing and proposed methods. The risk is FPR (top row) and $1-F1$ (bottom row).

in the frequency and complexity of anomalies, with some months exhibiting a higher occurrence or more challenging cases.

Figure 7 evaluates the performance of `DensityAD` in deployment under three training configurations: training on CSP A, training on CSP B, and training on a combination of data from both CSP plants. As expected, deploying a model trained on a different tower results in a performance decline. Furthermore, training on data from both plants does not yield any performance improvement, suggesting that information from one tower does not generalize well to another. Although thermal flow patterns are similar across CSPs, anomaly definitions vary due to site-specific factors such as geographic location and operational context. This limits cross-site generalization, indicating the need for per-site models or fine-tuning. Future work could address this through domain adaptation techniques. Although originally not designed for this purpose, `DensityAD` offers a general framework that can be extended to multivariate time series anomaly detection. In this work, we focus on its application to anomaly detection in CSPs, where the anomaly score is computed and subsequently processed through a thresholding mechanism. Finally, the results suggest that the proposed method supports practical deployment by enabling control over operational risk. For instance, it allows organizations to meet predefined detection targets—such

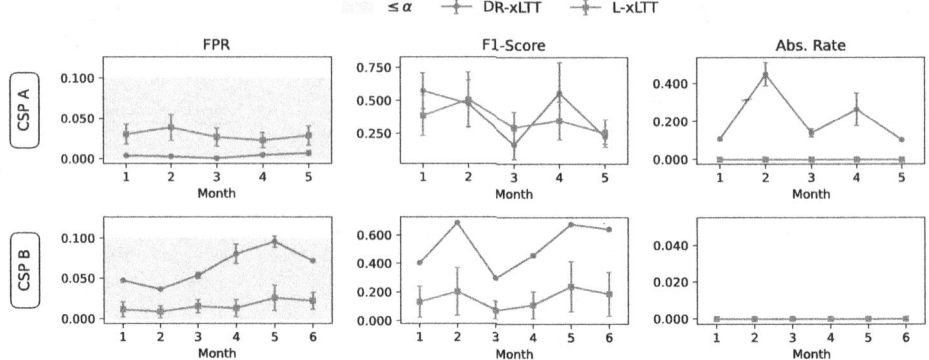

Fig. 6. FPR control for the proposed approaches in a deployment setting over multiple months, for the two CSP plants.

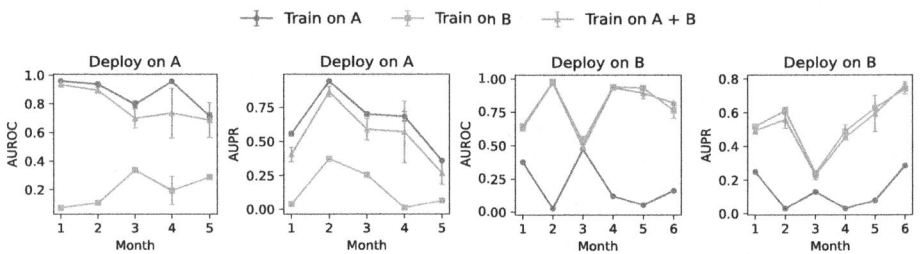

Fig. 7. AUROC and AUPR for the two CSP plants over multiple months using three different training settings (i.e. training on A, B, and $A+B$).

as identifying 90% of anomalies—thereby supporting compliance with regulatory or performance requirements.

8 Simulated Dataset

Building on the methodology described in [24], we construct a simulated dataset to facilitate the reproducibility and validation of our results. DensityAD enables exact likelihood computation while also allowing sampling from the learned distribution. Leveraging this capability, we generate high-quality samples using our proposed density-based model. The dataset simulates two distinct CSP setups, providing a valuable resource for advancing anomaly detection research in CSP plants. Further details are provided in the supplement.

Due to transformations applied during anonymization, we assessed the reliability of the generated images by comparing the average daily temperature profiles of both CSP plants. As shown in Fig. 8, temperature levels during the critical period (08:00 to 20:00) closely match between the simulated and original datasets. Temperatures outside this interval, which are notably lower, were regarded as trivial outliers and excluded from the simulated data.

9 Related Work

Unsupervised AD. Based on the assumption of a "clean" training dataset, i.e., containing only normal samples, unsupervised AD approaches have been proposed with the aim of training models that learn a "compact" representation of the normal behaviour. Then, anomalies are identified as deviations from this learned normality. Existing methods can be broadly categorized into four families [32]. First, both deep and shallow *one-class classifiers* [33,35] learn a decision boundary around normal samples with classical methods such as support vector data description. Second, *feature embedding-based* methods store or learn normal data representations using pre-trained models [19,31] or student-teacher networks [8,25,38]. Third, *reconstruction-based* methods use encoder-decoder architectures to map normal samples into a lower-dimensional bottleneck and reconstruct them with high fidelity. Lastly, *density-based* methods estimate the probability distribution of normal samples under the *concentration assumption*, where anomalies are expected to be in low-density regions. For a comprehensive survey, we refer readers to [20,32].

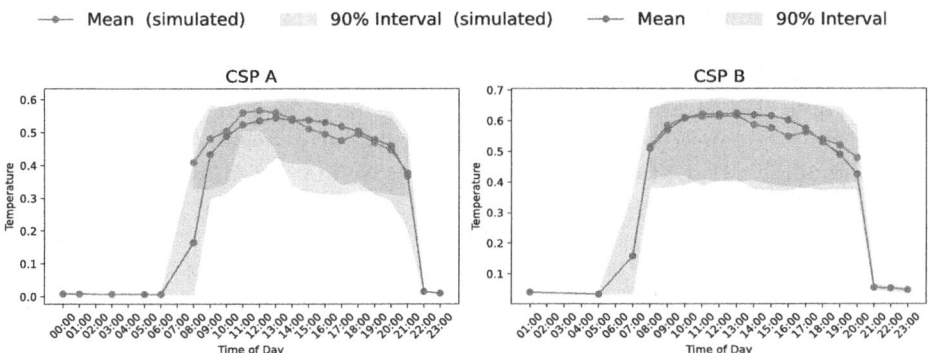

Fig. 8. Mean daily temperature for the original and simulated datasets. The shaded area represents the 90% temperature interval.

Beyond image-based AD, prior research also investigated AD in videos (VAD) [1,11,18], using historical sequences of observations to identify deviations. However, our setting differs in two key ways: (1) our IR images lack the semantic content of typical video frames, and (2) our solar dataset is captured at irregular intervals, while videos are captured at a fixed frame rate. Although [24] introduced a forecast-based AD approach for CSP plants, it lacks a reliable selection of AD threshold. Moreover, their study is limited to a single CSP plant, whereas our setting involves multiple plants, introducing additional heterogeinity.

Anomaly Detection Thresholds. To assign labels, AD methods typically threshold anomaly scores. Commonly used decision thresholds particularly relevant to our use case involve optimizing performance metrics, such as the F1-score

[2], G-Mean [17], or the area under the Precision-Recall Curve (PRC), on the validation set over a range of possible thresholds. Another class of methods builds on conformal prediction (CP) [36], a distribution-free framework for constructing prediction sets (e.g., those defined in our decision-making process) providing a finite-sample coverage guarantee. [7] introduces a method for computing conditionally valid conformal p-values for nonparametric outlier detection, framing the problem within a multiple hypothesis testing context. A key extension of CP, named *conformal risk control* [5], shifts the guarantee from coverage to managing any monotonically non-increasing risk function. The *Learn then Test* procedure [4] further allows us to extend this concept to any risk function, irrespective of its monotonicity, to generate risk-controlled prediction sets [6].

10 Conclusion

We introduced a principled and robust framework for anomaly detection (AD) designed to monitor CSP plants using infrared imagery captured at irregular intervals throughout the day. Our approach labels images as normal or anomalous by first assigning an anomaly score using a model trained on an unlabeled image dataset, followed by a thresholding procedure. To address the challenges of unsupervised AD for CSP plants, our contributions are fourfold. First, we proposed a framework for computing reliable anomaly detection thresholds with finite-sample risk coverage guarantees for any chosen risk function while allowing deferral to domain experts under high uncertainty. Second, to compute more robust anomaly scores for an observed image, we developed a density forecasting method that estimates its likelihood conditional on a sequence of previously observed images. Third, we conducted an extensive real-world deployment analysis over several months across two operational CSP plants, providing valuable insights for industrial maintenance. Lastly, we released a simulated dataset leveraging recent advancements in generative modeling, facilitating data-driven predictive maintenance (PdM) for critical infrastructure. By enhancing the reliability of renewable energy systems, our work supports the broader adoption of sustainable energy solutions for a greener future.

Acknowledgements. This research is funded by the project "Federated Learning and Augmented Reality for Advanced Control Centers." Special thanks to Thibault GEORGES and Adrien FARINELLE from John Cockerill for their assistance in analyzing the dataset and identifying related abnormal behaviors. We also acknowledge Victor DHEUR for his valuable feedback on the risk control approach.

References

1. Abdalla, M., Javed, S., Radi, M.A., Ulhaq, A., Werghi, N.: Video anomaly detection in 10 years: a survey and outlook. arXiv preprint arXiv:2405.19387 (2024)

2. Akcay, S., Ameln, D., Vaidya, A., Lakshmanan, B., Ahuja, N., Genc, U.: Anomalib: a deep learning library for anomaly detection. In: 2022 IEEE International Conference on Image Processing (ICIP), pp. 1706–1710. IEEE (2022)
3. Angelopoulos, A.N., Bates, S.: Conformal prediction: A gentle introduction. Found. Trends® Mach. Learn. **16**(4), 494–591 (2023)
4. Angelopoulos, A.N., Bates, S., Candès, E.J., Jordan, M.I., Lei, L.: Learn then test: Calibrating predictive algorithms to achieve risk control. Annals Appl. Stat. **19**(2), 1641–1662 (2025). https://doi.org/10.1214/24-AOAS1998
5. Angelopoulos, A.N., Bates, S., Fisch, A., Lei, L., Schuster, T.: Conformal risk control. arXiv [stat.ME] (Aug 2022)
6. Bates, S., Angelopoulos, A., Lei, L., Malik, J., Jordan, M.: Distribution-free, risk-controlling prediction sets. J. ACM (JACM) **68**(6), 1–34 (2021)
7. Bates, S., Candès, E., Lei, L., Romano, Y., Sesia, M.: Testing for outliers with conformal p-values. Ann. Stat. **51**(1), 149–178 (2023)
8. Batzner, K., Heckler, L., König, R.: EfficientAD: accurate visual anomaly detection at millisecond-level latencies. In: Proceedings of the IEEE/CVF Winter Conference on Applications of Computer Vision (WACV), pp. 128–138 (1 2024)
9. Bertasius, G., Wang, H., Torresani, L.: Is space-time attention all you need for video understanding? **2**(3), 4 (2021)
10. Bouman, R., Heskes, T.: Autoencoders for anomaly detection are unreliable. arXiv [cs.LG] (Jan 2025)
11. Chandrakala, S., Deepak, K., Revathy, G.: Anomaly detection in surveillance videos: a thematic taxonomy of deep models, review and performance analysis. Artif. Intell. Rev. **56**(4), 3319–3368 (2023)
12. Deepak, K., Chandrakala, S., Mohan, C.K.: Residual spatiotemporal autoencoder for unsupervised video anomaly detection. SIViP **15**(1), 215–222 (2021)
13. Dheur, V., Fontana, M., Estievenart, Y., Desobry, N., Taieb, S.B.: A unified comparative study with generalized conformity scores for multi-output conformal regression. arXiv [stat.ML] (Jan 2025)
14. Gudovskiy, D., Ishizaka, S., Kozuka, K.: CFLOW-AD: real-time unsupervised anomaly detection with localization via conditional normalizing flows. In: Proceedings - 2022 IEEE/CVF Winter Conference on Applications of Computer Vision, WACV 2022, pp. 1819–1828 (7 2021). https://doi.org/10.1109/WACV51458.2022.00188
15. Hasan, M., Choi, J., Neumann, J., Roy-Chowdhury, A.K., Davis, L.S.: Learning temporal regularity in video sequences. In: Proceedings of the IEEE Conference on Computer Vision and Pattern Recognition. pp. 733–742 (2016)
16. Kingma, D.P., Dhariwal, P.: Glow: Generative flow with invertible 1x1 convolutions. In: Advances in Neural Information Processing Systems, vol. 31 (2018)
17. Kubat, M., Matwin, S.: Addressing the curse of imbalanced training sets: one-sided selection. In: Proceedings of the 14th International Conference on Machine Learning, pp. 179–186 (1997)
18. Le, V.T., Kim, Y.G.: Attention-based residual autoencoder for video anomaly detection. Appl. Intell. **53**(3), 3240–3254 (2023)
19. Lee, S., Lee, S., Song, B.C.: CFA: coupled-hypersphere-based feature adaptation for target-oriented anomaly localization. IEEE Access **10**, 78446–78454 (6 2022). https://doi.org/10.1109/ACCESS.2022.3193699
20. Liu, J., et al.: Deep industrial image anomaly detection: a survey. Mach. Intell. Res. **21**(1), 104–135 (2024)

21. Lu, Y., Huang, B.: Structured output learning with conditional generative flows. In: Proceedings of the AAAI Conference on Artificial Intelligence, vol. 34, pp. 5005–5012 (2020)
22. Moore, A., Morelli, D.: ConDENSE: conditional density estimation for time series anomaly detection. J. Artif. Intell. Res. **79**, 801–824 (2024)
23. Novello, P., Dalmau, J., Andéol, L.: Exploring the link between out-of-distribution detection and conformal prediction with illustrations of its benefits (2025)
24. Patra, S., Sournac, N., Taieb, S.B.: Detecting abnormal operations in concentrated solar power plants from irregular sequences of thermal images. In: Proceedings of the 30th ACM SIGKDD Conference on Knowledge Discovery and Data Mining, pp. 5578–5589. KDD '24, Association for Computing Machinery, New York, NY, USA (2024https://doi.org/10.1145/3637528.3671623
25. Patra, S., Taieb, S.B.: Revisiting deep feature reconstruction for logical and structural industrial anomaly detection. Transactions on Machine Learning Research (2024)
26. Perini, L., Bürkner, P.C., Klami, A.: Estimating the contamination factor's distribution in unsupervised anomaly detection, pp. 27668–27679 (2023)
27. Perini, L., Davis, J.: Unsupervised anomaly detection with rejection. Adv. Neural. Inf. Process. Syst. **36**, 69673–69691 (2023)
28. Perini, L., Vercruyssen, V., Davis, J.: Quantifying the confidence of anomaly detectors in their example-wise predictions. In: Joint European Conference on Machine Learning and Knowledge Discovery in Databases, pp. 227–243. Springer (2020)
29. Perini, L., Vercruyssen, V., Davis, J.: Transferring the contamination factor between anomaly detection domains by shape similarity. In: Proceedings of the AAAI Conference on Artificial Intelligence **36**(4), 4128–4136 (6 2022). https://doi.org/10.1609/AAAI.V36I4.20331, https://ojs.aaai.org/index.php/AAAI/article/view/20331
30. Rezende, D., Mohamed, S.: Variational inference with normalizing flows. In: International Conference on Machine Learning, pp. 1530–1538. PMLR (2015)
31. Roth, K., Pemula, L., Zepeda, J., Schölkopf, B., Brox, T., Gehler, P.: Towards total recall in industrial anomaly detection. In: Proceedings of the IEEE/CVF Conference on Computer Vision and Pattern Recognition, pp. 14318–14328 (2022)
32. Ruff, L., et al.: A unifying review of deep and shallow anomaly detection. Proc. IEEE **109**(5), 756–795 (2021)
33. Ruff, L., et al.: Deep one-class classification. In: International Conference on Machine Learning, pp. 4393–4402. PMLR (2018)
34. Sudhakaran, S., Lanz, O.: Learning to detect violent videos using convolutional long short-term memory. In: 2017 14th IEEE International Conference on Advanced Video and Signal Based Surveillance (AVSS), pp. 1–6. IEEE (2017)
35. Tax, D.M., Duin, R.P.: Support vector domain description. Pattern Recogn. Lett. **20**(11-13), 1191–1199 (11 1999). https://doi.org/10.1016/S0167-8655(99)00087-2
36. Vovk, V., Gammerman, A., Shafer, G.: Algorithmic Learning In A Random World, 2005th edn. Springer, New York, NY (2005)
37. Zavrtanik, V., Kristan, M., Skočaj, D.: DRÆM - A discriminatively trained reconstruction embedding for surface anomaly detection. In: Proceedings of the IEEE International Conference on Computer Vision, pp. 8310–8319 (8 2021). https://doi.org/10.1109/ICCV48922.2021.00822
38. Zhang, J., Suganuma, M., Okatani, T.: Contextual affinity distillation for image anomaly detection, pp. 149–158 (2024)

Learning Topology Actions for Power Grid Control: A Graph-Based Soft-Label Imitation Learning Approach

Mohamed Hassouna[1,2](✉), Clara Holzhüter[1,2], Malte Lehna[1,2], Matthijs de Jong[3], Jan Viebahn[3], Bernhard Sick[2], and Christoph Scholz[1,2]

[1] Fraunhofer Institute for Energy Economics and Energy System Technology (IEE), Joseph-Beuys-Straße 8, Kassel 34117, Germany
[2] Intelligent Embedded Systems, University of Kassel, Kassel, Germany
mohamed.hassouna@iee.fraunhofer.de
[3] TenneT TSO B.V., Arnhem, The Netherlands

Abstract. The rising proportion of renewable energy in the electricity mix introduces significant operational challenges for power grid operators. Effective power grid management demands adaptive decision-making strategies capable of handling dynamic conditions. With the increase in complexity, more and more Deep Learning (DL) approaches have been proposed to find suitable grid topologies for congestion management. In this work, we contribute to this research by introducing a novel Imitation Learning (IL) approach that leverages soft labels derived from simulated topological action outcomes, thereby capturing multiple viable actions per state. Unlike traditional IL methods that rely on hard labels to enforce a single optimal action, our method constructs soft labels that capture the effectiveness of actions that prove suitable in resolving grid congestion. To further enhance decision-making, we integrate Graph Neural Networks (GNNs) to encode the structural properties of power grids, ensuring that the topology-aware representations contribute to better agent performance. Our approach significantly outperforms its hard-label counterparts as well as state-of-the-art Deep Reinforcement Learning (DRL) baseline agents. Most notably, it achieves a 17% better performance compared to the greedy expert agent from which the imitation targets were derived.

Keywords: Power Grids · Graph Neural Networks · Topology Control · Learning to Run a Power Network

1 Introduction

In recent years, Reinforcement Learning (RL) and Imitation Learning (IL) have emerged as powerful approaches for sequential decision-making in complex environments, including power grid management. In this context, agents must make rapid and informed topological adjustments to maintain grid stability under dynamic conditions. Recent advances in power grid control have demonstrated the effectiveness of RL-based agents, particularly when they are pre-trained using IL [5,11]. Prior work has applied IL for topology control using standard feed-forward neural networks with subsequent RL fine-tuning to improve decision-making policies [5,10,11]. Additionally, Graph Neural Networks (GNNs) have become popular as a structured way to encode power grid topology, enabling improved action representation and decision-making [6,19,21,28–30].

However, the existing IL methods often fail to capture the inherent uncertainty in the solution space and typically learn to mimic a single expert action per state, disregarding the fact that there are often multiple effective interventions that can ease congestion. This restrictive view can undermine policy robustness and adaptability, leading to rigid policies that struggle with generalization.

Grid2Op [3] provides a widely used framework for developing and evaluating RL-based grid control methods, particularly for topology optimization tasks such as substation reconfigurations [14]. In addition, RL agents have demonstrated strong performance in Learning to Run a Power Network (L2RPN) challenges [15–17,20], where the goal is to maintain grid operability under uncertainty and disturbances. In our experiments, we leverage the WCCI 2022 environment implemented in Grid2Op[1], thus allowing the benchmarking of our methods.

1.1 Main Contributions

To address the limitations of current approaches and enable more robust and adaptable policy learning for power grid control, we propose a soft-label imitation learning approach. Soft-label IL retains and exploits information about multiple effective actions for each grid state through a richer supervisory signal. This rich supervision guides the policy toward greater robustness and adaptability, reflecting the operational reality that power grid congestion can be resolved in more than one single way. Our approach thereby avoids overfitting to potentially sub-optimal expert decisions, reduces label noise, and guides the agent in learning a generalized policies that also are applicable for previously unseen grid states. Furthermore, soft labels enable us to naturally produce a ranking of candidate actions, which is especially valuable in power grid control, where the choice of multiple viable interventions can account for operational preferences, N-1 contingencies, or robustness criteria. This combination – retaining multiple desirable options alongside their respective confidence scores – ultimately results in a more reliable, adaptable, and realistic control policy.

Additionally, we leverage GNNs to account for the structural properties of power grids, reflecting their physical topology and power flow relationships. GNNs enable the policy to learn contextually rich representations for each grid component, which further improves decision-making. Our contributions can be summarized as follows:

1. Development of a novel soft-label approach for IL in power grid control, incorporating multiple viable actions into the learning signal.

---

[1] Grid2Op: https://grid2op.readthedocs.io/en/latest/ (last accessed 12/03/2025).

2. The integration of GNNs to effectively leverage the inherent graph structure of power grids and enhance decision-making.
3. A demonstration that our method outperforms two state-of-the-art RL approaches and particularly the greedy expert itself by utilizing soft action labels.

2 Related Work

The idea of congestion management through topology optimization has witnessed a surge in research interest, in part due to the L2RPN challenges by the french Transmission System Operator (TSO) RTE [15,17]. In many cases the proposed solutions consist of a model-free DRL algorithm that is restricted by rule-based or heuristic components [1,5,10,11,31]. Most of these DRL approaches are built with standard feed-forward Neural Network (FNN), however, [6] find in their survey that an increasing number of researchers use GNNs to incorporate the graphical nature of the power grid. As the number of topology actions increases drastically with grid size, there have further been different approaches to tackle the large action spaces. Some researchers propose a hierarchical agent strategy [13,29], or multi-agent approaches [18,19] to split the decision making process in smaller sub-tasks. Alternatively, [4] propose a Monte Carlo Tree Search (MCTS) to plan multiple steps ahead.

Moreover, IL has been explored for power grid control, motivated by the potential to accelerate computation through the imitation of rule-based and other expert agents. While there have been some application of IL by [5,10,11] to pre-train a feed-forward network on a greedy agent, they only used the models to jumpstart the DRL training process but didn't utilize the IL model as an agent for topolgy control directly. A further IL approach in this regard has been studied by [7,8]. In the first paper, [7] analyze both a greedy and a N-1 rule-based agent on the Grid2Op IEEE 14 environment and then use the experience of the agents to train a IL model. Several types of hybrid agents were constructed, which combined IL and simulation functionality. The hybrid agents showed similar performance with almost 100% completion of the scenarios, while reducing the inference duration of the agent. Even more interesting, [7] found that there occurs in some cases a confusion of the actions by the IL model, as some actions are not clearly distinguishable in some scenarios. In the second paper, [8] follow up on their IL framework and focus on applying (node-level) GNN prediction of the grid topology. They identify the busbar information asymmetry problem, where nodes on the same substation but different busbars remain unconnected in traditional graph representations, hindering GNN performance. They propose a heterogeneous GNN to address this by modeling inter-busbar connections, outperforming homogeneous GNNs and FNNs in accuracy and OOD generalization. Existing IL methods inherit expert biases by relying on deterministic policies that overlook diverse viable actions for overload mitigation, we highlight the need to capture all effective actions instead and address it through a richer representation of the labels.

3 Power Grid Setup

As mentioned earlier, we follow the previous researchers and use the Grid2Op environment, as it is the current benchmark for transmission grids [6] and allows the comparison with other approaches. Grid2Op is an open-source simulation platform designed for power grid operation research, particularly in the context of DRL and other Deep Learning (DL) control strategies. Since Grid2op was designed with RL in mind, we utilize the same terminology, though we do not apply RL in this work.

3.1 Environment

In this work, we utilize the L2RPN WCCI 2022 environment, which models the IEEE 118-bus transmission system with an expected 2050 electricity mix. As a result, the simulated fossil fuel generation accounts for less than 3%, and renewable energy sources are significantly increased [20]. At its core, the power grid can be represented as a graph where substations are nodes that are connected via transmission lines. Substations serve as connection points for grid components, including generators, loads, and power lines. This can be seen in Fig. 1, where we visualize the WCCI 2022 environment. This specific IEEE 118 transmission grid consists of 118 substations, 91 loads, 62 generators, and 7 battery storage units, all interconnected by 186 transmission lines. The observation space S of the contains 4,295 features such as active and reactive power flows, voltage magnitudes and angles, generator and storage injections, load demands, planned maintenance schedules, cooldown periods, and topology configurations. Among

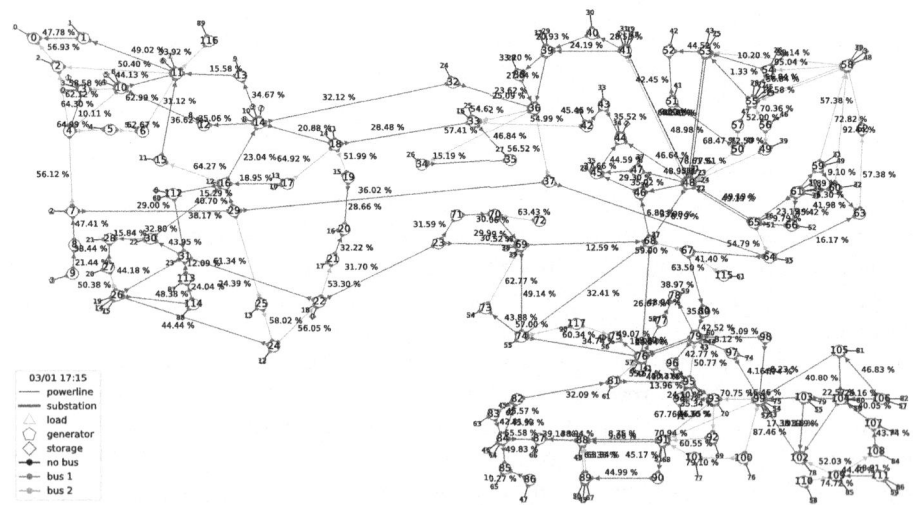

Fig. 1. Overview of the WCCI 2022 L2RPN environment, generated using Grid2Op's native visualization tools.

these, the most critical variable for this work is the line loading capacity, denoted as ρ_l for each line $l \in L$, with the maximum capacity across all lines given by $\rho_{max} = \max_l(\rho_l)$. Furthermore, a double busbar system is implemented. There, each substation consists of two busbars, with each component connected to either one of the busbars. However, power can only flow between elements connected to the same busbar within a substation. Thus, through the reassignment of grid components to a different busbar, one can substantially alter the power flow. For this reason, the topology optimization on a substation can provide a cost-effective and fast solution to tackle congestion issues in the transmission grid. Another feature of Grid2Op is the simulation function, obs.simulate(), which is essential for assessing the impact of proposed actions. It forecasts the grid's next state based on realistic generation and consumption data and computes the power flow.

Power flows can be simulated under the N-0 case, which assumes normal grid operation without any line outages. In contrast, the N-1 case involves simulating the failure of a single transmission line and calculating the resulting power flows, particularly focusing on the maximum line loadings to assess grid resilience. In the Grid2Op framework, a full N-1 contingency analysis is not conducted exhaustively. Instead, a softened version is used where an adversarial agent randomly disconnects one line from a predefined subset of lines deemed critical [14]. This simulates unexpected failures while maintaining computational feasibility and allowing learning-based agents to develop robust control strategies.

Grid2Op simulates power grid operations in 5-min. intervals, modeling fluctuations in demand, generation adjustments, and potential failures. Its goal is to maintain stability and prevent cascading failures due to line overloads using synthetic scenarios (*chronics*) based on historical data. An episode in Grid2Op can end in two ways: successful completion or early termination due to grid failure. A successful episode occurs when an agent manages the grid throughout all 2016 time steps (equivalent to one week). In contrast, early termination – often resulting in a blackout – happens when grid stability is compromised. A common cause is cascading failures triggered by the rule that disconnects a transmission line if its load remains above 100% for three consecutive time steps. Additionally, an episode ends immediately, in case a generator or load is disconnected, islanding occurs, or if the power flow solver fails to converge.

3.2 Action Space

The action space is divided into four different action types. The first action type includes line disconnection and reconnection, while the second type includes substation reconfiguration, which we interchangeably refer to as topology actions. The third action type includes generator redispatch as well as curtailment of renewable energies, while the fourth type relates to battery storage operations. In this work however, we only consider topology actions as they are the most cost-efficient action type. One simplified example substation reconfiguration action is shown in Fig. 2, which switches the line end 5 from the first to the second busbar. This completely changes the connection between the two substations, altering the power flow and mitigating the line overload. These discrete actions scale combinatorially with the number of substation elements, creating a large action space. Grid2Op restricts certain actions to maintain operational feasibility, ensuring that agents cannot take unrealistic or physically impossible steps. Nevertheless, the large action space still presents a significant challenge for control algorithms, hence an action space reduction is usually applied. Note that the line disconnection and reconnection also influences the busbar configuration, as non-connected elements can not be switched by topology actions. The resulting implications are later discussed in Sect. 4.4, as they influence the feasibility of topology actions. Nevertheless, all compared agents, including our own, do not explicitly learn line disconnection and reconnection, but instead automatically reconnect lines whenever possible to restore grid stability.

4 Methodology

We present a systematic approach to addressing grid overloads by combining simulation-based decision-making with advanced learning techniques. We begin by detailing the Greedy Expert Agent ($Greedy_{90\%}$), a reactive agent that selects the best corrective actions based solely on current grid conditions via load flow simulations. Then, we introduce the generation of soft labels, a strategy that leverages the full spectrum of simulated outcomes to create a richer supervisory signal. Additionally, we explain how the inherent graph structure of power grids is leveraged using GNNs to capture spatial dependencies. Lastly, the agent's architecture and practical enhancements, such as topology reversion and improved action feasibility is discussed.

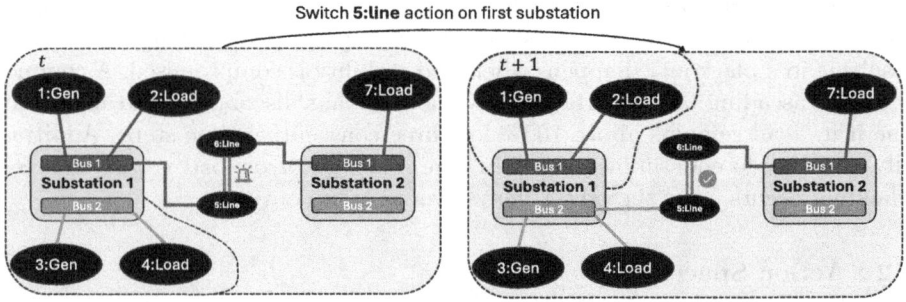

Fig. 2. Example of a substation reconfiguration action. Two substations are visualized, each with two busbars. Generators, loads, and line ends are represented as nodes that are interconnected via a busbar of a substation. From time step t to $t+1$, one end of line 5 is switched to the other busbar, altering the connection between the elements and mitigating the line overload.

4.1 Greedy Expert

The $Greedy_{90\%}$ performs an N-0 load flow simulation for all possible actions for one timestep and selects the one that has the lowest maximum line loading. For this, we utilize Grid2Op's env.simulate() method, which perform a power flow calculation based on forecasts of generation and loads. Specifically, the $Greedy_{90\%}$ is activated if any line loading exceeds 90%. In that case it simulates all actions and selects the action that provides the lowest maximum line loading ρ_{max}. This agent requires a lot of costly power flow simulations and is highly reactive, making decisions based solely on the current state of the grid without considering long-term implications or alternative strategies. Furthermore, it only considers the maximum line loading value and thus other lines with higher load are not regarded. Consequently, it is missing exploration and does not consider the holistic effect of actions.

4.2 Soft Labels

We begin the generation of soft labels by running the $Greedy_{90\%}$ agent through our environment. The details of the complete procedure for generating soft labels along with applying the greedy optimal action are described in Algorithm 1. However, instead of a simple greedy iteration through all actions and simulating the ρ_{max} for each action (line 4&5), we also compute an effectiveness score e_a based on the inverse maximum line loading $1 - \rho_{max}$ (line 5).[2] With this effectiveness score, we generate our soft labels that compare the impact of the action to all other actions. These soft labels are created by applying a temperature softmax function to the effectiveness score e_a (line 8). Note that we used a temperature parameter $\tau = 0.01$ via preliminary tests over several values to sharpen the softmax so that highly effective actions get substantial probability mass without excessive skew; a full sensitivity analysis could further validate this choice.

The remaining algorithm is then simply the greedy selection from the original $Greedy_{90\%}$ (line 11). Ultimately, this approach enables the agent to learn from all the simulations of possible actions that are otherwise discarded. Soft labels provide a relative measurement. A significantly higher value for a particular action indicates that this action is distinctly more effective in reducing line load compared to its counterparts and therefore, the model should be more confident in predicting this action. Conversely, if the effectiveness ratio is more evenly spread across several actions, it suggests that these actions have similar effects. Instead of rigidly following the best action, the agent is exposed to a richer supervisory signal.

---

[2] Note that we do not collect an effectiveness score if a grid failure is imminent, i.e., no action is able to resolve the congestion in the next step.

Algorithm 1. Soft Label Generation

Require: Environment env, Set of actions $\mathcal{A}$, temperature parameter τ
1: Initialize dataset $\mathcal{D} \leftarrow \emptyset$ and environment env
2: **for** each observation $s \in S$ **do** ▷ Iterate through environment and receive s
3:    **for** each action $a \in \mathcal{A}$ **do** ▷ Simulate maximum Line Loads
4:       Run env.simulate(a) to get $\rho_{max}(s,a)$
5:       Compute effectiveness score: $e_a = 1 - \rho_{max}(s,a)$
6:    **end for**
7:    **for** each action $a \in \mathcal{A}$ **do** ▷ Compute soft labels
8:       $\Psi(a \mid s) = \frac{\exp(e_a/\tau)}{\sum_{a' \in \mathcal{A}} \exp(e_{a'}/\tau)}$
9:    **end for**
10:   Store $(s, \Psi(a \mid s))$ in dataset $\mathcal{D}$
11:   Apply greedy optimal action $a^* = \arg\min_{a' \in \mathcal{A}} \rho_{max}(s,a')$ using env.step(a^*)
12: **end for**
13: **return** $\mathcal{D}$

4.3 Utilizing the Inherent Graph Structure of Power Grids

Power grids are inherently graph-structured systems, where substations, generators, loads, and transmission lines form interconnected nodes and edges. To leverage this structure, we transform the observations into a graph representation. This graph-based encoding allows GNNs to capture spatial dependencies and propagate congestion-reduction strategies across the grid.

Graph Construction. We treat each grid component – loads, generators, each end of a transmission lines, and storage – as an individual node. For every node, we aggregate features that capture the state of the grid component. To construct the graph, we first extract a range of features from the observation. These features include operational parameters like cooldown values, power injections, voltage measurements, and maintenance information. Each row in the graph's feature matrix corresponds to a grid asset, and each column captures a specific attribute, e.g., the power consumption of a load or the generation capacity of a generator. Missing values for features that do not apply to a particular component type are filled with zeros.

The edges in the graph are determined based on the physical connectivity of the grid. Specifically, nodes are connected according to the grid's topology, where edges represent electrical connections between components within the same substation or via transmission lines linking different substations. Importantly, transmission line features such as power flow, voltage, and loading are encoded directly into the nodes representing the respective line ends. This approach allows for a uniform node-based feature representation, ensuring that all relevant grid information is captured at the node level while maintaining a simple and efficient graph structure.

GNN Architecture. Our GNN architecture employs Graph Attention Network (GAT) [22] to model relationships between grid components, using attention mechanisms to weight the influence of neighboring nodes and thereby prioritizing critical connections, such as heavily loaded lines. Each observation is first transformed into a graph structure and processed through four GAT layers, which progressively refine the node representations. A global max pooling operation then aggregates these node-level features into a representation for graph-level prediction. This pooled output is subsequently passed through three feed-forward layers and an output layer whose dimensionality matches the size of the action space. The architecture search was conducted using Optuna's Tree-structured Parzen Estimator (TPE) algorithm [25], ensuring that the model's hyperparameters were optimally tuned for the task. Finally, the model is trained using Kullback-Leibler Divergence (KLDivLoss) to minimize the discrepancy between predicted output and soft labels derived according to Algorithm 1.

4.4 Agent

We construct the $SoftGNN_{90\%}$ agent using the GNN with specific mechanics to ensure adequate performance. First, we iterate through the environment and activate the agent only in case of an emergency, i.e., when the max line load ρ_{max} exceeds the threshold of 90%. In case the grid is stable ($\rho_{max} < 90\%$), we either execute a *DoNothing* action or revert the topology, as described below. Otherwise, we use the model's predictions to the current observation and sort the actions in descending order according to the model's output. The agent then iterates through the sorted list, validating each candidate action for feasibility and simulate its impact on the grid using the `env.simulate()` method to compute the post-action maximum line loading ρ_{max}. The first action that reduces ρ_{max} below the predefined threshold of 90% is executed. If no such action exists, the agent defaults to the *DoNothing* action. This process ensures that if an action is selected, it mitigates the grid congestion while adhering to operational constraints. We describe the ad-hoc enhancements as follows:

Topology Reversion. Reverting back to the base topology of the power grid in which all busbar couplers are closed, i.e., no substation is split, has been shown to enhance the performance of agents [10,11]. This is due to the fact that the base topology performs well for stable time steps such as during nights. Therefore, all agents discussed in this paper check for topology reversion when the activation threshold has not been reached. Whenever safely possible, i.e., when reversion doesn't cause ρ_{max} to increase beyond the threshold of 80%, the topology reversion is applied. The threshold value is adopted based on established literature [10], which has demonstrated that this value yields optimal performance.

Enhancing Topology Action Feasibility. In the context of applying substation reconfiguration actions in Grid2Op, we identified a critical limitation in the default behavior of the topology actions using the `set-bus` method: when an action is applied, it attempts to set busbar assignments for all elements, including those associated with currently disconnected lines. This behavior is problematic because it invalidates actions that are subsequently rejected by the environment. Particularly, all actions of both substations adjacent to the disconnected line are rendered invalid. This can be very critical when the disconnected line is adjacent to a large substation that accounts for a significant proportion of the action space. To address this issue, we introduce a pre-processing step that selectively removes bus assignments for all disconnected lines before applying an action. By doing so, the action retains valid bus assignments for connected components while ensuring that no invalid modifications are attempted for disconnected lines and hence significantly improving the feasibility of topology actions.

N-1 Load Flows at Inference Time. Lastly, to enhance robustness against potential line failures, we propose an extension agent $SoftGNN_{90\%}\ N-1$ that incorporates N-1 security criteria into its action selection. During inference, we first filter the top 10 actions from the sorted GNN output. For each candidate action, the agent simulates its impact under both N-0 (no failures) and N-1 (single-line failure) scenarios. It prioritizes actions that minimize this worst-case metric and selects the action with the lowest N-1 ρ_{max}. However, if all N-1 simulations result in overloads, i.e., $\rho_{max} \geq 100\%$, the agent falls back to the N-0 criterion, selecting the action that minimizes the baseline ρ_{max}. Consistent with the Grid2op framework and [10], we do not perform a full N-1 contingency analysis across all lines, but instead restrict simulations to the predefined subset of lines that can be attacked by the adversarial agent. Furthermore, we exclude line 93 from the N-1 analysis in accordance with the findings of [9], which show that disconnecting this line inevitably triggers a cascading failure within three time steps, regardless of the remedial action taken. Including such a pathological case would disproportionately distort the evaluation of otherwise effective actions.

5 Experiments

5.1 Experimental Setup

As outlined in Sect. 3.1, our study utilizes the WCCI 2022 L2RPN framework, visualized in Fig. 1. We train our agents on the publicly accessible environment data. All agents are trained for a maximum of 800 epochs, however, early stopping is applied based on validation performance to prevent overfitting. The early stopping criterion monitors the validation loss, and training halts if no improvement is observed for 20 consecutive epochs. The model with the best validation performance is selected for evaluation. Each agent is trained using the Adam optimizer, with learning rate adjustments managed by a learning rate scheduler that reduces the learning rate by a factor of 0.9 if no improvement in the validation loss is observed for 10 consecutive epochs. The batch size was fixed to 256 while all other hyperparameters were determined using optuna. Table 1 shows the selected hyperparameters for the GAT model of all *SoftGNN* agents

Table 1. Model architecture of the soft-label graph neural network used all *SoftGNN* agents. The architecture search was conducted using Optuna's TPE [25]. Additionally, the search range of the dropout parameter for all layers is [0, 0.5].

Component	Hyperparameters (Selected)	Search Range
GAT Layers (input, output, heads, dropout)		
Layer 0	GATConv(27, 16, 1, 0.177)	dim: {16, 32, 64, 128}, heads: {1,2,4,8}
Layer 1	GATConv(16, 32, 4, 0.139)	dim: {16, 32, 64, 128}, heads: {1,2,4,8}
Layer 2	GATConv(128, 64, 2, 0.174)	dim: {16, 32, 64, 128}, heads: {1,2,4,8}
Layer 3	GATConv(128, 128, 4, 0.096)	dim: {16, 32, 64, 128}, heads: {1,2,4,8}
Num. of Layers	4	{2, 3, 4, 5, 6}
Pooling	Global Max Pooling	{"max", "mean", "add"}
Linear Layers (input, output, dropout)		
Layer 0	Linear(128, 1024, 0.496)	dim: {128, 256, 512, 1024}
Layer 1	Linear(1024, 1024, 0.489)	dim: {128, 256, 512, 1024}
Layer 2	Linear(1024, 2030, 0.0)	–
Num. of Layers	3	{2, 3, 4}
Training		
Learning Rate	4.14×10^{-3}	$[10^{-5}\text{--}10^{-2}]$
Weight Decay	8.48×10^{-6}	$[10^{-6}\text{--}10^{-3}]$

as well as the respective search ranges. The GAT layers apply ELU as their activation function, while the subsequent linear layers apply ReLU. Hyperparameter search was conducted in a distributed setup on a computing cluster featuring 8 NVIDIA A100 GPUs, and training of the final model required approximately 8 h on a single GPU.

We evaluate our agents using the test environment of the 2022 challenge [20] provided by RTE France. The test environment comprises 52 scenarios, each spanning 2016 time steps. We follow the approach of [10] by employing 20 randomized master seeds to ensure statistical robustness and address variability across scenarios influenced by environmental seed differences. For comparability, we use the same master seeds. We further use the same action space of [10], which consists of 2000 actions from the L2RPN 2022 challenge winner [4]. Moreover, 30 expert actions selected by RTE were added, resulting in a total of 2030 actions.

The dataset, code, and trained models will be made publicly available in a dedicated GitHub repository[3], as well as to the *CurriculumAgent*[4] repository for compatibility with state-of-the-art RL approaches.

Ablation Study. Our ablation study evaluates the impact of soft labels and GNN models on agent performance by comparing four core variants, which allows

---

[3] https://github.com/AI4REALNET/soft_label_gnn.
[4] https://github.com/FraunhoferIEE/curriculumagent.

for a granular comparison. The variants include two hard-label approaches—an FNN model and a GNN model—termed *HardFNN* and *HardGNN*, respectively, as well as two soft-label approaches—*SoftFNN* and *SoftGNN*. Additionally, we analyzed the $SoftGNN_{90\%}\ N-1$ variant from Sect. 4.4 to assess the synergy between soft labels and N-1 safety-aware action selection. The agents were trained on the same data generated using Algorithm 1, with identical action spaces and the pre-processing fix for invalid bus assignments described in Sect. 4.4. We further compare the performance of these models to four benchmark agents. First the *DoNothing* baseline, second the expert greedy agent $Greedy_{90\%}$ with the pre-processing fix. Moreover, we re-evaluate two state-of-the-art agents from literature ($Senior_{95\%}$ [10] and $TopoAgent_{85-95\%}$ [10]) with the pre-processing fix in order to isolate the effects of the fix. We dub these agents $SeniorFix_{95\%}$ and $TopoAgentFix_{85-95\%}$, respectively.

The $Senior_{95\%}$ is a sophisticated DRL agent that performs topology actions when ρ_{max} exceeds a 0.95 threshold, ensuring safe and reliable intervention during extreme conditions, while the superior $TopoAgent_{85-95\%}$ activates under moderate instability and additionally employs a greedy search over pre-identified robust Target Topologies to sequentially combine actions and guide the grid toward a more stable configuration.

Metrics. Performance metrics include the L2RPN score (mean, median, quartiles) from the L2RPN 2022 challenge [20], a composite score that assesses the agent's ability to keep the power grid operational while minimizing operational costs. The score is computed by first calculating the total operational cost for each scenario – this includes energy losses, redispatch, curtailments, storage operations, and penalties for blackouts – and then applying a linear transformation to aid interpretability. It is calibrated by assigning the *DoNothing* baseline a score of 0. Agents performing worse than this baseline can receive scores as low as -100, while those that survive longer earn positive scores. The completion of every episode results in a score of 80 and for a 100 the agent must also minimize both energy loss and operational costs. Moreover, we measure the survival time with the median survival time and the Median Survival Time across Chronic Medians (MSTCM). The latter is less influenced by outlier performance since it averages over the chronics first [10].

5.2 Results

The experimental evaluation demonstrates the efficacy of our soft-label imitation learning approach combined with GNNs. We summarize the results in Table 2 and visualize in Fig. 3 the median survival time of each chronic across the 20 seeds. As expected, the *DoNothing* baseline achieved a score of 0 and median survival time of 229 steps, while the $Greedy_{90\%}$ agent improved performance with a mean L2RPN score of 37.91 and a median survival time of 1014 steps.

Re-evaluating previous state-of-the-art agents with the action feasibility fix (Sect. 4.4) yielded measurable gains. The $SeniorFix_{95\%}$ agent outperformed the

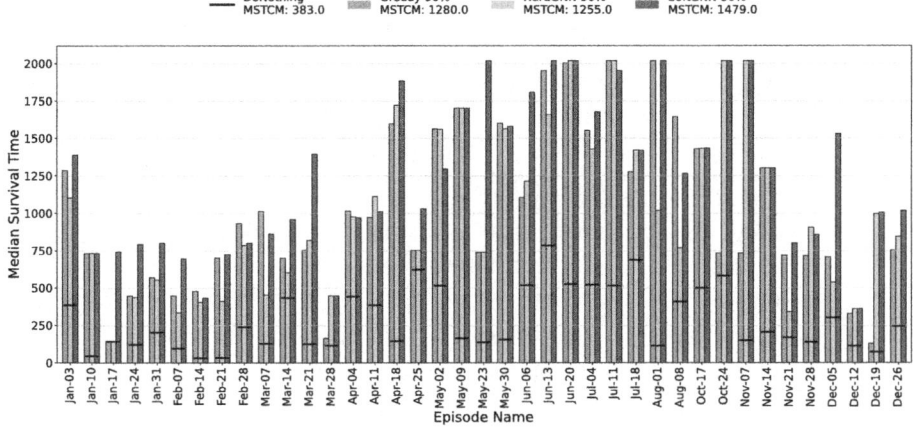

Fig. 3. Comparison of agent Median Survival Times across all test scenarios, calculated over 20 random seeds. The MSTCM is shown above the figure for reference. Chronics where all non-baseline agents survived (median survival time of 2017 steps) were excluded (13 in total) for clarity.

original $Senior_{95\%}$, increasing its median L2RPN score from 37.13 to 39.40 and MSTCM from 1160 to 1468. Similarly, $TopoAgentFix_{85-95\%}$ achieved higher performance across all metrics, though to a lesser extent. This clearly shows the effect of our preprocessing-fix.

With respect to the ablation study, both hard-label approaches perform similarly to the $Greedy_{90\%}$ agent with a small advantage of the $HardGNN_{90\%}$. This highlights the struggles to overcome imperfect teacher agents. In contrast, the soft-label models significantly surpass their hard-label counterparts. Among the soft-label agents, the GNN agent outperforms the FNN variant, indicating a synergy between the enhanced GNN feature representation and soft label learning. The $SoftGNN_{90\%}$ agent improved the L2RPN score by nearly 15% compared to its hard-label counterpart $HardGNN_{90\%}$. Particularly for very challenging runs, the $SoftGNN_{90\%}$ agent manages to outperform the hard-label variant and the expert and survives significantly longer. Similarly, for the FNN variants, the soft-label agent improved the score by 8%.

Finally, our $SoftGNN$ agents are able to outperform the state-of-the-art agents $Senior_{95\%}$ and $TopoAgent_{85-95\%}$ that employ more sophisticated simulation strategies and specifically optimize for long-term performance through RL. The $SoftGNN_{90\%}\ N-1$, incorporating N-1 security criteria during inference, achieved the highest overall performance with a mean L2RPN score of 44.43 and median survival time of 1299 steps. Notably, its MSTCM of 1566 surpassed even the $TopoAgentFix_{85-95\%}$ by 72 time steps, demonstrating the synergy between soft-label learning and safety-aware action selection.

We used Welch's t-test [26] to compare the $SoftGNN_{90\%}\ N-1$ agent against $Greedy_{90\%}$, $HardGNN_{90\%}$, $SoftFNN_{90\%}$, and $TopoAgentFix_{85-95\%}$, and in all

Table 2. Overview of the aggregated agent performance. The table provides the L2RPN score metric statistics as well as the median survival time and MSTCM.

Agent	L2RPN Score					Survival Time	
	$\bar{x}$	σ	$\tilde{x}$	Q_1	Q_3	$\tilde{x}$	**MSTCM**
DoNothing	00.00	0.00	00.00	00.00	00.00	229	383
Greedy$_{90\%}$	37.91	3.89	37.07	35.62	40.78	1014	1280
Senior$_{95\%}$ [10]	37.13	4.49	37.21	33.48	39.84	988	1160
SeniorFix$_{95\%}$	39.40	**2.98**	39.50	37.14	41.25	1026	1468
TopoAgent$_{85-95\%}$ [10]	41.26	3.01	40.41	39.41	43.69	1232	1436
TopoAgentFix$_{85-95\%}$	41.81	3.11	42.17	40.33	44.00	1263	1494
HardFNN$_{90\%}$	37.54	3.87	37.08	35.06	40.22	1020	1114
SoftFNN$_{90\%}$	40.73	4.16	40.54	36.60	43.64	1113	1316
HardGNN$_{90\%}$	38.28	3.58	37.95	35.85	40.08	1048	1255
SoftGNN$_{90\%}$	43.84	3.60	**43.96**	41.40	46.09	1293	1479
SoftGNN$_{90\%}$ $N-1$	**44.43**	3.27	43.49	**42.33**	**47.34**	**1299**	**1566**

cases rejected the null hypothesis ($p < 0.05$; see Table 3), indicating significant differences. D'Agostino's test [2] confirmed that the data adhered to normality.

These results underscore three key trends: (1) Soft-label IL significantly outperforms hard-label IL, (2) GNNs exploit the grid topology to improve decision-making, and (3) post-hoc N-1 evaluation further elevates performance by prioritizing N-1 resilient actions.

6 Discussion

The experimental results demonstrate that our soft-label IL approach, which leverages soft scores over viable topology actions, consistently outperforms both hard-label IL methods and the expert agent itself. This section synthesizes the key insights and contextualizes them within the landscape of IL.

Conventional hard-label IL methods inherit and amplify the flaws of the expert by enforcing rigid, deterministic policies. Our results show that both the

Table 3. Test Results of the Welch's t-test [26] with the hypothesis $H_0 : \mu_i = \mu_j$ against the alternative hypothesis $H_1 : \mu_i \neq \mu_j$.

H_0 Hypothesis	p-value
$H_0 : \mu_{Greedy_{90\%}} = \mu_{SoftGNN_{90\%}\ N-1}$	1.4×10^{-6}
$H_0 : \mu_{HardGNN_{90\%}} = \mu_{SoftGNN_{90\%}\ N-1}$	1.6×10^{-6}
$H_0 : \mu_{SoftFNN_{90\%}} = \mu_{SoftGNN_{90\%}\ N-1}$	0.003
$H_0 : \mu_{TopoAgent_{85-95\%}} = \mu_{SoftGNN_{90\%}\ N-1}$	0.013

$HardFNN_{90\%}$ and $HardGNN_{90\%}$ agents are on par with the $Greedy_{90\%}$ agent while performing significantly worse than their soft-label counterparts. This gap underscores how hard labels propagate the expert's biases, such as favoring inoptimal actions that might mitigate overloads for singular grid states but lead to unstable topologies for following states and hence disrupt long-term performance.

In contrast, soft labels enable the agent to generalize across states by learning structural patterns in the action space rather than memorizing individual decisions. By learning from soft scores, the model observes which actions are effective for each scenario and infer which actions are universally effective. This also reduces the label noise and the chance of overfitting to singular sub-optimal actions. We argue that the soft labels work like a confidence score, where the confidence decreases whenever there are many viable actions. This avoids overfitting to the action with the highest – yet not far off – score. Especially in these low confidence situations where the scores are distributed among multiple effective actions, the exact order of the actions is less important for the model to predict. This is consistent with the use of the KL divergence loss which doesn't account for the order of the predictions but rather the element-wise deviations from the target. Hence, the overall viability of actions is assigned more importance than the exact order according to the labels. This fits our use case perfectly, since it is merely important to bring line loads below a certain threshold. Because the model is able to observe the richer soft label, it is able to assess the general effectiveness of actions, resulting in a tendency to rank actions higher that contribute to reducing line loads in the training set more frequently.

It is even desired to output multiple action recommendations, which can be evaluated with more scrutiny, such as to their impact on the N-1 load flows. Our $SoftGNN_{90\%} N-1$ agent does exactly that for the top 10 actions and achieves a higher score and longer survival time. The flexibility of having multiple recommendations for operators is critical for power grids, where topology optimization must not only reduce line load, but also consider other optimization tasks, such as N-1 security or the topology depth [23].

Bridging our results to recent advances in IL, [27] demonstrated that confidence scores which indicates the quality of demonstrations enable IL agents to recover optimal policies from imperfect data. Similarly, our soft labels can be interpreted as such confidence scores. They show that reweighting imperfect demonstrations using confidence signals improves policy robustness. By borrowing this principle to power grid control, we show that soft labels surpass the performance of the imperfect expert by synthesizing a richer understanding of effective actions. By encoding uncertainty through soft labels, the agent avoids over-committing to suboptimal decisions and is therefore more robust to unseen grid states. It's noteworthy to point that the same phenomenon, of students models outperforming expert models as agents, was also confirmed by [8].

The integration of GNNs amplifies the benefits of soft labels by explicitly modeling the topological structure of the power grid. While the soft-label FNN agent improved performance over its hard-label counterpart, adding a GNN achieved the highest scores and median survival times. GNNs enhance decision-making by propagating congestion reduction strategies across interconnected substations and lines, ensuring that physical grid constraints are considered. This result is consistent with recent studies [6,8].

Applying Machine Learning (ML) techniques in real-world control rooms as decision support for (topological) remedial actions is still in its infancy. For example, the GridOptions tool [24] is one of the first AI-based decision-support tools deployed in a TSO control room. However, the scope of the first version of the GridOptions tool has been limited in several ways [12]. In particular, the optimization approach does not exploit ML yet, and, hence, is slow and inflexible. Consequently, our method's success has direct relevance to real-world grid operations. By training on diverse action soft scores, the agent becomes resilient to unexpected grid disturbances, e.g., equipment failures or renewable volatility. Our approach maximizes the utility of topology actions by identifying high-impact reconfigurations and therefore reduces the need for costly redispatch. Since we deal with critical infrastructure, our system is developed solely as a decision-support tool that provides action recommendations while leaving the final decision-making authority to qualified human operators.

While our approach marks a significant advancement, several challenges remain. Future work could explore action sampling strategies as well hybrid approaches applying RL fine-tuning to IL models to capture true long-term dependencies. Scaling to real-world sized power grids with different topologies will validate the method's broader applicability.

7 Conclusion

In this study, we introduce a novel imitation learning framework that leverages soft labels – derived from comprehensive load flow simulations – to capture multiple effective topology actions in power grid control. Our approach overcomes the limitations of traditional hard-label methods, which tend to rigidly follow a single expert decision and propagate its biases. By integrating graph neural networks, our agent learns to capture the grid's inherent spatial structure, leading to an improved performance. The impact of the proposed agent was studied on a benchmark IEEE 118-Bus transmission system. We find that the proposed method outperforms state-of-the-art RL agents and the greedy expert itself, showing the potential of soft-label imitation learning.

Acknowledgements. This work was supported by: (i) AI4REALNET founded by the European Union's Horizon Europe Research and Innovation program under the Grant Agreement No 101119527. Views and opinions expressed are however those of the author(s) only and do not necessarily reflect those of the European Union. Neither the European Union nor the granting authority can be held responsible for them. (ii) Graph Neural Networks for Grid Control (GNN4GC) founded by the Federal Ministry for Economic Affairs and Climate Action Germany (03EI6117A).(iii) Reinforcement Learning for Cognitive Energy Systems (RL4CES) founded by the German Federal Ministry of Education and Research (01|S22063B).

Disclosure of Interests. The authors have no competing interests to declare that are relevant to the content of this article.

References

1. Chauhan, A., Baranwal, M., et al.: Powrl: A reinforcement learning framework for robust management of power networks. arXiv preprint arXiv:2212.02397 (2022)
2. D'Agostino, R., Pearson, E.S.: Tests for departure from normality. empirical results for the distributions of b2 and b1. Biometrika **60**(3), 613–622 (1973). http://www.jstor.org/stable/2335012
3. Donnot, B.: Grid2op- A testbed platform to model sequential decision making in power systems . https://GitHub.com/rte-france/grid2op (2020). Accessed 22 Jan 2023 on Github
4. Dorfer, M., Fuxjäger, A.R., et al.: Power grid congestion management via topology optimization with alphazero. arXiv preprint arXiv:2211.05612 (2022)
5. EI Innovation Lab, Huawei Cloud, Huawei Technologies: NeurIPS Competition 2020: Learning to Run a Power Network (L2RPN) - Robustness Track. https://github.com/AsprinChina/L2RPN_NIPS_2020_a_PPO_Solution (2020). Accessed 22 Jan 2023 on Github
6. Hassouna, M., Holzhüter, C., Lytaev, P., Thomas, J., Sick, B., Scholz, C.: Graph reinforcement learning for power grids: a comprehensive survey (2024). https://arxiv.org/abs/2407.04522
7. de Jong, M., Viebahn, J., Shapovalova, Y.: Imitation learning for intra-day power grid operation through topology actions (2024). https://arxiv.org/abs/2407.19865
8. de Jong, M., Viebahn, J., Shapovalova, Y.: Generalizable graph neural networks for robust power grid topology control (2025). https://arxiv.org/abs/2501.07186
9. Lehna, M., Hassouna, M., Degtyar, D., Tomforde, S., Scholz, C.: Fault detection for agents on power grid topology optimization: a comprehensive analysis. arXiv preprint arXiv:2406.16426 (2024)
10. Lehna, M., Holzhüter, C., Tomforde, S., Scholz, C.: Hugo-highlighting unseen grid options: Combining deep reinforcement learning with a heuristic target topology approach. Sustainable Energy, Grids Netw. **39**, 101510 (2024)
11. Lehna, M., Viebahn, J., et al.: Managing power grids through topology actions: a comparative study between advanced rule-based and reinforcement learning agents. Energy and AI (2023)
12. Leyli-abadi, M., et al.: A conceptual framework for AI-based decision systems in critical infrastructures (2025). https://arxiv.org/abs/2504.16133
13. Manczak, B., Viebahn, J., et al.: Hierarchical reinforcement learning for power network topology control. arXiv preprint arXiv:2311.02129 (2023)
14. Marchesini, E., et al.: RL2grid: Benchmarking reinforcement learning in power grid operations (2024). https://openreview.net/forum?id=7J2C4QnQrl
15. Marot, A., Donnot, B., et al.: Learning to run a power network challenge for training topology controllers. Electric Power Systems Research (2020a)
16. Marot, A., Donnot, B., et al.: Learning to run a power network with trust. Electric Power Systems Research (2022)
17. Marot, A., Guyon, I., et al.: L2rpn: Learning to run a power network in a sustainable world neurips2020 challenge design (2020b)
18. de Mol, B., Barbieri, D., Viebahn, J., Grossi, D.: Centrally coordinated multi-agent reinforcement learning for power grid topology control (2025). https://arxiv.org/abs/2502.08681

19. van der Sar, E., Zocca, A., Bhulai, S.: Multi-agent reinforcement learning for power grid topology optimization. arXiv preprint arXiv:2310.02605 (2023)
20. Serré, G., Boguslawski, E., et al.: Reinforcement learning for energies of the future and carbon neutrality: a challenge design. arXiv preprint arXiv:2207.10330 (2022)
21. Taha, S., Poland, J., Knezovic, K., Shchetinin, D.: Learning to run a power network under varying grid topology. In: 2022 IEEE 7th International Energy Conference (ENERGYCON), pp. 1–6. IEEE (2022)
22. Veličković, P., Cucurull, G., Casanova, A., Romero, A., Liò, P., Bengio, Y.: Graph attention networks (2018). https://arxiv.org/abs/1710.10903
23. Viebahn, J., et al.: GridOptions Tool: Real-world day-ahead congestion management using topological remedial actions. CIGRE Science & Engineering (2024)
24. Viebahn, J., Kop, S., et al.: Gridoptions tool: Real-world day-ahead congestion management using topological remedial actions. CIGRE 2024 Paris Session (2024)
25. Watanabe, S.: Tree-structured parzen estimator: Understanding its algorithm components and their roles for better empirical performance (2023)
26. Welch, B.L.: The generalization of 'student's' problem when several different population variances are involved. Biometrika **34**(1/2), 28–35 (1947). http://www.jstor.org/stable/2332510
27. Wu, Y.H., Charoenphakdee, N., Bao, H., Tangkaratt, V., Sugiyama, M.: Imitation learning from imperfect demonstration. In: International Conference on Machine Learning, pp. 6818–6827. PMLR (2019)
28. Xu, P., et al.: Active power correction strategies based on deep reinforcement learning-part i: a simulation-driven solution for robustness. CSEE J. Power Energy Syst. **8**(4), 1122–1133 (2021)
29. Yoon, D., Hong, S., Lee, B.J., Kim, K.E.: Winning the l2rpn challenge: power grid management via semi-markov afterstate actor-critic. In: International Conference on Learning Representations (2021)
30. Zhao, Y., Liu, J., Liu, X., Yuan, K., Ren, K., Yang, M.: A graph-based deep reinforcement learning framework for autonomous power dispatch on power systems with changing topologies. In: 2022 IEEE Sustainable Power and Energy Conference (iSPEC), pp. 1–5. IEEE (2022)
31. Zhou, B., Zeng, H., et al.: Action set based policy optimization for safe power grid management. In: Machine Learning and Knowledge Discovery in Databases. Applied Data Science Track: European Conference, ECML PKDD 2021 (2021)

Progressive Decomposition-Enhanced Time-Varying Graph Neural Network for Traffic Forecasting

Jianuo Ji[1], Hongbin Dong[1(✉)], and Xiaoping Zhang[2]

[1] College of Computer Science and Technology, Harbin Engineering University, Harbin, China
`{jijianuo,donghongbi}@hrbeu.edu.cn`
[2] Traditional Chinese Medicine Data Center, China Academy of Chinese Medical Sciences, Beijing, China
`zhangxp@ndctcm.cn`

Abstract. Traffic forecasting, a core technology in intelligent transportation systems, has a broad range of applications. The fundamental challenge in traffic prediction lies in effectively modeling the complex spatio-temporal dependencies inherent in traffic data. Spatio-temporal graph neural network (GNN) models have emerged as one of the most promising approaches to address this challenge. However, GNN-based models for traffic forecasting have two significant limitations: i) Most methods model spatial dependencies in a static manner (predefined or self-learning), which fails to capture the time-varying nature of spatial dependencies in real-world scenarios; ii) It is unreliable to capture temporal and spatial dependencies in entangled temporal patterns. To this end, we propose a **P**rogressive **D**ecomposition-enhanced **T**ime-**V**arying **G**raph **N**eural **N**etwork, namely PDTVGNN, for accurate traffic forecasting. Specifically, we design a time-varying graph generator that incrementally generates a series of adjacency matrices to capture the time-varying spatial relationships. Moreover, we adopt a novel progressive decomposition idea where the decomposition blocks are embedded as internal blocks to decouple the entangled temporal patterns gradually. The decoupled trend and seasonal parts are modeled via the proposed spatio-temporal normalization module and attention mechanism, respectively. Extensive experimental results on four real-world public traffic datasets demonstrate that the proposed method outperforms state-of-the-art baselines.

Keywords: Graph neural network · Traffic forecasting · Seasonal-trend Decomposition

1 Introduction

Traffic management systems are facing growing pressure as vehicles on road networks increase. There is a pressing need to develop Intelligent Transportation

Systems (ITS) to achieve efficient traffic control. As a core technology and essential prerequisite for ITS implementation, traffic forecasting is pivotal in enabling effective traffic management [1].

The primary challenge in traffic forecasting is effectively capturing and modeling the complex and dynamic spatio-temporal dependencies in traffic data [2]. Over the years, researchers have explored various approaches, with deep learning techniques increasingly being adopted to uncover these spatio-temporal correlations. Graph neural networks (GNN) have gained popularity for spatial correlation modeling due to their strong capability in handling graph-structured data [3–5].

However, traffic forecasting has its characteristics in modeling temporal correlations within time series and capturing spatial dependencies between time series. Despite the effectiveness of existing methods, GNN-based models still have two significant limitations in traffic prediction. On the one hand, in real-world scenarios, the spatial dependencies between traffic sensors are highly dynamic, and the change of spatial relationships in a one-time step is closely related to the spatial relationships in the time step before it, which we call time-varying. For example, as shown in Fig. 1(b), the correlation between nodes A and B decreases in the morning and becomes more potent at other times. Existing methods mainly model spatial dependencies in a static way (predefined or self-learning), which obviously cannot handle such dynamic changes. Therefore, existing work does not fully harness the potential of graph neural networks on this problem. On the other hand, most existing methods capture potential dependencies directly from traffic sequences, which fails to uncover the intricate spatio-temporal dependencies masked under entangled temporal patterns. Specifically, they ignore that traffic data are composed of complex periodic patterns coupled with trend components in real-world scenarios, as shown in Figs. 1(c) and (d). This entanglement limits the capability of existing methods and is a performance bottleneck for traffic forecasting.

To address the above limitations, we propose a **P**rogressive **D**ecomposition-enhanced **T**ime-**V**arying **G**raph **N**eural **N**etwork, namely PDTVGNN, for traffic forecasting. Unlike previous methods, this paper introduces a novel progressive decomposition idea to disentangle complex temporal patterns by gradually decomposing the hidden sequences using the time series decomposition module throughout the forecasting process. For the seasonal part obtained after decoupling, we use the Fourier temporal attention to capture the temporal correlations. Additionally, we propose a time-varying graph generation module to construct a series of adjacency matrices that model the time-varying nature of the spatial structure, rather than maintaining a static graph structure. Subsequently, we employ a time-varying graph convolution module to extract the spatial dependencies. For the trend part obtained after decoupling, we propose a spatio-temporal normalization module to address the temporal and spatial non-stationarity information in the trend data. In summary, the main contributions are as follows:

– To cope with the intricate spatio-temporal dependencies masked by the entangled temporal patterns, we embed the decomposition blocks as internal blocks to progressively decouple the entangled temporal patterns. Moreover, the trend and seasonal parts obtained after decoupling are modeled separately.

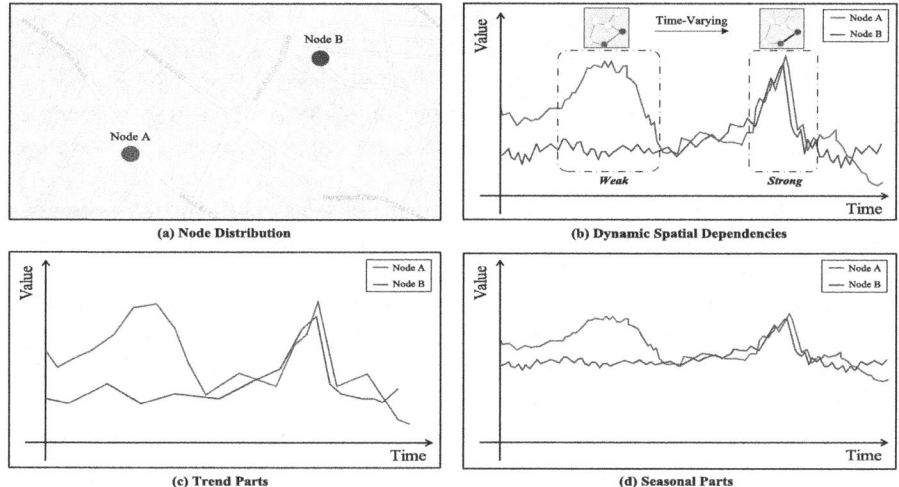

Fig. 1. The findings about traffic prediction.

– We propose a time-varying graph generator that produces a series of recurrent adjacency matrices to capture the dynamic and time-varying nature of spatial relationships.
– We validate the effectiveness of our method through extensive experiments on four real-world datasets, demonstrating its superior performance and significantly outpacing competitive baseline methods.

2 Related Work

2.1 Traffic Forecasting

Traffic forecasting has been extensively studied in intelligent transportation systems [6]. Early work focused on statistical methods like ARIMA [7] to predict traffic indicators. Later, machine learning models, such as VAR [8], were introduced with some success but were limited by assumptions of static conditions, hindering their ability to capture the complex nonlinear relationships in traffic data. Furthermore, these models neglected spatial dependencies, restricting their accuracy. Unlike earlier methods, deep neural networks, which capture both temporal and spatial features, have become popular. For example, FC-LSTM [9] combines CNNs with LSTM for traffic prediction. However, these models remain less effective in graph-based node data scenarios.

2.2 Spatio-Temporal Graph Neural Networks

In recent years, Graph Neural Networks have gained increasing attention due to their advanced performance. Therefore, researchers have begun to incorporate them into traffic prediction models to enhance predictive accuracy. Models such as DCRNN [10] and STGCN [11] are among the most prominent works in this area. These models capture spatial dependencies between nodes through predefined graph structures and temporal dynamics through CNNs or RNNs. However, these approaches heavily rely on manually defined graph structures, with the quality of the predefined graph structure directly influencing model performance. To address this limitation, frameworks such as Graph WaveNet [12], MTGNN [3], and AGCRN [13] have been proposed. These frameworks generate graph structures adaptively in a data-driven manner and have demonstrated remarkable results as a result. In recent work, PDFormer [14] utilizes three attentions to form spatial-temporal feature extraction blocks, which can model local geographic and global semantic information from neighbors, thus improving prediction accuracy. However, maximizing its performance depends to some extent on these three features. STPGNN [5] defines pivotal nodes based on the aggregation and distribution capabilities of traffic nodes and proposes a pivotal graph convolutional network to predict traffic. However, the performance of the model depends on how accurately the pivotal nodes are identified. In addition, DGCRN [15] designs hypernetworks that utilize and extract dynamic features of node attributes and dynamic filters to generate dynamic graphs. In general, traffic data contains strong dynamic spatio-temporal correlations. Therefore, modeling dynamic nonlinear spatio-temporal correlation is crucial for accurately predicting traffic flow. The dynamic generation of dynamic graphs has become a new research direction.

3 Preliminaries

In this section, we first present the task definition and then briefly review the core idea of attention mechanism.

3.1 Definition and Problem Statement

Traffic Topology Graph. A traffic topology graph is defined as $\mathcal{G} = (\mathcal{V}, \mathcal{E}, \mathcal{A})$ within certain road network. Where $\mathcal{V}$ denotes the set of nodes($|\mathcal{V}| = N$) and each node corresponds to a road sensor; $\mathcal{E}$ denotes the set of edges, which represents the physical connectivity of the sensors; and $\mathcal{A}$ denotes the adjacency matrix of the graph, whose elements are the connectivity between any pair of nodes in the graph.

Traffic Signal Tensor. The traffic signal tensor of N nodes over P time steps is denoted as $\mathcal{X} = (X_1, ..., X_t, ..., X_P) \in \mathbb{R}^{P \times N \times C}$. Here, $X_t \in \mathbb{R}^{N \times C}$ denotes the traffic signal of N nodes in the road network at time step t, and C is the number of traffic features (e.g., C = 3 for features traffic flow, speed, and occupy.). The traffic forecasting problem can be formalized as Eq. (1). Given a series of observations from N sensors in the graph $\mathcal{G}$ over the past P time steps, our goal is to predict the traffic signals at the next Q time steps via a mapping function $\mathcal{F}$:

$$[X_{P+1}, ..., X_{P+Q}] = \mathcal{F}([X_1, ..., X_P; \mathcal{G}]). \tag{1}$$

3.2 Attention Mechanism

The attention mechanism is a fundamental operation frequently employed in various modeling tasks. Its core principle involves assigning distinct weights to different segments of the input data, thereby emphasizing relevant information while disregarding less important details [16]. In essence, the attention mechanism operates by mapping a query and a set of key-value pairs to an output, where the query, keys, values, and output are represented as vectors. The output is computed as a weighted sum of the values, with each weight being determined by the interaction between the corresponding key and the query. These weights reflect the degree of association between the query and each key-value pair. In this work, we employ Scaled Dot-Product Attention [17], a widely used variant of the attention mechanism, specifically:

$$Attention(Q, K, V) = softmax(\frac{QK^T}{\sqrt{d_k}})V. \tag{2}$$

where Q, K, V, and d_k are the query, key, value, and their dimensions, respectively.

4 Methodology

4.1 Model Overview

The framework of our PDTVGNN is illustrated in Fig. 2. This section provides a detailed discussion of its technical components. It consists of stacked L spatio-temporal layers and an output layer. For each layer, this paper adopts a novel progressive decomposition idea, where the series decomposition module gradually disentangles hidden series throughout the forecasting process. This enables the model to separate complex temporal patterns and generate predictions based on the more predictable seasonal and trend components. For the seasonal part, we extract temporal correlations using Fourier temporal attention, as shown in Fig. 2(b). Furthermore, we utilize the time-varying graph generator, as shown in Fig. 2(c), along with the time-varying graph convolution module to capture spatial correlations over time. For the trend component, we develop a spatio-temporal normalization module to address the temporal and spatial non-stationarity in the trend component. The extracted trend information is progressively accumulated and serves as the final trend representation learned by the model. Each spatio-temporal layer is skip-connected to the output layer. The computation process for layer $l \in \{1, ..., L\}$ can be formalized as follows:

$$\begin{aligned}
\mathcal{S}_1^l, \mathcal{T}_1^l &= \text{SeriesDecomp}(\mathcal{X}^{l-1}) \\
\mathcal{S}_2^l, \mathcal{T}_2^l &= \text{SeriesDecomp}(\text{FFT-Attention}(\mathcal{S}_1^l)) \\
\mathcal{S}_3^l, \mathcal{T}_3^l &= \text{SeriesDecomp}(\text{Time-VaryingGCN}(\mathcal{S}_2^l)) \\
\mathcal{S}_3^l &= \text{FeedForward}(\mathcal{S}_3^l) + \mathcal{S}_3^l \\
\mathcal{X}^l &= \mathcal{S}_3^l + \text{STNorm}(\mathcal{T}_1^l) + \text{STNorm}(\mathcal{T}_2^l) + \text{STNorm}(\mathcal{T}_3^l)
\end{aligned} \tag{3}$$

where $\mathcal{X}^l$ denotes the output of layer l. $\mathcal{S}_i^l$ and $\mathcal{T}_i^l$ denote the seasonal and trend components obtained from the i-th time series decomposition module of layer l. The first layer input data $\mathcal{X}^0 \in \mathbb{R}^{P \times N \times D}$ is the high-dimensional spatial projection of the historical traffic observation data $\mathcal{X} \in \mathbb{R}^{P \times N \times C}$ through the linear layer, and D is the dimension of the hidden state.

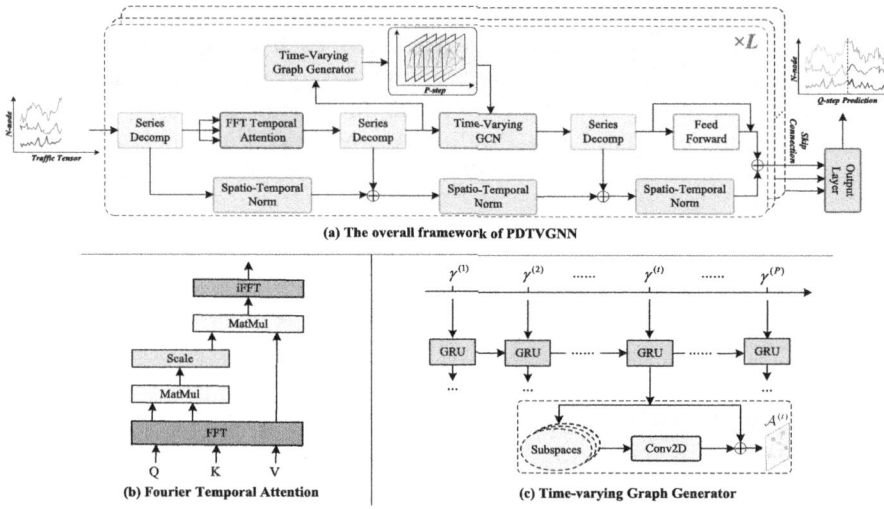

Fig. 2. Detailed framework of PDTVGNN.

4.2 Series Decomposition Module

Series decomposition [18], has been applied to time-series forecasting models such as the Autoformer [19] and FEDformer [20] to capture complex temporal patterns. To improve accuracy, we decompose the traffic series into trend and seasonal parts, which represent the long-term trend and potential periodicity of the traffic series, respectively. Specifically, moving averages is used to smooth out cyclical fluctuations, and the seasonal part is obtained by subtracting the trend from the original time series. As in Eq. (4), for input data $\mathcal{X} \in \mathbb{R}^{P \times N \times C}$ of length P, the trend and seasonal parts $\mathcal{X}_{sea}, \mathcal{X}_{tre} \in \mathbb{R}^{P \times N \times C}$ are obtained, respectively.

$$\begin{aligned} \mathcal{X}_{tre} &= AvgPool(padding(\mathcal{X}), w), \\ \mathcal{X}_{sea} &= \mathcal{X} - \mathcal{X}_{tre}. \end{aligned} \quad (4)$$

$AvgPool(\cdot)$ is a moving average operation with window size w and uses the operation *padding* to keep the length of the series constant.

4.3 Temporal Correlation Extraction

The series decomposition module decomposes the input of the P time steps into trend parts and seasonal parts. For the decomposed results, the seasonal part and the trend part are modeled using Fourier temporal attention and spatio-temporal normalization module.

Fourier Temporal Attention for Seasonal Parts. The seasonal component of the time series corresponds to high-frequency values. The Softmax operation amplifies larger values and diminishes smaller ones, concentrating attention on dominant frequencies and improving seasonal information capture [21]. In contrast to time-domain attention, frequency-domain attention offers superior performance, as the primary frequency patterns are directly accessible in the frequency domain. Consequently, as illustrated in Eqs. (5) and (6), Fourier attention is first computed in the frequency domain by transforming the query, key, and value through Fourier transformation. The result is then mapped back to the time domain through an inverse Fourier transformation.

$$\begin{aligned} Q_f &= FFT(Q) = FFT(\mathcal{X}_{sea}W_Q), \\ K_f &= FFT(K) = FFT(\mathcal{X}_{sea}W_K), \\ V_f &= FFT(V) = FFT(\mathcal{X}_{sea}W_V), \end{aligned} \quad (5)$$

$$\hat{\mathcal{X}}_{sea} = iFFT(softmax(Q_f K_f^T)V_f). \quad (6)$$

where W_Q, W_K, W_V are learnable parameters. With the help of Fast Fourier Transform (FFT), the computational complexity can be reduced from $O(n^2)$ to $O(n \log n)$.

Spatio-Temporal Normalization for Trend Parts. The attention mechanism fundamentally operates by modifying and adding to the contextual history, resulting in the inevitable loss of temporal information and poor generalization of trend data [21]. This limitation motivates the decomposition of time series into trend and seasonal parts. To address real-world scenarios where traffic data series exhibit non-stationarity and dynamic changes in data distribution, we propose a spatio-temporal normalization method (STNorm), which includes both temporal and spatial normalization. This method is designed to handle the temporal and spatial non-stationarity of the trend part, respectively.

Specifically, for the given trend input $\mathcal{X}_{tre} = \{\{X_{tre(t,v)}\}_{t=1}^{P}\}_{v=1}^{N}$, the mean and standard deviation of the particular instance along the time axis are computed as follows:

$$\begin{aligned} \mu_T[X_{tre(t,v)}] &= \frac{1}{P}\sum_{i=1}^{P} X_{tre(i,v)}, \\ \sigma_T^2[X_{tre(t,v)}] &= \frac{1}{P}\sum_{i=1}^{P}(X_{tre(i,v)} - \mu_T[X_{tre(t,v)}])^2, \end{aligned} \quad (7)$$

We then normalize the trend input across the time dimension as follows:

$$\mathrm{X}^T_{tre(t,v)} = \alpha_T \left(\frac{\mathrm{X}_{tre(t,v)} - \mu_T[\mathrm{X}_{tre(t,v)}]}{\sqrt{\sigma_T^2[\mathrm{X}_{tre(t,v)}] + \varepsilon}} \right) + \beta_T, \tag{8}$$

where α_T, β_T are learnable parameter vectors and ε is a small constant that maintains numerical stability. Similarly, we compute the mean and standard deviation of a particular instance along the spatial axis and then perform spatial normalization:

$$\mu_S[\mathrm{X}_{tre(t,v)}] = \frac{1}{N} \sum_{j=1}^{N} \mathrm{X}_{tre(t,j)},$$

$$\sigma_S^2[\mathrm{X}_{tre(t,v)}] = \frac{1}{N} \sum_{j=1}^{N} (\mathrm{X}_{tre(t,j)} - \mu_S[\mathrm{X}_{tre(t,v)}])^2, \tag{9}$$

$$\mathrm{X}^S_{tre(t,v)} = \alpha_S \left(\frac{\mathrm{X}_{tre(t,v)} - \mu_S[\mathrm{X}_{tre(t,v)}]}{\sqrt{\sigma_S^2[\mathrm{X}_{tre(t,v)}] + \varepsilon}} \right) + \beta_S, \tag{10}$$

With spatio-temporal normalization, the model extracts non-stationary information while preserving a consistent distribution for forecasting. The two normalized inputs are then combined and passed through a two-layer MLP to predict future trends:

$$\hat{\mathcal{X}}_{tre} = MLP([\mathcal{X}^T_{tre}, \mathcal{X}^S_{tre}]). \tag{11}$$

4.4 Time-Varying Graph Structure Generator

In real-world scenarios, the spatial correlations between nodes are not always constant, and the graph structure changes smoothly over time. To account for this inherent property, we propose a time-varying graph structure generator (TVGG) to capture the dynamic correlations between nodes. This module takes into account both the dependencies on the current input values and the graph structure from the previous time step, which is modeled recurrently:

$$\mathcal{A}^{(t)} = \mathcal{F}^d(\mathcal{A}^{(t-1)}, \gamma^{(t)}). \tag{12}$$

where $\mathcal{A}^{(t)} \in \mathbb{R}^{N \times N}$ denotes the adjacency matrix representing the spatial correlations at time step t, $\gamma^{(t)}$ refers to the node features, and $\mathcal{F}^d$ is the function for extracting change correlations. For simplicity, we omit the subscript l, which denotes the layer number, both in this equation and throughout the rest of this subsection.

However, directly parameterizing the adjacency matrix $\mathcal{A}$ and the mapping function $\mathcal{F}^d$ introduces significant computational overhead. To address this issue, we assume that the nodes have a time-varying representation e over time, and the time-varying graph structure can be derived from this dynamic node representation.

We use the Gated Recurrent Unit (GRU), a simple but powerful variant of recurrent neural networks, to model the dynamics of time-varying representations. Define $e^{(t)} \in \mathbb{R}^{N \times D_e}$ as the hidden state and the update process of the GRU as:

$$\begin{aligned}
z^{(t)} &= \sigma(W_z[\gamma^{(t)}, e^{(t-1)}] + b_z), \\
r^{(t)} &= \sigma(W_r[\gamma^{(t)}, e^{(t-1)}] + b_r), \\
\tilde{e}^{(t)} &= tanh(W_e[\gamma^{(t)}, (r^{(t)} \odot e^{(t-1)})] + b_e), \\
e^{(t)} &= z^{(t)} \odot e^{(t-1)} + (1 - z^{(t)}) \odot \tilde{e}^{(t)},
\end{aligned} \quad (13)$$

where $r^{(t)}$ and $z^{(t)}$ denote the reset gate and update gate, respectively, $\odot$ represents the Hadamard product, W_z, W_r and W_e are the learnable parameters, and σ is the sigmoid function.

Inspired by [22], we adopt a spatial embedding method to extract node features as the initial state of the GRU. First, an additional embedding vector is assigned to each node, and then a graph convolution layer is applied for Laplace smoothing. This process enhances the representation of each node by incorporating information from its neighbors, explicitly modeling the spatial structure while reflecting the graph structure information. The resulting spatial representation, $e \in \mathbb{R}^{N \times D_e}$, encapsulates the rich features of the nodes, which are then combined with a fully connected layer to form the initial hidden state $e^{(0)}$.

$$\begin{aligned}
\hat{\mathcal{A}}_{ij,v}^{(t)} &= \frac{(W_v e_i^{(t)} \cdot W_v e_j^{(t)})}{\delta}, \\
\mathcal{A}_{ij,v}^{(t)} &= \text{conv2D}(\hat{\mathcal{A}}_{ij,v}^{(t)}) + \hat{\mathcal{A}}_{ij,v}^{(t)},
\end{aligned} \quad (14)$$

where $\mathcal{A}_{ij,v}^{(t)}$ denotes the value of the graph structure learned by the v-th subspace at time step t in the i-th row and j-th column. W_v is the learnable matrix that maps the spatial correlation information to the v-th subspace. The operation $\cdot$ represents the inner product of vectors, and δ is used to prevent the correlation values from deviating excessively. In the above formulation, we introduce a 2D convolutional layer along with residual connections to enhance the information exchange between different subspaces, where the number of channels in the convolutional kernel corresponds to the number of subspaces. Finally, the matrices of all subspaces are summed:

$$\mathcal{A}_{ij}^{(t)} = f(\sum_{v=1}^{V} \mathcal{A}_{ij,v}^{(t)}). \quad (15)$$

where $f(\cdot)$ represents a normalization process designed to prevent training instability, it yields the time-varying graph structure $\mathcal{A}^{(t)}$ at time step t.

4.5 Time-Varying Graph Convolution Module

Formally, the output γ_l of the l-th layer of temporal attention is passed into the l-th TVGG, as presented in Sect. 4.4, generating a series of adjacency matrices as follows:

$$[\mathcal{A}_l^{(1)}, \mathcal{A}_l^{(2)}, ..., \mathcal{A}_l^{(P)}] = \mathcal{F}_l^a(\gamma_l). \tag{16}$$

where $\mathcal{A}_l = [\mathcal{A}_l^{(1)}, \mathcal{A}_l^{(2)}, ..., \mathcal{A}_l^{(P)}]$, P is the historical time step.

After learning the adjacency matrices, spatial dependencies are extracted using a graph convolution-based spatial propagation method. First, initial residual connections [23] are employed in graph convolution. By emphasizing the initial features, the learned features become more discriminative after multiple graph convolution layers. The layer-wise propagation rule can be expressed as:

$$H^{(m)} = (\partial H^{(0)} + (1-\partial)\mathcal{A}H^{(m-1)})W^{(m-1)}, \tag{17}$$

where $H^{(0)} = \gamma_l$ denotes the initial node features and ∂ is a hyperparameter that controls the proportion of initial information. Then, the component achieves the "changing locality" property by adaptively aggregating information from neighbors at different hops [24]. The output of the graph convolution is the combination of the representations obtained from all previous layers:

$$H^{(M)} = \sum_{m=0}^{M-1} H^{(m)}. \tag{18}$$

5 Experiments

This section presents a comprehensive evaluation of our proposed PDTVGNN framework. Specifically, we aim to address the following research questions:
- **RQ1.** How does PDTVGNN perform in the traffic prediction task?
- **RQ2.** How does each component of PDTVGNN contribute to the prediction?
- **RQ3.** How do key hyperparameters influence model performance?
- **RQ4.** Does PDTVGNN provide interpretability in the spatial dimension?

5.1 Setting

Datasets and Processing. To evaluate the performance of the PDTVGNN method, we conducted comparative experiments on four real-world datasets. Table 1 provides detailed information on the selected datasets, including the Los Angeles PEMS series (PEMS-BAY, PEMS04, PEMS08) and the California Metro Traffic Los Angeles (METR-LA). These datasets were chosen due to their distinct characteristics. Given the differences in sampling periods and regions, each dataset has unique time spans and node sizes, making them representative in their own right. Traffic flow data is aggregated at 5-minute intervals, resulting in 12 sample points per hour. The datasets are divided into training, validation, and test sets. In line with the most contemporary solution, METR-LA and PEMS-BAY are split in a 7:1:2 ratio, while PEMS04 and PEMS08 are split in a 6:2:2 ratio. Additionally, we utilize data from the previous hour (12 time steps) to predict traffic flow for the following hour (12 time steps), thereby performing multi-step prediction.

Table 1. Datasets description.

Datasets	Time steps	Nodes	Time windows	Data Type
METR-LA	34272	207	5 min	speed
PEMS-BAY	52116	325	5 min	speed
PEMS04	16992	307	5 min	flow
PEMS08	17856	170	5 min	flow

Baselines. We selected 13 baselines and categorized them into 4 classes: **(1)** Methods that do not consider spatial correlation: VAR [8], SVR, FC-LSTM [9]. **(2)** Methods based on predefined graphs: DCRNN [10], STGCN [11], STSGCN [4]. **(3)** Methods considering dynamic spatial correlation: GWnet [12], AGCRN [13], MTGNN [3], DGCRN [15]. **(4)** Other superior methods based on spatio-temporal graphs: GMAN [25], PDFormer [14], STPGNN [5].

Evaluative Metrics. Three commonly used evaluation metrics are employed: Mean Absolute Error (MAE), Root Mean Square Error (RMSE), and Mean Absolute Percentage Error (MAPE). All experiments are repeated five times, and the results were averaged.

Implementation Details. The implementation environment for PDTVGNN is Python 3.8 and PyTorch 2.2.1. The evaluation environment is a server equipped with a V100-PCIe-32. To train our model, an Adam optimization is used with an initial learning rate of 0.001, a batch size of 16, and a maximum of 60 epochs. Hyperparameters and their optimal values are determined on the validation set: the model dimension is 64, the number of attention heads is 8, and the number of model layers is [3, 3, 5, 5], respectively.

5.2 Predictive Performance (RQ1)

Tables 2 and 3 show the results, where the bolded values are optimal and the underlined values are suboptimal.

We find the following observations. **(1)** PDTVGNN outperforms all other state-of-the-art baselines on all datasets. We note that PDTVGNN's MAPE results on PEMS04 are slightly lower, but all other metrics are more favorable, such as the 0.38% decrease under MAE metrics. **(2)** The traditional statistical model performs poorly because it only considers temporal correlation

Table 2. Performance comparison of different methods on PEMS-BAY and METR-LA.

Datasets	Methods	15 min			30 min			60 min		
		MAE	RMSE	MAPE	MAE	RMSE	MAPE	MAE	RMSE	MAPE
PEMS-BAY	VAR	1.74	3.16	3.60%	2.32	4.25	5.00%	2.93	5.44	6.50%
	SVR	1.85	2.59	3.80%	2.48	5.18	5.50%	3.28	7.08	8.00%
	FC-LSTM	2.05	4.19	4.80%	2.20	4.55	5.20%	2.37	4.96	5.70%
	DCRNN	1.38	2.95	2.90%	1.74	3.97	3.90%	2.07	4.74	4.90%
	STGCN	1.36	2.96	2.90%	1.81	4.27	4.17%	2.49	5.69	5.79%
	STSGCN	1.44	3.01	3.04%	1.83	4.18	4.17%	2.26	5.21	5.40%
	GWNet	1.30	2.74	2.73%	1.63	3.70	3.67%	1.95	4.52	4.63%
	AGCRN	1.37	2.87	2.94%	1.69	3.85	3.87%	1.96	4.54	4.64%
	MTGNN	1.32	2.79	2.77%	1.65	3.74	3.69%	1.94	4.49	4.53%
	GMAN	1.34	2.91	2.86%	1.63	3.76	3.68%	_1.86_	_4.32_	_4.37%_
	DGCRN	_1.28_	_2.69_	_2.66%_	_1.59_	_3.63_	_3.55%_	1.89	4.42	4.43%
	PDFormer	1.32	2.83	2.78%	1.64	3.79	3.71%	1.91	4.43	4.51%
	STPGNN	1.35	2.88	2.85%	1.72	3.83	3.90%	2.10	4.72	5.03%
	PDTVGNN	**1.26**	**2.67**	**2.62%**	**1.55**	**3.53**	**3.48%**	**1.85**	**4.30**	**4.34%**
	Improv.	1.59%	0.75%	1.53%	2.58%	2.83%	2.01%	0.54%	0.47%	0.69%
METR-LA	VAR	4.42	7.89	10.20%	5.41	9.13	12.70%	6.52	10.11	15.80%
	SVR	3.99	8.45	9.30%	5.05	10.87	12.10%	6.72	13.76	16.70%
	FC-LSTM	3.44	6.30	9.60%	3.77	7.23	10.90%	4.37	8.69	13.20%
	DCRNN	2.77	5.38	7.30%	3.15	6.45	8.80%	3.60	7.60	10.50%
	STGCN	2.88	5.74	7.62%	3.47	7.24	9.57%	4.59	9.40	12.70%
	STSGCN	3.31	7.62	8.06%	4.13	9.77	10.29%	5.06	11.66	12.91%
	GWNet	2.69	5.15	6.90%	3.07	6.22	8.37%	3.53	7.37	10.01%
	AGCRN	2.87	5.58	7.70%	3.23	6.58	9.00%	3.62	7.51	10.38%
	MTGNN	3.31	7.62	8.06%	4.13	9.70	10.29%	5.06	11.66	12.91%
	GMAN	2.80	5.55	7.41%	3.12	6.49	8.73%	_3.44_	7.35	10.07%
	DGCRN	_2.62_	_5.01_	_6.63%_	_2.99_	_6.05_	_8.19%_	_3.44_	_7.19_	_9.73%_
	PDFormer	2.83	5.45	7.77%	3.20	6.46	9.19%	3.62	7.47	10.91%
	STPGNN	2.83	5.52	7.73%	3.25	6.59	8.91%	3.72	7.61	10.66%
	PDTVGNN	**2.59**	**4.93**	**6.51%**	**2.96**	**6.02**	**8.10%**	**3.39**	**7.15**	**9.62%**
	Improv.	1.16%	1.62%	1.84%	1.02%	0.50%	1.11%	1.47%	0.56%	1.14%

Table 3. Performance comparison of different methods on PEMS04 and PEMS08.

Datasets	Metric	VAR	SVR	FC-LSTM	DCRNN	STGCN	STSGCN	GWnet	AGCRN	MTGNN	GMAN	DGCRN	PDFormer	STPGNN	OURS	Improv.
PEMS04	MAE	24.44	26.18	23.60	24.42	23.90	21.52	19.91	19.36	19.50	19.25	18.80	_18.32_	18.34	**18.25**	0.38%
	RMSE	37.76	38.91	37.11	37.48	36.43	34.14	31.06	31.28	32.00	30.85	30.65	29.97	_29.64_	**29.59**	0.17%
	MAPE	17.27%	22.84%	16.17%	16.86%	13.67%	14.50%	13.62%	12.81%	14.04%	13.00%	12.82%	**12.10%**	12.49%	_12.14%_	-0.33%
PEMS08	MAE	19.83	20.92	21.18	18.49	18.79	17.88	15.57	15.65	15.31	14.87	14.60	_13.58_	13.90	**13.50**	0.59%
	RMSE	29.94	31.23	31.88	27.30	28.20	27.36	24.32	24.99	24.42	24.06	24.16	23.51	_23.05_	**22.59**	2.04%
	MAPE	13.08%	14.24%	13.72%	11.69%	10.55%	11.71%	10.32%	10.17%	10.70%	9.77%	9.33%	9.05%	_9.01%_	**8.98%**	0.33%

and ignores spatial dependence. (3) In GNN-based models, those that account for dynamic spatial correlations in time series, such as MTGNN and DGCRN, demonstrate more competitive performance than static graph embeddings. However, these models still rely on static graph structures and do not consider the spatial structure as time-varying and dynamic. In contrast, our PDTVGNN model incorporates the time-varying graph convolution module, which effectively captures the dynamic correlations among nodes by generating a series of time-varying graph structures, resulting in improved performance. (4) Most models utilizing attention mechanisms improve significantly over traditional time series and GNN-based models. Among them, GMAN and PDFormer outperform other baselines across different dataset metrics. However, our PDTVGNN model surpasses both, achieving superior performance. We attribute this to the intrinsic progressive decomposition capability provided by the series decomposition module in PDTVGNN, which effectively untangles entangled temporal patterns and enhances the model's ability to capture spatio-temporal dependencies.

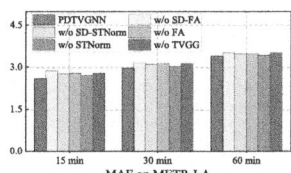 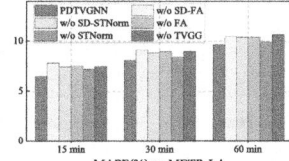 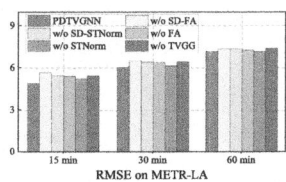

Fig. 3. Ablation study on METR-LA.

5.3 Ablation Study (RQ2)

To further evaluate the effectiveness of modules of PDTVGNN, we compare it with the following variants on the METR-LA dataset.
- **w/o SD-FA** removes the series decomposition and uses only the STNorm module to extract temporal features from the entangled traffic series.
- **w/o SD-STNorm** removes the series decomposition module and uses only the Fourier temporal attention to extract temporal features from the entangled traffic series.
- **w/o FA** replaces the Fourier temporal attention with the STNorm for seasonal parts.
- **w/o STNorm** replaces the STNorm with the Fourier temporal attention for trend parts.
- **w/o TVGG** removes time-varying graph generator and directly uses a predefined geographic adjacency matrix for graph convolution.

From the results presented in Fig. 3, all components contribute to the final result to some extent, and we draw the following conclusions. (1) The significant drop in performance for w/o SD-FA and w/o SD-STNorm emphasizes the importance of progressive decomposition and separately modeling trend and seasonal parts. **(2)** PDTVGNN outperforms w/o FA, demonstrating the effectiveness of the STNorm module in modeling trend components accurately. **(3)** PDTVGNN further improves performance over w/o STNorm, suggesting that the Fourier temporal attention aids the model in capturing seasonal information better. **(4)** w/o TVGG, which relies on static geographic distance-based graphs, exhibits large standard deviations, highlighting the need for dynamic spatial dependencies modeling.

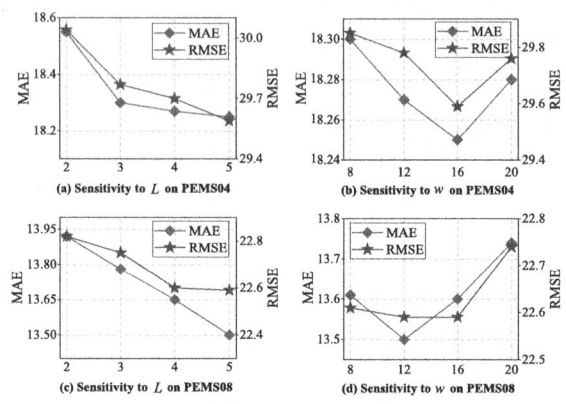

Fig. 4. The effect of model layers L and window size w on PEMS04 and PEMS08.

5.4 Parameter Sensitivity (RQ3)

A key advantage of the PDTVGNN model is its ability to disentangle complex temporal patterns progressively, thanks to the progressive decomposition capabilities provided by its embedded decomposition blocks. The model ensures robustness and accuracy by modeling the different components separately. In the series decomposition module, the parameter w represents the window size for the moving average operation. Smaller window sizes tend to overfit short-term fluctuations and neglect long-term trends, while larger window sizes may excessively smooth the data, diminishing sensitivity to rapid fluctuations. In our experiments, we set the values of w to 8, 12, 16, and 20 on the PEMS04 and PEMS08 datasets, respectively. The specific experimental results are shown in Figs. 4(b) and (d). We found that the optimal performance on PEMS04 is achieved with $w = 16$ and on PEMS08 with $w = 12$.

We also examined the impact of the number of layers L on model performance by varying L from 2 to 5. The experimental results in Figs. 4(a) and (c) show that performance improves as the model depth increases, with the best results achieved when $L = 5$ for both datasets.

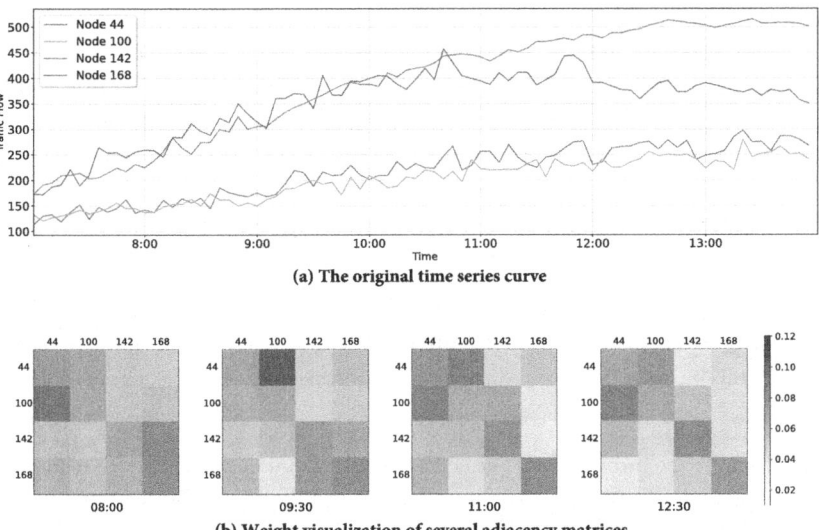

Fig. 5. Case study of time-varying graph (from traffic flow on PEMS08 dataset). (Color figure online)

5.5 Case Study (RQ4)

To further validate the effectiveness of the time-varying graph structure generator and provide spatial interpretability, we selected four nodes numbered 44, 100, 142, and 168 from the PEMS08 dataset on August 14, 2016, for a case study. Figure 5(b) shows the adjacency matrices at 8:00, 9:30, 11:00, and 12:30, visualized as heatmaps. The intensity of the purple grids indicates larger weights. Figure 5(a) also presents the original time series curves. As the relationships are one-way, we did not enforce symmetry in the adjacency matrix.

For node 142, before 11:00 and especially at 9:00, we observe a strong correlation between node 168 (represented by the red line) and node 142 (represented by the green line), with similar magnitudes of change. However, after 11:00, node 168 shows a decreasing trend while node 142 continues to increase. Adjacency matrixes effectively capture this shift in correlation, with corresponding matrix values decreasing over time. This supports our hypothesis that the spatial correlation of traffic data is time-varying. In contrast, when comparing the series trends of nodes 44 and 100, the correlation between them remains relatively stable and generally stronger, as reflected in the matrices. These observations provide compelling evidence for the effectiveness of the time-varying graph structure generator.

6 Conclusion

In this work, we propose a novel traffic forecasting model named PDTVGNN. Specifically, we adopt a progressive decomposition idea throughout the forecasting process, where decomposed blocks are embedded as internal modules to gradually decouple the entangled temporal patterns. The trend and seasonal parts obtained after decoupling are then modeled separately. Additionally, we introduce a time-varying graph generation module that constructs a series of adjacency matrices that process the current inputs and retain hidden information from the historical graph structure, capturing the time-varying nature of spatial relationships. Extensive experiments conducted on four real-world datasets demonstrate our proposed model's superiority and highlight each module's effectiveness.

Acknowledgements. This work is supported by National Natural Science Foundation of China No. 82374621.

Ethics Statement. The data used in this paper (PEMS04, PEMS08, PEMS-BAY, and METR-LA) are public open-sourced benchmark datasets, which are wildly used in academic research. No personally identifiable information was obtained and people can not infer personal information through the data. This work is not potentially a part of policing or military work. The authors of this paper are committed to ethical principles and guidelines in conducting research and have taken measures to ensure the integrity and validity of the data. The use of the data in this study is in accordance with ethical standards and is intended to advance knowledge in the field of traffic forecasting.

References

1. Tedjopurnomo, D.A., Bao, Z., Zheng, B., Choudhury, F., Qin, A.K.: IEEE Trans. Knowl. Data Eng. **34**(4), 1544–1561 (2020)
2. Yin, X., Wu, G., Wei, J., Shen, Y., Qi, H., Yin, B.: Deep learning on traffic prediction: methods, analysis, and future directions. IEEE Trans. Intell. Transp. Syst. **23**(6), 4927–4943 (2022)
3. Wu, Z., Pan, S., Long, G., Jiang, J., Chang, X., Zhang, C.: Connecting the dots: multivariate time series forecasting with graph neural networks. In: Proceedings of the 26th ACM SIGKDD International Conference on Knowledge Discovery and Data Mining, pp. 753–763 (2020)
4. Song, C., Lin, Y., Guo, S., Wan, H.: Spatial-temporal synchronous graph convolutional networks: a new framework for spatial-temporal network data forecasting. In: AAAI Conference on Artificial Intelligence, pp. 914-921 (2020)
5. Kong, W., Guo, Z., Liu, Y.: Spatio-temporal pivotal graph neural networks for traffic flow forecasting. In: AAAI Conference on Artificial Intelligence, pp. 8627–8635 (2024)
6. Jin, G., et al.: Spatio-temporal graph neural networks for predictive learning in urban computing: a survey. IEEE Trans. Knowl. Data Eng. **36**(10), 1–20 (2024)
7. Williams, B.M., Hoel, L.A.: Modeling and forecasting vehicular traffic flow as a seasonal Arima process: theoretical basis and empirical results. J. Transp. Eng. **129**(6), 664–672 (2003)
8. Zivot, E., Wang, J.: Vector autoregressive models for multivariate time series. In: Modeling Financial Time Series with S-Plus®, pp. 385–429. Springer, New York (2006). https://doi.org/10.1007/978-0-387-21763-5_11

9. Sutskever, I., Vinyals, O., Le, Q.V.: Sequence to sequence learning with neural networks. In: NeurIPS, pp. 3104-3112 (2014)
10. Li, Y., Yu, R., Shahabi, C., Liu, Y.: Diffusion convolutional recurrent neural network: data-driven traffic forecasting. In: ICLR (2018)
11. Yu, B., Yin, H., Zhu, Z.: Spatio-temporal graph convolutional networks: a deep learning framework for traffic forecasting. In: IJCAI, pp. 3634–3640 (2017)
12. Wu, Z., Pan, S., Long, G., Jiang, J., Zhang, C.: Graph WaveNet for deep spatial-temporal graph modeling. In: IJCAI, pp. 1907–1913 (2019)
13. BAI, L., Yao, L., Li, C., Wang, X., Wang, C.: Adaptive graph convolutional recurrent network for traffic forecasting. In: NeurIPS, pp. 17804–17815 (2020)
14. Jiang, J., Han, C., Zhao, W.X., Wang, J.: PDFormer: propagation delay-aware dynamic long-range transformer for traffic flow prediction. In: AAAI Conference on Artificial Intelligence, pp. 4365–4373 (2023)
15. Li, F., et al.: Dynamic graph convolutional recurrent network for traffic prediction: benchmark and solution. ACM Trans. Knowl. Discov. Data **17**(1), 1–21 (2023)
16. Bahdanau, D., Cho, K., Bengio, Y.: Neural Machine Translation by Jointly Learning to Align and Translate. arXiv preprint arXiv:1409.0473 (2014)
17. Vaswani, A., et al.: Attention is all you need. In: NeurIPS, pp. 5998–6008 (2017)
18. Cleveland, R.B., Cleveland, W.S., McRae, J.E., Terpenning, I.: STL: a seasonal-trend decomposition. J. Off. Stat. **6**(1), 3–73(1990)
19. Wu, H., Xu, J., Wang, J., Long, M.: Autoformer: decomposition transformers with auto-correlation for long-term series forecasting. In: Proceedings of the Advances in Neural Information Processing Systems (NeurIPS) (2021)
20. Zhou, T., Ma, Z., Wen, Q., Wang, X., Sun, L., Jin, R.: Fedformer: frequency enhanced decomposed transformer for long-term series forecasting. In: Proceedings of the International Conference on Machine Learning (ICML) (2022)
21. Zhang, X., et al.: First De-Trend then Attend: Rethinking Attention for Time-Series Forecasting. arXiv preprint arXiv:2212.08151 (2022)
22. Guo, S., Lin, Y., Wan, H., Li, X., Cong, G.: Learning dynamics and heterogeneity of spatial-temporal graph data for traffic forecasting. IEEE Trans. Knowl. Data Eng. **34**(11), 5415–5428 (2021)
23. Chen, M.,Wei, Z., Huang, Z., Ding, B., Li, Y.: Simple and deep graph convolutional networks. In: International Conference on Machine Learning, pp. 1725–1735 (2020)
24. Xu, K., Li, C., Tian, Y., Sonobe, T., Kawarabayashi, K., Jegelka, S.: Representation learning on graphs with jumping knowledge networks. In: Proceedings of the International Conference on Machine Learning (ICML), pp. 5453-5462 (2018)
25. Zheng, C., Fan, X., Wang, C., Qi, J.: GMAN: a graph multi-attention network for traffic prediction. In: AAAI Conference on Artificial Intelligence, pp. 1234–1241 (2020)

CESI: Sparse Input Spatial Interpolation for Heterogeneous and Noisy Hybrid Wireless Sensor Networks

Chaofan Li[✉], Till Riedel, and Michael Beigl

TECO Lab, Karlsruhe Institute of Technology, Karlsruhe, Germany
{chaofan.li,till.riedel,michael.beigl}@kit.edu

Abstract. Hybrid wireless sensor networks (HWSNs) combine sensors of varying costs to balance budget and deployment density. However, their data products often exhibit high heterogeneity and noise, presenting new challenges for spatial interpolation models. Traditional spatial interpolation models take dense input. When working on HWSN datasets, a large part of the dense input must be obtained through imputation, leading to feature distribution changes and error accumulation. To address these challenges, we propose the Context Encoder Spatial Interpolation (CESI) Model, designed to work directly with sparse, narrow-format input. CESI integrates a GraphSAGE-based backbone with a Transformer-based context embedding module, leveraging probabilistic encoding for better generalization to unseen coordinates and a self-supervised signal to balance inductive biases between the two modules. Experimental results demonstrate that CESI consistently outperforms baseline models across several publicly available real-world datasets.

Keywords: Spatial Interpolation · Graph Neural Network · Sparse Data

1 Introduction

In-situ sensor networks are crucial in many fields, offering high temporal coverage and robustness to interference. Modern sensor networks increasingly combine sensors of varying costs to balance budget and deployment density, enabling finer-grained data collection for more detailed modeling. We hereafter refer to them as hybrid wireless sensor networks (HWSNs) [13,20].

Low-cost sensors, while economical, often compromise accuracy and reliability, leading to highly heterogeneous and noisy HWSN datasets. This poses significant challenges for spatial interpolation models, which are traditionally designed based on homogeneous, high-quality sensor data [2,7,12,15,18]. These methods typically require dense, wide-format input (Fig. 1 left), which is increasingly incompatible with modern IoT protocols like OGC SensorThings API [16] that favor narrow, sparse data formats (Fig. 1 right) to cope with the heterogeneity of HWSN. Consequently, there is a pressing need for spatial interpolation models tailored to sparse input in HWSNs, which will introduce the following potential benefits:

Location X	Location Y	Humidity	Wind Speed	Temperature
25	25			
75	30	20%	2	
80	69	17%		10
121	105	14%	4	
...	...	...	...	...

Location X	Location Y	Property	Value
75	30	Humidity	20%
75	30	Wind Speed	2
80	69	Humidity	17%
80	69	Temperature	10
121	105	Humidity	14%
121	105	Wind Speed	4
...	...	...	...

Fig. 1. An example of the wide format (left) and narrow format (right) of the same input data entry of spatial interpolation models.

First, dense input models require extensive imputation to handle missing values in HWSN datasets. While traditional spatial interpolation methods also discuss data imputation, the causes of missing values in HWSNs differ significantly, resulting in much higher imputation workloads. In traditional sensor networks, missing values are mainly caused by occasional sensor failures. With high-quality sensors, such issues are infrequent. Thus, recent spatial interpolation studies still consider simple techniques like linear interpolation [8] or removing incomplete rows/columns [23] acceptable. In contrast, HWSNs face far more frequent failures from low-cost sensors, compounded by heterogeneity in sensor types, where sensors at different locations may only measure subsets of the observed properties. For instance, applying PE-GNN [12] to the SmartAQnet dataset [13] required imputing over 50% of the inputs, with all rows containing missing cells. In such cases, removing incomplete data is infeasible, while excessive imputation alters feature distributions and accumulates errors, degrading model performance. By using sparse input, we can prevent the data imputation step and the above-mentioned disadvantages (see Fig. 1 as an example).

Second, dense input models typically encode all properties at the same location (a row in Fig. 1 left) and focus on location-level correlations. In contrast, sparse input models encode each observation (a row in Fig. 1 right), directly capturing observation-level correlations. This allows sparse models to learn fine-grained relationships more efficiently.

Despite these benefits, sparse input introduces challenges. The high dimensional nature of the sparse input makes it harder for models to learn generalizable representations, and direct exposure to noisy observations makes sparse input models more sensitive to the high noise in HWSN datasets. In contrast, for dense input models, the imputed values that occupy a considerable part of input are obtained by referring to multiple observations. This helps neutralize the noise from individual sensors, making the dense input models more robust to noise.

Based on the above insights, we propose the Context Encoder Spatial Interpolation (CESI) Model with the following contributions:

- CESI is among the first spatial interpolation models tailored for narrow-format sparse input, effectively addressing the heterogeneity in HWSN datasets and achieving significant performance gains.
- We designed a self-supervised context embedding module to handle the sparse input series. This module uses variational inference to learn the probabilistic encoding of the input observations and uses a self-supervised loss signal to achieve an adaptive balance of inductive bias with other modules. Thus, the model's robustness against noise and universality across different tasks is significantly improved.
- We tested our model on three publicly available real-world HWSN datasets from different fields and with different characteristics. Compared to the baselines, whose performance is shaky across different datasets, our model consistently outperforms baselines on all three datasets.

2 Related Work

2.1 Challenges in HWSN Datasets

HWSN datasets are heterogeneous and noisy in several ways, typically including but not limited to the following:

- **Heterogeneity from various sensor models**: HWSNs are usually a mix of multiple sensor models. They may not observe all properties at the same location, which is often one of the underlying assumptions of studies based on traditional sensor networks.
- **Heterogeneity from dynamic sensor network topology**: Unlike the long-lived traditional measuring stations, the lifespan of low-cost sensors is unstable. Sometimes, deploying new ultra-low-cost sensors is even more affordable than retrieving and repairing old ones. These factors keep the spatial structure of HWSNs changing. Figure 2a illustrates how the total device amount of one of such sensor networks changes over time, while Fig. 2b shows when sensors in this network successfully returned data and when did not. It is easy to figure out that the topology of HWSNs is dynamic. Furthermore, in addition to stationary sensors, some sensor networks also partially [4,13] or fully [14] employ moveable sensors, which further enhances the heterogeneity of the spatial structure of the sensor network.
- **Heterogeneity due to low-power wireless communication protocols**: Deployment of traditional sensors often faces administrative difficulties, such as applying for land, power supply, and network access from local administrations. As a result, many HWSNs turn to using low-power wireless communication technologies such as LoRaWAN, Zigbee, BLE, etc. These communication protocols allow sensors to operate on batteries alone for a considerable period and send their observations to the data center wirelessly. The cost of this is usually a restricted uplink bandwidth and transmission time window. Even if the network delivers complete data at the end, the real-time heterogeneity induced by these protocols must be considered when considering the actual deployment of the model for real-time usage.

- **Uncertainty in sensor readings**: The accuracy of a sensor, not only in terms of its accuracy on its observed properties but also its position recorded by the mounted GPS module, is generally related to its price level. Some studies have also pointed out that how low-cost sensors are assembled and the environment they operate in can also harm their measurements. In severe cases, it can even return only qualitative results [3]. Moreover, maintaining HWSNs is a complex, long-term task requiring much manual logging during the installation, repair, and transfer of sensors. Considering that the operation period of HWSNs is often measured in years, human errors are almost unavoidable, and a significant portion of them are challenging to identify and fix in quality checks.

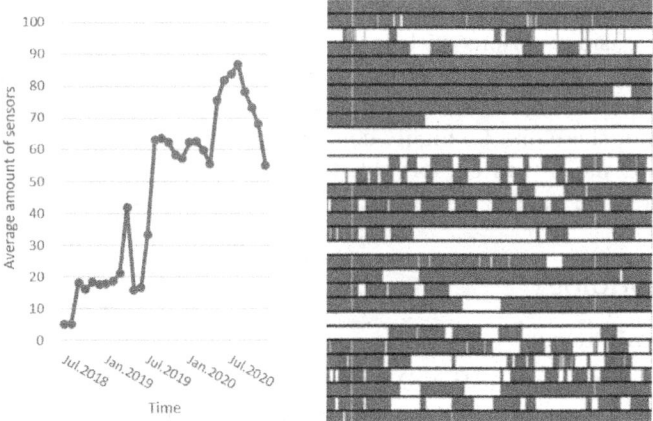

Fig. 2. (a). The curve of the monthly average active sensors in the SmartAQnet dataset [13] (Jul. 2018 to Dec. 2020). (b). Daily activity status of low-cost sensors in the SmartAQnet dataset (2021.01.01 to 2022.01.01). Each row represents a sensor, with white indicating no readings collected in the day and black indicating the opposite. (Color figure online)

2.2 Spatial Interpolation

Spatial interpolation aims to predict values of a target property at any location (mostly locations without historical observations) according to known observations. It is an essential spatial data analysis task widely used in atmosphere, geology, and urban studies.

Early machine learning approaches, such as K-Nearest Neighbors and Random Forest, are simple statistical models and struggle to capture complex and dynamic correlations [10]. Gaussian Processes (GP, also Kriging) [5,17] offer greater flexibility with custom kernel functions and provide reliable probabilistic estimates.

Deep learning methods have gained popularity in spatial interpolation, with two prominent families: Graph Neural Networks (GNNs) and Transformers. GNN-based models treat locations with known observations as graph nodes, capturing patterns of information transfer through message-passing mechanisms. Numerous GNN models [9,11,22] have been migrated to the field with promising results. Researchers have also improved these GNN models regarding the specific needs of the spatial interpolation task [1,12,18].

Transformer-based models interpret the input as a sequence of tokens. They adaptively extract the correlation between input tokens with the multi-head self-attention mechanism. However, we also note that existing transformer-based spatial interpolation models still use dense input that takes all known observations of the same location as a token, benefiting from its homogeneity to learn stable representations. For example, Fan et al. [7] put known observations on grid maps and processed them with Vision Transformer, Yu et al. [23] removes all sensing stations with more than 25% missing data, and Feng et al. [8] interpolates the missing data with linear interpolation. However, we believe that Transformer could also treat sparse observations as variable-length token sequences and, therefore, be highly compatible with the heterogeneity of HWSN datasets. This paper will explore whether we can extract stable, generalizable representations for spatial interpolation tasks from the sparse HWSN data.

3 Methodology

3.1 Preliminaries

Notations. We regard a HWSN dataset $D = \{F_j \mid j = 1, 2, ..., n\}$ as a collection of Frames F_j. Each Frame $F_j = \{O_i \mid i = 1, 2, ..., m\}$ contains all the Observations O_i recorded at a same time, which an example is illustrated as the table in Fig. 1 (right). Each Observation $O_i = (P, C, V)$ is a triplet of a one-hot encoded Property P, a two- or three-dimensional Coordinate C, and a Value V, which an example is illustrated as a row in Fig. 1 (right).

We refer to the Property that needs to be interpolated as the Target Property, abbreviated as P_{tgt}. For our model, we only consider one Target Property at a time. Since the spatial distribution of the Target Property is usually not only affected by spatial correlation but also correlated with some other Properties, HWSN datasets also observe these correlated Properties. They are called Support Properties, abbreviated as P_{sup}. Thus, a Frame F can be further divided into two parts: Target Sequence F_{tgt} includes all the Observations of P_{tgt} and Support Sequence F_{sup} includes all the Observations of P_{sup}.

Spatial Interpolation Task. Given an input Frame F' (F' may not in D), the spatial interpolation task is to predict the value V' of the P_{tgt} at any arbitrary target location C'. The basis for interpolation comes from the spatial correlation with the known values in F'_{tgt} and the effect of F'_{sup} on this correlation, which can be learned from Frames provided in D.

3.2 Framework

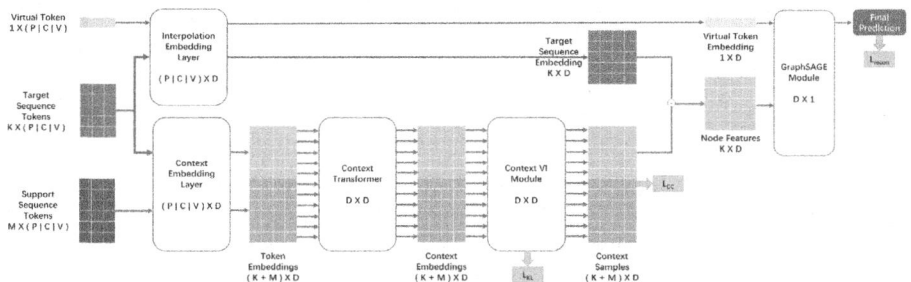

Fig. 3. An overview of the CESI model. The upper half is the GI Module, which mainly models the spatial correlations. The bottom half shows the TCE Module, which models the influence of the Support Sequence on the spatial correlations.

The main challenge of sparse input models on HWSN datasets is the contradiction between the requirement of adaptively discovering complex correlations and defective datasets, mainly manifested in low spatial coverage limited by the amount of the sensor and high noise due to the introduction of low-cost sensors. Such problems are usually solved in other fields by obtaining more data sources or using data augmentation approaches. However, in spatial interpolation tasks, such methods are generally limited. We can no longer return to the past to collect data from more locations, and we also lack prior knowledge of those Target Properties affected by complex systems for artificially creating more data. It's worth noting that some heuristics widely used in other fields, such as translation and transposition, are also risky in fields like meteorology, where spatial correlations are significantly affected by longitude, latitude, and azimuth.

These challenges necessitate a robust model design. Models with weak inductive biases, like Transformers [21], excel at capturing complex correlations but heavily depend on data quality and quantity, making their results unstable on HWSN datasets. Conversely, models with strong inductive biases, such as KCN [1] or even Inverse Distance Weighting Interpolation, while based on simple assumptions, perform surprisingly strongly on specific datasets. Nevertheless, they also risk their inductive biases being mismatched with the dataset. To address this, we propose a hybrid strategy: a strong inductive bias module serves as the backbone, complemented by a weak inductive bias module as an auxiliary component. A self-supervised signal dynamically balances the two modules, enabling better adaptation to different tasks.

Transformer-Based Context Embedding (TCE) Module. We design a Transformer-based module as our auxiliary component, whose structure is illustrated as the bottom part of Fig. 3. It learns the observation-level influence of the Support Properties on the spatial correlation of the Target Property. This influence is eventually encoded as Context Samples, which are subsequently used to correct the inputs of the GraphSAGE Module.

The TCE Module starts with input centering, that is, replacing the absolute coordinates in each observation of the input Frame F with its relative coordinates to the target location C':

$$F_{cen} = \{(P_i, C_i - C', V_i) \mid i = 1, 2, ..., m\} \tag{1}$$

With input centering, we hide the information of specific coordinates in the input Frame, forcing the TCE Module to concentrate on more generalizable spatial correlations. F_{cen} is then embedded by a multi-layer perceptron (MLP) and further processed by the Context Transformer. The Context Transformer is without positional embedding, making it order-independent for the input sequence. With the multi-head self-attention mechanism, each output token of the Context Transformer is obtained after referring to the information of all tokens in F_{cen}. In our design, the underlying intuition here is: for each input token, assuming that all other tokens are noise-free, how much should we adjust its embedding?

The output of the Context Transformer is a deterministic encoding that maps each token to a specific point in the latent space. As the reconstruction error decreases, the model risks overfitting noise in the dataset, leading to degraded performance. We use Variational Inference (VI) to learn a smooth, probabilistic latent space to address this. In probabilistic encoding, the data with noise is treated as a sample of the learned distribution. We construct a continuous and smooth latent space by repeatedly sampling from the learned distribution and ensuring these samples yield consistent outputs. This approach significantly enhances the model's generalization ability while providing meaningful uncertainty estimates for the final output. Specifically, we assume the posterior distribution in the latent space $q(z|x)$ follows a Gaussian distribution. The deterministic encoding x is passed through two MLPs to predict the mean μ and variance σ^2 of $q(z|x)$, respectively. Using the reparameterization trick, we sample a random Context Sample from $q(z|x)$:

$$z = \mu + \sigma\epsilon, \epsilon \sim \mathcal{N}(0, \mathbf{I}) \tag{2}$$

To align the learned posterior $q(z|x)$ with the standard normal prior $p(z) \sim \mathcal{N}(0, \mathbf{I})$, we minimize their KL divergence:

$$L_{KL} = D_{KL}(q(z|x) \,\|\, p(z)) \tag{3}$$

GraphSAGE-Based Interpolation (GI) Module. We select GraphSAGE as our backbone module, whose structure is illustrated as the upper part of Fig. 3. GraphSAGE assumes that the message-passing process follows the graph's topology, exchanging information within local neighborhoods through shared aggregation and update functions. This represents a relatively strong inductive bias. First, we construct a Virtual Token representing the target location in the format of an observation, in which the Value is filled as zero:

$$O_v = (P_{tgt}, C', 0) \tag{4}$$

The Virtual Token, along with the tokens in F_{tgt}, is then encoded by an MLP, which is the Interpolation Embedding Layer in Fig. 3, resulting in the Virtual Token Embedding and the Target Sequence Embeddings. Next, we use the Context Samples from the TCE Module to correct their corresponding Target Sequence Embeddings, resulting in Node Features. The Virtual Token Embedding and the Node Features are then together treated as the node feature matrix of the input graph. The adjacency matrix of the input graph is constructed using the k-nearest neighbors heuristic. Then, GraphSAGE is applied to process this graph. Finally, the GraphSAGE output corresponding to the Virtual Token is fed into an MLP Head to produce the interpolation result V'. We use the mean absolute error between V' and the label L as part of the supervisory signal for model training, named reconstruction loss:

$$L_{recon} = MAE(V', L) \tag{5}$$

Context Correction Loss. In addition to L_{recon} and L_{KL}, we introduce another self-supervision loss signal, named Context Correction Loss L_{CC}, to automatically balance the inductive bias of the two modules. It is the average of the L1 Norm of all Context Samplings:

$$L_{CC} = \frac{1}{n} \sum_{i=1}^{n} \|CS_i\|_1 \tag{6}$$

Introducing L_{CC} can bring the following benefits that stabilize the model's performance. First, since the input of the GraphSAGE Module is a linear combination of Target Sequence Embeddings and Context Samples, by limiting the Context Samples to the global minimum, the L_{CC} can make sure that the GraphSAGE Module dominates the training when backpropagating the L_{recon}. This ensures that the GraphSAGE module keeps being the central component of the pipeline, restricting the Transformer's strong trend of overfitting as a module with weak inductive bias. Second, since the Context Samples are sampled from a Gaussian distribution q learned by the Context VI Module, minimizing L_{CC} can constrain the standard deviation of q, preventing the model from identifying the major part of the input as noise and converging to suboptimal results. Third, the L_{CC} encourages the TCE Module to correct the inputs with the minimum possible corrections. This can be thought of as an Occam's razor-based heuristic. When a simple and a complex correction achieves similar results on a poorly sampled dataset, we will prefer the simpler one, thus reducing the overfitting.

The final loss Signal of the model pipeline is a linear combination of L_{recon}, L_{KL}, and L_{CC}:

$$L = L_{recon} + L_{KL} + L_{CC} \tag{7}$$

Table 1. Comparison of Datasets Included in this Study

Name	Sensor Type	Noise Level	P_{sup} Channels	Average F Length	Spatial Coverage Rate[1]	Missing rate[2]
SAQN	All fixed-location	High	8	200.31	12.30%	52.54%
ABO	All movable	Low	2	460.52	4.68%	0.38%
Marine	mixed	Pass quality inspection	5	339.62	97.96%	21.15%

1. How many grids have been observed at least once in the entire dataset 2. How many input cells are missing when expressed as dense input

4 Experiments

4.1 Experimental Setup

Datasets. We evaluate CESI on three publicly available real-world datasets: the SmartAQnet dataset (SAQN) [13], the NOAA Aircraft Based Observation dataset (ABO) [19], and the Copernicus In-situ Marine Observation dataset (Marine) [4]. Table 1 provides detailed dataset information.

The SAQN dataset is a typical fixed-location HWSN dataset that monitors urban air quality and meteorological conditions. It is characterized by a high missing rate and considerable noise due to deploying numerous low-cost sensors. Furthermore, its spatial coverage is limited as it relies exclusively on fixed-location sensors. In contrast, the ABO and Marine datasets reflect the trend of incorporating movable sensors in HWSN datasets for higher spatial coverage, which leads to more complex sensor topologies. The ABO dataset, which monitors meteorological parameters using sensors mounted on commercial aircraft, is distinguished by its low noise and extremely low missing rate. However, despite its larger number of observations in each Frame, the ABO dataset still exhibits limited spatial coverage as it is the only three-dimensional dataset included in our analysis. The Marine dataset, on the other hand, measures hydrological and meteorological parameters. Its use of a wide array of movable sensors results in high spatial coverage. This dataset also resembles a traditional dataset, given its relatively low missing data rate and the implementation of strict quality inspection processes. Experiments using the Marine dataset also provide an opportunity to evaluate the effectiveness of our model on more conventional datasets.

Baselines. We involve GraphSAGE [9] and Transformer [21] into baselines, as they are the base components of our model. From the GNN-based spatial interpolation models, we involve GAT [22], KSAGE [1], PE-SAGE [12], LSPE [6], and SPONGE [18]. From the attention-based spatial interpolation models, we involve SSIN [15], and SMACNP [2]. Experiment codes are provided in the additional materials.

Data Preprocessing. The SAQN dataset uses SmartAQnet data from January 1, 2017, to December 31, 2021. The time interval of the Frame is 1 h. The observed area is a rectangular area within 14 km north and east from 10.7992° E and 48.421° N. The target OP is PM10. Support OPs include PM2.5, temperature, relative humidity, air pressure, longitudinal wind speed, latitudinal wind speed, precipitation, and solar radiation.

For the ABO dataset, we selected all observations in this dataset from July 1, 2001, to April 1, 2004, located in the range of 74° W to 77° W, and 39° N to 42° N. The time interval of the Frame is 1 h. The target variable is air temperature, and the support variables include wind speed and wind direction.

For the Marine dataset, we selected all observations in this dataset from January 1, 1900, to December 31, 2010, located in the range of 36.0° W to 11.0° W, and 31.0° N to 56.0° N. The time interval of the Frame is 4 h. The target variable is water temperature, and the support variables include air temperature, air pressure, dew point, wind speed, and wind direction.

The following preprocessing steps are common to all the datasets:

- **Step 1**: Exclude outliers. In this step, we use the threshold method to exclude outliers that do not comply with physical laws. The preprocessing code provides further detail.
- **Step 2**: Split the Frames. We split the observations in the dataset into different Frames according to the time intervals mentioned above.
- **Step 3**: Spatial aggregation. We further partition the horizontal space into a 250 × 250 grid for each Frame. Then, we aggregate the readings with the same coordinates by averaging.
- **Step 4**: Filter the Frames. We only retain Frames that provide at least 5 nodes for training and one node for evaluation. For datasets that still have more than 20,000 Frames after filtering, we retain the 20,000 Frames with the latest timestamps.

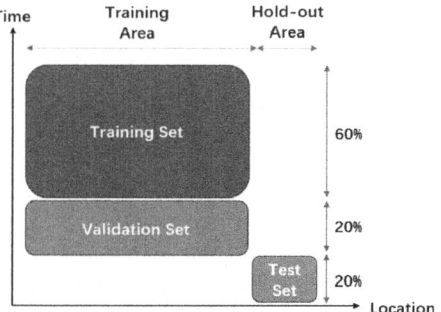

Fig. 4. Our strategy for dividing the dataset. With this strategy, we ensure that the models are tested only at times and locations that have never been seen during training and validation.

Evaluation Strategy. Figure 4 illustrates our strategy for dividing the dataset.

In the temporal dimension, we divide all the Frames into three parts according to their temporal order: 60%, 20%, and 20% each, which are used in the model's training, validation, and testing, respectively.

In the spatial dimension, we divided the study area into four equal parts by dividing the length and width of the horizontal area equally. We adopt the leave-one-area-out cross-validation method and, in turn, use four areas as holdout areas. The training and validation of the model are performed only with the label within the three non-hold-out regions, while the model is tested only with the label in the hold-out region. With the above evaluation strategy, we ensure that the models are tested only at times and locations that have never been seen during training and validation.

Further, test locations might be densely surrounded by other sensors, making it hard to evaluate whether the model performs well in the target locations that are very remote. Therefore, when testing the model, for each target location, in addition to testing with the complete Frame, we also use two other Frames that remove all nodes within 20 or 50 pixels by Manhattan distance of the target location, simulating the situation that target locations of different levels of remoteness.

As in other literature in the field, we choose the mean absolute error (MAE) and coefficient of determination (R^2) between the model output and the label as the metrics to evaluate the model performance. We first calculate the performance of four-fold leave-one-area-out cross-validations under each random seed and then calculate the mean and standard deviation of the results between different random seeds.

Environments. We conduct our experiments on an HPC cluster. Models that demand lower computational resources, including GCN, GraphSAGE, KCN, and PE-GNN, are trained on CPU nodes equipped with 20 Intel Xeon Gold 6230 CPUs and 192 GB of memory. Other models are trained on GPU nodes equipped with 20 Intel Xeon Gold 6230 CPUs, 192 GB of CPU memory, 2 NVIDIA Tesla V100 GPUs, and 64 GB of GPU memory.

The system used for all nodes is Red Hat Enterprise Linux (RHEL) 8.4. The training environment is based on Python 3.10.12, Pytorch 2.1.0 + CUDA 12.1, Pytorch-geometric 2.4.0, DGL 2.2.1, Numpy 1.26.1, Pandas 2.1.1, Scikit-learn 1.3.1, and Scipy 1.11.3.

4.2 Overall Performance

After random searches on hyperparameters, each model was evaluated with four-fold leave-one-area-out cross-validations and five random seeds (1, 2, 3, 4, and 5). Table 2 shows the overall performance.

Q1: Which model demonstrates the best overall performance? A1: CESI achieves the best average MAE and R^2 on all datasets. On the ABO dataset, Transformer and SMACNP rank second and third, respectively, while Transformer and SSIN occupy these positions on the Marine dataset. On the SAQN dataset, however, KSAGE and GraphSAGE take second and third place, as the above models experience significant degradation. In conclusion, CESI

Table 2. Overall Result of all models. Bold indicates the best performer, underline indicates the second place

Model	ABO		SAQN		Marine	
Metrics	MAE	R^2	MAE	R^2	MAE	R^2
GraphSAGE	10.293 ± 0.044	0.451 ± 0.004	5.863 ± 0.048	<u>0.317 ± 0.009</u>	1.993 ± 0.038	0.631 ± 0.012
Transformer	<u>1.811 ± 0.639</u>	<u>0.972 ± 0.025</u>	6.041 ± 0.437	0.184 ± 0.104	<u>0.971 ± 0.144</u>	<u>0.903 ± 0.027</u>
KSAGE	14.268 ± 0.021	0.012 ± 0.002	<u>5.535 ± 0.048</u>	0.301 ± 0.010	3.128 ± 0.018	0.198 ± 0.007
PE-SAGE	3.302 ± 0.258	0.927 ± 0.008	6.115 ± 0.243	0.217 ± 0.047	1.315 ± 0.042	0.835 ± 0.011
LSPE	13.844 ± 0.424	-0.390 ± 0.409	6.205 ± 0.115	0.171 ± 0.030	1.660 ± 0.084	0.721 ± 0.026
SPONGE	3.918 ± 0.296	0.913 ± 0.013	6.388 ± 0.138	0.249 ± 0.019	1.593 ± 0.071	0.768 ± 0.023
SSIN	18.800 ± 0.469	-0.420 ± 0.062	6.197 ± 0.084	0.167 ± 0.034	1.035 ± 0.052	0.893 ± 0.014
SMACNP	3.241 ± 0.281	0.884 ± 0.025	6.237 ± 0.337	0.201 ± 0.062	1.741 ± 0.044	0.287 ± 0.127
CESI	**1.426 ± 0.040**	**0.987 ± 0.001**	**5.362 ± 0.110**	**0.334 ± 0.008**	**0.944 ± 0.036**	**0.910 ± 0.009**

consistently outperforms all baselines across all three datasets, highlighting its adaptability.

Q2: Is sparse input a beneficial choice for spatial interpolation? A2: Sparse input is beneficial but presents challenges. On ABO and Marine datasets, even the Vanilla Transformer surpasses dense input baselines on average performance. However, sparse input models are more sensitive to noise and bias in lower-quality datasets, such as the Transformer failure on the SAQN dataset, and its performance is volatile on all the datasets. CESI effectively addresses this challenge, with MAE standard deviations 93.7%, 74.8%, and 75.0% lower than Transformer on ABO, SAQN, and Marine datasets, respectively. CESI's stability is competitive even against dense input models.

Q3: Why do many models degrade performance on the SAQN dataset? A3: First, the SAQN dataset only contains fixed-location sensors, coupled with a low spatial coverage rate, resulting in a high location-related bias in the dataset. Models that employ learnable location-based encodings (e.g., PE-SAGE, LSPE, SPONGE, SSIN) are particularly susceptible to these biases, leading to significant performance degradation. Second, the SAQN dataset has the highest heterogeneity and noise level. Models lacking stable inductive bias (Transformer and SMACNP) tend to overfit the noise, resulting in volatile performances. Our model, on the contrary, successfully overcomes these challenges.

Q4: Why is the performance on the ABO dataset so polarized? A4: Models like GraphSAGE, KSAGE, and SSIN use Euclidean distance-based heuristics for encoding spatial relationships, and unlike PE-SAGE and CESI, they do not incorporate additional location-based embeddings. The hidden inductive bias of such heuristics is the spatial isotropy of the Euclidean distance. However, on the ABO dataset, the Target Property (air temperature) has an evident stratification along the altitude dimension. This reminds us again that we should be cautious when introducing inductive bias into model design. When the inductive bias of the model is consistent with the actual situation of the dataset, we can learn a good model with less and worse data. However, when the model's inductive bias conflicts with the dataset's actual situation, the model's performance will be negatively affected.

4.3 Ablation Study

Table 3. Result of Ablation Study. Bold indicates the best performer, underline indicates the second place

Model	ABO		SAQN		Marine	
Metrics	MAE	R^2	MAE	R^2	MAE	R^2
CESI	**1.426 ± 0.040**	**0.987 ± 0.001**	**5.362 ± 0.110**	**0.334 ± 0.008**	0.944 ± 0.036	0.910 ± 0.009
CESI w/o L_{KL}	2.020 ± 0.187	0.972 ± 0.005	6.018 ± 0.156	0.170 ± 0.030	0.900 ± 0.025	0.915 ± 0.008
CESI w/o L_{CC}	<u>1.489 ± 0.045</u>	<u>0.986 ± 0.001</u>	6.044 ± 0.500	<u>0.214 ± 0.108</u>	0.980 ± 0.019	0.896 ± 0.008
CESI Null	2.285 ± 0.064	0.968 ± 0.002	8.548 ± 1.170	-0.672 ± 0.654	**0.865 ± 0.031**	0.922 ± 0.005

We use the following ablation models to study the effectiveness of each module: CESI w/o L_{KL} model removes the probabilistic encoding and its associated L_{KL}, CESI w/o L_{CC} model removes the Context Correction Loss L_{CC}, and CESI Null model simultaneously removes the both. All experiment settings are the same as above. Table 3 shows the results of the ablation study.

On the ABO dataset, both modules contribute to performance improvement. The main contribution comes from probabilistic encoding, while L_{CC} further refines the performance. On the SAQN dataset, the contribution on average MAE from both modules is roughly the same, and L_{CC} provides more stability improvement than probabilistic encoding.

However, our modules had a slight adverse effect on the Marine dataset. The probabilistic encoding and L_{CC} are designed to address bias and noise in datasets. However, these occurred less in the Marine dataset. First, the dataset has undergone strict quality checks, making it generally noise-free. Second, it boasts exceptionally high spatial coverage (up to 97.96%), minimizing location-related bias. This led to misattributions of our modules, where the probabilistic encoding mistakenly interpreted some genuine correlations as noise, resulting in the significant performance drop of CESI w/o L_{CC}. From the performance of CESI and CESI w/o L_{KL}, we observed that L_{CC} effectively served its intended purpose of constraining such misattributions yet did not fully mitigate the performance decline. Nevertheless, as the overall results demonstrated, this did not prevent the model from achieving state-of-the-art performance. This highlights that our model's competitive edge relies not solely on exploiting flawed datasets but also on learning fine-grained observation-level correlations.

We conducted additional experiments on robustness to missing rates and noise using the Marine dataset to validate our explanation.

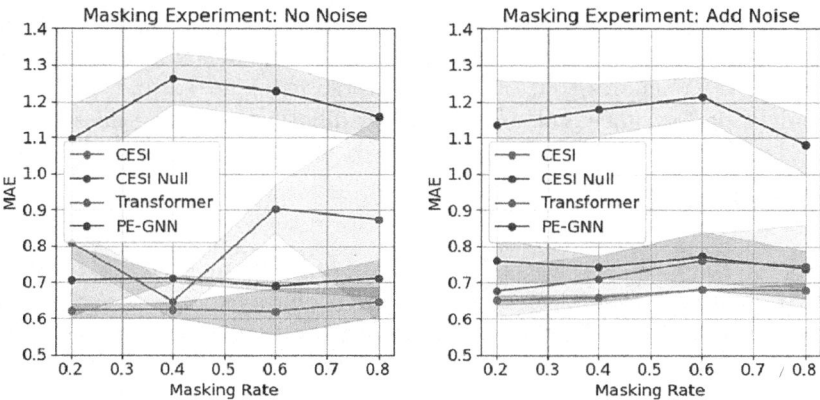

Fig. 5. Result of Robustness Experiment, the shaded area marks the standard deviation

4.4 Experiments on Robustness

Table 4. Result of Robustness Experiment. Bold indicates the best performer, underline indicates the second place

Masking Rate	20%		40%		60%		80%	
Metrics	MAE	R^2	MAE	R^2	MAE	R^2	MAE	R^2
Without additional noise								
CESI	**0.622 ± 0.019**	**0.874 ± 0.005**	**0.623 ± 0.021**	**0.878 ± 0.006**	**0.619 ± 0.064**	**0.878 ± 0.026**	**0.645 ± 0.041**	**0.872 ± 0.017**
CESI Null	0.705 ± 0.097	0.850 ± 0.040	0.710 ± 0.009	0.843 ± 0.005	0.690 ± 0.014	0.857 ± 0.008	0.711 ± 0.053	0.848 ± 0.019
Transformer	0.809 ± 0.040	0.797 ± 0.013	0.646 ± 0.048	0.864 ± 0.025	0.903 ± 0.067	0.722 ± 0.042	0.874 ± 0.281	0.690 ± 0.234
PE-GNN	1.095 ± 0.094	0.631 ± 0.066	1.263 ± 0.071	0.508 ± 0.054	1.228 ± 0.075	0.525 ± 0.067	1.158 ± 0.065	0.589 ± 0.045
With additional noise								
CESI	**0.651 ± 0.012**	**0.869 ± 0.003**	**0.658 ± 0.009**	**0.867 ± 0.001**	**0.679 ± 0.001**	**0.862 ± 0.001**	**0.678 ± 0.021**	**0.856 ± 0.004**
CESI Null	0.760 ± 0.063	0.834 ± 0.025	0.742 ± 0.031	0.840 ± 0.012	0.771 ± 0.071	0.829 ± 0.028	0.737 ± 0.051	0.841 ± 0.018
Transformer	0.676 ± 0.070	0.859 ± 0.028	0.709 ± 0.069	0.845 ± 0.032	0.761 ± 0.076	0.823 ± 0.033	0.745 ± 0.114	0.826 ± 0.051
PE-GNN	1.134 ± 0.124	0.603 ± 0.089	1.178 ± 0.073	0.594 ± 0.049	1.212 ± 0.057	0.559 ± 0.057	1.080 ± 0.080	0.651 ± 0.047

In the robustness experiment, we randomly mask 20%, 40%, 60%, and 80% of the observations from each Frame in the Marine Dataset to increase its missing rate, and we randomly add multiple Gaussian noise with different standard deviations to varying proportions of data. Then, we train CESI, CESI Null, Transformer, and PE-GNN models on these datasets. We train with random seeds 1, 2, and 3 for each model, respectively. The results are summarized in Table 4 and Fig. 5.

Obviously, (1). the CESI model performs best in all experiments. (2). Although we added noise with different standard deviations to different proportions of data, the noise didn't significantly affect the performance of the CESI model. Since the Gaussian noise added is consistent with the preset of probabilistic encoding, after getting rid of the misattribution, the stability of the model is even improved. (3). Dense input models represented by PE-GNN are hardly affected by the missing rate and noise because the model and data augmentation provide very stable inductive biases. However, as a price, it sacrifices the ability to discover fine-grained correlations, so the overall performance is the worst.

The above concludes that our design works as expected and can maintain the model's performance and stability under different noise and missing rates.

5 Conclusion

We propose the CESI Model for HWSN datasets. Our model directly takes the narrow format sparse input and learns their correlations. Since HWSN datasets usually exhibit small-scale, low spatial sampling rates and considerable noise, we use probabilistic encoding and a self-supervision signal named Context Correction Loss to extract encodings conducive to better generalizing to coordinates not present in the training set. As a result, we effectively improve the model's performance and stability. Experiments across several publicly available real-world HWSN datasets with different characteristics show the CESI Model holds significant potential for broader applications, such as enhancing data-driven decision-making in environmental monitoring, urban planning, and other domains reliant on sparse spatial data.

Acknowledgments. We thank the Helmholtz European Partnership for Technological Advancement (HEPTA) for supporting this study. The state of Baden-Württemberg also supported this work through bwHPC.

References

1. Appleby, G., Liu, L., Liu, L.P.: Kriging convolutional networks. In: Proceedings of the AAAI Conference on Artificial Intelligence, vol. 34, pp. 3187–3194 (2020)
2. Bao, L.L., Zhang, J.S., Zhang, C.X.: Spatial multi-attention conditional neural processes. Neural Netw. **173**, 106201 (2024)
3. Budde, M., et al.: Potential and limitations of the low-cost sds011 particle sensor for monitoring urban air quality. ProScience **5**(6), 12 (2018)
4. CDS: Global marine surface meteorological variables from 1851 to 2010 from comprehensive in-situ observations. Copernicus Climate Change Service (C3S) Climate Data Store (CDS) (2021), https://cds.climate.copernicus.eu/cdsapp#!/dataset/10.24381/cds.27f643d7, https://doi.org/10.24381/cds.27f643d7
5. Cui, T., Pagendam, D., Gilfedder, M.: Gaussian process machine learning and kriging for groundwater salinity interpolation. Environ. Modell. Softw. **144**, 105170 (2021)
6. Dwivedi, V.P., Luu, A.T., Laurent, T., Bengio, Y., Bresson, X.: Graph neural networks with learnable structural and positional representations. In: International Conference on Learning Representations (2022). https://openreview.net/forum?id=wTTjnvGphYj
7. Fan, H., Cheng, S., de Nazelle, A.J., Arcucci, R.: An efficient vit-based spatial interpolation learner for field reconstruction. In: International Conference on Computational Science, pp. 430–437. Springer (2023)

8. Feng, Y., et al.: Spatiotemporal informer: a new approach based on spatiotemporal embedding and attention for air quality forecasting. Environ. Pollut. **336**, 122402 (2023)
9. Hamilton, W., Ying, Z., Leskovec, J.: Inductive representation learning on large graphs. In: Advances in Neural Information Processing Systems, vol. 30 (2017)
10. Hu, J., Liang, Y., Fan, Z., Chen, H., Zheng, Y., Zimmermann, R.: Graph neural processes for spatio-temporal extrapolation. arXiv preprint arXiv:2305.18719 (2023)
11. Kipf, T.N., Welling, M.: Semi-supervised classification with graph convolutional networks. arXiv preprint arXiv:1609.02907 (2016)
12. Klemmer, K., Safir, N.S., Neill, D.B.: Positional encoder graph neural networks for geographic data. In: International Conference on Artificial Intelligence and Statistics, pp. 1379–1389. PMLR (2023)
13. Li, C., et al.: Smartaqnet 2020: a new open urban air quality dataset from heterogeneous pm sensors. Proscience **8** (2022)
14. Li, J.J., Faltings, B., Saukh, O., Hasenfratz, D., Beutel, J.: Sensing the air we breathe—the opensense zurich dataset. In: Proceedings of the AAAI Conference on Artificial Intelligence, vol. 26, pp. 323–325 (2012)
15. Li, J., Shen, Y., Chen, L., Ng, C.W.W.: SSIN: self-supervised learning for rainfall spatial interpolation. Proc. ACM Manage. Data **1**(2), 1–21 (2023)
16. Liang, S., et al.: Ogc sensorthings api part 1: Sensing version 1.1. In: Open geospatial consortium (2021)
17. Lucas, M.P., et al.: Optimizing automated kriging to improve spatial interpolation of monthly rainfall over complex terrain. J. Hydrometeorol. **23**(4), 561–572 (2022)
18. Njifon, M.A., Schuhmacher, D.: Graph convolutional networks for spatial interpolation of correlated data. Spatial Stat. **60**, 100822 (2024)
19. NOAA: Aircraft based observation (abo) dataset (2023). https://madis.ncep.noaa.gov/madis_acars.shtml
20. Petrova-Antonova, D., Jelyazkov, J., Pavlova, I.: Air quality monitoring platform with multiple data source support. Energy Sources, Part A: Recovery, Utilization, and Environmental Effects pp. 1–17 (2021)
21. Vaswani, A., et al.: Attention is all you need. In: Advances in Neural Information Processing Systems, vol. 30 (2017)
22. Veličković, P., Cucurull, G., Casanova, A., Romero, A., Lio, P., Bengio, Y.: Graph attention networks. arXiv preprint arXiv:1710.10903 (2017)
23. Yu, M., Masrur, A., Blaszczak-Boxe, C.: Predicting hourly pm2.5 concentrations in wildfire-prone areas using a spatiotemporal transformer model. Sci. Total Environ. **860**, 160446 (2023)

Enhancing Traffic Accident Classifications: Application of NLP Methods for City Safety

Enes Özeren[1], Alexander Ulbrich[1], Sascha Filimon[2], David Rügamer[1,3], and Andreas Bender[1,3](✉)

[1] Department of Statistics, LMU Munich, Munich, Germany
{enes.oezeren,a.ulbrich}@campus.lmu.de
[2] City of Munich, Munich, Germany
[3] Munich Center for Machine Learning (MCML), Munich, Germany
andreas.bender@stat.uni-muenchen.de

Abstract. A comprehensive understanding of traffic accidents is essential for improving city safety and informing policy decisions. In this study, we analyze traffic incidents in Munich to identify patterns and characteristics that distinguish different types of accidents. The dataset consists of both structured tabular features, such as location, time, and weather conditions, as well as unstructured free-text descriptions detailing the circumstances of each accident. Each incident is categorized into one of seven predefined classes. To assess the reliability of these labels, we apply NLP methods, including topic modeling and few-shot learning, which reveal inconsistencies in the labeling process. These findings highlight potential ambiguities in accident classification and motivate a refined predictive approach. Building on these insights, we develop a classification model that achieves high accuracy in assigning accidents to their respective categories. Our results demonstrate that textual descriptions contain the most informative features for classification, while the inclusion of tabular data provides only marginal improvements. These findings emphasize the critical role of free-text data in accident analysis and highlight the potential of transformer-based models in improving classification reliability.

Keywords: Few-Shot Learning · Topic Modeling · City Safety

1 Introduction

Traffic accidents pose a substantial risk to human life and incur high economic costs. Understanding their underlying causes and patterns is essential - not only to mitigate their consequences but also to develop effective preemptive strategies in the context of city safety and city planning. Numerous studies have investigated various aspects of traffic accidents, from identifying their root causes to

E. Özeren and A. Ulbrich—Contributed equally to this work.

assessing their severity using data analysis techniques [6,14,19,27]. The foundation of such studies is the availability of high-quality accident data. However, real-world accident records are often affected by inconsistencies and human error during data collection. These issues can lead to inaccuracies in how accidents are categorized, potentially obscuring important insights and limiting the effectiveness of data-driven safety measures.

Table 1. Classification of accidents and their explanations.

Code	Classification	Explanation
A1	Driving Accident	Loss of control of vehicle.
A2	Turning / Crossing Accid.	Conflict between turning vehicle and one moving in parallel direction.
A3	Turning Accident	Conflict betw. (turning) vehicle and another moving perpendicularly.
A4	Crossing Accident	Conflict between vehicle and crossing pedestrian.
A5	Stationary Accident	Conflict where at least one party must be stationary/parking.
A6	Longitudinal Accident	Conflict between parties moving in parallel, none of above applicable.
A7	Other Accident	None of the above applicable.

In the city of Munich, Germany, policemen record accident information at the location of the incident, which includes general information like date, time and location, person-specific characteristics (age, drug involvement, injury severity) as well as free-text description of the events leading up to the incident. The specific dataset used in this study is comprised of 105,217 unique traffic accidents recorded between 01.01.2017 and 31.12.2022, of which 102,569 contain free-text. Additionally, on-site, the policemen classify the accidents into one of seven distinct accident types (A1 – A7), listed in Table 1. This is done by (mentally) matching the course of events to the definition of the respective accident types. In order to avoid confusion later on, we define the following terms:

- *label definition*: A textual definition for each of the seven accident types (A1 - A7).
- *example text* or *accident description*: The free-text description of the accident recorded by the policemen on-site.
- *human label*: The label (A1 - A7) assigned to an accident on-site by the policemen.
- *ground truth*: 236 additional labels created by expert labelers for a small subset of accidents.

In our data set, almost 50% of the human labels fall within the fallback category A7. Given the high proportion of accidents in this category, a high misclassification rate is suspected. This is further supported by comparison to the city of Berlin, where only 25% of accidents fall into this fallback category. While there may be inherent differences between the two cities, the large proportion of accidents in the fallback category (A7) indicates a potentially high amount of mislabeling.

In this work, we aim to gain insights into the reasons for mislabeling and to improve the current classification system. This could lead to the implementation of better and more accurate safety measures. To this end, we utilize multimodal data, comprising free-text incident descriptions as well as tabular data.

Using advanced Natural Language Processing (NLP) techniques that have been successfully applied in various domains, including medical records, legal documents, and police reports [8,20,28], we gain insights about missclassification by applying transformer-based methods. Furthermore, we develop a classification model that achieves high accuracy in correctly assigning accidents. We make the code publicly available.[1]

2 Related Work

2.1 Traffic Accident Analysis

With the growing popularity of NLP methods, recent research has increasingly explored their application in accident data analysis [14,19,27]. While structured data has been extensively studied (see, e.g., [6,12]), the use of unstructured free-text features has gained traction only in recent years. Free-text descriptions can encode nuanced information that structured numerical data cannot fully capture, offering deeper contextual insights [27]. Early approaches to leveraging free-text descriptions often relied on simple word-count-based methods, such as [14], where text features were extracted based on keyword frequencies. Beyond traffic accidents, similar methods have been applied in legal text analysis. For instance, [13] achieved strong results using LSTMs for petition analysis and suggested exploring transformer-based methods as a next step. Recent research has increasingly focused on using word embeddings to capture richer semantic information. In this context, [19] employ BERT to incorporate free-text accident descriptions, demonstrating promising performance in a classification setting. Their findings suggest that further integrating free-text features could unlock significant potential, as such descriptions are widely used across different countries [19]. Their work focuses on extracting specific information from the accident descriptions and to compare classical and modern NLP approaches for classification, assuming the human labels to represent ground truth. In contrast, we investigate potential mislabeling of accident types and use multiple data modalities for classification compared to text-based inputs only.

2.2 Large Language Models

The Transformer architecture, proposed in 2017 for machine translation tasks [24], quickly became the dominant paradigm in the NLP domain [15]. The original design consists of an encoder-decoder structure, but both components are also independently used. While encoder-only models are utilized primarily for

---

[1] https://github.com/enesozeren/enhancing-traffic-accident-classifications.

learning text representations [3,4], encoder-decoder and decoder-only models are employed for text generation tasks [16,17].

These models, often referred to as Large Language Models (LLMs), have a large number of parameters and are trained on massive text corpora [2–4,16,22]. They can be fine-tuned for specific tasks, allowing for domain adaptation and improved performance [4,16]. Alternatively, techniques such as few-shot and chain-of-thought prompting have enabled the application of these models with good performance without requiring any additional parameter updating [2,25]. In this project, we utilized both approaches, few-shot classification for creating a second opinion about accident categories, and also fine-tuning for predictive modeling.

2.3 Topic Modeling

Topic models are designed to extract semantic themes from large volumes of unstructured text [1]. Traditional approaches such as latent dirichlet allocation (LDA) and non-negative matrix factorization (NMF) have been widely used for topic modeling. However, their performance is limited by a lack of semantic understanding, as they rely solely on bag-of-words representations and fail to capture contextual information [5]. Therefore, novel methods incorporating text-embeddings have been increasingly applied to topic modeling. In [5], BERTopic is proposed, a framework to perform topic modeling by creating dense vector representations of each document, which are then used for clustering. The framework makes use of Sentence-BERT [18], a time-efficient alternative of BERT [4] enabling to compare embeddings with cosine similarity. The resulting embeddings are dimensionally reduced and clustered. Finally, text representations for each cluster are chosen by modifying the TF-IDF approach proposed by ([7]) in a way that all documents within one cluster are treated as a single document [5]. This allows to extract class-related representative keywords. In our study, topic modeling is used to identify relevant topics within misclassified accidents.

3 Semantic Clustering

To investigate potential mislabeling, we first evaluate what semantic characteristics the free-text descriptions of accidents in a certain category show. This enables us to discover patterns within each accident type, notably which topics show up frequently within the fallback category A7.

3.1 Methods

In order to perform semantic clustering, we apply BERTopic [5] to extract topics present in the text corpus. Clustering is performed in an unsupervised way using the free-text accident descriptions only and without taking into account their human labels (A1-A7).

The first step is to convert all texts into dense vector representations. While BERTopic allows for direct usage without specifying a specific model, it is also possible to encode the text independently and pass the resulting vectors as an additional argument. One requirement for a suitable Sentence-Transformer is a context window of at least 2000 tokens, as this is the maximal text length in the dataset. Furthermore, the model is required to have German capabilities. For the study and given the two requirements, jiina-embeddings-v3 [21] is chosen from the MTEB benchmark ranking [11]. The model performs mean-pooling by default for combining all token-vectors into a single vector for each text.

Since the resulting embedding-vectors are 1024-dimensional, their dimensionality can be reduced. UMAP has shown to be able to reduce the amount of dimensions while maintaining more of the global structure than competing methods like t-SNE or PCA [10]. Four hyper-parameters have to be specified when using UMAP [10]. *Number of dimensions* controls the number of dimensions the reduced vector should have. *Number of neighbors* influences the locality of approximation patterns. If the parameter is increased, more global structures will be captured. In the context of this study, if one would be interested in many fine-grained topics, *number of neighbors* can be decreased. *Minimal distance* is mainly important for plotting since it controls how densely points can be packed together. It can be increased to avoid overplotting.

Next, the reduced embedding vectors can be clustered. For the study HDBSCAN is used, an extension of DBSCAN which allows for capturing clusters with varying densities [9]. As a hyper-parameter, a minimal cluster size can be fixed. Finally, for each cluster, representations have to be generated. The goal is to find words which are relevant for certain clusters. In [5] it is proposed to employ a variation of TF-IDF, such that documents within each cluster are considered as single documents, giving rise to the c-TF-IDF approach.

$$W_{t,c} = \text{tf}_{t,c} \cdot \log\left(1 + \frac{\mu}{\text{tf}_t}\right) \quad (1)$$

Here the term frequency $\text{tf}_{t,c}$ indicates the frequency of word t in cluster c. μ is the average number of words per class while tf_t is the frequency of term t across all classes. $W_{t,c}$ can therefore be interpreted as an estimated importance score for word t within class c. It needs to be stressed that this formula does not take into account word embeddings, but is only based on word frequencies. Therefore it might fail to accurately capture the true semantic meaning of each extracted topic [5].

3.2 Results

Due to computational constraints, we limited our analysis to a random subset of 50,000 accident descriptions. The topic model extracts 18 different topics, listed in Table 2. It can be seen that multiple topics about parking accidents have been extracted. Despite looking similar according to representative documents and the selected c-TF-IDF representations, different nuances are captured within some of those topics. To give one example, "Parking 3" has a relatively high cosine similarity to the topic "Intox." which is about accidents related to drug influence. Considerations like this can give an idea of what different subtleties the seemingly identical topics show.

Table 2. Topics extracted by BERTopic (outliers excluded). Topic (column 1) shows subjectively labeled topic names, based on representative documents and the extracted c-TF-IDF terms for better readability. Topics are ordered in descending order with regards to their counts (column 2), i.e., the number of observations per topic. The third column includes the content of each topic.

Topic	Count	Content
Parking 1	13,846	Parking accidents
Bicycle	8,293	Bike accidents, falling from bikes
Crossroad/Crash	4,376	Accidents mostly in crossroads, many with crashes
Parking 2	2,374	Parking accidents
Parking 3	2,212	Parking accidents
Parking 4	1,457	Parking accidents
Truck	1,242	Truck accidents, mostly damaging parked vehicles
Parking 5	999	Parking accidents, damaged side mirrors
Bus	828	Bus accidents
Damaged city obj.	645	Damaged objects like traffic lights, fences or traffic signs
Scooter	540	Scooter- and motorcycle accidents
Landsbergerstr.	422	Accidents in spacial proximity to Landsbergerstreet
Schleißheimerstr.	418	Accidents in spacial proximity to Schleißheimerstreet
Intox.	399	Accidents connected to drug influence
Fürstenriederstr.	394	Accidents in spacial proximity to Fürstenriederstreet
Dachauerstr.	366	Accidents in spacial proximity to Dachauerstreet
Parking 6	305	Parking accidents
Tram	301	Tram accidents

As one objective of the study is to understand what kind of accidents tend to get the fallback label A7 (other accident), the resulting topics can now be compared to the human labels. To do this, the text corpus is clustered in two different ways:

1. The texts are divided as suggested by the topic model, giving rise to 18 clusters.
2. The texts are divided as suggested by the human labels, i.e., the class assignment to one of the 7 categories is used as cluster indicator. This yields 7 clusters (A1 – A7).

Both clustering schemes are used in the following way. After encoding all texts with the same model used for clustering, representative embedding vectors are generated by applying mean-pooling within each cluster defined above. After this, their cosine similarity can be calculated and summarized as depicted in Fig. 1.

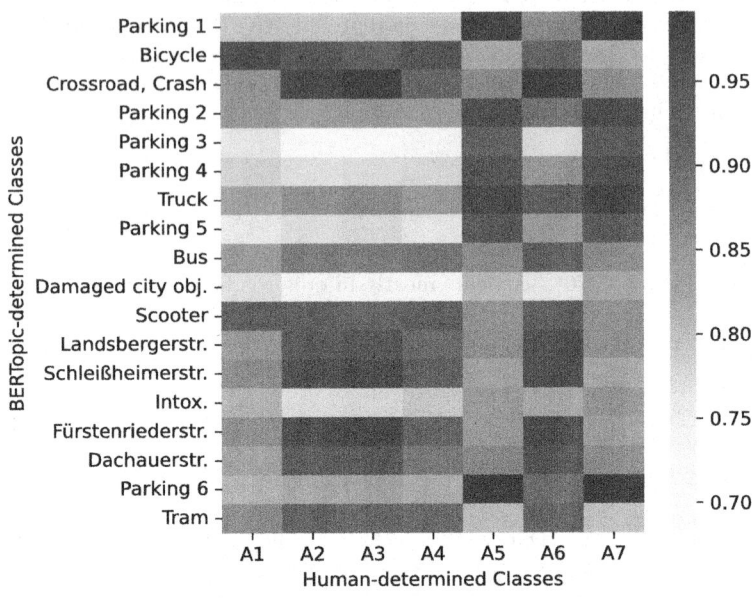

Fig. 1. Cosine similarity between BERTopic-generated and human-determined clusters.

First, we note that the lowest cosine similarity value is around 0.7, indicating generally high similarity, as this measure ranges up to a maximum of 1. This might be due to the fact that all texts are similar in the way that they all deal with traffic accidents. What can also be seen, for instance, is a high similarity between accident type A1 (driving accident), and the bicycle topic from the topic model (column 1). In fact, this accident type represents the class among all 7 with the highest proportion of bikes involved. Looking at column five, which includes accident type A5 (stationary accidents), a relatively high similarity to all six extracted parking topics is visible. Finally, column seven, which represents the fallback category A7 (other accidents) shows almost exactly the same color pattern as column five. In other words, accidents labeled as "other accident" seem to be similar to what our topic model identifies as parking accidents.

4 Classification with Few-Shot Prompting

In this section, labels are generated based on few-shot prompting techniques, designed to mimic the human labeling process in that it matches an accident description to the label definition of an accident type. The results are compared to the human labels, revealing potential anomalies in the labeling behavior.

4.1 Methods

Few-shot prompting is performed by conditioning the LLM on a given task description and a small set of examples to solve a task [2]. This approach has been proven to work better than zero-shot prompting, which relies only on task description without examples [2]. Unlike fine-tuning, few-shot prompting does not involve updating model parameters and a small number of examples (typically 2–10) is sufficient for effective task adaptation. This makes it more efficient than fine-tuning, which generally requires hundreds or even thousands of labeled examples for language tasks.

To apply few-shot prompting for our accident classification, a suitable LLM is selected based on three requirements. First, the model should be open-source to ensure it can process confidential data locally. Second, it needs to have strong proficiency in German, as all our text data is in German. Lastly, a technical requirement is that the model should run on available hardware (two Nvidia RTX A6000 GPUs with 48 GB memory in each). Based on these criteria, we choose the Gemma-2-27B-Instruct model by Google [22] as it meets our requirements and demonstrated strong performance in five widely used German language benchmarks [23].

4.2 Results

For our analyses, we use the label definitions that provide a high-level, representative description of each accident type and select six exemplary accident descriptions (with verified labels) for each non-fallback accident type (categories A1 to A6) from our data set. We intentionally exclude an example for accident type A7, which is the fallback category, to prevent the model from becoming biased towards a specific instance of category A7 (e.g., an accident involving a deer). We also refrained from including multiple examples per accident type to maintain a manageable prompt length, given hardware constraints (two Nvidia RTX A6000 GPUs). This decision was necessary to keep the inference time feasible for classifying all the accidents in the dataset, which already required approximately 24 h with our current setup. The (shortened) prompt is given in Fig. 2.

We apply the few-shot prompting for each accident description individually using the Gemma model and compare the results with human labels, as shown in Fig. 3. Overall, 44% of the LLM few-shot labels match the human labels. The anti-diagonal indicates a high agreement ratio for most accident types, but the large bubbles outside of the diagonal serve as an important signal for deeper analysis.

There are three bubbles larger than 20% outside the anti-diagonal in Fig. 3. The first case represents 49% of accidents labeled as type A2 by humans but classified as type A3 by LLM few-shot approach. Since A2 and A3 accident types are

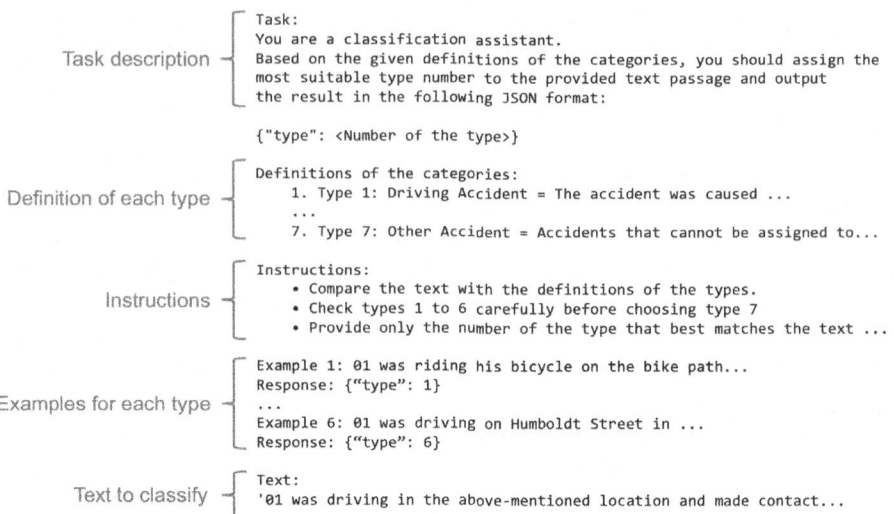

Fig. 2. Few-shot prompt for classifying accidents. Some components of the prompt shortened for illustration. The last part (text to classify) is changed for each accident text and inference is performed with the Gemma-2-27B-Instruct model. This is the translated English version; the original prompt is in German since accident texts are also in German.

both variations of turning accidents with a small difference (the driving direction of vehicles), we observe that LLM confused them easily. Upon reviewing examples, we find that humans could distinguish these cases more accurately than the LLM few-shot approach, potentially because they have a physical view of the accident scene which is not represented accurately in the textual description. The second case represents 21% of accidents labeled as type A6 (longitudinal accident) by humans but classified as type A3 (turning/crossing accident) by the LLM few-shot approach. Similar to the first case, human judgment is more reliable as they can interpret the temporal nature of events, whereas the LLM misclassifies those longitudinal accidents occurring just after turning maneuvers.

The third and most notable case is where 69% of accidents labeled as A7 (other accidents) by humans are classified as A5 (stationary accident) by the LLM. This case accounts for 34% of all traffic accidents. We observe that these accidents consistently contain parking-related keywords such as 'garage', 'parking', etc., as well as misspelled variations of them, indicating that they are related to damaged parked vehicles (which is in line with our findings from Sect. 4.2). This finding helps reduce uncertainty about accident characteristics in the fallback category A7. Before, 49% of all accidents in Munich fell into the fallback category, "Other accident (A7)", meaning their specific nature is unknown. Our analysis reveals that most of these accidents involve damages to parked vehicles. As a result, the proportion of accidents of unknown nature can be reduced substantially. This has practical implications. Only accidents of a known nature can be counteracted by city planning. For example, if an accident of types A1-A6 occurs frequently within a specific time span and location, countermeasures (e.g., traffic signs, etc.) can be implemented. For the fallback-category, this is not the case, as accidents could be of heterogeneous nature. However, our analysis helps to identify a large proportion of those as parking related, which can be mitigated accordingly.

5 Predictive Modeling

In this section, we describe our approach to building predictive models for accident classification. Given the potential for mislabeling in the training data, we explore different strategies for constructing training sets to improve label quality. Since both tabular and text data are available, we investigate these modalities individually and in combination to assess their contributions to predictive performance. Finally, we evaluate the models on an expert-labeled, ground-truth test set to provide a reliable assessment of their accuracy.

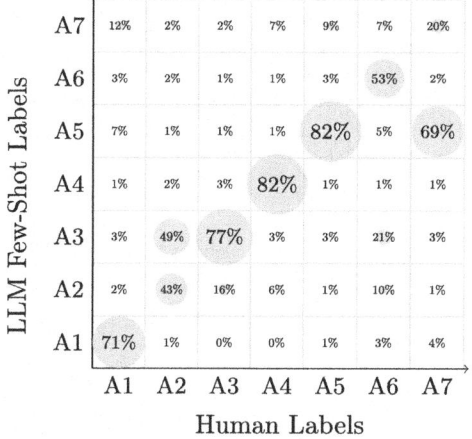

Fig. 3. Distribution of LLM few-shot labels vs. human labels. Each column sums to 100%, and bubble sizes correspond to the intersection ratio between LLM few-shot and human labels. The anti-diagonal represents the agreement ratio between the two.

5.1 Methods

Evaluation Strategy.

Training Set. One of the key motivations of this study is to detect mislabeled data. Therefore, relying solely on human labels is not ideal for this purpose. Instead, we explore two approaches to construct the training set, as illustrated in Fig. 4. The main objective is to select accident labels that are more likely to be correct. To achieve this, we compare human labels with those generated by an LLM using a few-shot approach (explained in Sect. 4).

Our first strategy assumes that all human-labeled instances for accident types A1–A6 are correct, while for A7, only labels agreed upon by both humans and the LLM are considered valid. This approach results in approximately 62,000 training labels, which we refer to as presumably low-quality labels since the assumption about human labels being entirely correct is relatively weak. The second strategy is more conservative, considering only those labels where both the human annotators and the LLM agree. This produces a smaller but more reliable set of approximately 45,000 labels, which we refer to as presumably high-quality labels.

We train supervised models using both training sets and compare their performance to assess the impact of label quality on model accuracy.

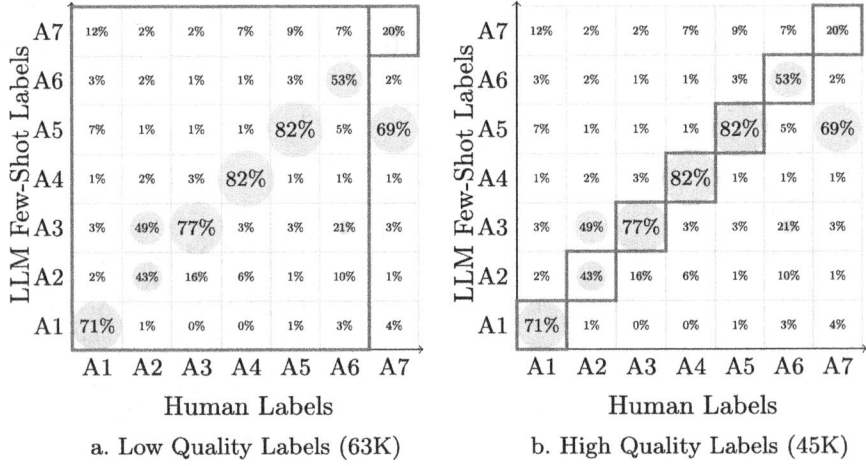

Fig. 4. Two strategies for constructing the training set. The accidents used to create the training set are highlighted in red. (a) Assuming all human-labeled instances for types A1–A6 are correct, while for type A7, only labels agreed upon by both humans and the LLM few-shot approach are considered correct. Due to the weaker assumption in this approach, we name these 62K labels as low-quality. (b) Considering only labels where both humans and the LLM few-shot approach agree as correct, resulting in 45K high-quality labels. (Color figure online)

Test Set. To ensure reliable evaluation of model performances, we ask domain specialists from the city of Munich to carefully label 236 traffic accidents. We use these expert-labeled examples as our test set to report results.

Models and Training Details.

MLP Model. Without using any text data, we employ a multi-layer perceptron (MLP) model to predict accident types based solely on tabular data. The model consists of feed-forward layers with skip connections and layer normalization. This model has 42 million parameters and is initialized randomly. The input is a fixed-size vector derived from the tabular features of the accident, and the model utilizes a softmax head to predict the accident type.

We train the MLP model on two Nvidia RTX A6000 GPUs. The optimization is performed using AdamW with an initial learning rate of 0.001, which decreases linearly by a factor of 0.9 every 5 epochs. We apply dropout with a probability of 0.1 and use a weight decay of 0.01 for regularization. The model is trained for 50 epochs, and we report the results from the best checkpoint based on the lowest validation loss.

LLM Few-shot Labeling. We use the Gemma Few-shot labels for comparison with the other supervised trained models. The details of few-shot labeling are given in Sect. 4.

Finetuned XLM-R. To predict accident types using text data, we employ an encoder-only LLM. XLM-RoBERTa-Large (XLM-R), a multilingual model with 550 million parameters [3], serves as our backbone. We use a pre-trained version of the model for transfer learning, fine-tuning it on our dataset. The model takes the accident text description as input and predicts the accident type through a softmax classification head with the model having 560 million parameters in total.

For fine-tuning XLM-R, we use Hugging Face [26]. The model is fine-tuned on two Nvidia RTX A6000 GPUs. We use an initial learning rate of 5×10^{-5}, a weight decay of 0.01, and train for 6 epochs. The effective batch size is set to 128. As before, we select the best checkpoint based on the lowest validation loss.

Multimodal Model. To effectively handle both tabular and text data modalities, we design a multimodal model that integrates information from both sources. The architecture follows a two-branch structure:

- **Textual Input Pathway:** The accident description is processed using the XLM-R model, which transforms the text into a text embedding via mean pooling.
- **Tabular Input Pathway:** The numerical and categorical accident-related features are fed into a multi-layer perceptron (MLP) model, which encodes them into a tabular feature embedding.
- **Fusion and Prediction:** The text embedding and tabular feature embedding are concatenated and passed through another MLP model, which acts as the final classifier with a softmax output layer to predict the accident type.

The XLM-R model is initialized with pretrained weights to leverage prior knowledge from multilingual text data, while the MLP components are randomly initialized. During training, all model parameters are updated.

The multimodal model is trained on two Nvidia RTX A6000 GPUs for 5 epochs with a batch size of 64. We use an initial learning rate of 1×10^{-5}, which decreases linearly by a factor of 0.7 every epoch. We apply a dropout rate of 0.2 and a weight decay of 0.01. The differnt models are summarized in Table 3.

Table 3. Comparison of predictive models for accident classification using different data sources and corresponding model sizes.

Model	Data Modality	Parameter Size
MLP	Tabular	42 M
LLM Few-shot Labeling	Text	27B
Finetuned XLM-R	Text	560 M
Multimodal Model	Tabular + Text	603 M

Model Comparisons. To assess the different approaches and data modalities for accident classification, we compare the models using accuracy and weighted F1 score metrics calculated on the test set. Accuracy measures the proportion of correct predictions over all predictions. Weighted F1 score is computed as the weighted mean of F1 scores for each accident type

$$\text{Weighted } F_1 \text{ Score} = \sum_{i=1}^{7} w_i \cdot F_{1,i}$$

where $F_{1,i}$ is the F1 score of class i, calculated as the harmonic mean of precision and recall, and $w_i = n_i / (\sum_{j=1}^{7} n_j)$ with n_i the number of samples in class i.

5.2 Results

Label Quality Effect. As discussed above, we constructed two training datasets: a larger one with lower-quality labels, containing approximately 62,000 accidents, and a smaller one with higher-quality labels, consisting of around 45,000 accidents. To examine the trade-off between dataset size and label quality, we trained three supervised models (MLP, Finetuned XLM-R, and Multimodal model) with the settings given in Sect. 5.1. We excluded the LLM few-shot approach from this comparison, as it does not involve parameter updates during training.

Table 4 presents the performance of models trained on either low- or high-quality labels, evaluated on a test set of 236 expert-labeled accidents. Despite the smaller size of the high-quality label dataset, models trained on it achieve comparable performance to those trained on the larger low-quality label dataset. This highlights the importance of high-quality labels in model training. However, one should take into account the additional cost associated with generating high-quality labels—specifically, the computational expense of applying LLM few-shot labeling to a larger set of accidents. In our case, this was not an additional burden, as the few-shot labeling had already been applied to the full dataset for the preceding analysis.

Table 4. Test set accuracy and weighted F1 scores for different models trained with datasets containing either low-quality (Low-Q) or high-quality (High-Q) labels. LLM Few-Shot Labeling is not explicitly trained, therefore presented in the center of both columns. Best accuracy and weighted F1 score values are highlighted in bold.

Model	Data Modality	Test Set Performance			
		Accuracy		W. F1 Score	
		Low-Q	High-Q	Low-Q	High-Q
MLP	Tabular	0.53	0.53	0.49	0.48
LLM Few-Shot Labeling	Text	0.61		0.58	
Finetuned XLM-R	Text	0.72	0.72	0.68	**0.70**
Multimodal Model	Text + Tabular	**0.73**	0.70	0.68	0.68

Model Comparisons. Comparing the different models and modalities, the results indicate that the MLP model, which relies solely on tabular data, performs the worst among all approaches (53% accuracy, 0.49 weighted F1 score). In contrast, all models incorporating text data—whether alone or in combination with tabular features—demonstrate better performance ($\geq 61\%$ accuracy, ≥ 0.58 weighted F1 score). This suggests that textual information is the primary source of information for this classification task, whereas tabular data alone lacks the necessary detail for accurate accident classification.

When comparing the LLM Few-Shot approach (61% accuracy) to the finetuned XLM-R model (72% accuracy), we observe that finetuning leads to superior performance. Even though Gemma is a much larger model, with 27 billion parameters in a decoder-only architecture, it underperforms relative to the 560-million-parameter encoder-only XLM-R model. Two key factors likely contribute to this outcome. First, encoder-only models like XLM-R leverage a bidirectional attention mechanism, which is inherently more effective for text classification tasks compared to the autoregressive nature of decoder-only models. Second, finetuning allows the model to better adapt to domain-specific data, whereas few-shot prompting, even with six examples, does not provide the same level of task specialization.

Finally, comparing the Multimodal Model to the Finetuned XLM-R shows no large difference in performance when both text and tabular data are used. This suggests that textual data carries the most relevant information for accident classification in our predictive models.

6 Conclusion and Future Directions

In this study, we analyzed Munich traffic accidents using multiple data modalities to uncover meaningful patterns. Through semantic clustering, we identified distinct topics across seven accident categories, providing deeper insights into their characteristics. To further investigate accident categorization, we employed an LLM with a few-shot approach and compared its results with human labels. Disagreements between the two revealed that many cases in the "other accidents" category involved damaged parked vehicles, supporting our findings from semantic clustering.

We also explored predictive modeling. Our results showed that models using text data outperformed those relying solely on tabular data, demonstrating the value of textual information for accident classification. Overall, our findings highlight the importance of NLP techniques in understanding traffic accidents. By leveraging textual data and machine learning, this approach offers valuable insights that can inform safety measures and contribute to the development of safer cities.

Future developments could focus on improving and incorporating data-based classification into practice, for example by deploying such a model to make real-time suggestions to human labelers (human-in-the-loop) and use active learning approaches to improve model-based classification over time.

Acknowledgements. We thank the City of Munich for supporting this project and providing access to the dataset.

References

1. Blei, D.M.: Probabilistic topic models. Commun. ACM **55**(4), 77–84 (2012)
2. Brown, T., et al.: Language models are few-shot learners. Adv. Neural. Inf. Process. Syst. **33**, 1877–1901 (2020)
3. Conneau, A., et al.: Unsupervised cross-lingual representation learning at scale. arXiv preprint arXiv:1911.02116 (2019)
4. Devlin, J., Chang, M.W., Lee, K., Toutanova, K.: Bert: pre-training of deep bidirectional transformers for language understanding. In: Proceedings of the 2019 conference of the North American chapter of the association for computational linguistics: human language technologies, volume 1 (long and short papers), pp. 4171–4186 (2019)
5. Grootendorst, M.: Bertopic: neural topic modeling with a class-based TF-IDF procedure. arXiv preprint arXiv:2203.05794 (2022)
6. Hossain, M.M., Zhou, H., Das, S.: Data mining approach to explore emergency vehicle crash patterns: a comparative study of crash severity in emergency and non-emergency response modes. Accident Anal. Prevent. **191**, 107217 (2023)
7. Joachims, T., et al.: A probabilistic analysis of the rocchio algorithm with tfidf for text categorization. In: ICML, vol. 97, pp. 143–151. Citeseer (1997)
8. Li, L., et al.: A scoping review of using large language models (LLMs) to investigate electronic health records (ehrs). arXiv preprint arXiv:2405.03066 (2024)

9. McInnes, L., Healy, J., Astels, S., et al.: hdbscan: hierarchical density based clustering. J. Open Source Softw. **2**(11), 205 (2017)
10. McInnes, L., Healy, J., Melville, J.: Umap: Uniform manifold approximation and projection for dimension reduction. arXiv preprint arXiv:1802.03426 (2018)
11. Muennighoff, N., Tazi, N., Magne, L., Reimers, N.: Mteb: Massive text embedding benchmark. arXiv preprint arXiv:2210.07316 (2022). https://doi.org/10.48550/ARXIV.2210.07316, https://arxiv.org/abs/2210.07316
12. Nassereddine, H., Santiago-Chaparro, K.R., Noyce, D.A.: Evaluating right-turn flashing yellow arrow for vehicle-pedestrian interactions using a non-probabilistic regression approach. Transp. Res. Rec. **2678**(2), 212–222 (2024)
13. Noguti, M.Y., Vellasques, E., Oliveira, L.S.: Legal document classification: an application to law area prediction of petitions to public prosecution service. In: 2020 International joint conference on neural networks (IJCNN), pp. 1–8. IEEE (2020)
14. Park, S., Park, S., Jeong, H., Yun, I., So, J.: Scenario-mining for level 4 automated vehicle safety assessment from real accident situations in urban areas using a natural language process. Sensors **21**(20), 6929 (2021)
15. Patwardhan, N., Marrone, S., Sansone, C.: Transformers in the real world: a survey on NLP applications. Information **14**(4), 242 (2023)
16. Radford, A., Narasimhan, K., Salimans, T., Sutskever, I., et al.: Improving language understanding by generative pre-training (2018)
17. Raffel, C., et al.: Exploring the limits of transfer learning with a unified text-to-text transformer. J. Mach. Learn. Res. **21**(140), 1–67 (2020)
18. Reimers, N., Gurevych, I.: Sentence-BERT: sentence embeddings using Siamese BERT-networks. In: Inui, K., Jiang, J., Ng, V., Wan, X. (eds.) Proceedings of the 2019 Conference on Empirical Methods in Natural Language Processing and the 9th International Joint Conference on Natural Language Processing (EMNLP-IJCNLP), pp. 3982–3992. Association for Computational Linguistics, Hong Kong, China (Nov 2019https://doi.org/10.18653/v1/D19-1410, https://aclanthology.org/D19-1410/
19. Seo, Y., Park, J., Oh, G., Kim, H., Hu, J., So, J.: Text classification modeling approach on imbalanced-unstructured traffic accident descriptions data. IEEE Open J. Intell. Transport. Syst. **4**, 955–965 (2023)
20. Siino, M., Falco, M., Croce, D., Rosso, P.: Exploring LLMs applications in law: a literature review on current legal NLP approaches. IEEE Access (2025)
21. Sturua, S., et al.: jina-embeddings-v3: Multilingual embeddings with task lora (2024). https://arxiv.org/abs/2409.10173
22. Team, G., et al.: Gemma 2: Improving open language models at a practical size. arXiv preprint arXiv:2408.00118 (2024)
23. Thellmann, K., et al.: Towards multilingual LLM evaluation for European languages. arXiv preprint arXiv:2410.08928 (2024)
24. Vaswani, A., et al.: Attention is all you need. In: Advances in Neural Information Processing Systems, vol. 30 (2017)
25. Wei, J., et al.: Chain-of-thought prompting elicits reasoning in large language models. Adv. Neural. Inf. Process. Syst. **35**, 24824–24837 (2022)
26. Wolf, T., et al.: Huggingface's transformers: State-of-the-art natural language processing. arXiv preprint arXiv:1910.03771 (2019)
27. Wu, J., Heydecker, B.: Natural language understanding in road accident data analysis. Adv. Eng. Softw. **29**(7–9), 599–610 (1998)
28. Xing, X., Chen, P.: Entity extraction of key elements in 110 police reports based on large language models. Appl. Sci. **14**(17), 7819 (2024)

Low Visibility Forecasting Using Numerical Weather Prediction Data

Topon Paul[1(✉)], Vidhisha Reddy[2], Sai Prem Kumar Ayyagari[2], Ryusei Shingaki[1], Kaneharu Nishino[1], and Yoshiaki Shiga[1]

[1] Corporate Laboratory, Toshiba Corporation, Kanagawa 212-8582, Japan
{toponkumar.paul,ryusei1.shingaki,kaneharu1.nishino, yoshiaki1.shiga}@toshiba.co.jp
[2] R&D Division, Toshiba Software (India) Pvt. Ltd., Bangalore 560034, KA, India
{vidhisha.reddy,saipremkumar.ayyagari}@toshiba-tsip.com

Abstract. Low visibility is a critical factor affecting aviation and transportation safety, often leading to operational disruptions, delays, and potential hazards. Weather phenomena, such as fog, rain, and snow, significantly contribute to reducing visibility, making accurate prediction essential for mitigating risks. Conventional forecasting methods with time-series visibility and meteorological data often struggle with data imbalance and censored data issues, which impact forecasting accuracy, particularly in the low visibility range. In this paper, we propose a new approach by employing Censored Quantile Regression Neural Network and Light Gradient-Boosting Machine to forecast visibilities in the low and high visibility ranges and combining the forecast values by using a probabilistic classifier model built with Logistic Regression. We show the effectiveness of the proposed approach by performing experiments with two datasets of observed and forecast meteorological data from Japan and evaluating it in terms of forecasting errors and the accuracy of forecasting of low visibility. Experimental results suggest that our approach is well-suited to forecast low visibility with high accuracy up to 24 h ahead.

Keywords: Visibility forecasting · Censored data · Imbalanced data · Meteorological data

1 Introduction

Visibility, a fundamental meteorological parameter, refers to the distance at which an object or light can be clearly perceived by the human eye in the atmosphere. Low visibility is a critical factor affecting aviation and transportation safety, often leading to operational disruptions, delays, and potential hazards. Weather phenomena, such as fog, heavy precipitation, snow, dust, and smoke, significantly contribute to reducing visibility, making accurate prediction of low visibility essential for mitigating risks. The definition of low visibility depends on the application; for example, in aviation, it is in kilometer range while in road transportation, it is in meter range.

There have been proposed a number of methods for visibility forecasting using time-series visibility datasets with weather data in literature. These methods include regression-based methods, deep learning-based methods, and physical models, which combine pre-processing of visibility data, addition of features required for better prediction, and selection of important features. For example, in [11], XGBoost and Light Gradient-Boosting Machine (LightGBM) are used to train a multimodal fusion model for visibility prediction. In [12], six machine learning methods: linear discriminant analysis, decision tree, Naïve Bayes, linear SVM, kNN, and neural network are used for visibility prediction. In [4], the authors have used two deep learning models: a Multilayer Perceptron (MLP) and a Convolutional Neural Network (CNN) to forecast one-step ahead visibility; they have concluded that the forecasting errors are affected by the lagged values used in building the forecasting models using the methods. In [13], the authors have used MLP to create 28 different prediction models of dominant visibility; these models are designed to forecast dominant visibility using different combinations of historical visibility data over various time-periods. They have concluded that inclusion of other meteorological data can stabilize forecasting accuracy. The authors in [9] have used a forward feature selection algorithm based on evolutionary computation to determine the optimal meteorological variables and deep learning as well as conventional machine learning methods to build forecasting models. In [5], the authors have utilized deep learning and conventional regression-based methods to forecast peak values accurately by utilizing the learning capabilities of these methods on time-series data. However, these traditional prediction models often struggle with censored (clipped) data, imbalanced data, and peak-shift issues, which impact forecasting accuracy, particularly in the low visibility range.

To handle censored data effectively, several state-of-the-art methodologies, such as Tobit exponential smoothing, quantile regression neural networks, and censored regression models, have been proposed to enhance prediction accuracy of a regression model. In [8], the authors have proposed Tobit Exponential Smoothing (Tobit ETS), an enhancement of traditional time-series forecasting for censored observations; this method incorporates Kalman filtering to dynamically update state vectors based on observed values and imposes censoring thresholds. In [7], the authors have proposed Censored Quantile Regression Neural Networks (CQRNN), a neural network-based learning framework designed to estimate conditional quantiles in censored datasets. Unlike traditional regression methods, CQRNN provides a fuller representation of the distribution of the target variable. In [2], the authors have extended censored regression methodologies by introducing a penalized Tobit likelihood approach to handle high-dimensional censored data. It employs Generalized Coordinate Descent (GCD) to iteratively optimize the Tobit likelihood function, and a soft-thresholding rule based on quadratic majorization to minimize penalized loss functions. In [1], the authors have applied Multi-Output Censored Quantile Regression Neural

Networks (Multi-CQNN) to mobility demand forecasting; they have integrated Bayesian modeling for improved interpretability. In it, a multi-output CQNN is trained with an asymmetric Laplace likelihood function to model censored data, and the network applies a tilted loss function to refine predictions under censoring constraints. The major problem of these approaches is that they can handle censored data properly but in the case of visibility forecasting, their forecast values are biased toward high visibility ranges due to imbalanced data.

To address these issues, one attempt is made in [6] by employing multiple forecasting models; however, though the method obtains better forecasting accuracy in the low visibility range, the forecasting accuracy in the high visibility range is low, making many false alarms. Moreover, in it, the weights of low and high visibility ranges are set manually; determination of appropriate weights at various observation stations might be difficult.

1.1 Main Contributions

To overcome the limitations of existing technologies to handle imbalanced and censored data properly and forecast low visibility with high accuracy, we propose a new approach by combining forecasting methods CQRNN and LightGBM with a probabilistic model employing Logistic Regression after selecting and transforming relevant meteorological variables. This new approach aims to enhance forecasting accuracy by leveraging advanced machine learning techniques and optimizing feature selection and provides a more comprehensive assessment of extreme low visibility events. We show the effectiveness of the proposed approach by performing experiments with two datasets of observed weather data and Numerical Weather Prediction (NWP) data, sourced from Japan Meteorological Agency (JMA).

2 Methods

In our proposed approach, to deal with the censored data and imbalanced data, we learn two forecasting models by employing CQRNN, and LightGBM with Kernel Density Estimation (KDE) weights. The issue of censored data is dealt with CQRNN, and the issue of imbalanced data is dealt with LightGBM with KDE weights. These models are tuned in such a way that CQRNN focuses in the low visibility range while LightGBM with KDE weights focuses in both visibility ranges. The forecast values by these two models are ensembled through Logistic Regression classifier, which gives the probabilities of visibility in the low and high ranges given the observed and forecast weather data. The outline of the proposed approach is shown in Fig. 1.

2.1 Selection of Meteorological Variables

Selection of the most relevant meteorological variables is very important because the irrelevant variables act as noises to input data and reduce the forecasting accuracy.

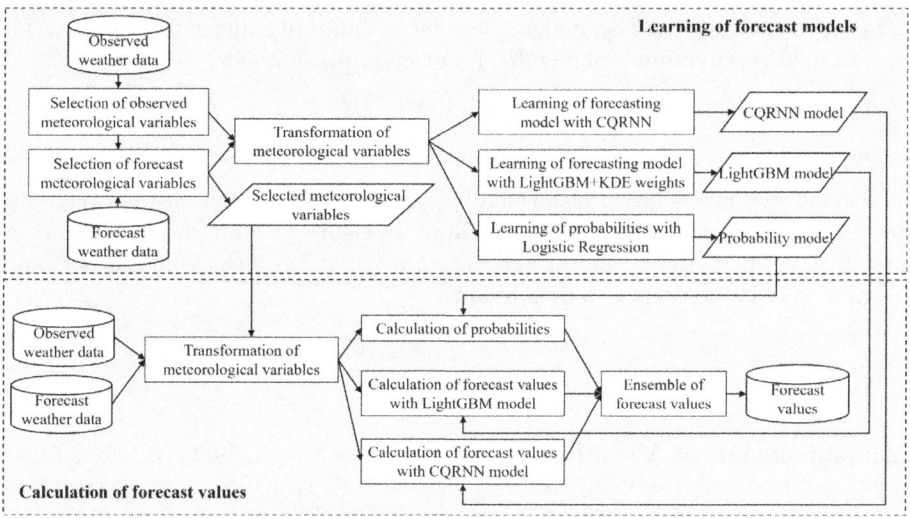

Fig. 1. Outline of proposed approach

Selection of Observed Meteorological Variables. To select the observed meteorological variables, we use the correlation coefficient between a meteorological variable and the target variable (visibility). Meteorological variables having higher correlation coefficients are selected. Then, correlation coefficients among the meteorological variables are calculated and only one from each group of highly correlated variables is selected. For example, sunshine hours and solar radiation are highly correlated; in this case, only sunshine hours is selected and solar radiation is discarded.

Selection of Forecast Meteorological Variables. Instead of using correlation between the target variable (visibility) and a meteorological variable, we use the quality of the forecast data as a selection criterion. If the quality of the forecast data is bad, the forecasting accuracy will fall. We use the correlation between the observed and forecast data of a meteorological variable as the selection criterion. The higher the correlation coefficient, the higher the quality of the meteorological variable. Meteorological variables having higher correlation coefficients are selected.

2.2 Transformation of Meteorological Variables

The transformation of meteorological variables is applied to improve the quality of the data and make it more suitable for predictive modeling. By normalizing and stabilizing the variance of the variables, we aim to enhance the performance of our models and obtain more accurate predictions.

To transform Relative Humidity (RH) and Precipitation (PR), a square root transformation is applied. This transformation is intended to normalize the data and reduce skewness; it also makes the relative humidity linear to visibility. The transformed relative humidity (RH_{tr}) and precipitation (PR_{tr}) are as follows:

$$RH_{tr} = \sqrt{100 - RH}; \tag{1}$$

$$PR_{tr} = \sqrt{100 - PR}. \tag{2}$$

Pressure variables are transformed by calculating the difference between Surface Pressure (SP, station pressure)/Vapor Pressure (VP) and Sea Level Pressure (SLP). The Differential Surface Pressure (DSP), and the Differential Vapor Pressure (DVP) are calculated as follows:

$$DSP = SP - SLP; \tag{3}$$

$$DVP = VP - SLP. \tag{4}$$

Transformation of Visibility Variable. Since the visibility values are censored, and low visibility values are rare events, logit transformation of the target variable might be helpful to build a stable model and to handle rare events. The steps to transform the target variable (visibility, y) using logit transformation are as follows.

1. Find y_{min} and y_{max}: determine the minimum (y_{min}) and maximum (y_{max}) values of the target variable.
2. Adjust y_{min} and y_{max}: adjust the minimum and maximum values slightly to avoid boundary issues:

$$y_{min} = y_{min} - 0.0001; \tag{5}$$

$$y_{max} = y_{max} + 0.0001. \tag{6}$$

3. Scale the target variable: scale the target variable y using the formula:

$$y_s = (y - y_{min})/(y_{max} - y_{min}). \tag{7}$$

4. Perform logit transformation: apply the logit transformation to the scaled variable:

$$logit(y_s) = \log\left(\frac{y_s}{1 - y_s}\right) \tag{8}$$

During calculation of forecast values, a forecast value (y_p) is transformed back to the original scale using the following steps.

1. Get the adjusted y_{min} and y_{max} values, calculated during transformation of the target variable using logit transformation.
2. Apply the reverse logit transformation to the forecast value:

$$y_l = \frac{\exp(y_p)}{1 + \exp(y_p)}. \tag{9}$$

3. Convert the reverse logit value back to the original scale:

$$y_f = y_{min} + y_l * (y_{max} - y_{min}). \tag{10}$$

2.3 Learning of Models

Here, we describe the learning of various forecasting models as well as the probabilistic model. The input and output data to these models are shown in Fig. 2. The input data consists of lagged values of the observed meteorological variables and the values of forecast meteorological variables up to the forecast horizon. The output data are the lead values of the target variable up to the forecast horizon. The pseudocode of learning of forecast models is given in Algorithm 1.

Algorithm 1: Pseudocode of learning of forecast models

Data: Observed weather data: $\boldsymbol{X}_o(t)$, observed data of target variable: $\boldsymbol{y}(t)$, forecast weather data: $\boldsymbol{X}_f = [\boldsymbol{X}_f(t+1), \ldots, \boldsymbol{X}_f(t+\Delta)]$
Result: $Model_{\text{CQRNN}}$, $Model_{\text{LightGBM}}$, $Model_{\text{prob}}$, NP
// l: lag size, Δ: forecast horizon, lv: threshold of LV

1. Transform meteorological variables of $\boldsymbol{X}_o(t)$ and $\boldsymbol{X}_f$;
2. Normalize $\boldsymbol{X}_o(t)$, $\boldsymbol{X}_f$, $\boldsymbol{y}(t)$ and get normalization parameters (NP);
3. Create lag values of $\boldsymbol{X}_o(t)$: $\boldsymbol{X}_{ol} = [\boldsymbol{X}_o(t-l), \ldots, \boldsymbol{X}_o(t-1), \boldsymbol{X}_o(t)]$;
4. Create lag values of $\boldsymbol{y}(t)$: $\boldsymbol{Y}_l = [\boldsymbol{y}(t-l), \ldots, \boldsymbol{y}(t-1), \boldsymbol{y}(t)]$;
5. Set $Model_{\text{CQRNN}} = \{\}$, $Model_{\text{LightGBM}} = \{\}$, $Model_{\text{prob}} = \{\}$;
6. **for** $s \in \{1, 2, \ldots, \Delta\}$ **do**
7.   Create lead values of $\boldsymbol{y}(t)$: $\boldsymbol{y}_s = \boldsymbol{y}(t+s)$;
8.   Extract forecast weather data: $\boldsymbol{X}_{fs} = \{\boldsymbol{X}_f(t+1), \ldots, \boldsymbol{X}_f(t+s)\}$;
9.   Create model input data by merging: $\boldsymbol{X}_s = [\boldsymbol{X}_{ol}, \boldsymbol{Y}_l, \boldsymbol{X}_{fs}]$;
10.   Calculate KDE weights $\boldsymbol{w}_s$ of $\boldsymbol{X}_s$ using $\boldsymbol{y}_s$;
11.   Learn models: $mc = CQRNN(\boldsymbol{X}_s, \boldsymbol{y}_s)$, $ml = LightGBM(\boldsymbol{X}_s, \boldsymbol{y}_s, \boldsymbol{w}_s)$, $pm = LogisticRegression(\boldsymbol{X}_s, \boldsymbol{y}_s > lv)$;
12.   Append models to $Model_{\text{CQRNN}}$, $Model_{\text{LightGBM}}$, $Model_{\text{prob}}$;
13. **end**

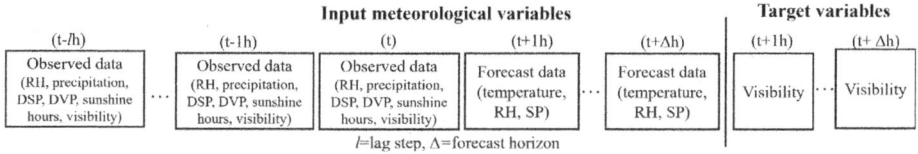

Fig. 2. Illustration of input and output data of various models

Learning of Forecasting Model with CQRNN. Among the regression models proposed to deal with censored data, we select CQRNN because it is a non-parametric regression model and can capture non-linear relationships among the variables. The CQRNN model estimates the conditional quantiles of the target variable given the input variables. Unlike Ordinary Least Squares (OLS) regression, which focuses only on estimating the mean of the target variable, quantile regression provides insights into the entire distribution. By predicting different quantiles, CQRNN enables a more comprehensive understanding of uncertainty and variability in the target variable. Figure 3 illustrates the forecast values of visibility at various quantiles. In CQRNN, the model is initialized with multiple quantiles to estimate, a neural network is trained using a loss function that accommodates both observed and censored data, and censored observations are re-weighted iteratively based on predicted quantiles to refine estimates.

Instead of relying on predefined weights as in [6], the introduction of CQRNN provides a data-driven approach to estimate different quantile predictions. Now, by leveraging the 0.1-quantile predictions from the CQRNN model, the approach ensures that the model captures lower-bound estimates (low visibility) effectively. This modification enhances the model's ability to account for uncertainty, leading to more reliable and flexible predictions.

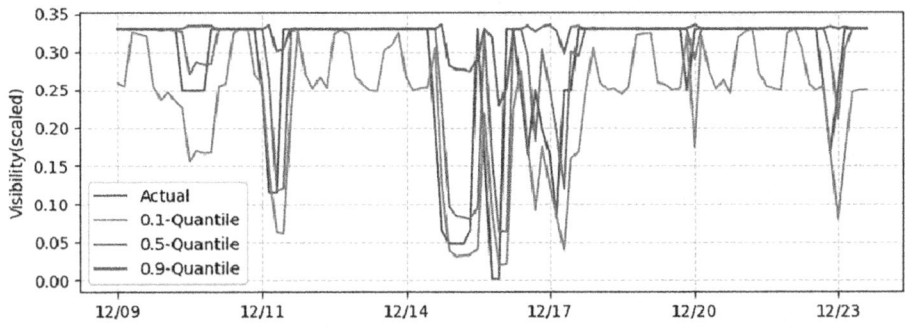

Fig. 3. Illustration of forecasting by CQRNN at various quantiles

Learning of Forecasting Model with LightGBM+KDE Weights. The problem at hand revolves around the challenge posed by imbalanced data on the performance of machine learning algorithms. Imbalanced data occurs when certain classes or categories within the dataset are under-represented, often leading to sub-optimal model performance, especially in cases where the focus is on rare occurrences within the data. To deal with this issue, we build another forecast model with LightGBM [3] with KDE weights [10] assigned to the input data.

LightGBM is a regression method based on decision trees and XGBoost. It utilizes various characteristics, such as sparse optimization, parallel training, multiple loss functions, regularization, bagging, and early stopping of XGBoost. It has faster training speed and better accuracy than other gradient boosting frameworks.

The steps to calculate KDE-based weights to the input data are as follows.

1. Determining density function of the target variable: To address the issue of imbalanced data, the first step involves calculating a measure of rarity for the target variable. This is achieved by determining the density function ($p(y)$)

of the target variable. The density of the data points is computed using the KDE method:

$$p(y) = \frac{1}{Nh} \sum_{i-1}^{N} K\left(\frac{y - y_i}{h}\right) \quad (11)$$

where N is the number of visibility values, h is the bandwidth of KDE, and K is the kernel function (Gaussian distribution).

2. Normalizing density points: The density points obtained in the previous step are then normalized using the min-max normalization technique:

$$p\prime(y) = \frac{p(y) - \min(p(Y))}{\max(p(Y)) - \min(p(Y))} \quad (12)$$

where Y is the set of N visibility values in the dataset.

3. Assigning sample weights: The final step involves assigning sample weights ($weight(y)$) based on the normalized density points as follows.

$$weight(y) = \max(1 - \alpha p\prime(y), \epsilon) \quad (13)$$

where $\alpha (0 \leq \alpha \leq 1.0)$ is a user-defined parameter that controls the influence of the density points on the sample weights; a lower value of α assigns greater importance to rare occurrences, while a higher value prioritizes common occurrences. $\epsilon(0 \leq \epsilon \leq 1.0)$ is a user-defined constant value; it serves as a threshold to ensure that the adjusted sample weight does not drop below a certain minimum value, thereby preventing excessively low weights. In this paper, we set α and ϵ to 0.7, and 0.4, respectively, based on some preliminary experiments, which ensures that the model learned by LightGBM with KDE weights focuses in both regions of visibility.

Learning of Probabilities with Logistic Regression. The probabilities of low and high visibility are calculated by using Logistic Regression (Logit Regression) classifier. This model is chosen for its effectiveness in binary classification tasks, where the goal is to categorize input data into one of two groups: low or high visibility range. Here, group 0 represents instances where visibility is less than or equal to lv (threshold of low visibility), while group 1 represents instances where visibility exceeds lv. The low visibility threshold is specific to a dataset; in this paper, we set lv to 1 km which is the threshold of visibility distance for fog. The classifier assigns probabilities to each group based on the input data, indicating the likelihood of belonging to each group. These probabilities are then utilized in calculation of forecasting values. By considering the probabilities assigned to each group, the model can make more informed forecasting, considering the uncertainty inherent in the classification task.

2.4 Calculation of Forecast Values

The pseudocode of calculation of forecast values is given in Algorithm 2. Given the observed and forecast meteorological variables, the variables are transformed and then forecast values are calculated with the CQRNN model and LightGBM model, and probabilities of low and high visibility is calculated with the learned Logistic Regression model.

Algorithm 2: Pseudocode of calculation of forecast values

Data: $Model_{\text{CQRNN}}$, $Model_{\text{LightGBM}}$, $Model_{\text{prob}}$, NP,
observed weather data: $X_{ol} = [X_o(t-l), \ldots, X_o(t-1), X_o(t)]$,
observed data of target variable: $Y_l = [y(t-l), \ldots, y(t-1), y(t)]$,
forecast weather data: $X_f = [X_f(t+1), \ldots, X_f(t+\Delta)]$
// l: lag size, Δ: forecast horizon
Result: Forecast values $\hat{\boldsymbol{y}}_f$

1 Transform meteorological variables of X_{ol} and X_f;
2 Normalize X_{ol}, X_f, Y_l using normalization parameters (NP);
3 Set $\hat{\boldsymbol{y}}_f = \{\}$;
4 **for** $s \in \{1, 2, \ldots, \Delta\}$ **do**
5   Extract forecast weather data $X_{fs} = [X_f(t+1), \ldots, X_f(t+s)]$;
6   Create model input data by merging: $X_s = [X_{ol}, Y_l, X_{fs}]$;
7   Calculate forecast values: $\hat{y}_{CQRNN} = Model_{\text{CQRNN},s}(X_s)$,
    $\hat{y}_{LightGBM} = Model_{\text{LightGBM},s}(X_s)$;
8   Caculate probabilities: $p_l, p_h = Model_{\text{prob},s}(X_s)$;
9   Calculate $\hat{y}_s = \hat{y}_{CQRNN} \times p_l + \hat{y}_{LightGBM} \times p_h$;
10   Transform $\hat{y}_s$ to original scale by using NP and append it to $\hat{\boldsymbol{y}}_f$;
11 **end**

Then, the final forecast value ($\hat{y}$) is calculated though the ensemble of the two forecast values as follows:

$$\hat{y} = \hat{y}_{CQRNN} \times p_l + \hat{y}_{LightGBM} \times p_h \qquad (14)$$

where $\hat{y}_{CQRNN}$ and $\hat{y}_{LightGBM}$ are the forecast values calculated by employing the CQRNN model and LightGBM model, respectively, p_l and $p_h (= 1 - p_l)$ are the probabilities of the low and high visibility, respectively. The rationale behind assigning the probability of low visibility to the forecast value by the CQRNN model and that of high visibility to the forecast value by the LightGBM model is as follows. Since the CQRNN model with a 0.1 quantile is specifically designed to predict the lower quantile of the distribution, it focuses on estimating the lowest range of the target variable. That means CQRNN model makes a prediction for low visibility; that is why the probability of low visibility is assigned to the forecast value by the CQRNN model. On the other hand, when the probability of high visibility is higher, we want to a make a prediction by emphasizing more on the forecast values by the LightGBM model because it is tuned to make better prediction in the high visibility range than CQRNN; that is why the probability of high visibility is assigned to the forecast values by the LightGBM model.

2.5 Evaluation Metrics

To evaluate the forecasting methods, we use forecasting errors: RMSE (Root Mean Square Error) and MAE (Mean Absolute Error) in the low visibility range and the accuracy of classification (F1 score, AUC) of visibilities in the low and high ranges. The lower the RMSE and MAE values, the better the performance of the forecasting model while the higher the F1 score and AUC, the better the performance of the forecasting model.

3 Experiments and Results

3.1 Datasets

To show the effectiveness of the proposed approach, we perform experiments with two datasets with observed and forecast weather data provided by JMA at Sendai and Akita weather stations in Miyagi and Akita Prefectures in Japan. We selected these two weather stations because they have diverse climatic conditions due to their geographical locations. The observed weather data is publicly available for download at the JMA website: https://www.data.jma.go.jp/risk/obsdl/index.php. The data is recorded at hourly interval. The observed meteorological variables are visibility, relative humidity, precipitation, temperature, dew-point temperature, vapor pressure, sea level pressure, surface pressure (station pressure), wind speed, snow cover, solar radiation, sunshine hours, and weather condition (sunny, cloudy, rainy, etc.).

As forecast weather data, we use Meso-Scale Model (MSM) forecast data of numerical weather prediction provided by JMA. The horizontal resolution of the MSM is 5km, and it provides 39-hour ahead forecast at 00, 03, 06, 09, 12, 15, 18, 21 UTC. The data is recorded at 3-hour interval with hourly interval in the forecast horizon. The forecast meteorological variables are pressure reduced to mean sea level, surface pressure, U and V components of wind, temperature, relative humidity, low cloud cover, high cloud cover, total cloud cover, accumulated precipitation, downward shortwave radiation flux. Temperature is converted from Kelvin scale to Celsius scale. We collect the data of both observed and forecast meteorological variables during the period 2020–2024. We use the data of 2020–2022 as the training data and 2023–2024 as the evaluation data.

3.2 Selected Meteorological Variables

Observed Meteorological Variables. From the observed weather data, we select precipitation, differential surface pressure, differential vapor pressure, sunshine hours and relative humidity having higher correlation with visibility.

Forecast Meteorological Variables. Using correlation coefficients (CC) of the actual and forecast meteorological variables, temperature, relative humidity, and surface pressure (see Fig. 4) are selected from the MSM forecast data as their CC are (0.96, 0.66, 0.95) and (0.97, 0.62, 0.80) respectively in the Sendai and Akita datasets, with all CC being greater than 0.50.

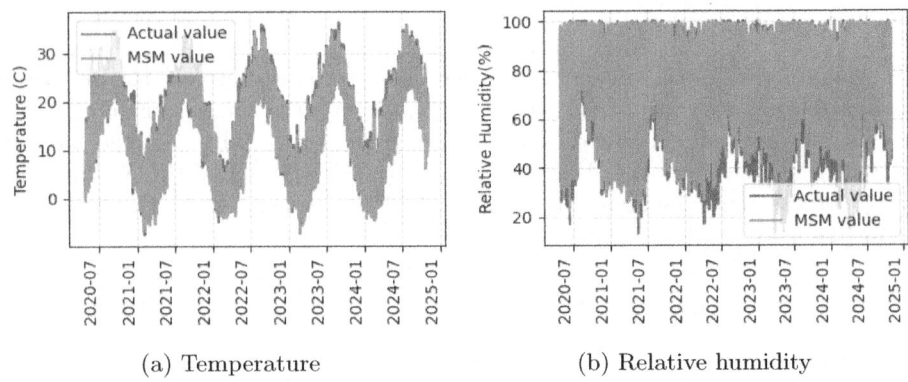

(a) Temperature   (b) Relative humidity

Fig. 4. Selected two meteorological variables from MSM forecast data

3.3 Experimental Setup

We perform experiments using various forecasting methods for forecast horizon of 1, 3, and 24 h. As a baseline method, we use LightGBM. For LightGBM, we use the defaults settings of the parameters of the python package. For CQRNN, the settings of the parameters are as follows: quantiles = [0.1, 0.2, 0.5, 0.7, 0.9, 1.0]; number of epochs = 50; batch size = 128; number of hidden units=100; and activation=relu. For CQRNN, we use 0.1-quantile forecast values. For Sendai dataset, we use the lag step of 6 for all observed variables; for Akita, it is set to 1. Logistic Regression is learned with balanced class weight.

3.4 Experimental Results

Comparison Between Baseline Method and Proposed Approach. First, we perform experiments with the lag values of the selected observed meteorological variables after transforming the values and applying the baseline method and the proposed approach. The experimental results are shown in Table 1. From the evaluation scores, we find that the proposed approach is consistently better than the baseline method in all evaluation metrics. In terms of accuracy of forecasting the values in the low and high visibility ranges, the proposed approach is significantly better.

Effects of Using Forecast Data. It is expected that by using forecast meteorological variables, the performance of the forecasting methods might improve by mitigating the problem of peak shift. However, since the quality of the forecast data might affect the performance of forecasting of visibility, here, we use the lead values of the observed meteorological variables as the forecast data. We perform experiments with the lag values of the selected observed meteorological variables merged with the forecast data created in this way. Here, we do not use the transformed values of the target variable. The experimental results are

Table 1. Comparative results of baseline method and proposed approach

Dataset	Forecast step	Baseline Method				Proposed Approach			
		RMSE	MAE	F1 score	AUC	RMSE	MAE	F1 score	AUC
Sendai	1	5.18	3.59	0.20	0.56	**4.42**	**2.36**	**0.51**	**0.69**
	3	7.22	6.22	0.10	0.53	**5.71**	**3.99**	**0.32**	**0.63**
	24	14.29	13.94	0.01	0.50	**13.10**	**12.26**	**0.05**	**0.52**
Akita	1	9.76	8.26	0.13	0.53	**5.89**	**3.32**	**0.37**	**0.75**
	3	11.64	10.39	0.04	0.51	**7.09**	**4.65**	**0.28**	**0.66**
	24	14.82	14.35	0.00	0.50	**9.87**	**8.20**	**0.15**	**0.56**

Table 2. Comparative results of the proposed approach under various conditions of input data to forecast models

Dataset	F. Step	Lag data only				Lag and forecast data				Target transformation			
		RMSE	MAE	F1 score	AUC	RMSE	MAE	F1 score	AUC	RMSE	MAE	F1 score	AUC
Sendai	1	4.42	2.36	0.51	0.69	**3.17**	**1.84**	**0.68**	**0.77**	4.56	2.25	0.53	0.72
	3	5.71	3.99	0.32	0.63	**3.72**	2.68	**0.37**	**0.66**	4.46	**2.63**	0.33	0.63
	24	13.10	12.26	0.05	0.52	**5.45**	**4.53**	**0.22**	**0.57**	7.84	6.12	0.15	0.55
Akita	1	5.89	3.32	0.37	0.75	**1.42**	0.85	**0.49**	0.81	1.52	**0.71**	0.48	**0.86**
	3	7.09	4.65	0.28	0.66	**1.91**	1.22	**0.43**	0.75	2.24	**1.21**	0.42	**0.79**
	24	9.87	8.20	0.15	0.56	**3.67**	**2.67**	0.29	0.62	5.65	3.47	**0.34**	**0.66**

shown in Table 2. From the evaluation scores, we find that by adding forecast data, the performance of the proposed approach is significantly improved.

Effects of Transformation of Target Variable. Next, we investigate whether transformation of the target variable improves the performance of forecasting approach or not. In this case, we perform experiments with transformation of the target variable. The experimental results are shown in Table 2. From the experimental results, we find that though transformation of the target variable produces better AUC on the Akita dataset, its performance in terms of other evaluation metrics is worse. Moreover, it produces worse scores on the Sendai dataset. Therefore, it is better not to transform the target variable.

Effects of Using MSM Forecast Data. In the previous subsection, we have observed that by adding the lead values of the observed meteorological variables as the forecast data improves forecasting performance significantly; however, in the real world, we must use real forecast data. In this context, we perform exper-

Table 3. Effects of using MSM forecast data

Dataset	Forecast step	Lag+lead forecast data				Lag+MSM forecast data			
		RMSE	MAE	F1Score	AUC	RMSE	MAE	F1Score	AUC
Sendai	1	**3.17**	**1.84**	**0.68**	**0.77**	4.64	2.58	0.57	0.72
	3	**3.72**	**2.68**	**0.37**	**0.66**	5.94	4.18	0.32	0.64
	24	**5.45**	**4.53**	**0.22**	**0.57**	10.83	9.78	0.05	0.52
Akita	1	**1.42**	**0.85**	**0.49**	**0.81**	5.48	3.16	0.39	0.74
	3	**1.91**	**1.22**	**0.43**	**0.75**	6.32	4.02	0.32	0.69
	24	**3.67**	**2.67**	**0.29**	**0.62**	8.79	7.45	0.13	0.56

iments with MSM forecast data instead of the lead values. The experimental results are shown in Table 3. From the experimental results, we find that using MSM forecast data instead of the lead values results in slightly lower evaluation scores, which is expected because the quality of MSM forecast data is inferior to lead values of the variables. The forecast values using observed and forecast data of meteorological variables are shown in Fig. 5. From the experimental results, we find that for short-term forecasting, such as rolling 3-hour forecast, the proposed approach produces forecast values with very high accuracy. As the forecasting horizon becomes longer, the forecasting accuracy falls, and the forecast values shift away from the actual values.

Forecasting of Visibility Under Various Weather Conditions. Next, we investigate the performance of the proposed approach under various weather conditions: fog, snow, and rain at Sendai weather station. Here, we perform experiments with the proposed approach by using lag values of the selected observed meteorological variables and MSM forecast data. We focus on those days (11 d) when visibility drops below 1 km. The weather conditions on three of those days are shown in Table 4. The forecast values on those selected days are shown in Figs. 6, 7, and 8. In the figures, 3-hour rolling forecast means the forecasting is scheduled at 00:00, 03:00, 06:00, 09:00, 12:00, 15:00, 18:00, 21:00 and at each scheduling time, values are forecast for 1–3 hours ahead. Similarly, in the case of 24-hour rolling forecast, forecasting is made at 00:00 every day.

Form the experimental results of 3-hour rolling forecast, we find that the proposed method can produce forecast values with very high accuracy. In the case of 24-hour rolling forecast, as the forecasting horizon increases, the forecasting

Table 4. Weather condition during poor visibility

Timestamp	Visibility(km)	Weather	Timestamp	Visibility(km)	Weather
2023/3/23 3:00	0.2	Fog	2023/6/2 18:00	0.5	Rain
2023/3/23 6:00	0.3	Fog	2024/2/21 12:00	1.0	Snow

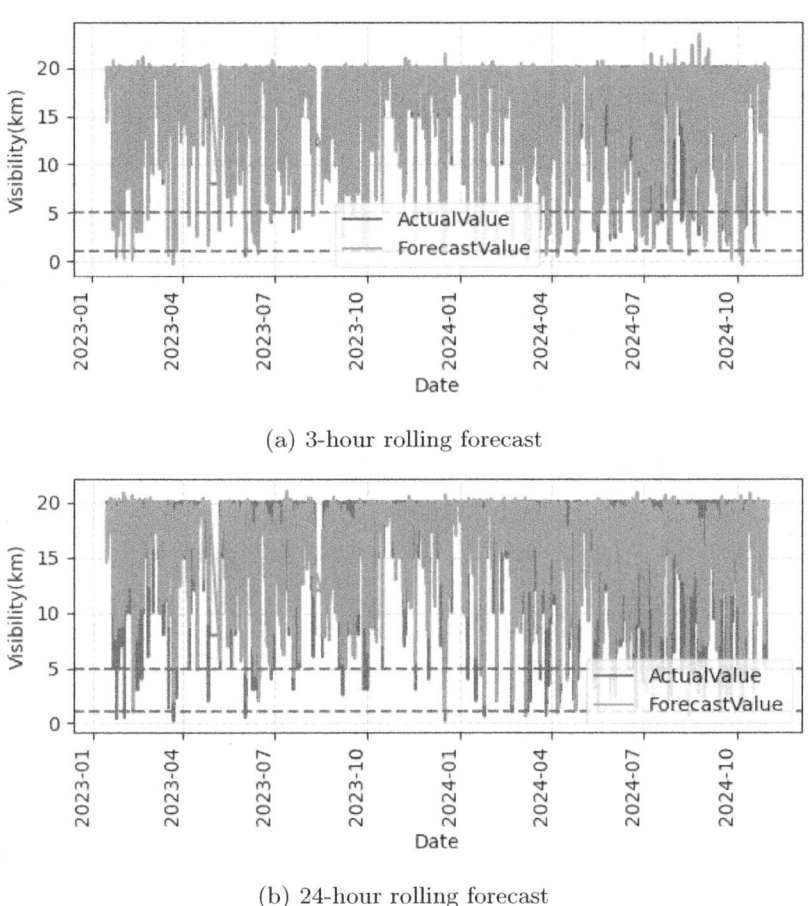

(a) 3-hour rolling forecast

(b) 24-hour rolling forecast

Fig. 5. Forecasting using observed and forecast data of meteorological variables

accuracy falls; however, using these forecast values it is possible to issue warning by the transportation and aviation authorities that in the following days visibility will drop below 5km, which might be helpful for the flight operators to reschedule their flights.

Execution Time. The training time of a 3-hour ahead forecast model is around 144 s, and the time required to calculate forecast values is 159 milliseconds on a computer with Intel® Core™ i7-1165G7@2.80 GHz processor and 16 GB of RAM running on Windows 11 Pro operating system.

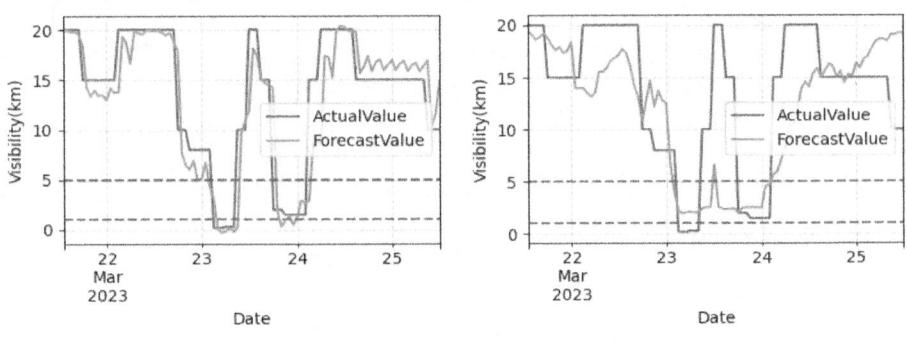

(a) 3-hour rolling forecast   (b) 24-hour rolling forecast

Fig. 6. Forecasting of low visibility caused by fog

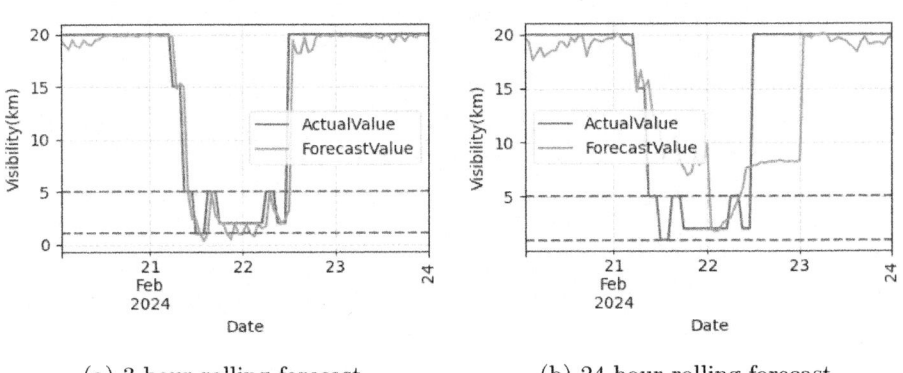

(a) 3-hour rolling forecast   (b) 24-hour rolling forecast

Fig. 7. Forecasting of low visibility caused by snow

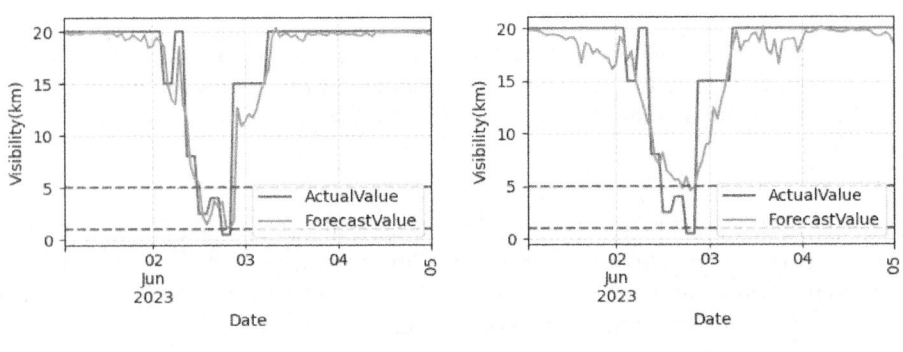

(a) 3-hour rolling forecast   (b) 24-hour rolling forecast

Fig. 8. Forecasting of low visibility caused by rain

4 Conclusion

In this paper, we have proposed a new approach to forecast low visibility with high accuracy and shown the effectiveness of the proposed approach by performing experiments with two datasets from Japan. From the experimental results, we have found that our proposed approach is better than the baseline method and can produce forecast values with very high accuracy for short-term forecasting, and for mid-term forecasting, it is possible to tell the trend of low visibility in the next day, which might be helpful for the transportation and aviation authorities to adjust their operation schedules.

Since we have confirmed the performance of the proposed approach using real-world datasets, we want to incorporate it into a traffic control system and perform field test in coming days. Moreover, we want to investigate the acceptable level of accuracy for forecasting of low visibility in various real-world applications in our future work.

References

1. Huttel, F., Peled, I., Rodrigues, F., Pereira, F.: Modeling censored mobility demand through censored quantile regression neural networks. IEEE Trans. Intell. Transp. Syst. **23**(11), 21753–21765 (2022)
2. Jacobson, T., Zou, H.: High-dimensional censored regression via the penalized tobit likelihood. J. Business Econ. Stat. **42**(1), 286–297 (2024)
3. Ke, G., et al.: LightGBM: a highly efficient gradient boosting decision tree. In: NIPS'17: Proceedings of the 31st International Conference on Neural Information Processing Systems, pp. 3149–3157 (2017)
4. Ortega, L.C., Otero, L.D., Solomon, M., Otero, C.E., Fabregas, A.: Deep learning models for visibility forecasting using climatological data. Int. J. Forecast. **39**(2), 992–1004 (2023)
5. Paul, T., et al.: Forecasting of reservoir inflow by the combination of deep learning and conventional machine learning. In: 2021 International Conference on Data Mining Workshops (ICDMW), pp. 558–565 (2021)
6. Paul, T., Reddy, V., Ayyagari, S.P.K., Shingaki, R., Nishino, K.: Forecasting of low visibility using weather and air quality data for safe and smooth transportation operation. In: Proceedings of ICMLA 2024 : 23rd International Conference on Machine Learning and Applications (2024)
7. Pearce, T., Jeong, J.H., Jia, Y., Zhu, J.: Censored quantile regression neural networks for distribution-free survival analysis. In: Advances in Neural Information Processing Systems, NeurIPS (2022)
8. Pedregal, D.J., Trapero, J.R., Holgado, E.: Tobit exponential smoothing, towards an enhanced demand planning in the presence of censored data (2024). https://arxiv.org/abs/2407.17920
9. Peláez-Rodríguez, C., Pérez-Aracil, J., Casanova-Mateo, C., Salcedo-Sanz, S.: Efficient prediction of fog-related low-visibility events with machine learning and evolutionary algorithms. Atmos. Res. **295**, 106991 (2023)
10. Steininger, M., Kobs, K., Davidson, P., Krause, A., Hotho, A.: Density-based weighting for imbalanced regression. Mach. Learn. **110**(8), 2187–2211 (2021). https://doi.org/10.1007/s10994-021-06023-5

11. Zheng, C., et al.: Weather visibility prediction based on multimodal fusion. IEEE Access **7**, 74776–74786 (2019)
12. Zhang, Y., Wang, Y., Zhu, Y., Yang, L., Ge, L., Luo, C.: Visibility prediction based on machine learning algorithms. Atmosphere **13**(7) (2022)
13. Zhu, L., Zhu, G., Han, L., Wang, N.: The application of deep learning in airport visibility forecast. Atmosph. Climate Sci. **7**, 314–322 (2017)

Curriculum RL Meets Monte Carlo Planning: Optimization of a Real World Container Management Problem

Abhijeet Pendyala[✉] and Tobias Glasmachers

Ruhr-University Bochum, Bochum, Germany
{abhijeet.pendyala,tobias.glasmachers}@ini.rub.de

Abstract. In this work, we augment reinforcement learning with an inference-time collision model to ensure safe and efficient container management in a waste-sorting facility with limited processing capacity. Each container has two optimal emptying volumes that trade off higher throughput against overflow risk. Conventional reinforcement learning (RL) approaches struggle under delayed rewards, sparse critical events, and high-dimensional uncertainty–failing to consistently balance higher-volume empties with the risk of safety-limit violations. To address these challenges, we propose a hybrid method comprising: (1) a *curriculum-learning* pipeline that incrementally trains a PPO agent to handle delayed rewards and class imbalance, and (2) an *offline pairwise collision model* used at inference time to proactively avert collisions with minimal online cost. Experimental results show that our *targeted inference-time collision checks* significantly improve collision avoidance, reduce safety-limit violations, maintain high throughput, and scale effectively across varying container-to-PU ratios. These findings offer actionable guidelines for designing safe and efficient container-management systems in real-world facilities.

Keywords: Reinforcement learning · Curriculum learning · Inference-time planning · Industrial control · Collision avoidance

1 Introduction

Waste-sorting facilities increasingly rely on data-driven methods to meet strict energy efficiency and sustainability goals, due in part to regulatory directives for responsible recycling of packaging waste. Modern plants must deal with fluctuating material types, unpredictable daily volumes, and stringent safety constraints. This work is inspired by the final stage of a waste-sorting facility where n containers (*bunkers*) accumulate various types of material at unique stochastic rates. These materials are subsequently transported to a processing unit (PU) for compaction into bales or products[1] during which PU is unavailable for further

---
[1] In this study the terms bunker/container and processing unit (PU)/press are used interchangeably.

processing. In addition, each container has a strict maximum capacity and overflowing beyond a threshold requires halting the facility for corrective measures, incurring steep penalties. In this context, *container management* emerges as a critical bottleneck: Emptying these containers too late risks overflow; emptying them too early or too frequently undermines throughput and raises energy costs.

Recent work has modeled container management as a reinforcement learning (RL) problem, notably through *ContainerGym* [9], providing a real-world benchmark where an RL agent decides *when* to empty each container. However, naive Proximal Policy Optimization (PPO) agents frequently fail in this domain, as *delayed rewards*, *sparse critical events*, and a *single shared PU* create complex scheduling dynamics. For instance, some containers have a "higher peak" volume (around 60–75% capacity) for optimal throughput and a "lower peak" (around 30–40%) as a fallback. Emptying containers at the peak volumes yields optimal products, hence emptying at other volumes is undesirable. The prime reason for missing a peak volume is unavailability of the PU caused by a *collision* of two or more containers reaching peak volume around the same time. Prior work showed that *curriculum learning* helps mitigate early overflows and improves PPO's learning curve [10]. Still, the problem of handling collisions remains unsolved, especially at higher container-to-PU ratios.

On the other hand, despite the installation of sophisticated sensors in these facilities and real-time monitoring, most waste sorting design layouts remain fixed once built, even if data points to major bottlenecks. This reveals a broader gap: leveraging RL not only to optimize day-to-day operations but also to guide *facility design decisions* such as how many containers can safely share a PU before collisions dominate. In other industries–like robotics or warehouse logistics–RL insights have influenced layout reconfiguration, helping systems adapt hardware choices to software-derived constraints. Yet in waste-sorting, this feedback loop remains largely unexplored.

To address these gaps, we present a *hybrid RL* method that integrates curriculum learning with a domain-specific *collision model* at inference time. Our approach (1) reduces collision-induced overflows and throughput losses, and (2) closes the loop between software-driven scheduling and hardware design insights. Specifically, we:

- Propose a three-phase *curriculum learning* strategy to tackle delayed rewards and dual-volume targets (higher vs. lower peak).
- Introduce an *offline-trained collision model* for on-the-fly inference checks, overriding risky "no-op" actions when multiple containers approach critical volumes.
- Systematically evaluate varying *container-to-PU ratios* (7:1 to 12:1), providing actionable guidelines on how many containers a single PU can realistically handle without causing excessive collisions.

Empirical results demonstrate that the proposed hybrid RL framework significantly cuts collisions, reduces safety limit violations, maintains higher throughput, and yields design insights for scaling container management (Fig. 1).

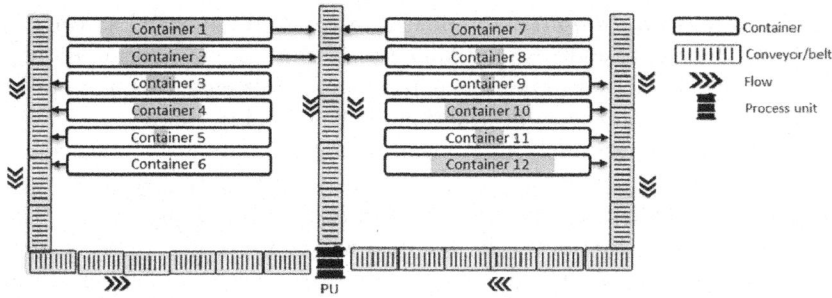

Fig. 1. Layout sketch of a facility with 12 containers and a PU, connected with conveyor belts. The containers are filled from above, with their current fill states indicated by the shaded areas.

2 Related Work

Reinforcement learning has proliferated in industrial and logistics applications, moving beyond canonical benchmarks to real-world applications. We categorize related literature under the following three key themes:

Curriculum Learning in Industrial RL. Curriculum learning (CL) systematically organizes the training tasks, typically starting with simpler sub-problems before moving to more challenging ones [1,2]. In industrial domains, where critical actions are rare and reward signals can be delayed or sparse, CL helps agents gather meaningful experience without being overwhelmed by complex dynamics from the outset. Prior work in container management [10] showed that a curriculum-based PPO significantly reduces early overflows compared to naive baselines. We build on this by designing a multi-phase reward curriculum–enabling the agent to master *dual-peak* emptying targets and maintain stable performance under varying inflows.

Inference-Time Planning and Collision Avoidance. While a trained RL policy provides baseline decisions at deployment, *inference-time planning* augments these decisions with lookahead logic or heuristic checks, often through Monte Carlo methods. Techniques vary in whether they update the agent's parameters or remain "stateless." Prominent examples include Monte Carlo simulations in game-playing AI [3,8], but similar ideas have surfaced in robotics [4,5], energy systems control [7] and autonomous driving [6]. In our context, we adopt a *collision model* that is trained offline to predict when multiple containers are poised to exceed safe volumes simultaneously. This model supplements a curriculum-trained policy by overriding risky no-operation actions–preventing multi-container collisions. By decoupling real-time safety checks from the offline-trained policy, our method maintains policy stability and adds minimal inference overhead, which is essential for deployment in high-throughput industrial environments.

RL-Driven Design Insights. An emerging trend in industrial settings is the use of RL not merely to control a dynamic process but also to inform insights into *design* decisions. In large warehouse environments, multi-agent RL has optimized the assignment of "chutes" to destinations [12], reducing robot congestion and improving throughput. Similar approaches in factory automation focus on workstation placement [13], where RL-driven layout designs outperform handcrafted alternatives. Meanwhile, open-source platforms like "Storehouse" show that RL can outperform heuristic policies in dynamic warehouse slotting [14]. These successes underscore how AI insights can *redesign* processes for higher efficiency, paralleling our goal of using RL not just to operate container management but to shape decisions on how many containers a PU can handle effectively.

Context of our Contribution. By integrating a *predefined curriculum* for delayed rewards with an *offline collision predictor*, our hybrid **PPO-CL-CM** approach targets both throughput optimization and collision avoidance in container management. Offline pairwise simulations yield a lightweight collision classifier, which can be queried at each time step to override the policy when collision risk is high. The result is a system that meets key challenges–dual-peak scheduling, sparse rewards, and collision hazards–while also generating real-world design insights. In the following sections, we present the formal environment setup, detail our curriculum learning phases, and then describe how we integrate collision checks at inference.

3 Environment and RL Formulation

In this section, we provide details of the considered container management environment. Building on the scenario described in Sect. 1, we reiterate the central design optimization criterion; each container has two preferred or "ideal" volumes at which emptying yields the highest-quality output. These correspond to a *Higher peak* offering better overall throughput if the container can safely reach this point and a *Lower peak*, providing a reasonable fallback when waiting longer could risk overflow or collide with the PU's availability window. In practice, larger volumes generally improve efficiency, as the PU operates more effectively when processing bigger batches at once. However, strictly aiming for the higher peak can provoke collisions or safety limit breaches if the single PU is not available in time.

Markov Decision Process (MDP) Setup. We model the container-management scenario as an MDP $(\mathcal{S}, \mathcal{A}, p, r, \gamma)$:

- **State s_t:** Comprises volumes $\{v_{i,t}\}_{i=1}^{n}$ for each container, a PU-availability counter p_t (time until the processing unit becomes available), and auxiliary signals such as ideal volumes. This provides the agent with both physical constraints (capacity, current usage) and strategic cues (optimal targets).

- **Action $a_t \in \{0, \ldots, n\}$**: Either do nothing ($a_t = 0$) or attempt to empty container i. If $p_t > 0$ (the PU is busy), an emptying request fails, and container i continues to fill. This design highlights collision risks when multiple containers approach peak volumes simultaneously.
- **Volume Dynamics**: Each container i grows according to a *random walk with drift*:
$$v_{i,t+1} = \max(0, v_{i,t} + \alpha_i + \epsilon_{i,t}), \tag{1}$$
where α_i is the average fill rate, and $\epsilon_{i,t} \sim \mathcal{N}(0, \sigma_i^2)$ captures stochastic fluctuations. Overflow occurs if $v_{i,t} > 40$, triggering a heavy penalty and episode termination.
- **PU Overhead**: Emptying container i with volume v imposes a busy time $g_i(v)$. The busy time consists of a material-dependent part that is proportional to the volume, and a constant offset for conveyor belt transport of the material from the container to the PU. During this period, p_t counts down to zero, after which the PU is free again. Requests made while $p_t > 0$ are effectively lost, emphasizing scheduling constraints.
- **Rewards**: The agent receives reward for emptying containers close to their peak volumes, since that behavior results in high quality output. Rewards are designed so that emptying at the higher peak is preferable. Container overflow is a terminal state with an episode reset. *Invalid* or wasteful empties (e.g., container already empty or PU busy) incur a negative penalty r_{pen}, while the *do-nothing* action yields zero.

Collision State. A *collision* arises when one or more containers simultaneously approach or exceed their higher-peak volumes, but the PU remains busy processing another container. This can rapidly push volumes over physical capacity if not addressed promptly. Although we first train the agent without a collision-specific mechanism, Sect. 5 discusses how we incorporate a collision model at inference time.

Objective. The agent must *schedule empties* near either the higher or lower volume peak to maximize efficiency, while preventing overflows and avoiding collisions on the shared PU. The tension between delaying emptying for higher-volume payoffs versus frequent empties for safety and reduced collisions creates a challenging RL problem under delayed rewards and a scarce PU bottleneck.

Key Challenges

- **Stochastic inflow and sensor noise:** Each container's fill rate depends on material type, density, and unpredictable external factors (e.g., time of day, seasonal fluctuations). Sensor noise further obscures volume estimates, making it difficult to predict precisely when a container will reach a target volume.
- **Delayed rewards and class imbalance:** Some containers fill slowly, requiring hours of in-simulation time to reach the target volume. Consequently,

episodes contain many "do nothing" steps, during which the state changes steadily but rewards from emptying remain sparse. As emptying actions are rare, reward-bearing moves are infrequent, creating skewed action distributions that challenge many reinforcement learning algorithms.
- **Dual-peak design and Collisions:** Having two ideal emptying peaks per container creates a nuanced trade-off: waiting for the higher peak boosts efficiency but risks collisions and overflow if multiple containers converge while the PU is busy. Alternatively, settling too often for the lower peak increases emptying frequency, raising energy costs and volume deviations. Balancing these opposing factors–alongside scheduling constraints to avoid collisions and safety violations–poses a central challenge.

Algorithm 1: Three-Phase Reward Computation

Input : Phase $ph \in \{1, 2, 3\}$, current volume v_t, action a_t, penalty r_{pen}, peaks $(v_{\text{low}}, v_{\text{high}})$, Gaussian params (h, w) or (h_1, h_2, w_1, w_2)
Output: Immediate reward r_t

if $a_t = 0$ then // No-op
  $r_t \leftarrow 0$;
else
  if (invalid conditions) then // Invalid empty
    $r_t \leftarrow r_{\text{pen}}$;
  else
    if $ph = 1$ then // Phase 1
      $r_t \leftarrow (h - r_{\text{pen}}) \exp\left(-\frac{(v_t - v_{\text{high}})^2}{2 w^2}\right) + r_{\text{pen}}$;
    else if $ph = 2$ then // Phase 2
      $r_t \leftarrow r_{\text{pen}} + \sum_{i \in \{\text{low}, \text{high}\}} \left[h_i - r_{\text{pen}}\right] \exp\left(-\frac{(v_t - v_i)^2}{2 w_i^2}\right)$;
    else // Phase 3
      if $|v_t - v_{low}| \leq 1 \lor |v_t - v_{high}| \leq 1$ then
        $r_t \leftarrow 1.0$
      else
        $r_t \leftarrow 0$

---

4 Methodology

In this section, we detail our complete pipeline for training PPO-based agents to manage containers. We begin with a *naive PPO* baseline, highlighting its struggles with sparse, multimodal rewards and the tendency toward premature empties. To address these issues, we then propose a *curriculum learning* scheme (PPO-CL) that incrementally shapes the agent's reward landscape. This two-stage progression–naive PPO followed by PPO-CL–lays the groundwork for an inference-time *collision model*, which further mitigates overflow risks when multiple containers compete for the PU.

4.1 Naive PPO Baseline and Its Shortcomings

A straightforward approach is to train a PPO agent directly on the final (multimodal) reward that encourages emptying containers at either the higher or lower peak. However, as outlined in Sect. 3, this environment poses multiple challenges: rewards are delayed and infrequent, containers fill at varying rates, and collisions can arise when the PU services multiple containers simultaneously. Without additional structure or foresight, empirical results (see Table 2) show that a naive PPO agent tends to:

- **Ignore long-term returns.** Driven by sparse rewards, the agent often performs multiple partial empties rather than waiting for the larger peak. This short-sighted strategy blocks the PU more frequently, increasing energy usage and leaving less capacity for containers that are about to overflow.
- **Struggle with skewed action distributions.** With many "do-nothing" steps before a container reaches its target volume, the agent fails to learn precise timing to consistently hit higher-volume empties.
- **Overlook future collisions.** Having no explicit mechanism to anticipate bottlenecks on the PU, the agent may wait too long and face simultaneous arrivals at near-peak volumes, risking overflow or forced early empties.

4.2 Curriculum Learning with PPO

These shortcomings motivate a more structured approach to handle delayed rewards, skewed actions, and collision risks. We therefore present a *curriculum learning* strategy that gradually refines the agent's timing and decision-making. We train a PPO agent with a *three-phase reward curriculum*, gradually introducing complexity over successive training segments. In each phase, the agent follows the same *state* and *action* definitions, but the reward function evolves to guide the agent toward better timing of empties:

- **Phase 1 (Unimodal Reward):** We place a single Gaussian peak at the higher peak volume and no reward at the lower peak, helping the agent learn to avoid excessively early empties.
- **Phase 2 (Multimodal Reward):** Two Gaussian peaks (higher and lower), letting the agent discover a fallback if waiting for the higher peak is unsafe or if the PU is unavailable.
- **Phase 3 (Step Reward):** A strict scheme awarding positive reward only when the emptied volume is within a narrow window (± 1) around *either* peak, refining precision once the agent learned to handle both targets.

As in [10,11], we further stabilize training by *freezing* the policy network in parts of Phase 2, updating only the value estimator to account for changes in reward structure. During Phase 3, we *unfreeze* the policy network but apply a stricter KL-divergence constraint, ensuring the agent does not deviate too aggressively from the policy learned in earlier phases. Algorithm 1 presents the logic for all three phases. By stepping through these phases with carefully tuned budgets, the agent (*PPO-CL*) acquires more robust scheduling behaviors than a naive single-stage approach. In particular, it learns to occasionally pick the lower peak to avert overflow. However, PPO-CL alone remains largely myopic about *collisions* across containers, motivating our inference-time mitigation strategy in the next section.

5 Collision Model and Inference Pipeline

Although PPO-CL improves emptying behavior, it still shows no signs of successfully learning about collision risks. We mitigate the problem by designing a mechanism to handle situations where multiple containers simultaneously approach their peak volumes. We address this by introducing a *collision model (CM)* trained offline on pairwise container data, then integrating it with the PPO-CL agent at inference time to form **PPO-CL-CM**. This approach balances high-volume empties with timely overrides to avert collisions, all at minimal run-time overhead.

Monte Carlo Rollouts for Pairwise Collisions: For efficient inference-time planning, we generate a large offline dataset of pairwise collision scenarios. By simulating isolated or small groups of containers, we capture diverse collision states with minimal run-time cost. We simulate each container pair (i, j) under stochastic filling (1). Two million repetitions across a container configuration yield a comprehensive offline data set of near-capacity, overflow, and collision events, minimizing deployment computation. For each pair, we perform:

1. Random initialization: Sample means and standard deviations $\mu_i, \mu_j, \sigma_i, \sigma_j$ for filling rates.
2. Stochastic evolution: Evolve volumes $v_i(\tau), v_j(\tau)$ over timesteps τ.
3. Collision bookkeeping: Record collisions when both containers near peaks while the PU is busy.

Feature Extraction and Training. At each simulation timestep, we extract collision-predictive features:

- Volumes: Container states (v_i, v_j)
- Proximity to peaks: $\Delta v_i = p_i - v_i, \Delta v_j = p_j - v_j$
- Filling parameters: $(\mu_i, \sigma_i, \mu_j, \sigma_j)$
- Time-lag context: Optional short-volume histories $\{v_i(\tau - 1), v_j(\tau - 1)\}$

Each timestep receives a *collision label* $\{0, 1\}$, creating a supervised dataset {features, collision label} for training. From this dataset, we train an XGBoost classifier to estimate collision probabilities: $P(C_{i,j} \mid s_t, a_t) = f_{\text{col}}(\text{features}_{i,j})$. XGBoost's gradient-boosted trees efficiently model complex relationships between volumes, fill rates, and near-capacity states. Tuned XGBoost offers fast, accurate pairwise collision risk predictions.

Inference-Time Integration with PPO-CL: Once trained, the collision model f_{col} is invoked at each decision step to assess pairwise collision probabilities. The *baseline* PPO-CL agent first proposes an action a_t. If it decides to empty a specific container ($a_t \neq 0$), we accept that choice directly. However, if PPO-CL proposes *no operation* ($a_t = 0$), the system queries f_{col} for all container pairs to estimate near-future collision risks. If any container at high volume is flagged with a collision probability above a threshold θ, we *override* the no-op by forcing an empty action on the most at-risk container. Algorithm 2 details the procedure.

Action Override Rationale. By limiting overrides to the no-op action, we minimally disturb PPO-CL's learned preference for waiting until containers reach higher volumes. Only when the model detects a high probability of overflow or severe collisions do we *force* an empty on a likely-to-clash container. This blend of *offline collision modeling* and *selective inference-time planning* yields a more collision-aware agent.

Algorithm 2: Integrated Inference-Time Decision with Pairwise Collision Prediction

---

Input : State s_t, PPO-CL policy π_{CL}, collision model f_{col}, threshold θ, peak volumes $\{p_i\}$
Output: Final action $a_{\text{final}} \in \{0, 1, \ldots, n\}$

1. PPO-CL Action: $a_t \sim \pi_{\text{CL}}(a_t \mid s_t)$;
if $a_t \neq 0$ **then**
  return $a_{\text{final}} \leftarrow a_t$;   // Accept non-zero action

2. Collision Assessment:
foreach *pair* (i, j) **do**
  $P(C_{i,j}) \leftarrow f_{\text{col}}(\text{features}_{i,j})$;
Assemble matrix $P_t[i, j] = P(C_{i,j})$;

3. Check Potential Collision Overrides:
$\mathcal{C} \leftarrow \{ i \mid v_i(t) \geq p_i - \delta \}$;
if $\mathcal{C} \neq \emptyset$ **then**
  foreach $i \in \mathcal{C}$ **do**
    $\text{CollisionRisk}(i) \leftarrow \text{RiskScore}(i, P_t)$
  $i^\star \leftarrow \arg\max_{i \in \mathcal{C}} \left[\text{CollisionRisk}(i)\right]$;
  if $\text{CollisionRisk}(i^\star) \geq \theta$ **then**
    $a_{\text{final}} \leftarrow i^\star$;   // Override with container $i^\star$
  else
    $a_{\text{final}} \leftarrow 0$;   // Retain no-op
  return a_{final}

return $a_{\text{final}} \leftarrow 0$;   // No containers at risk, do nothing

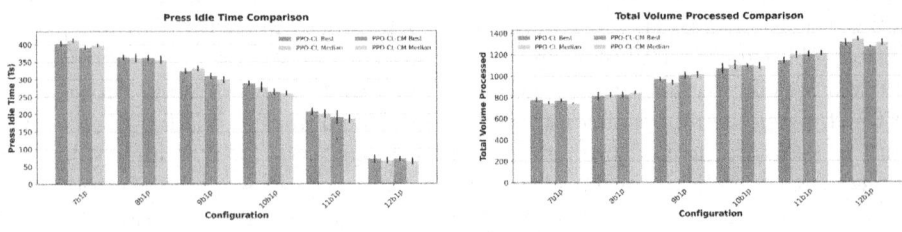

(a) Press idle time comparison.   (b) Total volume processed comparison.

Fig. 2. Performance metrics comparison between PPO-CL and PPO-CL-CM methods across different container configurations (7b1p to 12b1p). The bars show mean values and error bars indicate standard deviation. Left: Press idle time shows the duration the press remains inactive. Right: Total volume processed indicates the amount of material handled during one inference episode of 600 timesteps.

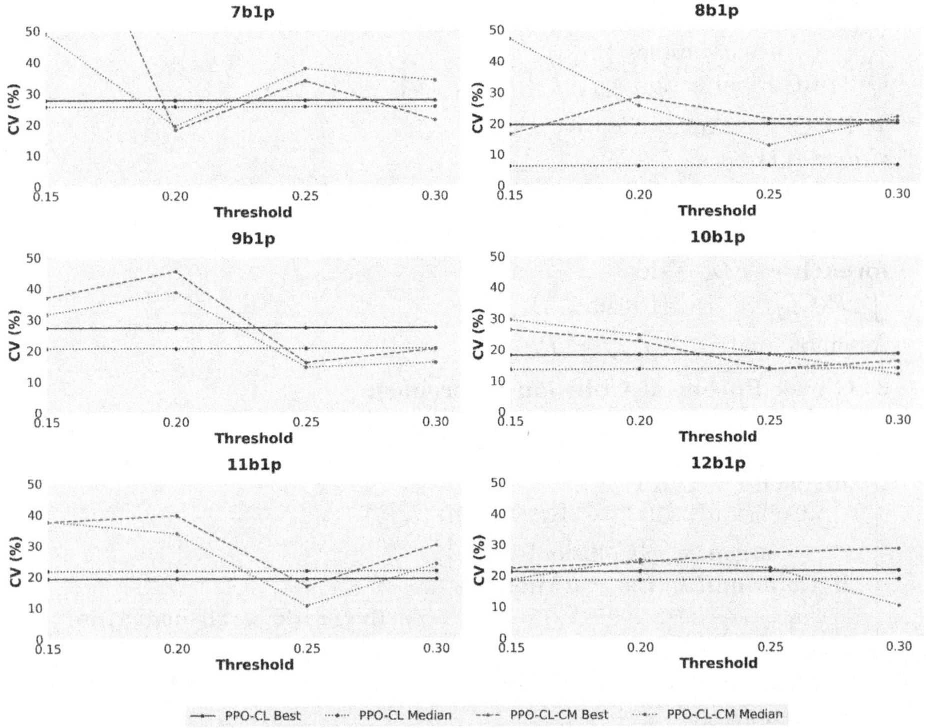

Fig. 3. Comparison of Coefficient of Variation (CV%) across different collision probability thresholds for all container configurations. Each subplot shows the performance of PPO-CL and PPO-CL-CM methods for a specific configuration. Lower CV% indicates more consistent performance.

6 Experimental Evaluation

In this section, we present a quantitative evaluation of the three agents naive PPO, PPO-CL, and PPO-CL-CM across multiple container-to-PU configurations. Our analysis addresses the following research questions (**RQs**):

1. **RQ1:** Is the inference-time collision model (*PPO-CL-CM*) effective compared to PPO-CL and naive PPO in terms of achieved reward?
2. **RQ2:** How effectively does the collision model reduce safety-limit violations (i.e., empties above the critical volume limit)?
3. **RQ3:** How do these findings inform real-world design choices, such as the ideal ratio of containers to processing units?

In the spirit of open and reproducible research, we make our source code available via an ***anonymous repository***.[2] The repository contains a script for reproducing all results presented in this section.

6.1 Experimental Setup

We evaluate our methods on environments with *7 to 12* containers and a single PU (labeled "7b1p" through "12b1p"). Following [9] we use an episode length of 600 timesteps, with a 60-second granularity. For each agent, we conduct *15* independent training runs using distinct random seeds. During inference, we run each seed-based policy in *5* rollouts and collect statistics. We present results for both the *best* and *median* performing seeds of each method, ensuring a fair and comprehensive comparison. Specifically, the *best seed* is selected based on the smallest number of *collision timesteps*, while the *median seed* is chosen from the remaining seeds in terms of the same metric.

Metrics: The reward signal aggregates many different subgoals. To obtain a fine-grained picture of algorithm performance, we monitor the following performance metrics:

- *Press Idle Time* (Fig. 2a): total timesteps during which the PU is not processing any container.
- *Total Volume Processed* (Fig. 2b): material throughput in one 600-step inference episode.
- *Collisions in time-steps*: the total number of timesteps in which a *collision state* occurs; that is, at least two containers simultaneously approach or exceed their ideal volumes (especially the higher peak) while the PU is busy and thus unable to service them.
- *Coefficient of Variation (CV%) (Fig. 3):* a normalized measure of variability in performance under different collision thresholds.
- *Total Volume Deviation*: the average (over all containers and timesteps) of the absolute difference between a container's actual volume and its nearest ideal peak, gauging how well empties align with target volumes.

---

[2] https://gitlab.com/anonymousppocl_cm1/anonymous_collisions_paper.

- *Actions per Container, Reward per Action, and Peak-Usage Ratios*: drawn from Tables 1 and 2.
- *Safety-Limit Violation Percentage* (Fig. 4): the fraction of emptying actions during inference where a container volume exceeds a fixed ***critical volume limit***, set 5 units above that container's higher ideal emptying peak.

All agents are tested under the same environmental conditions to isolate the impact of curriculum training and collision modeling. Moreover, the results shown in Figs. 2 and 4 and in Tables 1 and 2 are reported using the threshold values that yield the lowest CV% in Fig. 3, reflecting the most collision-stable configurations in our analysis.

6.2 Impact of Collision Model (RQ1)

From Table 2, we note that naive PPO often fails to empty containers at the *higher* ideal peak altogether (*e.g.*, ratio close to zero), indicating it resorts to early or sub-optimal empties. This behavior leads to more frequent episodes ending prematurely due to overflow (especially in the larger "12b1p" setup) or consistently high volume deviations. While PPO-CL capitalizes on the multi-phase reward shaping to handle delayed feedback and class imbalance, collisions can still occur if multiple containers simultaneously converge on their higher peaks. This is where incorporating *inference-time collision checks* to yield PPO-CL-CM has an edge.

As shown in Fig. 3, PPO-CL-CM achieves lower variability (CV%) across different collision probability thresholds, meaning it more consistently avoids hazardous states. From Fig. 2a, we see PPO-CL-CM generally reduces press idle time compared to PPO-CL, indicating fewer deadlocks where containers are left unemptied until near-overflow conditions. Meanwhile, Fig. 2b shows that *total volume processed* remains at least on par with (and often surpasses) PPO-CL, demonstrating that collision avoidance does not compromise overall throughput in an inference episode.

Table 1 reveals that *collision timesteps* drop systematically for *PPO-CL-CM*, and its *volume deviation* is also slightly lower on average. The *higher/lower peak ratio* in Table 2 confirms that PPO-CL-CM empties containers earlier (lower peak) only when the collision model flags imminent risk, thereby balancing high-throughput empties with safety. Hence, **RQ1** is answered: adding an inference-time collision model mitigates bottlenecks and collisions beyond what curriculum-based RL can achieve alone.

6.3 Safety-Limit Violations (RQ2)

Figure 4 summarizes the frequency of empties that exceed the safety critical volume limit, thus posing a higher risk of overflow and breach of physical limit. We observe that **PPO-CL-CM** consistently maintains a smaller fraction of risky empties overall than PPO-CL for all bunker-to-PU setups from *7b1p* through *12b1p*. This indicates that the collision model not only reduces direct collisions but also prompts timely empties before containers venture into risky volume ranges. Hence, we conclude **RQ2** by confirming that inference-time collision checks can effectively mitigate dangerous critical empties, supporting safer operation without sacrificing throughput.

6.4 Real-World Implications and Design Guidance (RQ3)

Figure 2a illustrates that as we move from "7b1p" up to "12b1p," *press idle time* diminishes significantly, reflecting how the PU becomes fully utilized with rising container counts. On the other hand, in extremely large configurations (e.g., 12 containers to 1 PU), collisions inevitably remain because a single resource cannot realistically handle multiple near-peak arrivals at once. While PPO-CL-CM can curb severe collisions, it cannot eliminate them entirely when the resource ratio is unfavorable. Thus for *Moderate Ratios:* Up to around 7–11 containers per PU, collision avoidance measures like PPO-CL-CM yield strong improvements without saturating the system. But for *High Ratios:*, beyond a certain limit (e.g., 12b1p), press idle time becomes negligible, and collision events dominate. An additional PU may be necessary for higher container configurations. Addressing **RQ3**, in practice, operators can apply these findings when deciding how many containers can be feasibly connected to a single processing unit, and whether advanced collision checks are cost-effective. Importantly, applying a collision model allows to safely operate more containers with the same number of expensive PUs.

Table 1. Main performance metrics (Best/Median) for each bunker configuration, all rounded to one decimal place. Each cell shows *Best* ± std. / *Median* ± std. in one line. We boldface the **better** result in PPO-CL-CM whenever it outperforms PPO-CL (lower collisions/dev or higher reward).

Config	Agent	Collisions (Ts)	Tot. vol. dev (%)	Reward/action
7b1p	PPO-CL	72.4 ± 20.0 / 81.6 ± 20.9	7.3 ± 2.1 / 6.9 ± 1.2	0.4 / 0.4
	PPO-CL-CM	**22.0 ± 3.9** / **34.4 ± 6.7**	**5.1 ± 0.7** / **6.1 ± 0.6**	**0.7** / **0.8**
8b1p	PPO-CL	77.2 ± 15.1 / 98.6 ± 6.1	7.4 ± 0.8 / 7.3 ± 0.9	0.3 / 0.4
	PPO-CL-CM	**66.2 ± 14.0** / **80.6 ± 10.2**	**6.7 ± 1.2** / **7.0 ± 0.7**	**0.6** / **0.5**
9b1p	PPO-CL	117.0 ± 31.7 / 153.4 ± 31.4	6.5 ± 1.4 / 7.5 ± 1.1	0.4 / 0.3
	PPO-CL-CM	**89.8 ± 14.4** / **117.0 ± 17.0**	**6.3 ± 1.4** / **7.6 ± 0.7**	**0.6** / **0.4**
10b1p	PPO-CL	154.6 ± 28.1 / 189.8 ± 25.8	6.8 ± 1.2 / 8.7 ± 0.9	0.4 / 0.2
	PPO-CL-CM	**138.2 ± 18.5** / **145.4 ± 26.3**	**6.4 ± 0.4** / **6.8 ± 0.9**	**0.5** / **0.5**
11b1p	PPO-CL	130.8 ± 25.0 / 156.4 ± 33.8	8.0 ± 1.3 / 6.9 ± 0.5	0.3 / 0.3
	PPO-CL-CM	**83.2 ± 13.9** / **148.4 ± 15.4**	**7.6 ± 1.2** / 6.8 ± 0.7	**0.5** / **0.5**
12b1p	PPO-CL	126.4 ± 26.8 / 195.8 ± 36.0	11.8 ± 2.1 / 10.2 ± 1.3	0.3 / 0.3
	PPO-CL-CM	**117.4 ± 31.9** / **175.6 ± 38.9**	13.0 ± 2.2 / 11.2 ± 1.6	**0.5** / **0.4**

Table 2. Comparison of Higher/Lower Peak Percentage Ratio and Mean Actions per container (single decimal precision). For each configuration, "Best" / "Median" rows show mean ± standard deviation where applicable.

Config	Type	Higher/Lower Peak % Ratio			Actions/Container		
		Naive PPO	PPO-CL	PPO-CL-CM	Naive PPO	PPO-CL	PPO-CL-CM
7b1p	Best	0.0	45.7	1.0	32.7 ± 8.9	20.0 ± 3.4	25.6 ± 2.6
	Median	0.0	18.6	0.8	29.6 ± 12.3	19.6 ± 2.8	24.4 ± 3.1
8b1p	Best	0.0	8.4	2.2	31.0 ± 10.0	18.9 ± 3.8	20.8 ± 3.9
	Median	0.0	14.0	2.9	31.2 ± 8.6	18.8 ± 3.1	20.9 ± 4.7
9b1p	Best	0.0	16.5	4.5	33.3 ± 9.0	19.4 ± 3.4	21.2 ± 2.7
	Median	0.0	19.6	3.3	34.8 ± 9.9	18.3 ± 4.1	21.4 ± 3.1
10b1p	Best	0.0	30.5	3.3	33.2 ± 10.3	18.9 ± 2.5	20.8 ± 4.2
	Median	0.0	11.7	3.1	31.6 ± 8.0	19.1 ± 2.8	20.7 ± 5.0
11b1p	Best	0.0	3.1	1.8	34.1 ± 6.3	20.6 ± 4.6	22.5 ± 4.3
	Median	0.0	6.7	2.9	32.9 ± 7.6	20.3 ± 2.7	21.7 ± 3.5
12b1p	Best	N/A	1.9	1.6	N/A	23.1 ± 7.0	23.2 ± 8.1
	Median	N/A	2.6	2.4	N/A	22.1 ± 4.8	22.1 ± 6.1

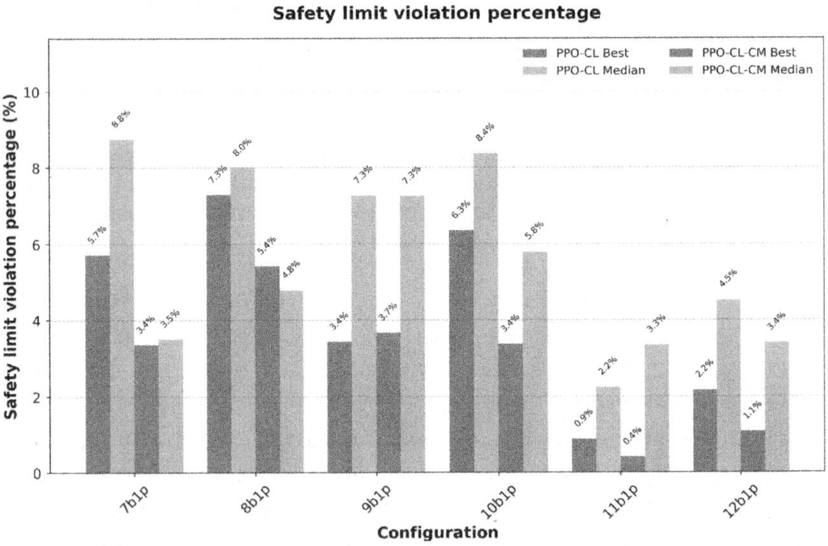

Fig. 4. Comparison of safety limit violation percentages across different bunker configurations. Bars show the percentage of emptying actions that exceeded the safety limit for each bunker configuration using PPO-CL and PPO-CL-CM methods.

7 Conclusion

We have presented a hybrid strategy for container management in a waste-sorting facility in a constrained resource scenario, where each container has two preferred "ideal" emptying volumes. The first component, *PPO-CL*, addresses the challenges of sparse rewards and dual-volume targets through a curriculum-learning approach that teaches the agent to empty containers near either a lower or higher peak. The second component, a *collision model* integrated at inference time (*PPO-CL-CM*), provides targeted overrides when containers risk colliding at peak volumes. This combination effectively balances the key design criteria: prioritizing the higher peak for optimal throughput while resorting to the lower peak only when collisions or safety violations become imminent.

Empirical results across various container-to-PU ratios (7:1 to 12:1) demonstrate that *PPO-CL-CM* reduces both collision episodes and empties above a critical safety threshold, *without sacrificing total processed volume*. By explicitly modeling future collision risk, it prevents premature empties that might otherwise occur if the agent tried to avoid collisions by abandoning the higher peak too soon. From an operational standpoint, these findings suggest that facility managers can confidently scale up container counts to a point, relying on our framework to avoid overflows and to ensure safe, high-volume empties. Beyond that point, collisions become unavoidable, but our method still lessens their severity.

A notable advantage of this framework is that the collision model is trained entirely offline via Monte Carlo simulations, adding only minimal overhead during inference. This approach stands in contrast to computationally intensive online planners like Monte Carlo Tree Search, making it better suited for large, stochastic industrial environments with real-time decision needs. Looking ahead, we envision several avenues to extend this work: integrating multiple PUs (or more complex resource constraints) within the same collision-avoidance framework, dynamically tuning collision thresholds based on time-of-day inflows or real-time capacity data, and more tightly fusing offline collision insights with online RL updates to further refine scheduling decisions. Our findings highlight that a domain-aware collision model, combined with carefully shaped RL curricula, can yield safer, more efficient container management, establishing a robust framework for broader industrial adoption and more complex resource-allocation tasks.

Acknowledgements. This work was funded by the German federal ministry of economic affairs and climate action through the "ecoKI" grant.

References

1. Narvekar, S., Peng, B., Leonetti, M., Sinapov, J., Taylor, M.E., Stone, P.: Curriculum learning for reinforcement learning domains: a framework and survey. J. Mach. Learn. Res. **21**, 1–50 (2020)

2. Wang, X., Chen, Y., Zhu, W.: A survey on curriculum learning. IEEE Trans. Pattern Anal. Mach. Intell. **44**(9), 4555–4576 (2022)
3. Browne, C.B.: A survey of monte carlo tree search methods. IEEE Trans. Comput. Intell. AI Games **4**(1), 1–43 (2012)
4. Romero, A., Zhang, Y., Gibon, K., Goy, M., Boulet, M., Pineau, J., Labbé, M.: Actor-Critic Model Predictive Control: Differentiable Optimization Meets Reinforcement Learning. arXiv preprint arXiv:2306.09852 (2023)
5. Wang, Z., Wei, W., Xie, A., et al.: Hybrid bipedal locomotion based on reinforcement learning and heuristics. Micromachines **13**(10), 1688 (2022)
6. Hoel, C.-J., Driggs-Campbell, K., Wolff, K., Laine, L., Kochenderfer, M.J.: Combining planning and deep reinforcement learning in tactical decision making for autonomous driving. IEEE Trans. Intell. Veh. **5**(2), 294–305 (2020)
7. Eseye, A.T., Zhang, X., Knueven, B., et al.: A Hybrid Reinforcement Learning–MPC Approach for Distribution System Critical Load Restoration. IEEE Power and Energy Society General Meeting (PESGM), In Proc (2022)
8. Silver, D., et al.: Mastering the game of go with deep neural networks and tree search. Nature **529**(7587), 484–489 (2016)
9. Pendyala, A., Dettmer, J., Glasmachers, T., Atamna, A.: ContainerGym: a real-world reinforcement learning benchmark for resource allocation. In: Machine Learning, Optimization, and Data Science, pp. 78–92. Springer Nature Switzerland (2024)
10. Pendyala, A., Atamna, A., Glasmachers, T.: Solving a real-world optimization problem using proximal policy optimization with curriculum learning and reward engineering. In: Machine Learning and Knowledge Discovery in Databases. Applied Data Science Track, pp. 150–165. Springer Nature Switzerland (2024)
11. Wang, X., et al.: SCC: an efficient deep reinforcement learning agent mastering the game of StarCraft II. arXiv preprint arXiv:2012.13169 (Dec 2020)
12. Shen, Y., McClosky, B., Durham, J.W., Zavlanos, M.M.: Multi-agent reinforcement learning for resource allocation in large-scale robotic warehouse sortation centers. In: 2023 62nd IEEE Conference on Decision and Control (CDC), 2023, pp. 7137–7143 (2023)
13. Ikeda, H., Nakagawa, H., Tsuchiya, T.: Towards automatic facility layout design using reinforcement learning. In: Communication Papers of the 17th Conference on Computer Science and Intelligence Systems, vol. 32, Annals of Computer Science and Information Systems, 2022, pp. 11–20 (2022)
14. Cestero, J., Quartulli, M., Metelli, A.M., Restelli, M.: Storehouse: a reinforcement learning environment for optimizing warehouse management. In: International Joint Conference Neural Networks (IJCNN), pp. 1–9 (2022)

Urban Verticalization and Water Consumption: A Data-Driven Approach for São Paulo

Arthur Hiratsuka Rezende[✉] and André P. de L. F. de Carvalho

Institute of Mathematical and Computer Sciences, University of São Paulo, São Paulo, Brazil
arthurhr@usp.br, andre@icmc.usp.br

Abstract. Concurrent trends of urbanization and population growth in Brazil can exert high pressure on the (already degraded) environment. In the city of São Paulo, in particular, there is a clear trend towards verticalization of real estate, increasing population density. To attend demands due to this rapid change in a particular area, water consumption, it is necessary to understand the aspects related with domestic water demand. The main objective of this study is to analyze the monthly water consumption in high-rise residential properties, and investigate the descriptive power of building related variables using machine learning. For such, real consumption data from the past three years (provided by the water and sewage company Sabesp) were obtained, along with two databases containing detailed information on high-rise apartment buildings in the city of São Paulo. After a meticulous integration of these databases, reliable information were obtained for 3,299 high-rise buildings, totalizing 276,670 apartments, described by 21 variables. One potential weakness in commonly used estimates (e.g., demographic, financial) is that they may be outdated or biased. In contrast, the physical characteristics of buildings are easily verifiable, and simple to obtain. The study's hypothesis is that relying solely on the building features may preserve a similar descriptive power, while eliminating uncertainties and biases. A contribution of this study is the estimation of the monthly consumption per unit, which can be used for modeling urban water distribution systems. In the experiments carried out, fourteen different regression algorithms for consumption prediction are investigated, and the predictive performance of the induced models is comparable with similar studies that use building characteristics alongside population estimates and water/sewage features in the building, partially confirming the research hypothesis.

Keywords: Water Consumption · Urban Infrastructure · Urban Verticalization · Machine Learning

1 Introduction

The rational management of natural resources is crucial for humanity. The United Nations[1] estimates that the global population reached 8 billion in 2022, with projections of nearly 10 billion by 2050–25% increase in just 28 years. According to the report, approximately 58.3% of the global population, including 54.3% in less developed regions, is expected to live in cities by 2025. These proportions are projected to rise to 68.4% and 65.6%, respectively, by 2050.

Additionally, according to the 2023 SNIS report[2], national water losses reached 37.8%, with São Paulo reporting a loss rate of 27.9%[3]. In this context, accurate consumption estimates are essential for realistic system modeling and simulation. These tools can support loss reduction efforts through improved leak detection.

Regarding water distribution (WD) in Brazil, demographic trends significantly influence water consumption patterns, as demonstrated in the Sect. 4.1. This study is part of a preliminary investigation supporting the revision of the Technical Standard for Residential Building Design by Sabesp, the water and sewage company that serves the city of São Paulo, in São Paulo state, Brazil. The study includes a diagnostic assessment of the current predictor's performance and presents preliminary results on the development of a new regressor.

1.1 Urbanization and Its Effects on Water Consumption

The relationship between water consumption and urban density has been verified in the city of Barcelona, Spain [6], due to population shifts from the central to peripheral areas. Urban areas in the city of Hawassa, Ethiopia [13], increased from 7.2% of the territory in 1991 to 26.5% in 2021, estimated to reach 45.9% by 2051. This expansion is expected to drive a 20% increase in water consumption.

A simulation of land-use changes in Brazil [3] projects an urban area expansion of over 4 km^2 in the city of Campina Grande, Brazil (an 8% increase) at the expense of rural areas. This transformation is expected to lead to a 7% rise in water consumption in the city between 2020 and 2050. In Tehran, Iran [30], deteriorated areas—characterized by structurally unstable buildings and streets with limited accessibility—show a negative correlation with water consumption, which may be attributed to outdated and inefficient distribution infrastructure.

Another factor that can affect urban WD, without increasing built-up areas, is the retrofitting of abandoned buildings into affordable housing, as studied by [7] in São Paulo. The city also has a housing policy of creating apartments of up to 50m^2 for social housing, and its 2014 Directive Plan promotes densification near public transport, driving the population to live closer to their working places, which is highly concentrated around the city center.

Since 1929, the city of São Paulo has seen a fast increasing number of high-rise apartment buildings (verticalization) [2] which accelerated during the 1960 s and

---

[1] UN-Habitat report - 2022.
[2] Sistema Nacional de Informações sobre Saneamento.
[3] Sabesp report on water losses.

1970s, and, since the 2000s, has seen an average of more than 250 new high-rise apartment buildings launched per year. By looking at the relationship between affordability and urban verticalization in the city, [18], it also be observed a paradigm shift in the recent constructions: a transition from low-to-mid-rise buildings to mid-to-high-rise developments, influencing both property prices and housing affordability.

1.2 Main Contributions

The main contribution from this study is to characterize the consumption of large consumers, defined as high-rise residential buildings. Water consumption data from the past three years in São Paulo was obtained with the support of Sabesp, and 21 building characteristics are integrated. The dataset includes 3,299 buildings, covering 276,670 apartments. The results may support WD simulations, with potential Smart City applications such as leakage detection and monitoring population density shifts and their impacts on water consumption.

The research hypothesis is that building characteristics provide strong descriptive and predictive power, reducing reliance on population, demographic, and income estimates, which may carry uncertainties and potential biases. After data integration and preprocessing, the most relevant variables for the water consumption in São Paulo are explored. An estimation of the consumption in high-rise buildings is presented, along with an analysis of the prediction errors.

2 Related Work

2.1 Related Studies on Water Comsumption

The related studies found by the authors investigate the demand profile of whole cities [10,13,14], explore and define consumption profiles, based on either hourly/daily patterns [13,15,16,20,22,24] or appliance usage [17,19,27,34]. Other works explored the average consumption of dwellings [4,11,21,31] or per building [5,9,29], with the latter being the focus of this study.

Regarding the techniques used, identification of statistical correlation, distribution analysis, and significance tests are employed to identify relevant variables. To estimate consumption, multiple linear regressions are commonly used [6,11,13,24,29,31,33]. The use of this easily explainable models is particularly interesting, as they provide coefficients that help assess the contribution of each variable to water consumption. GIS techniques [3,4,13,15,16,21,23,24,30] were also widely used, particularly considering Moran's I statistic and Spatial Lag/Correlation, in order to analyze spatial dependencies.

2.2 Variables Used to Explaining Urban Water Consumption

The selected variables are grouped into different domains. A subset of the variables proposed in the literature was used, since some of them are difficult to collect and may be unfeasible to collect, such as considering the type of plants in gardens [6]. Other variables may be biased, such as differentiating foreigners from residents [30,33] or considering religion [1].

Climatic Variables: In the context of climate data usage, it is common to find studies that investigate relationships with temperature, humidity, wind, and precipitation [10,12,14,16,22,31], as well as indirect influences through the presence of rainwater reuse systems [34] or alternative water supply systems [8]. Correlations with thermal sensation have also been observed [10,31].

Analyzing data from 38 Chinese cities [16], it was concluded that availability, tariff pricing, and the adoption of water-saving technologies become more significant compared to climatic factors. Notably, when consumers were grouped and a regression was performed [22], building characteristics and consumption related variables—such as hourly consumption, previous week's consumption at the same hour, and day of the week—were more influential than temperature.

Variables Related to Appliances: There are uncertainties regarding the consideration of equipment consumption (e.g., faucets, showers). Different usage habits [6,8,11,17,19,20,27,34] have been observed, aiming to define hourly consumption profiles. Some influencing factors include the age of residents [6], habits such as cooking at home versus dining out [20], the presence of efficient appliances [34], or the use of water reuse systems [8,17].

A challenge in considering appliance consumption is the need for *in loco* measurements [19,34] by residents, or the use of estimatives. Additionally, cultural specificities exist, such as in India (the most populous country), where 67% of the population uses traditional bucket baths instead of showers [25].

Population Variables: Common considerations include population estimates [10,12,19,20,23,31,33], the urban/rural resident ratio [13,16,31], and population density [13,24,30,31,33]. The distinction between daytime and nighttime inhabitants [26] and the proportion of people per household, room, or bathroom [24,29] are also used. A potential limitation is the necessity of conducting surveys and questionnaires, which restricts both reach and the number of observations.

A widely recognized finding is that the higher the number of residents in a household, the lower the *per capita* water consumption [6,8,11,26,27,31,33,34]. This is expected, as the property itself remains the same, and when more people share it, the "maintenance cost" is distributed among them [26,27,31].

Census data is commonly used, although it is sometimes outdated [3,33]. A notable observation, as pointed out by [32] for Spain's coastal region, is that cities with high tourism influx, seasonal population variations, or large number of short-term rental properties, can distort data. Only [15,32] consider this factor, which can present challenges and limitations in certain locations.

Consumption as a Variable: The variability of consumption depending on temporal factors, such as the day of the week and time of day, has been observed [14,15,20,22], as well as a reduction in consumption during nighttime hours [14,15,20]. Regarding the inclusion of property-related variables, [22] argues that they are not highly effective, but it is important to note that their approach relies on smart metering for determining hourly consumption.

In Brazil, [5] identifies the regression components that most contribute to estimating consumption as sewage collection and alternative water sources (for estimating property-level consumption), with piped water access also being considered [4,23]. The effects of water supply interruptions have been recognized as an important variable [4,8,24] in studies conducted in Mexico City, Mexico.

Demographic Variables: These are widely considered [6,8,15,25–27]. Although they represent universal characteristics, gender, age, type of employment among adults, and level of formal education exhibit different distributions depending on the level of development of a city or country. More developed regions face an aging population and generally provide higher levels of formal education.

Additionally, there is evidence of potential negative bias propagation, such as the questionable use of the female gender to explain increased consumption. There is assumptions that women spend more time at home [6], caring for the household and children [11]. Arguing that areas with a higher male-to-female ratio tend to have higher income levels, [31] uses gender as a proxy for income.

Financial Variables: The integration with the financial domain is widely explored, with the most common approach being the use of residents' income [4,6,8,11,19,20,25–27,31,34]. The value of the tariff charged for consumption is also considered [6,15,16,31], as well as property ownership [8,27], Gross Domestic Product (GDP) [12,16,24,31], and property prices [22,25,29].

In Brazil, [3] conducts a spatial analysis in Campina Grande, finding differences of more than 10% between low- and high-income neighborhoods. A similar approach is used by [21], on a national level, focusing on the city of Fortaleza. Both studies conclude that income inequality is reflected in water consumption, with wealthier areas consuming more.

In Aveiro, Portugal, [27] observes a statistical difference between the lowest income group and others, particularly in households with 3–4 people, where consumption in the lowest income group is approximately 37% lower. Finally, in Seville, Spain, [33] uses the property tax as a proxy for income. It is observed that high-income populations revitalize areas previously occupied by low-income groups, specifically in central regions, while the poor move further away. This situation affects the dynamics of the WD within the city.

Building Variables: Various studies aim to relate the characteristics of buildings to explain water consumption by their residents. The most commonly explored conditions include the number of rooms, especially bedrooms and bathrooms [6,8,11,25,29], presence of a swimming pool [6,8,29], constructed area [11,22,29,30,33], age of the building [8,22,27,29], and building type (single-story or vertical) [8,26,29,33].

According to [8,11,30], built area is typically associated with higher consumption levels, and [26] finds a difference of over 30% between properties larger than $100m^2$ and those smaller than $50m^2$. Also, the number of bedrooms and bathrooms figures as two of the most important variables [6,8,11,25,29]. The first reflects an estimate of how many people occupy the property, and the second is one of the areas linked to water consumption.

Table 1. Taxonomy of Studies on Water Consumption and Socio-Economic Factors. The highlighted variables are the most important in the study. Exploratory analysis are highlighted in purple, while regression tasks are highlighted in green. **Smp** Sample size; Domains: **Clm** Clima, **Dem** Demographic, **Bld** Building, **Ppl** Populational, **Eqp** Equipment, **Fnn** Financial, **Cns** Consumption

Ref	Focus	Smp	Source	Clm	Dem	Bld	Ppl	Eqp	Fnn	Cns
[25]	WEU	248	Survey	✓	✓				✓	✓
[30]	WD-D	-	BD	✓		✓	✓			
[14]	WDP-C	-	Meter	✓						✓
[10]	WDP-C	-	Meter	✓			✓			
[12]	WDP-C	-	BD	✓			✓		✓	
[23]	WDP-C	-	BD				✓			✓
[15]	WDP-C	-	BD		✓				✓	✓
[22]	CP-H	90	Meter	✓		✓				✓
[31]	Cpc	-	BD	✓	✓	✓	✓	✓	✓	✓
[6]	Cpc	532	Survey	✓	✓			✓	✓	
[34]	Cpc	151	Survey		✓			✓	✓	
[26]	Cpc	900	Survey	✓	✓			✓		
[8]	**HWC**	108	Survey	✓	✓			✓	✓	
[19]	WEU	36	Survey				✓	✓	✓	
[17]	WEU	48	Survey					✓	✓	
[24]	WD-D	-	BD			✓			✓	✓
[3]	WD-D	-	BD	✓	✓		✓	✓	✓	
[20]	CP-pc	36	Survey					✓		
[33]	Cpc	-	BD	✓	✓	✓				
[27]	Cpc	53	Survey	✓	✓				✓	✓
[21]	Cpc	-	BD						✓	
[16]	Cpc	-	BD	✓			✓	✓	✓	✓
[4]	Cpc	-	BD				✓		✓	✓
[11]	HWC*	380	Survey	✓	✓			✓	✓	
[9]	**HWC**	394	Survey	✓	✓	✓	✓	✓		
[29]	**HWC**	78	Survey	✓	✓					✓
[5]	**HWC**	89	Survey	✓	✓					✓
Ours	**HWC**	3299	BD		✓				✓*	

Regarding building characteristics, [27] finds no impact on consumption when considering the age of the building in Aveiro, Portugal. However, in Joinville, Brazil, [8] concludes that older buildings tend to have higher consumption, a hypothesis related to damaged pipes, lack of sustainable technologies.

In Summary, the variables considered and the focus of the research are compiled in Table 1. The themes of the research include Per Capita Consumption (Cpc), Household Water Consumption (HWC), Water Demand Profiling of Cities (WDP-C), Consumption Profiling of Households (CP-H), Consumption Profiling per Capita (CP-pc), Water Demand Distributions (WD-D), and Water End Use (WEU).

In the present analysis, data characterizing vertical residential buildings are obtained. The reason for the asterisk in the Financial domain in Table 1 is due to the consideration of the price and construction standards of the apartments and land, which can serve as a proxy variable for the residents' purchasing power.

There is a predominance of the financial domain (18) and building construction characteristics (15), indicating good coverage in the literature on related topics. Despite this, few recent studies focus on estimating urban domestic water consumption. Some distinguishing aspects of the present study include the number of collected observations and its specific focus on high-rise buildings.

3 Water Consumption and Buildings Characteristics

3.1 Data Acquisition and Integration

With the support of Sabesp, consumption data for the last three years in the city of São Paulo is obtained. Integration is performed with public municipal property tax data (IPTU) and data from Embraesp (Empresa Brasileira de Estudos de Patrimônio). The Embraesp database contains building characteristics such as the number of blocks, elevators, penthouses, apartment types, and floor levels. It also includes unit attributes such as the number of bedrooms, bathrooms, parking spaces, square footage, and price (adjusted to December 2024 values). From the IPTU database, data on land size and price, built area, and price per square meter, as well as the building quality standard, are obtained.

The lack of standardization between addresses is a challenge. The Sabesp data includes the provisional address of the building, the Embraesp data is the result of data collection, and the IPTU database contains official data. Furthermore, there are cases (Fig. 1) that more than one numbering was adopted, for convenience or practicality. Given the name of a street or ZIP code, variations in numbering are accepted within a margin (related to the land frontage).

Fig. 1. Problematic case in database integration - Google Earth/Maps

To validate the data, the building's age, number of floors, number of apartments, and land size with street frontage are cross-referenced. Finally, a web-scraping approach using Google Maps is implemented to resolve discrepancies in cases with multiple possibilities, using the building's name (when available).

3.2 Challenge in Consumption Estimation

It is assumed that large consumers, such as vertical residential buildings, have a non-negligible impact on the urban water distribution. In this scenario, data from the municipal tax database is used to assess the trend of the built area of new apartments in São Paulo, Brazil. Consumption estimation (m³/month/building) is performed using Eq. 1 from Sabesp's technical standard NTS181 [28]. The Mean Absolute Error (MAE) between the estimative and the real consumption is calculated, as shown by the dashed line in Fig. 2.

$$Consumption = -21.1 + 0.0177 \cdot A + 2.65 \cdot B + 3.97 \cdot D - 50.2 \cdot P_D + 46 \cdot V_G \quad (1)$$

The monthly *Consumption* (m³/month/building) is related to the Constructed Area A, number of Bathrooms B, and Bedrooms D, where P_D is 1 if $D > 3$, and 0 otherwise, as well as the number of Garage Spaces per apartment V_G.

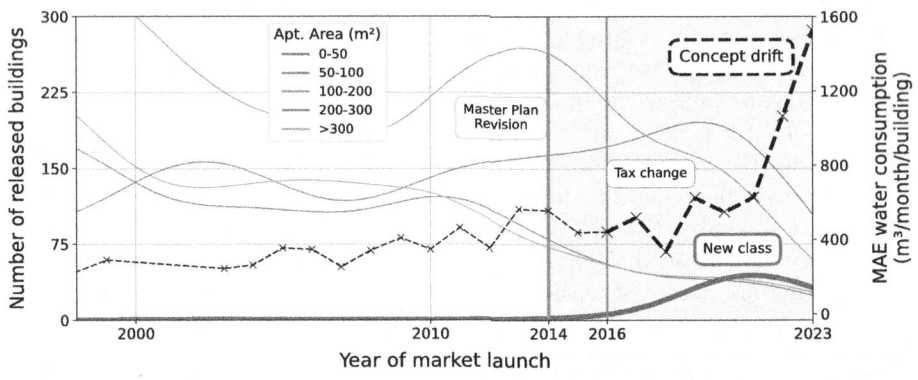

Fig. 2. Relationship between Real Estate Developments and Concept Drift in Sabesp's Regressor – Building Data (IPTU) and Consumption Data (Sabesp)

In 2014, the city master plan started encouraging the construction of small-sized apartments near public transport. In 2016, the local government issued a decree that altered the classification of these properties, which in turn affected the taxes paid. This legislative change gave rise to a new class of properties with up to 50m² of constructed area, that affects the consumption estimation.

Analyzing the consumption estimation error from Sabesp (dashed line), it is evident that, alongside the emergence of the new class, the average annual errors increase dramatically. This analysis allows for the identification of the effect (explosion in error) and the cause (new class) of a Concept Drift. This scenario motivates the search for a regression model that better explains water consumption using only building-related variables, as in the Sabesp model. The results of this study will support the revision of the NTS181 technical standard.

4 Experiments

For the experiments, a preliminary treatment of the consumption data was carried out. Based on experimental results, thresholds were adopted for the data preprocessing. Outliers corresponding to exceptionally high deviations (18 times) from a client's moving average were removed. To avoid strong variations, a smoothing technique was applied to consumers with a minimum consumption of $2 \text{ m}^3/\text{month}$. A smoothing operator was applied using median values over the last five months when consumption exceeds five times the limit.

Regarding outliers in the building features, automating the process and removing them using standard deviation seemed to lose valuable information. Therefore, manual removal was performed on the long tails distributions. For instance, entries with more than 400m^2 (<1% of cases), values above U\$1,000,000.00 (<2%) or U\$4,000.00/m^2 (<2%) are removed. These are exceptions in the dataset, and the estimation of high-end properties may be a subject for future studies.

4.1 Exploratory Analysis

To illustrate the relationship between variables and consumption by unit, an experiment using the UMAP is conducted. This technique transforms the data from a high-dimensional space into a lower-dimensional (latent) space. Its key feature is the preservation of neighborhood relationships, meaning points that were close in the original space tend to be neighbors in the latent space.

The attributes selected include the number of bathrooms/bedrooms/garage spaces, the value per square meter of the land, the number of apartments per floor, and the area of the apartments. For comparison, Principal Component Analysis (PCA) is also used, and the results are shown in Fig. 3. A good separation between different consumption levels is observed, and taking advantage of this observation, regression techniques are trained in the latent space.

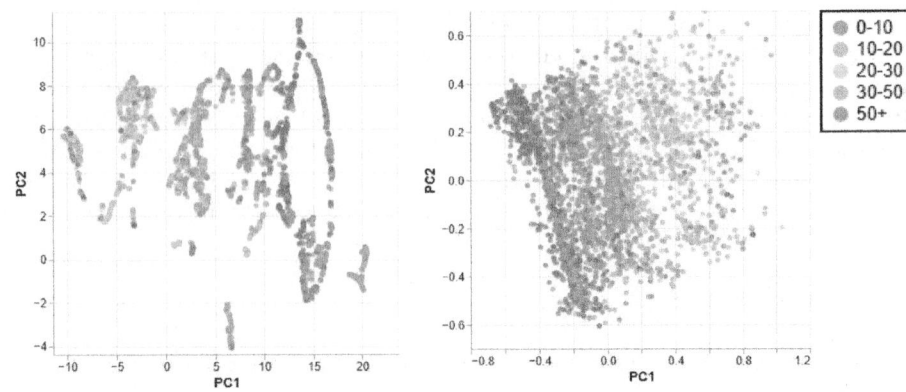

Fig. 3. Latent space - UMAP   Latent space - PCA

To analyze the relationship between multiple variables and consumption, parallel coordinate visualization is used. Min-Max normalized values are employed, meaning values close to 1 represent the maximum and values close to 0 represent the minimum for each variable. As shown in Fig. 4, for the top 25% highest consumers, there is an almost direct relationship between consumption and the number of bedrooms, bathrooms, and garage spaces, as well as the area and price of the apartment. It is worth noting that the land area and units per floor are associated with the bottom 20%. In other words, the larger consumers are buildings with relative few units, large square footage, and small plots of land.

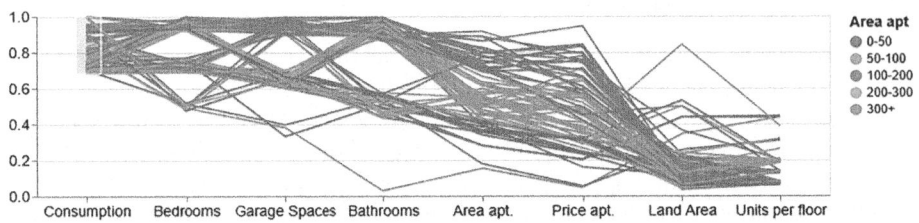

Fig. 4. Relationship between consumption and 7 selected variables

In the distributions shown in Fig. 5, the situation is similar to what has been observed in the literature, with a positive correlation between water consumption and the size of the residence [8,11,26,30] as well as the number of bathrooms [6,8,11,25,29]. This characterization is important because, as already observed, changes are occurring in the real estate market of São Paulo. It is noteworthy that apartments up to 50 m^2 have significantly lower consumption.

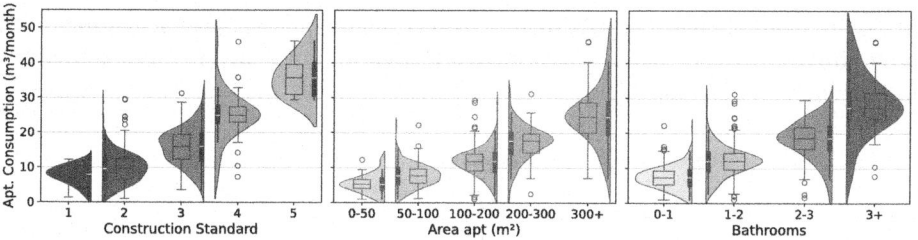

Fig. 5. Consumption distributions related to different variables

Furthermore, the financial variable related to the construction standard (CS) shows that units with CS 1 and 2 (more modest) have a consumption of around 10m^3/month, while units with high standards consume nearly three times as much. A positive correlation between consumption and income has been observed [3,8,21], and the CS may serve as a proxy for the residents' purchasing power.

4.2 Apartment Consumption Estimation

The dataset is splited into training and testing sets in an 80–20 ratio, and the data is normalized using the MinMax technique. The only categorical variable is the Construction Standard of the property, with 5 distinct classes, and Ordinal Encoding is applied. All implementations used are from the Sklearn library.

Different variable sets are tested, ranging from 4 to 21 variables. For feature selection, Recursive Feature Elimination (RFE) is used. In this method, the importance of each variable in the set is calculated, and the least important variables are recursively eliminated until the desired number is reached.

Fourteen different algorithms are tested, including Linear Regression and the regularized variants Ridge and Lasso Regression. Also tested are cases that transform the data into a new latent space and then apply regression, such as Principal and Independent Component Regression. The first uses Principal Component Analysis (PCA) to create the latent space, while the second uses Independent Component Analysis (ICA). One difference of ICA is the relaxation of the orthogonality condition of PCA when creating new components.

Various tree-based strategies are chosen, including Decision Tree (DT) and ensemble tree methods such as Random Forest and Extremely Randomized Trees. The use of DT with boosting strategies is employed with Gradient Boosting and AdaBoost. Finally, algorithms that use distances, such as K-Nearest Neighbors, or hyperplanes, such as Support Vector Machine, are also chosen.

Hyperparameter optimization is performed using grid search. Instead of splitting the training set into training and validation sets, 5-fold cross-validation is used for optimization, with Negative Mean Absolute Error adopted as the scoring parameter (the implementation always aims to maximize the score).

To illustrate the methodology, Fig. 6 compares four cases: (i) without data preprocessing, outlier removal, feature selection and regressor optimization (Baseline); with preprocessing the consumption data (anomaly detection and smoothing) and (ii) using only the Sabesp model variables (Sabesp) or (iii) using all available features (All feats); and (iv) with preprocessing and manually removing outliers, feature selection using RFE and hyperparameter optimization using GridSearch (Optimized).

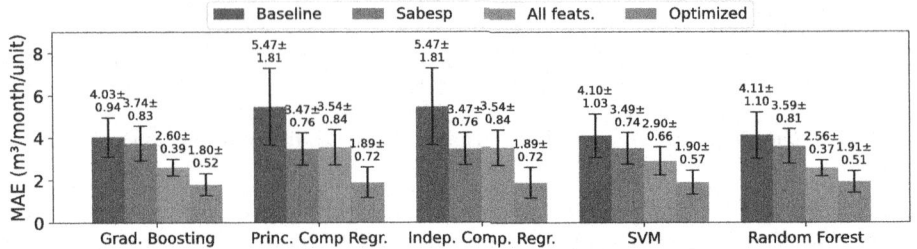

Fig. 6. Comparisson between regressors and methods

Preprocessing yields benefits mainly for linear regressors (PCR and ICR). Notably, Sabesp variables have good prediction power, but there is improvement when all features are included. Manual outlier removal, combined with feature selection and hyperparameter optimization, leads to considerable gains across all cases. Sensitivity analyses on outlier removal will be explored in future work.

The evaluation of the results is carried out using 10-fold cross-validation. The metrics considered, aiming for comparability with previously cited studies, include Mean Absolute Percentage Error (MAPE), Root Mean Squared Error (RMSE), Mean Absolute Error (MAE), and R^2. The regression algorithms used are listed in Table 2, along with the evaluation metrics.

Table 2. Regression Results. Highlighted in green the Tree models and in purple the Linear Regression models - limited to the top 5

Model	MAE	MAPE	RMSE	R^2
Gradient Boosting (**GB**)	**1.80 ± 0.52**	0.22 ± 0.08	**2.31 ± 0.91**	**0.68 ± 0.25**
Principal Component (**PC**)	1.89 ± 0.72	**0.21 ± 0.09**	2.54 ± 1.02	0.61 ± 0.33
Independent Component (**IC**)	1.89 ± 0.72	**0.21 ± 0.09**	2.54 ± 1.02	0.61 ± 0.33
Support Vector Machine	1.90 ± 0.57	0.23 ± 0.08	2.59 ± 0.82	0.62 ± 0.27
Random Forest	1.91 ± 0.51	0.25 ± 0.10	2.60 ± 0.86	0.59 ± 0.36
Huber Regression	1.92 ± 0.80	0.22 ± 0.10	2.54 ± 1.06	0.61 ± 0.33
Extr. Trees	1.93 ± 0.66	0.24 ± 0.11	2.67 ± 1.12	0.59 ± 0.33
Ridge Regression	1.94 ± 0.73	0.23 ± 0.09	2.58 ± 1.04	0.61 ± 0.32
Bayesian Ridge Reg.	1.95 ± 0.81	0.22 ± 0.10	2.60 ± 1.10	0.60 ± 0.36
AdaBoost	1.96 ± 0.45	0.25 ± 0.11	2.63 ± 0.79	0.59 ± 0.33
K-Nearest Neighbors	2.02 ± 0.49	0.25 ± 0.09	2.83 ± 0.85	0.57 ± 0.23
Linear Regression	2.03 ± 0.86	0.23 ± 0.11	2.71 ± 1.09	0.57 ± 0.35
Lasso Regression	2.09 ± 0.57	0.25 ± 0.07	2.83 ± 0.91	0.57 ± 0.28
Decision Tree	2.17 ± 0.76	0.27 ± 0.09	2.80 ± 0.89	0.51 ± 0.38

The use of trees and boosting showed better performance, as well as the strategy of creating a latent space and then performing linear regression. Significance testing between GB and PC/IC is conducted pairwise using the Wilcoxon Signed-Rank Test. A statistical difference (p-value < 0.01) is found for MAE, RMSE, and R^2, indicating that GB outperformed the others.

A residual analysis is performed. Normality tests are conducted using the Kolmogorov-Smirnov and Shapiro-Wilk tests, and homoscedasticity is assessed using the Breusch-Pagan Test. At a 5% significance level, normality and homoscedasticity are confirmed. By selecting the largest errors (Fig. 7), it is observed that they are related to apartments with few bathrooms and small built areas, but with high density (total number of units in the building).

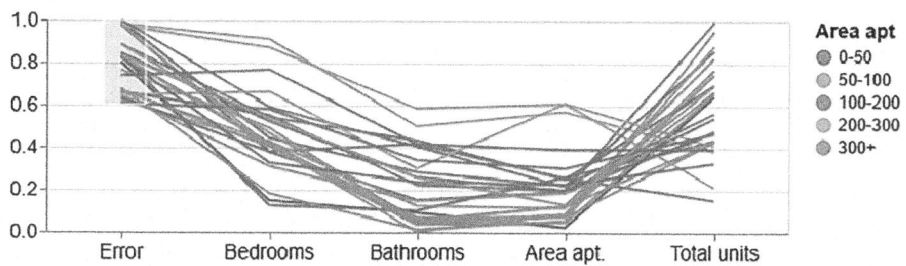

Fig. 7. Relationship between regression residuals and selected variables

It is worth noting the transformation applied to the target variable. To estimate total building consumption and compare it with the Sabesp regressor MAE, better performance was achieved by modeling consumption per unit rather than for the entire building. In older buildings without individual metering, only total consumption is available, and average per-unit consumption is estimated. Where individual measurements exist, the mean of actual unit consumption is used for estimation. For comparison with Sabesp's regressor, individual units errors are summed, and the Mean Absolute Error is computed at the building level.

5 Discussion

The careful cross-referencing of datasets allows the data from Sabesp to be linked with property characteristics with a high degree of reliability, given the checks described. In this context, integrating data from IPTU and Embraesp proves extremely fruitful, providing important variables related with consumption.

The relative ease of obtaining reliable data is considered an advantage for this approach and is thus adopted in this research. This statement can be justified by the ease of accessing real estate registry databases, such as those used in the present study, or even collecting data through questionnaires—measuring the number of rooms/area is considered simpler than measuring the flow rate of individual appliances (faucets, showers, etc.) for each use.

It is noted that selected variables create latent spaces in which the Consumption per unit (in m^3/month) have representations of the classes in well-defined regions for each class. It is observed that variables such as the number of bedrooms and bathrooms, as well as the unit area and land size, are good descriptors of consumption. Naturally, these are attributes correlated with the number of occupants in the property and the number of sanitary appliances, considering that maintenance and cleaning are proportional to the unit and land area.

Across the top five models—GB, PCR, ICR, SVM, and RF—seven features were consistently selected: number of Bedrooms, Bathrooms, and Garage Spaces; Unit Area; Units per Floor; Building Age; and Land Price per m^2. These variables appear to be the most informative building characteristics for predicting water consumption. Notably, the first four are also included in Sabesp's regressor.

Estimating monthly consumption in Brazil, [9] uses Univariate Regression Trees with acceptable results, achieving an RMSE of 5.90 m^3/month/household, whereas the present study reached values of 2.31 m^3/month/household. Using multiple linear regressions, [5] reports a MAPE of 16.78%, considering population variables and the availability of water and sewage services. This may explain why their results were better than the 22% obtained. However, it should be noted the heterogeneity among 3,299 buildings considered in this study.

Also using linear regression, [29] achieves a MAE of 1.23 m^3/month, a value comparable to the 1.80 m^3/month obtained in the present study. Regarding Sabesp's regressor, for the entire building, it presents an average MAE of 620 m^3/month (considering concept drift). Even before the emergence of the new class, the MAE values were around 350-400 m^3/month, and the strategy of estimating the consumption per apartment and then estimating the total consumption resulted in an MAE of 202.46 m^3/month.

6 Conclusion

Population growth puts pressure on the (already degraded) environment. Furthermore, another aspect to consider is the transition of rural populations to urban centers, adding stress to the infrastructure of cities. In this scenario, with the increase in population and the expected concentration of people in urban centers over the coming decades, it is imperative to seek solutions that promote quality of life while preserving natural resources.

Focusing on large water consumers, represented by vertical residential buildings, three datasets are integrated, with real consumption data provided by Sabesp–the largest sanitation company in Latin America. Data from 3,299 buildings, encompassing approximately 276,670 apartments, with 21 variables describing the properties, are gathered from the city of São Paulo. A possible concept drift is detected in Sabesp's model, potentially related to changes in the city's master plan and subsequent impacts on real estate development.

The research hypothesis is that only variables describing the characteristics of the buildings are sufficient to generate a good estimate of urban residential consumption in vertical buildings. This is partially verified, with performance similar to models that use population-related variables (population estimates, residents per household, etc.), financial variables (income estimates, GDP, etc.), or demographic variables (age, gender, educational level, etc.).

To confirm this, it is necessary to quantify the impact of considering the variables described above. Additionally, the influence of neighbors can be explored using GIS, and the impact of seasonality and the percentage of vacant units can be examined. These are relevant considerations that could improve models for estimating monthly water consumption, which are topics of ongoing work.

Acknowledgments. The study has the support of the São Paulo Research Foundation (FAPESP), by an undergraduate scholarship for scientific research (Grant 2024/08236-8) and by the Brazilian Applied Research Center on Smart and Sustainable Cities IARA (Grant 2020/09835-1). This study also had the support of the Water and Sewage Company (Sabesp), by providing the data used in the experiments.

Disclosure of Interests. The authors have no competing interests to declare that are relevant to the content of this article.

References

1. Ahmed Kalifa, Alanoud Al-Maadid, I.K., Makropoulos, C.: Individual water consumption behavior in relation to urban residential dynamics: the case of qatar. Urban Water J. **18**(10), 806–816 (2021). https://doi.org/10.1080/1573062X.2021.1941135
2. Alves, M., Appert, M., Montès, C., Tapia Martín, C.: Producing and living the high-rise New contexts, old questions? Series in Built Environment Bridging Languages and Scholarship, pp. 175–196 (03 2024)
3. Brito, H.C.d., Rufino, I.A.A., Barros Filho, M.N.M., Meneses, R.A.: Use of spatial data in the simulation of domestic water demand in a semiarid city: the case of campina grande, brazil. Urban Sci. **7**(4) (2023). 10.3390/urbansci7040120
4. Medina-Rivas, C.M., Morales-Novelo, J.A., Rodríguez-Tapia, L., Revollo-Fernández, D.A.: Mexico city's decline in per capita domestic water use: a comprehensive spatial-temporal study. Urban Water J. **22**(1), 1–15 (2025). https://doi.org/10.1080/1573062X.2024.2423400
5. Dias, T.F., Kalbusch, A., Henning, E.: Factors influencing water consumption in buildings in southern brazil. J. Clean. Prod. **184**, 160–167 (2018). https://doi.org/10.1016/j.jclepro.2018.02.093
6. Domene, E., Saurí, D.: Urbanisation and water consumption: influencing factors in the metropolitan region of Barcelona. Urban Stud. **43**, 1605–1623 (08 2006). https://doi.org/10.1080/00420980600749969
7. D'Ottaviano, C., Bossuyt, D.M.: Vertical incremental housing in são paulo. the case of minha casa minha vida – entidades. Int. J. Housing Policy **0**(0), 1–26 (2024). 10.1080/19491247.2024.2308716
8. Garcia, J., Salfer, L.R., Kalbusch, A., Henning, E.: Identifying the drivers of water consumption in single-family households in Joinville, southern Brazil. Water **11**(10) (2019). https://doi.org/10.3390/w11101990
9. Grespan, A., Garcia, J., Brikalski, M.P., Henning, E., Kalbusch, A.: Assessment of water consumption in households using statistical analysis and regression trees. Sustain. Cities Soc. **87**, 104186 (2022). https://doi.org/10.1016/j.scs.2022.104186

10. Haque, M.M., de Souza, A., Rahman, A.: Water demand modelling using independent component regression technique. Water Resour. Manage **31**(1), 299–312 (2016). https://doi.org/10.1007/s11269-016-1525-1
11. Alharsha, I., Memon, F.A., Farmani, R., Hussien, W.E.A.: An investigation of domestic water consumption in Sirte, Libya. Urban Water J. **19**(9), 922–944 (2022). https://doi.org/10.1080/1573062X.2022.2105239
12. Joseph, N., Ryu, D., Malano, H.M., George, B., Sudheer, K.P.: Estimation of statewide and monthly domestic water use in India from 1975 to 2015. Urban Water J. **18**(6), 421–432 (2021). https://doi.org/10.1080/1573062X.2021.1893362
13. Kassay, A.B., Tuhar, A.W., Ulsido, M.D.: Integrated modelling techniques to implication of demographic change and urban expansion dynamics on water demand management of developing city in lake hawassa watershed, ethiopia. Environ. Res. Commun. **5**(5), 055012 (May 2023). https://doi.org/10.1088/2515-7620/acd512
14. Kavya, M., Mathew, A., Shekar, P.R., P, S.: Short term water demand forecast modelling using artificial intelligence for smart water management. Sustain. Cities and Society **95**, 104610 (2023). https://doi.org/10.1016/j.scs.2023.104610
15. Loureiro, D., Coelho, S.T., Machado, P., Santos, A., Alegre, H., Covas, D.: Profiling Residential Water Consumption, pp. 1–18. https://doi.org/10.1061/40941(247)44
16. Lu, S., Gao, X., Li, W., Jiang, S., Huang, L.: A study on the spatial and temporal variability of the urban residential water consumption and its influencing factors in the major cities of china. Habitat Int. **78**, 29–40 (2018). https://doi.org/10.1016/j.habitatint.2018.05.002
17. Marinoski, A.K., Vieira, A.S., Silva, A.S., Ghisi, E.: Water end-uses in low-income houses in southern Brazil. Water **6**(7), 1985–1999 (2014). https://doi.org/10.3390/w6071985
18. Marques, E., Minarelli, G.: Verticalization and residential affordability in são paulo. Available at SSRN 4930980
19. Matos, C., Teixeira, C.A., Bento, R., Varajão, J., Bentes, I.: An exploratory study on the influence of socio-demographic characteristics on water end uses inside buildings. Sci. Total Environ. **466–467**, 467–474 (2014). https://doi.org/10.1016/j.scitotenv.2013.07.036
20. Matos, C., Teixeira, C.A., Duarte, A., Bentes, I.: Domestic water uses: characterization of daily cycles in the north region of Portugal. Sci. Total Environ. **458–460**, 444–450 (2013). https://doi.org/10.1016/j.scitotenv.2013.04.018
21. Xavier de Melo Lopes, T.M., Oliveira da Silva, S.M., de Sousa Sampaio, L., Barbosa Soares, R.: Water and socioeconomic inequalities: spatial analysis of water consumption in Brazil. Urban Water J. **21**(9), 1056–1070 (2024). https://doi.org/10.1080/1573062X.2024.2397791
22. Pesantez, J.E., Berglund, E.Z., Kaza, N.: Smart meters data for modeling and forecasting water demand at the user-level. Environ. Modell. Softw. **125**, 104633 (2020). https://doi.org/10.1016/j.envsoft.2020.104633
23. Ramos-Bueno, A., Galeana-Pizaña, J.M., Perevochtchikova, M.: Urban water consumption analysis through a spatial panel modeling approach: a case study of Mexico city, 2004–2022. Water Supply **24**(9), 3179–3195 (2024). https://doi.org/10.2166/ws.2024.191
24. Ramos-Bueno, A., Perevochtchikova, M., Chang, H.: Socio-spatial analysis of residential water demand in Mexico city. Tecnología y ciencias del agua **12**(2), 59–110 (2021). https://doi.org/10.24850/j-tyca-2021-02-02
25. Ramsey, E., Berglund, E.Z., Goyal, R.: The impact of demographic factors, beliefs, and social influences on residential water consumption and implications

for non-price policies in urban India. Water **9**(11) (2017). htttps://doi.org/10.3390/w9110844
26. Rondinel-Oviedo, D.R., Sarmiento-Pastor, J.M.: Water: consumption, usage patterns, and residential infrastructure. a comparative analysis of three regions in the lima metropolitan area. Water Int. **45**(7-8), 824–846 (2020). https://doi.org/10.1080/02508060.2020.1830360
27. S. Costa, I.M., Sousa, V.: Understanding residential water demand: insights from a survey in a Mediterranean city. Urban Water J. **21**(4), 521–537 (2024). https://doi.org/10.1080/1573062X.2024.2312501
28. Sabesp: Norma Técnica Sabesp NTS 181, revisão 4 edn. (Novembro 2017)
29. Silva, K.P.T.D., Kalbusch, A., Henning, E., Menezes, G.A.L.: Modeling water consumption in multifamily buildings: a case study in southern Brazil. Urban Water J. **18**(10), 783–795 (2021). https://doi.org/10.1080/1573062X.2021.1934040
30. Tayebi, S., Feizizadeh, B., Esfandi, S., Aliabbasi, B., Ali Alavi, S., Shamsipour, A.: A neighborhood-based urban water carrying capacity assessment: Analysis of the relationship between spatial-demographic factors and water consumption patterns in Tehran, Iran. Land **11**(12) (2022). https://doi.org/10.3390/land11122203
31. Fabiano da Veiga, A.K., Henning, E.: Drivers of urban water consumption in brazil: a countrywide, cross-sectional study. Urban Water J. **20**(10), 1462–1470 (2023). https://doi.org/10.1080/1573062X.2022.2041049
32. Villar-Navascués, R.A., Pérez-Morales, A.: Factors affecting domestic water consumption on the spanish mediterranean coastline. Prof. Geogr. **70**(3), 513–525 (2018). https://doi.org/10.1080/00330124.2017.1416302
33. Villarín, M.C.: Methodology based on fine spatial scale and preliminary clustering to improve multivariate linear regression analysis of domestic water consumption. Appl. Geogr. **103**, 22–39 (2019). https://doi.org/10.1016/j.apgeog.2018.12.005
34. Willis, R.M., Stewart, R.A., Giurco, D.P., Talebpour, M.R., Mousavinejad, A.: End use water consumption in households: impact of socio-demographic factors and efficient devices. J. Cleaner Product. **60**, 107–115 (2013). https://doi.org/10.1016/j.jclepro.2011.08.006 special Volume: Water, Women, Waste, Wisdom and Wealth

Order Acquisition Under Competitive Pressure: A Rapidly Adaptive Reinforcement Learning Approach for Ride-Hailing Subsidy Strategies

Fangzhou Shi[✉][iD], Xiaopeng Ke[iD], Xinye Xiong[iD], Kexin Meng[iD], Chang Men[iD], and Zhengdan Zhu[iD]

Didi Chuxing, Beijing, China
{arkshifangzhou,kexiaopeng,cintiaxiong,
kexinmeng,menchang,zhuzhengdan}@didiglobal.com

Abstract. The proliferation of ride-hailing aggregator platforms presents significant growth opportunities for ride-service providers by increasing order volume and gross merchandise value (GMV). On most ride-hailing aggregator platforms, service providers that offer lower fares are ranked higher in listings and, consequently, are more likely to be selected by passengers. This competitive ranking mechanism creates a strong incentive for service providers to adopt coupon strategies that lower prices to secure a greater number of orders, as order volume directly influences their long-term viability and sustainability. Thus, designing an effective coupon strategy that can dynamically adapt to market fluctuations while optimizing order acquisition under budget constraints is a critical research challenge. However, existing studies in this area remain scarce.

To bridge this gap, we propose FCA-RL, a novel reinforcement learning-based subsidy strategy framework designed to rapidly adapt to competitors' pricing adjustments. Our approach integrates two key techniques: Fast Competition Adaptation (FCA), which enables swift responses to dynamic price changes, and Reinforced Lagrangian Adjustment (RLA), which ensures adherence to budget constraints while optimizing coupon decisions on new price landscape. Furthermore, we introduce RideGym, the first dedicated simulation environment tailored for ride-hailing aggregators, facilitating comprehensive evaluation and benchmarking of different pricing strategies without compromising real-world operational efficiency. Experimental results demonstrate that our proposed method consistently outperforms baseline approaches across diverse market conditions, highlighting its effectiveness in subsidy optimization for ride-hailing service providers.

Keywords: Reinforcement Learning · Ride-Hailing · Subsidy Strategy

---

Supplementary Information The online version contains supplementary material available at https://doi.org/10.1007/978-3-032-06129-4_15.

© The Author(s), under exclusive license to Springer Nature Switzerland AG 2026
I. Dutra et al. (Eds.): ECML PKDD 2025, LNAI 16022, pp. 246–262, 2026.
https://doi.org/10.1007/978-3-032-06129-4_15

1 Introduction

The rise of ride-hailing aggregators [1]—platforms integrating various third-party ride-hailing services—has grown alongside the ride-hailing industry [12]. These platforms enhance demand realization and social welfare by increasing market thickness and reducing matching frictions, allowing smaller ride-service providers to boost order volume and gross merchandise value (GMV). As depicted in the Fig. 1, key stakeholders include the *Passenger, Ride-Hailing Aggregators (RHA)*, and *Ride-Service Providers (RSP)*. The prices quoted by each RSP are sorted and displayed on the passenger's interface (demonstrated in Fig. 1). To improve user experience, RHAs typically automatically select the top-K lowest-priced options. This mechanism strongly motivates RSPs to lower their price to fall within this range, as the majority of passengers tend to maintain this default range when sending orders due to inherent inertia.

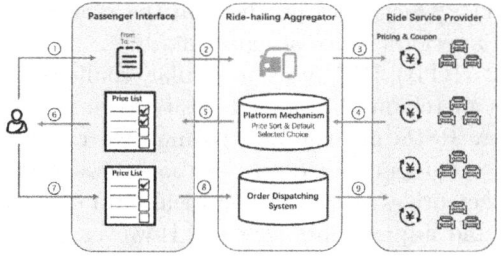
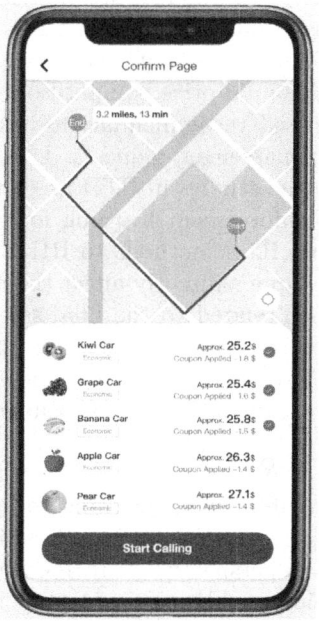

① - ③ The passenger inputs the origin and destination, prompting the aggregator to request price quotes from all service providers.
④ - ⑥ Service providers submit their quoted prices after applying coupons. The aggregator ranks them and auto-selects certain options based on its mechanism before presenting the price list to the passenger.
⑦ - ⑨ The passenger send an order with the chosen options, and the aggregator dispatches it to the most suitable driver from the selected service providers.

(a) **The interaction process between a passenger, a ride-hailing aggregator, and ride service providers**.

(b) **A demonstration of the passenger's interface form on the ride-hailing aggregator**.

Fig. 1. The ride-hailing aggregation process and passenger interface.

Once an order is sent, it will be dispatched to one of the most suitable drivers of the RSPs selected by the passenger. This means that, for a RSP, the fewer ride-service options a passenger selects in a request, the less competition for order completion it will face. Therefore, competing on price (i.e., the travel fare) with other RSPs essentially prompts passengers to select and send orders, thereby increasing the likelihood of order completion. Unlike other studies that discuss long-term base price pricing strategies [15,19], or dynamic price surging [4] under extreme supply & demand conditions, this paper focuses on RSPs that use instant coupons to granularly adjust prices in response to price competition in RHA, a topic that has been underexplored in previous research.

The limited budget of each RSP necessitates the development of efficient coupon allocation strategies for competitive effectiveness, which presents a significant research challenge. Traditional methods borrow ideas from user marketing [20], using uplift modeling [6] techniques to model the individual treatment effect in the passenger's willingness to send an order, after which the duality method with Lagrangian multiplier is applied to solve the maximization problem of order volume (or GMV) under budget constraints. However, these methods usually assume a stable distribution of features, treating the data as Independent and Identically Distributed (IID), which does not hold in the real world, especially when other RSPs perform aperiodic price adjustments.

The field of Real-Time Bidding (RTB) [17] faces a similar challenge of dynamic price competition. In RTB, merchants bid for ad positions in personalized recommendations, akin to how RSPs use coupons to improve rankings in passenger requests. Dynamic price competition occurs in both areas, with some studies in RTB predicting market prices [10] from historical data or using reinforcement learning for real-time bid adjustments [2,9,14]. However, applying RTB methods to RHA is complicated by two main differences. First, RSP coupons directly affect the rank and the final travel fare, whereas RTB bids are not related to the final sales price. Second, order completion in RHA depends on the number of selected RSPs, real-time supply status, and the RHA dispatch algorithm, which introduces significant uncertainty. In contrast, the conversion rate in RTB depends primarily on the item price and user interest. These differences complicate the design of coupon strategies in the RHA environment.

We propose FCA-RL, a framework that uses Bayesian posterior updates and reinforcement learning to dynamically mitigate the adverse effects of competitors' aperiodic price adjustments on coupon efficiency and budget control. From the perspective of RSPs, we formulate this budget-constrained order maximization problem as a Markov Decision Process (MDP). To solve this MDP under aperiodic price adjustments by competitors, we introduce a **Fast Competition Adaptation (FCA)** module that quickly tracks the evolving price landscape, and a **Reinforced Lagrangian Adjustment (RLA)** module that optimizes coupon allocation according to the updated market conditions. The integration of these two modules ensures sustained efficiency and accurate budget execution in a dynamic RHA environment.

Evaluating coupon strategies in real time is risky due to potential declines in GMV and order volume. To overcome this, we developed **RideGym**, an offline simulation system that emulates the ride-hailing process and allows for flexible configurations, including supply factors and competition levels. In addition, this system serves as an interactive environment for training our reinforcement learning agent. Our evaluations show that our algorithm significantly outperforms baseline models by reducing budget control errors and improving the Finish Return on Investment.

Our main contributions are threefold: **(1) The first work focuses on the coupon strategies of RSPs in RHA.** To the best of our knowledge, we are the first study to explore using coupons for instant price competition in RHAs from the perspective of a RSP. **(2) A novel dynamic RL subsidy framework.** We propose FCA-RL, a novel reinforcement learning-based coupon strategy framework configured with a module for rapid market response in RHA, which enables precise budget control in dynamic markets without compromising coupon efficacy. **(3) A Full-Chain RHA Simulator.** We have developed a simulation system, **RideGym**, that models the complete lifecycle of an order within the RHA, facilitating comprehensive analysis of coupon strategies under various algorithmic and environmental variations.

2 Related Works

Coupon Strategy in Industry. Coupon strategies are widely employed in e-commerce to enhance customer purchasing willingness while adhering to budget constraints. Zou et al. [20] formulate this problem as a constrained optimization task based on uplift estimation and solve it using a duality method with Lagrangian relaxation, under the assumption of a stable distribution. Dai et al. [5] introduced a PID controller to dynamically adjust the Lagrangian multiplier for real-time traffic control but did not account for the optimality. Xiao et al. [16] define a model-based constrained Markov decision process (CMDP) and propose a joint optimization of both λ and the policy. Zhang et al. [18] utilize offline reinforcement learning to allocate personalized discounts under a predefined budget, leveraging offline dataset augmentation with multiple λ choices; however, their offline approach is unsuitable for scenarios where market conditions are unpredictable and evolve irregularly. Chen et al. [3] design an optimal instant discount strategy for multiple products on ride-hailing aggregators, but their focus on aggregator profitability diverges from our approach.

Online Advertising Bidding. The optimal coupon strategy of RSP in RHA is similar to advertisers bidding in RTB, where merchants compete for prime placements. Zhang et al. [17] model the winning function and advertisers' private values under specific formulations, deriving an optimal bidding strategy. Recently, reinforcement learning has gained traction in bidding. Cai et al. [2] model request distribution transitions in advertising as an MDP, using dynamic programming for optimal bidding. He et al. [9] propose a general bidding framework using the dual Lagrangian method and reinforcement learning for budget control under traffic fluctuations but remains ineffective for market price dynamics. Wang et al. [13,14] model the problem as a Partial Observable Markov Decision Process

(POMDP), leveraging Transformers and variational inference to capture market price uncertainties, achieving better adaptability.

3 Problem Formalization

3.1 Original Problem

Notation. Suppose M RSPs participate in the RHA. From the perspective of a single RSP, we define a budget rate $B \in [0,1]$ and a coupon set $\mathbf{d} = \{d_0, \ldots, d_{H-1}\} \subseteq [0,1]$, where a 20% discount corresponds to $d_j = 0.2$. Over the period $[t_{start}, t_{end}]$, we collect a dataset $\mathcal{D}_{t_{start}}^{t_{end}} = \{(\mathbf{x}_i, g_i, d_{i,j}, y_i^{I,j}, y_i^{C,j})\}_{i=0}^{N-1}$, which includes contextual features $\mathbf{x}_i$ (e.g., supply-demand conditions and order distance), base prices $g_i \in \mathbb{R}_+^1$ before coupon application, the applied coupon $d_{i,j}$, and two binary variables: $y_i^{I,j} \in \{0,1\}$, indicating whether the RHA automatically selects the RSP in the passenger's form (Fig. 1-⑤) with coupon $d_{i,j}$, and $y_i^{C,j} \in \{0,1\}$, indicating the order completion status after applying $d_{i,j}$. Notably, $y_i^{I,j}$ and $y_i^{C,j}$ are sampled from the corresponding potential outcome distributions $P_{\mathbf{x}_i}^{I,(j)}$ and $P_{\mathbf{x}_i}^{C,(j)}$ for coupon $d_{i,j}$. Additionally, we introduce a new dataset $\mathcal{D}_{t_{end}+1}^{t_{end}+L}$, where the potential outcome distributions $P_{\mathbf{x}}^{I,(j)}$ and $P_{\mathbf{x}}^{C,(j)}$ for each coupon d_j are influenced by competitors' sporadic price adjustments, leading to distributions that differ from those in $\mathcal{D}_{t_{start}}^{t_{end}}$.

Original Formulation. Given $\mathcal{D}_{t_{start}}^{t_{end}}$, let $z_{ij} \in [0,1]$ represent the counterfactual estimation of $y_i^{C,(j)}$, which can be derived from a model trained on this dataset by uplift modeling techniques [6], indicating the order completion probability for opportunity i when applying coupon d_j over $[t_{start}, t_{end}]$. We define $v_{ij} \in \{0,1\}$ as the decision variable indicating whether coupon d_j is applied to opportunity i, ensuring exactly one coupon per request: $\mathbf{v}_i = (v_{i0}, \ldots, v_{i(H-1)})^\mathsf{T} \in \{0,1\}^H$. Our objective is to optimize $\{\mathbf{v}_i\}_{i=0}^{N-1}$ to maximize order completions while adhering to a predetermined budget rate, ensuring that the total coupon expenditure does not exceed the product of total earned GMV and the budget rate. Additionally, we aim to develop an adjustment algorithm to enable rapid adaptation to new data distributions in $\mathcal{D}_{t_{end}+1}^{t_{end}+L}$. We begin by formulating a constrained optimization problem on the original dataset $\mathcal{D}_{t_{start}}^{t_{end}}$

$$\min_{\mathbf{v}} - \sum_{i=0}^{N-1} \sum_{j=0}^{H-1} z_{ij} v_{ij}$$

$$s.t. \sum_{i=0}^{N-1} \sum_{j=0}^{H-1} g_i z_{ij} v_{ij} d_j \leq \sum_{i=0}^{N-1} \sum_{j=0}^{H-1} g_i z_{ij} v_{ij} \cdot B \quad (1)$$

$$v_{ij} \in \{0,1\}, \quad \sum_{j=0}^{H-1} v_{ij} = 1$$

$$\forall i \in \{0, \cdots, N-1\}, \quad \forall j \in \{0, \cdots, H-1\}$$

3.2 Optimal Decision Function

The integrality constraint on v is removed by applying linear relaxation. Other constraints are relaxed using the Lagrange multiplier, and the problem is then reformulated in its dual form (see Appendix C.1 for details):

$$\max_{\lambda \geq 0} \min_{\mathbf{v}} L(\mathbf{v}, \lambda) = \sum_{i=0}^{N-1} \sum_{j=0}^{H-1} z_{ij}(\lambda g_i d_j - \lambda g_i B - 1) v_{ij} \quad (2)$$

This Lagrangian dual transformation preserves the optimal value of the original problem through the strong duality (see Appendix C.2 for proof). From Eq. 2, the optimal discount $j^*(\lambda)$ for each opportunity i, given a fixed λ, is:

$$j^*(\lambda) = \underset{j}{argmin} \; z_{ij}(\lambda g_i d_j - \lambda g_i B - 1) \quad (3)$$

where $v_{ij} = 1$ for $j = j^*$ and $v_{ij} = 0$ otherwise (see Appendix C.3 for details). Given this formulation, the maximum of Eq. 2 is obtained by tuning λ over a sum of piecewise linear convex functions. To handle non-differentiable points, we apply a ternary search to iteratively determine λ^*.

However, competitors' aperiodic price adjustments lead to continuous changes in the distributions of $\mathbf{z}$, making the optimized λ^* from $\mathcal{D}_{t_{start}}^{t_{end}}$ non-generalizable. To address this, we decompose the order completion probability z_{ij} (Eq. 4) into $f_{ij}^{(in)}$ (completion probability when auto-selected) and $f_{ij}^{(out)}$ (when not auto-selected). We explicitly model the RSP's In-Range Rate (*IRR*, Def. 1) as w_{ij}, representing the probability of entering the auto-selection range for each coupon, since the *IRR* is the most sensitive part affected by the competitors' sporadic price changes, unlike $f_{ij}^{(in)}$ and $f_{ij}^{(out)}$. Thus, tracking and calibrating the *IRR* distribution in real-time and applying adaptive optimization are critical to maintaining efficiency in $\mathcal{D}_{t_{end}+1}^{t_{end}+L}$. We model this as a Markov Decision Process (MDP) [11], allowing reinforcement learning to adjust λ at each time step in response to the real-time *IRR* changes.

$$z_{ij} = w_{ij} f_{ij}^{(in)} + (1 - w_{ij}) f_{ij}^{(out)} \quad (4)$$

Definition 1. *(In-Range Rate, IRR). For a ride-hailing opportunity i, the IRR represents the probability that an RSP's quoted price is auto-selected by the RHA to maximize user satisfaction. The number of In-Range RSPs depends on the opportunity's context $\mathbf{x}_i$ and follows a top-$K(\mathbf{x}_i)$ lowest-price rule, where $K : \mathcal{X} \to \mathbb{N}^+$ maps features to the number of auto-selections.*

4 Method

In this section, we introduce FCA-RL, a reinforcement learning-based coupon strategy framework tailored for competitive RHA environments. We define a MDP as outlined in Sect. 4.1 and propose to solve it through our proposed **Reinforced Lagrangian Adjustment (RLA)**, with an online module, **Fast Competition Adaptation (FCA)**, integrated to monitor and adapt to the evolving IRR landscape influenced by competitors' sporadic price adjustments. An overview of our framework is demonstrated in Fig. 2.

4.1 Reinforced Lagrangian Adjustment (RLA)

Markov Decision Process. We model the λ adaptation process as a finite-horizon MDP $(\mathcal{S}, \mathcal{A}, \mathcal{T}, \mathcal{R}, \mathcal{P}, \mathcal{F}, \gamma)$ with the state space $\mathcal{S}$, the action set $\mathcal{A}$, the transition function $\mathcal{T}$, the reward function $\mathcal{R}$, the penalty function $\mathcal{P}$, the full-achievement function $\mathcal{F}$, and the discount factor γ. In our study, we equate the long-term impact by setting $\gamma = 1$.

State. Each state $s \in \mathcal{S}$ at time step t encapsulates: a normalized time slot index, the previous Lagrangian multiplier λ_{t-1}, the coupon campaign status up to t (including the executed budget rate, gap to target, gained GMV, and Finish ROI), and statistics of the latest IRR distribution. This state representation supports effective decision-making based on IRR changes.

Action. At each time step t, the action $\mathbf{a}_t \in \mathcal{A}$ adjusts λ_{t-1} via Eq. 5, with η controlling the extent of the adjustment. The updated λ_t is then used in Eq. 3 for coupon assignment. lb and up are set to be the lower bound and the upper bound of λ.

$$\lambda_t = \min(\max(\lambda_{t-1} \cdot \eta \cdot a_t, lb), ub) \tag{5}$$

Transition Function. In this study, state transitions $\mathcal{T} : \mathcal{S} \times \mathcal{A} \to P(s_{t+1}|s_t, a_t)$ are integrated in **RideGym** and are not explicitly modeled in our method.

Reward Function. After calculating the coupon assignment j^* for each passenger's request by Eq. 3 with λ_t at step t, the reward function $r \in \mathcal{R} : \mathcal{S} \times \mathcal{A} \to \mathbb{R}$ is defined in Eq. 6, which reflects the order completions resulting from this coupon assignment.

$$r_t(s_t, a_t) = \sum_{i=0}^{N_t - 1} z_{ij^*(\lambda_t(s_t, a_t))}^t \tag{6}$$

Penalty Function. At each time step t, issuing coupons increases the probability of order completions, while also consuming the budget. We thus define a penalty function $p \in \mathcal{P} : \mathcal{S} \times \mathcal{A} \to \mathbb{R}$, demonstrated in Eq. 7, to record the budget consumption.

$$p_t(s_t, a_t) = \sum_{i=0}^{N_t - 1} z_{ij^*(\lambda_t(s_t, a_t))}^t g_i^t d_{j^*(\lambda_t(s_t, a_t))} \tag{7}$$

Full-Achievement Function. In our scenario, the constraint is a predetermined budget rate over a specified period $[t_{start}, t_{end}]$, rather than a fixed budget amount. Compliance with this constraint depends not only on the expenditure, but also on the total GMV achieved by our coupon allocation strategy. Therefore, we employ Eq. 8 to integrate past cumulative subsidy expenditures, GMV gains (from t_{start} to t), and forecasts up to t_{end} to assess adherence to the budget rate constraint. We propose a Full-Achievement function, demonstrated in Eq. 10, to balance the total achievement of order completions and budget rate compliance.

Note that the total order completions for the entire period are normalized by the previously solved optimal order completions using the ternary search method in $[t_{start}, t_{end}]$, denoted by R^*.

$$CR_t = \frac{\sum_{s=0}^{t-1} p_s^{obs} + \sum_{s=t}^{T-1} p_s(s_s, a_s)}{\sum_{s=0}^{t-1} r_s^{obs} + \sum_{s=t}^{T-1} r_s(s_s, a_s)} \quad (8)$$

$$Constraint\_Penalty = e^{max(\frac{CR_t}{CR^*}-1,\, 0)} - 1 \quad (9)$$

$$F_t = \frac{\sum_{s=0}^{t-1} r_s^{obs} + \sum_{s=t}^{T-1} r_s(s_t, a_t)}{R^*} - Constraint\_Penalty \quad (10)$$

Parameters Initialization of Decision Function. First, we pretrain the fundamental models and initialize λ on the dataset $\mathcal{D}_{t_{start}-L}^{t_{start}-1}$. The fundamental models, $\mathcal{W}$, $\mathcal{F}^{(in)}$ and $\mathcal{F}^{(out)}$, are used to estimate the parameters w_{ij}, $f_{ij}^{(in)}$, and $f_{ij}^{(out)}$, respectively, in Eq. 3 during decision making. This allows us to solve for λ^* on $\mathcal{D}_{t_{start}-L}^{t_{start}-1}$ via ternary search to maximize Eq. 2. The resulting λ^* is then used by the actor to adjust the system at the initial time step.

Actor and Critic. In this study, we adopt the Actor-Critic framework [7]. At each time slot t, the actor π_θ, parameterized by θ, is a neural network that takes the current state s_t as input and outputs the mean μ_t and standard deviation σ_t of a Gaussian distribution. An action a_t is then sampled from this distribution. The action a_t adjusts the previous λ_{t-1} by Eq. 5. To stabilize λ updates, we adjust λ using Eq. 11, where $\delta\lambda_{t-1}$ denotes the previous change margin and λ_t^o represents the λ originally modified by a_t; this adjusted value is then utilized in Eq. 3 to determine the optimal coupon allocation for each request in the current time slot. The critic $Q_\gamma(\cdot, \cdot)$ estimates the Full-Achievement F_t based on the state-action pair (s_t, a_t).

$$\lambda_t = \lambda_{t-1} + (\lambda_t^o - \lambda_{t-1})/(1 + \delta\lambda_{t-1}) \quad (11)$$

4.2 Fast Competition Adaption (FCA)

At each time step t, to promptly respond to fluctuations in (IRR) induced by sporadic price adjustments by competitors, we propose modeling the initial IRR landscape for each candidate coupon as a set of Beta distributions. This facilitates capturing dynamic changes through Bayesian posterior updates. Under the Homogeneous Competitors Assumption (Assumption 1), Proposition 1 holds, validating the use of Beta distributions to model the initial IRR distribution.

Assumption 1 *(Homogeneous Competitor Assumption). All RSPs belong to the same service category (e.g., economy), which implies that when they join the RHA at $t = 0$, the prices $p_m(\mathbf{x})$ offered by all RSPs for requests with identical characteristics $\mathbf{x}$ follow an independent and identically distributed continuous distribution with a cumulative distribution function (CDF) F_X.*

Proposition 1. *Let M denote the total number of RSPs for a given request i. The CDF of the $K(\mathbf{x}_i)$-th lowest price, denoted as $F_{X_{(K(\mathbf{x}_i))}}$ follows a Beta distribution (proof provided in Appendix D). It follows directly that the IRR for request i at $t = 0$ is governed by:*

$$Pr(p_m(\mathbf{x}_i) \leq X_{(K(\mathbf{x}_i))}) \sim Beta(K(\mathbf{x}_i), M + 1 - K(\mathbf{x}_i)). \tag{12}$$

In the following, we demonstrate how the conjugate properties of the Beta distribution facilitate rapid Bayesian posterior updates at time step t, enabling swift adaptation to competitors' price adjustments at the previous time step.

Clustering. A key challenge is that samples are not identical across time steps, so the observed In-Range outcomes at time $t-1$ cannot be directly applied to individual samples at time t. To address this, we employ the K-Means algorithm [8] to cluster requests with similar features, establishing a mapping $f : \mathbb{X} \to \mathbb{C} = \{0, \ldots, S-1\} \subseteq \mathbb{N}$ from the feature space to the cluster labels. This allows us to implement a Bayesian posterior update at time t based on observations from the corresponding cluster at $t-1$. We denote the most recent parameters of the Beta distribution for cluster c as $\alpha_{c,d}$ and $\beta_{c,d}$, for each $d \in \mathbf{d}$.

Initialization of IRR Prior. In our framework, the tracking of the IRR distribution commences at time step t_{start}. We average the predictions from model $\mathcal{W}$ over the dataset $\mathcal{D}_{t_{start}-L}^{t_{start}-1}$, stratified by the previously defined clustering labels and coupon levels. This yields the initial parameters $\alpha_{c,d}^{t_{start}}$ and $\beta_{c,d}^{t_{start}}$ for each cluster c and coupon d. We store these in a dictionary $\mathcal{I}$, with the cluster centers as keys and the corresponding $(\alpha_{c,d}^{t_{start}}, \beta_{c,d}^{t_{start}})$ as values to track the IRR landscape.

Bayesian Posterior Update. Assuming intra-cluster homogeneity during the FCA process (with an acceptable loss of precision), we model the number of In-Range samples in each cluster under each candidate coupon as a binomial. Specifically, let $N_{c,d}^{t-1}$ denote the number of samples in cluster c at time $t-1$ that received coupon d, and $N_{c,d}^{in,t-1}$ the number of those samples that are In-Range. Given the Binomial–Beta conjugacy, the posterior at time t also follows to a Beta distribution (proof provided in Appendix E). As a result, the parameters at t can be updated by

$$\begin{aligned} \alpha_{c,d}^t &= N_{c,d}^{in,t-1} + \alpha_{c,d}^{t-1} \\ \beta_{c,d}^t &= N_{c,d}^{t-1} - N_{c,d}^{in,t-1} + \beta_{c,d}^{t-1}. \end{aligned} \tag{13}$$

To address potential stochastic noise in Beta distribution updates due to limited samples per time step, we introduce a window size parameter, l, aggregating In-Range observations from the preceding l time steps (Setting $l = 1$ is consistent with Eq. 13).

4.3 Integration of FCA in RLA

This section describes the integration of FCA into the RLA actor's decision-making process. FCA influences two key aspects of decision-making:

Augmentation of s_t. At time step t, the general *IRR* status tracked by FCA under coupon d, represented by $\frac{1}{S}\sum_c \alpha_{c,d}^t$ and $\frac{1}{S}\sum_c \beta_{c,d}^t$, is incorporated into the state vector s_t. This allows the actor to adjust λ_{t-1} to λ_t based on the updated *IRR* information.

Refinement of w. To preserve heterogeneity across samples, the original predictions, denoted as $\alpha_{(\mathcal{W}(\mathbf{x},d))}^{t,ori}$ and $\beta_{(\mathcal{W}(\mathbf{x},d))}^{t,ori}$, from $\mathcal{W}$ for each individual sample are retained but adjusted using the latest parameters tracked by FCA. The refined predictions for a sample in cluster c at time step t are as follows:

$$\begin{aligned}\alpha_{\mathbf{x},d}^t &= \alpha_{(\mathcal{W}(\mathbf{x},d))}^{t,ori} + \alpha_{c=f(x),d}^t \\ \beta_{\mathbf{x},d}^t &= \beta_{(\mathcal{W}(\mathbf{x},d))}^{t,ori} + \beta_{c=f(x),d}^t\end{aligned} \quad (14)$$

These updated estimates, along with the new λ_t, are incorporated into Eq. 3 to determine the coupon allocation at time step t.

After the coupons are issued, **RideGym** returns the actual In-Range and order completion results for that time step. FCA collects the $N_{c,d}^{in,t}$ and $N_{c,d}^t$ to update $\alpha_{c,d}$ and $\beta_{c,d}$ for each cluster and observed coupon. Any unexpected price adjustments by competitors are captured by the updated values of $\alpha_{c,d}$ and $\beta_{c,d}$. The complete process of our FCA-RL is demonstrated in Algorithm 1.

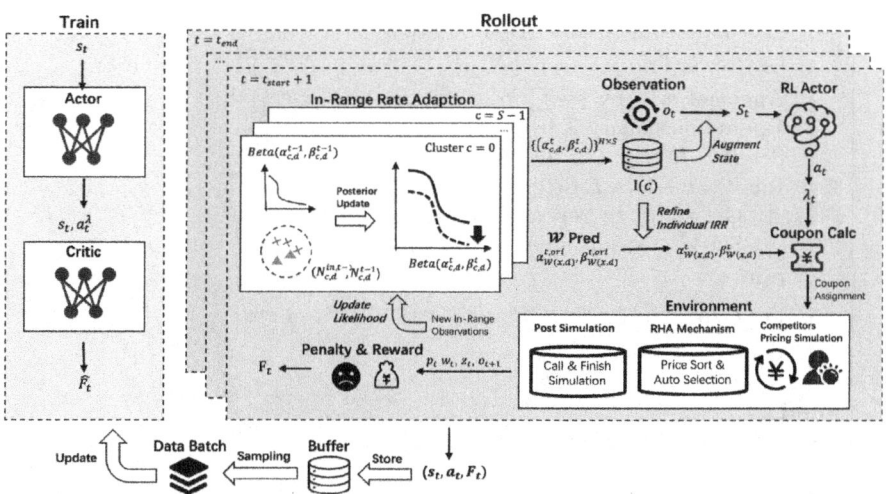

Fig. 2. An overview of our FCA-RL framework which detailing the integration of FCA and RLA at each rollout step. After several rollouts, a batch of tuples (s_t, a_t, F_t) is sampled for reinforcement learning training.

5 RideGym

Implementing new subsidy strategies directly in online environments carries the risk of financial loss. To mitigate this risk, we propose the **RideGym** simulation system, which models the complete operations of a ride-hailing aggregator. As depicted in Fig. 3, RideGym consists of three core components: the Basic Pricing Engine, the Strategy Engine, and the Post-Pricing Engine. This simulation framework enables the evaluation of different subsidy strategies under diverse market conditions without the potential losses associated with real-world implementation.

Algorithm 1: FCA-RL Algorithm

Input: B; $\mathcal{W}$; $\mathcal{F}^{(in)}$; $\mathcal{F}^{(out)}$; λ_0^*; R^*; CR^*; $\mathcal{I}$; RideGym $\mathcal{E}$; $\mathbf{d}$; Batch size b;
Output: π_θ; Q_γ; $\mathcal{I}$

1 **while** *not convergent* **do**
2   Set $\lambda_0 = \lambda_0^* + \epsilon$;
3   Observe state $\mathbf{s}_0$ from $\mathcal{E}$;
4   Set $R = 0$; $C = 0$;
5   **for** $t = 0$ *to* T **do**
6   Get an action $\mathbf{a}_t \sim \pi_\theta(\mathbf{s}_t)$;
7   Get λ_t by Eq. 5;
8   Get $\alpha^{t,ori} \in \mathcal{R}^{N_t \times |\mathbf{d}|}$ and Get $\beta^{t,ori} \in \mathcal{R}^{N_t \times |\mathbf{d}|}$ estimated by $\mathcal{W}$;
9   Get $\mathbf{f}^{(in)} \in \mathcal{R}^{N_t \times |\mathbf{d}|}$, $\mathbf{f}^{(out)} \in \mathcal{R}^{N_t \times |\mathbf{d}|}$ estimated by $\mathcal{F}^{(in)}$ and $\mathcal{F}^{(out)}$;
10   Update $\alpha^t \in \mathcal{R}^{N_t \times |\mathbf{d}|}$ and $\beta^t \in \mathcal{R}^{N_t \times |\mathbf{d}|}$ by Eq. 14;
11   Sample $\mathbf{w}^t \in \mathcal{R}^{N_t \times |\mathbf{d}|}$ from $\mathbf{Beta}(\alpha^t, \beta^t)$;
12   Calculate coupon allocation by Eq. 3;
13   Get reward r_t, p_t, s_{t+1}, $\{N_{c,d}^t\}^{|\mathbb{C}| \times |\mathbf{d}|}$ and $\{N_{c,d}^{in,t}\}^{|\mathbb{C}| \times |\mathbf{d}|}$ from $\mathcal{E}$;
14   Augment s_{t+1} by $\{\frac{1}{S}\sum_c \alpha_{c,d}^t\}^{|\mathbf{d}|}$ and $\{\frac{1}{S}\sum_c \beta_{c,d}^t\}^{|\mathbf{d}|}$;
15   Update dictionary $\mathcal{I}$ by Eq. 13 ;
16   Set $R = R + r_t$; $C = C + p_t$; Set $V = 0$; Set $Z = 0$;
17   **for** $k = t+1$ *to* T **do**
18   Get r_k, p_k by repeat execution of line 6 to 14;
19   Set $V = V + r_k$; Set $Z = Z + p_k$;
20   **end**
21   Set $CR_t = \frac{C+Z}{R+V}$; Set $CP = e^{max(\frac{CR_t}{CR^*} - 1, 0)} - 1$;
22   Set $F_t = \frac{(R+V)}{R^*} - CP$;
23   Store (s_t, a_t, F_t) in $\mathcal{M}$;
24   **end**
25   Sample b of tuples from $\mathcal{M}$;
26   Update Critic by minimizing the loss $L_{Critic} = \frac{1}{b}\sum_i (F^i - Q(s^i, a^i))^2$
27   Update Actor by maximizing the PPO loss
       $L^{\text{CLIP}}(\theta) = \hat{\mathbb{E}}_t \left[\min \left(r_t(\theta)\hat{F}_t, \text{clip}(r_t(\theta), 1-\epsilon, 1+\epsilon)\hat{F}_t \right) \Big| r_t(\theta) = \frac{\pi_\theta(a_t|s_t)}{\pi_{\theta_{\text{old}}}(a_t|s_t)} \right]$
28 **end**

Basic Pricing Engine. In this engine, the base price of each order is determined by a configurable price per mile. Price adjustments by one RSP affect others within the RHA. To simulate market competition, we introduce a stochastic price adjustment mechanism by configuring the frequency, lower and upper bounds of each competitor's price adjustment. The actual adjustment amount is sampled from a uniform distribution defined by these bounds. The adjusted price for the m-th RSP is calculated as: $p_m^{\text{aft}} = p_m \times (1+a)$, where a is the sampled adjustment amount.

Strategy Engine. The Strategy Engine generates orders for each time slot, maintaining the desired order count distribution by using multiple normal distributions to approximate the actual distribution. Each RSP can then apply its configurable coupon strategy to assign coupons to the generated orders.

Post-Pricing Engine. The post-pricing engine processes the quoted prices from all RSPs, ranks them in ascending order, and simulates both automatic and passenger selection. Automatic selection by RHA employs a top-K mechanism, while the number of RSPs selected by a passenger, denoted by K', is calculated as follows: given a list of quoted prices $(p_1, p_2, ..., p_M)$ for M RSPs,

$$K' = \text{Clip}\left(K + \log_b\left(\text{density}(p_1, ..., p_M) + b^{-K}\right), 1, M\right)$$

where K is the number of RSPs selected by default, b is an adjustable base, and density($\cdot$) calculates the density of the price list. The clipping function ensures that K' stays within the range $[1, M]$. After the order is sent by passengers with selected RSPs, each order is assigned a random supply factor $s \in [0, 1]$ to model supply conditions. Assuming service capabilities $(tp_1, tp_2, ..., tp_M)$ for the M RSPs, the probability of the i-th RSP answering an order is: $P(\text{answer} = i \mid s) = s \cdot \frac{tp_i}{\sum_{j=1}^{M} tp_j}$. The no answer rate of an order is: $P(\text{no answer} \mid s) = 1 - \sum_{j=1}^{M} P(\text{answer} = j \mid s)$. Finally, the simulation includes a random normal distribution to model potential order cancellations.

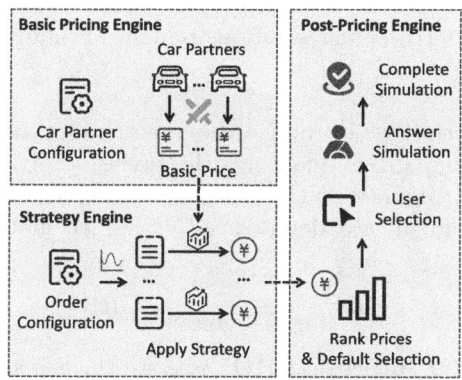

Fig. 3. The pipeline of RideGym.

6 Evaluation

6.1 Evaluation Setup

Dataset Detail. Our RideGym platform generates four different scenarios (referred to as Scenes 1 to 4) under varying configurations. Each scenario consists of three datasets: Pre-train, Train, and Test, with the Pre-train and Train datasets being consistent across all scenarios. In Scenes 1 to 3, price adjustments by other RSPs through changes in base prices occur with increasing frequency. These adjustments directly influence an RSP's ranking within the RHA form and affect the IRR. To assess the robustness of our method in stable pricing environments, we introduce Scene-4, where no RSPs change their prices. See Appendix B for more details on the configuration of the different scenes.

Training and Evaluation Details. In this section, we first describe the training details for each scene. For the FCA-RL model, both $\mathcal{W}$ and $f^{(in)}$ are MLPs trained on the Pre-train dataset. In our implementation, we omit the prediction of $f_{ij}^{(out)}$, assuming that RSPs placed Out-Range have a negligible probability of being selected by passengers. These pre-trained models are then used to infer the Test dataset without further weight optimization. Further details can be found in Appendix A.1.

Baseline Details. We introduce three baselines to analyze the coupon strategy in RHA: (i) **Optimal Method(OPT)**: This approach utilizes the ground truth of the completion label to derive the optimal solution. (ii) **Primal-Dual Method-A(PDM-A)**: A traditional technique that implements uplift modeling the predictions of the completion probability z_{ij} in an end-to-end fashion. It then solves a constrained optimization problem using the Primal-Dual Method. (iii) **PDM-S**:This method explicitly models w_{ij} and $f_{ij}^{(in)}$, similar to our FCA-RL approach. However, it employs the Primal-Dual Method to derive the solutions without real-time adjustments to the IRR and λ. To construct proper estimates for the parameters in their optimal decision function, we train MLPs to predict w_{ij}, $f_{ij}^{(in)}$ for PDM-S, and z_{ij} for PDM-A. All baselines are solved on the same Train dataset as FCA-RL. Their solutions remain unchanged during evaluation on the Test set.

Evaluation Metric. Here, we introduce three metrics for analyzing algorithms.

Cost Rate Error, CRE quantifies the precision of a coupon strategy in controlling costs. It is defined as the difference between the actual coupon cost rate and the target budget rate, denoted as CR^*. Mathematically, the total CRE is expressed as:

$$CRE = \left| \frac{\sum_i \text{cost}_i}{\sum_i \text{gmv}_i} - CR^* \right| \tag{15}$$

Finish Return Of Interest, FROI assesses the effect of coupon strategies on increasing order volumes, where F, F_0 are the count of finished orders with-/without strategy, C is the subsidy cost of the subsidy strategy, A and A_0 are the Average Selling Price (ASP) with/without strategy.

$$FROI = \frac{F - F_0}{\frac{A_0}{A}C} \tag{16}$$

Reinforcement Learning Reward, RLR gauges the order increasing effect and the control ability at the same time:

$$RLR = \frac{\sum_{i=1}^{T} r_i^{obs}}{R^*} - (e^{max(\frac{CR}{CR^*}-1,0)} - 1) \tag{17}$$

6.2 Empirical Results

Here, we summarize our evaluation target to the following research questions. Experiments run on a machine with a 16-core Intel CPU, 40GB RAM, and GeForce RTX 2080 Ti GPU. Results are averaged over five random seeds.

RQ1: How does FCA-RL Compare to the Other Baselines in Terms of Performance? We present three key metrics for Scene-1 to 3 across all baselines. Since the ground truth for In-Range and order completion results is generated by our RideGym, we obtain the optimal λ^* using ternary search. As shown in Table 1, our FCA-RL significantly outperforms all baselines on these metrics. It achieves smaller budget rate errors, indicated by the CRE column (up and down arrows correspond to over- and underspending), and higher money efficiency in scenarios with different price adjustment frequencies. In competitive pricing scenarios such as Scene-2 and Scene-3, FCA-RL limits budget rate errors to within 0.3 percentage points (pp), surpassing the second-best method, PDM-S, by reductions of 0.6 pp and 0.4 pp. While occasionally overspending compared to PDM-S, FCA-RL demonstrates higher efficiency, with FROI increases of 0.1% in Scene-1 and 3.6% in Scene-3, defying the typical economic principle that marginal benefits decrease as costs increase.

Table 1. Strategy Performance on Three Scenes

Method	Scene-1			Scene-2			Scene-3		
	CRE	FROI	RLR	CRE	FROI	RLR	CRE	FROI	RLR
Optimal	0.000	1.663	0.48	0.001	1.388	0.283	0.000	1.366	0.476
PDM-A	(↑)0.023	1.305	−0.111	(↑)0.032	1.016	−0.499	(↑)0.020	1.062	−0.149
PDM-S	(↓)0.002	1.575	0.127	(↑)0.012	1.228	0.040	(↓)0.007	1.262	0.104
RL-FCA	(↓)**0.001**	**1.578**	**0.168**	(↓)**0.006**	**1.454**	**0.167**	(↓)**0.003**	**1.308**	**0.208**

RQ2: What is the Effect of the FCA Component? We conducted ablation experiments on FCA modules across various scenarios (Scene-1 to Scene-4, shown in Table 2). Additionally, we analyzed the impact of window size on FCA effectiveness in the most competitive pricing scenario (Scene-3), with results presented in Table 3. Table 2 shows that the FCA module reduces budget rate execution errors in all scenes. It outperforms standard RL without *IRR* adaptation in competitive scenarios (Scene-2 and 3) by 32.2% and 77.4% in RLR. However, in stable price scenarios (Scene-1 and 4), FCA offers no advantage, as the stable distribution may hinder RL training convergence. As shown in Table 3, testing different window lengths in Scene-3 revealed that longer windows improve RL training, with minimal differences beyond a length of 20. We therefore chose a final window length of 24.

RQ3: How does our FCA-RL Outperform the Others? Our FCA-RL adapts to market changes by adjusting the Lagrange multiplier (λ) in real-time. Figure 4 illustrates how the true *IRR* distribution shifts due to price adjustments and compares our method's quick adaptation to others relying on training set distribution. To highlight FCA's response to *IRR* distribution changes, we show results with a window size of 1, where FCA is more sensitive but also introduces greater fluctuations in RL training. Figure 5 illustrates how the RL agent adjusts the λ parameter at each time step in response to changes in the *IRR* distribution (first two columns). The third column displays the budget rate implementations

Table 2. Ablation Study for FCA

	FCA	CRE	FROI	RLR
Scene-1	w	($\downarrow$)**0.001**	1.578	0.168
	w/o	($\downarrow$)0.003	**1.653**	**0.197**
Scene-2	w	($\downarrow$)**0.001**	1.316	**0.119**
	w/o	($\downarrow$)0.011	**1.500**	0.090
Scene-3	w	($\downarrow$)**0.003**	1.308	**0.208**
	w/o	($\downarrow$)0.02	**1.466**	0.117
Scene-4	w	($\downarrow$)**0.002**	1.362	0.125
	w/o	($\downarrow$)0.008	**1.453**	**0.195**

Table 3. Study for the Window Size

WS	CRE	FROI	RLR
1	($\downarrow$)0.017	1.398	0.133
3	($\downarrow$)0.019	1.397	0.143
10	($\downarrow$)0.007	1.346	0.182
15	($\downarrow$)0.005	1.325	0.192
20	($\downarrow$)0.003	1.308	0.203
24	($\downarrow$)**0.003**	1.308	**0.208**
30	($\downarrow$)**0.003**	1.308	**0.208**

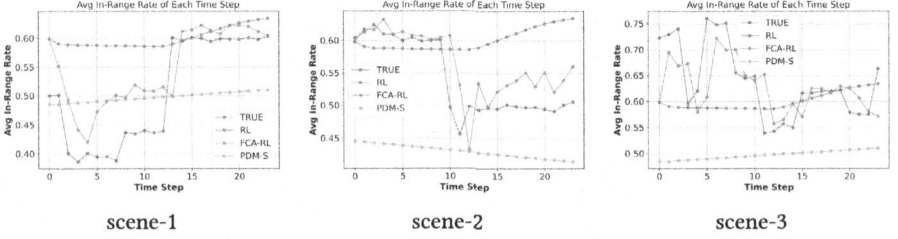

Fig. 4. Average *IRR* adjustment for each method over each time step

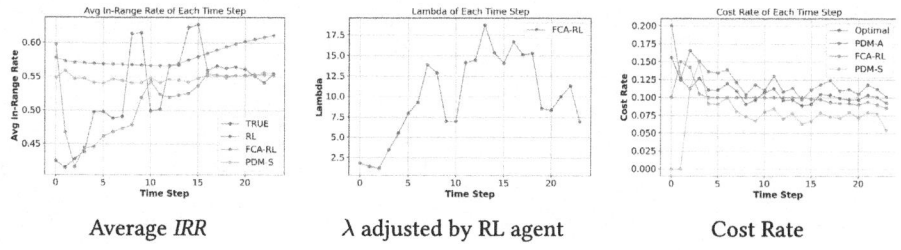

Fig. 5. Visualization of the performance of our FCA-RL method in Scene-3

for each method. FCA-RL promptly adjusts λ, achieving a smoother budget rate and a spending profile that closely aligns with the optimal strategy compared to other methods.

7 Conclusion

We propose FCA-RL, a reinforcement learning-based approach to optimize order acquisition for RSPs under price competition in RHA. Its effectiveness is demonstrated through experiments on RideGym, our self-developed simulation system for managing the full lifecycle of ride requests. In this study, we primarily address temporary data distribution shifts caused by price competition. However, the potential passenger response to coupons and long-term supply-demand dynamics remain underexplored, which we aim to address in future work.

References

1. Bao, Y., Zang, G., Yang, H., Gao, Z., Long, J.: Mathematical modeling of the platform assignment problem in a ride-sourcing market with a third-party integrator. Transport. Res. Part B: Methodol. **178**, 102833 (2023)
2. Cai, H., Ren, K., Zhang, W., Malialis, K., Wang, J., Yu, Y., Guo, D.: Real-time bidding by reinforcement learning in display advertising. In: Proceedings of the tenth ACM International Conference on Web Search and Data Mining, pp. 661–670 (2017)
3. Chen, J., Xiong, J., Chen, G., Liu, X., Yan, P., Jiang, H.: Optimal instant discounts of multiple ride options at a ride-hailing aggregator. Eur. J. Oper. Res. **314**(2), 718–734 (2024)
4. Chen, M.K., Sheldon, M.: Dynamic pricing in a labor market: surge pricing and flexible work on the uber platform. Ec **16**, 455 (2016)
5. Dai, J., Li, H., Zhu, W., Lin, J., Huang, B.: Data-driven real-time coupon allocation in the online platform. arXiv preprint arXiv:2406.05987 (2024)
6. Gutierrez, P., Gérardy, J.Y.: Causal inference and uplift modelling: a review of the literature. In: International Conference on Predictive Applications and APIs, pp. 1–13. PMLR (2017)
7. Haarnoja, T., Zhou, A., Abbeel, P., Levine, S.: Soft actor-critic: Off-policy maximum entropy deep reinforcement learning with a stochastic actor. In: International Conference on Machine Learning, pp. 1861–1870. PMLR (2018)

8. Hartigan, J.A., Wong, M.A.: Algorithm as 136: A k-means clustering algorithm. J. Royal Stat. Society. series c (applied statistics) **28**(1), 100–108 (1979)
9. He, Y., et al.: A unified solution to constrained bidding in online display advertising. In: Proceedings of the 27th ACM SIGKDD Conference on Knowledge Discovery and Data Mining, pp. 2993–3001 (2021)
10. Ren, K., Qin, J., Zheng, L., Yang, Z., Zhang, W., Yu, Y.: Deep landscape forecasting for real-time bidding advertising. In: Proceedings of the 25th ACM SIGKDD International Conference on Knowledge Discovery and Data Mining, pp. 363–372 (2019)
11. Szepesvári, C.: Algorithms for reinforcement learning. Springer nature (2022)
12. Wang, H., Yang, H.: Ridesourcing systems: a framework and review. Transport. Res. Part B: Methodol. **129**, 122–155 (2019)
13. Wang, H., Du, C., Fang, P., He, L., Wang, L., Zheng, B.: Adversarial constrained bidding via minimax regret optimization with causality-aware reinforcement learning. In: Proceedings of the 29th ACM SIGKDD Conference on Knowledge Discovery and Data Mining, pp. 2314–2325. KDD '23, ACM (Aug 2023). https://doi.org/10.1145/3580305.3599254, http://dx.doi.org/10.1145/3580305.3599254
14. Wang, H., et al.: Roi-constrained bidding via curriculum-guided Bayesian reinforcement learning. In: Proceedings of the 28th ACM SIGKDD Conference on Knowledge Discovery and Data Mining, pp. 4021–4031. KDD '22, Association for Computing Machinery, New York, NY, USA (2022). https://doi.org/10.1145/3534678.3539211
15. Wang, X., He, F., Yang, H., Gao, H.O.: Pricing strategies for a taxi-hailing platform. Transport. Res. Part E: Logist. Transport. Rev. **93**, 212–231 (2016)
16. Xiao, S., et al.: Model-based constrained MDP for budget allocation in sequential incentive marketing (2023). https://arxiv.org/abs/2303.01049
17. Zhang, W., Yuan, S., Wang, J.: Optimal real-time bidding for display advertising. In: Proceedings of the 20th ACM SIGKDD International Conference On Knowledge Discovery and Data Mining, pp. 1077–1086. Association for Computing Machinery, New York, NY, USA (2014)
18. Zhang, Y., et al.: Bcorle (λ): an offline reinforcement learning and evaluation framework for coupons allocation in e-commerce market. Adv. Neural. Inf. Process. Syst. **34**, 20410–20422 (2021)
19. Zhou, J., Xu, R.: Long-term pricing strategy based on network externalities. J. Intell. Fuzzy Syst. **40**(2), 3035–3043 (2021)
20. Zou, W.Y., Du, S., Lee, J., Pedersen, J.: Heterogeneous causal learning for effectiveness optimization in user marketing (2020). https://arxiv.org/abs/2004.09702

Ordinal Aligned Domain Generalization for Sensor-Based Time Series Regression

Yunchuan Shi, Wei Li[✉], and Albert Y. Zomaya

The University of Sydney, Sydney, Australia
{yshi7084,weiwilson.li,albert.zomaya}@sydney.edu.au

Abstract. Time series data powers sensor systems in health, cities, and beyond, demanding robust analysis for real-world impact. While deep learning models excel in this field, their performance degrades in new environments due to data distribution shifts. Domain generalization (DG) aims to enhance model performance in new environments, but current methods primarily focus on discrete data, assuming a discrete, fixed label space, and addressing distribution shifts by extracting common features from inputs across all source domains. However, sensor-based tasks involve real-valued data with diverse input and label spaces. Existing approaches overlook the continuity between data and labels, mapping input data with similar labels to scattered feature spaces, making models susceptible to distribution shifts. Additionally, variations in the label space cause predictive features to change across domains, complicating the identification of stable, generalizable features. This work introduces a new DG framework tailored for sensor-based tasks, operating without access to target domain data or post-deployment adjustments. Our approach learns Ordinal-Aligned Task-Specific (OATS) features that capture stable relationships between continuous labels and input features while maintaining domain independency under input and label space shift. This enables the model to make accurate predictions across unseen domains and continuous label spaces. Experiments on multiple real-world time series regression datasets show that our method outperforms 14 baselines, reducing prediction error by 13% on average.

Keywords: Domain Generalization · Time Series Regression · Ordinal Alignment · Label Space Shift

1 Introduction

Time series analysis is crucial for understanding and predicting sequential data in sensor-based systems, with applications in smart grids [3], environmental monitoring [28], and healthcare [7]. Deep neural networks excel in capturing complex patterns in such data [15,27]. However, building these models requires large, labeled datasets [14], which are costly and impractical to collect in all deployment environments. Traditional model-building process assumes that the training and testing data share the same statistical distributions, called independent and identically distributed (i.i.d.) data [3]. Under this assumption, the trained models can generalize to new, unseen data in new environments. In practice, sensor data vary across geographic locations and environments due to factors like sensor configurations and environmental conditions [13], forming distinct *domains*. For example, seismic sensor data in one area forms a domain, while data collected in a different area forms another domain. These variations lead to shifts in both input and the label distributions, known as *domain shifts* [33]. As a result, models trained on training (source) domains may perform poorly on new, unseen (target) domains, leading to a significant drop in predictive accuracy and limiting the model's reliability in real-world applications. To mitigate distribution shifts, transfer learning [24] and domain adaptation [8] have been proposed, but they require auxiliary data from target domains for model adjustment before or after deployment, which is impractical in time-sensitive and resource-limited sensor settings such as earthquake monitoring and emergency health monitoring [15].

Domain generalization (DG) [39] offers a solution that enables models to learn knowledge from multiple source domains that generalize well to unseen domains without requiring auxiliary data or post-deployment adjustments [2,33]. While DG has shown promise in sensor-based classification tasks like activity recognition and fault diagnosis, its application to regression remains underexplored. Classification tasks typically have a fixed label space where all domains share the same discrete labels. Many DG methods primarily address distribution shifts in the input space, learning domain-invariant features by identifying stable predictive patterns across source domains. However, many sensor-based applications, such as environmental monitoring, energy management, and health assessment, have real-valued data with diverse continuous input and label spaces across domains, leading to *label space shifts*. This variability affects model generalization in two ways. First, it complicates the identification of stable predictive features, as label space shifts alter the distribution of predictive patterns across domains. Crucial label-associated features may only appear in certain domains. For example, seismic activity in low-intensity regions lacks high-intensity earthquake signatures. This challenges DG methods that assume a shared predictive structure across all domains. In extreme cases, label space shifts create domain-exclusive label ranges, preventing label overlap and hindering the extraction of stable, transferable patterns. As a result, learning informative features while eliminating domain dependencies becomes difficult. Second, the target domain may contain unseen labels with no corresponding features in the source domain, making accurate predictions in the new label space difficult. Existing DG methods are often ineffective under these conditions, leading to inaccurate or suboptimal features for generalization. Furthermore, they overlook the continuous nature of label spaces and the subtle relationships between labels and input patterns. In regression tasks, small changes in labels correspond to gradual, continuous changes in input patterns. Methods designed for discrete labels fail to capture these relationships, mapping continuous patterns into discrete features [34]. This limitation becomes particularly problematic under domain shifts, where small variations in input features can cause large prediction deviations, making models that learn fragmented features highly sensitive to domain shifts.

To address these challenges, we propose a new DG framework for time series regression tasks in sensor-based applications. Our approach learns **O**rdinal **A**ligned **T**ask **S**pecific (OATS) to enhance generalization across unseen domains by learning stable features aligned with labels while remaining independent of domain variations. *Ordinal aligned* ensures that features capture continuous label relationships, reflecting smooth, gradual changes in regression tasks. *Task-specific* removes domain-dependent information, enabling models to generalize effectively across different environments. Together, these properties improve robustness to distribution shifts and allow extrapolation to unseen domains. Our framework leverages contrastive learning [37], which helps the model distinguish relevant features without additional annotation by contrasting similar and dissimilar examples. We extract two key feature types using regression labels as a reference: (1) Ordinal aligned features, which consistently correspond with labels across domains and capture continuous variations as labels change. We encourage an ordered and consistent alignment by enforcing signal pairs with closer regression labels to have higher similarity across domains. This structured alignment improves robustness to distribution shifts and helps the model discern which features are truly associated with label variations and how changes in feature space correspond to label variations, and vice versa. Using this relationship, the model can recognize patterns in unseen label ranges that lie near or between familiar patterns from training by extrapolating from learned continuous structures. (2) Domain-dependent features, which encode domain variations unrelated to the regression task by contrasting pairs of signal from same domain with different labels. These features help eliminate domain dependencies from the ordinal aligned features, ensuring task specificity through a loss function designed to explicitly minimize the mutual information between ordinal aligned features and domain-dependent features. This approach addresses the challenge of removing domain-dependent information from predictive representations when label space shifts occur. The contributions of this paper are summarized as follows:

1. We propose a new DG framework for sensor-based time series regression that aligns features with the ordinal nature of continuous labels, moving beyond the distributional assumptions of existing methods.
2. Our framework learns OATS features that capture essential predictive information while stable with respect to labels and independent of domain variations, enhancing generalization across domains.
3. We conducted extensive experiments on four real-world sensor applications, comparing our approach with 14 DG methods. The results demonstrate that our framework outperforms SOTA approaches, achieving improved performance and reliability under domain shifts.

2 Preliminaries and Problem Setting

2.1 Domain Generalization

DG is a subfield of transfer learning that aims to develop models capable of performing well on unseen domains with distinct data distributions from the training domain [33]. Unlike domain adaptation [3,35], DG does not rely on target domain information during training, making it particularly challenging. Initially prominent in computer vision, DG now gains traction in time-series and signal processing, such as human activity recognition [25], industrial automation [22], and healthcare [7]. Existing DG methods fall into three categories [33]. 1) Data augmentation approaches, such as Mixup and GAN-based techniques [11,13] generate synthetic data to improve generalization. 2) Learning strategies include meta-learning [18,22], which simulates domain shifts by splitting source tasks to enhance adaptability, invariant risk minimization (IRM) [10], which encourages consistent predictive rules across varying domains, and distributionally robust optimization (DRO) [9], which optimizes model performance in worst-case scenarios. 3) Representation learning seeks domain-invariant features through distribution alignment methods by reducing maximum mean discrepancy (MMD) [13] or correlation [1], domain-adversarial learning (DANN) [15,16], and feature disentanglement [2,4,25] to separate domain-specific factors from robust, transferable representations. Despite these advances, most DG methods assume discrete, consistent label spaces and focus primarily on classification. This limits their effectiveness in time-series regression, where label space shifts introduce challenges that disrupt stable predictive patterns across domains. As a result, existing approaches often degrade when label distributions vary between source and target domains. Some recent studies have explored regression, [16] tackles time-series forecasting with temporal shifts where distributions evolve within a single domain but do not address domain shifts across environments. [8,14,30,35] tackle regression task under label drift, they rely on extra target-domain information, such as unlabeled samples, do not strictly conform to the DG setting where the target domain is entirely unknown. As a result, developing robust regression models that handle continuously shifting label distributions in unseen domains remains an open and pressing challenge in DG research. In Appendix A, we further discuss the limitations of DG methods in regression with continuous label space shifts. Propositions 1 and 2 show that domain-invariant feature extraction can lose critical predictive information and fail to remove domain dependency.

2.2 Problem Setting of DG Regression

Let $\mathcal{X} \subseteq \mathbb{R}^{M \times T}$ be the input space and $\mathcal{Y} \subseteq \mathbb{R}$ be the label space of real numbers. where T represents the length of the time series, and M is the number of dimensions in each input sample. A domain is defined over the product space $\mathcal{X} \times \mathcal{Y}$ and is represented by a joint probability distribution $\mathcal{P}(X, Y)$. For each domain d, we have a set of data samples $D_d = \{(x_i^d, y_i^d)\}_{i=1}^{N_d}$, where each sample

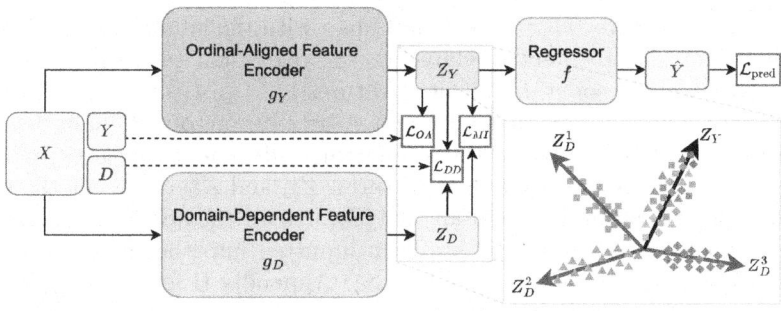

Fig. 1. The overview of our proposed framework

(x_i^d, y_i^d) is drawn from the distribution $\mathcal{P}_d(X, Y)$. Here, N_d is the number of samples in domain d. We use X_d and Y_d to represent the input set and label set, respectively, in domain d. To represent multiple source domains, we define a set $\mathcal{S} = \{1, \ldots, S\}$, where each element corresponds to a source domain with its joint distribution $\mathcal{P}_s(X, Y)$. Let D_S represent the combined data from all source domains, with X_S and Y_S denoting the full set of inputs and labels across these domains. The unseen target domain, where we will evaluate the model's generalization ability, is represented by a separate distribution, $\mathcal{P}_t(X, Y)$. Label space shift may exist between domains, which is defined as occurring between domains j and k when the possible values or ranges of their label distributions, denoted as $\mathcal{P}(Y_j)$ and $\mathcal{P}(Y_k)$, differ. This shift is characterized by the inequality of their support sets, $\mathcal{S}_{Y_j} \neq \mathcal{S}_{Y_k}$. To measure the generalization capability of a model $f : \mathcal{X} \to \mathcal{Y}$, we calculate its empirical risk on a given domain d, defined as:

$$R(f, \mathcal{P}(X, Y)) = \mathbb{E}_{x, y \sim \mathcal{P}(X, Y)} \|y - f(x)\|_2^2 \tag{1}$$

This risk measure calculates the average Mean Squared Error (MSE) loss between the model's predictions $f(x)$ and the actual labels y for samples from domain d. The goal of DG is to train a model f using data from the source domains that minimizes the risk in the unseen target domain, denoted $R(f, \mathcal{P}_t(X, Y))$.

3 Our Approach

We propose a framework for time series regression that learns Ordinal Aligned, Task-Specific (OATS) features by extracting both ordinal-aligned features and domain-dependent features, and minimizing the mutual information between them to enforce task specificity. Fig. 1 provides an overview of our framework, which includes three main components: an ordinal-aligned feature encoder g_Y, a domain-dependent feature encoder g_D, and a regressor f. Both encoders, g_Y and g_D, share the same network architecture but are trained to extract different feature representations from the input data x. Specifically, g_Y extracts ordinal-aligned features $z_Y = g_Y(x)$ that align with the labels in an ordinal way, capturing information directly related to the regression task. In contrast, the domain-dependent encoder g_D extracts features $z_D = g_D(x)$ that capture unique characteristics of each domain and assist g_Y in filtering out domain-dependent influences. We use Z_D to denote the set of domain-dependent features, and Z_Y to denote the set of domain-dependent features. Z_D^i and Z_Y^i represent the subsets of domain-dependent and ordinal-aligned features for the domain i, respectively. The ordinal-aligned features Z_Y are then inputted into the regressor f, which outputs the final prediction $\hat{y} = f(Z_Y)$. See Appendix B for the pseudocode of training and inference. Below, we formally define ordinal aligned features and domain dependent features:

Definition 1. Ordinal Aligned Features: Let x_i, x_j, x_k be three data samples from different source domains, with labels y_i, y_j, j_k satisfying $|y_i - y_j| < |y_i - y_k|$, indicating that y_i is closer to y_j than to y_k. Ordinal aligned features are $z_i, z_j, z_k \in Z_Y$ consistent across domain given label and satisfying $sim(z_i, z_j) < sim(z_i, z_k)$, where $sim(\cdot, \cdot)$ represents a similarity measure between two features (i.e. euclidean distance or cosine similarity).

These features encode the smooth, gradual relationships inherent in regression tasks. For instance, in seismic analysis, waveform characteristics change gradually from a magnitude 3 to a magnitude 6 earthquake. A waveform for magnitude 4 falls between those for magnitudes 3 and 6 but more closely resembles magnitude 3. Similarly, in clinical pain assessments, physiological signals respond gradually as pain levels increase. Moving from "no pain" to "severe pain" involves intermediate stages like "mild pain" and "moderate pain," with each stage marked by subtle changes in physiological signals. Such gradual shifts in labels produce a smooth, continuous effect on the associated features. This ordinal continuity implies that inputs contain features reflecting a progression of label values, where adjacent labels are associated with more similar features. By identifying these features, the model captures representations that encode the stable relationship between labels and feature variations across domains, effectively modeling this relationship based on label distances. This enables the model to approximate and align features smoothly across neighboring labels, improving generalization to unseen label ranges by leveraging the learned similarity structure among features. To remove domain-dependency from ordinal aligned features while preserving task specificity, we identify these features from each domain that remain stable even as labels change, formally defined as follows:

Definition 2. Domain Dependent Features: Let x_i, x_j be two data samples from the same domain X_d with different labels y_i, y_j, and let x_k be a sample from a different domain $X_{d'}$. The Domain Dependent Features $z_i, z_j, z_k \in Z_D$ capture domain-specific variations while remaining independent of the labels by maximizing the similarity between z_i and z_j, while minimizing their similarity to z_k from other domains and the ordinal aligned features $z_y \in Z_Y$.

To extract these features effectively, our framework uses contrastive learning [4,37] to identifies shared patterns in data. We design contrastive objectives for both encoders, g_Y and g_D, helping them specialize in their respective roles. As shown in Fig. 1 (bottom right), our framework organizes the feature space by separating ordinal-aligned features Z_Y from domain-dependent features Z_D and aligning Z_Y features according to label values to form an ordinal structure.

3.1 Ordinal Aligned Feature for Regression

To achieve ordinal alignment of features, as defined in Definition 1, we aim to train the ordinal-aligned encoder g_Y to prioritize similarity between feature pairs based on the closeness of their labels. Specifically, for any two features $g_Y(x_i)$ and $g_Y(x_j)$ with labels y_i and y_j, we aim for their similarity to be greater than that of any pair $g_Y(x_i)$ and $g_Y(x_k)$, where $|y_i - y_j| < |y_i - y_k|$. This approach adapts recent advances in learning features through contrastive learning [37] to address the unique challenges of multi-domain generalization with shifting continuous label spaces. To guide g_Y in learning these ordinal aligned features, we introduce a loss function $\mathcal{L}_{OA}$, which increases the similarity between features with closer labels. The loss function is defined as:

$$\mathcal{L}_{OA} = -\frac{1}{N} \sum_{x_i, x_j \in X_S, i \neq j} \log \frac{e^{\text{sim}(g_Y(x_i), g_Y(x_j))/\tau_{OA}}}{\sum_{x_k \in \Phi(i,j)} e^{\text{sim}(g_Y(x_i), g_Y(x_k))/\tau_{OA}}} \quad (2)$$

In this setup, we evaluate all pairs of input features in the source domain. For each pair x_i and x_j, the numerator measures the similarity between their encoded features, while the denominator sums similarities between $g_Y(x_i)$ and all features x_k in $\Phi(i,j)$. Here, $\Phi(i,j) = \{x_k \in X_S \mid |y_i - y_j| < |y_i - y_k|\}$ includes features with label distances to y_i greater than the distance between y_i and y_j, ensuring closer labels are prioritized. The temperature parameter τ_{oa} adjusts the sensitivity to similarity: lower values sharpen the focus on more similar pairs, while higher values smooth the distribution. The exponential scaling further emphasizes pairs with higher similarity scores, amplifying their influence on the loss function. By minimizing $\mathcal{L}_{OA}$, the encoder is encouraged to produce feature pairs with smaller label distances that are more similar than pairs with larger label distances. This optimization enforces ordinal alignment across the feature space, helping the encoder capture the continuous nature of the labels. Additionally, this objective aligns features with similar labels from different domains, allowing the model to learn consistent patterns in diverse environments. By focusing on stable, label-consistent features, our approach enhances generalization across domains by capturing elements that remain invariant despite domain variations.

3.2 Minimizing Domain Dependency

To address the presence of non-overlapping label ranges that may exist exclusively in a single source domain, and to ensure that the ordinal-aligned encoder g_Y learns features free from domain-dependent information, we introduce a domain-dependent encoder, g_D, along with two contrastive loss functions. The domain-dependent encoder captures label unrelated characteristics unique to each domain, allowing us to remove these features from the ordinal-aligned ones, enforcing task-specificity. The encoder g_D is designed to ensure that features with different labels from the same domain are similar, maximizing their intra-domain similarity. Specifically, for two data points x_i^s and x_j^s from the same domain s, we aim to maximize their similarity in the feature space. Conversely, for data points x^s and x^t from different domains s and t, we minimize their similarity. To encourage the removal of domain-dependent features from ordinal-aligned feature, we also minimize the similarity between the features generated by ordinal-aligned encoder g_Y and domain-dependent encoder g_D. These optimization objectives are collectively achieved through a contrastive loss function, $\mathcal{L}_{DD}$. In this setting, Z_Y, the features extracted by g_Y, represent one category, while Z_D^s, the domain-dependent features extracted by g_D for each domain s, form separate categories. The aim is to ensure high similarity within each category and low similarity across categories. The contrastive loss function is defined as:

$$\mathcal{L}_{\mathrm{DD}} = -\sum_{z_i \in Z_Y \cup Z_D} \frac{1}{|\mathring{P}(z_i)|} \sum_{z_j \in \mathring{P}(z_i)} \log \frac{e^{\mathrm{sim}(z_i, z_j)/\tau_{\mathrm{DD}}}}{\sum_{z_k \in \mathring{N}(z_i)} e^{\mathrm{sim}(z_i, z_k)/\tau_{\mathrm{DD}}}} \qquad (3)$$

$\mathring{P}(z_i) = \{z_j \in Z_Y \cup Z_D \mid \mathrm{category}(z_j) = \mathrm{category}(z_i), z_j \neq z_i\}$ denotes features from the same category as z_i, and $\mathring{N}(z_i) = \{z_k \in Z_Y \cup Z_D \mid \mathrm{category}(z_k) \neq \mathrm{category}(z_i)\}$ denotes features from different category. The temperature parameter τ_{DD} controls the sensitivity to similarity differences. Minimizing $\mathcal{L}_{\mathrm{DD}}$ promotes high similarity among features within the same category (numerator) while reducing similarity among features from different categories (denominator). This encourages g_D to identify domain-dependent features within each domain. However, there remains a possibility that Z_Y and Z_D may still be correlated. We aim to minimize their mutual information to remove their dependency: $I(Z_Y, Z_D) = D_{KL}(\mathcal{P}(Z_Y, Z_D) \parallel \mathcal{P}(Z_Y)\mathcal{P}(Z_D))$. Minimizing mutual information is equivalent to minimizing the Kullback-Leibler (KL) divergence between the joint probability distribution $\mathcal{P}(Z_Y, Z_D)$ and the product of the marginal distributions $\mathcal{P}(Z_Y)\mathcal{P}(Z_D)$ by definition. However, directly computing the KL divergence between high-dimensional distributions is challenging due to its intractability. To address this challenge, we propose an contrastive objective and a discriminating head h to approximate the KL divergence with feature similarity. We construct a set of feature pairs $\{(Z_Y, Z_D)\}$ by concatenating ordinal-aligned and domain-dependent feature along the feature dimension to represent joint distribution $\mathcal{P}(Z_Y, Z_D)$. Additionally, we create another set of feature pairs $\{(Z_Y, Z_D')\}$, where Z_D' is obtained by shuffling the indices of Z_D, ensuring independence between concatenated ordinal-aligned and domain-dependent features to simulate samples from the product of the marginals $\mathcal{P}(Z_Y)\mathcal{P}(Z_D)$. The discriminating head h is a network designed to project $\{(z_Y, z_D)\}$ and $\{(z_Y, z_D')\}$

into distinct feature spaces. The proposed objective function is defined as:

$$\mathcal{L}_{\mathrm{MI}} = -\frac{1}{N} \sum_{z_i, z_j \in Z_J, i \neq j} \log \frac{e^{\mathrm{sim}(h(\mathrm{GRL}(z_i)), h(z_j))/\tau_{\mathrm{MI}}}}{\sum_{z_k' \in Z_M} e^{\mathrm{sim}(h(z_i), h(z_k'))/\tau_{\mathrm{MI}}}} \\ - \frac{1}{N} \sum_{z_i', z_j' \in Z_M, i \neq j} \log \frac{e^{\mathrm{sim}(h(z_i'), h(z_j'))/\tau_{\mathrm{MI}}}}{\sum_{z_k \in Z_J} e^{\mathrm{sim}(h(z_i'), h(z_k))/\tau_{\mathrm{MI}}}} \quad (4)$$

Here, Z_J represent the set of features drawn from the joint distribution $\mathcal{P}(Z_Y, Z_D)$, and Z_M represent the set of features drawn from the marginal distribution $\mathcal{P}(Z_Y)\mathcal{P}(Z_D)$. Minimizing this objective function encourages the discriminative head h to map feature pairs from the same distribution to be closer together while pushing apart those from different distributions, enable h effectively distinguish between concatenated feature pairs drawn from the joint versus marginal distributions, thus assessing the similarity between the two distributions and approximating the KL divergence. To minimize the KL divergence and reduce the mutual information, we employ adversarial learning by applying a gradient reversal layer (GRL) to Z_Y before it is passed to h. This approach reverse the gradient sign been prepackaged, guiding the encoder to learn patterns that make h unable to differentiate the features belonging to the joint distribution or the marginal distributions, thereby minimizing the KL divergence and reducing their mutual information. By integrating these strategies, we ensure that the ordinal-aligned encoder g_Y focuses on learning features pertinent to the task while being robust to domain-dependent variations, thus enhancing generalization across domains.

3.3 Selection of Similarity Measurements

The choice of similarity measurements is critical to optimizing our framework. Specifically, $\mathcal{L}_{OA}$ aims for ordinal-aligned features to be more similar when conditioned on their corresponding labels, while $\mathcal{L}_{DD}$ seeks to minimize the similarity between ordinal-aligned dependent and domain-dependent features from each domain. This setup introduces a potential conflict in contrasting ordinal-aligned features, as they are simultaneously pushed to align closely with each other and to diverge from domain-dependent features. To resolve this potential conflict, we employ distinct similarity metrics for each objective: L2 distance for $\mathcal{L}_{OA}$ and cosine similarity for $\mathcal{L}_{DD}$. This strategic choice positions the ordinal-aligned features in different orientations within a high-dimensional space relative to domain-dependent features, while aligning the ordinal-aligned features along a similar axis but at varying positions (see Fig. 1 - bottom right).

3.4 Overall Loss Function

The overall objective function for training the model is:

$$\mathcal{L}_{\mathrm{ALL}} = \mathbb{E}_{x,y \sim \mathcal{P}_s(X,Y)} \|y - f(g_Y(x))\|_2^2 + \lambda_1 \mathcal{L}_{OA} + \lambda_2 \mathcal{L}_{DD} + \lambda_3 \mathcal{L}_{MI} \quad (5)$$

The first term represents the mean squared error between the predicted outputs and the actual labels. The remaining terms are weighted components of the loss function that manage domain-dependent and ordinal label aligned representation constraints. The parameters λ_1, λ_2, λ_3 are regularization weights that balance the influence of constraints relative to the primary regression task. By jointly optimizing these losses, the model learns to extract OATS features that align with label order while simultaneously removing domain-dependent characteristics. This enables the model to generalize effectively across different domains and make accurate predictions for the regression task. Our generalization method operates solely during training, using f, g_Y and g_D with their respective loss functions to guide learning. During inference, only the ordinal-aligned encoder g_Y and regressor f are used to make predictions on unseen data. A few more discussions on our design can be found in Appendix C.

4 Experiments

4.1 Datasets and Setup

We tested our method on real-world time series data from biomedical, seismology, and energy systems with distribution shifts. The Pain Assessment dataset (BioVid) [32] predicts pain intensity levels using physiological sensor data collected from 87 subjects in response to heat-induced pain. Pain intensity includes levels ranging from 0 (no pain) to 4 (severe pain). Each subject was treated as a distinct domain due to individual biological and psychological variations that affect data distribution, following established practices [36]. This setup allowed us to evaluate the ability of the model to generalize to new patients. To assess the impact of label space shifts, we modified the original dataset, which features uniformly distributed labels, by randomly removal some range of labels from each subject's label distribution. These conditions tested the robustness of our method and other DG approaches under varying degrees of label space shift. The Air Quality Prediction dataset (PRSA) [5], consists of hourly air pollution index measurements and meteorological data collected from multiple air monitoring stations in Beijing. The objective is to predict future air pollution index variations based on meteorological data. The Earthquake Detection dataset (LEN-DB) [21], contains three-component seismic data captured along vertical, north-south, and east-west axes. Each recording is labeled with earthquake magnitude. Data from ten countries were treated as separate domains. The magnitude distributions vary across stations due to geological and geographical factors. This dataset includes 22,207 sequences, providing a diverse evaluation setting for domain generalization under label space shifts. The Energy Disaggregation dataset (REFIT) [23] records household energy use at 8-second intervals over two years. The data includes whole-house aggregate consumption and individual appliance loads. Our task involves short-term Non-Intrusive Load Monitoring (NILM), where the goal is to predict the power consumption of a target appliance at the midpoint of a sequence based on the overall household energy usage. We selected eight houses and targeted four appliances: washing machines, microwaves, fridges, and dishwashers. Each appliance is treated as a distinct regression task, and data from each house represents a unique domain. Each appliance-specific dataset includes 64,000 sequences. For a comprehensive description of the used datasets, refer to Appendix D. In our experiments, we employed a Leave-One-Domain-Out (LODO) strategy to evaluate our method. Under this approach, one domain was held out as the target domain while the remaining domains were used for training. Each domain was sequentially excluded, ensuring that all domains were evaluated as target domains. We conducted 15 trials per experiment, averaging the results to ensure a robust evaluation. Appendix E gives details on implementation and hyperparameter settings. The code is available at https://github.com/yshi22/OATSDG.

4.2 Baselines

We evaluated our model against 14 recent and widely used DG approaches for sensor-based data to assess its effectiveness comprehensively. Empirical Risk Minimization (ERM) [31] serves as a baseline, representing conventional training by minimizing loss on source domains without additional generalization strategies. We compared our model with widely adopted DG methods, including Coral [29], MMD [26], DANN [6], MLDG [12], DRO [9], and Mixup [38], which have been applied to many time series tasks [1,13,15,18]. Additionally, we included recent methods that perform well in image-based applications but remain underexplored for time series data. VREx [10] applies variance regularization to stabilize performance across diverse environments, improving domain resilience. mDSDI [2] combines meta-learning with feature disentanglement, and CDDG [4] incorporates contrastive learning to learn invariant features. We also evaluated recent approaches that address time series data. Diversify [16] leverages domain adversarial learning to extract domain-invariant features from time sequences. GILE [25] employs feature disentanglement to identify stable components in sensor signals. Fixed [17] enhances generalization by augmenting stable features, with evaluations conducted explicitly on time series data. MAMR [19] applies weighted meta-learning tailored for regression tasks.

4.3 Results

The experiments evaluated the robustness and effectiveness of our DG framework across the datasets, with a particular focus on the challenges posed by domain shifts in regression tasks. As detailed in Table 1, our framework outperforms others, achieving the lowest Mean Absolute Error (MAE) and Root Mean Squared Error (RMSE) in most target domains. For Biovid tests, existing domain-invariant representation learning methods, MMD, Coral, DANN and Diversify outperformed ERM when label spaces are consistent across domains (reduced generalization errors). However, their performance degraded significantly under label space shifts, consistent with our Proposition 1. In some cases, their performance was even worse than ERM. This is likely because ERM, while

Table 1. The performance comparison of various DG methods on BioVid, LEN-DB, PRSA and REFIT datasets using LODO testing. The table shows average MAE and RMSE across all target domains for each method (mean ± standard deviation). Results are in bold if our model has the best performance.

| | Biovid | | | | REFIT | | | |
| | No LSS | | Under LSS | | Microwave | | Washing Machine | |
	MAE	RMSE	MAE	RMSE	MAE	RMSE	MAE	RMSE
ERM [31]	1.132 ± 0.004	1.569 ± 0.004	1.136 ± 0.010	1.585 ± 0.010	34.56 ± 01.50	158.26 ± 03.25	41.16 ± 02.03	184.03 ± 05.19
MMD [26]	1.127 ± 0.014	1.540 ± 0.012	1.143 ± 0.001	1.558 ± 0.002	44.65 ± 00.89	158.32 ± 01.52	52.64 ± 01.33	188.15 ± 02.98
Coral [29]	1.131 ± 0.016	1.541 ± 0.017	1.139 ± 0.008	1.560 ± 0.006	32.53 ± 00.31	159.73 ± 00.94	42.65 ± 00.73	191.19 ± 02.45
DANN [6]	1.147 ± 0.004	1.560 ± 0.003	1.178 ± 0.010	1.598 ± 0.013	30.74 ± 02.91	143.31 ± 05.84	58.52 ± 04.18	193.51 ± 09.66
Mixup [38]	1.116 ± 0.009	1.533 ± 0.013	1.135 ± 0.013	1.557 ± 0.012	33.15 ± 01.50	156.26 ± 03.69	40.00 ± 02.31	181.10 ± 07.02
MLDG [12]	1.152 ± 0.010	1.577 ± 0.029	1.167 ± 0.010	1.600 ± 0.012	49.12 ± 13.34	150.66 ± 13.94	48.48 ± 18.40	176.69 ± 23.35
DRO [9]	1.120 ± 0.005	1.515 ± 0.004	1.167 ± 0.018	1.799 ± 0.020	41.18 ± 02.21	171.46 ± 05.09	44.60 ± 01.85	192.65 ± 06.02
VREx [10]	1.130 ± 0.011	1.544 ± 0.012	1.136 ± 0.012	1.558 ± 0.013	35.97 ± 01.64	160.82 ± 04.03	41.71 ± 01.63	187.17 ± 04.98
mDSDI [2]	1.116 ± 0.006	1.527 ± 0.007	1.126 ± 0.006	1.543 ± 0.009	32.45 ± 01.79	146.85 ± 04.99	42.36 ± 02.81	179.92 ± 06.49
GILE [25]	1.228 ± 0.008	1.606 ± 0.009	1.251 ± 0.013	1.637 ± 0.016	39.64 ± 09.19	157.06 ± 10.42	47.68 ± 11.18	185.75 ± 25.20
Fixed [17]	1.172 ± 0.007	1.588 ± 0.005	1.193 ± 0.013	1.618 ± 0.010	31.00 ± 01.85	143.63 ± 01.55	55.43 ± 01.92	190.61 ± 05.49
MAMR [19]	1.183 ± 0.012	1.618 ± 0.019	1.182 ± 0.013	1.612 ± 0.012	43.50 ± 09.14	150.18 ± 12.04	53.70 ± 14.54	179.62 ± 16.91
Diversify [16]	1.124 ± 0.004	1.532 ± 0.005	1.138 ± 0.011	1.550 ± 0.014	31.27 ± 02.58	152.69 ± 03.74	43.53 ± 03.78	176.06 ± 03.55
CDDG [4]	1.129 ± 0.005	1.547 ± 0.007	1.158 ± 0.003	1.575 ± 0.005	38.07 ± 01.97	158.88 ± 04.33	41.08 ± 01.58	180.61 ± 05.48
Ours	**1.107 ± 0.008**	**1.504 ± 0.009**	**1.123 ± 0.002**	**1.540 ± 0.004**	**29.26 ± 02.90**	146.71 ± 05.16	**35.78 ± 02.91**	**174.43 ± 07.13**

| | LENDB | | PRSA | | REFIT | | | |
| | | | | | Fridge | | Dishwasher | |
	MAE	RMSE	MAE	RMSE	MAE	RMSE	MAE	RMSE
ERM [31]	0.422 ± 0.035	0.707 ± 0.046	30.79 ± 4.05	45.97 ± 5.21	37.97 ± 00.84	50.66 ± 00.86	36.99 ± 01.40	202.27 ± 04.16
MMD [26]	0.449 ± 0.037	0.698 ± 0.047	30.40 ± 1.15	45.57 ± 1.19	39.67 ± 00.20	50.32 ± 00.25	47.06 ± 00.49	194.53 ± 01.41
Coral [29]	0.489 ± 0.008	0.744 ± 0.009	31.48 ± 0.09	45.77 ± 0.20	**36.94 ± 00.26**	58.38 ± 00.18	51.31 ± 00.33	197.34 ± 00.77
DANN [6]	0.455 ± 0.024	0.706 ± 0.032	33.85 ± 1.62	48.92 ± 2.54	41.90 ± 00.64	53.72 ± 07.80	37.06 ± 01.02	207.80 ± ?
Mixup [38]	0.464 ± 0.028	0.710 ± 0.036	38.47 ± 1.39	56.19 ± 1.96	37.84 ± 00.72	50.40 ± 00.72	36.67 ± 01.04	201.47 ± 02.23
MLDG [12]	0.506 ± 0.109	0.794 ± 0.120	31.45 ± 1.59	46.85 ± 2.41	37.56 ± 02.14	56.46 ± 02.32	51.58 ± 13.85	196.57 ± 11.88
DRO [9]	0.480 ± 0.029	0.730 ± 0.034	31.11 ± 2.37	45.53 ± 2.97	41.93 ± 00.98	57.74 ± 01.40	39.88 ± 01.39	207.55 ± 03.41
VREx [10]	0.474 ± 0.035	0.720 ± 0.043	31.14 ± 2.67	45.84 ± 2.88	38.20 ± 00.88	51.03 ± 00.94	38.30 ± 01.67	204.39 ± 04.03
mDSDI [2]	0.415 ± 0.025	0.697 ± 0.032	31.04 ± 4.49	46.02 ± 5.41	39.90 ± 01.37	49.98 ± 01.17	39.73 ± 02.20	201.73 ± 04.78
GILE [25]	0.440 ± 0.029	0.695 ± 0.036	30.55 ± 1.32	44.35 ± 1.99	41.52 ± 00.81	49.89 ± 00.85	39.11 ± 05.18	199.68 ± 09.19
Fixed [17]	0.492 ± 0.047	0.747 ± 0.056	38.81 ± 0.80	56.70 ± 1.40	41.67 ± 00.30	51.03 ± 03.36	37.68 ± 01.93	193.36 ± 05.44
MAMR [19]	0.542 ± 0.102	0.824 ± 0.116	38.47 ± 4.15	55.19 ± 5.96	42.44 ± 03.77	53.34 ± 04.36	51.46 ± 17.26	193.05 ± 18.63
Diversify [16]	0.457 ± 0.050	0.698 ± 0.054	30.81 ± 0.85	46.55 ± 2.03	39.69 ± 01.17	52.46 ± 05.15	36.59 ± 03.36	205.30 ± 01.32
CDDG [4]	0.423 ± 0.031	0.707 ± 0.041	33.34 ± 7.90	49.10 ± 9.73	38.03 ± 01.01	50.97 ± 01.11	39.42 ± 01.38	204.59 ± 03.93
Ours	**0.386 ± 0.025**	**0.666 ± 0.032**	**28.98 ± 0.72**	**43.72 ± 1.37**	38.35 ± 01.48	**49.84 ± 01.12**	**35.83 ± 00.61**	202.86 ± 01.34

retaining some domain-dependent noise, also preserves essential predictive features of different label spaces. Conversely, mDSDI, which attempts to adapt domain-specific information after learning domain-invariant features, preserve more label-related information, making it less susceptible to label shifts compared to other baselines. However, it struggles to align features from different domains with labels and fails to capture continuous relationships between features and labels, resulting in lower performance than our approach. Our framework shows robust, stable performance under label shifts, with consistently low standard deviations. It also outperforms across most metrics on the LEN-DB, PRSA and REFIT datasets. MLDG, MAMR, DRO, and VREx, while different in their treatment of domain shifts, struggle to meet the diverse predictive challenges across different labels within domains. Their performance is limited under variable domain conditions, impacted by the distinct prediction difficulties and variances among labels. Data augmentation techniques also fail to bridge

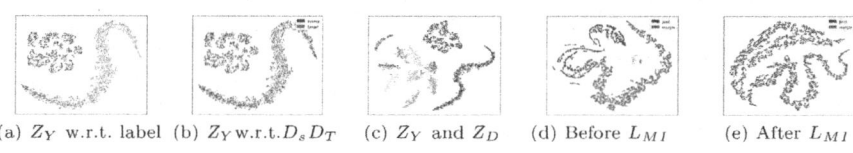

(a) Z_Y w.r.t. label (b) Z_Y w.r.t. $D_s D_T$ (c) Z_Y and Z_D (d) Before L_{MI} (e) After L_{MI}

Fig. 2. t-SNE visualization of features extracted by our approach.

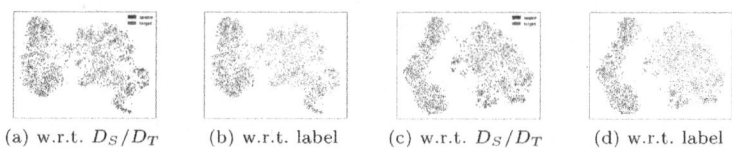

(a) w.r.t. D_S/D_T (b) w.r.t. label (c) w.r.t. D_S/D_T (d) w.r.t. label

Fig. 3. t-SNE visualization of features extracted by ERM (a,b) and Domain-Invariant Feature Learning (c,d)

the domain gap effectively, largely due to the inherent noise and discrepancies present in time-series data across domains. These results demonstrate the effectiveness of our framework in handling the complexities of domain generalization in regression tasks, particularly its ability to adapt to diverse real-world scenarios. See Appendix F for the significance analysis and detailed results of each method across the leave-out domains for each dataset.

4.4 Visualization of Extracted Features

We used t-SNE [20] to visualize the extracted features and validate the effectiveness of ordinal alignment. Figures 2a and 2b showcase the alignment of ordinal-aligned features with label values (blue for lower, yellow for higher) and between source and target domains (purple and red, respectively). The visualizations highlight our ability to maintain a correct ordinal relationship with respect to label values (monotonous blue-to-yellow gradient), and the overlapping colors in Fig. 2b indicate successful domain generalization. Figure 2c demonstrates effective learning of domain-dependent features, with each domain represented by distinct colors and clear separation, without overlap. Figure 2d and 2e validates the effectiveness of minimizing domain-dependency in Sect. 3.2, shows the mutual information between ordinal-aligned and domain dependent features via distributional divergence between $\mathcal{P}(Z_Y, Z_D)$(purple points) and $\mathcal{P}(Z_Y)\mathcal{P}(Z_D)$(red points) before and after applying $\mathcal{L}_{MI}$. Before applying $\mathcal{L}_{MI}$ (Fig. 2d), a large distance between samples of $\mathcal{P}(Z_Y, Z_D)$ and $\mathcal{P}(Z_Y)\mathcal{P}(Z_D)$ indicates high KL divergence, suggesting considerable mutual information between ordinal-aligned and domain-dependent features. After applying $\mathcal{L}_{MI}$ (Fig. 2e), the distributions are aligned, indicating a lower KL divergence and reduced mutual information between the ordinal-aligned and domain-dependent features. We also provide visualization results of features learned through ERM and domain-invariant feature learning methods. Figure 3a and 3b shows the alignment results for ERM, where target domain features (red points) do not align well with source domain

Table 2. Ablation study showing the effect of different loss components and distance metrics across four datasets.

	REFIT		Biovid		LEN-DB		PRSA	
	MAE	RMSE	MAE	RMSE	MAE	RMSE	MAE	RMSE
ERM	37.67 ± 01.44	148.77 ± 03.37	1.136 ± 0.010	1.585 ± 0.010	0.422 ± 0.035	0.707 ± 0.046	30.79 ± 4.05	45.97 ± 5.21
$\mathcal{L}_{OA}$	35.34 ± 01.29	145.79 ± 03.67	1.133 ± 0.008	1.549 ± 0.007	0.391 ± 0.034	0.670 ± 0.018	30.04 ± 1.21	44.98 ± 1.78
$\mathcal{L}_{ALL}$	**34.71 ± 01.91**	**143.33 ± 03.78**	**1.126 ± 0.005**	**1.536 ± 0.006**	**0.386 ± 0.025**	**0.666 ± 0.032**	**28.98 ± 0.72**	**43.72 ± 1.37**
Cosine	35.71 ± 02.17	144.42 ± 04.48	1.129 ± 0.005	1.545 ± 0.007	0.392 ± 0.027	0.676 ± 0.032	29.69 ± 1.41	44.56 ± 1.83
L2	35.90 ± 02.18	145.22 ± 04.15	1.130 ± 0.006	1.549 ± 0.006	0.389 ± 0.024	0.674 ± 0.027	29.06 ± 0.92	43.86 ± 1.65

features (purple points), as indicated by a significant number of red points (target) located outside the purple points (source). This indicates that ERM fails to learn features that generalize across domains. Additionally, the learned features do not capture the ordinal relationships between labels, as the distribution of label values around the features does not show a gradient transition (label values are indicated by color). Figure 3c and 3d shows the alignment results using DANN [6]. The target and source domain distributions align, with red points mostly covered by purple areas. However, the features still fail to capture the ordinal relationships between labels, and label relationships are incorrectly learned. This issue is observed in areas with smaller label values (darker points), where unexpectedly high label values (brighter points) appear. These t-SNE visualizations support the effectiveness and robust generalization capabilities of our approach. More visualization results and comparisons with different DG approaches are given in Appendix G.

4.5 Ablation Study

Our ablation study examines the contributions of different components in our framework, as shown in Table 2. The baseline ERM model (without DG), shows high MAE and RMSE, indicating its poor generalization. Each additional component in our framework progressively improves the model's ability to generalize. The inclusion of ordinal alignment $\mathcal{L}_{OA}$ shows a definite improvement in performance, and combining $\mathcal{L}_{DD}$ and $\mathcal{L}_{MI}$ to minimize domain-dependency further enhances performance ($\mathcal{L}_{all}$ in the table). These results demonstrate the effectiveness of our method. We also analyzed the effect of different distance metrics, Cosine and L2, used within the contrastive objectives $\mathcal{L}_{DD}$ and $\mathcal{L}_{OA}$. We compared separate uses of each metric, as well as a hybrid approach: Cosine similarity for $\mathcal{L}_{DD}$ and L2 distance for $\mathcal{L}_{OA}$. The hybrid approach ($\mathcal{L}_{all}$ in the table) achieved the best performance and stability. It effectively resolves potential conflicts between metrics and positions ordinal-aligned features optimally within the feature space. This ensures that while these features are aligned, their magnitudes can vary, ultimately leading to improved model generalization.

5 Discussion

Our framework is broadly applicable to various sensor-based applications, including environmental monitoring, medical diagnostics, and industrial process control. Importantly, it introduces no additional computational cost during inference. The latency, memory footprint, and overall complexity of the deployed model remain identical to a model with the same architecture trained using conventional methods. The only added overhead arises during training, where the g_D requires one additional forward pass, and the contrastive losses require pairwise feature similarity computations, leading to quadratic complexity with respect to batch size. In practice, this burden is mitigated by performing training on dedicated high-performance machines, while deployment is carried out on resource-constrained edge or embedded devices. A key assumption of the framework is the existence of stable label-aligned features across domains. In cases where label-feature relationships vary significantly, such as when similar labels correspond to distinct sensor reading patterns due to concept drift, or when non-linear or non-monotonic dependencies violate the assumption of gradual label transitions, the effectiveness of ordinal alignment may be reduced.

6 Conclusion and Future Work

This paper presented a new framework for improving domain generalization in time-series regression by learning ordinal-aligned, task-specific features. Our method aligns representations with label order while explicitly disentangling domain-dependent variations. Extensive experiments across diverse real-world sensor datasets demonstrate that the framework reliably models subtle variations in sensor readings, preserves ordinal continuity across domains, and consistently outperforms existing approaches. For future work, we plan to conduct pilot studies in real-world deployment settings to further evaluate and refine the framework's performance. A key objective is to extend the method to accommodate complex, non-linear, and non-monotonic relationships between features and labels, which may violate the assumption of gradual label–feature alignment. We will also optimize the model architecture and training pipeline for improved efficiency, introduce a more compact loss formulation to simplify hyperparameter tuning, and adapt the framework to multi-dimensional regression targets. These developments will expand its applicability across a broader range of sensor reading characteristics and label distributions, advancing robust domain generalization for complex regression tasks in dynamic, real-world environments.

Acknowledgment. The authors acknowledge support from Australia-China Centre for Energy Informatics and Demand Response Technologies through Department of Industry, Innovation and Science, Australia (ACRIII000004). Dr. Wei Li acknowledges the support of the Australian Research Council (ARC) through the Discovery Early Career Researcher Award (DE210100263). Professor Zomaya and Dr. Wei Li acknowledge the support of an ARC Discovery Project (DP200103494).

References

1. Avendano, D.N., Deschrijver, D., Van Hoecke, S.: Unsupervised transfer learning across different data modalities for bearing's speed identification. Inter. J. Acoust. Vibrat. **29**(2) (2024)
2. Bui, M.H., Tran, T., Tran, A., Phung, D.: Exploiting domain-specific features to enhance domain generalization. Adv. Neural. Inf. Process. Syst. **34**, 21189–21201 (2021)
3. Chang, X., Li, W., Shi, Y., Zomaya, A.Y.: Taming the domain shift in multi-source learning for energy disaggregation. In: Proceedings of the 29th ACM SIGKDD Conference on Knowledge Discovery and Data Mining, pp. 3805–3816 (2023)
4. Chen, H., Zhang, Q., Huang, Z., Wang, H., Zhao, J.: Towards domain-specific features disentanglement for domain generalization. arXiv preprint arXiv:2310.03007 (2023)
5. Du, Y., et al.: Adarnn: adaptive learning and forecasting of time series. In: Proceedings of the 30th ACM International Conference on Information & Knowledge Management, pp. 402–411 (2021)
6. Ganin, Y., et al.: Domain-adversarial training of neural networks. J. Mach. Learn. Res. **17**(59), 1–35 (2016)
7. Guan, Z., et al.: Dynamic graph transformer network via dual-view connectivity for autism spectrum disorder identification. Comput. Biol. Med. **174**, 108415 (2024)
8. He, H., Queen, O., Koker, T., Cuevas, C., Tsiligkaridis, T., Zitnik, M.: Domain adaptation for time series under feature and label shifts. In: International Conference on Machine Learning, pp. 12746–12774. PMLR (2023)
9. Huang, Z., et al.: Robust generalization against photon-limited corruptions via worst-case sharpness minimization. In: Proceedings of the IEEE/CVF Conference on Computer Vision and Pattern Recognition, pp. 16175–16185 (2023)
10. Krueger, D., et al.: Out-of-distribution generalization via risk extrapolation. In: International Conference on Machine Learning, pp. 5815–5826. PMLR (2021)
11. Lee, B.T., Kwon, J.m., Jo, Y.Y.: Tada: Temporal adversarial data augmentation for time series data. arXiv preprint arXiv:2407.15174 (2024)
12. Li, D., Yang, Y., Song, Y.Z., Hospedales, T.: Learning to generalize: meta-learning for domain generalization. In: Proceedings of the AAAI Conference on Artificial Intelligence, vol. 32 (2018)
13. Li, D., Liu, L., Qi, Y., Liu, S., Luo, Z.: A cross-domain short-term power prediction method based on multiple environmental sensors in photovoltaic systems and domain generalisation theory. IEEE Sensors J. (2024)
14. Li, J., Yang, Y., Chen, Y., Zhang, J., Lai, Z., Pan, L.: Dwlr: domain adaptation under label shift for wearable sensor. In: Proceedings of the Thirty-Third International Joint Conference on Artificial Intelligence, pp. 4425–4433 (2024)
15. Liu, Z., Yang, X.: A generalization model for arrhythmia classification based on spectral feature extraction and domain generalization. In: the 5th International Symposium on Artificial Intelligence for Medicine Science, pp. 378–384 (2024)
16. Lu, W., et al.: Diversify: a general framework for time series out-of-distribution detection and generalization. IEEE Trans. Pattern Anal. Mach. Intell. (2024)
17. Lu, W., et alk.: Fixed: frustratingly easy domain generalization with mixup. In: Conference on Parsimony and Learning, pp. 159–178. PMLR (2024)

18. Luo, C., et al.: Laserkey: eavesdropping keyboard typing leveraging vibrational emanations via laser sensing. IEEE Trans. Mobile Comput. (2025)
19. Ma, N., Liu, F., Wang, H., Zhou, S., Bu, J., Han, B.: Domain generalization in regression (2024)
20. Van der Maaten, L., Hinton, G.: Visualizing data using t-sne. J. Mach. Learn. Res. **9**(11) (2008)
21. Magrini, F., Jozinović, D., Cammarano, F., Michelini, A., Boschi, L.: Len-db - local earthquakes detection: A benchmark dataset of 3-component seismograms built on a global scale. Zenodo (2020). https://zenodo.org/records/3648232, data set
22. Meng, Y., Dong, Z., Lu, K.C., Li, S., Shao, C.: Meta-learning-based domain generalization for cost-effective tool condition monitoring in ultrasonic metal welding. IEEE Trans. Indust. Inform. (2024)
23. Murray, D., Stankovic, L., Stankovic, V.: An electrical load measurements dataset of united kingdom households from a two-year longitudinal study. Sci. Data **4**(1), 1–12 (2017)
24. Otović, E., et al.: Intra-domain and cross-domain transfer learning for time series data–how transferable are the features? Knowl.-Based Syst. **239**, 107976 (2022)
25. Qian, H., Pan, S.J., Miao, C.: Latent independent excitation for generalizable sensor-based cross-person activity recognition. In: Proceedings of the AAAI Conference on Artificial Intelligence. vol. 35, pp. 11921–11929 (2021)
26. Qin, T., Wang, S., Li, H.: Evolving domain generalization via latent structure-aware sequential autoencoder. IEEE Trans. Pattern Anal. Mach. Intell. **45**(12), 14514–14527 (2023)
27. Shi, Y., Li, W., Chang, X., Yang, T., Sun, Y., Zomaya, A.Y.: On enabling collaborative non-intrusive load monitoring for sustainable smart cities. Sci. Rep. **13**(1), 6569 (2023)
28. Shi, Y., Li, W., Zomaya, A.Y.: Domain generalization for time-series forecasting via extended domain-invariant representations. In: 2024 IEEE Annual Congress on Artificial Intelligence of Things (AIoT), pp. 110–116. IEEE (2024)
29. Sun, B., Saenko, K.: Deep coral: correlation alignment for deep domain adaptation. In: Hua, G., Jégou, H. (eds.) ECCV 2016. LNCS, vol. 9915, pp. 443–450. Springer, Cham (2016). https://doi.org/10.1007/978-3-319-49409-8_35
30. Sun, Q., Murphy, K.P., Ebrahimi, S., D'Amour, A.: Beyond invariance: test-time label-shift adaptation for addressing" spurious" correlations. Adv. Neural. Inf. Process. Syst. **36**, 23789–23812 (2023)
31. Vapnik, V.N., Vapnik, V., et al.: Statistical learning theory (1998)
32. Walter, S., et al.: The biovid heat pain database data for the advancement and systematic validation of an automated pain recognition system. In: IEEE International Conference on Cybernetics, pp. 128–131. IEEE (2013)
33. Wang, J., et al.: Generalizing to unseen domains: a survey on domain generalization. IEEE Trans. Knowl. Data Eng. (2022)
34. Wang, Y., et al.: Contrastive-ace: domain generalization through alignment of causal mechanisms. IEEE Trans. Image Process. **32**, 235–250 (2022)
35. Yang, H.R., Ren, C.X., Luo, Y.W.: Cod: Learning conditional invariant representation for domain adaptation regression. arXiv preprint arXiv:2408.06638 (2024)
36. Zamzmi, G., et al.: Convolutional neural networks for neonatal pain assessment. IEEE Trans. Biometrics Behav. Identity Sci. **1**(3), 192–200 (2019)

37. Zha, K., Cao, P., Son, J., Yang, Y., Katabi, D.: Rank-n-contrast: learning continuous representations for regression. Adv. Neural Inform. Process. Syst. **36** (2024)
38. Zhang, H., Cisse, M., Dauphin, Y.N., Lopez-Paz, D.: mixup: beyond empirical risk minimization. arXiv preprint arXiv:1710.09412 (2017)
39. Zhang, W., Deng, L., Zhang, L., Wu, D.: A survey on negative transfer. IEEE/CAA J. Automatica Sinica **10**(2), 305–329 (2022)

Social Sciences (Social Good, Psycology, History, ...)

Density-Aware Walks for Coordinated Campaign Detection

Atul Anand Gopalakrishnan[1], Jakir Hossain[1], Tuğrulcan Elmas[2], and Ahmet Erdem Sarıyüce[1]( )

[1] University at Buffalo, Buffalo, USA
{atulanan,mh267,erdem}@buffalo.edu
[2] University of Edinburgh, Edinburgh, UK
telmas@ed.ac.uk

Abstract. Coordinated campaigns frequently exploit social media platforms by artificially amplifying topics, making inauthentic trends appear organic, and misleading users into engagement. Distinguishing these coordinated efforts from genuine public discourse remains a significant challenge due to the sophisticated nature of such attacks. Our work focuses on detecting coordinated campaigns by modeling the problem as a graph classification task. We leverage the recently introduced Large Engagement Networks (LEN) dataset, which contains over 300 networks capturing engagement patterns from both fake and authentic trends on Twitter prior to the 2023 Turkish elections. The graphs in LEN were constructed by collecting interactions related to campaigns that stemmed from ephemeral astroturfing. Established graph neural networks (GNNs) struggle to accurately classify campaign graphs, highlighting the challenges posed by LEN due to the large size of its networks. To address this, we introduce a new graph classification method that leverages the density of local network structures. We propose a random weighted walk (RWW) approach in which node transitions are biased by local density measures such as degree, core number, or truss number. These RWWs are encoded using the Skip-gram model, producing density-aware structural embeddings for the nodes. Training message-passing neural networks (MPNNs) on these density-aware embeddings yields superior results compared to the simpler node features available in the dataset, with nearly a 12% and 5% improvement in accuracy for binary and multiclass classification, respectively. Our findings demonstrate that incorporating density-aware structural encoding with MPNNs provides a robust framework for identifying coordinated inauthentic behavior on social media networks such as Twitter.

Keywords: Random weighted walks · Coordinated campaigns · Graph density

1 Introduction

Social media platforms like Twitter (now X) provide a space for people to express their opinions and stay informed about trending topics. However, like other social media platforms, Twitter is vulnerable to manipulation by malicious actors. These actors often engage in coordinated attacks that artificially amplify trends using fake accounts and bots. They can operate in a synchronized manner while concealing their identities, misleading users, journalists, and policymakers about what is genuinely trending. Such tactics also coerce users into engaging with fabricated trends, making it increasingly difficult to distinguish between organic trends and those driven by manipulation. Prior research has shown that coordinated campaigns are prevalent in several countries, including Turkey, Pakistan, and India [10,20,21].

Gopalakrishnan et al. [16] recently introduced a new graph classification dataset, LEN, consisting of engagement networks including some coordinated campaigns within Turkey's Twitter sphere during the 2023 Turkish elections. To identify ground-truth campaign graphs, they focus on ephemeral astroturfing, a tactic where a coordinated network of bots rapidly generates a large volume of tweets to manipulate Twitter's trending list, only to delete them shortly afterward. In each engagement graph, nodes represent users, while edges represent user interactions in the form of retweets, quotes, or replies.

The problem of coordinated campaign detection can be considered as a graph classification task, making it well-suited for message-passing neural networks (MPNNs) [18,22,36,40]. However, Gopalakrishnan et al.'s analysis using established MPNNs highlights the challenges posed by LEN due to its large network sizes. MPNNs are often designed for domains with significantly smaller graphs, such as molecular structures. In contrast, LEN contains approximately ten times more edges, on average, than typical datasets of graphs, such as ogbn-ppa, one of the largest biological graph datasets.

Present Work. In this paper, we exploit the fact that campaign-related engagement graphs tend to be denser. We aim to accurately identify coordinated campaigns using our method, called **DE**nsity-aware walks for **CO**ordinated campaign **DE**tection (**DECODE**). We incorporate network density into node embeddings by leveraging node-level density properties, such as degree, core number, and truss number, using random weighted walks (RWWs). For the RWW, we sample a new node using the current node's density, ensuring that each node maintains a similar local density throughout the walk. These RWWs are converted to density-aware embeddings embeddings using Skipgram [26]. We then train a message-passing neural network (MPNN) using these embeddings as input features, enabling the model to leverage density awareness for improved classification. Figure 1 provides a descriptive diagram of our framework. The key contributions of our work can be summarized as follows:

- We leverage multiple density measures, namely degree, core numbers and truss numbers, to distinguish campaign and non-campaign networks based on local density.
- We introduce DECODE, which uses RWWs to encode each node such that its embedding closely resembles those of neighboring nodes with similar densities.
- We train MPNNs on the LEN dataset using the the density-aware embeddings to identify campaigns and their subtypes. To evaluate their effectiveness, we compare our models with the baselines from [16].

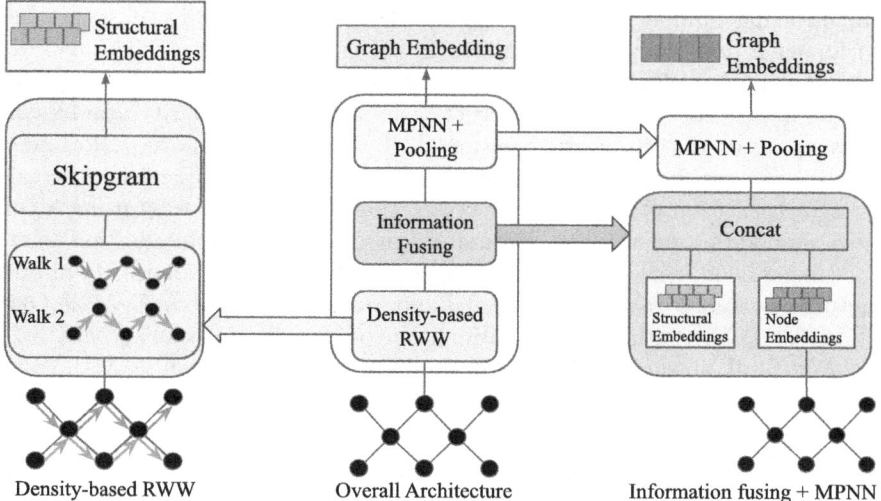

Fig. 1. An overview of DECODE. Density-based random weighted walk captures the local densities around a node. This representation is then concatenated with the input node feature available in the dataset. The concatenated embedding is encoded using an MPNN and subsequently aggregated to form the graph embedding, which is used for downstream classification.

The rest of the paper is structured as follows. In Sect. 2, we review related work, while Sect. 3 introduces the dataset and essential terminologies. In Sect. 4, we present our methodology, including the random weighted walk algorithm and its density-awareness encoding using degrees, core numbers, and truss numbers. We verify and discuss the performance improvements using the density-aware embeddings to demonstrate their importance in Sect. 5. Finally, we conclude by summarizing our findings and addressing potential limitations and future directions in Sect. 6. The code for DECODE is available at https://github.com/erdemUB/ECMLPKDD25.

2 Related Work

In this section we discuss related work in the domain of structural and positional encoding and its relevance in MPNNs and graph transformers (Sect. 2.1), and coordinated campaigns on social media platforms (Sect. 2.2).

2.1 Structural and Positional Encoding

Structural encoding is the process of ensuring that nodes with similar structural roles in a graph have similar embeddings. Positional encoding captures the proximity between two nodes in a graph. Both of these encodings can be obtained using random weighted walks. In Deepwalk, random walks are generated for each node [30]. These walks are converted to node embeddings using Skipgram [26]. Node2Vec biases the random walks to preserve both local (BFS) and global structure (DFS) [17]. Struct2Vec constructs similarity graphs using time-warping as the similarity function [33]. Random-walks are performed on the similarity graphs to generate node embeddings. Modularized non-negative matrix factorization (M-NMF) preserves community structure by using a community embedding matrix and community modularity score in addition to random walk embeddings [38]. Random walk features have also been used to improve structural awareness of MPNNs [43,44] and graph transformers [6,7,32]. Other commonly used structural and positional encoding include heat kernel [13,23], subgraphs [3,4], shortest distance [24], and node degree centralities [41]. In this work, we devise a new random-walk that captures the local density around nodes.

2.2 Coordinated Campaigns on Social Media

The process by which users on a social media platform coordinate in large groups to engage in malicious behavior is known as a coordinated campaign (also known as influence operations) [29]. These coordinated campaigns are often designed to mislead users by disseminating misinformation or by propagating falsified ideologies. Examples of coordinated campaigns include, using advertisements and influencers to dominate trends [27], deploying bots to boost user popularity [8,9], and state-sponsored influence operations, such as Russia's interference in the 2016 US elections [42] and alleged coordinated attacks by the Chinese Communist Party to sway public opinion [19]. Our work leverages coordinated campaigns driven by ephemeral astroturfing, where bots flood Twitter with random tweets to bypass filters and then delete them immediately [10,16]. Since Twitter updates trends in windows, deleted tweets remain unaccounted for until the next update, allowing adversaries to exploit the illusion of organic engagement.

Over the years, methods have been developed to counter coordinated efforts on Twitter. These include techniques such as tweet and hashtag similarity [25,28], temporal methods focusing on tweet frequency [28,37], shared URLs and articles [15], and detecting other coordination signals [12,31,39]. Recent approaches have explored centrality-based node pruning on similarity networks [25], and graph neural networks [11,15] for detecting these attacks. Our work attempts to identify coordinated campaigns by modeling it as a graph classification problem. Additionally, we encode density-based properties using RWWs. Incorporating density-aware embeddings into MPNN training leads to improved performance in classification compared to using only the raw node features from the dataset.

3 Preliminaries

In this section, we describe our dataset and the key terminologies required for this work. We first provide details on the LEN dataset in Sect. 3.1. Then we

Table 1. Statistics of the engagement networks for LEN, containing 314 networks.

	Sub-types	# G	# nodes			# edges			Explanation
			Max	Min	Avg.	Max	Min	Avg.	
Campaign	Politics	62	50,286	100	6,570	71,704	203	10,210	Political content including slogans, and misinformation camps.
	Reform	58	19,578	131	1,229	1,105,918	540	25,268	Organized movements advocating political changes.
	News	24	54,996	581	10,368	80,784	942	15,582	News amplified through bot and troll activity.
	Finance	14	9,976	273	1,802	10,725	243	2,334	Financial promotions, primarily cryptocurrency-related.
	Noise	9	55,933	454	12,180	48,937	473	10,882	Content that does not fit into any specific category.
	Cult	6	7,880	313	2,303	11,615	637	3,431	Slogans from a cult leveraging bots.
	Entertainment	3	4,220	678	2,237	132,013	3,806	48,767	Celebrities using bots for self-promotion.
	Common	3	9,974	3,487	5,919	9,470	2,818	7,066	Frequently used phrases forming trends organically.
	Overall	179	55,933	100	5,157	1,105,918	203	16,006	
Non-Campaign	News	52	95,575	818	24,834	213,444	709	43,201	Coverage of news not sourced from Twitter.
	Sports	30	75,653	469	9,530	101,656	403	12,948	Discussions around major sports events.
	Festival	17	119,952	885	35,466	199,305	803	55,947	Trends related to holidays, festivals, and special occasions.
	Internal	11	87,720	4,188	33,061	196,103	4,374	54,442	Events primarily generated within Twitter's ecosystem.
	Common	10	64,320	1,214	17,079	99,306	1,270	24,869	Frequently used phrases forming trends organically.
	Entertainment	8	20,060	1,477	7,289	45,211	1,712	12,578	Engagement with popular TV shows and online videos.
	Announ. cam.	4	26,358	6,650	13,382	50,864	14,362	24,817	Officially launched political campaigns.
	Sports cam.	3	4,661	2,880	3,654	7,367	4,451	5,534	Hashtags initiated by professional sports teams.
	Overall	135	119,952	469	20,632	213,444	403	33,765	

give a brief overview of the notation, the density metrics used (degree, k-core, k-truss) and message passing neural networks in Sect. 3.2.

3.1 Large Engagement Networks (LEN) Dataset

Large Engagement Networks (LEN) is graph dataset that contains coordinated campaigns related to Turkish Twitter. It focuses on the 2023 elections in Turkey when this issue was prevalent. The campaign graphs in the dataset are an outcome of ephemeral astroturfing. The dataset comprises of 314 engagement networks, where each network is associated to a trend. There are 179 campaign graphs and 135 non-campaign graphs. These graphs are further divided into sub-types such as politics, news, finance and more, as shown in Table 1. The nodes represent users and edges represents engagements between the users. A directed edge from node X to Y, signifies that X engaged with (retweeted, replied to, or quoted) Y. The graphs also consist of node and edge features. The features used for the node attributes include user description (bio), follower count, following count, user's total tweet count, and user's verification status. The edge attributes include the type of engagement (retweet, reply, or quote), engagement count (e.g., number of retweets), impression count, text, number of likes, whether the tweet is labeled as sensitive or not, and the timestamp of the tweet. Gopalakrishnan et al. provides three benchmarks for the LEN dataset: (1) binary classification to classify the networks into campaign and non-campaign networks; (2) multi-class classification to categorize campaigns into one of the 7 sub-types as shown in Table 1; and (3) binary classification of news networks into campaign and non-campaign. We use the LEN dataset as it is the only ground-truth graph classification dataset that identifies if a trend's popularity is driven by coordinated campaigns.

3.2 Notation, Density Metrics, and MPNNs

A graph is a collection of vertices and edges. It is depicted as $G = (V, E)$, where V is the number of vertices and E is the number of edges. A graph can also be represented as $G = (A, X, y)$, where A is the adjacency matrix, X is the feature matrix for the nodes, and y is the graph's label.

Degree, k-Core and k-Truss: The degree of a node is the number of edges connected to it, providing a simple measure of its local connectivity [14]. A k-core is a subgraph in which every node has at least k connections within the subgraph [35]. The core number of a node represents the largest k-core to which it belongs. Computing core numbers of all the nodes in a graph has a linear cost, $O(|E|)$. Similarly, a k-truss is defined as a subgraph where each edge is part of at least $k - 2$ triangles within the subgraph [5]. The truss number of an edge indicates the highest k-truss to which it belongs. Computing truss numbers is a bit costly, $O(|E|^{1.5})$, but is still polynomial and practical for large networks. Since truss numbers are edge-based, we compute a node's truss number by averaging the truss numbers associated to the connected edges. Degree, core number, and truss number all measure graph density, with degree indicating direct connections, and core and truss numbers reflecting a node's role in dense substructures.

We use three local density measures for a node: (1) degree of the node, (2) core number of the node, and (3) average truss numbers of all edges incident to the node (we simply refer them as degree, core, and truss number of a node in the rest of the paper). Note that we ignore the edge directions in the engagement networks, hence we use the original definitions of k-core and k-truss for undirected graphs.

Message Passing Neural Networks: MPNNs consist of two steps, aggregate and update, as shown in Eq. 1, where $\mathcal{N}(v)$ is used to represent the neighborhood of node v.

$$h_v^{(l+1)} = \text{UPDATE}\left(h_v^{(l)}, \text{AGGREGATE}\left(\{h_u^{(l)} \mid u \in \mathcal{N}(v)\}\right)\right) \quad (1)$$

In the aggregate step, each node gathers information from its neighbors. This typically involves summing, averaging, or applying more complex functions (e.g., attention mechanisms) to the neighbors' feature vectors. In the update step, the aggregated information is combined with the node's own features to update its representation. To do so, a neural network (example, an MLP) or a simple transformation (example, a weighted sum) is applied. Therefore, the nodes refine their representations based on the information received. MPNNs generally differ in the aggregation strategy used. GCN uses dual-degree normalization to account for the varying number of neighbors each node may have [22]. GAT uses attention weight to assign varying weights to each neighbor [36]. GIN uses an MLP to perform aggregation using a trainable parameter (ϵ) to determine the amount of importance given to the ego node, as compared to its neighbors [40].

Table 2. Descriptive statistics to indicate the average degree, core number and truss numbers of the nodes across different sub-types spanning campaign and non-campaign graphs. Overall, campaign graphs exhibit higher local densities than the non-campaign ones.

	Sub-types	Mean Degree	Mean Core number	Mean Truss number
Campaign	Politics	3.108 ± 1.483	1.635 ± 0.872	0.384 ± 1.595
	Reform	16.258 ± 12.118	9.067 ± 7.067	17.104 ± 10.545
	News	3.015 ± 0.990	1.598 ± 0.481	0.172 ± 0.365
	Finance	2.590 ± 1.512	1.414 ± 0.823	0.287 ± 0.977
	Noise	2.080 ± 0.790	1.214 ± 0.342	0.261 ± 0.370
	Cult	2.981 ± 0.690	1.580 ± 0.409	0.569 ± 0.919
	Entertainment	11.477 ± 0.264	6.180 ± 0.171	2.311 ± 1.920
	Common	2.391 ± 1.586	1.380 ± 0.793	0.572 ± 0.751
	Overall	**3.941 ± 10.459**	**2.120 ± 6.083**	**5.057 ± 7.933**
Non-Campaign	News	3.443 ± 0.845	1.778 ± 0.412	0.179 ± 0.106
	Sports	2.718 ± 0.581	1.428 ± 0.242	0.155 ± 0.150
	Festival	2.867 ± 0.501	1.526 ± 0.239	0.245 ± 0.157
	Internal	3.293 ± 0.901	1.705 ± 0.438	0.184 ± 0.110
	Common	2.913 ± 0.650	1.529 ± 0.305	0.109 ± 0.068
	Entertainment	3.453 ± 0.941	1.816 ± 0.471	0.651 ± 0.491
	Announced Camp.	3.711 ± 1.135	1.925 ± 0.588	1.309 ± 0.970
	Sports Camp.	3.029 ± 0.191	1.590 ± 0.100	0.037 ± 0.012
	Overall	**3.210 ± 0.81**	**1.672 ± 0.387**	**0.219 ± 0.261**

GraphSAGE is an inductive graph representational learning model that has the ability to generalize to unseen nodes, unlike transductive models [18]. This is done by learning a message-passing model on a sampled set of nodes in the given graph.

4 Methodology

We propose DECODE, a random weighted walk (RWW) approach for learning density-aware node embeddings. Here, node densities are used to determine transition probabilities in the RWWs. This emphasis on density is because campaign graphs in LEN are denser than non-campaign graphs. Specifically, we use degree, core number, and truss number as density metrics due to their widespread use and computational efficiency [2,34]. Table 2 provides detailed statistics showcasing the density metrics across campaign and non-campaign graphs. Notably, the densest campaign graphs belonged to the reform sub-type, which constitutes a large portion of the dataset, as shown in Table 1.

Algorithm 1 provides a formal overview of DECODE. In our algorithm, ϕ represents the density function, where $\phi(v)$ returns the normalized density of a given node v. The function ϕ is defined based on the chosen density metric for

Algorithm 1. Density-aware random weighted walk (DECODE)

Input: Graph $G = (V, E)$, walk length L, density func. $\phi : V \to [0, 1]$, threshold τ
Output: List of walks W
Initialize $W \leftarrow []$
for each node $v \in V$ **do**
  Initialize walk $w \leftarrow [v]$
  for $t = 1$ to L **do**
    $v_t = \text{Top}(w)$
    Let $N(v_t) \leftarrow \{u \in V \mid (v_t, u) \in E\}$
    if $N(v_t) \neq \emptyset$ **then**
      if $\phi(v_t) > \tau$ **then**
        Set $w_u = \phi(u)$ for all $u \in N(v_t)$
      else
        Set $w_u = 1 - \phi(u)$ for all $u \in N(v_t)$
      end if
      Sample $v_{t+1} \sim P(u) = w_u / \sum_{u' \in N(v_t)} w_{u'}$
      Push v_{t+1} to w
    end if
  end for
  Append w to W
end for
return W

RWWs. It can be set to return the degree, core number, or truss number of a node.

Additionally, we introduce τ, a scalar threshold parameter that differentiates between high and low-density nodes in RWWs. The threshold is set to one of the following values: 0.5, the median node density in the graph, or the midpoint of node densities, as detailed in Sect. 5.1. The steps for collecting RWWs in our algorithm are as follows:

1. At each step of the RWW, the next node is selected based on the density of the current node.
2. If the current node's density exceeds the threshold τ, transitions to higher-density neighbors are preferred, with sampling weights defined as ($w_u = \phi(u)$), where w_u represents the weight assigned to node u
3. Conversely, if the current node's density is below τ, transitions to lower-density neighbors are favored by inverting the sampling weights ($w_u = 1 - \phi(u)$).
4. The transition probabilities for the neighbors are obtained by normalizing the sampling weights and new nodes are sampled using them at each step.
5. Once we obtain the RWWs, we use Skipgram to encode them, following prior methods [17,30].

These density-aware embeddings and node feature are fed into the MPNNs for downstream classification. The MPNNs used in this paper include GCN,

GAT, GIN, and GraphSAGE. In the following section we discuss the experimental setup used in this paper and discuss our results for binary and multiclass classification by comparing our method to the results provided in [16].

5 Experimental Evaluation

We evaluate the performance of DECODE on the LEN dataset using two tasks: (i) campaign vs. non-campaign classification in engagement networks (binary classification) and (ii) campaign sub-type classification, where the sub-types are provided in Table 1 (multi-class classification). Section 5.1 details the experimental setup. Sections 5.2 and 5.3 present the experimental results for binary and multi-class classification, respectively.

5.1 Experimental Setup

We run our model on two input configurations: (i) density-aware embeddings and (ii) a concatenation of density-aware embeddings with the input node features available in the dataset. We consider each of the three density-based features in our random walks—degrees, core numbers, and truss numbers—and provide comparisons. To contextualize the empirical results of DECODE, we compare our method against four baselines: GCN, GAT, GIN, and GraphSAGE. These models are trained solely on the input node features available in the dataset. This comparison allows us to evaluate the importance of density-aware embeddings over existing node features. To construct the RWW embeddings, we set the walk length to 100. For encoding the nodes using Skipgram, we use a window length of 4, meaning each node is encoded using its four neighboring nodes in the random weighted walks. The walk embedding size is set to 128. We set the threshold parameter (τ) to the following values:

- **0.5**: A fixed value of 0.5.
- **Median**: The median of the list of the density-based features in a graph.
- **Mid-point (abbreviated as mid)**: This value is calculated as the average of the smallest and largest values of the density-based feature under consideration.

For MPNNs, we perform hyperparameter tuning over hidden layer sizes, $h \in \{128, 256, 512, 1024\}$, and learning rates, $l \in \{0.001, 0.0001, 0.00001\}$ as done in [16]. We also use mean pooling to produce graph embeddings.

5.2 Results for Campaign vs Non-campaign Classification

LEN consists of 179 campaign graphs and 135 non-campaign graphs. The results for accuracy and F1-score are presented in Tables 3 and 4, respectively. We observe the following key insights:

Table 3. Accuracy for binary classification. **NF** denotes the MPNN trained with node features and **RWW** denotes the one that used random-weighted walks. Best in each group is in bold. Underlined value denotes the best overall accuracy.

	Input	Degree		Core Numbers		Truss Numbers	
		τ	Accuracy	τ	Accuracy	τ	Accuracy
GCN	NF	–	0.702 ± 0.018	–	0.702 ± 0.018	–	0.702 ± 0.018
	RWW	mid	**0.810 ± 0.013**	0.5	0.787 ± 0.010	median	0.800 ± 0.019
	NF + RWW	mid	0.784 ± 0.006	median	**0.805 ± 0.018**	0.5	**0.803 ± 0.019**
GAT	NF	–	0.735 ± 0.015	–	0.735 ± 0.015	–	0.735 ± 0.015
	RWW	median	**0.795 ± 0.015**	mid	**0.808 ± 0.022**	median	**0.836 ± 0.016**
	NF + RWW	median	0.792 ± 0.022	0.5	0.785 ± 0.010	median	0.792 ± 0.030
GIN	NF	–	0.633 ± 0.065	–	0.633 ± 0.065	–	0.633 ± 0.065
	RWW	0.5	**0.756 ± 0.005**	median	0.766 ± 0.014	0.5	0.771 ± 0.006
	NF + RWW	0.5	0.751 ± 0.005	mid	**0.792 ± 0.014**	mid	**0.782 ± 0.019**
SAGE	NF	–	0.729 ± 0.006	–	0.729 ± 0.006	–	0.729 ± 0.006
	RWW	0.5	**0.852 ± 0.010**	mid	0.774 ± 0.025	0.5	**0.834 ± 0.052**
	NF + RWW	median	0.758 ± 0.010	0.5	**0.790 ± 0.017**	0.5	0.813 ± 0.018

Table 4. F1-score for binary classification. **NF** denotes the MPNN trained with node features and **RWW** denotes the one that used random-weighted walks. Best in each group is in bold. Underlined value denotes the best overall F1-score.

	Inp.	Degree		Core Numbers		Truss Numbers	
		τ	F1	τ	F1	τ	F1
GCN	NF	–	0.687 ± 0.021	–	0.687 ± 0.021	–	0.687 ± 0.021
	RWW	mid	**0.839 ± 0.004**	median	0.814 ± 0.008	median	0.806 ± 0.021
	NF + RWW	median	0.805 ± 0.011	median	**0.838 ± 0.017**	0.5	**0.824 ± 0.017**
GAT	NF	–	0.765 ± 0.018	–	0.765 ± 0.018	–	0.765 ± 0.018
	RWW	median	**0.825 ± 0.012**	mid	**0.840 ± 0.015**	median	**0.853 ± 0.011**
	NF + RWW	median	0.820 ± 0.020	0.5	0.824 ± 0.006	median	0.824 ± 0.030
GIN	NF	–	0.710 ± 0.037	–	0.710 ± 0.037	–	0.710 ± 0.037
	RWW	0.5	**0.807 ± 0.005**	median	0.800 ± 0.013	0.5	0.790 ± 0.003
	NF + RWW	mid	0.782 ± 0.006	mid	**0.816 ± 0.012**	mid	**0.795 ± 0.019**
SAGE	NF	–	0.713 ± 0.008	–	0.713 ± 0.008	–	0.713 ± 0.008
	RWW	0.5	**0.877 ± 0.010**	mid	0.789 ± 0.020	0.5	**0.857 ± 0.031**
	NF + RWW	median	0.803 ± 0.007	0.5	**0.820 ± 0.016**	0.5	0.834 ± 0.011

- Pairing GraphSAGE with degree-based RWW achieves the best performance, yielding an accuracy of 0.852 ± 0.010 and an F1-score of 0.877 ± 0.010, surpassing the best baseline in [16] by 0.117 and 0.112 for accuracy and F1-score, respectively. The value of τ is set to 0.5 in this case.
- RWW features consistently outperform LEN node features, achieving higher accuracy and F1-score in most cases.
- Embeddings learnt from degree-based RWW generally outperforms other density-aware variants, achieving the highest AUROC scores across all models. The only exception is when GCN and GraphSAGE are trained on embed-

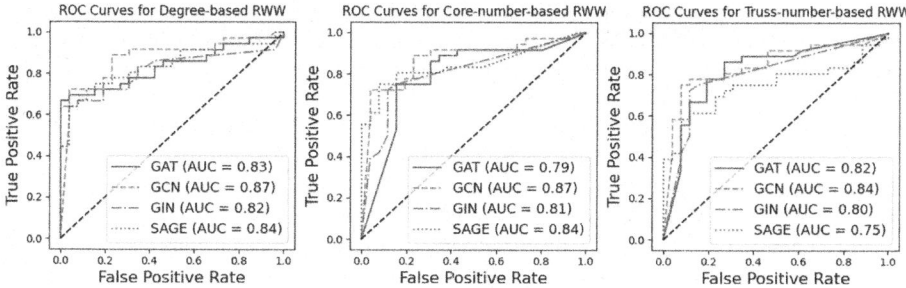

Fig. 2. Receiver Operating Characteristic (ROC) curves for campaign vs. non-campaign classification for degree, core-number and truss-number based random weighted walks. The best performing input format and threshold are taken into consideration for each model.

dings obtained from k-core-based RWW, where the AUC scores are identical. The results are illustrated in Fig. 2.
- The best-performing threshold varies depending on the model used. Median serves as the best threshold for GCN and GAT, while 0.5 is optimal for GIN and GraphSAGE.

The above insights suggest that RWW based methods yield improvements in performance for both accuracy and F1-score. Additionally, degree-based RWW generally outperforms core or truss-based RWWs. However the choice of threshold is model-dependent.

5.3 Results of Campaign-Type Classification

The goal here is to classify campaign graphs into one of the seven sub-types described in Table 1. Among these, the most common categories are Politics (62 graphs) and Reform (58 graphs). The results for accuracy and macro F1-scores are provided in Tables 5 and 6, respectively.

From these results, the following inferences can be made:

- Pairing GIN with degree-based RWW achieves the best performance, with an accuracy of 0.679 ± 0.001, surpassing the baseline in [16] by 0.045.
- The model accuracies benefit the most when input node features from the dataset are combined with density-aware embeddings, outperforming all the other setups in a majority of the scenarios.
- The best-performing thresholds are mid for GCN, 0.5 for GAT, and median for GIN and GraphSAGE, yielding the highest accuracy for each model.
- The highest macro-F1 score obtained by our work is 0.338 ± 0.051 (for GIN with truss-based RWW and τ set to 0.5) which is 0.013 less than the best performing baseline provided in [16]. We believe this happens due to label imbalance. Several campaign-type labels (example, finance, entertainment, cult) have very few samples, making them harder to classify.

Table 5. Accuracy results for multiclass classification. **NF** denotes the MPNN trained with node features and **RWW** denotes the one that used random-weighted walks. Best in each group is in bold. Underlined value denotes the best overall accuracy.

	Inp.	Degree		Core Numbers		Truss Numbers	
		τ	Acc.	τ	Acc.	τ	Acc.
GCN	NF	-	0.533 ± 0.041	-	0.533 ± 0.041	-	0.533 ± 0.041
	RWW	median	0.619 ± 0.019	0.5	0.614 ± 0.011	0.5	0.628 ± 0.000
	NF + RWW	0.5	**0.647 ± 0.009**	mid	**0.665 ± 0.011**	mid	**0.651 ± 0.015**
GAT	NF	-	0.567 ± 0.033	-	0.567 ± 0.033	-	0.567 ± 0.033
	RWW	0.5	**0.647 ± 0.009**	mid	0.670 ± 0.037	mid	0.623 ± 0.017
	NF + RWW	0.5	0.628 ± 0.025	0.5	**0.674 ± 0.001**	mid	**0.633 ± 0.027**
GIN	NF	-	0.633 ± 0.067	-	0.633 ± 0.067	-	0.633 ± 0.067
	RWW	mid	**0.679 ± 0.001**	median	0.647 ± 0.009	mean	0.637 ± 0.024
	NF + RWW	median	0.670 ± 0.009	median	**0.656 ± 0.017**	median	**0.679 ± 0.023**
SAGE	NF	-	0.583 ± 0.053	-	0.583 ± 0.053	-	0.583 ± 0.053
	RWW	0.5	0.637 ± 0.01	0.5	0.656 ± 0.027	median	**0.660 ± 0.011**
	NF + RWW	0.5	**0.665 ± 0.011**	median	**0.665 ± 0.065**	median	0.651 ± 0.001

Table 6. Macro F1-score results for multiclass classification. **NF** denotes the MPNN trained with node features and **RWW** denotes the one that used random-weighted walks. Best in each group is in bold. Underlined values denote the best overall Macro-F1 score.

	Inp.	Degree		Core Numbers		Truss Numbers	
		τ	Macro-F1	τ	Macro-F1	τ	Macro-F1
GCN	NF	-	**0.251 ± 0.022**	-	0.251 ± 0.022	-	0.251 ± 0.022
	RWW	median	0.249 ± 0.009	0.5	0.247 ± 0.018	0.5	0.250 ± 0.001
	NF + RWW	mid	0.249 ± 0.004	mid	**0.260 ± 0.007**	mid	**0.259 ± 0.006**
GAT	NF	-	**0.264 ± 0.014**	-	0.264 ± 0.014	-	**0.264 ± 0.014**
	RWW	0.5	0.255 ± 0.003	mid	**0.298 ± 0.024**	median	0.233 ± 0.006
	NF + RWW	mean	0.227 ± 0.01	mean	0.255 ± 0.028	median	0.247 ± 0.015
GIN	NF	-	**0.351 ± 0.09**	-	**0.351 ± 0.09**	-	**0.351 ± 0.09**
	RWW	0.5	0.317 ± 0.053	mean	0.260 ± 0.003	0.5	0.272 ± 0.030
	NF + RWW	median	0.305 ± 0.03	0.5	0.280 ± 0.028	mid	0.338 ± 0.051
SAGE	NF	-	**0.320 ± 0.061**	-	**0.320 ± 0.061**	-	**0.320 ± 0.061**
	RWW	0.5	0.266 ± 0.03	median	0.282 ± 0.025	mid	0.274 ± 0.019
	NF + RWW	0.5	0.295 ± 0.011	median	0.267 ± 0.026	median	0.254 ± 0.003

- We also provide confusion matrices for the models across various RWW methods in Fig. 3, where we display the confusion matrix for the best-performing configuration of each model-RWW pair. From this, we again observe that models struggle to accurately classify labels with fewer graphs.

The insights above suggest that RWW-based methods improve performance in terms of accuracy. Additionally, we find that degree is an effective parameter for random weighted walks, and the median is a suitable threshold. However,

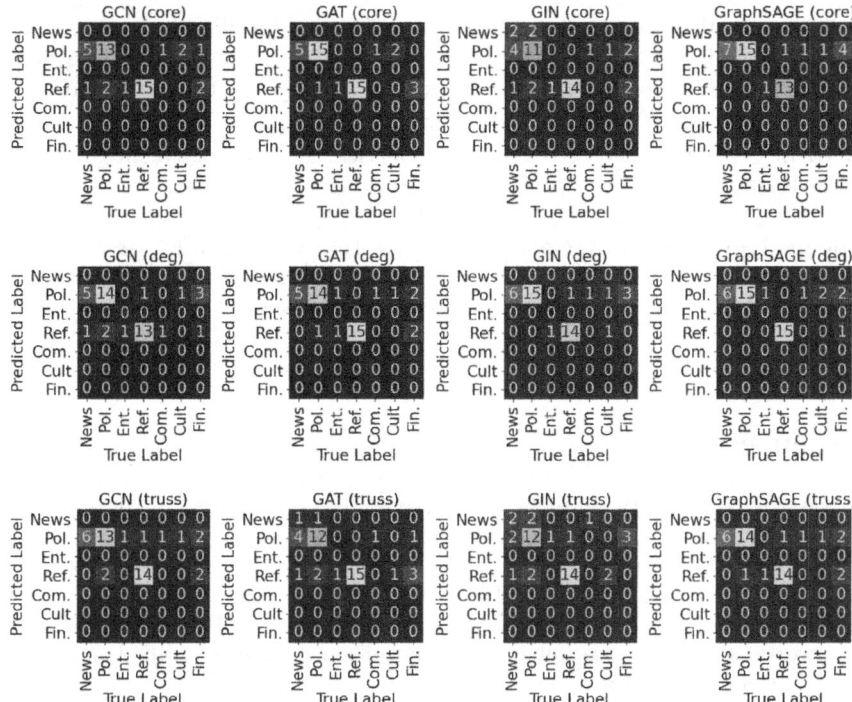

Fig. 3. Confusion matrices for multi-class classification. The best performing configuration is considered for each model and density pair is displayed here.

we observe a drop in F1-scores, likely due to the models' difficulty in classifying graphs associated with labels that have fewer samples.

6 Conclusion

We propose DECODE, a density-based random weighted walk (RWW) approach that leverages local density metrics such as degree, core number, and truss number to detect coordinated campaigns in engagement networks. We prioritize density over other structural properties, as campaign graphs are consistently denser than non-campaign graphs, exhibiting higher mean degree, core number, and truss number. DECODE learns density-aware embeddings using RWWs, where node transitions are guided by local density, ensuring that neighboring nodes have similar density characteristics. These RWWs are then converted into density-aware embeddings using Skipgram. We train an MPNN using these embeddings on the LEN dataset and observe performance improvements, surpassing the accuracy of [16] by 11% and 4.5% in binary and multiclass classification, respectively. Additionally, we outperform their F1-score for binary classification by 0.112. However, our highest macro-F1 score for campaign type classification is 0.013 lower than the best-performing baseline from Gopalakrishnan et al. This is due to the label disparity issues in the campaign classification problem. For future work, we aim to explore alternative RWW methods, such as nearest-neighbor RWW, instead of thresholding approaches. Additionally, we plan to incorporate other structural properties, such as betweeness centrality and clustering coefficient, to further refine the RWW process.

Acknowledgements. A. A. Gopalakrishnan, J. Hossain, and A. E. Sariyuce are supported by NSF awards OAC-2107089 and IIS-2236789, and this research used resources from the Center for Computational Research at the University at Buffalo (CCR 2025) [1].

References

1. Center for computational research, university at buffalo (2025). http://hdl.handle.net/10477/79221. Accessed 14 April 2025
2. Batagelj, V., Zaversnik, M.: An o (m) algorithm for cores decomposition of networks. arXiv preprint cs/0310049 (2003)
3. Bouritsas, G., Frasca, F., Zafeiriou, S., Bronstein, M.M.: Improving graph neural network expressivity via subgraph isomorphism counting. IEEE Trans. Pattern Anal. Mach. Intell. **45**(1), 657–668 (2022)
4. Chen, D., O'Bray, L., Borgwardt, K.: Structure-aware transformer for graph representation learning. In: International Conference on Machine Learning, pp. 3469–3489. PMLR (2022)
5. Cohen, J.: Trusses: Cohesive subgraphs for social network analysis. National Security Agency Technical Report **16**(3.1), 1–29 (2008)
6. Dwivedi, V.P., Bresson, X.: A generalization of transformer networks to graphs. arXiv preprint arXiv:2012.09699 (2020)
7. Dwivedi, V.P., et al.: Long range graph benchmark. Adv. Neural. Inf. Process. Syst. **35**, 22326–22340 (2022)
8. Elmas, T.: Analyzing activity and suspension patterns of twitter bots attacking turkish twitter trends by a longitudinal dataset. In: Companion Proceedings of the ACM Web Conference 2023, pp. 1404–1412 (2023)
9. Elmas, T., Overdorf, R., Aberer, K.: Characterizing retweet bots: the case of black market accounts. In: Proceedings of the International AAAI Conference on Web and Social Media, vol. 16, pp. 171–182 (2022)
10. Elmas, T., Overdorf, R., Özkalay, A.F., Aberer, K.: Ephemeral astroturfing attacks: the case of fake twitter trends. In: 2021 IEEE European Symposium on Security and Privacy (EuroS&P), pp. 403–422. IEEE (2021)
11. Elmas, T., Randl, M., Attia, Y.: # teamfollowback: detection & analysis of follow back accounts on social media. In: Proceedings of the International AAAI Conference on Web and Social Media, vol. 18, pp. 381–393 (2024)
12. Erhardt, K., Pentland, A.: Hidden messages: mapping nations' media campaigns. Comput. Math. Organ. Theory **30**(2), 161–172 (2024)
13. Feldman, O., Boyarski, A., Feldman, S., Kogan, D., Mendelson, A., Baskin, C.: Weisfeiler and leman go infinite: Spectral and combinatorial pre-colorings. Trans. Mach. Learn. Res.

14. Freeman, L.C.: Centrality in social networks conceptual clarification. Soc. Netw. **1**(3), 215–239 (1978)
15. Gabriel, N.A., Broniatowski, D.A., Johnson, N.F.: Inductive detection of influence operations via graph learning. Sci. Rep. **13**(1), 22571 (2023)
16. Gopalakrishnan, A.A., Hossain, J., Elmas, T., Sariyuce, A.E.: Large engagement networks for classifying coordinated campaigns and organic twitter trends (2025). https://api.semanticscholar.org/CorpusID:276742534
17. Grover, A., Leskovec, J.: node2vec: scalable feature learning for networks. In: Proceedings of the 22nd ACM SIGKDD International Conference on Knowledge Discovery and Data Mining, pp. 855–864 (2016)
18. Hamilton, W., Ying, Z., Leskovec, J.: Inductive representation learning on large graphs. Adv. Neural Inform. Process. Syst. **30** (2017)
19. Jacobs, C.S., Carley, K.M.: # whatisdemocracy: finding key actors in a chinese influence campaign. Comput. Math. Organ. Theory **30**(2), 127–147 (2024)
20. Jakesch, M., Garimella, K., Eckles, D., Naaman, M.: Trend alert: a cross-platform organization manipulated twitter trends in the indian general election. Proc. ACM Human-Comput. Interact. **5**(CSCW2), 1–19 (2021)
21. Kausar, S., Tahir, B., Mehmood, M.A.: Towards understanding trends manipulation in pakistan twitter. arXiv preprint arXiv:2109.14872 (2021)
22. Kipf, T.N., Welling, M.: Semi-supervised classification with graph convolutional networks. In: International Conference on Learning Representations (2017)
23. Kreuzer, D., Beaini, D., Hamilton, W., Létourneau, V., Tossou, P.: Rethinking graph transformers with spectral attention. Adv. Neural. Inf. Process. Syst. **34**, 21618–21629 (2021)
24. Li, P., Wang, Y., Wang, H., Leskovec, J.: Distance encoding: design provably more powerful neural networks for graph representation learning. Adv. Neural. Inf. Process. Syst. **33**, 4465–4478 (2020)
25. Luceri, L., Pantè, V., Burghardt, K., Ferrara, E.: Unmasking the web of deceit: Uncovering coordinated activity to expose information operations on twitter. In: Proceedings of the ACM Web Conference 2024, pp. 2530–2541 (2024)
26. Mikolov, T., Chen, K., Corrado, G., Dean, J.: Efficient estimation of word representations in vector space. arXiv preprint arXiv:1301.3781 (2013)
27. Ong, J.C., Cabañes, J.V.: Architects of networked disinformation: Behind the scenes of troll accounts and fake news production in the philippines (2018)
28. Pacheco, D., Flammini, A., Menczer, F.: Unveiling coordinated groups behind white helmets disinformation. In: Companion Proceedings of the Web Conference 2020, pp. 611–616 (2020)
29. Pamment, J., Smith, V.: Attributing information influence operations: Identifying those responsible for malicious behaviour online. NATO Strategic Communication Centre of Excellence (2022)
30. Perozzi, B., Al-Rfou, R., Skiena, S.: Deepwalk: online learning of social representations. In: Proceedings of the 20th ACM SIGKDD International Conference on Knowledge Discovery and Data Mining, pp. 701–710 (2014)
31. Pote, M., Elmas, T., Flammini, A., Menczer, F.: Coordinated reply attacks in influence operations: Characterization and detection. In: Proceedings of the International AAAI Conference on Web and Social Media, vol. 19, pp. 1586–1598 (2025)
32. Rampášek, L., Galkin, M., Dwivedi, V.P., Luu, A.T., Wolf, G., Beaini, D.: Recipe for a general, powerful, scalable graph transformer. Adv. Neural. Inf. Process. Syst. **35**, 14501–14515 (2022)

33. Ribeiro, L.F., Saverese, P.H., Figueiredo, D.R.: struc2vec: Learning node representations from structural identity. In: Proceedings of the 23rd ACM SIGKDD International Conference on Knowledge Discovery and Data Mining, pp. 385–394 (2017)
34. Sariyüce, A.E., Seshadhri, C., Pinar, A., Çatalyürek, Ü.V.: Nucleus decompositions for identifying hierarchy of dense subgraphs. ACM Trans. Web (TWEB) **11**(3), 1–27 (2017)
35. Seidman, S.B.: Network structure and minimum degree. Soc. Netw. **5**(3), 269–287 (1983)
36. Veličković, P., Cucurull, G., Casanova, A., Romero, A., Liò, P., Bengio, Y.: Graph attention networks. In: International Conference on Learning Representations (2018)
37. Vishnuprasad, P.S., Nogara, G., Cardoso, F., Cresci, S., Giordano, S., Luceri, L.: Tracking fringe and coordinated activity on twitter leading up to the us capitol attack. In: Proceedings of the International AAAI Conference on Web and Social Media, vol. 18, pp. 1557–1570 (2024)
38. Wang, X., Cui, P., Wang, J., Pei, J., Zhu, W., Yang, S.: Community preserving network embedding. In: Proceedings of the AAAI Conference on Artificial Intelligence, vol. 31 (2017)
39. Weber, D., Neumann, F.: Amplifying influence through coordinated behaviour in social networks. Soc. Netw. Anal. Min. **11**(1), 1–42 (2021). https://doi.org/10.1007/s13278-021-00815-2
40. Xu, K., Hu, W., Leskovec, J., Jegelka, S.: How powerful are graph neural networks? In: International Conference on Learning Representations
41. Ying, C., et al.: Do transformers really perform badly for graph representation? Adv. Neural. Inf. Process. Syst. **34**, 28877–28888 (2021)
42. Zannettou, S., Caulfield, T., De Cristofaro, E., Sirivianos, M., Stringhini, G., Blackburn, J.: Disinformation warfare: Understanding state-sponsored trolls on twitter and their influence on the web. In: Companion Proceedings of the 2019 World Wide Web Conference, pp. 218–226 (2019)
43. Zeng, D., Chen, W., Liu, W., Zhou, L., Qu, H.: Rethinking random walk in graph representation learning. In: ICASSP 2023-2023 IEEE International Conference on Acoustics, Speech and Signal Processing (ICASSP), pp. 1–5. IEEE (2023)
44. Zhou, C., Wang, X., Zhang, M.: Facilitating graph neural networks with random walk on simplicial complexes. Adv. Neural. Inf. Process. Syst. **36**, 16172–16206 (2023)

Fairness is in the Details : Face Dataset Auditing

Valentin Lafargue[1,2,3]✉, Emmanuelle Claeys[4], and Jean-Michel Loubes[2,3]

[1] IMT, Toulouse, France
valentin.lafargue@math.univ-toulouse.fr
[2] INRIA, Toulouse, France
[3] ANITI 2, Toulouse, France
[4] IRIT, Toulouse, France

Abstract. Auditing involves verifying the proper implementation of a given policy. As such, auditing is essential for ensuring compliance with the principles of fairness, equity, and transparency mandated by the European Union's AI Act. Moreover, biases present during the training phase of a learning system can persist in the modeling process and result in discrimination against certain subgroups of individuals when the model is deployed in production. Assessing bias in image datasets is a particularly complex task, as it first requires a feature extraction step, then to consider the extraction's quality in the statistical tests. This paper proposes a robust methodology for auditing image datasets based on so-called "sensitive" features, such as gender, age, and ethnicity. The proposed methodology consists of both a feature extraction phase and a statistical analysis phase. The first phase introduces a novel convolutional neural network (CNN) architecture specifically designed for extracting sensitive features with a limited number of manual annotations. The second phase compares the distributions of sensitive features across subgroups using a novel statistical test that accounts for the imprecision of the feature extraction model. Our pipeline constitutes a comprehensive and fully automated methodology for dataset auditing. We illustrate our approach using two manually annotated datasets. (Code and datasets available at https://github.com/ValentinLafargue/FairnessDetails).

Keywords: Audit · Images · Bias · Distribution · Statistical test · Uncertainty · Classification · Fitzpatrick · Gender · Age

1 Introduction

The widespread adoption of machine learning (ML) systems in industrial applications has heightened concerns about fairness, transparency, and accountability.

Supplementary Information The online version contains supplementary material available at https://doi.org/10.1007/978-3-032-06129-4_18.

The issue of bias in algorithmic decision-making has emerged as a critical concern within the machine learning community. A substantial body of research has examined how such biases can adversely impact algorithmic outcomes, potentially leading to violations of fundamental rights, as highlighted in the European AI Act. This legislation highlights the need to prevent AI systems from perpetuating or exacerbating existing societal inequities through systematic bias analysis. These biases not only compromise fairness but also raise ethical and legal challenges, underscoring the need for rigorous detection through systematic audit processes to ensure accountability and mitigate unintended harms. We refer for instance to [3,36], [19], [8,16,23,38] or [26]. Beyond decision-making contexts, we know that algorithmic biases often stem from biases present in the training datasets themselves. Auditing an image dataset is a challenge in itself. Firstly, it is necessary to determine which variables to consider and how to extract them from an image. The importance of auditing image datasets is amplified by the fact that every image inherently encodes explicit features. Unlike text or numerical datasets, which can omit or abstract sensitive details, images visually represent specific characteristics, often revealing cues about sensitive features such as ethnicity, age, and gender. Manual labeling of such features is prohibitively expensive when dealing with large-scale datasets or when conducting extensive audits across multiple variables. To address this issue, convolutional neural networks (CNNs) can be employed to predict sensitive features, although they require annotated data for their training (lesser amount). Once trained, the network can predict the sensitive feature of the remaining data in the dataset (with a certain error relative to it). In our context, we define bias in an image dataset as statistically significant difference of distributions (e.g., an ethnicity or an age group under-represented). Statistical tests usually do not take into account the uncertainty of the labels (false predictions). We propose a prediction-aware testing pipeline that evaluates the underlying characteristic of a dataset while accounting for the model's imprecision during statistical analysis. Considering the model's accuracy in our testing pipeline helps minimize the required manual labeling, enabling large-scale auditing. The Sect. 2 presents the literature review about the sensitive feature extraction method and about the error-robust statistical testing. The Sect. 3 introduces the datasets used and our manual annotation procedure, the Sect. 4 explains our feature extraction and classification methodology, the Sect. 5 presents our error-aware testing protocol, then the Sect. 6 highlights our results. Section 7 concludes with some perspectives and future work.

2 Related Works

Assessing bias in image datasets requires careful consideration of several aspects. First, the dataset contains potentially sensitive variables. Some features must be extracted to serve as proxy estimates for these variables. Based on these features, an auditing pipeline generates reports on diversity and representativeness using selected metrics or statistical tests. The following subsections provide an overview of general concepts from the literature related to each of these aspects.

2.1 Choice of Possible Sensitive Variables

Ethnic classification refers to the classification of individuals into distinct groups based on perceived physical characteristics, such as skin color, hair texture, and facial shape. Many academic datasets separate images into at least five categories: Latino, Asian, White, Black, and Other. This classification is common in many reference datasets such as the Adult dataset [7] and is derived from the US Census 2000 classification. In [25], the authors criticize methodologies that rely exclusively on race as a variable, arguing that this approach is overly restrictive.

An alternative to the Census 2000 classification is to use medical skin analysis criteria. In [9], the authors presented a method using the ITA (Individual Typology Angle) algorithm [34,41] to estimate skin tone in the context of classifying skin lesions and to normalize the impact of lighting variations on facial images. Similarly, the Fitzpatrick classification, introduced by [20], classifies individuals based on their skin's reaction to sun exposure. This classification has six classes and takes into account features such as skin color, the presence of freckles, hair and eye color, and reactions to sun exposure (precise definition and the demographic distribution are in the Appendix). Inspired by [11], we believe that the Fitzpatrick scale is well-defined as it stems from its dermatology origin. This thorough definition paired is with its popularity justify in our opinion its usage in the context of auditing.

The authors of [39] recommend considering ethnicity as a color shade, in particular to use the newly created Monk Skin Tone Scale [35]. However, the wide range of shades makes it challenging to separate groups and, consequently, to identify bias. Once the features are selected, the next step is to automate their extraction from the image dataset.

2.2 Model for Dataset Labelisation

Depending on the size of the dataset, manual extraction may be time-consuming and challenging, prompting the use of a classifier to automatically annotate part of the dataset. CNNs are particularly well suited to images, as they can extract visually identifiable features. From a face image, CNNs can capture skin tone as a set of pixel colors or as ITA. However, this information alone omits ethnic features [41] such as hair texture or face shape, which can reduce the accuracy of ethnic classification. This highlights the need for image segmentation. Therefore, the chosen architecture should identify areas that contain these features, while excluding irrelevant areas such as the background. Among existing methods [21], the FairFace architecture [31] detects faces and classifies age and gender using a ResNet34 architecture [27]. A variant approach in [37] employs a nested U-Net architecture called U^2-Net. Finally, interest has brewed around understanding and guiding the CNNs by understanding how the networks treat facial characteristics [44]. A segmentation of the skin region can be achieved using DeepLabv3 [14] with a MobileNetV3 Large Backbone model [28] pretrained on Celeb-HQ [32]. An extension proposed by [34,41] estimates ITA values. More precisely, after smoothing the image and applying a skin mask, the authors applied a K-means clustering on the pixels values and kept the one with the highest luminosity to extract the ITA values. Finally, [2] trained a CNN from scratch to classify skin pixel shades into 10 classes. However, none of these methods explore the impact of training dataset size which is crucial when auditing, as underlined in [15], or provide specific configurations for the Fitzpatrick classification.

2.3 Metrics and Statistical Tests

Once features have been extracted from the dataset and transformed into variables, they are used to group individuals based on these variables. The fairness auditing process then evaluates whether certain groups are over- or underrepresented in comparison to predefined parameters, which may include equal or official proportions. This parameter ensures the preservation of the so-called *diversity* [17], such as maintaining almost equal frequencies between different groups. Consider a dataset $\mathcal{D}$ of observations composed of p variables: $X^0, \ldots, X^{p-1}$. Let X^0 be a variable that may convey bias (e.g., ethnicity or age), and X^j be a variable that may induce disparity or the bias representation (e.g., gender). We focus on the conditional distribution of X^0 given X^j, denoted as $\mathcal{L}(X^0|X^j)$ or when no ambiguity is possible $\{X^0|X^j\}$.

The first measure of fairness aims at quantifying the diversity in the dataset. For this, a diversity loss is introduced in [43]. Given classes $\{1, \ldots, k\}$ with target frequencies $f_i \left(\sum_{i=1}^{k} f_i = 1\right)$, and real frequencies $f'_1, \ldots, f'_k$, the diversity loss Δ is defined as $\Delta := 1 - \inf_{f_i > 0} f'_i / f_i$. Hence, it computes a ratio $\Delta \in [0, 1]$ where a value of Δ close to 1 means that at least one group is highly under-represented. Unfortunately, this metric focuses solely on one unrepresented group. For discrete categorical variables, diversity can be evaluated using Conditional Shannon entropy. The Conditional Shannon entropy distribution $C(S)$ of a subset $S \subseteq X^0$ is defined as:

$$C(S) = -\sum_{i=1}^{k} f_i \log f_i$$

where x_i^j is a possible modality of X^j and $s_i = \frac{|S| \cap |X^j = x_i^j|}{|S|}$ is the probability to observe S according $X^j = x_i^j$. Equally distributed entropy according to X^j corresponds to good diversity. Both of the aforementioned metrics cannot be extended to cases where the space of conditional observations is large and are not related to a statistical test [12].

The second main measure of fairness for such problems comes from a volumetric perspective comparison. Actually, Geometric diversity [17] provides a meaningful similarity measure for observations in multiple dimensions. Consider each data point of the dataset $x \in X$, represented by a variable vector v_x. The geometric diversity of a subset $S \subseteq X$ is defined as the n-volume of the parallelotope spanned by the p variable vectors $\{v_x : x \in S\}$, where $n = |S|$ is the size of the subset. Denoting the data matrix of the subset S as $\mathbf{D} \in \mathbb{R}^{p \times n}$, the (squared) n-volume of the n parallelogram embedded in p dimensional space can be computed by means of the determinant of the Gramian matrix $\mathbf{G} = \mathbf{D}^T\mathbf{D}$ (with variable vectors as columns in $\mathbf{D}$). Thus, the geometric diversity can be measured by :

$$G(S) = \sqrt{\mathrm{Det}(\mathbf{D}^T\mathbf{D})}$$

The larger $G(S)$, the more diverse is S in the variable space. However, Geometric Diversity cannot be applied if one aims to compare variable distributions using statistical hypothesis testing [13]. The Disparate Impact (DI) is one of the most used fairness metric, defined for a binary model $\hat{Y} = f(X)$ by the ratio

$$DI(f, S) := \frac{\min\left(\mathbb{P}(\hat{Y}=1 \mid S=0), \mathbb{P}(\hat{Y}=1 \mid S=1)\right)}{\max\left(\mathbb{P}(\hat{Y}=1 \mid S=0), \mathbb{P}(\hat{Y}=1 \mid S=1)\right)}$$

This quantity is equal to 1 when there is probabilistic independence between the model's decision $\hat{Y}$ and the sensitive variable S. The smaller the DI is, the more discrimination towards the minority class exist. Hence, several norms or regulations impose that a model should have its disparate impact greater than 0.8 as detailed in [24] or [42].

This metric generally used to evaluate the discrimination of a model, can be applied to evaluate the probabilistic bias of two sensitive variables. We choose to include it only in the Appendix (1) not to confuse the reader and make him think that we evaluate our model's fairness (for the instance the bias in the CNN predicting the Fitzpatrick Class), (2) homogeneity between the parity test (about one sensitive variable) where the DI is not applicable and the equal representation test (about two sensitive variables) where one might use the DI and (3) while relevant, we believe that testing a null hypothesis with multiple statistical tests is a more robust approach.

Rather than relying on high-level metrics or aggregated scores, our approach evaluates biases by directly comparing the distributions of sensitive variables across subgroups. To quantify the distance between distributions with large, high-dimensional samples, one may measure the general Wasserstein distance, given by:

$$W_{\tilde{p}}(\mu, \nu) = \left(\inf_{\pi \in \Gamma(\mu,\nu)} \int_{M \times M} d(x,y)^{\tilde{p}} d\pi(x,y)\right)^{1/\tilde{p}}$$

where $\tilde{p} \geq 1$, $W_{\tilde{p}}$ is the $\tilde{p}^{\text{th}}$ Wasserstein distance, $\Gamma(\mu, \nu)$ denote all joint distributions π that have marginals μ and ν, $d()$ is the distance function between points x and y that matched and M is a given metric space. Using the Wasserstein distance, a classical distance-based test, such as the two-sample test (i.e. variables following the same distribution), can be applied following the tests proposed in [5] using the limit distributions developed in [4] or [6,40]. Other statistical tests, such as those based on averages or conditional averages, may also provide insights into the proximity of variable distributions [17]. Traditional statistical tests, such as Pearson's R, the t-test, and ANOVA, are commonly used. For non-normal data distributions, non-parametric tests, such as the χ^2 test, the Kolmogorov-Smirnov (KS) test, or the Central Limit Theorem (CLT) based test, serve as an alternative.

The previously mentioned metrics and tests do not account for the classification accuracy of feature extraction. Since feature extraction is performed automatically, as highlighted by [1], who evaluated how varying levels of label error

Fig. 1. Fitzpatrick classification (5 class) from the left to right Phototype I, II, III-IV, V, VI. The first row is from the GAN dataset, while the second is from the CelebA dataset, both dataset are released to the community.

(simulated through label flipping) affected the disparity metrics, it is essential to consider the model's accuracy in the bias detection task. Permutation methods have long been used in pursuit of robustness, as demonstrated by [18], who introduced a permutation-based fairness framework with labelled data. Although an extensive body of work has addressed label errors in the training set, to the best of our knowledge, no specific test for bias detection, that accounts for errors in the automated extraction of variables, has been proposed.

Our contribution, therefore, is to propose a full pipeline that starts with a variable extraction step and extends to robust statistical tests designed to consider the fairness according to the accuracy of the model's annotations. The following section details our complete methodology and introduces robust statistical techniques to highlight biases in images datasets.

3 Datasets and Manual Annotation

3.1 Datasets

To illustrate our pipeline, we rely on two datasets as guidelines, using them as the starting point of our process. These datasets are academic benchmark datasets of two different types. Generated Photos dataset [10,22] is a synthetic images dataset sourced from a commercial platform and are generated using a GAN-based model [30]. The dataset intentionally encompasses a broad range of demographic features, including gender and ethnicity, with the GAN's hyperparameters calibrated to represent individuals with appearances associated with diverse ethnicities. Each image has been generated with Census 2000 labeling, ensuring an almost equal proportion of Caucasian, Asian, Hispanic or Latino, and Black populations. For our work, we utilized the academic version of this dataset, which contains 10,000 generated facial images. We also work on a well-known benchmark: The CelebA dataset [33] for comparative analysis. The CelebA dataset has approximately 200,000 celebrity images sourced from the Internet, annotated with multiple facial features. From this dataset, we randomly sampled 1,500 images to assess how our test performs on a smaller dataset.

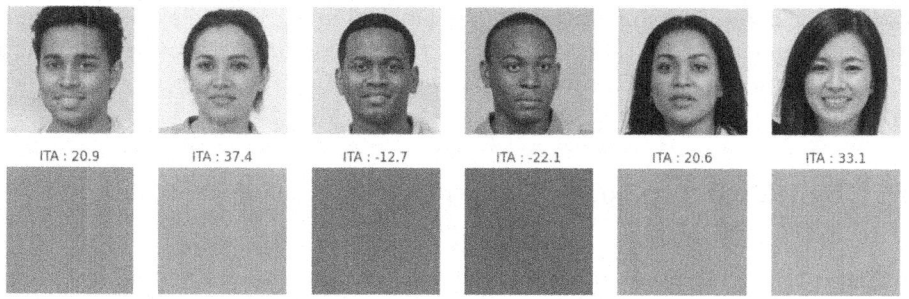

Fig. 2. Skin color extracted and Individual Typology Angle (ITA) of the GAN dataset.

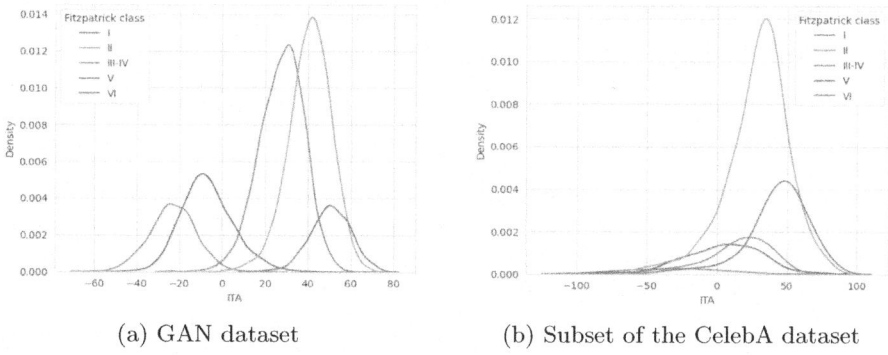

Fig. 3. Probability density of ITA given the Fitzpatrick class.

3.2 Manual Annotation

All images were manually labeled by three non-expert individuals according to the Fitzpatrick classification. This manual annotation helps assess how well our model aligns with a fully manual annotation. However, Phototypes III and IV are hardly distinguishable for non-experts and rarely reach full agreement. Thus, we chose to merge them. Figure 1 gives some examples of our manual classification. As with ethnicity, a person's gender is determined by the majority vote of our three annotators. Even when considering the reflected gender, our dataset did not adequately represent the transgender or the bi-gender community, just to name a few, leading the annotators to classify the portrayal of gender to the limited view of gender binary notion that includes only men and women. In this regard, we view our work as part of initial studies towards auditing gender representation, which should further be extended in this direction in the future.

4 Sensitive Variable Classification Using Neural Network

Manual auditing is not cost-effective for high- or medium-level auditing of large-scale datasets. This underscores the need for neural networks to predict sensitive variables accurately. Numerous manually labelled image datasets exist for binary gender classification - although we regret the lack of datasets with more diverse gender representations - facilitating the use of highly effective pre-trained networks for gender estimation.

4.1 Individual Typology Angle (ITA) Estimation and Link with Fitzpatrick

To improve the accuracy of the Fitzpatrick classification, we add an Individual Typology Angle (ITA) estimation step to our model, which can be seen as an enrichment of pixel information. ITA values are computationnaly derived from skin regions (isolated by pre-trained DeepLabv3). The estimate of the ITA value is based on 2 colorimetric parameters: the luminance $L*$ and the yellow/blue component $b*$. The ITA is defined as follows:

$$\text{ITA} = \arctan\left(\frac{L*-50}{b*}\right) \times \frac{180}{\pi} \quad (1)$$

where a perceptual lightness at value 50 corresponds to a maximum chroma. We extracted the mean and standard deviation of the ITA values and of other colometric parameters. Figure 2 presents examples of extracted ITA.

Figure 3 gives the ITA distribution according the Fitzpatrick class and confirm the clear correlation between the Fitzpatrick classes and ITA values. Higher Fitzpatrick class numbers correspond to lower mean ITA values. However, as a single ITA score can be assigned to several Fitzpatrick classes, there is no one-to-one correspondence between the two. We further research the difference between the ITA and the Fitzpatrick class in the Appendix.

4.2 Gender, Age and Fitzpatrick Scale Classification

We used the FairFace [29] method to classify gender and age, as its architecture provides the best results for these tasks. Despite certain limitations—such as detecting undesirable background faces- it achieved the best accuracy. Since our classification task relies primarily on facial features, especially skin, we studied the effect of applying masks to images before training our fine-tuned CNN. We tested three approaches: (1) using the original images, (2) removing the background, and (3) isolating only the segmented skin region. The extracted ITA and skin-related information are incorporated as additional features in the latent layer of the neural network architecture.

In most of our experiments, we added a custom classification head to ResNet-50 or ResNet-101 embeddings [27] and fine-tuned these models on our labeled dataset, eliminating the need for full CNN training. The impact of training set size is analyzed in Sect. 6. We use two feature extraction configurations: (1) the final dense layer's output (1,000-dimensional) and (2) the preceding layer's output (2,048-dimensional). Figure 4 present an overview of our classification pipeline. More details on the architecture, optimizer, early stopping, compute

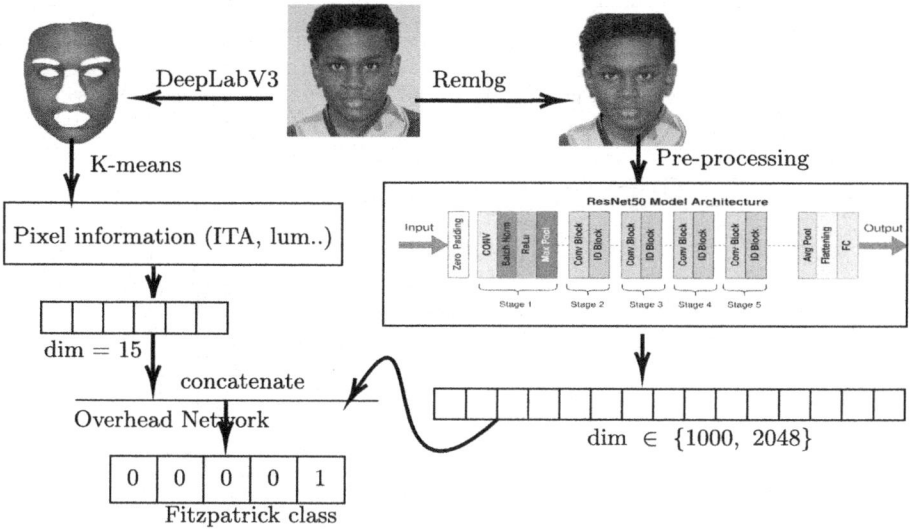

Fig. 4. Pipeline for our Fitzpatrick classification.

time, and transfer learning method are provided in the Appendix. We created a Neural Network architecture to accurately predict the Fitzpatrick class with as few manually labeled image as possible, however, this part was not mandatory to our auditing framework thanks to the following section, which explains how we calibrate our testing pipeline given a model's accuracy.

5 Uncertainty Aware Statistical Test

Statistical Test Used. We find rejection based on variable distributions more meaningful, hence, $\mathcal{H}_0$ assumes that both groups are drawn from the same underlying distribution. In our proposed methodology, we use a modified version of well-known statistical tests to compare two distributions, including the χ^2 test, the CLT-based mean test and the Wasserstein-based test. Note that categorical multimodal variables are treated as binary variables in a one-vs-all approach, which can be considered a limitation to our work. Two tests are presented here: the parity test and the equal representation test.

Parity Test (One Sensitive Variable). To audit the bias according to a tested variable X^0 (gender, age or Fitzpatrick), it is necessary to compare the observed distribution of X^0 with its expected distribution. When X^0 is *gender*, this process involves comparing X^0 observed values with a Bernoulli distribution of $p = \frac{1}{2}$ (i.e. testing $H_0 : X^0 \sim \mathcal{B}(p)$). While the assumption of a uniform distribution for the binary gender may appear reasonable, it is important to recognize the limitations of such an assumption when considering age groups or the Fitzpatrick class. To this end, a chosen parameter reflecting a real mondial distribution was

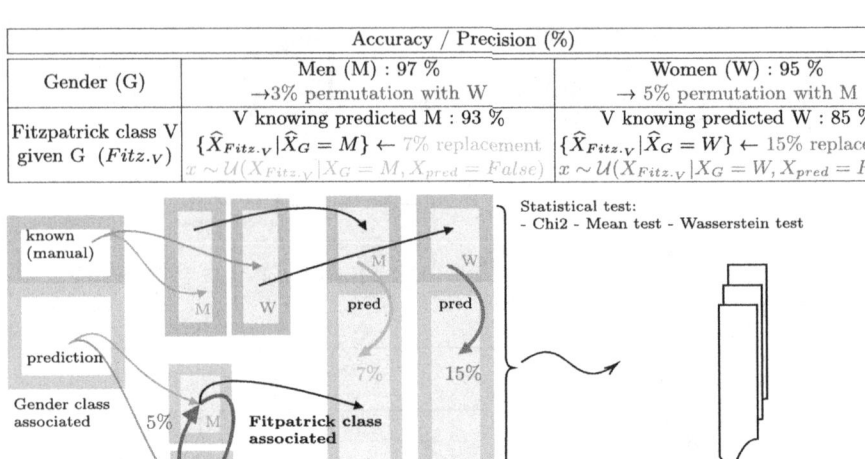

Fig. 5. Diagram explaining our error-aware testing pipeline in an equal representation test of the Fitzpatrick class V conditioned by the gender.

utilized for comparison, the recorded parameters are available in the Appendix. Hence, we test, respectively for when X^0 is the age ($H_0 : X^0 \sim RealDistr(Age)$) and for when X_0 is the Fitzpatrick class ($H_0 : X^0 \sim RealDistr(Fitzpatrick)$).

Equal Representation (Two Sensitive Variables). We test whether the distribution of a variable X^0 (a Fitzpatrick skin type or age interval) differs significantly given another variable X^j (gender 'men' or 'women'). Let's consider $x_{i'}^0 \in 1, \cdots, K'$ the K' modalities of X^0 and $x_i^j \in 1, \cdots, K$ the K modalities of X^j. To perform this analysis, we first partition the dataset based on X^j (one-versus-all according to x_i^j) and then compare the distribution of X^0 across the two resulting partitions of X^j. We define the variable $W^0 \in \{0,1\}^{K'}$ such as $W^0 = (W_1^0, \cdots, W_{K'}^0)$ and the $W_{i'}^0$ are defined as followed:

$$\forall i' \in 1, \cdots, K' \quad W_{i'}^0 := \begin{cases} 1 & \text{if } X^0 = x_{i'}^0 \\ 0 & \text{otherwise.} \end{cases} \quad (2)$$

a condition notation of $W_{i'}^0$ on a subspace S according X^j is given by:

$$\forall i \in 1, \cdots, K \quad W_{i',i}^{0,j} := \begin{cases} 1 & \text{if } X^0 = x_{i'}^0 \text{ in } S \in \{X^j = x_i^j\} \\ 0 & \text{if } X^0 \neq x_{i'}^0 \text{ in } S \in \{X^j = x_i^j\} \end{cases} \quad (3)$$

$$W_{i',\bar{i}}^{0,j} := \begin{cases} 1 & \text{if } X^0 = x_{i'}^0 \text{ in } S \in \{X^j \neq x_i^j\} \\ 0 & \text{if } X^0 \neq x_{i'}^0 \text{ in } S \in \{X^j \neq x_i^j\} \end{cases} \quad (4)$$

We test the following assumption on the distributions, $H_0 : W_{i',i}^{0,j} \sim W_{i',\bar{i}}^{0,j}$.

Uncertainty Aware. To ensure reliability, the auditing process must be robust to variations in model annotation accuracy. Consequently, the test must be robust to prediction errors and minimize false negatives for the null hypothesis, $\mathcal{H}_0$. As permutation tests, we randomly invert the automatic annotation modality of some predicted variables while keeping manual annotations unchanged. This procedure serves to reduce the discrepancy between distributions and minimize false negatives in test decisions. The model prediction is denoted by $\widehat{W}_i^0$, and the true value by W_i^0. These tests are modified according to the following methodology:

- Parity test:
  1. We calculate the model's accuracy $A^{W_{i'}^0} := \mathbb{P}[\widehat{W}_{i'}^0 = W_{i'}^0]$ for each of the estimated variables $\widehat{W}_{i'}^0$.
  2. We randomly replace $100 \times (1 - A^{W_{i'}^0})\%$ of $\widehat{W}_{i'}^0$ by values simulated according to the expected parameter (for example $\mathcal{B}(\frac{1}{2})$ for gender).
- Representation test:
  1. We calculate the prediction's precision $P^{W_i^j} := \mathbb{P}[W_i^j = 1 | \widehat{W}_i^j = 1]$ for each of the variables $\widehat{W}_i^j$.
  2. We randomly permute $100 \times (1 - P^{W_i^j})\%$ between $\widehat{W}_i^j$ and $\widehat{W}_{\neg i}^j$ values (e.g., transforming predicted women into predicted men and vice versa)
  3. We compute $A^{W_{i'}^0, W_i^j=1} := \mathbb{P}[\widehat{W}_{i'}^0 = W_{i'}^0 | W_i^j = 1]$ which represents the classification model's accuracy for the modality $x_{i'}^0$ conditioned on x_i^j.
  4. We randomly replace $100 \times (1 - A^{W_{i'}^0, W_i^j=1})\%$ of the automatically annotated variables $\widehat{W}_{i',i}^{0,j}$ and $\widehat{W}_{i',\neg i}^{0,j}$ respectively with manually annotated variables $W_{i',i}^{0,j}$ and $W_{i',\neg i}^{0,j}$.

Note that the accuracies and precisions above are calculated on the validation set. We conduct multiple statistical tests across several simulations and aggregate the results by taking the median p-value of all simulations. This framework is illustrated in Fig. 5.

6 Results

We report results on the two datasets described in Sect. 3.1. Our auditing process consists of: (1) assessing whether there is a significant difference in the observed proportions across three sensitive attributes—gender, age, and Fitzpatrick classification; and (2) evaluating whether significant differences exist in the observed proportions of age and Fitzpatrick classification, **conditioned on gender**.

6.1 Ablation Study of the Fitzpatrick Classification

As shown in Fig. 6, the size of the manually annotated training dataset has a significant influence on model accuracy. Using the GAN dataset, our model achieves a 76% correct Fitzpatrick classification prediction rate on the test set, with at

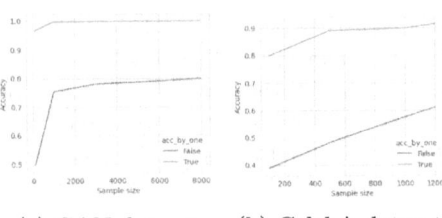

(a) GAN dataset (b) CelebA dataset

Fig. 6. Learning sample size impact on the Network accuracy (Fitzpatrick classification). The by-one-accuracy includes predictions for the true class as well as the directly adjacent classes.

Table 1. Impact of hyperparameters and architecture for neural network designed to classify the Fitzpatrick scale on the GAN and CelebA datasets.

Hyperparameter	GAN	CelebA
Skin information (ITA..)	+0.6	+0.2
Overhead network choice	+3.7	+4.2
Skin mask	−1.7	+1.2
Removing background	+0.1	+1.8
Latent space size (2048)	+1.9	+2.7

least 12.5% manual annotation. However, with CelebA, the accuracy of the model does not exceed 65%, despite hyperparameter tuning. It highlights the necessity of accounting for model errors in the tests to avoid the need for a full retraining of the CNN. Age and gender are provided by a trained FairFace model, so there is no training step, and the model achieved respectively a 97.17% and a 94.46% accuracy on *CelebA* and *GAN* for the gender classification. Without age labels, to verify the consistency of FairFace's age prediction, we compared its prediction with another network prediction and obtained a 72.77% classification similarity for the GAN dataset. Table 1 provides an ablation study examining the impact of each hyperparameter in the CNN architecture for Fitzpatrick classification. A high-dimensional latent space, the incorporation of ITA into the model, and the removal of image backgrounds significantly enhance the learning process. However, the use of a skin mask has a negative effect on the results. This can be explained by the removal of features such as hair color, which are essential for Fitzpatrick classification. The addition of ITA showed a notable improvement for small training datasets with an embedding size of 1000 dimensions. We believe that skin-related features are sufficiently captured for the embedding of size 2048 but lost during dimensionality reduction (embedding of size 1000).

6.2 Ablation Study of the Error-Aware Method

To study the impact of the error-aware approach, we evaluated the statistical tests with and without taking into account the imprecision of the neural network's predictions. The colored cell on Table 2 and Table 3 show the effect of adding the uncertainty aware corrections to the statistical tests. For the parity test (1), for over the 135 tests, the aggregation of test accepted $\mathcal{H}_0$ 20 times with the error-aware approach, and only six times without it. For the equal representation test (2), the error-aware method affected the result of 88 of the 126 aggregations of tests: for 84 out of the previously mentioned 88, the uncertainty aware corrections made the audit result more tolerant.

Table 2. Statistical test on the parity of Gender ($\mathcal{H}_0: p = 0.5$) and the real distribution for the Fitzpatrick class and Age ($\mathcal{H}_0$: marginal and global distributions are equivalent). The test used were the Wasserstein test, the Mean test and the χ^2 test. ✓, ✓$_{2/3}$ and × respectively means that 0, 1 or at least 2 tests rejected $\mathcal{H}_0$. Colored cell means that the test result are different because of the error-aware protocol: ■ means that, thanks to the error-aware method, less test rejected $\mathcal{H}_0$.

Sensitive Variable	(a) GAN Sample Size					(b) CelebA Sample Size			
	100	500	1000	3000	8000	100	500	1000	1200
Gender	×	×	×	×	×	×	×	×	×
Age									
0-2	✓	✓	✓	✓	✓	✓	✓	✓	✓
3-9	×	×	×	×	×	×	×	×	×
10-19	×	×	×	×	×	×	×	×	×
20-29	×	×	×	×	×	×	×	×	×
30-39	×	×	×	×	×	×	×	×	×
40-49	×	×	×	×	×	✓	✓	✓	✓
50-59	×	×	×	×	×	✓	✓	✓	✓
60-69	×	×	×	×	×	×	×	×	×
70+	×	×	×	×	×	×	×	×	×
Fitzp. class									
I	×	×	×	×	×	×	×	×	×
II	×	×	×	×	×	×	×	×	×
III- IV	×	×	×	×	×	×	×	×	×
V	×	×	×	×	✓	×	×	×	✓
VI	×	×	×	×	×	×	×	×	✓$_{2/3}$

6.3 Sample Size Impact on Statistical Test Results

Here, we assess whether both test methodologies produce the same conclusions as those obtained from the fully annotated dataset, which serves as the ground truth without annotation errors, given different amounts of manually annotated data. The parity test (1), for the *GAN* dataset resulted in only four false rejections out of the 75 tested hypotheses, with the error associated with Fitzpatrick category V (Table 2a). For the *CelebA* dataset, we observed two modalities with false rejection out of the 15 tested (see Table 2b). In both datasets, our parity test demonstrates robustness to the *sample size* effect. The equal representation test (2) is more sensitive to sample size effect. For the *GAN* dataset, it produced eleven false rejections out of 70 tests (Table 3a). It seems that sample size $\geq$ 1000 is enough to get stabilized results. For the *CelebA* dataset, Our equal representation test (Table 3) produced three false negative and three false positives among 56 tests.

6.4 Auditing Result

Parity Test Results (1). For the *GAN* dataset, the parity tests of our audit (Table 2a) reveal that the observed proportions for gender, age, and Fitzpatrick

Table 3. Equal representation statistical test on the for the Fitzpatrick class and the Age, with respect to each reflected closest binary gender subgroup. $\mathcal{H}_0$: The Fitzpatrick or Age distribution of the reflected men subgroup is the same as the reflected women subgroup. The tests used were the Wasserstein test, the Mean test, and the χ^2 test. ✓, ✓$_{2/3}$ and × respectively means that 0, 1 or at least 2 tests rejected $\mathcal{H}_0$. Colored cell means that the test result are different because of the error-aware protocol: ▨ and ▨ respectively mean that, because of the error-aware method, less test or respectively more test rejected $\mathcal{H}_0$

Sensitive Variable	(a) GAN Sample Size					(b) CelebA Sample Size			
	100	500	1000	3000	8000	100	500	1000	1200
Age									
0-2	✓	✓	✓	✓	✓	✓	✓	✓	✓
3-9	✓	✓	×	✓	✓	✓	✓	✓	✓
10-19	✓	✓	✓	✓	✓	✓	✓	✓	✓
20-29	✓$_{2/3}$	✓	×	✓	✓$_{2/3}$	×	×	×	×
30-39	✓	✓	✓	✓	✓	✓	✓$_{2/3}$	✓	✓
40-49	✓	✓	✓	✓	✓	✓	✓	✓	✓
50-59	✓	✓	✓	✓	✓	✓	✓	✓	✓
60-69	✓	✓	✓	✓	✓	✓	✓	✓	✓
70+	✓	✓	✓	✓	✓	✓	✓	✓	✓
Fitz. class									
I	✓$_{2/3}$	✓$_{2/3}$	×	×	×	✓$_{2/3}$	✓$_{2/3}$	×	×
II	×	×	✓$_{2/3}$	✓$_{2/3}$	✓	×	×	×	×
III- IV	×	×	×	×	✓$_{2/3}$	✓	✓	✓	✓
V	×	×	✓	×	✓$_{2/3}$	×	×	✓$_{2/3}$	✓
VI	×	×	×	×	×	✓	×	✓$_{2/3}$	✓$_{2/3}$

scale features do not align with the proportions recorded in the general population. For the *CelebA* dataset, the population aged 40 to 59 is the only age group representative of the recorded parameter.

Equal Representation Test Result (2). For the *GAN* dataset, our auditing reveals a strong gender-related bias with ethnicity, for example, a woman is 1.37 times more likely to be in the Fitzpatrick class I compared to a man. Contrariwise, a man is 1.41 times more likely to be in the Fitzpatrick class VI (For all values, see in the Appendix). No gender-related biases with age are present in the *Gan* dataset. In *CelebA*, the age group 20–29 is overrepresented among women (73% of women are in this age group against 36% for men). There also exist a strong Fitzpatrick-gender bias: while 66% of women are of Fitzpatrick class II, 52% of men are. On the contrary, men are 12.5 times more likely to be in the Fitzpatrick class I.

7 Conclusion

We have proposed a new bias auditing method that minimizes the need for manual annotation (requiring between 100 and 1000 annotations) and is robust to errors in automated annotation. When rejecting the null hypothesis, data fluctuations mean that not all statistical tests necessarily yield the same conclusions. For instance, the χ^2 test appeared more lenient compared to the Wasserstein test. To address this, we consider the majority vote of the results from our three tests. We are also aware that our method tends to accept the null hypothesis ($\mathcal{H}_0$) more readily in the equal representation test. However, we aim to avoid discouraging users from adopting our method due to an excessive number of false rejections. Our primary goal is to encourage users to utilize our tool rather than to achieve a high recall rate (sensitivity). We emphasize the importance of assessing the representativity of individuals before using an image dataset for training, in order to mitigate potential discrimination. In the context of the AI Act, which will require companies to certify the compliance of training data for machine learning models, we hope that this audit will serve as a first tool at their disposal. Our future work will aim to monitor bias in generative models in online mode.

Acknowledgments. The authors are partially supported by the AI Interdisciplinary Institute and ANR Regulia, which is funded by the French "Investing for the Future – PIA3" program under the Grant agreement n°ANR-23-IACL-0002. We extend our thanks to Diallo Mohamed, Oumou Hawa Bah and Djiguinée Mamady for their efforts in the labeling process.

Disclosure of Interests. The authors have no competing interests.

References

1. Adebayo, J., Hall, M., Yu, B., Chern, B.: Quantifying and mitigating the impact of label errors on model disparity metrics (2023)
2. Alifia, R.V., Ayu, M.A.: Preprocessing with skin segmentation to improve monk skin tone (MST) classification. In: 11th International Conference on EECSI (2024)
3. Barocas, S., Hardt, M., Narayanan, A.: Fairness and machine learning: limitations and opportunities (2023)
4. del Barrio, E., González-Sanz, A., Loubes, J.M.: Central limit theorems for general transportation costs (2024)
5. del Barrio, E., Gordaliza, P., Loubes, J.M.: A central limit theorem for LP transportation cost on the real line with application to fairness assessment in machine learning. J. IMA **8**, 817–849 (2019)
6. del Barrio, E., Loubes, J.M.: Central limit theorems for empirical transportation cost in general dimension. Ann. Probab. **47**, 926–951 (2019)
7. Becker, B., Kohavi, R.: Adult. UCI machine learning repository (1996)
8. Besse, P., del Barrio, E., Gordaliza, P., Loubes, J.M., Risser, L.: A survey of bias in machine learning through the prism of statistical parity (2022)
9. Bevan, P.J., Atapour-Abarghouei, A.: Detecting melanoma fairly: Skin tone detection and debiasing for skin lesion classification (2022)
10. Boddeti, V.N., Sreekumar, G., Ross, A.: On the biometric capacity of generative face models (2023)
11. Buolamwini, J., Gebru, T.: Gender shades: Intersectional Accuracy Disparities in Commercial Gender Classification. In: 1st Conference on FAccT (2018)

12. Celis, L.E., Deshpande, A., Kathuria, T., Vishnoi, N.K.: How to be fair and diverse? CoRR (2016)
13. Celis, L.E., Keswani, V., Straszak, D., Deshpande, A., Kathuria, T., Vishnoi, N.K.: Fair and diverse DPP-based data summarization. CoRR (2018)
14. Chen, L.C., Papandreou, G., Schroff, F., Adam, H.: Rethinking atrous convolution for semantic image segmentation (2017)
15. Chen, M., Zhang, Z., Wang, T., Backes, M., Zhang, Y.: FACE-AUDITOR: data auditing in facial recognition systems. In: 32nd USENIX Security Symposium (USENIX Security 23), pp. 7195–7212. USENIX Association, Anaheim, CA (2023). https://www.usenix.org/conference/usenixsecurity23/presentation/chen-min
16. Chouldechova, A.: Fair prediction with disparate impact: a study of bias in recidivism prediction instruments. Big Data **5**, 153–163 (2017)
17. Clemmensen, L.K.H., Kjærsgaard, R.D.: Data representativity for machine learning and AI systems. ArXiv (2022)
18. DiCiccio, C., Vasudevan, S., Basu, K., Kenthapadi, K., Agarwal, D.: Evaluating fairness using permutation tests. In: 26th ACM SIGKDD International Conference on Knowledge Discovery & Data Mining (2020)
19. Feldman, M., Friedler, S.A., Moeller, J., Scheidegger, C., Venkatasubramanian, S.: Certifying and removing disparate impact (2015)
20. Fitzpatrick, T.B.: The validity and practicality of sun-reactive skin types I through VI. Arch Dermatol. **124**, 869–871 (1988)
21. Gatis, D.: REMBG (2022). https://github.com/danielgatis/rembg
22. Generated, photos, team: generated dataset (2024). https://generated.photos/solutions/academic-research
23. Gordaliza, P., del Barrio, E., Fabrice, G., Loubes, J.M.: Obtaining fairness using optimal transport theory. In: International Conference on Machine Learning (2019)
24. Groves, L., Metcalf, J., Kennedy, A., Vecchione, B., Strait, A.: Auditing work: exploring the New York city algorithmic bias audit regime. In: Proceedings of the 2024 ACM Conference on Fairness, Accountability, and Transparency, pp. 1107–1120 (2024)
25. Hanna, A., Denton, E., Smart, A., Smith-Loud, J.: Towards a critical race methodology in algorithmic fairness. In: 2020 Conference on FAccT (2020)
26. Hardt, M., Price, E., Price, E., Srebro, N.: Equality of opportunity in supervised learning. In: Advances in Neural Information Processing Systems (2016)
27. He, K., Zhang, X., Ren, S., Sun, J.: Deep residual learning for image recognition (2015)
28. Howard, A., et al.: Searching for MobileNetV3 (2019)
29. Karkkainen, K., Joo, J.: FairFace: face attribute dataset for balanced race, gender, and age for bias measurement and mitigation. In: Proceedings of the IEEE/CVF Winter Conference on Applications of Computer Vision (2021)
30. Karras, T., Laine, S., Aila, T.: A style-based generator architecture for generative adversarial networks (2019)
31. King, D.E.: Max-margin object detection (2015)
32. Lee, C.H., Liu, Z., Wu, L., Luo, P.: MaskGAN: towards diverse and interactive facial image manipulation. In: IEEE Conference on CVPR (2020)
33. Liu, Z., Luo, P., Wang, X., Tang, X.: Deep learning face attributes in the wild. In: ICCV (2015)
34. Merler, M., Ratha, N., Feris, R.S., Smith, J.R.: Diversity in faces (2019)
35. Monk, E.: The monk skin tone scale (2023)
36. Oneto, L., Chiappa, S.: Fairness in machine learning (2020)

37. Qin, X., Zhang, Z., Huang, C., Dehghan, M., Zaiane, O.R., Jagersand, M.: U2-net: going deeper with nested u-structure for salient object detection. Pattern Recognit. **106**, 107404 (2020)
38. Risser, L., Sanz, A., Vincenot, Q., Loubes, J.M.: Tackling algorithmic bias in neural-network classifiers using Wasserstein-2 regularization (2022)
39. Schumann, C., Olanubi, G.O., Wright, A., Jr., E.M., Heldreth, C., Ricco, S.: Consensus and subjectivity of skin tone annotation for ml fairness (2024)
40. Taskesen, B., Blanchet, J., Kuhn, D., Nguyen, V.A.: A statistical test for probabilistic fairness. In: 2021 ACM Conference FAccT (2021)
41. Thong, W., Joniak, P., Xiang, A.: Beyond skin tone: a multidimensional measure of apparent skin color (2023)
42. Wright, L., et al.: Null compliance: Nyc local law 144 and the challenges of algorithm accountability. In: Proceedings of the 2024 ACM Conference on Fairness, Accountability, and Transparency, pp. 1701–1713 (2024)
43. Zameshina, M., et al.: Fairness in generative modeling: do it unsupervised! In: GECCC (2022)
44. Zhang, Q., Wang, W., Zhu, S.C.: Examining CNN representations with respect to dataset bias (2017). https://arxiv.org/abs/1710.10577

Sports

On Identifying Fast Road Races: Decomposing Race Conditions and Individual Performance Level

Klaus Brinker[✉]

Department Hamm 1, Hamm-Lippstadt University of Applied Sciences, Hamm, Germany
klaus.brinker@hshl.de

Abstract. We address the question of how to identify fast road races in running by automatically decomposing race results into athlete performance and race condition components. Our approach does not require explicit modeling of influencing factors such as course terrain profiles. Favorable conditions have a substantial impact on race results in road running, and can be critical for meeting championship qualifying standards or for achieving personal bests. We frame this problem as an instance of weighted nonnegative matrix factorization and validate our approach using 6,000 real-world 10k race results from recent local to regional level races. Extensive experiments on both this real-world data and simulated data demonstrate the robustness of this method to high missing value rates and its ability to reduce bias in estimating race conditions compared to mean- or median-based approaches. Our approach also successfully recovered seasonal patterns in race conditions. The number of races and the rate of missing values were found to be the most important properties affecting accuracy, while the number of athletes had less impact.

Keywords: Endurance Sports · Nonnegative Matrix Factorization

1 Introduction

In many endurance sports, athletic performance is measured in terms of the time required for completing a given course, or the distance covered within a given time. In both cases, a single value summarizes a complex interplay of underlying factors that affect each athlete's overall performance in a particular race. Unraveling running performance has been approached in the literature from a variety of perspectives, among others, using environmental properties, physiological measurements, training statistics, and course characteristics.

Supplementary Information The online version contains supplementary material available at https://doi.org/10.1007/978-3-032-06129-4_19.

We study a related yet distinct problem: distinguishing general race conditions from individual performance levels. General race conditions encompass factors that vary between races but remain approximately constant within each race, such as weather or course topology. In contrast, individual performance levels pertain to characteristics specific to each athlete. This distinction allows us to separately analyze the impact of external race conditions and individual athletic abilities on performance outcomes.

We propose an automatic data-driven method based on solving an associated optimization problem for unpacking these two groups of components. In the most basic model instantiation, we unpack race results as the product of two particular values, one of them linked to the race and the other one to the athlete. Our approach is suitable for endurance sports where *individual performance* is the dominant factor, and components such as team tactics and race dynamics are less important. While this assumption is met for typical road races in running and time trial competitions in cycling, it is not met in cycling road races. Note that naive approaches for quantitatively capturing race conditions, such as mean or median race results, dependent heavily on the athlete performance distribution within races and are easily biased. We provide experimental evidence that our approach is less prone to this problem as it *simultaneously* conducts race and athlete unpacking.

Several interesting applications are facilitated by decomposing race condition and performance level, such as estimating and comparing race results of athletes who did not compete in the same race in a sound manner [11], or computing flat equivalent distances for comparing race courses [12]. If we assume that static race conditions, such as elevation profile or surface properties, are dominant, more favorable race conditions may be identified based on associated condition values for future race schedule planning, among others. More technically, both [11,12] build on a general matrix factorization solved by alternating least squares optimization, while our approach is based on nonnegative matrix factorization [7], a matrix decomposition technique which has received increasing attention and has been considered in a variety of fields, among those are astrophysics [10] and bioinformatics [5].

Our main contributions include a practical, entirely data-driven, and parameter-free method for effectively separating race conditions and athlete performance using nonnegative matrix factorization as the core computational technique. This approach is well-suited to real-world race data and handles missing values in a principled way with limited computational demands. We introduce an intuitive and interpretable normalization method for practitioners and compiled a real-world dataset of approximately 6,000 recent 10k race results from local to regional level running road races in Germany (2022–2023) using publicly available data sources. To evaluate the performance of our method and study the impact of specific dataset properties on estimation accuracy, we conducted extensive experiments on both this real-world dataset and an additional simulated one. Furthermore, nonnegative matrix decomposition provides a general data-driven framework for analyzing race properties and athlete profiles without explicit feature modeling.

This paper is structured as follows: We discuss related research from the fields of sports performance science and machine learning in the following section. In Sect. 3, we introduce our approach both from a technical perspective, including the underlying mathematical optimization problem and the solution strategy based on weighted nonnegative matrix factorization, and from a conceptual perspective with respect to interpreting the decomposition results and practical applications. We discuss experimental results on real-world road running races and simulation data in Sect. 4 to provide a comprehensive empirical analysis of the properties of our approach. Finally, in Sect. 5, we summarize our findings and discuss promising directions for future research.

2 Related Work

A related matrix factorization method has been considered in [11] for *race pace* results in multi-distance running races as an initial processing step. Beyond directly utilizing decomposition values for race pace prediction for known races, the authors employ race characterization vectors as targets in a linear regression model. Here, the inputs are distance and elevation features computed from global navigation satellite system (GNSS) route data. The final combined model allows for race pace prediction for races not included in the initial dataset. While adopting a similar factorization step for race time or covered distance, we focus on race condition estimation for fixed-distance or fixed-time races. Building upon [11], the authors in [12] incorporate a physiological model for adjusting different race distances beyond a straightforward average pace approach. The aim of this approach is to compute hypothetical flat equivalent distances for running routes.

Several studies have addressed the impact of ambient weather conditions on endurance performance in road running, including air temperature [1,8,15], relative humidity [1,15], air pressure [8,15], solar radiation [1], precipitation [8], and wind [8]. In addition to these typically highly variable features, more stable properties correlated with performance have been studied as well, among these are altitude [15] and course terrain profile [13], which includes elevation profile and the number and type of turns. In contrast to this, physiological and technological differences between athletes may be considered as an orthogonal dimension of overall performance. Physiological features include age and sex [16], among the technological ones is advanced footwear technology [9]. In this paper, we do not aim to study individual factors but rather to separate both groups of components in a data-driven manner. This setting allows for a substantially broader application range, as no measurements beyond basic race results are required.

3 Race Result Decomposition

In this section, we propose a model for decomposing endurance race results into two distinct components: those associated with the race itself and those associated with the individual athletes. First, we elaborate on the underlying motivation and assumptions, before we introduce technical details of our decomposition model. Then, we proceed by discussing its implication on analyzing race data.

We focus on endurance race results where individual performance is the predominant factor in races and components, such as team tactics, race dynamics, and drafting, are less important. While this may be considered a reasonable assumption for typical road races in running and time trial competitions in cycling, among others, it is less so in typical cycling road races. From a data perspective, we consider races where outcomes are measured by a single value, typically by a time or distance measurement. Hence, we start of a straightforward race results collection comprising a set of races and athletes: For each athlete-race combination, this dataset contains either a valid race result or a special flag, if the athlete did not compete in this particular race. This type of dataset can be compiled for a variety of endurance sports easily, and we will present real-world results for regional running road races in the experimental results section.

We assume each athlete's fitness level to remain *approximately* constant for the analyzed period of time, hence, multi-season datasets are less suitable for our approach. Drawing on this assumption, race results from athletes competing in *multiple competitions* can be used for estimating race conditions, as athlete performances in races correlate with more or less favorable race conditions. Obviously, race data from athletes competing in a single race only does not provide meaningful information for this purpose. As races are not deterministic processes, we have to consider a random component which impacts race results and captures incomplete knowledge of the overall process. Starting from a potentially large dataset comprising results from multiple athletes and races, we aim at limiting the impact of this inherent randomness in each individual result.

As noted above, separating race- and athlete-related components in this type of data becomes much simpler once we have access to either one. However, since neither is known *a priori*, the major challenge is to unpack both simultaneously.

3.1 Decomposition Model

Assume we are given an overall number of m athletes competing in n races. We proceed from a $m \times n$ nonnegative real matrix of race results $X \in \mathbb{R}_+^{m \times n}$, with $X_{ij} \geq 0$ storing the outcome for athlete i in race j. In this setting, race outcomes X_{ij} typically represent a time measurement for a given race course, or the distance covered within a fixed period of time on a given race course.

We consider an unsupervised approach by applying nonnegative matrix factorization (NMF) [7] to the race result matrix X to solve the decomposition problem. Hence, we aim at solving the following optimization problem for a given rank d with $1 \leq d \leq \min(m, n)$:

$$\arg\min_{A,R} \frac{1}{2} \sum_{ij} (X_{ij} - \sum_k A_{ik} R_{kj})^2 = \arg\min_{A,R} \frac{1}{2} \sum_{ij} (X - AR)_{ij}^2 \qquad (1)$$

where $A \in \mathbb{R}_+^{m \times d}$ and $R \in \mathbb{R}_+^{d \times n}$. Hence, NMF computes an approximation AR of rank d of the race result matrix X:

$$X \approx AR. \qquad (2)$$

In practice, we typically need to account for a significant number of missing values in X, as only a subset of athletes competes in a particular given race. Weighted nonnegative matrix factorization (WNMF) [14] is an extension of NMF, which allows to consider missing data by adding a binary $m \times n$ matrix P in the optimization problem, where $P_{ij} = 0$, if X_{ij} is missing, otherwise $P_{ij} = 1$:

$$\arg\min_{A,\,R} \frac{1}{2} \sum_{ij} P_{ij}(X - AR)_{ij}^2. \qquad (3)$$

Note that solutions are not unique as simultaneously permuting columns of A and rows of R, or rescaling both matrices, yields the same objective value.

While it is obvious that the race data matrix X contains only nonnegative values, it is less obvious why we should restrict our solution to nonnegative decomposition matrices A and R. Other decomposition techniques, such as principal component analysis (PCA) and vector quantization (VQ), do not impose this constraint. However, as has been demonstrated in the seminal paper [7], PCA and VQ tend to learn linear combinations that typically involve complex cancellations and where many basis elements lack intuitive meaning. In contrast, in NMF no subtractions can occur and more intuitive, parts-based representations are learned, an appealing property which has led to increasing attention in recent years in several application fields, among those are astrophysics [10] and bioinformatics [5]. From a statistical perspective, solutions of (3) are maximum likelihood estimators for A and R, if we assume additive i.i.d. Gaussian noise with mean 0 and standard deviation σ for race results X_{ij} [2].

From a computational perspective, it was proved in [3] that the optimization problem (3) is NP-hard, even for rank $d = 1$. Computing the global optimum solution is therefore not realistic in general, and we have to resort to approximation algorithms. As a side note, for the rank $d = 1$ case *without* missing data, the global minimizer can be computed in a straightforward manner based on singular value decomposition [4]. For our experiments, we implemented a straightforward multiplicative update approach [6] to compute approximate solutions based on the matrix update rules for WNMF given in [4]. While more sophisticated optimization techniques are available, this straightforward approach proved to be both efficient and robust in our race data experiments.

3.2 Interpreting Decomposition Results

In this section, we will elaborate more on interpreting matrix decompositions for race results. For a given rank value d, the $X \in \mathbb{R}_+^{m \times n}$ race result matrix is factorized into $X \approx AR$, where m and n correspond to the number of athletes and races, respectively. Here, the $m \times d$ matrix A is associated with *athletes*, and more precisely, row k stores a d-dimensional nonnegative characterization for athlete k. Likewise, the $d \times n$ matrix R is linked to *races*, and column l stores a d-dimensional nonnegative characterization of race l. The choice of the rank d is the only hyperparameter in our model and controls the length of the athlete and race characterizations. We focus on the case $d = 1$. Here, the approximation of a race result X_{ij} for athlete i in race j simplifies to the product of two values, $X_{ij} \approx A_i R_j$, where $A_i \stackrel{\text{def}}{=} A_{i1}$ and $R_j \stackrel{\text{def}}{=} R_{1j}$. Therefore, the value A_i can be interpreted as the basic fitness level for athlete i, while R_j integrates all performance-related properties of race j. These race-related properties typically vary between races, but remain roughly constant for all athletes in the same race. As stated above, typical factors relevant in many endurance races are:

- weather (temperature, humidity, precipitation, wind)
- course terrain profile (elevation profile, surface, number / type of turns)
- altitude

As noted above, there exists a scaling degree of freedom for solutions of the optimization problem (3). We propose the following average race normalization[1]:

$$R^{\text{avg}} \stackrel{\text{def}}{=} \frac{1}{n} \sum_j R_j \tag{4}$$

$$A_i^{\text{norm}} \stackrel{\text{def}}{=} A_i \cdot R^{\text{avg}} \quad \text{and} \quad R_j^{\text{norm}} \stackrel{\text{def}}{=} \frac{R_j}{R^{\text{avg}}} \tag{5}$$

Normalization yields better interpretability of the decomposition results:

$$X_{ij} \approx A_i^{\text{norm}} \cdot R_j^{\text{norm}} \tag{6}$$

While A_i^{norm} represents a reference race result for athlete i assuming average race conditions, R_j^{norm} is normalized such that a value of 1.0 corresponds to *average* race conditions in the dataset.

3.3 Applications

In this section, we elaborate more on applications for the decomposition matrices A^{norm} and R^{norm} and rank value $d = 1$. First of all, R^{norm} allows to compare general race conditions for two races k and l in a principled quantitative manner. For example, suppose that $R_k^{\text{norm}} = 1.03$ and $R_l^{\text{norm}} = 0.99$, then race results in race k will typically be approximately 4% higher compared to l. In contrast to simple race statistics, such as mean or median results, race decomposition approaches are potentially more robust with respect to the athlete performance distribution and allow comparing races with more or less elite level participation as has been noted in [11,12], as long as there is some participation overlap. In the experimental section, we will demonstrate this problem on real-world data.

Conceptually, our approach is of retrospective nature and aims at analyzing past race results, since environmental conditions may change in the future.

---
[1] Median-based normalization is another straightforward option.

However, R^{norm} may allow identifying more favorable races, assuming that static race conditions, such as the course terrain profile, are dominant. In [12], a two-step approach is considered for computing hypothetical equivalent flat distances for comparing races, where race result matrix factorization is combined with an elevation profile regression step.

As A^{norm} encodes general athlete fitness levels, we can compare two athletes k and l by their associated values A_k^{norm} and A_l^{norm}, even though they did not compete in the same race (see [11]). Beyond ranking athletes by their fitness level, our normalization method allows for a quantitative comparison as fitness levels represent hypothetical race results for an average race. Moreover, assuming that athlete i did not compete in race j, a hypothetical race result can be estimated by $\hat{X}_{ij} \stackrel{\text{def}}{=} A_i^{\text{norm}} \cdot R_j^{\text{norm}}$, which technically is a data imputation approach for missing results. For actual race results, residual values

$$D_{ij} \stackrel{\text{def}}{=} X_{ij} - A_i^{\text{norm}} \cdot R_j^{\text{norm}} = X_{ij} - \hat{X}_{ij}$$

provide some insight into whether the outcome for athlete i in race j is above or below the expected level.

In many endurance sports, scoring systems are used to aggregate results over a series of races. Here, race condition normalization X_{ij}/R_j^{norm} may be considered as a preprocessing step for result aggregation as an alternative to uncalibrated and rank-based approaches.

4 Experimental Results

In this section, we present empirical results of our approach on race data decomposition. Our first study is devoted to real-world running race data, while our second study considers simulated data to provide a more fine-grained analysis of the properties of our approach.

In our experimental studies, we focus on the case rank $d = 1$, where race results are approximated by

$$X_{ij} \approx A_i^{\text{norm}} \cdot R_j^{\text{norm}}.$$

As stated above, normalized matrix decomposition values have a straightforward interpretation for $d = 1$, since A^{norm} represents reference race results for athletes under average race conditions and R^{norm} encodes race-related performance components. As we will discuss below, missing data is a major issue in our real-world experimental study.

As stated in Sect. 3.1, solving the underlying WNMF problem is computationally very demanding as it is NP-hard. For our experimental study, we used an iterative approximation approach based on multiplicative updates [6] using the WNMF update rules derived in [4] for the weighted sum of squared differences loss function. The matrices A and R were initialized randomly by sampling elements from a uniform distribution over $[0, 1]$. The factorization algorithm stopped once the relative loss change between two subsequent iterations fell below a tolerance value of 10^{-8}. Normalization, i.e., computing A^{norm} and R^{norm}, was conducted as a postprocessing step (see Eqs. (4) and (5)).

4.1 Real-World Data for Road Running

Data Preparation and Characterization. We conducted a study on results from regional road races in running. The dataset consists of publicly available results[2] from local to regional level 10k road races in Westphalia, a region of northwestern Germany and a regional district of the German Athletics Association (DLV), for the years 2022 and 2023. The raw dataset was compiled on 2024/11/06 using regional district (= *Westfalen*) and race category (= *road race*) as filter criteria. Note that these races are characterized by relatively flat to moderately hilly courses with limited elevation change. Hence, altitude level can be neglected as a relevant performance impacting factor for these races.

The raw dataset contains 6784 individual results for 50 races in 2022 and 9565 results for 52 races in 2023 with valid entries for the considered fields, i.e., result time, name, sex, year of birth. Since this dataset does not include any unique identifier for athletes, such as a national athlete ID, we consider results to originate from the same athlete, if all of the following three records are identical: name, sex, and year of birth. After matching records, we applied the following two-step filtering process to compose a common dataset for all experiments. Step one consists of removing athletes who competed in a single race only, as we assume these records to provide limited information for the decomposition process. In step two, we removed races with less than 10 valid result entries remaining after the athlete removal step.

After preprocessing, the final dataset for 2022 consists of 2302 result records for 904 athletes in 40 races, and 3832 result records for 1309 athletes in 47 races (see Table 1 for more details on the dataset properties). For each year, we composed a m-by-n nonnegative matrix $X \in \mathbb{R}_+^{m \times n}$ for all combinations of athletes and races, where X_{ij} stores the result for athlete i in race j. Note that 93.6% and 93.8% of the matrix entries are missing for 2022 and 2023, respectively, due to the fact that athletes competed in a subset of races only. Hence, dealing with missing data is of particular importance here.

Results on Algorithmic Stability. We conducted an initial set of experiments on this dataset to analyze algorithmic initialization sensitivity by solving the decomposition problem for 100 random initializations of A and R. Despite the huge number of missing values, the algorithm was rather robust, as indicated by the *maximum* standard deviation for matrix entries in A^{norm} and R^{norm} of $4.08 \cdot 10^{-1}$ and $8.58 \cdot 10^{-5}$ for 2022, and $9.09 \cdot 10^{-2}$ and $2.96 \cdot 10^{-5}$ for 2023. Moreover, robustness with respect to random initialization can be further increased by reducing the termination tolerance value.

Results on Race-Factors. We computed race result decompositions for 2022 and 2023 (detailed results are given in the supplementary section in Tables 8

---

[2] See https://ladv.de/westfalen/ergebnisse or as an alternative source https://ergebnisse.leichtathletik.de, as part of the official website of the German Athletics Association.

Table 1. Race dataset properties (after preprocessing).

		Year	
		2022	2023
Results		2302	3832
Races		40	47
Athletes		904	1309
Race results (in minutes)	min	31:03	31:18
	max	1:21:33	1:26:26
	mean	48:33	48:52
	median	47:56	48:16
	SD	8:20	8:36
Result entries (per race)	min	15	10
	max	168	328
	mean	57.5	81.5
	median	49.0	53.0
	SD	38.9	75.7
Result entries (per athlete)	min	2	2
	max	13	14
	mean	2.5	2.9
	median	2.0	2.0
	SD	1.1	1.6

and 9). The race factors R_j^{norm} are compared with normalized mean and median results, i.e., a normalized mean or median value of 1.0 corresponds to a global dataset mean or median race result.

The Pearson correlation coefficients calculated between mean / median race results and R_j^{norm} are 0.509 and 0.432 for the year 2022, and 0.226 and 0.148 for the year 2023. These results indicate a rather limited positive linear correlation between the r-factors and both the mean and median race outcomes, hence, providing initial evidence that these approaches for capturing race-related components are conceptually different.

As most of the race courses in this dataset are characterized by limited elevation change and took place at a similar low altitude level, we hypothesized that weather conditions are of particular importance for differences in race conditions and hence in race results. Therefore, we grouped the races into monthly bins and computed normalized mean and median results, and mean r-factors. There are some important observations to be pointed out in Tables 3 and 4. The overall range of normalized mean and median values is substantially larger. Moreover, we can observe a seasonal pattern for r-factor values both in 2022 and 2023, while this pattern is much less pronounced, if at all visible, for mean and median values. Figure 1 provides bar chart visualizations for this seasonal pattern. With respect to r-factors, the best race conditions could be observed in April and October for 2022, and in February and October for 2023.

Apart from seasonal patterns, race-specific comparisons provide some evidence that r-factor values are less biased with respect to more or less elite level athlete distribution: In 2023, races 9 and 10 overlap as the state road championships (race 10) have been conducted as part of race 9 (see Table 9 in the supplementary section). Here, the mean and median for both athlete subsets are substantially different (mean: 0.963 vs. 0.846 and median: 0.935 vs. 0.824), presumably due to the fact that the state championship (sub-)race comprises a more competitive athlete subset. When interpreted as a race condition characterization, mean and median values are obviously misleading here, as both races have been conducted simultaneously on the same course. In contrast, the r-factor values for these races are considerably less impacted by the athlete performance distribution (1.006 vs. 1.000).

Imputation Results. We conducted an additional experiment focusing on data imputation only. In each subexperiment, we removed a single valid result entry X_{ij} from the data matrix, computed both decomposition matrices A^{norm} and R^{norm} using the remaining entries, and estimated this additional missing entry (see (6)). We compared each estimated entry with the ground truth one using the well-known mean absolute error (MAE) and the mean relative error (MRE) measures as evaluation measures, and averaged the results over all subexperiments for non-missing result entries in X. As alternative imputation methods, we considered athlete-based mean and median value imputation.

The imputation results are shown in Table 2, where for both 2022 and 2023, mean and median achieve comparable estimation accuracy, while WNMF-based imputation is the most accurate method in this evaluation. As stated in the dataset properties Table 1, the mean number of result entries per athlete is 2.5 and 2.9, respectively. Moreover, the mean standard deviation per athlete is 71.0 and 73.3, respectively. Hence, considering this typically very small number of highly variable data points per athlete (out of which one is masked out in the

Table 2. Evaluation of imputation error for WNMF-imputation and athlete-based mean and median imputation. Year-wise column-normalized background coloring is added to emphasize differences.

Year	Imputation Method	MAE	MRE
2022	WNMF	106.3	0.0354
	mean	117.6	0.0391
	median	117.9	0.0391
2023	WNMF	107.4	0.0352
	mean	112.9	0.0370
	median	112.7	0.0368

Table 3. Normalized mean, median, and r-factors for races grouped by month for 2022. Note that the dataset does not include outdoor race results for 1/2022. Column-normalized background coloring is added to emphasize differences.

Month	Athletes	mean	median	r-factor
2	204	1.017	1.020	1.008
3	256	0.957	0.952	0.996
4	169	1.030	1.039	0.990
5	180	0.988	0.993	0.992
6	102	0.980	0.974	1.003
7	235	1.032	1.043	1.016
8	156	1.018	1.009	1.016
9	273	1.049	1.046	1.014
10	252	0.963	0.968	0.985
11	182	1.004	0.992	0.992
12	293	0.972	0.974	1.004

Table 4. Normalized mean, median, and r-factors for races grouped by month for 2023. Column-normalized background coloring is added to emphasize differences.

Month	athletes	mean	median	r-factor
1	507	1.010	1.009	0.991
2	212	1.013	1.013	0.981
3	239	0.983	0.979	0.994
4	201	1.040	1.048	0.990
5	308	1.022	1.014	1.009
6	260	1.001	0.977	1.019
7	409	1.021	1.031	0.996
8	820	0.969	0.966	0.995
9	353	1.031	1.047	0.994
10	176	0.930	0.925	0.978
11	63	0.953	0.969	0.983
12	284	1.010	1.005	1.011

above stated evaluation process), we should not expect a high level of accuracy when estimating individual results. In a secondary evaluation, we confirmed that imputation accuracy generally increases for all methods with the number of results available for the considered athlete.

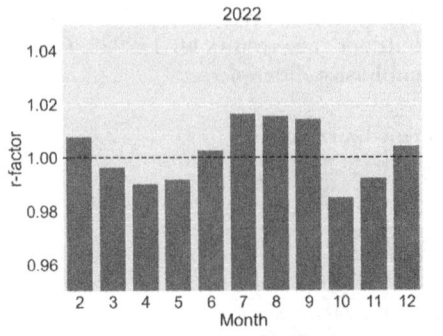 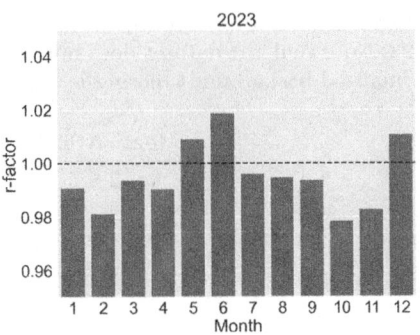

Fig. 1. Average r-factors for races grouped by month for 2022 and 2023. Note that the dataset does not include outdoor race results for 1/2022. The reference line corresponds to the mean r-factor among all races for the considered year.

4.2 Simulated Data

In addition to experiments on real-world data, we conducted a series of experiments on simulated race data in order to analyze the algorithmic sensitivity with respect to the missing value rate, the number of races, and the number of athletes. The conceptual difference between real-world data and simulated data is that the data-generating process is known for the latter one, and more specifically the ground truth matrix entries $\hat{A}_i^{\text{norm}}$ and $\hat{R}_j^{\text{norm}}$. Hence, we are able to quantitatively evaluate the accuracy of our approach in estimating these matrices given noisy race data $\hat{X}$.

The ground truth athlete-related entries $\hat{A}_i^{\text{norm}}$ were randomly sampled from a uniform distribution over $[1800, 2700]$ corresponding to reference race times between 30 min and 90 min. The race-related entries $\hat{R}_j^{\text{norm}}$ were randomly sampled from a uniform distribution over $[0.9, 1.1]$. Both choices are based roughly on the observed real-world value ranges. Race results $\hat{X}_{ij}$ were computed as

$$\hat{X}_{ij} = \hat{A}_i^{\text{norm}} \cdot \hat{R}_j^{\text{norm}} + \epsilon_{ij},$$

where the additive noise components ϵ_{ij} were randomly sampled from a Gaussian distribution with mean $\mu = 0$ and standard deviation $\sigma = 70$.

We used the following approach for simulating missing values in $\hat{X}$: In each row, one entry is randomly selected as a valid data element (which corresponds to the requirement that each athlete has to compete in at least one race). Likewise, we randomly select one entry in each column to be a valid data element (which corresponds to the requirement that each race is associated with at least one result). Note that these two steps are conducted independently of each other. All remaining entries are randomly assigned to the valid and missing data categories in order to match the required overall missing data rate. For each choice of parameters, we computed average MAE and MRE values over 100 repeated simulation runs.

Table 5. Error evaluation (MAE, MRE) for A^{norm} and R^{norm} using simulated race data with varying missing value rates. Column-normalized background coloring is added to emphasize differences.

missing values	A^{norm} MAE	MRE	R^{norm} MAE	MRE
0.00	18.4	0.0082	0.0075	0.0075
0.10	18.0	0.0081	0.0072	0.0072
0.20	17.3	0.0077	0.0067	0.0067
0.30	17.5	0.0078	0.0067	0.0067
0.40	16.5	0.0074	0.0059	0.0059
0.50	17.4	0.0078	0.0059	0.0059
0.60	20.0	0.0090	0.0071	0.0071
0.70	19.7	0.0088	0.0061	0.0061
0.80	23.1	0.0103	0.0066	0.0066
0.90	30.4	0.0137	0.0069	0.0070
0.91	31.8	0.0143	0.0067	0.0067
0.92	33.7	0.0152	0.0069	0.0069
0.93	36.6	0.0165	0.0077	0.0077
0.94	38.0	0.0171	0.0068	0.0068
0.95	42.0	0.0189	0.0077	0.0076
0.96	46.8	0.0211	0.0085	0.0085
0.97	53.4	0.0240	0.0104	0.0104

Missing Values. In a first experimental evaluation, we fixed the number of athletes (=1000) and the number of races (=50), while varying the fraction of missing values from 0.0 to 0.8 in equal steps of 0.1, and between 0.90 and 0.97 with a step size of 0.01. Note that there is a limit for the fraction of missing values of 0.97 here, as for 0.98, which corresponds to 1000 missing values, all missing entries would already be required for ensuring the minimum valid data constraint for athletes only.

The results shown in Table 5 indicate that up to a missing value fraction of roughly 0.9 there is a continuous, but limited increase in the estimation error measures for A, while for R the estimation error is at a rather stable level up to a missing value fraction of 0.96. Then, all error measures increase substantially at the final missing value fraction of 0.97.

Number of Athletes. A second experimental evaluation is devoted to the number of athletes. Here, we fixed the number of races (=50) and the missing value rate (=0.9), while the number of athletes varied between 100 and 10,000,000 with a multiplicative step factor of 10. Note that our missing value model requires the number of athletes to be greater than 50.

Table 6. Error evaluation (MAE, MRE) for A^{norm} and R^{norm} using simulated race data with varying numbers of athletes. Column-normalized background coloring is added to emphasize differences.

athletes	A^{norm} MAE	MRE	R^{norm} MAE	MRE
100	32.0	0.0144	0.0114	0.0114
1000	30.5	0.0137	0.0070	0.0070
10000	30.9	0.0139	0.0067	0.0067
100000	31.0	0.0139	0.0069	0.0069
1000000	30.2	0.0136	0.0064	0.0064
10000000	30.6	0.0137	0.0065	0.0065

Table 7. Error evaluation for simulation race data with varying numbers of races. Column-normalized background coloring is added to emphasize differences.

races	A^{norm} MAE	MRE	R^{norm} MAE	MRE
20	49.0	0.0220	0.0103	0.0104
30	40.6	0.0182	0.0090	0.0090
40	35.0	0.0157	0.0081	0.0081
50	31.2	0.0140	0.0075	0.0076
60	27.4	0.0123	0.0062	0.0062
70	25.8	0.0116	0.0064	0.0064
80	23.5	0.0105	0.0055	0.0055
90	22.6	0.0101	0.0056	0.0056
100	21.0	0.0094	0.0052	0.0052

The results shown in Table 6 indicate that the error measures are at a rather stable level over a very large range of the number of athletes, except for the initial number of 100 athletes.

Number of Races. A third experimental evaluation is devoted to the number of races. Here, we fixed the number of athletes (=1000) and the missing value rate (=0.9) while varying the number of races between 20 and 100 with a step size of 10. Note that our missing value model requires the number of races to be greater than 10.

The results given in Table 7 show a continuous error decrease with an increasing number of races. While for 20 and 30 races, the associated error values are comparatively high, error values decrease at a substantially lower rate starting at 40 .

Discussion. In our experimental evaluations on simulated data, the missing value rate and the number of races had the largest impact on the considered error measures. For the missing value rate, the impact on A^{norm} seems to be more pronounced, while the estimation accuracy was more stable for R^{norm}. The impact of the number of races on A^{norm} and R^{norm} seems to be on a similar scale.

In contrast to these findings, there seems to be only a minor impact of the number of athletes on the estimation performance, as suggested by our experiments which cover a large range of values.

5 Conclusions

We propose a novel data-driven approach for separating two essential groups of components from a set of race results: Race conditions and individual performance level. Based on nonnegative matrix factorization for dimensionality reduction, we unpack results into race- and athlete-related quantitative characterizations. Their dimensionality is the only hyperparameter of our method.

We focus on the one-dimensional case in our experimental evaluation, where the normalized values associated with athletes and races have a straightforward interpretation: The athlete component represents a reference race result assuming average conditions and hence a quantification of the individual performance level, while the race value integrates general factors such as weather and course terrain profile.

In the experimental section, we conduct a series of evaluations on real-world race data for local to regional level 10k road running races and simulated race data. We demonstrate that our approach is a practical method for real-world data, and in particular is a mathematically sound and well-suited method for dealing with a high missing value rate. We show that our method provides more robust estimates for race conditions with respect to the particular athlete distribution competing in a race, while simple mean- or median-based techniques suffer from obvious drawbacks and compute biased race estimates. Moreover, we were able to recover seasonal patterns from race-data only, which is consistent with the fact that weather conditions are of particular importance for the considered races which are characterized by limited elevation change and a similar altitude level. A series of experiments on simulated race data suggests that our approach provides stable estimates over a wide range of dataset properties. More precisely, in our experiments, the missing value rate and the number of races had a larger impact on the estimation accuracy, while the number of athletes had less impact. The computational complexity of our approach is rather low and should not be a limiting factor for typical applications.

Unpacking race conditions and individual performance levels provides a variety of interesting applications, such as comparing results of athletes who did not compete in the same race in a sound quantitative manner, comparing past race conditions and potentially identifying favorable future ones, and scoring systems for race series.

We focused on the case $d = 1$, where all components related to particular races and athletes were integrated into associated scalar values. However, for d $>$1 this approach provides a framework for computing multidimensional characterizations as well, which, due to the nonnegativity constraint (see Sect. 3.1), facilitates feature interpretability. From a conceptual and terminological point of view, it is more appropriate to refer to multidimensional race and athlete characterizations as race condition and athlete profiles rather than race condition values and athlete performance levels. Then $\sum_k A_{ik}R_{kj}$ can be interpreted as matching race and athlete *profiles* against each other. It will be interesting to analyze and potentially link individual components of these profiles to known performance factors or explore novel ones. These more fine-grained characterizations may provide an interesting starting point for better understanding the strengths and weaknesses of athletes with respect to race conditions, and allow for better matching those to specific race demands in the future.

Disclosure of Interests. The authors have no competing interests to declare that are relevant to the content of this article.

References

1. Ely, M.R., Cheuvront, S.N., Roberts, W.O., Montain, S.J.: Impact of weather on marathon-running performance. Med. Sci. Sports Exerc. **39**(3), 487–493 (2007)
2. Gillis, N.: Nonnegative Matrix Factorization. Society for Industrial and Applied Mathematics, Philadelphia, PA (2020)
3. Gillis, N., Glineur, F.: Low-rank matrix approximation with weights or missing data is NP-hard. SIAM J. Matrix Anal. Appl. **32**(4), 1149–1165 (2011)
4. Ho, N.D.: Nonnegative matrix factorization - Algorithms and applications. Ph.D. thesis, Université catholique de Louvain (2008)
5. Jagadeesh, K.A., et al.: Identifying disease-critical cell types and cellular processes by integrating single-cell RNA-sequencing and human genetics. Nat. Genet. **54**(10), 1479–1492 (2022)
6. Lee, D., Seung, H.S.: Algorithms for non-negative matrix factorization. In: Leen, T., Dietterich, T., Tresp, V. (eds.) Advances in Neural Information Processing Systems, vol. 13. MIT Press (2000)
7. Lee, D.D., Seung, H.S.: Learning the parts of objects by non-negative matrix factorization. Nature **401**(6755), 788–791 (1999)
8. Nikolaidis, P.T., Di Gangi, S., Chtourou, H., Rüst, C.A., Rosemann, T., Knechtle, B.: The role of environmental conditions on marathon running performance in men competing in Boston marathon from 1897 to 2018. Int. J. Environ. Res. Public Health **16**(4), 614 (2019)
9. Ortega, J.A., Healey, L.A., Swinnen, W., Hoogkamer, W.: Energetics and biomechanics of running footwear with increased longitudinal bending stiffness: a narrative review. Sports Med. **51**(5), 873–894 (2021)
10. Ren, B., Pueyo, L., Zhu, G.B., Debes, J., Duchêne, G.: Non-negative matrix factorization: robust extraction of extended structures. Astrophys. J. **852**(2), 104 (2018)
11. de Smet, D., Verleysen, M., Francaux, M.: Running race times prediction and runner performances comparison using a matrix factorization approach. In: Proceedings of the 5th International Congress on Sport Sciences Research and Technology Support (icSPORTS 2017), pp. 96–101 (2017)

12. de Smet, D., Verleysen, M., Francaux, M., Baijot, L.: Long-distance running routes' flat equivalent distances from race results and elevation profiles. In: Proceedings of the 6th International Congress on Sport Sciences Research and Technology Support - Volume 1: icSPORTS, pp. 56–62. INSTICC, SciTePress (2018)
13. Snyder, K.L., Hoogkamer, W., Triska, C., Taboga, P., Arellano, C.J., Kram, R.: Effects of course design (curves and elevation undulations) on marathon running performance: a comparison of breaking 2 in Monza and the INEOS 1:59 challenge in Vienna. J. Sports Sci. **39**(7), 754–759 (2021)
14. Srebro, N., Jaakkola, T.: Weighted low-rank approximations. In: Proceedings of the 20th International Conference on Machine Learning (ICML), vol. 3, pp. 720–727 (2003)
15. Wang, S., Gao, M., Xiao, X., Jiang, X., Luo, J.: Wasted efforts of elite marathon runners under a warming climate primarily due to atmospheric oxygen reduction. NPJ Climate Atmospheric Sci. **7**(1), 97 (2024)
16. Zavorsky, G.S., Tomko, K.A., Smoliga, J.M.: Declines in marathon performance: sex differences in elite and recreational athletes. PLOS ONE **12**(2), 1–17 (02 2017)

Trajectory Imputation in Multi-agent Sports with Derivative-Accumulating Self-ensemble

Han-Jun Choi[1], Hyunsung Kim[2,3], Minho Lee[4], Minchul Jeong[5], Changjo Kim[3], Jinsung Yoon[3], and Sang-Ki Ko[6(✉)]

[1] KETI, Seongnam, South Korea
hanjun_c@keti.re.kr
[2] KAIST, Daejeon, South Korea
hyunsung.kim@kaist.ac.kr
[3] Fitogether Inc., Seoul, South Korea
{hyunsung.kim,changjo.kim,jinsung.yoon}@fitogether.com
[4] Saarland University, Saarbrücken, Germany
minho.lee@uni-saarland.de
[5] Weflo Inc., Seoul, South Korea
mcjeong@weflo.ai
[6] University of Seoul, Seoul, South Korea
sangkiko@uos.ac.kr

Abstract. Multi-agent trajectory data collected from domains such as team sports often suffer from missing values due to various factors. While many imputation methods have been proposed for spatiotemporal data, they are ill-suited for multi-agent sports, where player movements are highly dynamic and interactions evolve over time. To address these challenges, we propose MIDAS (**M**ulti-agent **I**mputer with **D**erivative-**A**ccumulating **S**elf-ensemble), a data-efficient framework that imputes multi-agent trajectories with high accuracy and physical plausibility. It jointly predicts positions, velocities, and accelerations via a Set Transformer-based neural network and refines them by recursively accumulating predicted velocity and acceleration values. These predictions are then combined using a learnable weighted ensemble to produce final imputed trajectories. Experiments on three sports datasets show that MIDAS significantly outperforms existing baselines, with particularly large margins in limited-data settings. We also demonstrate its utility in downstream tasks such as estimating total distance and pass success probability. The source code is available at https://github.com/gkswns95/midas.git.

Keywords: Sports Analytics · Multi-Agent System · Trajectory Imputation · Deep Learning under Physical Constraints · Weighted Ensemble

---

H.-J. Choi and H. Kim—Contributed equally to the paper.

1 Introduction

Many spatiotemporal domains, such as transportation, robotics, surveillance, and sports, handle multi-agent trajectory data. While advances in computer vision and sensing technologies have facilitated large-scale trajectory data collection, acquiring complete data remains challenging due to various factors such as signal loss in wearable devices and limitations of the camera's field of view (Fig. 1). This prevalence of missing values calls for the development of effective imputation techniques that can accurately reconstruct missing trajectories.

Though various imputation methods have been proposed for spatiotemporal data, applying them to multi-agent sports remains challenging due to their dynamic nature. In particular, while many of them [1,5,16–18,24] have demonstrated their effectiveness in multi-sensor data, including traffic flow or air quality datasets, they do not account for dynamic interactions between agents. In such fixed-sensor networks, spatial relationships typically remain constant over time. In contrast, multi-agent domains such as team sports involve players with continuously changing positions, requiring a suitable architecture for explicitly modeling these dynamic inter-agent relationships while maintaining permutation-equivariance with respect to the agents.

Furthermore, player motion is governed by biomechanical constraints that impose physical limits on speed, acceleration, and directional change. To accurately model such constraints and generate physically plausible trajectories, imputation models must learn nuanced patterns in movement dynamics. This typically requires a large volume of high-quality training data. However, this poses a significant limitation in the sports domain, where player tracking data is often treated as confidential due to the competitive nature of professional leagues.

Addressing these challenges, this paper proposes MIDAS (**M**ulti-agent **I**mputer with **D**erivative-**A**ccumulating **S**elf-ensemble), a framework for multi-agent sports that imputes missing trajectories with high accuracy and data efficiency by explicitly enforcing the physical constraints that real player trajectories

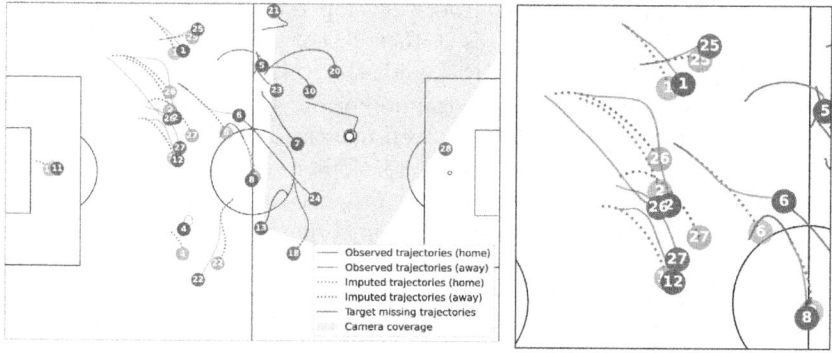

(a) Full-pitch view along with camera coverage   (b) Close-up view

Fig. 1. Example of imputing unobserved player trajectories from tracking data obtained in a soccer broadcast.

should satisfy. First, a neural network equipped with Set Transformers [13] and player-wise bidirectional LSTMs [9] predicts the positions, velocities, and accelerations of missing players. In addition to this *initial prediction* (IP), it generates alternative estimates through *derivative-accumulating prediction* (DAP), which recursively accumulates the predicted velocity and acceleration values from the nearest observed positions in both forward and backward directions. Finally, the learnable soft voting mechanism combines these three predictions, namely IP and forward/backward DAPs, to produce the final imputed trajectories.

The proposed MIDAS overcomes the aforementioned challenges in two aspects. First, by employing the Set Transformer, it models dynamic inter-agent relationships while ensuring permutation-equivariance with respect to agents. Second, MIDAS jointly predicts positions, velocities, and accelerations, and integrates them through a derivative-accumulating self-ensemble mechanism that explicitly enforces their physical consistency. This design enables the model to capture the underlying patterns of player motion, leading to improved data efficiency.

Experiments across three sports datasets demonstrate that MIDAS consistently outperforms existing baselines in terms of both positional accuracy and physical plausibility of imputed trajectories, with particularly large margins in low-data settings. In addition, we showcase real-world applications of MIDAS, including the approximation of physical (e.g., total distance covered) and contextual (e.g., pass success probability) metrics based on imputed trajectories.

2 Related Work

Numerous methods have been proposed for time series and spatiotemporal data imputation. Early models such as BRITS [1], GRU-D [4], and MRNN [28] relied on recurrent models, but suffered from compounding errors due to dependence on their previous predictions. Non-autoregressive frameworks such as NAOMI [16], CSDI [24], and SAITS [7] mitigated this issue by enabling parallel imputation across time steps, improving robustness and efficiency. More recently, methods like TIDER [15] and TimesNet [25] were developed to capture temporal patterns such as seasonality or local biases. Other recent approaches further leverage graph structures (GRIN [6], SPIN [17], and NRTSI [21]), information bottlenecks (TimeCIB [5]), or low-rank priors (ImputeFormer [18]) to enhance imputation performance. Although they perform well on static multi-sensor systems, they are not designed to handle dynamic interactions in multi-agent scenarios.

Meanwhile, several frameworks have proposed dedicated architectures for multi-agent imputation to capture shifting spatial relationships of agents. Notable examples include Graph Imputer [19], GC-VRNN [26], and TranSPORTmer [2], which employ dynamic graph or set attention [13] architectures to model time-varying player interactions. More recently, methods tailored for sports data with advanced architectures have been explored, such as U2Diff [3] and Event2Tracking [10]. However, the former suffers from high computational costs and low data efficiency inherent to diffusion models, while the latter requires manually annotated event data, which are not always available. Interaction modeling has been widely studied in future trajectory forecasting [8,12,14,23,27,29], but these methods are not directly applicable to missing trajectory imputation.

3 Proposed Framework

Our study about multi-agent trajectory imputation assumes a scenario where the missing time intervals of players could differ from one another. To elaborate, let the trajectories of K players be $X_{1:T} = \{\mathbf{x}^k_{1:T}\}^K_{k=1}$, where each player k's input features $\mathbf{x}^k_t$ at each time t consist of their (x,y) position $\mathbf{p}^k_t = (p^k_{t,x}, p^k_{t,y})$, velocity $\mathbf{v}^k_t = (v^k_{t,x}, v^k_{t,y})$, and acceleration $\mathbf{a}^k_t = (a^k_{t,x}, a^k_{t,y})$. Here, the velocity and acceleration are calculated from the position values by the following approximations:

$$\mathbf{v}^k_t \approx \frac{\mathbf{p}^k_t - \mathbf{p}^k_{t-1}}{\Delta t}, \quad \mathbf{a}^k_t \approx \frac{\mathbf{v}^k_{t+1} - \mathbf{v}^k_t}{\Delta t} \tag{1}$$

where Δt is the difference between adjacent time steps.

In our scenario, each $\mathbf{x}^k_{1:T}$ has missing parts identified by a masking sequence $\mathbf{m}^k_{1:T} = (m^k_1, \ldots, m^k_T)$ where $m^k_t = 1$ if $\mathbf{x}^k_t$ is *observed* and 0 if it is *missing*. Then, an imputation model aims to take the incomplete data $\{\mathbf{m}^k_{1:T} \odot \mathbf{x}^k_{1:T}\}^K_{k=1}$ as input and produce imputed trajectories $\{\hat{\mathbf{x}}^k_{1:T}\}^K_{k=1}$. Combining these with the observed fragments results in complete trajectories, i.e.,

$$\tilde{\mathbf{x}}^k_{1:T} = \mathbf{m}^k_{1:T} \odot \mathbf{x}^k_{1:T} + (\mathbb{1}_T - \mathbf{m}^k_{1:T}) \odot \hat{\mathbf{x}}^k_{1:T}, \quad k = 1, \ldots, K. \tag{2}$$

The novelty of the proposed framework lies in the mechanism of enhancing the model performance by combining positions directly predicted by a neural network and those resulting from accumulating predicted derivatives (i.e., velocity and acceleration values). To elaborate on the details of the proposed mechanism, the remainder of this section consists of the following four parts: Sect. 3.1 describes the neural network for initial prediction, Sect. 3.2 introduces the derivative accumulation process for alternative predictions, Sect. 3.3 describes the weighted ensemble mechanism to combine multiple predictions resulting from the previous sections, and Sect. 3.4 explains the loss function for model training. See Fig. 2 illustrating the overall architecture of our framework.

3.1 Neural Network-Based Initial Prediction

This section describes the neural network architecture that makes *initial prediction* (IP) of imputed trajectories. It takes partially observed trajectories $\{\mathbf{m}^k_{1:T} \odot \mathbf{x}^k_{1:T}\}^K_{k=1}$ as an input and predicts each player k's full trajectory

$$\hat{\mathbf{x}}^{k,i}_{1:T} = \{(\hat{p}^{k,i}_{t,x}, \hat{p}^{k,i}_{t,y}, \hat{v}^{k,i}_{t,x}, \hat{v}^{k,i}_{t,y}, \hat{a}^{k,i}_{t,x}, \hat{a}^{k,i}_{t,y})\}^T_{t=1}, \tag{3}$$

where the superscript i stands for "initial".

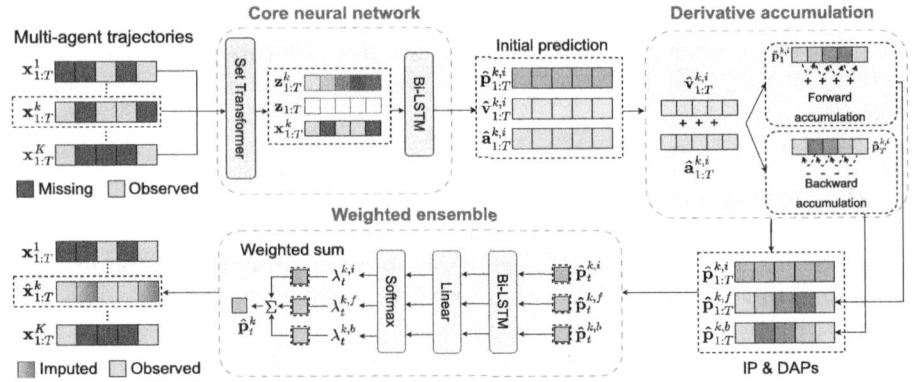

Fig. 2. Overview of the proposed framework.

Since there is generally no inherent order among players in team sports, modeling their movements requires ensuring *permutation-equivariance*. That is, permuting the input order should not affect each player's output, except for applying the same permutation in the output order. Following a recent study on the ball trajectory inference in team sports [11], we employ Set Transformer [13] to ensure the permutation-equivariance of outputs.

To be specific, we obtain permutation-equivariant player-wise embeddings $\{\mathbf{z}_t^k\}_{k=1}^K$ from the encoder of a Set Transformer and a single permutation-invariant embedding $\mathbf{z}_t$ from a full Set Transformer for each time step t:

$$(\mathbf{z}_t^1, \ldots, \mathbf{z}_t^K) = \text{ST-Encoder}(m_t^1 \mathbf{x}_t^1, \ldots, m_t^K \mathbf{x}_t^K),$$
$$\mathbf{z}_t = \text{SetTransformer}(m_t^1 \mathbf{x}_t^1, \ldots, m_t^K \mathbf{x}_t^K). \quad (4)$$

Frame-by-frame application of the Set Transformer to the input features yields embeddings $\{(\mathbf{z}_t^1, \ldots, \mathbf{z}_t^K, \mathbf{z}_t)\}_{t=1}^T$. Then, bidirectional LSTMs [9] sharing weights across players extract the sequential information from the concatenated sequence $\{(\mathbf{x}_t^k, \mathbf{z}_t^k, \mathbf{z}_t)\}_{t=1}^T$ per player k by updating joint hidden states:

$$\mathbf{h}_t^{k,f} = \text{LSTM}^f(\mathbf{x}_t^k, \mathbf{z}_t^k, \mathbf{z}_t; \mathbf{h}_{t-1}^{k,f}), \quad \mathbf{h}_t^{k,b} = \text{LSTM}^b(\mathbf{x}_t^k, \mathbf{z}_t^k, \mathbf{z}_t; \mathbf{h}_{t+1}^{k,b}) \quad (5)$$

Lastly, a fully-connected layer decodes the joint hidden state to output a prediction $\hat{\mathbf{x}}_t^{k,i} = \text{FC}(\mathbf{h}_t^{k,f}, \mathbf{h}_t^{k,b})$ at each time t. In later sections, we combine it with alternative predictions to get a more accurate final prediction.

3.2 Derivative-Accumulating Prediction

In this section, we start from the fact that players' acceleration values highly vary over time since they are directly related to their stochastic intents. In contrast, velocities are more correlated across neighboring time steps, and positions exhibit even stronger autocorrelation than their derivatives. This implies that accurately predicting acceleration values can lead to more stable and accurate position estimates, provided the physical relationships in Eq. (1) are maintained. However, since the model introduced in Sect. 3.1 does not enforce these relationships in its outputs $\{\hat{\mathbf{x}}_{1:T}^{k,i}\}_{k=1}^{K}$, accurate prediction of the derivatives does not necessarily lead to improved position accuracy.

Taking this into account, we make alternative *derivative-accumulating predictions* (DAP), which enforces the physical relationships in Eq. (1) for improved stability. Specifically, given a missing segment (t_s, t_e) for a player k, we recursively predict positions inside the segment by accumulating velocities and accelerations in either direction using the following equation derived from Eq. (1):

$$\mathbf{p}_{t+1}^k \approx \mathbf{p}_t^k + \mathbf{v}_{t+1}^k \Delta t, \quad \mathbf{v}_{t+1}^k \approx \mathbf{v}_t^k + \mathbf{a}_t^k \Delta t. \tag{6}$$

That is, along the forward direction, we start from the observed position $\mathbf{p}_{t_s}^k$ by setting $\hat{\mathbf{p}}_{t_s}^{k,f} = \mathbf{p}_{t_s}^k$ and recursively add predicted velocities and accelerations to obtain *forward predictions* $\hat{\mathbf{p}}_t^{k,f}$ for $t \in (t_s, t_e)$ as follows:

$$\hat{\mathbf{p}}_t^{k,f} \approx \hat{\mathbf{p}}_{t-1}^{k,f} + \hat{\mathbf{v}}_t^{k,i} \Delta t \approx \hat{\mathbf{p}}_{t-1}^{k,f} + (\hat{\mathbf{v}}_{t-1}^{k,i} + \hat{\mathbf{a}}_{t-1}^{k,i} \Delta t)\Delta t \tag{7}$$

Likewise, we start from the observed position $\mathbf{p}_{t_e}^k$ at the opposite endpoint and recursively subtract the predicted derivatives to obtain *backward predictions* $\hat{\mathbf{p}}_t^{k,b}$.

Adopting DAPs instead of initial prediction carries several advantages. First, since the loss between these DAPs and the ground truth penalizes unstable predictions of the velocity and acceleration, minimizing it improves the smoothness of the predicted derivatives. Considering that existing position-oriented imputation models suffer from fluctuating trajectories, these smooth derivatives have a clear advantage in that they result in more plausible positional predictions. Furthermore, enforcing the relationships between the physical quantities imposes an additional inductive bias on the model, making it more data-efficient.

3.3 Weighted Ensemble of Multiple Predictions

Alhough DAP introduced in Sect. 3.2 has clear advantages over IP resulting from Sect. 3.1, it also has a potential drawback known as the *error compounding problem*. Because DAP only relies on the observation at an endpoint as an anchor and the predicted derivatives that are accumulated on the anchor, prediction errors tend to grow as the number of iterations in Eq. (7) (or its backward counterpart) increases. In contrast, IP is robust to this problem since it is less sensitive to estimates at certain time steps.

To balance this trade-off, we take a hybrid approach that combines the strengths of both IP and DAP. Rather than exclusively relying on one prediction, it performs a soft voting ensemble by computing a weighted sum of three predictions, IP and forward/backward DAPs. These weights are dynamically learned through an additional player-wise Bi-LSTM, which adapts the contribution of each prediction at each time step.

More specifically, for each player k and time step t, we feed the three predictions $\hat{\mathbf{x}}_t^{k,i}, \hat{\mathbf{p}}_t^{k,f}, \hat{\mathbf{p}}_t^{k,b}$ along with the context embeddings $\mathbf{z}_t^k, \mathbf{z}_t$ from Eq. (4) into a Bi-LSTM that updates its hidden states:

$$\tilde{\mathbf{h}}_t^{k,f} = \text{LSTM}^f(\hat{\mathbf{x}}_t^{k,i}, \hat{\mathbf{p}}_t^{k,f}, \hat{\mathbf{p}}_t^{k,b}, \mathbf{z}_t^k, \mathbf{z}_t, \gamma_t; \tilde{\mathbf{h}}_{t-1}^{k,f}), \tag{8}$$

$$\tilde{\mathbf{h}}_t^{k,b} = \text{LSTM}^b(\hat{\mathbf{x}}_t^{k,i}, \hat{\mathbf{p}}_t^{k,f}, \hat{\mathbf{p}}_t^{k,b}, \mathbf{z}_t^k, \mathbf{z}_t, \gamma_t; \tilde{\mathbf{h}}_{t+1}^{k,b}). \tag{9}$$

where $\gamma_t = \exp(-\max\{0, \mathbf{W}_\gamma \delta_t + \mathbf{b}_\gamma\})$ is the temporal decay factor introduced in BRITS [1], indicating the distance of t from observed endpoints. We define $\delta_t = (t - t_s, t_e - t)$ to provide symmetric time gaps for weighting the bidirectional DAPs. Then, a fully-connected layer with a softmax activation returns

$$(\lambda_t^{k,i}, \lambda_t^{k,f}, \lambda_t^{k,b}) = \text{Softmax}(\text{FC}(\tilde{\mathbf{h}}_t^{k,f}, \tilde{\mathbf{h}}_t^{k,b})) \tag{10}$$

that add up to 1. Based on these weights, the model yields a final prediction

$$\hat{\mathbf{p}}_t^k = \lambda_t^{k,i} \hat{\mathbf{p}}_t^{k,i} + \lambda_t^{k,f} \hat{\mathbf{p}}_t^{k,f} + \lambda_t^{k,b} \hat{\mathbf{p}}_t^{k,b}. \tag{11}$$

Combining this final prediction with the observed fragments by Eq. (2) results in complete trajectories across the entire period:

$$\tilde{\mathbf{x}}_{1:T}^k = \mathbf{m}_{1:T}^k \odot \mathbf{x}_{1:T}^k + (\mathbb{1}_T - \mathbf{m}_{1:T}^k) \odot \hat{\mathbf{x}}_{1:T}^k, \tag{12}$$

where $\hat{\mathbf{x}}_t^k = (\hat{p}_{t,x}^k, \hat{p}_{t,y}^k, \hat{v}_{t,x}^{k,i}, \hat{v}_{t,y}^{k,i}, \hat{a}_{t,x}^{k,i}, \hat{a}_{t,y}^{k,i})$.

Figure 3 illustrates how MIDAS dynamically adjusts ensemble weights depending on the characteristics of the missing segment. For Player 2, who has a short and stable missing trajectory, the model assigns negligible weight to IP, relying more on DAPs for imputation. In contrast, Player 3's longer and more variable missing trajectory leads to higher IP weights, especially in the middle where DAP errors may accumulate. This highlights MIDAS's ability to improve the final prediction by adaptively combining its components.

3.4 Loss Function

In our framework, improving the accuracy of the prediction at each stage contributes to a more reliable ensemble output. Therefore, we minimize not only the loss between the final ensemble prediction and the true trajectories but also

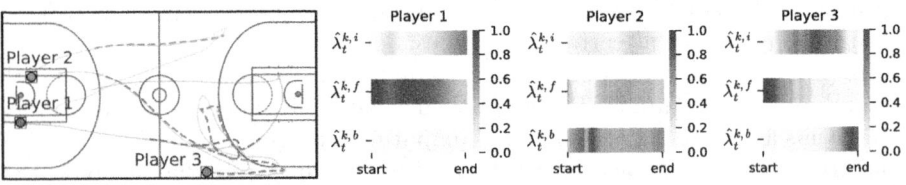

Fig. 3. Example of ensemble weights for individual imputed trajectories, where circles indicate each player's initial position.

Table 1. Details on the three sports datasets.

Split	Soccer		Basketball		A. Football	
	Matches	Frames	Matches	Frames	Matches	Frames
Training	2	65,014	70	1,621,835	—	425,000
Validation	0.5	20,104	10	216,118	—	52,150
Test	0.5	21,242	20	468,885	—	—

the loss of each auxiliary prediction. Specifically, we compute the mean absolute errors (MAEs) for the IP and DAPs as well as the ensemble prediction, respectively, and train the entire architecture by minimizing the sum of these MAEs. Formally, for the MAE losses $\mathcal{L}^i$ of the IP, $\mathcal{L}^f$ and $\mathcal{L}^b$ for the bidirectional DAPs, and $\mathcal{L}^h$ for the ensemble prediction, the model is trained by minimizing

$$\mathcal{L}^{\text{MIDAS}} = \mathcal{L}^i + \mathcal{L}^f + \mathcal{L}^b + \mathcal{L}^h. \tag{13}$$

4 Experiments

In this section, we conduct experiments on multiple sports datasets to evaluate the performance of MIDAS and its generalizability across different sports.

4.1 Data Preparation

In the experiments, we independently trained and evaluated models on three public datasets collected from popular team sports: soccer, basketball, and American football. The soccer dataset is provided by Metrica Sports[1] and contains tracking data for 22 players collected across three matches. For basketball, we use the first 100 matches of SportsVU NBA dataset[2], containing trajectories of 10 players per match. The American football dataset is from the Kaggle competition[3] and is based on NFL's Next Gen Stats. We adopt its preprocessed version[4] provided by the NRTSI paper [21], which contains 9,543 five-second time series of six offensive players. The original sampling rates of the three datasets are 25 Hz, 25 Hz, and 10 Hz, respectively, but we downsample all datasets to 10 Hz for consistency. As model inputs, we use 200 frames (20 s) per sequence for soccer and basketball and 50 frames (5 s) for American football.

4.2 Missing Scenarios

To evaluate the model performance on various missing patterns, we consider the following three scenarios that may occur during data acquisition processes:

---

[1] https://github.com/metrica-sports/sample-data.
[2] https://github.com/linouk23/NBA-Player-Movements.
[3] https://www.kaggle.com/competitions/nfl-big-data-bowl-2021.
[4] https://github.com/lupalab/NRTSI/tree/main/codes_stochastic.

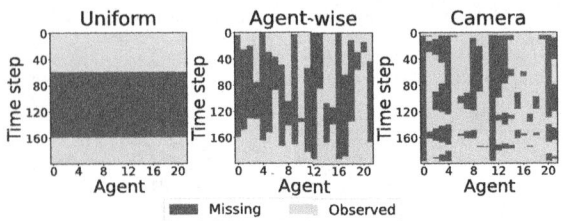

Fig. 4. Masking matrix examples for three different missing scenarios.

1. Uniform missing: All players have missing values at the same time interval. Note that among the baselines, NAOMI [16] and NRTSI [21] are designed to only handle this scenario and are not capable of the following other scenarios.
2. Agent-wise missing: Individual players have different missing intervals.
3. Broadcasting camera: A virtual camera follows the ball and only captures the players inside the camera view, resulting in missing values for the remaining players as shown in Fig. 1. Following Graph Imputer [19], we conduct experiments only on the soccer dataset for this scenario.

Figure 4 illustrates examples of masking matrices from the soccer dataset used in each missing scenario. Since our task is to impute trajectories given observed data before and after the missing intervals, we ensure that the first and last five frames of each sequence are always observable, following previous work [16,19,21]. During training, we apply a dynamic missing rate ranging from 0.1 to 0.9, while testing is conducted with a fixed missing rate of 0.5 to encourage the model to generalize across various missing rate scenarios. Additional evaluations with different missing rates are presented as the ablation study in Sect. 4.5.

4.3 Baseline Models and Evaluation Metrics

In the experiments, we compare the imputation performance of MIDAS with several baselines, including naive methods such as linear interpolation (LI) and cubic spline (CS), as well as deep learning models such as BRITS [1], NAOMI [16], NRTSI [21], CSDI [24], Graph Imputer (GI) [19], and ImputeFormer (IF) [18]. To evaluate the impact of our derivative-accumulating self-ensemble mechanism, we also implement a baseline that only uses the initial prediction (IP) described in Sect. 3.1 and is trained with the loss $\mathcal{L}^i$ from Sect. 3.4. For models such as BRITS, NAOMI, and CSDI that do not preserve permutation-equivariance of input players, we sort trajectories by the sum of their average x and y coordinates to ensure permutation robustness. We compare these baselines using two evaluation metrics: (1) *position error* (PE) indicating the average Euclidean distance between the true and predicted positions and (2) *step change error* (SCE) [16,21] defined as the average absolute difference between the variance of the true and predicted velocities to assess the trajectories' physical plausibility.

4.4 Main Experimental Results

The resulting Table 2 shows that the proposed MIDAS consistently outperforms other baselines in both positional accuracy (PE) and physical plausibility (SCE). Linear interpolation (LI) and cubic spline (CS) offer simple yet competitive results in some scenarios. Notably, deep learning baselines such as BRITS, NAOMI, and CSDI, which are not designed for multi-agent domains, often fail to exceed these naive baselines. Similarly, Graph Imputer (GI) performs worse than LI and CS in many cases, as previously reported in its original article [19].

By contrast, our model for initial prediction (IP) already surpasses most baselines, demonstrating its strength in modeling dynamic multi-agent interactions. Furthermore, comparing IP and MIDAS highlights the effectiveness of our self-ensemble mechanism. By effectively leveraging the complementary strengths of initial predictions and alternative derivative-accumulating predictions, it leads to superior performance even compared to state-of-the-art methods such as Impute-Former (IF) in most scenarios.

Table 2. Performance of imputation methods on different datasets and scenarios.

Scenario	Metric	Method									
		LI	CS	BRITS	NAOMI	NRTSI	CSDI	GI	IF	IP	MIDAS
Soccer											
Uniform	PE	3.8406	2.2085	7.4859	4.5343	3.1791	3.4295	4.6511	2.0898	1.4563	**1.3205**
	SCE	0.1299	0.0867	3.9089	3.9793	0.0854	0.1586	0.1191	0.0815	0.1488	**0.0516**
Agent-wise	PE	5.0752	11.4647	5.7266	—	—	4.0279	5.6011	2.5798	2.0755	**1.9832**
	SCE	0.1631	0.2939	2.9627	—	—	0.1305	0.1508	0.0976	0.1057	**0.0535**
Camera	PE	3.1083	1.9209	7.4208	—	—	3.5181	3.6512	2.2151	1.4879	**1.2296**
	SCE	0.0993	0.0547	4.1967	—	—	0.2132	0.0934	0.3149	0.1554	**0.0374**
Basketball											
Uniform	PE	3.3481	2.3114	2.9085	1.5254	2.5291	2.2558	2.8305	1.3622	0.9801	**0.9727**
	SCE	0.1483	0.1025	1.0521	0.3230	0.0734	0.0631	0.1066	0.0531	**0.0432**	0.0438
Agent-wise	PE	4.4992	10.3857	2.4238	—	—	2.3471	2.5859	**1.3345**	1.3832	1.3862
	SCE	0.1787	0.2715	0.5397	—	—	0.0563	0.0700	0.0485	**0.0373**	0.0381
American Football											
Uniform	PE	0.8897	0.7448	1.7990	0.9692	0.5158	0.5558	0.8899	0.3673	0.2073	**0.1542**
	SCE	1.1063	0.9463	10.9459	2.3112	0.2989	0.4905	1.1023	0.2858	0.1990	**0.1126**
Agent-wise	PE	1.5128	1.2041	1.7527	—	—	0.6182	1.5128	0.3944	0.2383	**0.2104**
	SCE	1.0641	0.5306	10.6807	—	—	0.4288	1.0631	0.1869	0.1180	**0.0967**

Such observations are also evident in Fig. 5, where LI, NRTSI, and CSDI often generate unrealistic trajectories, either overly linear or changing direction too frequently, resulting in erratic and implausible motion patterns. In contrast, IF and MIDAS produce trajectories that closely resemble true player movements, as indicated by the relatively low PEs over the missing interval.

Table 3. Performance of the top-3 methods on the basketball dataset when trained with full data (70 games) versus limited data (3 games).

Scenario	Metric	Limited Data			Full Data		
		IF	IP	MIDAS	IF	IP	MIDAS
Uniform	PE	1.6741	1.1868	**1.1438**	1.3622	0.9801	**0.9727**
	SCE	0.0628	0.1483	**0.0493**	0.0531	**0.0432**	0.0438
Agent-wise	PE	1.8876	1.6414	**1.5994**	**1.3345**	1.3832	1.3862
	SCE	0.0645	0.0452	**0.0439**	0.0485	**0.0373**	0.0381

Meanwhile, an interesting observation emerges in the basketball dataset, where IP and IF show performance comparable to or slightly better than MIDAS in some cases. We attribute this to the larger amount of training data available (70 games), which may reduce the relative advantage of MIDAS. In contrast, for soccer and American football, where training data are more limited, MIDAS's derivative-based self-ensemble mechanism demonstrates its data efficiency by significantly outperforming other methods.

To investigate whether this data efficiency holds for the basketball dataset, we measure model performance on an additional setting where models are trained using only 3 games (comparable in scale to the training data used for the soccer dataset). As shown in Table 3, all models experience a performance drop when trained on limited data. However, the degradation is much less severe for MIDAS, which eventually outperforms both IF and IP under this setting. This observation underscores the practical utility of MIDAS in real-world sports analytics, where obtaining large amounts of complete tracking data is often difficult due to the competitive and commercial nature of professional sports.

4.5 Ablation Studies

In addition to the main experiments, we conducted two ablation studies to further investigate the model's behavior across varying difficulties and the impact of its features and components on the performance.

Model Behavior Across Varying Difficulties. To better understand how MIDAS responds to varying levels of difficulty, we conduct an ablation study analyzing the model's behavior across different missing lengths. For the agent-wise missing scenario in the soccer and basketball datasets, we divide trajectory segments in the test set into three groups based on missing length.

As shown in Table 4, the position error increases with longer missing segments, and the advantage of DAP over IP diminishes. When the missing length is short, the DAP components outperform the initial prediction (IP) by a wide margin, resulting in substantial performance gains through the ensemble. However, as the missing length increases, the uncertainty of player motion makes DAP less reliable, reducing its advantage. This trend is reflected in the ensemble weights as well: $\hat{\lambda}_t^{k,i}$ increases and $\hat{\lambda}_t^{k,f}$ decreases as the missing length grows.

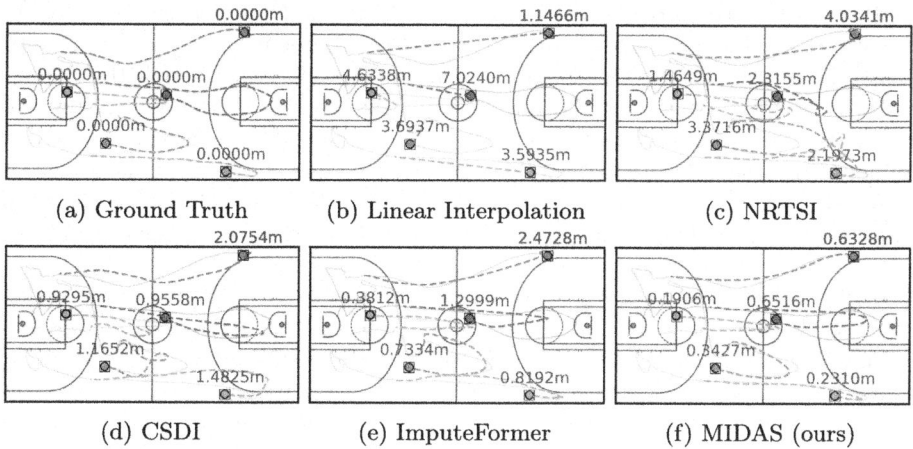

Fig. 5. Ground truth (solid) and imputed trajectories (dashed) for a uniform missing scenario in basketball. Circles indicate the players' initial positions, and the annotated values represent average position errors over the missing interval.

Table 4. Position errors and ensemble weights of each MIDAS component in Eq. (11) across different missing lengths within 200-frame (20 s) trajectory segments. Segments are grouped into the short, medium, and long thirds based on missing length, where the mean and standard deviation of the number of missing frames in each group are reported in the table.

Sports	Category	Missing Frames	$\hat{\mathbf{p}}_t^{k,i}$ ($\hat{\lambda}_t^{k,i}$)	$\hat{\mathbf{p}}_t^{k,f}$ ($\hat{\lambda}_t^{k,f}$)	$\hat{\mathbf{p}}_t^{k,b}$ ($\hat{\lambda}_t^{k,b}$)	$\hat{\mathbf{p}}_t^k$
Soccer	Short	33.30 ± 15.72	0.1379 (0.0001)	0.0742 (0.6501)	0.0783 (0.3498)	**0.0504**
	Medium	90.42 ± 19.17	0.7939 (0.0003)	0.7492 (0.6110)	0.7624 (0.3887)	**0.7004**
	Long	173.41 ± 21.70	2.7359 (0.0002)	2.7017 (0.5034)	2.7186 (0.4964)	**2.6082**
Basketball	Short	33.86 ± 16.11	0.0444 (0.1596)	0.0424 (0.5216)	0.0426 (0.3187)	**0.0376**
	Medium	90.65 ± 19.02	0.5395 (0.1783)	0.5483 (0.4809)	0.5482 (0.3406)	**0.5312**
	Long	172.60 ± 21.20	1.8104 (0.1801)	1.8288 (0.4313)	1.8258 (0.3985)	**1.8005**

Table 5. Position errors of each MIDAS component in Eq. (11), when trained using different subsets of features.

IP Features	DAP Features	$\hat{\mathbf{p}}_t^{k,i}$	$\hat{\mathbf{p}}_t^{k,f}$	$\hat{\mathbf{p}}_t^{k,b}$	$\hat{\mathbf{p}}_t^k$
Position	Velocity	4.0008	2.8203	2.8261	2.5549
Position	Vel. & accel.	2.9119	2.6973	2.6858	2.4954
Pos. & vel.	Velocity	1.6600	1.5742	1.5590	1.4025
Pos. & vel.	Vel. & accel.	1.6235	1.5731	1.5670	1.4013
All features	Velocity	1.6713	1.4985	1.5595	1.2644
All features	Vel. & accel.	**1.4963**	**1.4122**	**1.3982**	**1.2296**

In addition, the advantage of DAP over IP varies by sport. In soccer, DAP maintains its superiority over IP even for long segments, and the IP component receives almost zero weight in the ensemble, indicating that MIDAS relies entirely on DAP. In contrast, in basketball, IP surpasses DAP for medium and long segments. This is reflected in noticeably higher $\hat{\lambda}_t^{k,i}$, suggesting its greater influence in ensemble prediction. This difference likely stems from the nature of basketball, where the variability of player motion is higher relative to the small court size, making long-range accumulation of derivatives more error-prone.

Impact of Derivative Features. To empirically justify the use of derivative features in IP and DAP, we compared the performance of MIDAS on the broadcasting camera scenario in soccer with those trained without accelerations (i.e., using positions and velocities) and even without velocities (i.e., only using positions) of observed trajectories. Furthermore, we configured IP to predict only positions and velocities, and DAP to estimate positions only based on predicted velocities. We then compared these "velocity-only" DAP models with their counterparts that also incorporate predicted accelerations as in Eq. (7).

Table 5 shows that providing velocities and accelerations as input features for IP clearly improves the imputation performance. We attribute this to the neural network architecture for IP, where Set Transformers independently encode multi-agent contexts at each time step via Set Transformers, and player-wise Bi-LSTMs link temporal information. Providing derivatives as input allows the Set Transformers to utilize information of adjoining time steps, resulting in more comprehensive context embeddings compared to using positions alone.

In addition, we observe consistent performance improvements when predicted accelerations are incorporated into DAP alongside velocities (i.e., rows 2, 4, and 6 versus 1, 3, and 5, respectively). We attribute this to the fact that including accelerations enables DAP to capture the finer dynamics of player motion, mitigating the drift caused by error compounding in velocity-only DAP.

4.6 Time Complexity Analysis

While achieving high imputation accuracy is important, real-world deployment requires efficient processing without excessive computational overhead. To assess the feasibility of real-time use, we analyze both the theoretical and empirical time complexity of the proposed MIDAS framework.

From a theoretical standpoint, we consider three key parameters: the number of time steps T, the hidden dimension m, and the number of players K. It takes $O(TK^2m)$ for Set Transformer used in the initial prediction, $O(TKm^2)$ for Bi-LSTMs employed in the initial prediction and weighted ensemble. In total, $O(TK^2m + TKm^2) \approx O(TKm^2)$ as $m \gg K$. Since Bi-LSTM adopts a recurrent structure, the entire computation process proceeds over $O(T)$ steps, proportional to the length of the sequence.

In addition to this analysis, we empirically evaluated the inference time of MIDAS and several baseline models using an NVIDIA TITAN RTX GPU with 24 GB memory. As summarized in Table 6, although MIDAS is slightly slower

Table 6. Empirical analysis of time complexity on soccer and basketball data. Each row corresponds to an imputation method, with the number of parameters, average inference time per 20-second window, and total processing time for half a soccer match and a full basketball match in the test set described in Table 1.

Method	Soccer			Basketball		
	Params	**Inference**	Total	Params	Inference	Total
NRTSI	84,090,968	893.07 ms	84.40 s	84,017,192	906.74 ms	100.55 s
CSDI	414,209	394.44 ms	39.68 s	413,825	324.70 ms	37.68 s
ImputeFormer	1,290,978	6.19 ms	4.92 s	1,060,578	5.68 ms	3.85 s
MIDAS	3,945,579	24.32 ms	8.22 s	3,945,579	21.58 ms	5.71 s

than ImputeFormer [18], it can process an entire 40-minute game (half-match for soccer and full game for basketball) within 10 s. This demonstrates that MIDAS operates well within real-time constraints, enabling its potential use in practical scenarios such as live match analysis or broadcasting augmentation.

5 Applications

In Sect. 4, we evaluate model performance primarily based on metrics related to missing periods in sports data. In practice, however, what is more important in this domain is the quality of the trajectories for the entire period, as they can be utilized in diverse domain-specific downstream tasks. As examples, we present two promising applications in the soccer domain: approximating physical statistics and pass success probability from incomplete tracking data.

5.1 Approximation of Physical Statistics for Load Management

In this section, we explore how accurately our method can estimate statistics for a given period when imputed trajectories are combined with known observations. Specifically, we compare the *total distance* covered by a player and the *number of sprints* estimated by each method, as they are widely used as indicators for players' physical performance or fitness. We first compute velocities from the observed/imputed positions based on Eq. 1 and obtain speed values by calculating the norms of these velocity vectors. To make the best estimation from given positional predictions, we remove outliers whose speed is larger 12 m s^{-1} or whose norm of the acceleration exceeds 8 m s^{-2} and replace the values by linear interpolation. Also, we smoothen the resulting speed signal by applying a Savitzky-Golay filter [20]. After preprocessing speed signals, we compute the distance covered by each player by summing the speed values multiplied by $\Delta t = 0.1$ s. For the latter, if a player runs faster than 6 m s^{-1} for consecutive frames, we detect his/her movement during the frames as *sprint* and count the number of such sprints the player made during the given period.

Table 7. Players' physical statistics estimated by different models and their mean absolute percentage errors (MAPE) for the soccer test data.

Method	Distance (m)		Sprints	
	Mean	MAPE	Mean	MAPE
Ground Truth	11,093.5	—	41.49	—
Linear Interp.	10,167.8	8.46%	38.89	6.32%
Cubic Spline	10,686.3	3.73%	38.85	6.73%
BRITS	10,979.2	2.76%	59.89	53.62%
CSDI	11,343.0	2.77%	44.20	14.71%
Graph Imputer	8,972.1	19.15%	37.85	9.80%
ImputeFormer	11,441.7	3.22%	50.25	26.29%
MIDAS (ours)	**10,922.4**	**1.58%**	**40.71**	**4.95%**

For evaluation, we use the soccer test data consisting of the half of a match and assume the broadcasting camera scenario. Since players played for different time periods, we normalize each player's statistics by 90 min and calculate the averages of such normalized values estimated by MIDAS and other baselines, respectively. Note that players who ran fewer than two sprints during the half were excluded from every evaluation.

According to Table 7, MIDAS provides accurate estimates close to the ground truth. Especially considering that almost all baselines either suffer from inaccurate distance measures (linear interpolation, cubic spline, and Graph Imputer) or overestimate speed spikes (BRITS, CSDI, and ImputeFormer), it is obvious that our model takes clear advantage of smooth prediction of velocities. In a nutshell, our framework is practical in that it can provide reliable statistics with incomplete tracking data, which originally require complete player trajectories.

5.2 Approximation of Pass Success Probability for Spatial Analysis

One representative example of leveraging player tracking data for match analysis is Pitch Control [22], which estimates the probability that a pass to each location on the pitch would be successful. Such pass success probabilities for different destinations are typically visualized as a heat map overlayed on the pitch, so that domain experts can evaluate players' positioning and decision-making for both actual and hypothetical passes to different locations on the pitch.

Thus, to demonstrate the applicability of imputation models in actual match analysis, we compare the Pitch Control maps generated using the player positions imputed by different methods. In the situation in Fig. 6 as an example, player 23 of the blue team has the ball, while his teammates 22 and 26 are making forward runs towards the open spaces on the left flank and in the center behind the red defensive line, respectively. The ground truth map (Fig. 6a) indicates that the blue team has a slightly higher control probability in both areas, reflecting reasonable pass success opportunities to these players, who are

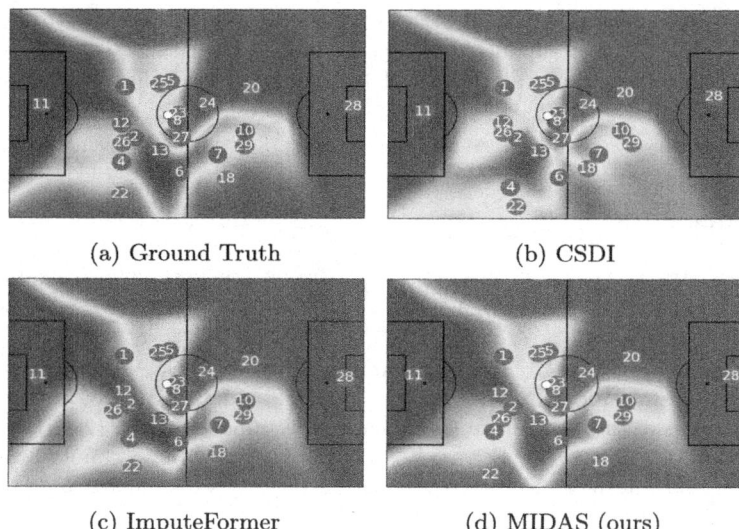

Fig. 6. Pass success probability maps based on true and imputed player positions resulting from different methods in a partially-observable camera setting. Darker red and blue regions indicate a higher probability of the left and right teams gaining possession, respectively, if the ball is passed to those areas. (Color figure online)

onside. However, inaccurate imputations by CSDI (Fig. 6b) and ImputeFormer (Fig. 6c) lead to issues such as players being mispredicted in offside positions or pass success probabilities being over- or underestimated in critical areas. In contrast, MIDAS (Fig. 6d) produces predictions that closely follow the actual player dynamics, resulting in probability maps that more accurately reflect the true game situation. This example instantiates how our framework facilitates more reliable downstream analysis by providing accurate imputation results.

6 Conclusions

This paper proposes MIDAS, a framework for imputing missing values in multi-agent trajectories with high accuracy and physical plausibility. MIDAS combines a permutation-equivariant neural network for initial trajectory prediction with a self-ensemble mechanism that incorporates derivative-based alternative predictions to refine imputation results and enforce physical consistency. Experiments on three team sports datasets under various missing scenarios demonstrate the effectiveness of our approach in generating trajectories with higher positional accuracy and improved reality than existing baselines. While this study focuses on team sports, we believe the proposed framework is applicable to other spatiotemporal domains. Future work will explore extending MIDAS to additional domains such as autonomous driving and crowd simulation, as well as its application to downstream tasks that require complete and reliable trajectory data.

Acknowledgments. Ko was supported by the NRF grant (RS-2023-00208094) funded by MSIT and Choi was supported by Institute of Information & Communications Technology Planning & Evaluation (IITP) grant funded by the Korea government (MSIT) (No. RS-2022-II220608).

References

1. Cao, W., Wang, D., Li, J., Zhou, H., Li, L., Li, Y.: BRITS: bidirectional recurrent imputation for time series. In: Advances in Neural Information Processing Systems, vol. 31 (2018)
2. Capellera, G., Ferraz, L., Rubio, A., Agudo, A., Moreno-Noguer, F.: TranSPORTmer: a holistic approach to trajectory understanding in multi-agent sports. In: Proceedings of the 17th Asian Conference on Computer Vision (2024)
3. Capellera, G., Rubio, A., Ferraz, L., Agudo, A.: Unified uncertainty-aware diffusion for multi-agent trajectory modeling. In: IEEE/CVF Conference on Computer Vision and Pattern Recognition (2025)
4. Che, Z., Purushotham, S., Cho, K., Sontag, D.A., Liu, Y.: Recurrent neural networks for multivariate time series with missing values. Sci. Reports **8** (2018)
5. Choi, M., Lee, C.: Conditional information bottleneck approach for time series imputation. In: Proceedings of the 12th International Conference on Learning Representations (2023)
6. Cini, A., Marisca, I., Alippi, C.: Multivariate time series imputation by graph neural networks. In: Proceedings of the 10th International Conference on Learning Representations (2022)
7. Du, W., Côté, D., Liu, Y.: SAITS: self-attention-based imputation for time series. Expert Systems with Appl. **219** (2023)
8. Gupta, A., Johnson, J., Fei-Fei, L., Savarese, S., Alahi, A.: Social GAN: socially acceptable trajectories with generative adversarial networks. In: IEEE Conference on Computer Vision and Pattern Recognition (2018)
9. Hochreiter, S., Schmidhuber, J.: Long short-term memory. Neural Comput. **9**(8), 1735–1780 (1997)
10. Hughes, H., et al.: Event2Tracking: reconstructing multi-agent soccer trajectories using long-term multimodal context. In: Proceedings of the 39th AAAI Conference on Artificial Intelligence (2025)
11. Kim, H., Choi, H., Kim, C., Yoon, J., Ko, S.: Ball trajectory inference from multi-agent sports contexts using set transformer and hierarchical Bi-LSTM. In: Proceedings of the 29th ACM SIGKDD Conference on Knowledge Discovery and Data Mining (2023)
12. Kipf, T.N., Fetaya, E., Wang, K., Welling, M., Zemel, R.S.: Neural relational inference for interacting systems. In: Proceedings of the 35th International Conference on Machine Learning (2018)
13. Lee, J., Lee, Y., Kim, J., Kosiorek, A.R., Choi, S., Teh, Y.W.: Set Transformer: a framework for attention-based permutation-invariant neural networks. In: Proceedings of the 36th International Conference on Machine Learning (2019)
14. Li, J., Yang, F., Tomizuka, M., Choi, C.: EvolveGraph: multi-agent trajectory prediction with dynamic relational reasoning. In: Advances in Neural Information Processing Systems, vol. 33 (2020)

15. Liu, S., Li, X., Cong, G., Chen, Y., Jiang, Y.: Multivariate time-series imputation with disentangled temporal representations. In: The 11th International Conference on Learning Representations (2023)
16. Liu, Y., Yu, R., Zheng, S., Zhan, E., Yue, Y.: NAOMI: non-autoregressive multiresolution sequence imputation. In: Advances in Neural Information Processing Systems 32 (2019)
17. Marisca, I., Cini, A., Alippi, C.: Learning to reconstruct missing data from spatiotemporal graphs with sparse observations. In: Advances in Neural Information Processing Systems 35 (2022)
18. Nie, T., Qin, G., Ma, W., Mei, Y., Sun, J.: Imputeformer: low rankness-induced transformers for generalizable spatiotemporal imputation. In: Proceedings of the 30th ACM SIGKDD Conference on Knowledge Discovery and Data Mining (2024)
19. Omidshafiei, S., et al.: Multiagent off-screen behavior prediction in football. Sci. Reports **12** (2022)
20. Savitzky, A., Golay, M.J.E.: Smoothing and differentiation of data by simplified least squares procedures. Analytical Chemistry **36**(8) (1964)
21. Shan, S., Li, Y., Oliva, J.B.: NRTSI: non-recurrent time series imputation. In: IEEE International Conference on Acoustics, Speech and Signal Processing (2023)
22. Spearman, W., Basye, A., Dick, G., Hotovy, R., Pop, P.: Physics-based modeling of pass probabilities in soccer. In: MIT Sloan Sports Analytics Conference (2017)
23. Sun, F., et al.: Interaction modeling with multiplex attention. In: Advances in Neural Information Processing Systems, vol. 35 (2022)
24. Tashiro, Y., Song, J., Song, Y., Ermon, S.: CSDI: conditional score-based diffusion models for probabilistic time series imputation. In: Advances in Neural Information Processing Systems 34 (2021)
25. Wu, H., Hu, T., Liu, Y., Zhou, H., Wang, J., Long, M.: TimesNet: temporal 2D-variation modeling for general time series analysis. In: Proceedings of the 11th International Conference on Learning Representations (2023)
26. Xu, Y., Bazarjani, A., Chi, H., Choi, C., Fu, Y.: Uncovering the missing pattern: unified framework towards trajectory imputation and prediction. In: IEEE/CVF Conference on Computer Vision and Pattern Recognition (2023)
27. Yeh, R.A., Schwing, A.G., Huang, J., Murphy, K.: Diverse generation for multi-agent sports games. In: IEEE/CVF Conference on Computer Vision and Pattern Recognition (2019)
28. Yoon, J., Zame, W.R., van der Schaar, M.: Estimating missing data in temporal data streams using multi-directional recurrent neural networks. IEEE Trans. Biomed. Eng. **66**(5), 1477–1490 (2019)
29. Yuan, Y., Weng, X., Ou, Y., Kitani, K.: AgentFormer: agent-aware transformers for socio-temporal multi-agent forecasting. In: IEEE/CVF International Conference on Computer Vision (2021)

A Scalable Approach for Unified Large Events Models in Soccer

Tiago Mendes-Neves[1,2(✉)], Luís Meireles[2], and João Mendes-Moreira[1,2]

[1] Faculdade de Engenharia da Universidade do Porto, Porto, Portugal
tiago.neves@fe.up.pt
[2] LIAAD - INESC TEC, Porto, Portugal

Abstract. Large Events Models (LEMs) are a class of models designed to predict and analyze the sequence of events in soccer matches, capturing the complex dynamics of the game. The original LEM framework, based on a chain of classifiers, faced challenges such as synchronization, scalability issues, and limited context utilization. This paper proposes a unified and scalable approach to model soccer events using a tabular autoregressive model. Our models demonstrate significant improvements over the original LEM, achieving higher accuracy in event prediction and better simulation quality, while also offering greater flexibility and scalability. The unified LEM framework enables a wide range of applications in soccer analytics that we display in this paper, including real-time match outcome prediction, player performance analysis, and game simulation, serving as a general solution for many problems in the field.

Keywords: Large Events Model · Sports Analytics · Deep Learning · Generative Model

1 Introduction

Large Events Models (LEMs) [11] are an innovative concept in soccer analytics, drawing inspiration from the success of Large Language Models (LLMs). Just as LLMs predict the next word in a sequence based on the context of previous words, LEMs are engineered to predict the next event in a soccer match, given the current game state. These events include discrete actions such as passes, shots, fouls, and more, collectively forming the "language" of soccer.

LEMs leverage deep learning techniques and are trained on extensive datasets of soccer event data. This training enables them to identify patterns and sequences in gameplay, allowing them to simulate entire soccer matches from a specified starting point or predict the likelihood of specific events occurring next. The goal of LEMs is to solve one of the long-standing limitations of traditional soccer analytics models: existing models often lack flexibility, i.e., they are designed for specific tasks and require redevelopment for new applications.

Supplementary Information The online version contains supplementary material available at https://doi.org/10.1007/978-3-032-06129-4_21.

In Mendes-Neves et al. [11], the authors employ a chain of classifiers approach to build a LEM. This method involves a sequence of multiple classifiers working together, where each classifier focuses on predicting a specific aspect of the upcoming event, using the outputs of the previous classifiers as additional input. The chain begins with predicting the next event type (such as a pass, shot, or foul) using the current game state (e.g., previous event, ball location, ...). The second classifier then takes the predicted event type plus the game state to determine the event's accuracy (whether it will be successful and whether it will result in a goal). Finally, the third classifier uses all prior predictions (event type, accuracy, and goal outcome) alongside the game state to forecast additional details, including the time elapsed until the event occurs, its location on the field (X and Y coordinates), and whether the home team will perform it. By structuring the prediction process this way, the chain of classifiers captures how the event type influences its likelihood of success and other attributes, leading to a more accurate model of soccer match dynamics.

Although the chain of classifiers architecture effectively captures the core elements of a soccer event, this approach exhibited several drawbacks. Firstly, the discontinuous nature made fine-tuning complex, as each classifier required individual adjustments [10], leading to a cumbersome process when adapting the model to specific teams or players. Secondly, scaling the model proved challenging. Different analytical tasks might necessitate different model sizes, but the chain structure required synchronized scaling across all modules. Finally, the parallel nature of some predictions within the architecture meant that specific components did not leverage the full context of the event sequence.

These limitations show the need for a more streamlined and integrated approach to modeling soccer event data. In this paper, we explore the potential of a unified LEM. Using a causal masking strategy, we unify the LEM by predicting the next event in a tabular format. The central idea driving this unified approach is to design a system capable of sequentially predicting each element of a soccer event. This sequential prediction process, even if it requires multiple inference steps for a single event, allows the model to incorporate the full context of preceding event elements. In the appendix of this paper, we also document a strategy to treat the problem as a language modeling task, with inferior results to our approach.

This paper is organized as follows. Section 2 reviews related work in soccer analytics and generative modeling, highlighting the gaps our approach addresses. Section 3 details our experimental setup, including data preparation and the methodology. Section 4 presents our results, evaluating model performance across prediction accuracy and simulation fidelity, with applications demonstrated in Sect. 5. Finally, Sect. 6 concludes with a summary of findings and directions for future work. Appendices provide supplementary details on datasets and alternative modeling approaches.

2 Related Work

Soccer analytics has witnessed a remarkable evolution, driven by models tailored to dissect various facets of the game, addressing a spectrum of tasks like valuing discrete actions, players, and teams. For example, expected goals (xG) models predict the likelihood of a shot resulting in a goal based on location, angle, and other contextual factors like defensive pressure [1,13]. Frameworks like Valuing Actions by Estimating Probabilities (VAEP) [4] and expected threat (xT) [8,15] extend this concept by assessing the broader impact of actions on scoring or conceding probabilities. Meanwhile, models leveraging tracking data analyze player movements offering insights into off-ball contributions and team formations [5,17]. This diversity underscores the complexity of soccer, necessitating specialized tools for distinct analytical objectives.

The advent of LLMs has demonstrated the power of large-scale, self-supervised models to address a wide range of tasks within a single framework [3,14]. LLMs learn data representations from vast, unlabeled datasets, enabling them to generalize across applications (e.g., text generation, translation, and question answering). This paradigm shift offers a compelling analogy for sports analytics. In soccer, current methods often rely on task-specific models. The success of LLMs suggests that a sequence model could serve as a "foundation" for soccer analytics, capable of modeling event sequences and adapting to diverse downstream tasks without specialist solutions.

Before the introduction of LEMs, generative modeling in soccer analytics was limited to narrow scopes. For instance, Seq2Event [16] employed transformers and recurrent neural networks to predict the next event in a match sequence but limited itself to passes, dribbles, crosses, and shots. TacticAI [20] utilized graph neural networks to model player interactions, predicting outcomes and suggesting tactical adjustments, but limited to corner kicks. There are other efforts [2], but all require a limited action set to compromise. These shortcomings set the stage for developing LEMs, which aim to provide a comprehensive generative framework.

LEMs was a pioneering approach to generatively model soccer events in a holistic manner. Inspired by LLMs, LEMs sought to learn the underlying probability distribution of event sequences, enabling realistic simulation and prediction. LEMs adopted a chain of classifiers to model multiple event attributes within a unified framework. This approach covered a significant portion of the SPADL schema [4] (excluding identifiers), offering a more complete representation of soccer dynamics than its predecessors while modeling 33 event types. This was a significant improvement over existing proposals.

Despite their innovations, LEMs exhibited several drawbacks that limit their effectiveness and scalability, which we seek to address in this paper. The reliance on a chain of classifiers introduces architectural complexity, requiring the training (and post-training) to be executed three times, upon which there is a necessity to verify if the models have learned coherent patterns among themselves. The context window of the model is also limited, only using a single event to predict the following.

3 Experimental Setup

3.1 Data

For training our models, we used data from the 2015–2016 to 2021–2022 seasons for the first and second leagues of Portugal, Spain, Germany, and France, as well as the first leagues of Denmark and Belgium. We selected these leagues due to their high level of competitiveness and availability. We used the 2022–2023 season of the same leagues for validation purposes, with 100 000 randomly sampled instances reserved for validation during model training and 15% of the remaining validation set used to evaluate the models. The 2023–2024 season is used for testing applications in Sect. 5. A more in-depth description of the datasets is available in Table 1.

The work is also reproducible using publicly available datasets, such as Pappalardo et al. [12] or Statsbomb Free Data[1]. However, because companies utilize different data standards to annotate events, there may be differences in how the models perceive these events. Nonetheless, the quality and depth of the underlying data has an effect on the model quality.

3.2 Deviations from the Original Dataset

In contrast to Wyscout's original grouping, with several event types under broad categories, we refined and expanded some of these event types. The changes we made are the following:

- Wyscout groups multiple types of duels under the "duels" event type. We split this category into five distinct types of duels: "defensive duel," "offensive duel," "aerial duel," "loose ball duel," and "dribble."
- We separated the "passes" category into three subcategories: "pass," "long pass," and "cross."
- For "shot," we differentiated based on the part of the body used: "right-footed shot," "left-footed shot," and "headshot."
- We differentiated the "shot against" event type by changing it to "save" when a goalkeeper made a save.
- Cards were previously associated with an "interruption" event. We now explicitly distinguish between "yellow card" and "red card" events.
- Some events also have an associated "carry." A carry occurs when a player moves the ball from where they received it to a new position before executing another action or being interrupted by a duel. To improve the accuracy of our models and given the importance of spatio-temporal aspects in soccer, we added an event each time a carry is associated with another event. The carry event follows the event with which it was initially associated.
- We also introduced two new event types: the "first half end" and "game end." These events help in modeling when game simulations should terminate, fixing the issue with the original proposal where all games ended exclusively based

---

[1] https://statsbomb.com/what-we-do/hub/free-data/.

on time. This extends the time limit where games are forced to end from 90 to 99 min, with the first half extending from 45 to 49 min.

To reduce the number of inputs in our model, we computed two new variables:

- Accurate: In the dataset, different event types have different indicators of success. Since they are independent, we merged them into a single variable to reduce the number of variables being forecasted. An event is considered accurate if it meets the following criteria:
  - the event is a pass and is accurate
  - a player is the first to touch the ball in an aerial duel
  - a player successfully progresses with the ball in an offensive duel
  - a player recovers possession in a ground duel
  - the event is a carry that leads to progression on the field
  - the event is a shot that results in a goal
- Time elapsed: Time in an event is described by two variables: minute and second. We compute the time difference in seconds between two events to reduce them to a single variable. Then, we clip the "time elapsed" variable to a maximum value of 100, ensuring that we do not require extra tokens to manage larger values. This extends from the original proposal that capped the "time elapsed" at 60 s.

The new "accurate" variable now carries both the information of the *isAccurate* and of *isGoal* from the original architecture [11]. This provides an improvement by reducing the number of variables to forecast from 7 to 6. While previously, in the chain of classifiers approach, this was not significant since both variables are predicted with a single step, in our new approach, reducing the number of variables is important as each variable is inferred individually.

3.3 Statistical Description of the Dataset

For the rest of this paper, we will use the following abbreviations for the variables included in the models.

3.4 Reshaping

We reshaped the dataset to fit in a tabular format. We created six copies of each event, each with a target for each of the h, e, x, y, t, and a variables. Some inputs will be masked as -1 depending on the target variable to hide future information from the model. For example, to predict the y variable, we mask y and all subsequent variables (t and a). When we aim to predict the first variable h, we mask all variables. Listing 1.1 shows a sample of the data in this format.

In addition to the event variables we aim to predict, we have contextual variables such as the current goals scored for home and away team (hg and ag), along with red and yellow cards (hr, ar, hy, ay). All other variables preceded by a c refer to contextual variables extracted from previous events.

hy → Home team yellow cards.
ay → Away team yellow cards.
hr → Home team red cards.
ar → Away team red cards.
hg → Home team goals scored.
ag → Away team goals scored.
p → True if period is second half.
m → Minute.
s → Second.
h → True if the event was made by the home team.
e → Event type.
x → x-coordinate of the event on the field.
y → y-coordinate of the event on the field.
t → Time elapsed since previous event.
a → Accurate.

Table 1. Descriptive statistics of the processed Wyscout dataset

Variable		Set		
		Train	Validation	Test
General				
Events	#	39,580,286	6,036,590	5,955,852
Matches	#	22,773	3,352	3,256
Events per Match	Mean	1,738	1,800	1,829
Home Team (h)				
Majority Class		1	1	1
Majority Class	%	0.51	0.51	0.51
Event Type (e)				
Unique Values	#	32	32	32
Majority Class		pass	pass	pass
Majority Class	%	0.36	0.38	0.38
Coordinates (x, y)				
Unique Values	#	101	101	101
x	Mean	47.58	47.13	47.07
y	Mean	49.63	50.33	50.19
Time (t)				
Unique Values	#	101	101	101
Majority Class		2	2	2
Majority Class	%	0.22	0.22	0.23
t	Mean	3.27	3.19	3.20
Action Type (a)				
Majority Class		1	1	1
Majority Class	%	0.51	0.5	0.51

Listing 1.1. A tabular dataset sample for sequence size 3. The first row indicates column headers while subsequent rows show example event records.

```
id,h,e,x,y,t,a,p,m,s,hg,ag,hr,ar,hy,ay,c1_h,c1_e,
    c1_x,c1_y,c1_t,c1_a,c2_h,c2_e,c2_x,c2_y,c2_t,
    c2_a,c3_h,c3_e,c3_x,c3_y,c3_t,c3_a,target
235200910,1,0,64,71,3,-1,0,40,42,0,0,0,0,0,0,0,6,
    13,36,2,0,1,18,100,100,29,0,1,12,100,68,9,0,1
192308161,1,0,29,25,-1,-1,1,69,13,0,1,0,0,1,1,1,0,
    10,61,5,1,1,24,0,0,5,0,0,0,27,43,3,0,4
...
```

3.5 Tabular Modeling with Multilayer Perceptrons

In our proposal, we model soccer events as a tabular problem, where each row represents an event and columns represent features of that event. The core idea is to autoregressively predict each event in a sequence, using the context of previous events and the current game state. We will refer to this approach as Multilayer Perceptrons Large Events Model (MLP LEM).

Data Flow. The data flow in MLP LEMs is presented in Fig. 1.

The input data for LEMs consists of three main components:

1. Game Context: represents the global state of the game at any given time. These features provide crucial context for the model, reflecting each team's overall performance and situation and influencing the likelihood of different events.
   It includes (hg, ag, hy, ay, hr, ar).
2. Previous Event Sequence: provides a localized context, capturing the immediate history leading to the current event. The model receives a fixed-length sequence of the n most recent events. Each event in the sequence is represented using a six-token format, just like the current event.
3. Event: represents the event being predicted at each step, containing the information of which tokens are masked and require prediction.

The LEM predicts each event autoregressively, one token at a time. Each token is a part of an event which is encoded to enable modeling. This means the model predicts each token of the current event sequentially, conditioning each prediction on the game context, previous events, and the previously predicted tokens. Initially, when all tokens of the current event are unknown, the current event vector is initialized with an "unknown" token (represented as −1 in our implementation) for each token. The prediction process then unfolds sequentially as follows: h, e, x, y, t, and a.

Like the original proposal [11], the model does not simply classify the most likely token at each step. Instead, it outputs a probability distribution over the

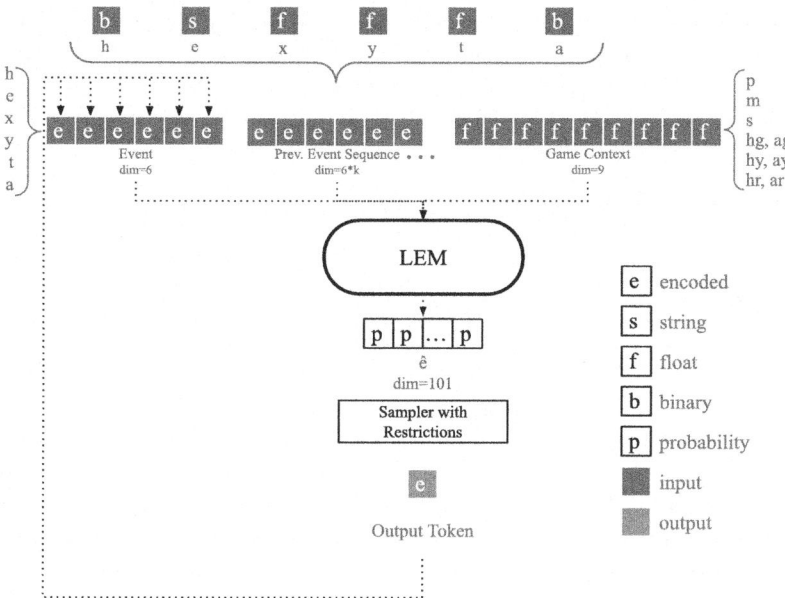

Fig. 1. Data flow in MLP LEMs. The model inputs the game context, previous events, and the current event to predict the next event in the sequence. Each event is represented by six tokens: Team, Event Type, Elapsed Time, Start X, Start Y, and Accuracy. The model predicts each token sequentially, updating the current event representation with each prediction.

possible values for each token. This allows us to incorporate randomness into the event-generation process through sampling.

Training Procedure. The raw event data is transformed into a numerical format suitable for the neural network using tokenization, where each feature of an event is mapped to a discrete numerical token. This tokenization process resulted in a vocabulary size of 101, tokenized as follows:

- The spatial features, x and y, representing the coordinates of an event on the field, were discretized into 101 tokens each, representing values from 0 to 100.
- The temporal feature, t was also discretized into 101 tokens. Since the original data could go up to 30 min without an event occurring, we condensed the range to reduce the vocabulary size while maintaining sufficient temporal resolution for normally occurring games.
- The e feature was encoded using 34 tokens, representing the different types of events in the dataset. We reused the tokens 0–33 to avoid increasing the output space.
- The t and a features were represented with two tokens (0 and 1).

We experimented with MLP architectures of varying depths and widths to explore the impact of model size on performance. After preliminary experiments, we selected 7 architectures that scale their parameter count exponentially (10k, 30k, 100k, 300k, 1M, 3M, and 10M). The configurations presented in Listing 1.2 were extensively tested.

Listing 1.2. Model architectures for MLP LEMs.

```
MLP(input_size=get_size(seq_len), hidden_sizes=[  80,              ], output_size=101)
MLP(input_size=get_size(seq_len), hidden_sizes=[  96,   96,   96], output_size=101)
MLP(input_size=get_size(seq_len), hidden_sizes=[ 196,  196,  196], output_size=101)
MLP(input_size=get_size(seq_len), hidden_sizes=[ 360,  360,  360], output_size=101)
MLP(input_size=get_size(seq_len), hidden_sizes=[ 682,  682,  682], output_size=101)
MLP(input_size=get_size(seq_len), hidden_sizes=[1200, 1200, 1200], output_size=101)
MLP(input_size=get_size(seq_len), hidden_sizes=[2220, 2220, 2220], output_size=101)
```

The models were trained using the Adam optimizer [9], with an initial learning rate of 0.01. We employed the binary cross-entropy with logits loss function, with a batch size of 1024. A dropout rate of 0.3 was used on every layer of all models for regularization. During training, we measured the model's performance in the validation set. Due to the computational cost of evaluating the entire validation set, a representative sample of 100 000 data points was used for evaluation. For scaling law experiments, we use 25% of the train data. Subsequently, the best models were trained using the entire dataset for 4 epochs. The code to reproduce our training process is available on Github[2].

4 Results

4.1 Scaling Laws

We conducted initial experiments to investigate the relationship between model size, sequence length, and performance using a subset of the training data. We trained a series of MLP models as described in Sect. 3.5. The validation loss curves for these models are presented in Fig. 2.

The results demonstrate that a sequence length of 3 consistently yielded the lowest validation loss across different model sizes. This suggests that capturing the immediate context of the three preceding events provides the most valuable information for predicting the subsequent event.

4.2 Training on the Full Dataset

Based on the insights gained from the scaling law experiments, we selected the 100k, 300k, 1M, 3M, and 10M models with a sequence length of 3 and trained them on the full dataset. The learning rate was reduced to 0.001 for this stage of training to prevent overshooting the optimal solution. The validation loss curves for these models are shown in Fig. 3.

The validation loss curves indicate that the models continued improving, achieving lower loss values than the scaling law experiments. The trend in the

---

[2] https://github.com/nvsclub/LargeEventsModel/.

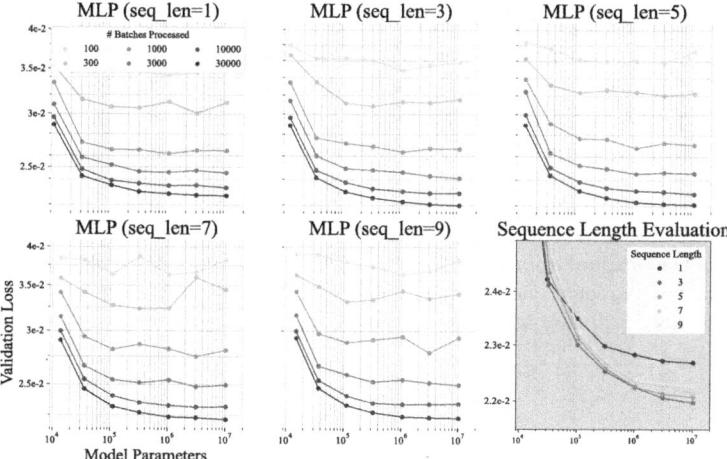

Fig. 2. Validation loss of MLPs trained with varying sequence lengths and model parameters. Each plot represents the test performed at a different sequence length, and each line represents the loss at different points during the training process.

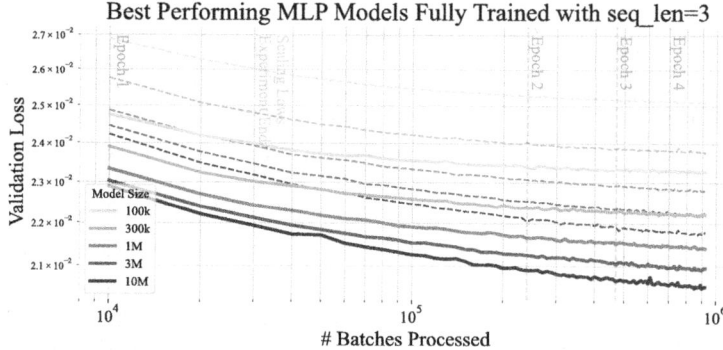

Fig. 3. Validation loss curves for the best-performing MLP models, all using a sequence length of 3. The validation loss continues decaying as the data increases past the previous scaling laws experiment, although the rate of decrease is shrinking. Dotted lines represent train losses.

validation loss curves suggests that the models might benefit from further training. It is possible that, with more training epochs, the models could achieve even better performance, as the slope of the curves indicates that we are yet to convergence. Nonetheless, the returns are diminishing as the scale of resources to increase performance increases exponentially. This decay in performance increase is observable in the performance metrics presented in Table 2.

MLP models can learn meaningful patterns from event data better than our original proposal. The larger models generally outperform the smaller ones, but the gains diminish with increasing size. The best model choice depends on the specific application and the acceptable trade-offs between performance, inference time, and computational resources. The largest model, 10M, provides the best overall performance across the board but at the cost of significantly higher inference times. A smaller model might be more suitable for applications where speed is critical, offering a good balance between performance and efficiency.

Table 2. Performance metrics for MLP models on the validation set. Our new approach outperforms the original approach (OG LEM) at nearly every scale. All variables where the performance increase is not visible reflect significant modifications on the new model that put our new proposal at a disadvantage.

	OG LEM	MLP 100k	MLP 300k	MLP 1M	MLP 3M	MLP 10M
Accuracy						
h (Team)	0.938[a]	0.855	0.864	0.871	0.873	0.874
e (Event Type)	0.557	0.644	0.656	0.664	0.667	0.670
a (Accuracy)	0.817[b]	0.852	0.856	0.860	0.860	0.861
F1-Score						
h (Team)	0.938[a]	0.855	0.864	0.871	0.873	0.874
e (Event Type)	0.499	0.577	0.591	0.603	0.608	0.612
a (Accuracy)	0.873[b]	0.852	0.856	0.859	0.860	0.861
R^2						
x	0.636	0.812	0.836	0.851	0.857	0.858
y	0.292	0.435	0.571	0.603	0.625	0.651
t (Time Elapsed)	0.552[c]	0.153	0.408	0.420	0.447	0.464
MAE						
x	8.5	6.945	6.308	5.919	5.775	5.695
y	15.6	13.526	11.330	10.648	10.233	9.804
t (Time Elapsed)	2.6[c]	1.735	1.515	1.475	1.427	1.401
Inference Time (seconds per 150 000 tokens)						
Any variable	0.023	0.011	0.019	0.048	0.130	0.419

[a] In the original proposal, the h variable was predicted in the last step and, in this iteration, is the first variable to be predicted, having less information to work with. Therefore, this value is inflated.
[b] In the original proposal, the a variable was predicted in the second step and, in this iteration, is the last variable to be predicted, having more information to work with. Integrating the goal variable into a also inflates the accuracy of our newer models.
[c] The time elapsed variable ranged between 0 and 60 in the original proposal, while it now ranges from 0 to 100.

4.3 Benchmarking Large Events Models

Evaluating the quality of our LEMs based on their accuracy in predicting individual tokens is not enough. Token-level accuracy alone does not fully capture the capabilities of a generative model, particularly for downstream tasks like simulating entire soccer matches. While a high token prediction accuracy is desirable, it does not guarantee that a model can generate coherent sequences of events that accurately reflect the dynamics of a real game. We evaluate our models' ability to simulate full soccer matches and compare the statistical properties of these simulated matches (10,000 simulations from kickoff to the end of the match) to real-world data, focusing on three key metrics: goals scored by the home team (Home Goals), by the away team (Away Goals) and the difference between the scores of each team (Goal Difference).

We compute a distance metric based on the element-wise differences to quantify the similarity. Specifically, for each metric (home goals, away goals, goal difference), we calculate the absolute difference between the corresponding elements of the predicted and expected distributions and then sum these differences. Formally, let $[p_1, p_2, ..., p_n]$ be the array representing the predicted distribution and $[e_1, e_2, ..., e_n]$ be the array representing the expected distribution. The distance D calculation is formalized in Eq. 1.

$$D = \sum_{i=1}^{n} |p_i - e_i| \tag{1}$$

Benchmarking Results. Table 3 presents the results on our benchmark.

Table 3. The simulation error of MLP models at their best epochs. The error is measured as the distance between simulated and actual soccer match outcomes. Lower distances indicate better simulation accuracy, reflecting a closer alignment.

Model	Epoch	Goal Delta Distance	Home Goal Distance	Away Goal Distance	Total Distance
MLP 100k	3	0.081	0.057	0.050	0.188
MLP 300k	3	0.076	0.022	0.067	0.165
MLP 1M	1	0.061	0.082	0.034	0.177
	2	0.088	0.045	0.136	0.269
MLP 3M	3	0.067	0.079	0.084	0.230
MLP 10M	1	0.117	0.354	0.322	0.793

Interestingly, we observe that the best performing MLP models (e.g., MLP 10M) according to Table 2 exhibit poor simulation capabilities despite achieving the best performance in token prediction. Their distance scores are significantly higher than small models, indicating a divergence between token-level accuracy and the ability to generate realistic match outcomes. On the other hand, smaller models exhibit the best overall simulation performance. These models show a good balance between token-level accuracy and generative capacity. Furthermore, the results suggest that, in some cases, earlier training epochs can yield better simulation results than later epochs. This might be because earlier epochs retain more "uncertainty" or stochasticity in their predictions, which can be beneficial for generating diverse and realistic sequences of events.

Figure 4 visualizes the distribution of goal differences for real matches and compares it to the simulated distributions. We observe a close alignment between almost all distributions, indicating that any model can generate realistic simulations of events in soccer matches.

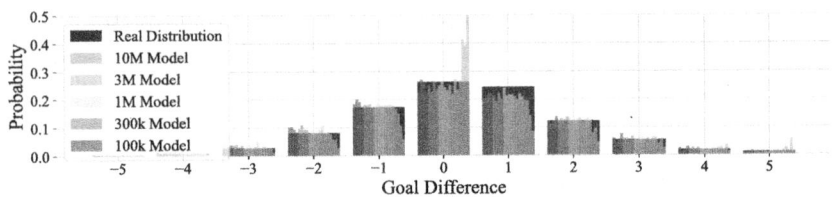

Fig. 4. Comparison of goal difference distributions between real matches and MLP simulations across different epochs (in order epoch 1, 2, 3, and 4). Each bar represents the number of simulations ending with the respective goal difference.

5 Applications of Large Events Models

The potential of LEMs lies in their broad applicability to various problems in soccer analytics. This section demonstrates applications, showcasing how LEMs can provide novel insights. All applications presented here utilize the MLP 100k model, the smallest fully-trained model introduced in this paper. These examples demonstrate that even a relatively small LEM can offer significant value.

5.1 Measuring Performance

Estimating Shot Efficiency. While xG models have become common in football analytics, they primarily focus on a single aspect of the shot. LEMs offer a more granular approach, allowing us to analyze more aspects of shots, like the shot efficiency. This metric assesses how effectively players convert their involvement in the game into shots taken, providing a complementary perspective to traditional expected goals analysis.

We mask the e and subsequent variables (x, y, t, and a) to estimate the probability of each event being a shot. By attributing this probability to each event, we calculate the chance of each event being a shot. Note that no fine-tuning is required in this approach. We are using the simulator to ask, "What is the probability that this situation leads to a shot?" for all actions in a soccer match. The answer contains a probability calculated using the average behaviors of our training set. To measure the behavior of specific players, we aggregate the probabilities across all events where the player was involved and compare it with the actual number of shots taken. These results are presented in Table 4, which analyzes individual player shot efficiency, contrasting the expected shot count with the actual shots taken during the 2023/24 Portuguese First League season. Jota Silva and Pedro Gonçalves exhibit the most significant positive deviations, with a delta of +35.38 and +32.97, suggesting an exceptionally high propensity to take shots. Similarly, V. Gyökeres takes approximately 16 more shots than anticipated, which is particularly noteworthy given his high line for expected shots. In opposition, players such as Pepê Aquino and João Mário have negative deltas of -11.34 and -13.01, respectively. This could indicate a more selective approach to shooting, possibly prioritizing higher-quality opportunities or reflecting a tendency to opt for passes or dribbles over shots in certain situations. It may also be associated with a lack of confidence in their finishing abilities.

Table 4. Player shot data for the 2023/24 season of the Portuguese First League. The delta column represents the difference between actual shots taken and the expected number of shots based on LEM predictions. A positive delta (highlighted in blue) suggests a player is taking more shots than expected, given their involvement in the game, potentially indicating a shoot-first mentality. Conversely, a negative delta (highlighted in red) could suggest a more hesitant approach to shooting.

Team Name	Player Name	Expected Shots	# Shots	Delta
Sporting CP	V. Gyökeres	86.18	102	15.82
Porto	Francisco Conceição	70.70	76	5.30
Benfica	Rafa Silva	66.34	83	16.66
Benfica	Á. Di María	65.00	92	27.00
Porto	Pepê Aquino	62.34	51	-11.34
Porto	Galeno	56.20	75	18.80
Vitória Guimarães	Jota Silva	55.62	91	35.38
Sporting CP	Pedro Gonçalves	54.03	87	32.97
Benfica	João Mário	54.01	41	-13.01
Vízela	S. Essende	51.81	76	24.19

Quantifying Accumulated Pass Risk. Traditional pass accuracy metrics often fail to capture the true value of a player's passing ability. A player can achieve high pass accuracy by playing safe passes in his half that contribute little to advancing the team's attack. Metrics like ball possession have been criticized as poor indicators of proactive or effective play.

LEMs offer a way to quantify pass risk by estimating the probability of success for each pass based on its contextual factors. This allows us to calculate a player's *Expected Passes Completed* (EPC), representing the number of passes a player is expected to complete successfully, given the difficulty of the passes attempted. By comparing a player's actual completed passes to their EPC, we obtain a more informative measure of their passing ability and risk-reward assessment that accounts for the risk and value associated with each pass.

Table 5. EPC results for the 2023/24 season of the Portuguese First League. EPC represents the number of passes a player is expected to complete, given the difficulty of their attempts. Delta highlights the difference between accurate passes and EPC.

Player Name	Team Name	EPC	Accurate Passes	Delta
João Neves	Benfica	1550	1688	138
A. Varela	Porto	1326	1446	120
António Silva	Benfica	1403	1519	116
João Mário	Benfica	1279	1395	116
João Moutinho	Sporting Braga	1299	1410	111
Gonçalo Inácio	Sporting CP	1920	2022	102
Diogo Nascimento	Vizela	1030	1132	102
N. Otamendi	Benfica	1456	1555	99
F. Aursnes	Benfica	1346	1440	94
O. Diomandé	Sporting CP	1425	1513	88

Table 5 presents the EPC and delta for players in the 2023/24 Portuguese League season. Players in this table consistently exceed their EPC, indicating they are completing more passes than expected for the risk they are taking. For instance, João Neves of Benfica has a delta of +138, demonstrating his ability to successfully execute passes on a risk-adjusted basis. The metric offers a more nuanced and insightful approach to evaluating passing performance, highlighting players who effectively balance risk and reward in their passing game.

5.2 Game Simulation

As introduced in the original proposal [11], a key application of LEMs is the simulation of soccer matches. We distinguish between two primary types of simulations: short-term and long-term. Short-term simulations focus on predicting events within a limited horizon, such as forecasting the likelihood of a goal within the following ten events. Conversely, long-term simulations aim to model an entire match from a specific point until its conclusion, enabling the estimation of match outcomes like the final score or the probability of a win.

Short-Term. Short-term simulations allow for a granular analysis of game dynamics by predicting the immediate consequences of specific in-game situations. At the most basic level, we can simulate a single subsequent event to understand the likely progression of play. By simulating the specified number of subsequent events numerous times and calculating the percentage of simulations in which a goal was scored, we can calculate the probability of a goal in the short term. Figure 5 demonstrates this capability by visualizing the short-term goal-scoring probability throughout a match. Note that these probabilities are crucial for action valuation methods such as VAEP [4].

Long-Term. LEMs can simulate full matches by iteratively feeding the model's output as input, allowing it to generate the next event in the sequence until a terminal state (e.g., the end of the match or a certain number of events). This opens a wide range of analytical possibilities. The generated event sequences are fully compatible with existing event data analysis workflows, provided they operate within the feature space encompassed by LEMs. A key application of long-term simulations is the real-time estimation of match outcome probabilities. In Fig. 6, we present examples of such estimations for three different matches. For each game, we initialized 10,000 simulations from each event. Each point in the plot represents the probability of each outcome at the time of each event.

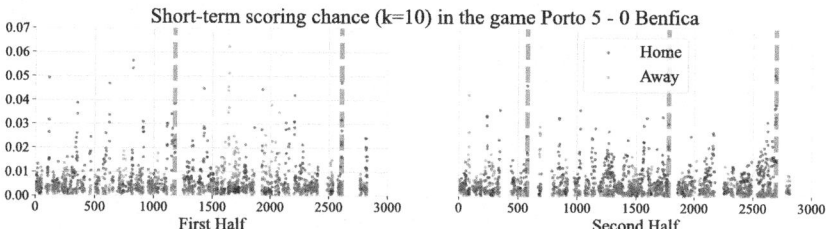

Fig. 5. Short-term probability forecasting, i.e., the chance of scoring within 10 events during the Porto - Benfica, 5–0, March 3, 2024.

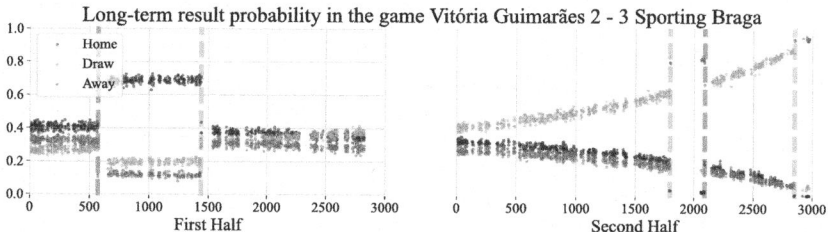

Fig. 6. Real-time long-term probabilities of home, draw, and away win outcomes for a selection of matches, generated using long-term simulations with LEMs. Vertical lines indicate the timing of goals. Vitória Guimarães - Sporting Braga, 2–3, May 11, 2024.

6 Conclusion

We introduced a unified LEM framework that advances soccer analytics by replacing the original chain-of-classifiers approach with a tabular autoregressive model. Our framework delivers superior predictive accuracy and simulation quality. Key findings show that our unified LEM not only outperforms its predecessor in event prediction and simulation fidelity but also achieves an optimal balance of performance and computational efficiency. The versatility of this approach shines through its practical applications, enabling real-time match outcome prediction, detailed player performance analysis and game simulations. By addressing previous limitations like synchronization and scalability with a single, flexible model, the unified LEM lays a robust foundation for the future of soccer analytics. Its adaptability suggests potential applications beyond soccer, extending to other sports or sequential event-driven domains. Future research on transformer-based architectures for further performance gains, and developing fine-tuning techniques to tailor the model to specific tasks or teams will increase the use cases of LEMs even more. This work marks a significant step forward in creating scalable, impactful tools for data-driven sports analysis.

Acknowledgements. This work is financed by National Funds through the Portuguese funding agency, FCT - Fundação para a Ciência e a Tecnologia, within project UIDB/50014/2020.

Disclosure of Interests. The authors have no competing interests to declare that are relevant to the content of this article.

References

1. Anzer, G., Bauer, P.: A goal scoring probability model for shots based on synchronized positional and event data in football (soccer). Front. Sports Active Living **3**, 624475 (2021). https://doi.org/10.3389/fspor.2021.624475
2. Baron, E., Hocevar, D., Salehe, Z.: A foundation model for soccer, Jul 2024. https://doi.org/10.48550/arXiv.2407.14558
3. Open AI: language models are few-shot learners (2020)
4. Decroos, T., Bransen, L., Van Haaren, J., Davis, J.: Actions speak louder than goals: valuing player actions in soccer. In: Proceedings of the 25th ACM SIGKDD International Conference on Knowledge Discovery & Data Mining, pp. 1851–1861. ACM, Anchorage AK USA, July 2019. https://doi.org/10.1145/3292500.3330758
5. Fernández, J., Bornn, L., Cervone, D.: A framework for the fine-grained evaluation of the instantaneous expected value of soccer possessions. Mach. Learn. **110**(6), 1389–1427 (2021). https://doi.org/10.1007/s10994-021-05989-6
6. Hoffmann, J., et al.: Training compute-optimal large language models. In: 36th Conference on Neural Information Processing Systems (NeurIPS 2022) (2022)
7. Kaplan, J., et al.: Scaling laws for neural language models, January 2020. https://doi.org/10.48550/arXiv.2001.08361
8. Singh, K.: Introducing expected threat (xT) (2018)
9. Kingma, D.P., Ba, J.: Adam: a method for stochastic optimization, January 2017. https://doi.org/10.48550/arXiv.1412.6980

10. Mendes-Neves, T., Meireles, L., Mendes-Moreira, J.: Estimating player performance in different contexts using fine-tuned large events models, April 2024. https://doi.org/10.48550/arXiv.2402.06815
11. Mendes-Neves, T., Meireles, L., Mendes-Moreira, J.: Towards a foundation large events model for soccer. Mach. Learn. (2024). https://doi.org/10.1007/s10994-024-06606-y
12. Pappalardo, L., et al.: A public data set of spatio-temporal match events in soccer competitions. Sci. Data **6**(1) (2019). https://doi.org/10.1038/s41597-019-0247-7
13. Pollard, R., Ensum, J., Taylor, S.: Estimating the probability of a shot resulting in a goal: the effects of distance, angle and space. Int. J. Soccer Sci. **2**(1) (2004)
14. Radford, A., Wu, J., Child, R., Luan, D., Amodei, D., Sutskever, I.: language models are unsupervised multitask learners. Open AI (2019)
15. Rudd, S.: A framework for tactical analysis and individual offensive production assessment in soccer using markov chains. New England Symposium on Statistics in Sports (2011)
16. Simpson, I., Beal, R.J., Locke, D., Norman, T.J.: Seq2Event: learning the language of soccer using transformer-based match event prediction. In: Proceedings of the 28th ACM SIGKDD Conference on Knowledge Discovery and Data Mining, ACM, August 2022. https://doi.org/10.1145/3534678.3539138
17. Spearman, W., Basye, A., Dick, G., Hotovy, R., Pop, P.: Physics-based modeling of pass probabilities in soccer (2017)
18. Touvron, H., et al.: LLaMA: open and efficient foundation language models, February 2023. https://doi.org/10.48550/arXiv.2302.13971
19. Vaswani, A., et al.: Attention is all you need. ArXiV (2017)
20. Wang, Z., et al.: Tacticai: an ai assistant for football tactics. Nat. Commun. **15**(1), 1906 (2024). https://doi.org/10.1038/s41467-024-45965-x

Web and Social Networks

Who is at Risk? Analyzing the Risk of Radicalization Among Reddit Users

Ece Calikus[1(✉)], Gianmarco De Francisci Morales[2], and Aristides Gionis[3]

[1] Department of Information Technology, Uppsala University, Uppsala, Sweden
ece.calikus@it.uu.se
[2] CENTAI, Turin, Italy
gdfm@acm.org
[3] Division of Theoretical Computer Science, KTH Royal Institute of Technology, Stockholm, Sweden
argioni@kth.se

Abstract. Online radicalization is a growing societal concern. Extremist groups actively exploit online media to reach wide audiences, spreading ideologies that incite hate and violence. The lack of transparency and conscious use of social media worsens this issue, as users often remain unaware of being targeted by disinformation or radical propaganda. This work analyzes the risk of online radicalization and provides insights for individuals, platforms, and policymakers to mitigate its harmful effects. We conduct a data-driven study to analyze Reddit users' radicalization risk. We build a temporal classification model using interpretable machine learning to predict the risk of radicalization with features based on RECRO, a recent social theory of Internet-mediated radicalization. Our findings reveal RECRO features are strong indicators, with features from later stages having greater influence. We also analyze risk distributions across communities, showing higher risk in controversial groups but also identifying extremists in generic and neutral communities. This result highlights the importance of critical thinking when engaging with online content.

Keywords: social media analysis · risk prediction · online safety

1 Introduction

Social media platforms and online forums have reshaped social communication and societal discourse in an unprecedented way. Despite initially being expected as a democratizing tool for information access and sharing, they have contributed to serious negative phenomena such as political polarization, echo chambers, disinformation and online segregation [9,11,14]. Over time, discourse on critical topics has become toxic, enabling extremists to influence public discussions, connecting with like-minded individuals [10] and radicalizing sympathizers [29].

Individuals engage with social media from different starting points. Some already hold extreme beliefs, while others may gradually accept radical views over time through their online interactions [28]. An important concern with online platforms is the lack of transparency regarding the activities and interactions of social media users. Many users are unaware of whether they are targeted by misinformation campaigns or trapped within echo chambers [7]. Therefore, they lack the necessary tools to employ prevention strategies before becoming deeply connected with controversial groups online.

In this paper, we conduct a data-driven analysis of radicalization risk among Reddit users and provide insights into their susceptibility to radicalization [39]. We develop a risk-prediction model that not only assesses radicalization risk but also elucidates the contributing factors.

Our approach begins by identifying relevant features associated with the risk of radicalization. To achieve this goal, we adopt the RECRO model, a social science framework for internet-mediated radicalization proposed by Neo [29]. RECRO is the acronym for the five stages of radicalization presented in this framework: *Reflection, Exploration, Connection, Resolution, and Operational*. Similar to other works [33,36], our study focuses on the first three phases of RECRO, which can be inferred from the users' online behaviors unlike the final two phases corresponding to real-world actions. The phases considered are: (*i*) *Reflection*: users' predisposition to radicalization; (*ii*) *Exploration*: the process of developing new viewpoints; and (*iii*) *Connection*: bonding with radicalized groups [29]. We hypothesize that an individual's radicalization risk evolves throughout these phases and is strongly correlated with the factors outlined within each phase. We empirically ground this theoretical framework via an exploratory analysis of Reddit data.

We consider the prediction of radicalization risk to be a high-stakes decision-making problem where inaccurate estimation can have important consequences. Misclassifying some groups of users or individuals as having a high risk of radicalization can potentially intensify societal biases, while failing to estimate radicalized groups may legitimize and reassure their behaviors. Therefore, our approach prioritizes developing a risk-prediction model that is highly intelligible and reliable.

To achieve our research goals, we use *generalized additive models* (GAMs) [18], which are effective for building inherently interpretable models [6]. A GAM is a linear combination of nonlinear submodels, each processing a single feature [46]. The contribution of each feature can be visualized, making them highly intelligible [5]. For our risk-prediction model, we use *explainable boosted machines* (EBM) [30], a GAM-based model offering accuracy comparable to more complex machine learning (ML) models, while remaining transparent.

To train our model, we annotate Reddit users as high and low risk based on their online activities. We obtain data from banned subreddits known to produce violent and hateful content and assume their users are at higher risk of radicalization. We also collect data from /r/neutralnews and /r/NeutralPolitics as proxies for low-risk individuals.

Our analysis shows that REC features are strong predictors of radicalization risk, thus supporting our hypothesis. Features from later RECRO phases have a stronger impact on predicted risk, and the average risk among high-risk users increases over time. These findings are consistent with social theories which describe radicalization as a gradual, multi-stage process [29,42].

In addition to feature analysis, we study the distribution of risk among users in various Reddit communities. Specifically, we compare users in non-banned but controversial communities (e.g., /r/MensRights, /r/AskTrumpSupporters) similar to those in banned ones (e.g., /r/incels, /r/The_Donald), their 'antipodal' communities (e.g., /r/AskFeminists, /r/hillaryclinton), and broader topic subreddits (e.g., /r/politics, /r/economics). While users in controversial communities are at higher risk, radicalization risk is also present in more general communities.

Our contributions can be summarized as follows:

- We propose a data-driven approach inspired by a social theory to analyze the risk of radicalization of Reddit users. We open-source anonymized data and code to facilitate reproducibility, with the potential for generalizing to all Reddit users.[1]
- We develop a risk-prediction model that uses an interpretable ML method, enabling an in-depth analysis of features contributing to radicalization risk. We empirically validate the RECRO theory on large-scale real-world data by analyzing the impact of REC features on predicting radicalization risk.
- We conduct a comprehensive study of Reddit users across diverse communities, revealing that no online platform offers a foolproof "safe space," highlighting the need for vigilance in online content consumption.

2 Related Work

Radicalization theories model how individuals shift from conforming viewpoints to extreme ideologies [29]. Social sciences offer multiple theories [29,42]. For example, the 3N approach [42] models the physiological factors in radicalization using three stages: (*i*) needs (drives behind radicalization), (*ii*) narratives (legitimating extreme behaviors), and (*iii*) networks (connections with like-minded individuals). In this work, we use the RECRO model [29], a pathway-based framework comprising five phases, as discussed in the introduction, and we exclusively focus on the first three stages (REC).

Computational Analysis of Online Extremism. The study of radicalization on the internet has attracted research from the area of computational science. Hosseinmardi et al. [20] examine the radical content on YouTube and discover that consumption of political videos is affected by both user preferences and platform features. Papadamou et al. [32] also analyze YouTube videos to investigate whether recommendation algorithms guide users towards Incel-related content, a movement known for hateful and misogynistic views. Garimella et al. [11] study the role of partisan users and gatekeepers in political echo chambers on social media. Rollo et al. [35] develop an "attention-flow" graph to track the shifting interests of Reddit users across subreddits, identifying potential gateways to radicalized communities.

---

[1] https://github.com/reguluslus/RedditRiskPrediction.

Relation to Prior Work. Some existing approaches also incorporate social theories in their models. Lerman et al. [24] use the 3N radicalization model [42] to study pro-anorexia communities on X. The most related works to ours by Phadke et al. [33] and Russo et al. [36] also incorporate the initial three stages of the RECRO model. Phadke et al. [33] study the impact of RECRO stages on conspiracy theory discussions by analyzing users in a single subreddit /r/conspiracy. Conversely, Russo et al. [36] operationalize RECRO parameters and analyze their impact on users migrating to a fringe platform after a community on Reddit is banned by studying two subreddits (/r/The_Donald and /r/fatpeoplehate).

Our study differs in several ways. First, previous work focuses on specific use cases (e.g., conspiracy communities and user migrations) and examines only a few subreddits. By contrast, we use RECRO to build a broader model predicting radicalization risk for all Reddit users. Second, we incorporate temporal information to track how risk and its contributing factors evolve. Third, while we use the same RECRO stages, we rely on different features, apart from some similar linguistic features during reflection. Finally, our experiments address distinct research questions: "Do later RECRO stages influence radicalization risk more?" and "Is risk prevalent outside controversial communities?".

3 Data

We download historical Reddit data from the PushShift repository [2], comprised of comments and posts from 1 January 2016 to 31 December 2020 taken from the most popular 20k subreddits. Reddit is organized into subreddits: forums for specific topics [27]. Users can join subreddits to share and receive information, while whether a user subscribes to a subreddit is not public. We can only collect data for users who have posted or commented on a subreddit. For our risk-prediction model, we categorize Reddit users as "high-risk" and "low-risk" cohorts based on the subreddits they actively participated in.

Over the years, numerous controversial subreddits have emerged to spread radical ideologies and hateful content [16,35]. Reddit introduced quarantining for subreddits violating their policies, eventually banning persistent violators [37]. In our study, we use these banned subreddits as proxies for communities with high radicalization risk. To identify banned subreddits, we scrape the homepages of all subreddits in the PushShift dataset [2] and send requests to each URL. If a subreddit is banned, the request returns a ban warning message. We retain only those banned for radicalization-related reasons (e.g., "promoting hate" or "inciting violence") and exclude subreddits banned for other reasons such as "graphic content" or "copyright violations"[2]. Ultimately, we retain 115 subreddits banned between Jan 1, 2016, and Dec 31, 2020. Following [27], users with at least five posts or 25 comments in a banned subreddit are labeled "high-risk."

For the "low-risk"' cohort, we select users from neutral communities (/r/neutralnews and /r/NeutralPolitics), focused on polite, empirical discussions of news and politics. Despite their intent, some users in these communities

---
[2] https://redditinc.com/policies/content-policy.

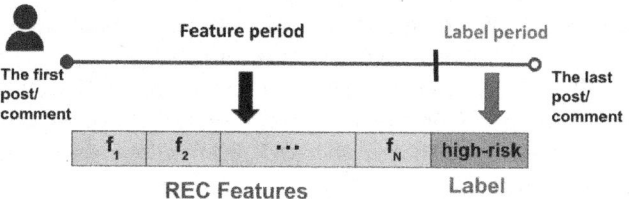

Fig. 1. Feature and label periods on user journeys.

are also active in banned ones. To ensure dataset integrity, we exclude such users and include the remaining neutral community users in the "low-risk"' cohort, applying the same cutoff as for "high-risk"' users.

We consider users' entire Reddit history including all the subreddits they participated in. Each user's historical data is split into an observation (feature) period and a subsequent label period (Fig. 1) [21]. Users posted or commented in banned subreddits during the label period are labeled "high-risk," others as "low-risk." This separation lets us predict future participation in banned subreddits, identifying users particularly at risk. Notably, even previously "high-risk" users are labeled "low-risk" if they never participated in a banned community during the label period. Consequently, risk scores are higher for users likely to engage in banned communities soon, and lower for those who never do or cease participating.

4 Measuring Radicalization Features

4.1 Reflection

The "reflection" phase is described as "the triggers, needs, and vulnerabilities that an individual may have, which increase one's susceptibility towards alternative belief systems" [29]. Personal traits, issues, and social life can shape one's openness to exploring new online viewpoints, including those supporting violent extremism. In this study, we use several language markers in Reddit posts and comments as proxies for psychological states and personality traits to analyze the reflection phase.

Linguistic Features. Psycho-linguistic features in users' online behavior, such as comments expressing anger, anxiety, and heightened emotions are markers of radicalization [16,33,38].

To extract linguistic features, we use Empath [8], an open-source tool that analyzes text through lexical categories. We include Empath scores for four pre-built categories: *anger, hate, nervousness, and positive emotion*. We calculate the average empath score for user u and a given category α as

$$R^\alpha_{\text{emp}}(u) = \frac{\sum_{i=1}^{m} e(p_i) + \sum_{j=1}^{n} e(c_j)}{m+n}, \qquad (1)$$

where $e(p_i)$ and $e(c_j)$ are the empath scores of the ith post and j^{th} comment, and m and n are the number of posts and comments.

We expect all factors except "positive emotion" to positively correlate with radicalization risk scores. Conversely, "positive emotion" is anticipated to negatively correlate, indicating that higher-risk users show less positivity in their Reddit posts and comments.

Moral Foundations. Moral judgments have shown to be important features for understanding political polarization [44], group formation [13], and radicalization [1]. We analyze the moral content in the text using the extended Moral Foundations Dictionary (eMFD) [19], which includes five core aspects of human morality according to Moral Foundations Theory [12,17]: *care/harm, fairness/cheating, loyalty/betrayal, authority/subversion, and sanctity/degradation.*

For a given text, the eMFD tool provides a moral foundation scoring in each category which suggests the probability of the text including annotations in that category [19]. To characterize the reflection phase of the use u, we compute the moral foundation scores in each category β as

$$R^{\beta}_{\text{moral}}(u) = \frac{\sum_{i=1}^{m} f(p_i) + \sum_{j=1}^{n} f(c_j)}{m+n}, \tag{2}$$

where $f(p_i)$ and $f(c_j)$ are the moral foundation scores of the ith post and j^{th} comment, and m and n are the number of posts and comments.

4.2 Exploration

In RECRO, the "exploration" phase is when individuals search online for alternative belief systems, exposing them to radical narratives and new worldviews [29]. We posit that the spread of radical ideas often relies on disinformation, thereby increasing individuals' vulnerability to exposure to misinformation. Studies also link conspiracy theories to extremism, suggesting conspiracy communities can serve as gateways to radicalization [33,35].

To incorporate misinformation and conspiracy features, we use Media Bias Fact Check (MBFC),[3] an independent organization rating media sources on political bias, factual reporting, and conspiracy levels. MBFC, the largest online news credibility evaluator, covers about 5300 web pages [4,43]. We crawl MBFC to collect factuality and conspiracy scores for news sources.

Exposure to Misinformation. We quantify exposure to misinformation by estimating the misinformation content in subreddits that the user engages with. If a user posts or comments in a subreddit, we assume they are likely exposed to its content, either directly through subscription or indirectly through algorithmic recommendations.

We adopt an approach similar to the one presented by [43]. We gather data from MBFC's Web pages, which are organized into various categories such as "left bias," "right bias," "questionable sources," and "conspiracy-pseudoscience."

---
[3] https://mediabiasfactcheck.com.

We collect the names, URLs, and factuality ratings of each news source. MBFC rates factual reporting on a 6-point Likert scale, from "very low" to "very high." We convert these categorical ratings to numerical values in the range $[-2, 3]$, where "very low" corresponds to -2 and "very high" to 3. We calculate the factuality score for a subreddit as the average score of all links shared there, excluding unrated links. Finally, we quantify the exposure to misinformation for a user, denoted as u, as follows:

$$E_{\text{mis}}(u) = -\frac{\sum_{i=1}^{k} f(s_i)}{k}, \quad (3)$$

where $f(s_i)$ is the factuality score of the ith subreddit and k is the number of subreddits that user u has posted or commented.

Seeking Conspiracy. We measure exposure to conspiracy-related content similarly to misinformation. We extract and annotate the news sources categorized under "Conspiracy-Pseudoscience" on the MBFC website. Additionally, we review sources in the "Questionable Source" category, annotating those with "conspiracy" as well. A subreddit's conspiracy score is the ratio of conspiracy-labeled links to all MBFC-categorized links posted in that subreddit. Finally, we quantify the exposure to misinformation for user u as

$$E_{\text{consp}}(u) = \frac{\sum_{i=1}^{k} c(s_i)}{k}, \quad (4)$$

where $c(s_i)$ is the conspiracy score of the ith subreddit and k is the total number of subreddits where user u has written.

4.3 Connection

During the "connection" phase, individuals deepen their radical perspective by interacting with like-minded communities [29]. We assume users who frequently post or comment in Reddit communities with hateful, offensive, or discriminatory discussions are more likely to bond with and adopt the views of those groups.

To identify problematic subreddits, one approach might involve using banned communities or those with similar discussions, often moderated for reasons like "promoting hate" or "inciting violence." However, since our training data for high-risk users comes exclusively from banned communities, and low-risk users never participate in them, using similar communities to characterize the connection phase risks data leakage.

Instead, we measure the language toxicity in the community to analyze whether its users frequently include abusive and harmful content in their posts and discussions. For this, we use Google's Perspective API,[4] a widely adopted tool for toxicity assessment [23,36]. The API provides scores (0 to 1) for attributes like "toxicity," "insult," "threat," and "sexually explicit." We focus on

---

[4] https://perspectiveapi.com.

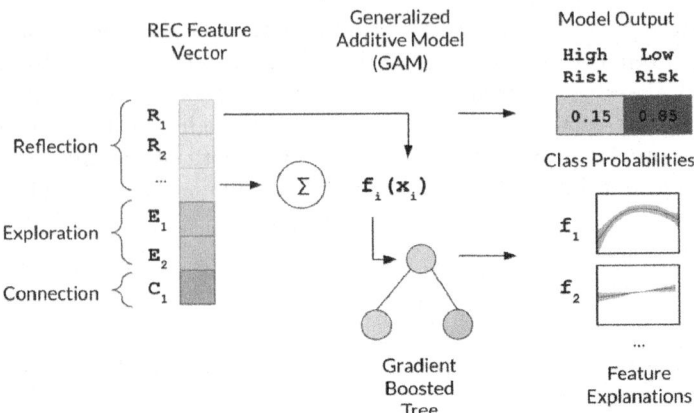

Fig. 2. Illustration of the risk-prediction model. It takes REC features as input, producing risk probabilities and feature attributions (adapted from [45]).

the "toxicity," attribute, defining a subreddit's toxicity level, $t(s_i)$, as the average toxicity score of all its posts and comments.

$$t(s_i) = \frac{\sum_{i=1}^{m} t(p_i) + \sum_{j=1}^{n} t(c_j)}{m + n}, \tag{5}$$

where $t(p_i)$ and $t(c_i)$ are the toxicity scores of the ith post and j^{th} comment and m and n are the total number of posts and comments published in subreddit s_i.

Finally, the engagement score of a given user u, is computed as the average number of posts and comments across the list of subreddits in which u participated, with each subreddit being weighted with its toxicity score

$$C_{\text{eng}}(u) = \frac{\sum_{i=1}^{k} t(s_i)(m_i + n_i)}{k}, \tag{6}$$

where $t(s_i)$ is the toxicity score of the ith subreddit, m_i and n_i are the number of posts and comments made by u in s_i respectively, and k is the total number of subreddits in which u has been active.

While Russo et al. [36] use user-level "language toxicity" to operationalize the reflection phase, we argue that toxic language does not inherently indicate vulnerability to radicalization. Instead, individuals adopt more toxic behavior after joining radical communities. Therefore, we focus on community-level toxicity to spot problematic subreddits likely to be radicalizing, thereby capturing the connection phase.

5 Risk-Prediction Model

Generalized additive models (GAMs) [18] are a category of models that offer greater flexibility and efficacy compared to linear models while still being more

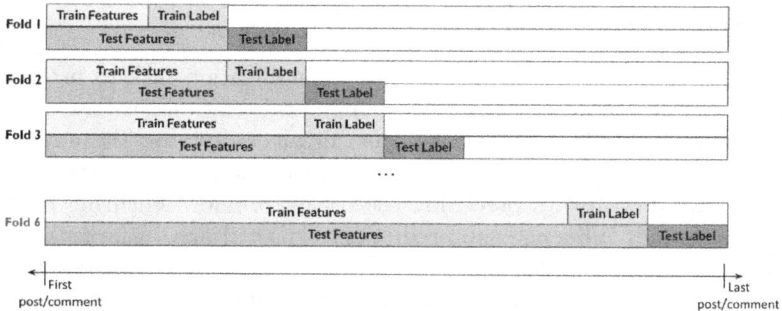

Fig. 3. Temporal cross-validation procedure.

interpretable than complex models such as neural networks [46]. A GAM models the target variable as the sum of non-linear functions of single input features [46]. The impact of each term on the final prediction can be visualized by plotting the target variable as the output of each function and the given term [6].

In particular, we employ Explainable Boosting Machines (EBMs) [30], which are based on the GA^2M algorithm [5,25], and belong to the family of GAMs of the following form

$$g(E[y]) = \beta_0 + \sum f_j(x_j) + \sum f_{ij}(x_i, x_j), \tag{7}$$

where $g(\cdot)$ is the link function depending on the ML task, x_j is the jth feature, f_j is the shape function for feature x_j, and f_{ij} is a function for pairwise interactions between x_i and x_j. Each input feature x_j is a REC feature (e.g., R_{tox} or E_{mis}) presented in Sect. 4. The shape function f_j is learned by using gradient-boosted ensembles of bagged trees. Since we formulate our problem as a binary classification model that predicts users' risk of radicalization as "high risk" or "low risk," the link function $g(\cdot)$ is a logit (inverse of the logistic function).

Figure 2 shows a depiction of the model. EBM improves on traditional GAM by capturing feature interactions and employing tree-based ensemble learning. It achieves performance on par with other tree-based boosting methods [30] while remaining highly interpretable by decomposing its prediction into each feature's contribution. We use the EBM implementation provided by InterpretML [30].

6 Results

This section presents results from the collected data and risk-prediction model. We first show performance comparisons between the EBM and other ML models. Next, we analyze how radicalization features influence user risk and their evolving importance over time. Finally, we compare risk distributions across communities with differing viewpoints.

6.1 Predictive Performance

We frame our problem as a temporal binary classification task to predict users' radicalization risk. To accurately capture temporal relations, we use a temporal cross-validation procedure [22,34,40]. This involves dividing the data into six temporal folds (see Fig. 3). Each fold contains a training and testing set, with the training window always preceding the testing window, ensuring that future information doesn't influence the prediction of past. Each training and testing split also has consecutive feature and label periods (explained in Sect. 3). REC features are generated from user posts and comments during the feature period, while users are labeled "high-risk" or "low-risk" based on their posting or commenting activity in banned subreddits during the label period. This setup allows for early prediction of radicalization risk.

As stated by Neo [29], the stages of RECRO are not distinctly separated and can occur simultaneously. Thus, all 12 features characterizing the REC phases are included in each fold. Reddit users in our data do not have uniform timelines regarding the first and last dates of their activity, total duration, and posting frequency. Therefore, we split the temporal folds based on the percentage of total time spent on Reddit, rather than specific dates. This approach allows us to track how risk changes for each user over their timeline, instead of focusing on specific calendar times.

For final predictions (Table 1) and feature analysis (Fig. 8), the first five folds are used to select the best parameters, while the last fold is held out to report final results.

Figure 4 shows the temporal-cross-validation results from EBM and three other classification models (Random Forest, XGBoost, and Logistic Regression) using the same set of REC features. Each fold shows the average ROC-AUC scores obtained from each hyperparameter tuned for that model. Additionally, Table 1 shows the final prediction performance on four metrics: ROC-AUC, accuracy, precision, and recall. In terms of prediction performance, EBM exhibits performance on par with state-of-the-art ML methods such as Random Forest and XGBoost. This result aligns with observations in previous studies [15,30]. All methods achieve a high classification performance, thus, showing that it is possible to automatically distinguish Reddit users at higher radicalization risk from the ones at lower risk over time by using the REC features.

Table 1. Risk prediction performance of different ML models.

Model	ROC-AUC	Accuracy	Precision	Recall
EBM	0.8179	0.8186	0.6223	0.8165
XGBoost	0.7978	0.7892	0.5741	0.8165
Random Forest	0.7649	0.7794	0.5673	0.7339
Logistic Regression	0.7846	0.8039	0.6090	0.7431

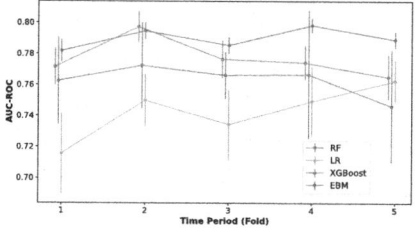 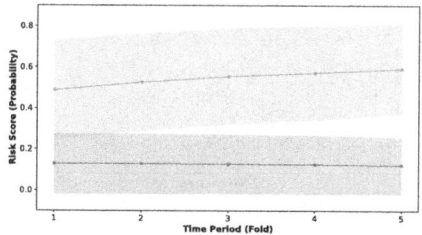

Fig. 4. Temporal cross-validation results for each method

Fig. 5. Average risk over time for high and low-risk cohorts.

Figure 5 shows how risks progress over time among different types of users. This figure presents the average risk scores for users from high- and low-risk cohorts, as described in Sect. 3. The risk scores of users in the high-risk cohort steadily increase on average, while they remain relatively stable among low-risk users. Note that users within the same cohort do not exhibit identical activity on Reddit, and we cannot assume they follow the stages of RECRO in the same manner. Some users may enter problematic communities at much earlier stages and then cease engaging with these communities, while others may experience a slower progression but become more deeply connected with these communities [26]. Nevertheless, the overall trend indicates that the risk of radicalization progressively advances on average during users' online journeys, aligning with the prevailing social theories about online radicalization [29,42].

6.2 Feature Analysis

The additive property of the EBM model enables measuring each input feature's contribution to the prediction. Each term $f(x_i)$ in the model returns a score (i.e., a log odds ratio), which is subsequently added to the users' predicted risk [5]. More specifically, $f(x_i) > 0$ implies that x_i contributes to a positive label (high risk), while $f(x_i) < 0$ implies that x_i contributes to a negative label (low risk).

Figure 6 displays the importance of REC features in models trained with temporal cross-validation. The y-axis shows the mean absolute value of feature importance scores across the training set [5,30], computed by scoring each data point using one feature at a time and averaging the absolute values. The figure illustrates how importance scores for different REC phases evolve over time.

The most influential feature is typically a connection phase feature measuring engagement with toxic communities, closely followed by an exploration feature quantifying exposure to misinformation. Since users experience REC phases simultaneously, some engage with banned communities early and are labeled high-risk, which may explain why the connection feature remains influential even in the early stages. In contrast, conspiracy seeking, the second exploration feature, behaves differently: it ranks third in importance during the first three periods but drops significantly to fifth by the end.

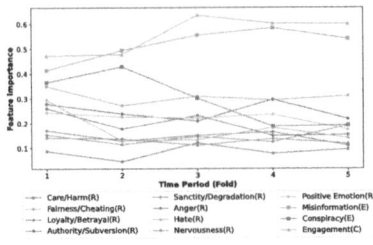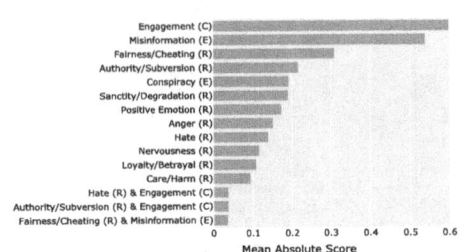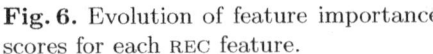

Fig. 6. Evolution of feature importance scores for each REC feature.

Fig. 7. Feature importance table of the final EBM model.

Initially, feature importance scores are closer to each other across all phases, but over time, the gap between the connection and reflection phase features widens. Combined with Fig. 5 showing an increasing trend among risk scores over time, this finding provides empirical support for RECRO, postulating that Internet-mediated radicalization is a process evolving over successive phases [29].

Figure 7 presents the ranking of REC features and their pairwise interactions in the final prediction model based on their importance. Engagement and misinformation remain the most influential features, followed by two morality features (fairness/cheating and authority/subversion), characterizing the reflection phase. Linguistic features, such as anger, hate, and nervousness, contribute significantly less to radicalization risk in comparison. This is notable as many previous studies have emphasized language signals as strong indicators of problematic behavior and have widely used them to analyze radicalization [31,38].

We further analyze the effect of REC features on risk by plotting their shape functions in Fig. 8. The y-axis delineates the scores (log odds ratios) predicted by the model, while the x-axis shows the values of the input REC feature [5]. The error bars represent the standard deviation of the risk score, determined via 100 rounds of bagging [5,30].

The first graph shows the risk scores concerning the connection feature (i.e., engagement), which stands out as the most influential feature in our model. It exhibits a near-logistic growth, with the growth rate peaking between the feature values of 0.11 and 0.17. That is, engagement scores lower and higher than these values push predictions toward low and high-risk classes, respectively.

Misinformation, as an exploration feature and the second most important factor, exhibits a mostly positive trend. This confirms our assumption that exposure to misinformation is significantly associated with radicalization. Such a finding should urge online platforms to enhance their tools and content moderation strategies to limit exposure to misinformation and fake news, thereby mitigating the progression of radicalization. Similarly, the conspiracy shape function, overall suggests an elevated risk for users who explore content from conspiracy-related subreddits and has a positive impact on the prediction target.

Most contributing reflection terms—fairness/cheating, authority/subversion, and positive emotions—exhibit inverse correlation with risk scores, showcasing

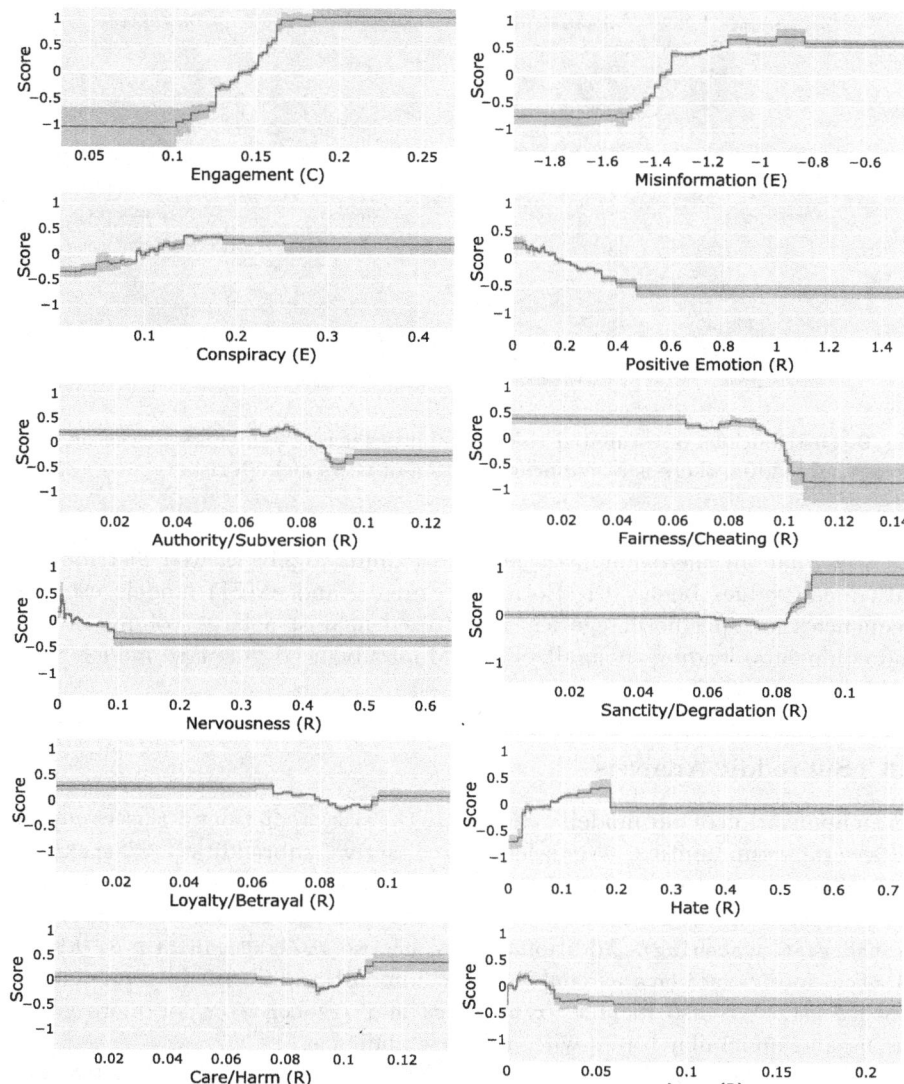

Fig. 8. Shape functions learned by the EBM model that each corresponding a REC feature.

high-risk users use less fairness and authority-related vocabularies and express less positive emotion in their posts and comments. Remarkably, other reflection terms such as loyalty (i.e., "us versus them" thinking) [19], care/harm, anger, hate, and nervousness, known to commonly permeate radical discourse in offline contexts [16,38], have lower impact on prediction results. Their respective shape plots reveal markedly low and frequently inconsistent effects in the logit space.

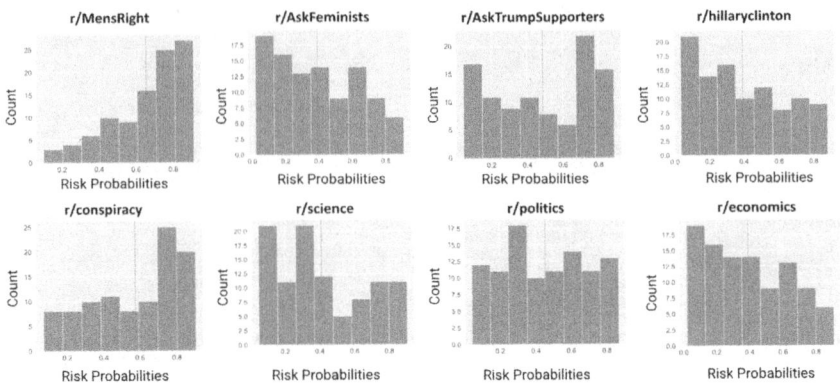

Fig. 9. Distributions of estimated risk probabilities across subreddits. Even on mainstream subreddits, there is a significant portion of users at high risk.

Note that all these linguistic features exhibit highly skewed distributions, with mean values below 0.1. Both the Empath and eMFD models use word frequencies for specific categories, normalized against a large volume of posts and comments, leading to small values. More advanced language models might yield different results.

6.3 Subreddit Analysis

As an application of our model, we compute the risk predictions for users engaged in several communities. We select three active subreddits (/r/MensRights, /r/AskTrumpSupporters, and /r/conspiracy) known for controversial opinions, resembling their banned counterparts (/r/incels, /r/The_Donald, and /r/thegreat-awakening). Additionally, we choose /r/AskFeminists, /r/hillary clinton, and /r/science as contrasting communities, informed by previous literature [41]. We also include /r/politics and /r/economics for more general discussions on similar topics with a diverse audience.

We randomly select 100 users from each subreddit among the 1000 most active users and predict their risk scores with our model. Figure 9 shows the distribution of their risk probabilities. The average risk is considerably higher among users in controversial communities compared to their antipodes or more general communities. However, a substantial number of users in communities such as /r/AskFeminists, /r/hillaryclinton, and /r/politics, are also at risk. This indicates that extreme views are not exclusive to banned or overtly controversial communities, but can be prevalent even in "neutral" or "generic" ones such as /r/science and /r/economics. These findings emphasize the importance of critical thinking when consuming online content and engaging with users.

7 Conclusion

In this paper, we studied the radicalization risk of Reddit users by combining a data-driven approach with a social theory framework, RECRO. We developed a risk-prediction model using a GAM-based machine-learning method, enabling detailed analysis of features contributing to risk. The model was trained on historical data, with users from banned and neutral communities selected and annotated using a temporal validation design.

Our study analyzed how features within the RECRO framework impact radicalization risk over time. Features from later RECRO phases have stronger predictive power, particularly during later periods of users' online journeys. We also examined risk in communities similar to banned ones, their opposite groups, and general topic subreddits. Results showed many users in controversial communities are at high risk, and even generic communities have notable numbers of at-risk users, highlighting the importance of critical thinking online.

Limitations. Radicalization risk is subjective and hard to quantify. We use banned communities as proxies for heightened risk, based on frequent violations of Reddit's rules against inciting violence or hate. However, "low risk" does not rule out radical beliefs, and "high risk" does not confirm actual radicalization.

We carefully prevent data leakage, ensuring none of the REC features rely on the target variable or future information. Still, the model relies on curated data from clearly distinct communities, and real-world risk distributions may not be so bimodal. Furthermore, radicalization can be a multifactorial process [3]. We frame it as a binary classification to leverage ML models for risk prediction. Future research should refine this approach.

Acknowledgments. This research was funded by the ERC Advanced Grant REBOUND (834862), and the Wallenberg AI, Autonomous Systems and Software Program (WASP) funded by the Knut and Alice Wallenberg Foundation.

Ethical Considerations. This research addresses the sensitive subjects of radicalization and online extremism, requiring careful use of ML models and interpretation of results. Our goal is to identify key factors that increase susceptibility to radicalization risk on online platforms and draw attention to safety and awareness. We strive to ensure our research outcomes are accurate, transparent, and framed to avoid perpetuating harmful narratives or stereotypes. Our dataset comes from the PushShift archive [2], a widely used public resource in over a hundred peer-reviewed studies. No personally identifiable information is used, and all analyses are aggregated to ensure user anonymity. This study involved no human interventions and required no IRB review.

References

1. Alizadeh, M., Weber, I., Cioffi-Revilla, C., Fortunato, S., Macy, M.: Psychology and morality of political extremists: evidence from twitter language analysis of alt-right and antifa. EPJ Data Sci. 8(1), 1–35 (2019)

2. Baumgartner, J., Zannettou, S., Keegan, B., Squire, M., Blackburn, J.: The pushshift reddit dataset. ICWSM **14**, 830–839 (2020)
3. Berger, J.M.: Extremism. MIT Press (2018)
4. Bozarth, L., Saraf, A., Budak, C.: Higher ground? how groundtruth labeling impacts our understanding of fake news about the 2016 us presidential nominees. In: ICWSM, vol. 14, pp. 48–59 (2020)
5. Caruana, R., Lou, Y., Gehrke, J., Koch, P., Sturm, M., Elhadad, N.: Intelligible models for healthcare: predicting pneumonia risk and hospital 30-day readmission. In: KDD, pp. 1721–1730 (2015)
6. Chang, C.H., Tan, S., Lengerich, B., Goldenberg, A., Caruana, R.: How interpretable and trustworthy are gams? In: KDD, pp. 95–105 (2021)
7. Cinelli, M., Francisci Morales, G., Galeazzi, A., Quattrociocchi, W., Starnini, M.: The echo chamber effect on social media. PNAS **118**(9), e2023301118 (2021)
8. Fast, E., Chen, B., Bernstein, M.: Empath: understanding topic signals in large-scale text. In: CHI, pp. 4647–4657, May 2016
9. Garimella, K., De Francisci Morales, G., Gionis, A., Mathioudakis, M.: Quantifying controversy in social media. In: WSDM (2016)
10. Garimella, K., De Francisci Morales, G., Gionis, A., Mathioudakis, M.: Reducing controversy by connecting opposing views. In: WSDM (2017)
11. Garimella, K., De Francisci Morales, G., Gionis, A., Mathioudakis, M.: Political discourse on social media: echo chambers, gatekeepers, and the price of bipartisanship. In: WWW (2018)
12. Graham, J., et al.: Moral foundations theory: the pragmatic validity of moral pluralism. In: Advances in Experimental Social Psychology, vol. 47, pp. 55–130. Elsevier (2013)
13. Graham, J., Haidt, J., Nosek, B.A.: Liberals and conservatives rely on different sets of moral foundations. J. Pers. Soc. Psychol. **96**(5), 1029 (2009)
14. Guess, A.M., Nyhan, B., Reifler, J.: Exposure to untrustworthy websites in the 2016 us election. Nat. Hum. Behav. **4**(5), 472–480 (2020)
15. Guldogan, E., Yagin, F.H., Pinar, A., Colak, C., Kadry, S., Kim, J.: A proposed tree-based explainable artificial intelligence approach for the prediction of angina pectoris. Sci. Rep. **13**(1), 22189 (2023)
16. Habib, H., Srinivasan, P., Nithyanand, R.: Making a radical misogynist: how online social engagement with the manosphere influences traits of radicalization. CSCW **6**(the CSCW2), 1–28 (2022)
17. Haidt, J.: The new synthesis in moral psychology. Science **316**(5827), 998–1002 (2007)
18. Hastie, T., Tibshirani, R.: Generalized additive models: some applications. J. Amer. Statist. Assoc. **82**(398) (1987)
19. Hopp, F.R., Fisher, J.T., Cornell, D., Huskey, R., Weber, R.: The extended moral foundations dictionary (emfd): development and applications of a crowd-sourced approach to extracting moral intuitions from text. Behav. Res. Methods **53**, 232–246 (2021)
20. Hosseinmardi, H., Ghasemian, A., Clauset, A., Mobius, M., Rothschild, D., Watts, D.: Examining the consumption of radical content on YouTube. PNAS **118**(32) (2021)
21. Hyndman, R.J., Athanasopoulos, G.: Forecasting: principles and practice. OTexts (2018)
22. Kumar, A., et al.: Using machine learning to assess the risk of and prevent water main breaks. In: KDD, pp. 472–480 (2018)

23. Kumar, D., Hancock, J., Thomas, K., Durumeric, Z.: Understanding the behaviors of toxic accounts on Reddit. In: WebConf, pp. 2797–2807 (2023)
24. Lerman, K., et al.: Radicalized by thinness: using a model of radicalization to understand pro-anorexia communities on Twitter. arXiv:2305.11316 (2023)
25. Lou, Y., Caruana, R., Gehrke, J., Hooker, G.: Accurate intelligible models with pairwise interactions. In: KDD, pp. 623–631 (2013)
26. Monti, C., Aiello, L.M., De Francisci Morales, G., Bonchi, F.: The language of opinion change on social media under the lens of communicative action. Sci. Rep. **12**, 17920 (2022)
27. Monti, C., D'Ignazi, J., Starnini, M., De Francisci Morales, G.: Evidence of demographic rather than ideological segregation in news discussion on Reddit. In: WebConf, pp. 2777–2786 (2023)
28. Necaise, A., Williams, A., Vrzakova, H., Amon, M.J.: Regularity versus novelty of users' multimodal comment patterns and dynamics as markers of social media radicalization. In: Hypertext, pp. 237–243 (2021)
29. Neo, L.S.: An internet-mediated pathway for online radicalisation: RECRO. In: Violent Extremism: Breakthroughs in Research and Practice (2019)
30. Nori, H., Jenkins, S., Koch, P., Caruana, R.: Interpretml: a unified framework for machine learning interpretability. arXiv preprint arXiv:1909.09223 (2019)
31. Nouh, M., Nurse, J.R., Goldsmith, M.: Understanding the radical mind: identifying signals to detect extremist content on Twitter. In: IEEE ISI, pp. 98–103. IEEE (2019)
32. Papadamou, K., et al.: "How over is it?" Understanding the incel community on YouTube. CSCW **5** (2021)
33. Phadke, S., Samory, M., Mitra, T.: Pathways through conspiracy: the evolution of conspiracy radicalization through engagement in online conspiracy discussions. In: ICWSM, vol. 16, pp. 770–781 (2022)
34. Ramachandran, A., et al.: Predictive analytics for retention in care in an urban hiv clinic. Sci. Rep. **10**(1), 6421 (2020)
35. Rollo, C., De Francisci Morales, G., Monti, C., Panisson, A.: Communities, gateways, and bridges: measuring attention flow in the reddit political sphere. In: SocInfo (2022)
36. Russo, G., Horta Ribeiro, M., Casiraghi, G., Verginer, L.: Understanding online migration decisions following the banning of radical communities. In: WebSci (2023)
37. Russo, G., Verginer, L., Ribeiro, M.H., Casiraghi, G.: Spillover of antisocial behavior from fringe platforms: The unintended consequences of community banning. In: ICWSM, vol. 17, pp. 742–753 (2023)
38. Shrestha, A., Kaati, L., Cohen, K.: Extreme adopters in digital communities. J. Threat Assess. Manag. **7**(1–2), 72 (2020)
39. Thompson, R.: Radicalization and the use of social media. J. Strateg. Secur. **4**(4), 167–190 (2011)
40. Vajiac, C., et al.: Preventing eviction-caused homelessness through ml-informed distribution of rental assistance. In: AAAI, vol. 38, pp. 22393–22400 (2024)
41. Waller, I., Anderson, A.: Quantifying social organization and political polarization in online platforms. Nature **600**(7888), 264–268 (2021)
42. Webber, D., Kruglanski, A.W.: Psychological factors in radicalization: a "3n" approach. In: The Handbook of the Criminology of Terrorism, pp. 33–46 (2016)
43. Weld, G., Glenski, M., Althoff, T.: Political bias and factualness in news sharing across more than 100,000 online communities. In: ICWSM, vol. 15, pp. 796–807 (2021)

44. Wolsko, C., Ariceaga, H., Seiden, J.: Red, white, and blue enough to be green: effects of moral framing on climate change attitudes and conservation behaviors. J. Exp. Soc. Psychol. **65**, 7–19 (2016)
45. Xenopoulos, P., Freeman, W.R., Silva, C.: Analyzing the differences between professional and amateur esports through win probability. In: WebConf, pp. 3418–3427 (2022)
46. Zhuang, H., et al.: Interpretable ranking with generalized additive models. In: WSDM, pp. 499–507 (2021)

Knowledge Distillation for Job Title Prediction and Project Recommendation in Open Source Communities

Xin Liu, Hang Su, and Xuesong Lu(✉)

East China Normal University, Shanghai, China
{xinliu,suhang}@stu.ecnu.edu.cn, xslu@dase.ecnu.edu.cn

Abstract. In the era of rapid digitalization, the demand for digital talents is surging and talent management in open source communities has become a crucial research area. This paper explores the application of large language models (LLMs) in two key talent management tasks within open source communities: project recommendation and job title prediction. First, we construct an evaluation dataset TM-Eval to assess the performance of LLMs on the two tasks. Second, we construct a QA dataset JA-QA from LinkedIn that describes the required APIs for each job title with job description. The dataset is used to distill knowledge pertaining to job-API correspondence of larger LLMs into smaller ones, in order to reduce computational overhead for the two tasks. We propose a hierarchical knowledge transfer method including logit-based distillation, feature-based distillation and task-specific fine-tuning with Low-Rank Adaptation. Experimental results show that larger LLMs outperform smaller ones on the two tasks. Moreover, the proposed distillation method can effectively enhance the performance of smaller LLMs, making them even surpass the original larger LLMs in some cases. This study provides a new approach for talent management in open source communities, which leverages the knowledge of LLMs to improve prediction and recommendation accuracy while reducing computational overhead. A replication package is available at https://github.com/DaSESmartEdu/KDJPPR.

Keywords: Knowledge Distillation · Large Language Models · Talent Management · Open Source Community

1 Introduction

As the digitalization process of various industries continues to evolve, their demand for digital talents is growing rapidly. A recent report by the National Skills Coalition analyzes 43 million online job postings and finds that 92% of jobs require some type of digital skills[1]. As a gathering place for digital talents, talent management in open source communities is gaining more and more attention,

---
[1] http://t.newsletterext.worldbank.org/r/?id=h23ec8764,c882dba,c88543a

including project recommendation [4,24,25], skill modeling [15,26], developer identification [2,8,17], job title prediction [16,18], and so on.

Existing studies mainly train deep learning models [16,24] or conduct surveys [15,27] to analyze and understand the behaviors of talents in open source communities. With the emergence of large language models (LLMs), it is very interesting to investigate the ability of LLMs on the problem. LLMs are trained with web-scale data and therefore should have a wealth of knowledge pertaining to digital talents, e.g., job titles and digital skills, as well as open source communities, e.g., software, APIs, projects and developers. As such, it is natural to mine the above knowledge of LLMs for talent management in open source communities. The advantages are that one does not have to collect and clean a bunch of data in order to train traditional models, which inevitably takes a lot of preparation time, and can interact with LLMs for talent management in a more semantic way, e.g., instructing an LLM or asking an LLM questions.

In this study, we investigate the ability of LLMs on talent management in open source communities. We particularly focus on two tasks in the literature, namely, project recommendation [4,25] and job title prediction [16,18]. The former aims to recommend suitable open source projects to talents and the latter aims to predict future job titles for talents, based on their past experience in open source communities and the job market. To achieve this, we first construct from the TOSE dataset [16] an evaluation dataset *TM-Eval*, which contains 2,000 data points. Each data point has a context of the historical job titles and API experience in open source projects of a talent, and a prompt that asks an LLM to determine whether the talent is likely to have the target job title (job title prediction) or API experience (project recommendation) in the future. We use TM-Eval to evaluate LLMs and obtain their performance on the two tasks. Second, we hope to reduce the computational overhead of LLMs for the two tasks and hence distill the knowledge of larger LLMs into smaller ones. We construct from LinkedIn[2] a QA dataset *JA-QA* containing 20,000 pairs, where each QA pair contains a question asking about the APIs required by a job title and the corresponding answer depicting a set of APIs. We use JA-QA to distill the knowledge of a teacher LLM into a student LLM by designing three loss functions. Then we use TM-Eval to evaluate the performance of the student LLM on the above two tasks. Experimental results show that 1) larger LLMs perform better as expected than smaller LLMs on the two tasks and 2) our proposed distillation method can effectively improve the performance of smaller LLMs, making them even surpass the original larger LLMs in some cases.

2 Related Work

2.1 Talent Management in Open Source Communities

The research of talent management in open source communities aims to help developers improve their experience and career, as well as improve efficiency and quality of open source software development. Representative problems include project recommendation, job title prediction and skill modeling.

---

[2] https://prospeo.io/api/social-url-enrichment.

Project recommendation focuses on leveraging user behaviors, content features, and social networks to suggest relevant repositories or projects tailored to developers' interests. For instance, Xu et al. [31] leverage developers' behaviors and project content, utilizing TF-IDF and cosine similarity to calculate project similarities. Sun et al. [25] integrate developer behaviors and project features for GitHub project recommendations. They use TF-IDF to extract characteristics from project descriptions and source code, and apply simulated annealing to optimize the parameters for generating top-N recommendations. Shao et al. [24] utilize text encoding and a graph convolutional network (GCN) to convert paper abstracts and GitHub repository descriptions/tags into vectors, helping users find relevant code repositories for academic papers. Dey et al. [4] employ Doc2Vec embeddings to represent developers, projects, and APIs in the skill Space. This model can predict developers' future API usage and project-joining behavior. Job title prediction aims to predict the job titles via developer expertise. For example, Liu et al. [16] explore the duality between job title prediction and API expertise prediction in open source communities, and propose a dual learning approach to predict job titles in the IT field. Montandon et al. [18] predict GitHub users' technical roles by extracting features like programming languages and project details. They employ Random Forest and Naive Bayes methods for multi-label classification. Skill modeling focuses on accurately representing developers' skill in open source software (OSS). For instance, Liang et al. [15] conduct a survey with 455 OSS contributors and identify relevant skills. They try to understand how contributors grow and share these skills, and derive design implications for incorporating skills into OSS tools and platforms. Sun et al. [26] construct a GitHub social network to integrate developers' social and development activity data, and use the heterogeneous graph neural network to learn developers' technical skill representations. Differently from existing studies, we try to mine the knowledge of LLMs for talent management in open source communities.

2.2 AI-Assisted Talent Management

In recent years, AI-driven techniques have significantly advanced talent management field [21]. Representative tasks include talent search [20,23], career mobility prediction [14,28,36], person-job fitting [22,33], job recommendation [5,10,30],and so on.

Talent search aims to identify qualified candidates by utilizing search queries defined by recruiters or hiring managers to enhance recruitment efficiency. Ozcag-lar et al. [20] propose a two-level ranking system for talent search, combining Generalized Linear Mixed models with Gradient Boosted Decision Tree. Ramanath et al. [23] transform recruiters' search queries and candidate features into semantic embeddings and employ learning-to-rank method to sort and identify the suitable candidates for recruitment. Career mobility prediction aims to provide talents' career development paths by analyzing extensive career trajectory data, including work experience, job transitions, skills development and more. Li et al. [14] propose a contextual LSTM model to predict next employer and job title of talent by integrating profile context and career trajectory dynamics. Zhang et al. [37] employ an attention-based heterogeneous graph embedding framework to predict the next employer and job title of talent. Zha et al. [36] employ a trajectory hypergraph to represent career mobility patterns and use attention mechanisms to integrate market features into career trajectory modeling. Person-job fit focuses on measuring the degree of matching between a job posting and a candidate's resume. Qin et al. [22] use LSTM to model the job requirements and candidates' semantic representation and apply ability-aware attention strategies to measure the importance of matching results. Bian et al. [1] construct a job-resume graph to capture implicit correlations between jobs and resumes, and propose a multi-view co-teaching network to integrate text- and relation-based matching module. Yao et al. [33] formulate person-job fit as a graph matching problem and propose a knowledge-enhanced approach that integrates skill extraction with a graph representation learning model. Yu et al. [34] employ contrastive learning to obtain an embedding representation of resumes and jobs, and alleviate data sparsity by data augmentation methods based on EDA [29] and ChatGPT [19]. Job recommendation task aims to provide each candidate with a list of suitable job opportunities derived from the candidate's profile and job postings. Dave et al. [3] utilize job transition, job-skill, and skill co-occurrence networks to jointly learn job and skill embeddings for effective job and skill recommendation. Yu et al. [35] disentangle hierarchical skill factors and model multi-level recruitment interactions to generate a personalized list of job recommendations for candidates. Differing from existing studies, we focus on talent management in open source communities.

3 Preliminaries

3.1 Task Description

Given a set of historical job titles and API experience in open source projects of a talent, our aim is to predict whether the talent is likely to have a job title (job title prediction) or API experience (project recommendation) in the future. For the latter task, we follow Dey et al. [4] and regard recommending suitable open source projects as predicting the main APIs of a project that the talent works on in the future.

3.2 Dataset Construction

First, to evaluate the ability of LLMs on the above two tasks, we leverage the TOSE dataset [16] and construct an evaluation dataset TM-Eval containing 2,000 data points. Each data point describes the historical job titles and API experience of a talent and then prompts an LLM to determine whether the talent is likely to take a target job title or use a set of target APIs. The data points are labeled with "Yes" or "No" according to the facts in TOSE. Figure 1(a) gives an example data point in TM-Eval.

Career history of user A:
['web developer', 'web developer', 'blockchain developer']
Project experience of user A :
[['tifffile', 'matplotlib.cm', 'pandas', 'sk image', 'PyQt5.QtGui', 'numpy', 'os','s ys', 'scipy','PyQt5.QtWidgets', 'collectio ns.Counter', 'xlwt.Workbook', 're', ...]].
Analyze user A's career history and project experience to determine whether user A is likely to work on the target job title:
[chief operating officer]

Return the answer strictly in the format "Yes" or "No".

Yes

(a) TM-Eval

Question:
What APIs are required for the role of {software architect}?
Here is the job description:
{Who is Recruiting from Scratch : Recruiting from Scratch is a premier talent firm that focuses on placing the best product managers, software, and hardware talent at innovative companies. Our team is 100% remote and we work with teams across the United States to help them hire...}
Answer:
The APIs are timeSeries, sql, compat, tasks, ServiceStack.DesignPatterns. Model, analytic, languages, mssql, solver.Solver, functional, System....

(b) JA-QA

Fig. 1. The example data points in TM-Eval and JA-QA.

You are a helpful assistant. Given Skill, you need to find the most relevant APIs from a candidate set of APIs.
Skill:
Deep learning
Candidates:
[tensorflow, tensorflow.keras, torch, torch.nn, torch.optim, sklearn, deoplete, Dense, deoplete, deepmerge,alexnet.AlexNet, ...]
Please output the the most relevant API(s) from Candidates based on the given Skill.
Output format:
{result:[candidate1, candidate2, ...] }

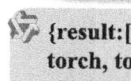
{result:[tensorflow, tensorflow.keras, torch, torch.nn, torch.optim, sklearn, alexnet.AlexNet, ...] }

(a) Replacing Skills with APIs

You are a helpful assistant. Given Job Title, you need to find the most relevant job title from a candidate set of standardized job titles.
Job Title:
Senior Software Engineer
Candidates:
[computer hardware engineer, embedded syste ms software developer, software architect, clou d engineer, software developer, knowledge engineer, embedded system designer, integratio n engineer, ICT network engineer, ICT security manager, ICT presales engineer...]

Please output the the most relevant job title from Candidates based on the given Job Title.
Output format: {result: candidate }

{result:software architect}

(b) Standardizing Job Titles

Fig. 2. The prompting template for replacing skills with APIs and standardizing job titles.

Second, to distill the knowledge from larger LLMs into smaller LLMs, we construct from LinkedIn a QA dataset JA-QA containing 20,000 QA pairs. Each pair contains a question asking about the required APIs for a job title with the job description, and the corresponding answer depicting a set of APIs. Figure 1(b) gives an example QA pair in JA-QA. We use the questions as input and the answers as output to distill the knowledge in larger LLMs.

It is worth mentioning that the original requirements listed in job descriptions on LinkedIn are skills rather than APIs. In order to better connect the job market and the open source experience in knowledge distillation, we replace the skills with APIs by prompting an LLM, which is depicted in Fig. 2(a). The candidate APIs have the most similar embeddings with that of the given skill, where the embeddings are obtained using gte-Qwen2-1.5B-instruct[3], a strong embedding model for semantic similarity measurement. Furthermore, the original job titles listed in job descriptions are not standardized. As such, we also prompt an LLM to standardize each job title, which is depicted in Fig. 2(b). The standardized job titles are collected from the ESCO taxonomy[4]. We also use gte-Qwen2-1.5B-instruct to embed the job titles and pick the most similar standardized job titles as the candidates of the given job title.

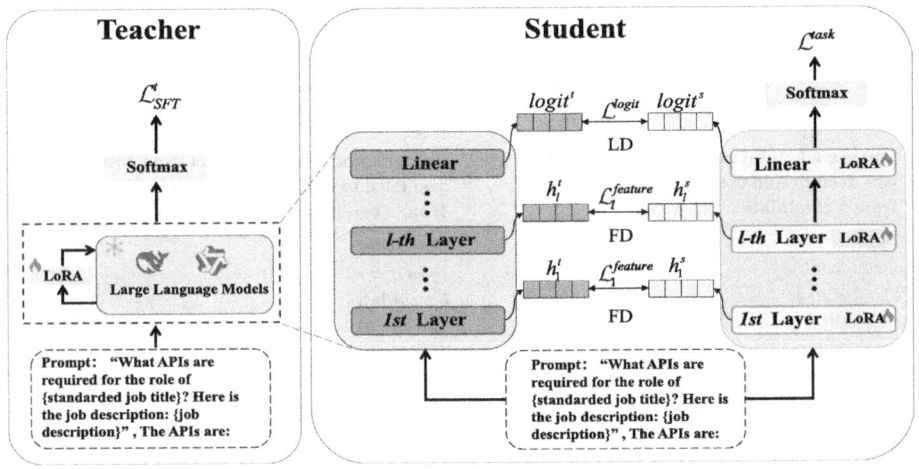

Fig. 3. The proposed method.

4 Knowledge Distillation for Job-API Correspondence

4.1 Overview

We propose a knowledge distillation method to distill the knowledge in larger LLMs pertaining to the correspondence between jobs and APIs into smaller LLMs, which is depicted in the right part of Fig. 3. We design a hierarchical

---
[3] https://huggingface.co/Alibaba-NLP/gte-Qwen2-1.5B-instruct.
[4] https://esco.ec.europa.eu/en/classification/occupation_main.

knowledge transfer mechanism through (1) logit-based distillation that aligns output probability distributions between teacher and student LLMs, and (2) feature-based distillation that transfers structural patterns from intermediate transformer layers. This dual distillation mechanism enhances the student LLM's capacity for capturing nuanced job-API associations while maintaining computational efficiency. To ensure the student LLM learns more precise knowledge, we employ Low-Rank Adaptation (LoRA) [13] to fine-tune the teacher model before distillation, which is depicted in the left part of Fig. 3. The fine-tune and distillation stages both use the JA-QA dataset.

4.2 Fine-Tuning the Teacher LLM

To enhance the knowledge of the teacher LLM pertaining to the correspondence between jobs and APIs, we adopt supervised fine-tuning (SFT) by LoRA. This approach preserves the teacher's reasoning capabilities while integrating domain-specific knowledge.

Particularly, we use the question and job description of each data pair in the JA-QA dataset as the input and the corresponding answer as the target to fine-tune the teacher LLM. The input sequence q is formulated as follows:

Prompt: "What APIs are required for the role of $\{job\ title\}$? Here is the job description: $\{job\ description\}$. The APIs are:___"

The target a is an API sequence $\{a_1, a_2, \ldots, a_n\}$, where n denotes the length of the API sequence. This structured formulation enables the teacher LLM to effectively capture the relationship between jobs and APIs.

To efficiently adapt the teacher LLM, we employ LoRA for weight matrix adaptation in the transformer layers. Instead of updating all model parameters, LoRA introduces trainable low-rank matrices $A \in \mathbb{R}^{r \times k}$ and $B \in \mathbb{R}^{d \times r}$ to adjust specific weight projections. Here, $r \ll \min(d, k)$ is the rank of the low-rank matrices, controlling the number of trainable parameters. For a given weight matrix $W \in \mathbb{R}^{d \times k}$, the adapted transformation is:

$$h = (W + \Delta W)q = (W + BA)q, \tag{1}$$

where h denotes the output of each transformer layer. At the final output layer, the teacher LLM minimizes the negative log probability for generating the target sequence a:

$$\mathcal{L}_{SFT}^t = -\sum_{i=1}^{n} \log P(a_i | a_{<i}, q; \theta_t, B, A), \tag{2}$$

where θ_t denotes the parameters of the teacher LLM and n is the API sequence length. This objective forces the teacher LLM to generate the correct API sequence while maintaining linguistic coherence.

4.3 Knowledge Distillation

While larger LLMs excel in semantic understanding, their high inference memory and latency often make them unsuitable for deployment in real-life systems. To address this issue, we propose to transfer the knowledge of a larger and more complex teacher LLM into a smaller and more efficient student LLM using knowledge distillation [7,12]. After distillation, the student LLM obtains the teacher's knowledge to map jobs to APIs while significantly reducing computational overhead, making it feasible for real-life deployment.

The student LLM shares a similar architecture with the teacher LLM and has fewer layers and smaller hidden dimensions. The input and the target output of the student LLM are the same as those of the teacher LLM, as depicted in Sect. 4.2. To transfer the teacher LLM's knowledge to the student LLM, we employ a multi-layer knowledge distillation approach, which distills both the low-level features and the logit distributions. Particularly, we design three loss functions for distillation, including logit-based distillation, feature-based distillation, and task-specific fine-tuning with LoRA.

Logit-Based Distillation. Logit-based distillation transfers the teacher's output distribution to the student by minimizing the Kullback-Leibler (KL) divergence between their logits. Let L^t and L^s denote the logits of the teacher and student LLMs, respectively. To stabilize the training process, we adopt a temperature scaling parameter τ for the logits, which softens the probability distributions. Then, the probability distributions p^t and p^s are obtained by applying the softmax function on the scaled logits. This process can be computed as:

$$p^t = \text{softmax}(\frac{L^t}{\tau}), \quad p^s = \text{softmax}(\frac{L^s}{\tau}). \tag{3}$$

To handle case where the teacher and student LLMs have different output dimensions (e.g., due to different vocabulary sizes), we introduce a padding mechanism. If the student LLM's output dimension is smaller than the teacher's, we pad the student logits with zeros to match the teacher's output dimension, and vice versa. This ensures that the KL divergence can be computed correctly. The padding operation is defined as:

$$\text{pad\_logits}(p^s, p^t) = \begin{cases} (\text{concat}(p^s, \mathbf{0}), p^t) & \text{if } \dim(p^s) < \dim(p^t), \\ (p^s, \text{concat}(p^t, \mathbf{0})) & \text{if } \dim(p^s) > \dim(p^t), \\ (p^s, p^t) & \text{otherwise,} \end{cases} \tag{4}$$

where $\mathbf{0}$ is a zero vector of appropriate size.

The logit-based distillation loss is then computed as the KL divergence between the teacher's and student's output distributions:

$$\text{KL}(p^t | p^s) = p^t(a|q) \log \frac{p^t(a|q)}{p^s(a|q)}. \tag{5}$$

To ensure more stable training, the logit-based distillation loss is scaled by the square of the temperature τ and normalized by the maximum sequence length n:

$$\mathcal{L}^{logit} = \text{KL}(p^t|p^s) \cdot \frac{\tau^2}{n}. \tag{6}$$

Feature-Based Distillation. Feature-based distillation aligns the intermediate representations (hidden states) of the teacher and student LLMs [38]. This approach ensures that the student LLM not only mimics the teacher's final output but also learns to replicate its internal representation.

Suppose that the student LLM has l intermediate layers. Feature-based distillation is conducted between the l layers and the first l layers of the teacher LLM, because the student LLM has fewer layers. Let h_i^t and h_i^s denote the hidden states of the teacher and student models at layer i, respectively. Since the teacher and student LLMs may have different sizes for the hidden states, we introduce an adaptation layer to project the student's hidden states into the teacher's representation space. At the ith layer, the adaptation layer contains a trainable linear transformation W_i that maps the student's hidden state h_i^s into the teacher's hidden state space. Similarly, we apply a temperature scaling parameter τ to the hidden states. The probability distributions at layer i p_i^t and p_i^s are obtained by applying the softmax function to the temperature-scaled hidden states:

$$p_i^t = \text{softmax}(\frac{h_i^t}{\tau}), \quad p_i^s = \text{softmax}(\frac{W_i \cdot h_i^s}{\tau}). \tag{7}$$

The feature-based distillation loss for layer i is then computed as:

$$\mathcal{L}_i^{feature} = \text{KL}(p_i^t|p_i^s) = p_i^t \log \frac{p_i^t}{p_i^s}. \tag{8}$$

The overall feature-based distillation loss is the average of the layer-wise losses:

$$\mathcal{L}^{feature} = \frac{1}{l} \sum_{i=1}^{l} \mathcal{L}_i^{feature}, \tag{9}$$

where l is the number of layers in the student LLM.

Task-Specific Fine-Tuning. In addition to distillation, the student LLM is also fine-tuned using the JA-QA dataset like the teacher LLM does. The task-specific loss is the negative log likelihood for generating the target API sequence a:

$$\mathcal{L}^{task} = -\sum_{i=1}^{n} \log P(a_i|a_{<i}, q; \theta_s), \tag{10}$$

where θ_s denotes the parameters of the student LLM.

The overall loss for training the student LLM is a weighted combination of the logit-based distillation loss, the feature-based distillation loss, and the task-specific fine-tuning loss:

$$\mathcal{L}^{student} = \alpha\mathcal{L}^{logit} + \beta\mathcal{L}^{feature} + \mathcal{L}^{task}, \tag{11}$$

where α and β are hyperparameters. During training, the student LLM minimizes $\mathcal{L}^{student}$ using LoRA.

5 Performance Evaluation

We aim to answer the following four research questions:

- **RQ1:** How do the latest representative LLMs perform on project recommendation and job title prediction for open source talents?
- **RQ2:** How do our fine-tuning and knowledge distillation approaches improve the performance of LLMs?
- **RQ3:** How do the different components influence the LLMs' performance?
- **RQ4:** How do the hyperparameters influence the LLMs' performance?

5.1 Datasets

We use the JA-QA dataset depicted in Sect. 3.2 to fine-tune and distill knowledge from the teacher LLMs, which contains 20,000 QA pairs. We use TM-Eval depicted in Sect. 3.2 to evaluate the performance of project recommendation and job title prediction, which contains 1,000 data points for each task.

5.2 Comparative Methods

We use four traditional models as baselines, including Skill-Space [4], NeuMF [11], APJFNN [39], and WEPJF [6]. We train these models using the TOSE dataset[5] except those used to construct TM-Eval. Skill-Space embeds users and APIs in a shared space and we use the embeddings for job title prediction and project recommendation. NeuMF leverages user-job title and user-API interactions for prediction and recommendation. APJFNN uses RNNs and attention mechanisms to capture key information and semantic relationships among job titles and API sequences. WEPJF models user preferences in job title and API sequences using contrastive learning. We cannot compare with DualJE [16] because we don't have the datasets to train the API and job title models. For LLMs, we evaluate the performance of Qwen2.5-14B, -7B and -3B [32], and DeepSeek-R1-Distill-Qwen-14B, -7B and -1.5B [9][6]. Then, we fine-tune Qwen2.5-14B and R1-Distill-Qwen-14B using JA-QA and use the fine-tuned models as the teachers, i.e., Qwen2.5-14B w/SFT and R1-Distill-Qwen-14B w/SFT. Finally,

---
[5] We convert the data format to adapt the data to our tasks.
[6] We omit 'DeepSeek' when necessary.

we use Qwen2.5-7B and -3B, and R1-Distill-Qwen-7B and -1.5B as the students and conduct knowledge distillation. The results models are Qwen2.5-7B w/KD, Qwen2.5-3B w/KD, R1-Distill-Qwen-7B w/KD and R1-Distill-Qwen-1.5B w/KD.

5.3 Hyperparameters and Evaluation Metrics

The training process is conducted in parallel on two NVIDIA A800 80G GPUs, with a batch size of 32 per GPU. The models are trained for 3 epochs with a learning rate of 1e-5, which is adjusted using a cosine decay strategy. The optimizer is AdamW, and the distillation temperature coefficient is set to 3, which regulates the influence of the teacher LLM's soft targets on the student LLM. The loss balance factors α and β are set to 1.0 and 0.5, respectively, after tuning.

Since the predicted results are binary, e.g. Yes/No, we adopt the following four evaluation metrics: Accuracy (Acc), Precision (Pre), Recall (Rec), and F1-score (F1).

Table 1. Main Results.

Methods	Job Title Prediction				Project Recommendation			
	Pre	Rec	F1	Acc	Pre	Rec	F1	Acc
Skill Space [4]	55.85	54.31	55.07	54.82	52.36	54.28	53.30	53.57
NeuMF [11]	56.22	57.13	56.67	56.85	55.69	54.06	54.86	55.59
APJFNN [22]	57.76	56.68	57.21	57.39	56.15	55.47	55.81	56.24
WEPJM [6]	59.23	61.12	60.16	60.31	58.35	59.57	58.95	59.46
Qwen2.5-14B	72.49	69.94	71.19	72.36	68.98	67.79	68.38	69.25
Qwen2.5-7B	64.45	62.87	63.56	66.58	62.85	61.30	62.07	64.46
Qwen2.5-3B	61.50	60.34	60.91	61.27	58.62	59.82	59.21	61.49
Qwen2.5-14B w/SFT	**74.78**	**72.66**	**73.70**	**73.95**	**72.24**	**71.15**	**71.69**	**72.67**
	(↑ 2.29)	(↑ 2.72)	(↑ 2.51)	(↑ 1.59)	(↑ 3.26)	(↑ 3.36)	(↑ 3.31)	(↑ 3.42)
Qwen2.5-7B w/KD	**69.72**	**68.65**	**69.18**	**70.45**	**66.39**	**65.72**	**66.05**	**67.35**
	(↑ 5.27)	(↑ 5.78)	(↑ 5.62)	(↑ 3.87)	(↑ 3.54)	(↑ 4.42)	(↑ 3.98)	(↑ 2.89)
Qwen2.5-3B w/KD	**65.83**	**65.39**	**65.61**	**66.15**	**63.54**	**63.89**	**63.71**	**64.02**
	(↑ 4.33)	(↑ 5.05)	(↑ 4.70)	(↑ 4.88)	(↑ 4.92)	(↑ 4.07)	(↑ 4.50)	(↑ 2.53)
R1-Distill-Qwen-14B	73.15	69.32	71.18	73.65	69.54	68.72	69.13	70.12
R1-Distill-Qwen-7B	66.62	64.45	65.52	67.79	63.39	64.08	63.73	65.38
R1-Distill-Qwen-1.5B	62.05	62.85	62.45	63.07	59.04	60.61	59.81	61.48
R1-Distill-Qwen-14B w/SFT	**75.09**	**73.48**	**74.27**	**75.41**	**71.43**	**72.15**	**71.79**	**73.75**
	(↑ 1.94)	(↑ 4.16)	(↑ 3.09)	(↑ 1.76)	(↑ 1.89)	(↑ 3.43)	(↑ 2.66)	(↑ 3.63)
R1-Distill-Qwen-7B w/KD	**70.25**	**69.91**	**70.08**	**71.32**	**67.82**	**67.31**	**67.56**	**69.03**
	(↑ 3.63)	(↑ 5.46)	(↑ 4.56)	(↑ 3.53)	(↑ 4.43)	(↑ 3.23)	(↑ 3.83)	(↑ 3.65)
R1-Distill-Qwen-1.5B w/KD	**66.34**	**65.23**	**65.78**	**66.53**	**63.52**	**64.47**	**63.99**	**65.81**
	(↑ 4.29)	(↑ 2.38)	(↑ 3.33)	(↑ 3.46)	(↑ 4.48)	(↑ 3.86)	(↑ 4.18)	(↑ 4.33)

5.4 RQ1: Performance of the Latest LLMs

The first part of Table 1 reports the performance of the four traditional models. The second part reports the performance of Qwen2.5 and the fourth part reports the performance of DeepSeek-R1-Distill-Qwen. We observe two points. First, the LLMs perform significantly better than the four traditional models, indicating that the LLMs have already been equipped with rich knowledge pertaining to talent management in open source communities. Second, for either Qwen2.5 or DeepSeek-R1-Distill-Qwen, the larger LLMs perform better than the smaller LLMs, indicating the former have richer knowledge. The observation is consistent with the scaling laws.

5.5 RQ2: Performance of the Fine-Tuned and Distilled LLMs

The third and fifth parts of Table 1 report performance of the fine-tuned and distilled Qwen2.5 and DeepSeek-R1-Distill-Qwen, respectively. We observe that all LLMs are improved on the two tasks on all metrics, compared to their original variants before fine-tuning or distillation. First, we observe that the teacher LLMs, i.e., Qwen2.5-14B and R1-Distill-Qwen-14B, are further improved after

Table 2. Ablation Study

Model	Method	Job Title Prediction				Project Recommendation			
		Pre	Rec	F1	Acc	Pre	Rec	F1	Acc
Qwen2.5-7B	SFT	65.81	63.92	64.85	67.29	64.94	62.88	63.89	65.41
	KD w/ Orig Teacher	66.37	65.25	65.81	68.13	65.59	65.01	65.30	65.68
	KD w/o feature	67.15	67.49	67.32	68.89	65.78	64.85	65.31	66.34
	KD w/o logit	67.34	66.95	67.14	69.58	66.13	65.48	65.80	66.64
	Ours	**69.72**	**68.65**	**69.18**	**70.45**	**66.39**	**65.72**	**66.05**	**67.35**
Qwen2.5-3B	SFT	63.46	62.98	63.22	64.17	60.15	62.42	62.16	62.43
	KD w/ Orig Teacher	63.69	63.14	63.41	64.58	61.88	62.95	62.41	63.14
	KD w/o feature	64.33	63.96	64.14	64.91	62.58	62.75	62.66	63.43
	KD w/o logit	64.76	64.91	64.83	65.25	62.92	63.27	63.09	63.61
	Ours	**65.83**	**65.39**	**65.61**	**66.15**	**63.54**	**63.89**	**63.71**	**64.02**
R1-Distill-Qwen-7B	SFT	67.75	65.59	66.65	68.52	65.02	64.61	64.81	67.29
	KD w/ Orig Teacher	67.68	66.13	66.90	68.76	65.59	65.01	65.30	67.38
	KD w/o feature	68.44	67.53	67.98	69.45	65.87	64.94	65.40	67.61
	KD w/o logit	68.67	68.16	68.41	69.96	66.79	67.41	67.10	68.32
	Ours	**70.25**	**69.91**	**70.08**	**71.32**	**67.82**	**67.31**	**67.56**	**69.03**
R1-Distill-Qwen-1.5B	SFT	62.96	63.33	63.14	63.85	60.45	61.24	60.84	62.27
	KD w/ Orig Teacher	63.47	64.03	63.75	64.11	61.11	62.28	61.69	62.93
	KD w/o feature	63.85	63.96	63.90	64.48	61.74	62.35	62.04	63.19
	KD w/o logit	64.29	64.58	64.43	65.47	62.34	63.12	62.73	64.11
	Ours	**66.34**	**65.23**	**65.78**	**66.53**	**63.52**	**64.47**	**63.99**	**65.81**

fine-tuning, due to the injection of domain knowledge. Second, the improvements of the four student LLMs are even larger, indicating the effectiveness of the proposed distillation method. Moreover, Qwen2.5-7B w/KD and R1-Distill-Qwen-7B w/KD perform close to the original Qwen2.5-14B and R1-Distill-Qwen-14B, and Qwen2.5-3B w/KD and R1-Distill-Qwen-1.5B w/KD surpass the performance of the original Qwen2.5-7B and R1-Distill-Qwen-7B, indicating that our distillation method makes smaller LLMs outperform the original larger LLMs.

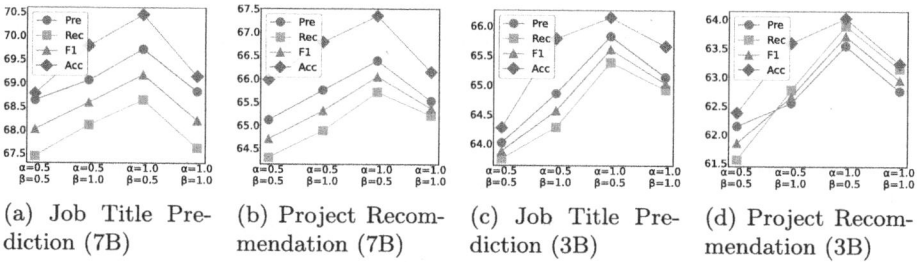

(a) Job Title Prediction (7B)   (b) Project Recommendation (7B)   (c) Job Title Prediction (3B)   (d) Project Recommendation (3B)

Fig. 4. Varying α and β for Qwen2.5.

5.6 RQ3: Ablation Study

For each student LLM, we design four ablation models. First, we directly fine-tune the LLM using the JA-QA dataset, which is denoted by SFT. Second, we distill from the original teacher LLM, i.e., the teacher LLM without fine-tuning on JA-QA, which is denoted by KD w/ Orig Teacher. Third, we remove the feature-based distillation loss and the logit-based distillation loss from the total distillation loss, respectively, which are denoted by KD w/o feature and KD w/o logit.

The results are reported in Table 2. We observe that all ablation models perform worse than our distilled student model in each LLM group, which indicates the effectiveness of the components in our proposed distillation method. Particularly, the significant performance gap between SFT and the distilled student LLM shows the effect of using both feature-based distillation and logit-based distillation.

5.7 RQ4: Hyperparameter Analysis

The most important hyperparameters in our distillation method are the loss balance factors α and β. We vary their values for both student LLMs. Figure 4 shows the results of Qwen2.5 on the two tasks. We observe that the best performance is achieved when $\alpha = 1.0$ and $\beta = 0.5$, for both tasks and both LLM sizes. This may indicate that the logit-based distillation loss is more important than the feature-based distillation loss. Figure 5 shows the results of DeepSeek-R1-Distill-Qwen on the two tasks, and we observe similar results with that of Qwen2.5.

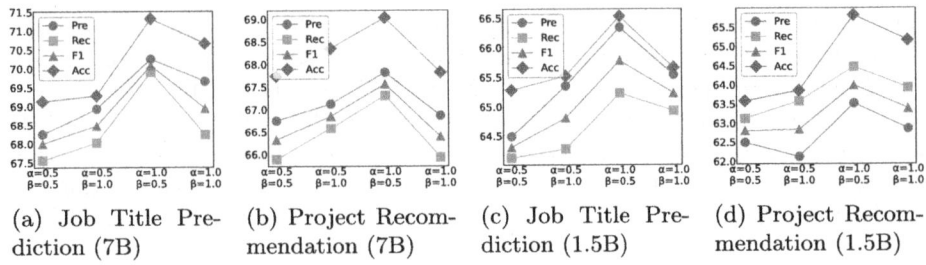

(a) Job Title Prediction (7B) (b) Project Recommendation (7B) (c) Job Title Prediction (1.5B) (d) Project Recommendation (1.5B)

Fig. 5. Varying α and β for DeepSeek-R1-Distill-Qwen.

6 Discussion and Conclusion

This research focuses on leveraging large language models (LLMs) for talent management in open source communities, specifically in the job title prediction and project recommendation tasks. By constructing the TM-Eval and JA-QA datasets, we evaluate the performance of the latest representative LLMs and propose a knowledge distillation method to transfer knowledge from larger LLMs to smaller ones. The experimental results lead to several significant findings. First, LLMs demonstrate remarkable superiority over traditional models in both tasks, and larger LLMs outperform smaller ones. Second, our fine-tuning and knowledge distillation approaches are highly effective. Fine-tuning injects domain-specific knowledge into teacher LLMs, while distillation enables student LLMs to significantly improve their performance.

However, there are still areas for improvement. For example, the datasets used may not comprehensively cover all aspects of talent management in open source communities, and the distillation method could be further optimized to handle more complex scenarios, such as distilling into different LLMs. In addition, the study primarily focuses on two tasks, which may lead to a relatively narrow research scope without considering more diverse scenarios. Future research could explore expanding the datasets, improving the distillation algorithm, and integrating more advanced techniques to enhance the performance and generalization ability of LLMs in open source talent management tasks. It could be valuable to explore other talent management tasks in open source communities beyond the current focus, such as contributor profiling, skill development tracking, and the attraction and retention of open source talents. Overall, this study offers a solid foundation for future research in this field.

Acknowledgements. This work is supported by the grant from the National Natural Science Foundation of China (Grant No. 62277017 and 62137001).

References

1. Bian, S., et al.: Learning to match jobs with resumes from sparse interaction data using multi-view co-teaching network. In: Proceedings of the 29th ACM International Conference on Information & Knowledge Management, pp. 65–74 (2020)
2. Bock, T., Alznauer, N., Joblin, M., Apel, S.: Automatic core-developer identification on GitHub: a validation study. ACM Trans. Softw. Eng. Methodol. **32**(6), 1–29 (2023)
3. Dave, V.S., Zhang, B., Al Hasan, M., AlJadda, K., Korayem, M.: A combined representation learning approach for better job and skill recommendation. In: Proceedings of the 27th ACM International Conference on Information and Knowledge Management, pp. 1997–2005 (2018)
4. Dey, T., Karnauch, A., Mockus, A.: Representation of developer expertise in open source software. In: 2021 IEEE/ACM 43rd International Conference on Software Engineering (ICSE), pp. 995–1007. IEEE (2021)
5. Du, Y., et al.: Enhancing job recommendation through LLM-based generative adversarial networks. In: Proceedings of the AAAI Conference on Artificial Intelligence, pp. 8363–8371 (2024)
6. Gong, Z., Song, Y., Zhang, T., Wen, J.R., Zhao, D., Yan, R.: Your career path matters in person-job fit. In: Proceedings of the AAAI Conference on Artificial Intelligence. vol. 38, pp. 8427–8435 (2024)
7. Gou, J., Yu, B., Maybank, S.J., Tao, D.: Knowledge distillation: a survey. Int. J. Comput. Vision **129**(6), 1789–1819 (2021)
8. Greene, G.J., Fischer, B.: CVExplorer: identifying candidate developers by mining and exploring their open source contributions. In: Proceedings of the 31st IEEE/ACM International Conference on Automated Software Engineering, pp. 804–809 (2016)
9. Guo, D., et al.: DeepSeek-R1: Incentivizing reasoning capability in LLMs via reinforcement learning. arXiv preprint arXiv:2501.12948 (2025)
10. Han, X., Zhu, C., Hu, X., Qin, C., Zhao, X., Zhu, H.: Adapting job recommendations to user preference drift with behavioral-semantic fusion learning. In: Proceedings of the 30th ACM SIGKDD Conference on Knowledge Discovery and Data Mining, pp. 1004–1015 (2024)
11. He, X., Liao, L., Zhang, H., Nie, L., Hu, X., Chua, T.S.: Neural collaborative filtering. In: Proceedings of the 26th International Conference on World Wide Web, pp. 173–182 (2017)
12. Hinton, G., Vinyals, O., Dean, J.: Distilling the knowledge in a neural network. arXiv preprint arXiv:1503.02531 (2015)
13. Hu, E.J., et al.: LoRA: Low-rank adaptation of large language models. In: International Conference on Learning Representations (2022)
14. Li, L., Jing, H., Tong, H., Yang, J., He, Q., Chen, B.C.: NEMO: next career move prediction with contextual embedding. In: Proceedings of the 26th International Conference on World Wide Web Companion, pp. 505–513 (2017)
15. Liang, J.T., Zimmermann, T., Ford, D.: Understanding skills for OSS communities on GitHub. In: Proceedings of the 30th ACM Joint European Software Engineering Conference and Symposium on the Foundations of Software Engineering, pp. 170–182 (2022)
16. Liu, X., Wang, Y., Dong, Q., Lu, X.: Job title prediction as a dual task of expertise prediction in open source software. In: Joint European Conference on Machine Learning and Knowledge Discovery in Databases, pp. 381–396. Springer (2024)

17. Montandon, J.E., Silva, L.L., Valente, M.T.: Identifying experts in software libraries and frameworks among GitHub users. In: 2019 IEEE/ACM 16th International Conference on Mining Software Repositories (MSR), pp. 276–287. IEEE (2019)
18. Montandon, J.E., Valente, M.T., Silva, L.L.: Mining the technical roles of GitHub users. Inf. Softw. Technol. **131**, 106485 (2021)
19. OpenAI: Introducing ChatGPT (2022). https://openai.com/blog/chatgpt
20. Ozcaglar, C., et al.: Entity personalized talent search models with tree interaction features. In: The World Wide Web Conference, pp. 3116–3122 (2019)
21. Qin, C., et al.: A comprehensive survey of artificial intelligence techniques for talent analytics. arXiv preprint arXiv:2307.03195 (2023)
22. Qin, C., et al.: Enhancing person-job fit for talent recruitment: an ability-aware neural network approach. In: The 41st international ACM SIGIR Conference on Research & Development in Information Retrieval, pp. 25–34 (2018)
23. Ramanath, R., et al.: Towards deep and representation learning for talent search at LinkedIn. In: Proceedings of the 27th ACM International Conference on Information and Knowledge Management, pp. 2253–2261 (2018)
24. Shao, H., et al.: paper2repo: Github repository recommendation for academic papers. In: Proceedings of The Web Conference 2020, pp. 629–639 (2020)
25. Sun, X., Xu, W., Xia, X., Chen, X., Li, B.: Personalized project recommendation on GitHub. Sci. China Inf. Sci. **61**, 1–14 (2018)
26. Sun, Y., et al.: Automatically deriving developers' technical expertise from the GitHub social network. In: Proceedings of the 39th IEEE/ACM International Conference on Automated Software Engineering, pp. 2462–2463 (2024)
27. Vadlamani, S.L., Baysal, O.: Studying software developer expertise and contributions in stack overflow and GitHub. In: 2020 IEEE International Conference on Software Maintenance and Evolution (ICSME), pp. 312–323. IEEE (2020)
28. Wang, C., Zhu, H., Hao, Q., Xiao, K., Xiong, H.: Variable interval time sequence modeling for career trajectory prediction: deep collaborative perspective. In: Proceedings of the Web Conference 2021, pp. 612–623 (2021)
29. Wei, J., Zou, K.: EDA: easy data augmentation techniques for boosting performance on text classification tasks. In: Proceedings of the 2019 Conference on Empirical Methods in Natural Language Processing and the 9th International Joint Conference on Natural Language Processing (EMNLP-IJCNLP), pp. 6382–6388 (2019)
30. Wu, L., Qiu, Z., Zheng, Z., Zhu, H., Chen, E.: Exploring large language model for graph data understanding in online job recommendations. In: Proceedings of the AAAI Conference on Artificial Intelligence. vol. 38, pp. 9178–9186 (2024)
31. Xu, W., Sun, X., Hu, J., Li, B.: REPERSP: recommending personalized software projects on GitHub. In: 2017 IEEE International Conference on Software Maintenance and Evolution (ICSME), pp. 648–652. IEEE (2017)
32. Yang, A., et al.: Qwen2. 5 technical report. arXiv preprint arXiv:2412.15115 (2024)
33. Yao, K., Zhang, J., Qin, C., Wang, P., Zhu, H., Xiong, H.: Knowledge enhanced person-job fit for talent recruitment. In: 2022 IEEE 38th International Conference on Data Engineering (ICDE), pp. 3467–3480. IEEE (2022)
34. Yu, X., Zhang, J., Yu, Z.: ConFit: improving resume-job matching using data augmentation and contrastive learning. In: Proceedings of the 18th ACM Conference on Recommender Systems, pp. 601–611 (2024)
35. Yu, X., et al.: DISCO: a hierarchical disentangled cognitive diagnosis framework for interpretable job recommendation. In: 2024 IEEE International Conference on Data Mining (ICDM), pp. 590–599 (2024)

36. Zha, R., et al.: Towards unified representation learning for career mobility analysis with trajectory hypergraph. ACM Trans. Inf. Syst. **42**(4), 1–28 (2024)
37. Zhang, L., et al.: Attentive heterogeneous graph embedding for job mobility prediction. In: Proceedings of the 27th ACM SIGKDD Conference on Knowledge Discovery & Data Mining, pp. 2192–2201 (2021)
38. Zhang, L., Shi, Y., Shi, Z., Ma, K., Bao, C.: Task-oriented feature distillation. Adv. Neural. Inf. Process. Syst. **33**, 14759–14771 (2020)
39. Zhu, C., et al.: Person-Job Fit: adapting the right talent for the right job with joint representation learning. ACM Trans. Manag. Inf. Syst. (TMIS) **9**(3), 1–17 (2018)

Collaborative Interest-Aware Graph Learning for Group Identification

Rui Zhao[1,2], Beihong Jin[1,2(✉)], Beibei Li[3], and Yiyuan Zheng[1,2]

[1] Institute of Software, Chinese Academy of Sciences, Beijing, China
Beihong@iscas.ac.cn
[2] University of Chinese Academy of Sciences, Beijing, China
[3] College of Computer Science, Chongqing University, Chongqing, China

Abstract. With the popularity of social media, an increasing number of users are joining group activities on online social platforms. This elicits the requirement of group identification (GI), which is to recommend groups to users. We reveal that users are influenced by both group-level and item-level interests, and these dual-level interests have a collaborative evolution relationship: joining a group expands the user's item interests, further prompting the user to join new groups. Ultimately, the two interests tend to align dynamically. However, existing GI methods fail to fully model this collaborative evolution relationship, ignoring the enhancement of group-level interests on item-level interests, and suffering from false-negative samples when aligning cross-level interests. In order to fully model the collaborative evolution relationship between dual-level user interests, we propose **CI4GI**, a **C**ollaborative **I**nterest-aware model for **G**roup **I**dentification. Specifically, we design an interest enhancement strategy that identifies additional interests of users from the items interacted with by the groups they have joined as a supplement to item-level interests. In addition, we adopt the distance between interest distributions of two users to optimize the identification of negative samples for a user, mitigating the interference of false-negative samples during cross-level interests alignment. The results of experiments on three real-world datasets demonstrate that CI4GI significantly outperforms state-of-the-art models.

Keywords: Recommender Systems · Group Recommendation · Graph Neural Networks · Contrastive Learning

1 Introduction

With the proliferation of social media, joining online groups has become a vital way for users to share experiences, explore interests and expand social connections. For example, on the game platform *Steam*, players participate in multiplayer battles by joining game groups. Similarly, on the travel community *Mafengwo*, users can join groups of interest, find travel partners within the groups and plan group trips. For users, group participation serves not only as an

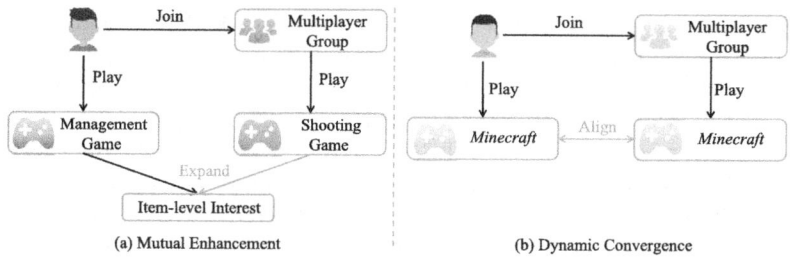

Fig. 1. Illustration of mutual enhancement and dynamic convergence.

effective channel for accessing vertical domain knowledge but also as a critical hub for establishing social bonds. For the platform, users' interests in groups can enhance their engagement and retention. Therefore, the group identification (GI) task, i.e., recommending groups to users becomes a topic that needs to be explored. Compared with directly recommending items to users, recommending groups to users can establish an emotional link between the platform and users and maintain long-term user stickiness. This paper focuses on the GI task.

We note that the essence of the GI task is to understand users' interests and find groups that attract them. Specifically, users are jointly influenced by two levels of interests when joining groups: group-level interests and item-level interests, which can be learned from their historical participation in groups and historical interactions with items, respectively. Most importantly, these dual-level interests are deeply intertwined and exhibit a collaborative evolution mechanism: users initially select groups based on existing item-level interests, while their group interactions subsequently expand their item-level interests, because the items interacted with by the group might become potential item-level interests for users. This item-level interest evolution drives users to join more relevant groups, ultimately leading to a dynamic alignment between the dual-level interests.

The collaborative evolution process between the dual-level interests plays a crucial role in accurately modeling user interests for the GI task. It can be modeled from two aspects: i) **Mutual Enhancement**: On the one hand, joining groups expands users' item-level interests. For example, in Fig. 1(a), a user who typically plays single-player management games also joins a group to participate in multiplayer shooting games. In this case, the user's interest in shooting games within the group becomes a part of the item-level interest. On the other hand, item-level interests also influence users' decisions to join groups. Considering users' item-wise preferences in GI helps uncover groups that users are interested in. ii) **Dynamic Convergence**: There is an overlap between users' group-level and item-level interests. As shown in Fig. 1(b), a user plays *Minecraft* both in single-player mode and within a group in multiplayer mode. At this point, the user's item-level and group-level interests are highly aligned. This property justifies constructing cross-level preference alignment via self-supervised learning, thereby enhancing representation quality and recommendation accuracy.

Existing methods fail to effectively solve the GI task. Traditional recommendation models focus on binary recommendation tasks, such as user-item recommendation, which only model users' item-level interests and are not suitable for group identification. Recently, several methods specifically designed for the GI task have been proposed, such as DiRec [15] and GTGS [17]. While these methods model both users' group-level and item-level interests, they fail to fully capture the collaborative evolution relationship between these dual-level interests. Specifically, they model users' group-level and item-level interests separately, overlooking the enhancement effect of group participation on users' item-level interests. What is worse, although these methods employ contrastive learning to align cross-level interests within a user and push away this user's interests from other users' interests, they overlook interest overlaps among similar users, crudely pushing away the representations of similar users, which adversely affects the representation learning and recommendation effectiveness.

To fully model the collaborative evolution relationship between users' dual-level interests, we propose a collaborative interest-aware graph learning model CI4GI. CI4GI leverages the hypergraph convolution network and graph attention network (GAT) to learn users' group-level and item-level interests from their historical user-group and user-item interactions. To model the mutual enhancement between these dual-level interests, we design an interest enhancement strategy with two key innovations: i) Item Representation Enhancement: we augment the item representation in the user-item interaction graph based on group-item interaction information. ii) Contextual Enhancement: The group a user joins is considered as the context of that user. We identify additional interests from items interacted with by the groups the user has joined and use them as a supplement to item-level interests. Furthermore, to mitigate false-negative interference in contrastive learning caused by users with similar interests, we propose a dynamic false-negative sample optimized self-supervised learning loss to effectively align users' group-level and item-level interests.

Our contributions are summarized as follows.

- We highlight that the key to the GI task lies in understanding users' dual-level interests (i.e., group-level and item-level interests) and capturing their collaborative evolution relationship. To address this, we propose a collaborative interest-aware graph learning model CI4GI.
- We design an interest enhancement strategy that supplements users' item-level interests through item representation enhancement and contextual enhancement.
- We propose a dynamic false-negative sample identification method based on the distance between interest distributions of two users to alleviate the problem of false-negative samples caused by overlapping interests of similar users.
- We conduct extensive experiments on three publicly available datasets, and the significant improvement of CI4GI on all datasets demonstrates its strength in completing the GI task.

The rest of the paper is organized as follows. Section 2 introduces the related work and Sect. 3 describes the model CI4GI in detail. Subsequently, Sect. 4 gives the experimental evaluation. Finally, the paper is concluded in Sect. 5.

2 Related Work

The group identification task is first proposed in CFAG [18], and there exist closely related tasks in the name of group recommendation. Therefore, we provide a brief introduction to these tasks and emphasize their differences.

The group recommendation aims to recommend items for a group of members [3,19,21]. Existing group recommendation models focus on aggregating the interests of different members to recognize their common interests. Multiple group recommendation models such as AGREE [1] and SoAGREE [2] propose different attention-based aggregation methods. Recently, ConsRec [16] models users and items as nodes, groups as hyperedges, and learns group representations through the hypergraph neural network. However, these methods mainly model the item-level interests of users, ignoring users' group-level interests.

In addition to recommending items to groups, the term 'group recommendation' in the literature is also used to denote the recommendation of groups to their potential members. Traditional approaches typically use various algorithms to reconstruct user-group membership matrices by utilizing additional auxiliary information, such as the semantic content of group descriptions in CCF [4], visual information from photos in JTM [11], and user behaviors across different time periods in DMF [13]. CFAG [18] is the first to define the GI task, which learns the interaction relationships among users, groups, and items through tripartite graph convolution layers. DiRec [15] classifies the user's intention of joining a group into social intention and personal interest intention, and then combines user and group representations under these two intention categories for recommendations. GTGS [17] models the user-group-item relationships using three hypergraphs: a group hypergraph from the user's perspective, a user hypergraph from the item's perspective, and a user hypergraph from the group's perspective. However, all of these approaches model users' group-level and item-level interests separately, not only ignoring the extension of group-level interests to item-level interests but also often improperly aligning two interests through contrastive learning.

On the other hand, our work is related to graph-based recommender systems (RSs), which can be broadly categorized into three classes from a modeling perspective: (i) graph convolutional network-based RSs [6,12,14]; (ii) graph attention network-based RSs [9,10]; and (iii) gated graph neural network-based RSs [5]. Most graph-based RSs focus only on user-item bipartite graphs, and directly applying these models to the group identification task is inappropriate due to the fact that they cannot capture the complex relationships among users, items, and groups. To realize the GI task, new graph-based models need to be developed.

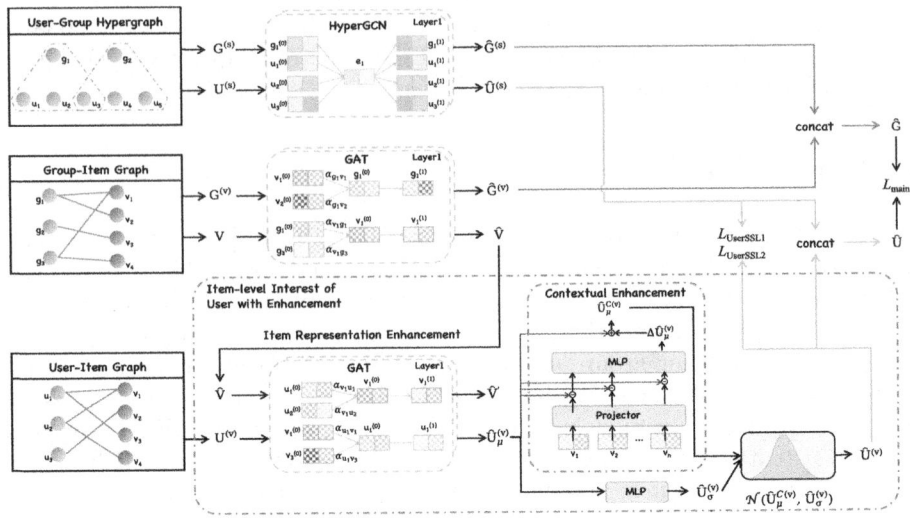

Fig. 2. Architecture of CI4GI.

3 Methodology

3.1 Model Overview

Let $\mathcal{U}$, $\mathcal{V}$ and $\mathcal{G}$ denote the user set, item set, and group set, respectively. There are three types of observed interactions among users, items, and groups, i.e., user-item interactions denoted as $\mathbf{X} \in \mathbb{R}^{|\mathcal{U}| \times |\mathcal{V}|}$, group-item interactions represented as $\mathbf{Y} \in \mathbb{R}^{|\mathcal{G}| \times |\mathcal{V}|}$, and user-group affiliations represented as $\mathbf{Z} \in \mathbb{R}^{|\mathcal{U}| \times |\mathcal{G}|}$. Given a user $u_i \in \mathcal{U}$, the goal of the group identification task is to predict the groups that user u_i has not yet joined but is highly likely to be interested in joining in the future.

For this task, we propose a collaborative interest-aware graph learning model CI4GI, whose architecture is shown in Fig. 2. CI4GI first employs a hypergraph to model user-group history interactions to learn group-level interests for users and groups. Then, CI4GI leverages two graph attention networks to model user-item and group-item interactions, capturing item-level interests for users and groups. To model the mutual enhancement between these dual-level interests, we design an interest enhancement strategy with two types of enhancements. First, item representation enhancement leverages group-item interaction information to augment item representations that have learned via the user-item interaction graphs. Second, contextual enhancement identifies additional interests of users from the items interacted with by the groups they have joined, serving as a supplement to users' item-level interests. Further, we propose a contrastive learning loss with dynamic false-negative sample optimization. It aligns users' group-level and item-level interests while alleviating the problem of false-negative samples caused by overlapping interests of similar users.

3.2 Embedding Layer

We maintain an embedding layer to initialize the learnable embeddings of users, items, and groups. For item set $\mathcal{V}$, the learnable item embedding matrix $\mathbf{V} \in \mathbb{R}^{|\mathcal{V}| \times d}$ is obtained after the embedding layer, where d is the embedding size. For the users, we represent group-level and item-level interests in two matrices, i.e., the group-level interest matrix $\mathbf{U}^{(s)} \in \mathbb{R}^{|\mathcal{U}| \times d}$ and the item-level interest matrix $\mathbf{U}^{(v)} \in \mathbb{R}^{|\mathcal{U}| \times d}$. Similarly, for groups, there are $\mathbf{G}^{(s)} \in \mathbb{R}^{|\mathcal{G}| \times d}$ and $\mathbf{G}^{(v)} \in \mathbb{R}^{|\mathcal{G}| \times d}$.

3.3 Group-Level Interest Learning

We employ a hypergraph to model user-group affiliations. CI4GI defines a user-group affiliation hypergraph as $H^{UG} = (\mathcal{N}, \mathcal{E}^{UG})$, where $\mathcal{N} = \mathcal{U} \cup \mathcal{G}$ denotes the node set, i.e., a node of H^{UG} is a user in $\mathcal{U}$ or a group in $\mathcal{G}$. The hyperedge set is denoted as $\mathcal{E}^{UG}$, where a hyperedge $e_k^{UG} \in \mathcal{E}^{UG}$, $k \in [1, |\mathcal{G}|]$ connects all user nodes in the group g_k along with the group node g_k. The association matrix $T^{UG} = [t_{ik}^{UG}] \in \mathbb{R}^{(|\mathcal{U}|+|\mathcal{G}|) \times |\mathcal{G}|}$ represents the connectivity between nodes and hyperedges in the hypergraph H^{UG}.

By modeling the hypergraph with a hyperedge connecting the group and all its members, we preserve the social relationships within the group. We then employ the classical hypergraph convolution for representation learning:

$$N^{(l)} = \sigma(D_\mathcal{N}^{-\frac{1}{2}} T^{UG} D_\mathcal{E}^{-1} T^{UG^T} D_\mathcal{N}^{-\frac{1}{2}} N^{(l-1)} \mathbf{W}^{UG}) \quad (1)$$

where $D_\mathcal{N} \in \mathbb{R}^{|\mathcal{N}| \times |\mathcal{N}|}$ and $D_\mathcal{E}^{|\mathcal{E}| \times |\mathcal{E}|}$ represent the degree matrices of the nodes and hyperedges, respectively. $N^{(l)} \in \mathbb{R}^{|\mathcal{N}| \times d}$ is the node representation of the l-th layer, $N^{(0)} = \text{Concat}(\mathbf{U}^{(s)}, \mathbf{G}^{(s)})$, $\mathbf{W}^{UG} \in \mathbb{R}^{d \times d}$ is a learnable matrix, σ is the sigmoid function.

Finally, the group-level interests of users and groups are obtained after L layers hypergraph convolution: $\hat{\mathbf{U}}^{(s)}, \hat{\mathbf{G}}^{(s)} = N^{(L)}$.

3.4 Item-Level Interest Learning

We learn the item-level interests of groups and users, respectively.

Item-Level Interest of Group. We define the group-item interaction graph as $G^{GV} = (\mathcal{N}^{GV}, \mathcal{E}^{GV})$, where $\mathcal{N}^{GV} = \mathcal{G} \cup \mathcal{V}$ denotes the node set, an edge $e_{jk}^{GV} \in \mathcal{E}^{GV}, j \in [1, |\mathcal{V}|], k \in [1, |\mathcal{G}|]$ denotes the group g_k interacting the items v_j. The association matrix $T^{GV} \in \mathbb{R}^{(|\mathcal{G}|+|\mathcal{V}|) \times (|\mathcal{G}|+|\mathcal{V}|)}$ represents the connectivity between nodes in G^{GV}. We use classical GAT [10] for representation learning:

$$\hat{\mathbf{G}}^{(v)}, \hat{\mathbf{V}} = \text{GAT}_{\Theta_{GV}}([\mathbf{G}^{(v)} || \mathbf{V}], T^{GV}) \quad (2)$$

where $\text{GAT}_{\Theta_{GV}}$ is a stack of L-layer graph attention networks, $\mathbf{G}^{(v)}$ and $\mathbf{V}$ are the initial groups' item-level interest representations and item representations, $\hat{\mathbf{G}}^{(v)} \in \mathbb{R}^{|\mathcal{G}| \times d}$ and $\hat{\mathbf{V}} \in \mathbb{R}^{|\mathcal{V}| \times d}$ are those learned from GAT.

Item-Level Interest of User with Enhancement. Similarly, CI4GI defines the user-item interaction graph as $G^{UV} = (\mathcal{N}^{UV}, \mathcal{E}^{UV})$. The association matrix $T^{UV} \in \mathbb{R}^{(|\mathcal{U}|+|\mathcal{V}|) \times (|\mathcal{U}|+|\mathcal{V}|)}$ denotes the connectivity between nodes in G^{UV}. We also apply a graph attention network to learn user-item interactions.

Further, we propose an interest enhancement strategy with two methods: item representation enhancement and contextual enhancement.

Item representation enhancement aims to enhance the item representation in user-item interaction graph with the group-item interaction information, thereby capturing the similarity between the item-level interest of the group and the user. This helps the model recognize the user's tendency to join a group based on their interests in the items. Specifically, we use the item representation $\hat{\mathbf{V}}$ learned from G^{GV} as the initial item representation for G^{UV}:

$$\hat{\mathbf{U}}_\mu^{(v)}, \hat{\mathbf{V}}' = \text{GAT}_{\Theta_{UV}}([\mathbf{U}^{(v)} || \hat{\mathbf{V}}], T^{UV}) \tag{3}$$

where $\text{GAT}_{\Theta_{UV}}$ is the graph attention network, $\mathbf{U}^{(v)}$ is the initial users' item-level interest representations and $\hat{\mathbf{V}}$ is the item representation learned from G^{GV}. $\hat{\mathbf{U}}_\mu^{(v)}$ and $\hat{\mathbf{V}}'$ are the user and item representations learned by the GAT.

In group identification scenarios, users' item-level interests are extended by joining groups, with items shared within these groups becoming potential interests for the user. Therefore, we propose a ***contextual enhancement*** that treats the groups the user has joined as their context information, identifying potential interests from the items that the user has historically interacted with by joining the group. Specifically, we first identify contextual items by the user-group affiliation matrix $\mathbf{Z}$ and the group-item interaction matrix $\mathbf{Y}$. Then, we project the contextual item representation $\hat{\mathbf{V}}$ into the same vector space as the user's representation $\hat{\mathbf{U}}_\mu^{(v)}$ using a projection matrix $\mathbf{W}^C$. Finally, we compute the distance between the user representation and the contextual items embeddings to obtain the increment $\Delta \hat{\mathbf{U}}_\mu^{(v)}$ with the following formula:

$$\Delta \hat{\mathbf{U}}_\mu^{(v)} = \text{MLP}(\hat{\mathbf{U}}_\mu^{(v)} - D_{ZY}^{-1} \mathbf{Z}\mathbf{Y} \times \hat{\mathbf{V}}\mathbf{W}^C) \tag{4}$$

where $D_{ZY} \in \mathbb{R}^{|\mathcal{U}| \times |\mathcal{U}|}$ is the row degree matrix of the matrix obtained after multiplying matrices $\mathbf{Z}$ and $\mathbf{Y}$, which is used for normalization. $\mathbf{W}^C \in \mathbb{R}^{d \times d}$ is the projection matrix.

The context-enhanced user representation is then obtained by adding the increment $\Delta \hat{\mathbf{U}}_\mu^{(v)}$:

$$\hat{\mathbf{U}}_\mu^{C(v)} = \hat{\mathbf{U}}_\mu^{(v)} + \gamma \Delta \hat{\mathbf{U}}_\mu^{(v)} \tag{5}$$

where γ is a hyperparameter indicating the weight of the increment.

Further, we represent the users' item-level interests as independent Gaussian distributions instead of fixed embeddings, which improves the robustness and flexibility of users' interest representations. Specifically, based on the user representation $\hat{\mathbf{U}}_\mu^{(v)}$ learned from Eq. 3 (which is regarded as the mean of the user interest distribution), the variance of the user interest distribution is computed by a multilayer perceptron: $\hat{\mathbf{U}}_\sigma^{(v)} = \text{MLP}(\hat{\mathbf{U}}_\mu^{(v)})$.

We sample user representations $\hat{\mathbf{U}}^{(v)}$ from independent Gaussian distributions $\hat{\mathbf{U}}^{(v)} \sim \mathcal{N}(\hat{\mathbf{U}}_\mu^{(v)}, \hat{\mathbf{U}}_\sigma^{(v)})$. Since direct sampling prevents gradient backpropagation, we apply the reparameterization trick as follows:

$$\hat{\mathbf{U}}^{(v)} = \hat{\mathbf{U}}_\mu^{C(v)} + \hat{\mathbf{U}}_\sigma^{(v)} \epsilon \qquad (6)$$

where ϵ is randomly sampled from the standard normal distribution $\mathcal{N}(0,1)$.

3.5 Cross-Level Interest Alignment

In this paper, we model users' group-level and item-level interests separately. Since these interests may overlap in real group identification scenarios, we propose using contrastive learning to align the cross-level interests. Additionally, similar users' interests can overlap, and vanilla contrastive learning may lead to false-negative samples. To address this, we introduce a dynamic false-negative sample optimized contrastive learning loss, using Wasserstein distance between user interest distributions to identify false-negative samples and improve the quality of cross-level interest alignment.

Vanilla Contrastive Learning. We align the cross-level interests of the same user by performing conventional contrastive learning on the user's group-level interest $\hat{\mathbf{U}}^{(s)}$ and item-level interest $\hat{\mathbf{U}}^{(v)}$ via the following InfoNCE [7] loss:

$$L_{\text{UserSSL1}} = -\sum_{u_i \in \mathcal{U}} \log \frac{\exp(sim(\hat{\mathbf{u}}_i^{(v)}, \hat{\mathbf{u}}_i^{(s)})/\tau)}{\exp(sim(\hat{\mathbf{u}}_i^{(v)}, \hat{\mathbf{u}}_i^{(s)})/\tau) + N_{\text{V1}}^U + N_{\text{S1}}^U} \qquad (7)$$

$$N_{\text{V1}}^U = \sum_{u_{i'} \in \mathcal{U}_i^-} \exp(sim(\hat{\mathbf{u}}_{i'}^{(v)}, \hat{\mathbf{u}}_i^{(s)})/\tau), \quad N_{\text{S1}}^U = \sum_{u_{i'} \in \mathcal{U}_i^-} \exp(sim(\hat{\mathbf{u}}_i^{(v)}, \hat{\mathbf{u}}_{i'}^{(s)})/\tau) \qquad (8)$$

where $\hat{\mathbf{u}}_i^{(s)}$ and $\hat{\mathbf{u}}_i^{(v)}$ form a pair of positive samples. $\mathcal{U}_i^-$ is the set of negative samples w.r.t. the user u_i, which is composed of other users (i.e., $u_{i'} \neq u_i$) within the same batch. $sim(\cdot)$ is to calculate the similarity of a pair of vectors, which refers to the cosine similarity in this paper. τ is the temperature parameter.

Dynamic False-Negative Sample Optimization. We dynamically identify false-negative samples by comparing users' item-level interest distributions. Specifically, for the item-level interest distribution $\hat{\mathbf{u}}_i^{(v)}$ of user u_i, we compute the Wasserstein distance to the distribution $\hat{\mathbf{u}}_j^{(v)}$ of any other user u_j. If the distance is less than or equal to a threshold μ, u_j is considered a false-negative sample of u_i. Only users with a Wasserstein distance greater than μ from u_i are included in the negative sample set.

$$\mathcal{N}eg_i = \{u_j \mid u_j \in \mathcal{U} \text{ and } d_{W2}(u_i, u_j) > \mu\} \qquad (9)$$

where d_{W2} denotes the Wasserstein distance, the higher the similarity of two users' distributions, the smaller the Wasserstein distance, μ is the threshold, and $\mathcal{N}eg_i$ is the set of negative samples w.r.t. the user u_i.

To ensure that the false-negative sample set remains adaptive, we dynamically update the set in each batch based on the latest interest distributions. This allows the contrastive learning process to continuously adjust to evolving user interests and prevents the model from being misled by static or outdated negative samples. Then, similar to conventional user contrastive learning, the following loss is used to align cross-level interest representations of the same user:

$$L_{\text{UserSSL2}} = -\sum_{u_i \in \mathcal{U}} \log \frac{\exp(sim(\hat{\mathbf{u}}_i^{(v)}, \hat{\mathbf{u}}_i^{(s)})/\tau)}{\exp(sim(\hat{\mathbf{u}}_i^{(v)}, \hat{\mathbf{u}}_i^{(s)})/\tau) + N_{V2}^U + N_{S2}^U} \quad (10)$$

$$N_{V2}^U = \sum_{u_{i'} \in \mathcal{U}_i^- \cap \mathcal{N}eg_i} \exp(sim(\hat{\mathbf{u}}_{i'}^{(v)}, \hat{\mathbf{u}}_i^{(s)})/\tau), \; N_{S2}^U = \sum_{u_{i'} \in \mathcal{U}_i^- \cap \mathcal{N}eg_i} \exp(sim(\hat{\mathbf{u}}_i^{(v)}, \hat{\mathbf{u}}_{i'}^{(s)})/\tau) \quad (11)$$

3.6 Model Optimization

After obtaining the group-level and item-level interest representations of users and groups, we can calculate the main loss of CI4GI by three steps. First, the two types of interests are concatenated for both users and groups to obtain the final user representation $\hat{\mathbf{U}}$ and group representation $\hat{\mathbf{G}}$:

$$\hat{\mathbf{U}} = [\hat{\mathbf{U}}^{(s)} || \hat{\mathbf{U}}^{(v)}], \quad \hat{\mathbf{G}} = [\hat{\mathbf{G}}^{(s)} || \hat{\mathbf{G}}^{(v)}] \quad (12)$$

Then, the dot product similarity is used to compute the probability score s_{ik} of a user u_i joining the group g_k:

$$s_{ik} = \hat{\mathbf{u}}_i \cdot \hat{\mathbf{g}}_k \quad (13)$$

where $\hat{\mathbf{u}}_i = \hat{\mathbf{U}}(i,:)$ is the final representation of the user u_i and $\hat{\mathbf{g}}_k = \hat{\mathbf{G}}(k,:)$ is the final representation of the group g_k. Subsequently, we calculate the BPR loss as the main loss:

$$L_{\text{main}} = \frac{1}{|\mathcal{T}|} \sum_{(u_i, g_k, g_{k'}) \in \mathcal{T}} -\log \sigma(s_{ik} - s_{ik'}) \quad (14)$$

where $\mathcal{T} = \{(u_i, g_k, g_{k'}) \mid z_{ik} = 1 \text{ and } z_{ik'} = 0\}$ is the training set, $z \in \mathbf{Z}$ is the element in the user-group affiliation matrix. σ is the sigmoid function.

Finally, we jointly optimize the main loss and auxiliary losses:

$$L = L_{\text{main}} + \lambda_1(\beta L_{\text{UserSSL1}} + (1-\beta) L_{\text{UserSSL2}}) + \lambda_2 ||\Theta||_2^2 \quad (15)$$

where Θ is all trainable parameters in CI4GI, $||\Theta||_2^2$ is the regularization loss, λ_1 and λ_2 are hyperparameters, and $\beta = 1/(1 + \exp(-k(epoch - E)))$ is the annealing parameter that controls the weight of the two types of contrastive learning loss, where k and E are hyperparameters.

Table 1. Statistics of datasets.

Dataset	# Users	# Items	# Groups	# User-Group participation	# User-Item interactions	# Group-Item interactions
Mafengwo	1,269	999	972	5,574	8,676	2,540
Weeplaces	1,501	6,406	4,651	12,258	43,942	6,033
Douban	11,099	2,351	1,085	57,654	444,776	23,318

3.7 Complexity Analysis

Space Complexity. In CI4GI, the learnable parameters mainly come from item embeddings, two user interest embeddings and two group interest embeddings. In addition, in the hypergraph convolution, the number of parameters of the L layer is Ld^2, and the number of parameters of the two L layers GAT is $2L(d^2 + 2d)$. The number of parameters in the MLP and the projection matrix is $O(d^2 + d)$. Therefore, the space complexity of CI4GI is $O(|\mathcal{V}|d + |\mathcal{U}|d + |\mathcal{G}|d + Ld^2 + Ld)$.

Time Complexity. The computational amount during the training of CI4GI is mainly concentrated on the hypergraph convolution and GAT. Assuming that $|T^{UG}|$ denotes the number of non-zero elements of the association matrix T^{UG}, the time complexity of hypergraph convolution is $O(L(|\mathcal{U}| + |\mathcal{G}|)d^2 + L|T^{UG}|d)$. Assuming that $|T^{GV}|$ and $|T^{UV}|$ denote the number of non-zero elements in the association matrices T^{GV} and T^{UV}, respectively, the time complexity of the two GATs is $O(L(|\mathcal{U}| + |\mathcal{G}| + |\mathcal{V}|)d^2 + L(|T^{GV}| + |T^{UV}|)d)$. Therefore, the time complexity of CI4GI is $O(Ld^2(|\mathcal{U}| + |\mathcal{V}| + |\mathcal{G}|) + Ld(|T^{UG}| + |T^{GV}| + |T^{UV}|))$.

4 Experiments

4.1 Experimental Setup

Datasets. We choose three public datasets to conduct experiments.

- **Mafengwo.** It records the travel history of users on the Mafengwo APP, where users can create or join groups, taking offline group trips. We use the dataset published by CFAG [18].
- **Weeplaces.** It records users' check-ins on location-based social networks in major cities of the U.S. We follow the same operations as in GroupIM [8] for constructing user-POI interactions and group-POI interactions.
- **Steam.** It records users' game preferences on the online gaming platform Steam, where users have their records of games they have played and can create or join a group. We use the dataset published by CFAG [18].

Table 1 lists the statistics of the three datasets. We randomly split the user participation in each dataset into training, validation, and test sets with a ratio of 7:1:2.

Baselines. The following baselines are chosen to compare with CI4GI:

Three recommendation models: **LightGCN**[1], which is a classical graph-based recommendation model [6]; **SGL**[2], which introduces contrastive learning into GNN-based recommendation by generating contrast views through node dropout, edge dropout, or random walk [14]; **SimGCL**[3], which presents an embedding-based enhancement method to construct positive sample pairs in contrastive learning by adding uniform noise to the embedding [20]. As DiRec [15] does, we apply them on the GI task by treating each group as an item and thus only utilizing user-group affiliations.

Two group recommendation models: **AGREE**[4], which is a classical group recommendation model using an attention mechanism for member aggregation [1]; **ConsRec**[5], the state-of-the-art model for group recommendation, which proposes a hypergraph neural network to learn member-level aggregation and captures the group consensus on three views [16]. As DiRec [15] does, we adapt them by replacing their initial group-item BPR loss with user-group BPR loss.

Three GI models: **CFAG**[6], a classical GI model, which constructs a group-user-item tripartite graph and designs a tripartite graph convolution layer [18]; **DiRec**[7], which divides the user's intention of joining a group into social intention and personal interest intention [15]; **GTGS**[8], which models the relationships between users, groups, and items by three hypergraphs, and proposes transition hypergraph convolution by using users' preferences for items as a prior knowledge [17].

Implementation Details. We implement our model in PyTorch. In our model, L is set to 2, the temperature τ is set to 1, the hyperparameter k in β is set to 0.1, and the threshold E in β is set as follows: 20 for Mafengwo, 30 for Weeplaces and Steam, and contextual enhancement representation weight γ is set as follows: 1 for Mafengwo and Steam, and 1.25 for Weeplaces, and the Wasserstein distance threshold μ is set as follows: 1.5 for Mafengwo, 2.0 for Weeplaces and Steam, λ_1 and λ_2 are set to $1 \times e^{-4}$. For the sake of fairness, we set the size of all embeddings d to 256, the batch size to 1024 and the learning rate to 0.005 in all the experiments. For all baselines, the hyperparameters are set to values corresponding to best performance reported in their respective papers. Experiments are conducted on NVIDIA RTX3090 GPU with 24G memory. The implementation code has been released[9].

---

[1] https://github.com/kuandeng/LightGCN.
[2] https://github.com/wujcan/SGL-Torch.
[3] https://github.com/Coder-Yu/QRec.
[4] https://github.com/LianHaiMiao/Attentive-Group-Recommendation.
[5] https://github.com/FDUDSDE/WWW2023ConsRec.
[6] https://github.com/mdyfrank/CFAG.
[7] https://github.com/WxxShirley/CIKM2023DiRec.
[8] https://github.com/mdyfrank/GTGS.
[9] https://github.com/ZhaoRui-7/CI4GI.

Table 2. Overall performance. The values in bold and underlined are the best and second best results in each column.

Dataset	Mafengwo				Weeplaces				Steam			
Metric	R@10	R@20	N@10	N@20	R@10	R@20	N@10	N@20	R@10	R@20	N@10	N@20
LightGCN	0.2925	0.3607	0.1865	0.2040	0.2490	0.3159	0.1465	0.1646	0.2411	0.3283	0.1333	0.1558
SGL	0.2957	0.3628	0.1937	0.2109	0.2511	0.3124	0.1456	0.1624	0.2327	0.3241	0.1289	0.1524
SimGCL	0.2943	0.3576	0.1890	0.2052	0.2486	0.3140	0.1466	0.1645	0.1872	0.2896	0.0930	0.1189
AGREE	0.1679	0.2302	0.1061	0.1222	0.2312	0.2957	0.1355	0.1529	0.1882	0.2977	0.0996	0.1275
ConsRec	0.3403	0.4312	0.2161	0.2382	0.3451	0.4379	0.2039	0.2288	0.2568	0.3608	0.1359	0.1626
CFAG	0.3007	0.4051	0.1698	0.1965	0.3848	0.4778	0.2251	0.2529	0.2328	0.3427	0.1224	0.1507
DiRec	0.3588	0.4636	0.2231	0.2500	<u>0.3904</u>	<u>0.4843</u>	<u>0.2341</u>	<u>0.2591</u>	<u>0.2738</u>	<u>0.3745</u>	<u>0.1436</u>	<u>0.1696</u>
GTGS	<u>0.3611</u>	<u>0.4672</u>	<u>0.2248</u>	<u>0.2520</u>	0.3813	0.4693	0.2308	0.2547	0.2225	0.3275	0.1110	0.1379
CI4GI	**0.3937**	**0.5016**	**0.2557**	**0.2829**	**0.4179**	**0.4990**	**0.2664**	**0.2879**	**0.2912**	**0.3823**	**0.1605**	**0.1840**
Inprov.(%)	9.02	7.36	13.74	12.26	7.04	3.03	13.79	11.11	6.35	2.08	11.76	8.49

Metrics. To evaluate the performance of recommending groups to users, we adopt two metrics, i.e., Recall@K and NDCG@K (R@K and N@K for short), where Recall focuses on whether the user actually chooses the recommended group, NDCG focuses on the ranking of the recommended groups and K is set to either 10 or 20.

4.2 Performance Comparison

Overall Performance. Table 2 lists the experimental results on the three datasets. From Table 2, we have the following observations.

Traditional recommendation models perform poorly because they typically represent user-group affiliations as graphs, capturing only users' group-level interests while overlooking their item-level interests. Similarly, group recommendation models are not well-suited for the GI task, as they lack the capability to model the complex user interests in GI scenarios.

In contrast, GI models achieve better performance as they are specifically designed for this task. However, while they capture both users' group-level and item-level interests, they overlook the collaborative relationship between the dual-level interests, limiting their effectiveness.

Our CI4GI outperforms all baselines on three datasets. Taking NDCG@10 as an example, compared to the best baseline on each of the three datasets, CI4GI shows improvements of 11.76%–13.79%, averaging at 13.09%.

Cold-Start Performance. We evaluate the cold-start performance of CI4GI on Mafengwo and Weeplaces. Specifically, we randomly remove user-group interaction history in the training set, ensuring that each user has joined at most k groups, where $k = 1, 2, 3, 4$. We choose DiRec, GTGS, ConsRec and SGL, the best models from different types of baselines, for comparison.

As shown in Fig. 3, CI4GI outperforms the baselines in all cases. In particular, CI4GI achieves the best performance even when $k = 1$, i.e., the user has

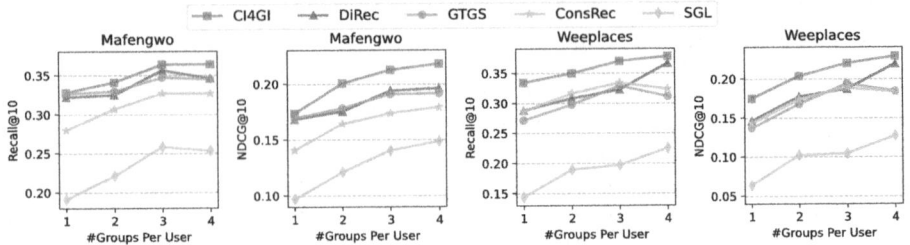

Fig. 3. Cold-start performance comparsion.

Table 3. Ablation study.

Model	Mafengwo		Weeplaces		Steam	
	R@10	N@10	R@10	N@10	R@10	N@10
CI4GI	**0.3973**	**0.2557**	**0.4179**	**0.2664**	**0.2912**	**0.1605**
(A) w/o group-level interests	0.3351	0.2135	0.3828	0.2349	0.2699	0.1443
(B) w/o item-level interests	0.3203	0.2074	0.3097	0.1954	0.2836	0.1529
(C) w/o enhancement	0.3687	0.2365	0.3873	0.2436	0.2820	0.1592
(D) w/o item enhancement	0.3817	0.2547	0.4069	0.2508	0.2866	0.1602
(E) w/o contextual enhancement	0.3697	0.2426	0.3894	0.2460	0.2838	0.1541
(F) w/o CL	0.3730	0.2484	0.3994	0.2549	0.2765	0.1547
(G) w/o $L_{UserSSL1}$	0.3818	0.2503	0.4134	0.2649	0.2837	0.1564
(H) w/o $L_{UserSSL2}$	0.3772	0.2514	0.4115	0.2626	0.2845	0.1565
(I) w/o β	0.3797	0.2525	0.4109	0.2597	0.2826	0.1527

only one interacted group in history. This could be because CI4GI applies an interest enhancement strategy in the user's item-level interest learning, which improves the representation of the user's item-level interest and alleviates the deficiency of the user's group-level interests in cold-start scenarios. As the threshold k increases from 1 to 3, the performance of all models improves, indicating that more historical user-group interactions are beneficial to interest learning. However, when k increases from 3 to 4, some models experience a decline in performance (e.g., DiRec on Mafengwo, GTGS and ConsRec on Weeplaces), while CI4GI continues to improve its performance. This may be because a higher number of user-group interactions introduce more complex user's interests, and CI4GI can capture these intricate interests by identifying the collaborative relationships between dual-level user interests, thus leading to superior performance.

4.3 Ablation Study

Effect of Dual-Level Interest Learning. We design two variants to observe the impact of dual-level interest learning in CI4GI on performance. Variant A removes group-level interests in CI4GI, i.e., only item-level interests of users and groups are used to compute similarity. Variant B removes item-level interests in CI4GI.

The experimental results on three datasets are listed in the top part of Table 3. Removing either interest leads to significant performance degradation, which illustrates the effectiveness of dual-level interest modeling in CI4GI. On Steam, the performance degradation of variant A is more significant, indicating that group-level interests play a more important role. In contrast, on Mafengwo and Weeplaces, the performance degradation of variant B is more significant, i.e., item-level interests play a more important role. This may be due to the fact that Weeplaces has a very low average number of users per group (fewer than 3), making it difficult to accurately characterize groups using only group-level interests, leading to a substantial performance drop.

Effect of Interest Enhancement Strategy. We build three variants to observe the effect of interest enhancement strategy during users' item-level interest learning in CI4GI. Variant C deletes the interest enhancement strategy, i.e., directly uses the user representation obtained through the GAT as the item-level interest representation of the user. Variant D removes the item representation enhancement, replacing the item representation in user-item GAT learning with random initialization. Variant E deletes the contextual enhancement.

The experimental results of these three variants on three datasets are listed in the middle part of Table 3. The performance of variants D and E is lower than that of CI4GI, indicating that removing any of the interest enhancement methods results in a decrease in performance. Among the two variants, variant E shows the most significant performance degradation, highlighting the effectiveness of contextual enhancement in improving group identification. This is likely because it identifies the item that motivates the user to join the group as a potential interest, effectively enriching the user's item-level preferences. Additionally, variant C exhibits a significant performance degradation, which suggests that the simultaneous deletion of the two interest enhancement methods has a significant negative impact on model performance.

Effect of Contrastive Learning. We build four variants to observe the effect of contrastive learning in CI4GI. Variant F deletes the entire contrastive learning(CL) module. Variant G removes the vanilla contrastive learning loss L_{UserSSL1}, variant H removes the contrastive learning loss with dynamic false-negative sample optimization L_{UserSSL2}, and variant I deletes the annealing parameter β used to balance the two contrastive learning losses, setting β to a constant value of 0.5.

The experimental results on three datasets are listed in the bottom part of Table 3. Both variants G and H underperform compared to CI4GI, indicating that removing either contrastive learning loss negatively impacts model performance. Variant I experiences a more significant performance degradation compare to variants G and H, as the absence of the annealing parameter prevents the model from properly balancing the two contrastive learning losses. This causes

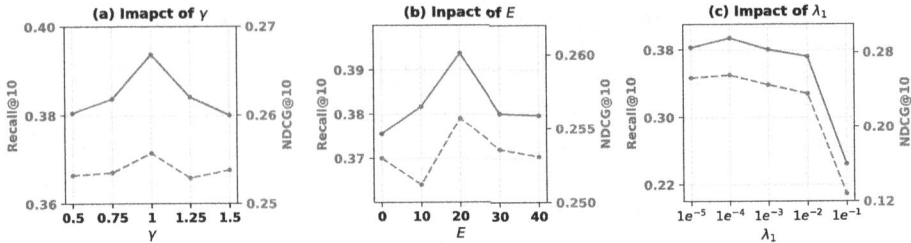

Fig. 4. Sensitivity analysis of hyperparameters γ, E and λ_1 on Mafengwo dataset.

the model to rely on the Wasserstein distance for identifying false-negative samples before it has sufficiently learned user interest patterns and distributional representations. As a result, the identified false-negative samples are heavily influenced by random initialization and lack meaningful guidance. Additionally, variant F shows a substantial performance decline, highlighting the crucial role of the contrastive learning module in CI4GI.

4.4 Hyperparameter Sensitivity Analysis

We perform experiments on Mafengwo datasets to explore the sensitivity of the weight of contextual enhancement γ, the thershold E in annealing parameters β and the wight of contrastive learning loss λ_1. We fix other hyper-parameters, and tune γ, E and λ_1 within $\{0.5, 0.75, 1, 1.25, 1.5\}$, $\{0, 10, 20, 30, 40\}$, $\{1e^{-5}, 1e^{-4}, 1e^{-3}, 1e^{-2}, 1e^{-1}\}$, respectively. From the results in Fig. 4, we can observe that as γ increases from 0.5 to 1, the performance of CI4GI shows an increasing trend, and when γ exceeds 1, the model performance starts to decrease. This suggests that appropriate contextual enhancement representation weight helps to improve the quality of the user representation, which in turn improves the model performance. The performance of CI4GI first rises and then falls as E increases. When E is too small, the model is prematurely subjected to unguided false negative sample identification before it has learned the basic user interests. Conversely, when E is too large, the weight of contrastive learning with negative sample optimization is consistently small and fail to guide model optimization. CI4GI achieves optimal performance when $\lambda_1 = 1 \times e^{-4}$. If λ_1 is too small, the contrastive learning loss has little impact, while if λ_1 is too large, the weight of the contrastive learning loss is almost equal to the weight of the main loss, leading to a decrease in effectiveness.

5 Conclusion

Group identification is a challenging recommendation task, as a user's decision on joining a group is jointly influenced by both group-level and item-level interests. Therefore, effectively capturing these two types of interests and their collaborative relationship is crucial for accurate group identification. We propose a model

CI4GI, which simultaneously models users' group-level and item-level interests, and designs an interest enhancement strategy to capture the mutual enhancement of the dual-level interests through item representation enhancement and contextual enhancement. Meanwhile, we design a contrastive learning strategy with dynamic false-negative sample optimization to improve the alignment of cross-level interests. Experimental results on public datasets show that CI4GI significantly improves the accuracy of group identification.

Acknowledgment. This work was supported by the National Natural Science Foundation of China under Grant No. 62072450.

References

1. Cao, D., He, X., Miao, L., An, Y., Yang, C., Hong, R.: Attentive group recommendation. In: The 41st International ACM SIGIR Conference on Research & Development in Information Retrieval, pp. 645–654 (2018)
2. Cao, D., He, X., Miao, L., Xiao, G., Chen, H., Xu, J.: Social-enhanced attentive group recommendation. IEEE Trans. Knowl. Data Eng. **33**(3), 1195–1209 (2019)
3. Chen, T., Yin, H., Long, J., Nguyen, Q.V.H., Wang, Y., Wang, M.: Thinking inside the box: learning hypercube representations for group recommendation. In: Proceedings of the 45th International ACM SIGIR Conference on Research and Development in Information Retrieval, pp. 1664–1673 (2022)
4. Chen, W.Y., Zhang, D., Chang, E.Y.: Combinational collaborative filtering for personalized community recommendation. In: Proceedings of the 14th ACM SIGKDD International Conference on Knowledge Discovery and Data Mining, pp. 115–123 (2008)
5. Cui, Z., Li, Z., Wu, S., Zhang, X.Y., Wang, L.: Dressing as a whole: outfit compatibility learning based on node-wise graph neural networks. In: The World Wide Web Conference, pp. 307–317 (2019)
6. He, X., Deng, K., Wang, X., Li, Y., Zhang, Y., Wang, M.: LightGCN: simplifying and powering graph convolution network for recommendation. In: Proceedings of the 43rd International ACM SIGIR Conference on Research and Development in Information Retrieval, pp. 639–648 (2020)
7. Oord, A.v.d., Li, Y., Vinyals, O.: Representation learning with contrastive predictive coding. arXiv preprint arXiv:1807.03748 (2018)
8. Sankar, A., Wu, Y., Wu, Y., Zhang, W., Yang, H., Sundaram, H.: GroupIM: a mutual information maximization framework for neural group recommendation. In: Proceedings of the 43rd International ACM SIGIR Conference on Research and Development in Information Retrieval, pp. 1279–1288 (2020)
9. Tao, Z., Wei, Y., Wang, X., He, X., Huang, X., Chua, T.S.: MGAT: multimodal graph attention network for recommendation. Inf. Process. Manag. **57**(5), 102277 (2020)
10. Veličković, P., Cucurull, G., Casanova, A., Romero, A., Lio, P., Bengio, Y.: Graph attention networks. arXiv preprint arXiv:1710.10903 (2017)
11. Wang, J., Zhao, Z., Zhou, J., Wang, H., Cui, B., Qi, G.: Recommending Flickr groups with social topic model. Inf. Retrieval **15**, 278–295 (2012)

12. Wang, X., He, X., Wang, M., Feng, F., Chua, T.S.: Neural graph collaborative filtering. In: Proceedings of the 42nd International ACM SIGIR Conference on Research and Development in Information Retrieval, pp. 165–174 (2019)
13. Wang, X., Donaldson, R., Nell, C., Gorniak, P., Ester, M., Bu, J.: Recommending groups to users using user-group engagement and time-dependent matrix factorization. In: Proceedings of the AAAI Conference on Artificial Intelligence. vol. 30 (2016)
14. Wu, J., et al.: Self-supervised graph learning for recommendation. In: Proceedings of the 44th international ACM SIGIR Conference on Research and Development in Information Retrieval, pp. 726–735 (2021)
15. Wu, X., Xiong, Y., Zhang, Y., Jiao, Y., Zhang, J.: Dual intents graph modeling for user-centric group discovery. In: Proceedings of the 32nd ACM International Conference on Information and Knowledge Management, pp. 2716–2725 (2023)
16. Wu, X., et al.: ConsRec: learning consensus behind interactions for group recommendation. In: Proceedings of the ACM Web Conference 2023, pp. 240–250 (2023)
17. Yang, M., et al.: Group identification via transitional hypergraph convolution with cross-view self-supervised learning. In: Proceedings of the 32nd ACM International Conference on Information and Knowledge Management, pp. 2969–2979 (2023)
18. Yang, M., Liu, Z., Yang, L., Liu, X., Wang, C., Peng, H., Yu, P.S.: Ranking-based group identification via factorized attention on social tripartite graph. In: Proceedings of the Sixteenth ACM International Conference on Web Search and Data Mining, pp. 769–777 (2023)
19. Yin, H., Wang, Q., Zheng, K., Li, Z., Yang, J., Zhou, X.: Social influence-based group representation learning for group recommendation. In: 2019 IEEE 35th International Conference on Data Engineering (ICDE), pp. 566–577. IEEE (2019)
20. Yu, J., Yin, H., Xia, X., Chen, T., Cui, L., Nguyen, Q.V.H.: Are graph augmentations necessary? Simple graph contrastive learning for recommendation. In: Proceedings of the 45th International ACM SIGIR Conference on Research and Development in Information Retrieval, pp. 1294–1303 (2022)
21. Zhao, R., Jin, B., Lv, Y., Zheng, Y., Lai, W.: Multiple hypergraph learning for ephemeral group recommendation. In: Joint European Conference on Machine Learning and Knowledge Discovery in Databases, pp. 89–105. Springer (2024)

MASTFM: Meta-learning and Data Augmentation to Stress Test Forecasting Models

Ricardo Inácio[1,2(✉)], Vítor Cerqueira[1,2], Marília Barandas[3], and Carlos Soares[1,2,3]

[1] Faculdade de Engenharia da Universidade do Porto, Porto, Portugal
{rcinacio,vcerqueira,csoares}@fe.up.pt
[2] Laboratory for Artificial Intelligence and Computer Science (LIACC), Porto, Portugal
[3] Fraunhofer Portugal AICOS, Porto, Portugal
marilia.barandas@aicos.fraunhofer.pt

Abstract. Time series forecasting is pivotal across industries, as it fosters data-driven decision-making, increasing the chances of successful outcomes. Yet, certain instances that feature adverse characteristics, may lead models to manifest stress through decreases in performance (e.g., large errors). Hence, the ability to preemptively identify such cases, while establishing their root causes, would be advantageous to elevate the understanding of forecasting processes, informing users about the trustworthiness of predictions. Hence, we propose MASTFM, a method based on meta-learning that leverages statistical characteristics of input time series, and estimations of forecasting performance from model outputs, to build a metamodel that learns conditions for stress. Given that such occurrences are naturally rare, data augmentation is employed to ensure balance during training. Moreover, SHapley Additive exPlanations (SHAP) are used to explain how features impact forecasting behaviour.

Keywords: Time Series Forecasting · Meta-learning · Data Augmentation · Stress Testing

1 Introduction

Time series forecasting remains highly practical for decision-makers, as it enables statistically-based procedures [2], increasing the chances of success. Forecasts can be carried out with considerable accuracy and certainty, by leveraging patterns found in past data. Nonetheless, data difficulties, such as missing values or outliers, are prone to arise [10]. Difficult instances, which can be described as stress-inducing, may impact the underlying model negatively, resulting in abnormal behaviours such as large errors, high uncertainty, or hubris (i.e., large errors and low uncertainty). Inevitably, these are only made apparent after the fact, which leads users to distrust predictions. Hence, being able to preemptively identify those cases, while establishing contributing factors, would substantially elevate the understanding of forecasting mechanisms. It could also foster responsible practices, for example, by informing users about poor forecasts to dismiss.

To this end, we present MASTFM, a Python package that leverages meta-learning to explain which time series might induce model stress. It relies on patterns derived from feature extraction methods, and estimations of forecasting performance based on model outputs. These are used to fit a metamodel, which learns to classify new instances as stress-inducing or not. Given that such cases are rare by nature, training a balanced, unbiased classifier might be challenging. Thus, resampling techniques, focused on data augmentation, are employed. The probabilities predicted by the metamodel are then used to explain the behaviour of the forecasting model. Moreover, SHAP [7] values are used to explain how features affect the metamodel, and consequently forecasting performance. A video demonstration[1] and the package[2], are available online.

2 MASTFM Specification

2.1 Forecasting Model

Our solution operates as a wrapper around forecasting models, as a way to identify which time series (and what specific feature values), might lead them to manifest stress. Any supervised regression algorithm that is compatible with the scikit-learn [8] API is also compatible with MASTFM. This implies that even those not belonging to the scikit-learn [8] library, are also supported, as long as compatibility with its API is ensured, such as LightGBM [6] or XGBoost [1].

2.2 Metamodel

A metamodel, in the form of a binary classifier based on meta-learning, is the central component of MASTFM. It leverages statistical features extracted from time series via tsfeatures [3], and data augmentation methods, either via over-sampling, or synthetic time series generation, to mitigate the effects of target imbalance. Forecasting performance is estimated via SMAPE by default.

The binary label in each task ($\delta \in \{\delta^E, \delta^U, \delta^H\} \rightarrow$ errors, uncertainty, and hubris, respectively), takes its corresponding threshold(s) in consideration: $\tau \rightarrow E$, $\beta \rightarrow U$, $(\tau, \beta) \rightarrow H$. These are defined by percentiles of forecasting performance estimates e_i, from a model f in a time series Y_i, comprising information of both errors (e_i^e) and uncertainty (e_i^u): $e_i = (e_i^e, e_i^u)$, to classify a time series $Y_i \in \mathcal{Y}$ as stress-inducing ($\hat{\delta}_i = 1$) as follows: $\delta_i^E = e_i^e > \tau$, $\delta_i^U = e_i^u > \beta$, and $\delta_i^H = (e_i^e > \tau) \wedge (e_i^u < \beta)$. Stress-inducing time series are identified using the above schemes for each task, and used as ground truths for the metamodel.

---

[1] https://www.youtube.com/watch?v=0bm99xHWBrs.
[2] https://pypi.org/project/mastfm/.

2.3 Performance

The quality of the metamodel, in terms of the trustworthiness of its predictions is measured in ROC AUC, which quantifies its ability to discern from the two established classes of instances: stress-inducing or not. A set of experiments which showcases the results of several variants of the metamodel, each leveraging a different augmentation technique, across six distinct datasets, is presented in the paper that introduces the theoretical foundations behind this work.[3]

Furthermore, analyses that compare how each metamodel variant performs both on average and on each dataset individually, across increasingly stricter stress settings, are also available on the paper. The reported outcomes indicate that the method is generally able to identify and characterise conditions for forecasting model stress, and that it performs more favourably when paired with data augmentation, mainly with methods that directly generate synthetic time series data, rather than generating features.

2.4 Explanations

The metamodel can then be applied to learn patterns present in time series features, which might be correlated to stress. The predicted probabilities can be used to explain forecasting behaviour, by employing explainability methods. MASTFM uses SHAP [7], to indicate which are the most important features in each meta-classification task (i.e., $E, U,$ or H), and how each contributes to the outcomes. Visual explanations are made available to the user, as shown in Fig. 1.

3 Applications

This package targets users who seek to identify conditions for stress in a time series dataset, which might lead a forecasting model to behave abnormally. Therefore, given a model f, a set of time series $\mathcal{Y}$, and the kind of stress to quantify $(E, U,$ or $H)$, MASTFM can automatically determine which series might cause it, explaining it via statistical features. Although many methods incorporate the modules that comprise this work, as far as we are aware, this is the first that integrates them in the context of stress testing based on meta-learning, to model the characteristics of challenging scenarios. This leads to a practical understanding of forecasting mechanisms, via state-of-the-art explainability approaches [7].

One use case is shown in Algorithm 1, where XGBoost is put to forecast time series captured in a monthly frequency, with seasonal periods of length 12. The user is interested in stress that manifests as large errors, and it considers those above the $80th$ percentile as significant. Besides point forecasts, the associated prediction intervals are computed, with a confidence level of 90%, via Conformal Prediction [9], quantifying uncertainty. Imbalance is mitigated by generating synthetic time series using Scaling [5], which adjusts data magnitude. It is also

---

[3] Meta-learning and Data Augmentation for Stress Testing Forecasting Models [4].

possible to apply data transformations (e.g., first differences), to ease modelling. The subsequent methods produce the explanations shown in Fig. 1, which not only illustrate the distribution of series across differing manifestations of stress, but also how feature values affect the outcomes of the metamodel, and consequently forecasting performance. In this example, time series showcasing low `trend` and `linearity` values, lead the metamodel to classify them as stress-inducing, meaning that the forecasting model struggles with that kind of data.

A practical example of how this method can be used, as showcased in the previously mentioned video demonstration[4], can also be found in the open repository of this project, in the form of a simple test notebook[5], which allows the use of diverse augmentation methods from the two aforementioned categories.

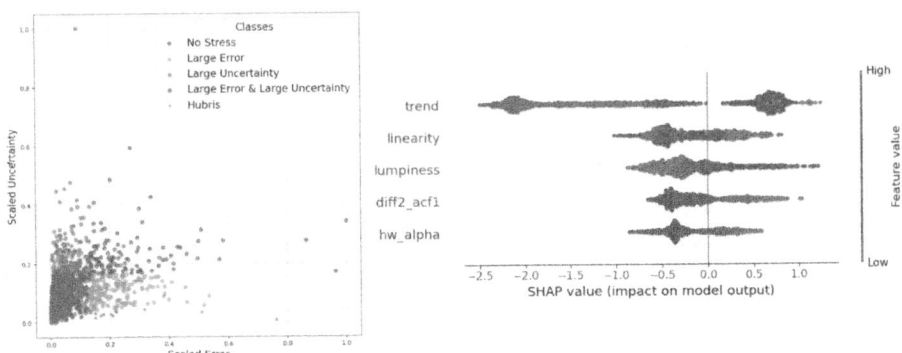

Fig. 1. Visual explanations. On the left, a scatter plot shows each series coloured by the respective stress class. On the right, SHAP values of the 5 most important features for the metamodel are shown. Values to the right of the vertical line contribute to a positive classification, and colour denotes the feature value (red = high, blue = low). (Color figure online)

Algorithm 1. Example of usage for the `MASTFM` package

```
mast = MASTFM(                              ▷ Initialize MASTFM class
    forecasting_model=XGBoost(),  ▷ Provide the forecasting regression model to wrap around
    seasonality=12,                ▷ Set the seasonality (e.g., 12 to monthly data)
    frequency="M",                          ▷ Set the time series frequency
    horizon=12,                             ▷ Set the forecast horizon
    target="errors",                        ▷ Set type of stress to gauge
    level=90,            ▷ Set confidence level between 0 and 100 for prediction intervals
    quantile=80,                     ▷ Set quantile for the threshold of stress
    augmentation_method="Scaling"          ▷ Set a valid data augmentation method
)
mast.fit(df=df, target_differences=1)    ▷ Fit the method and apply first differences
mast.plot_stress()         ▷ Plot each series, across the error and uncertainty dimensions
mast.explanations()           ▷ Explain how features affect the metamodel using SHAP
mast.show_large_errors_ids()              ▷ List series that lead to large errors
mast.show_large_uncertainty_ids()         ▷ List series that lead to high uncertainty
mast.show_hubris_ids()               ▷ List series that lead to overconfident predictions
```

---

[4] c.f. footnote 1.
[5] https://github.com/ricardoinaciopt/mastfm/tree/main/test.

Acknowledgments. This work was partially funded by projects AISym4Med (n.º 101095387) supported by Horizon Europe Cluster 1: Health, ConnectedHealth (n.º 46858), supported by Competitiveness and Internationalisation Operational Programme (POCI) and Lisbon Regional Operational Programme (LISBOA 2020), under the PORTUGAL 2020 Partnership Agreement, through the European Regional Development Fund (ERDF) and Agenda "Center for Responsible AI", nr. C645008882-00000055, investment project nr. 62, financed by the Recovery and Resilience Plan (PRR) and by European Union - NextGeneration EU, and also by FCT plurianual funding for 2020–2023 of LIACC (UIDB/00027/2020 UIDP/00027/2020).

References

1. Chen, T., Guestrin, C.: Xgboost: A scalable tree boosting system. In: Proceedings of the 22nd ACM SIGKDD (2016)
2. Hewamalage, H., Bergmeir, C., Bandara, K.: Global models for time series forecasting: a simulation study. Pattern Recogn. **124**, 108441 (2022)
3. Hyndman, R., et al.: tsfeatures: time series feature extraction (2024)
4. Inácio, R., Cerqueira, V., Barandas, M., Soares, C.: Meta-learning and data augmentation for stress testing forecasting models. In: International Symposium on Intelligent Data Analysis, pp. 343–357. Springer (2025)
5. Iwana, B.K., Uchida, S.: An empirical survey of data augmentation for time series classification with neural networks. PLoS ONE **16**(7), e0254841 (2021)
6. Ke, G., et al.: Lightgbm: A highly efficient gradient boosting decision tree. In: Advances in Neural Information Processing Systems, vol. 30 (2017)
7. Lundberg, S.: A unified approach to interpreting model predictions (2017)
8. Pedregosa, F., et al.: Scikit-learn: machine learning in python. J. Mach. Learn. Res. **12** (2011)
9. Vovk, V., Gammerman, A., Shafer, G.: Algorithmic learning in a random world, vol. 29. Springer (2005)
10. Wang, Y.: Robustness and reliability of machine learning systems: a comprehensive review. Eng. Open **1**(2), 90–95 (2023)

Time Series Machine Learning with Aeon: Classification and Regression

Matthew Middlehurst[1,2(✉)], Anthony Bagnall[1,3], Germain Forestier[4,5], Ali Ismail-Fawaz[4], and Antoine Guillaume[6]

[1] University of Southampton, Southampton, UK
m.b.middlehurst@gmail.com
[2] University of Bradford, Bradford, UK
[3] University of East Anglia, Norwich, UK
[4] IRIMAS, Université de Haute-Alsace, Mulhouse, France
[5] DSAI, Monash University, Melbourne, Australia
[6] Novahé, Saint-Cloud, France

Abstract. We present the classification and regression modules of `aeon`, a Python library for all machine learning tasks involving time series. `aeon` follows the `scikit-learn` API and is compatible with its utilities such as model selection and pipelines. The toolkit contains a wide range of algorithms, including the state-of-the-art and popular benchmarks for each time series learning task. We demonstrate how to use the `aeon` toolkit for these tasks and give an example of where these algorithms may be useful. More information and an introductory video of the toolkit modules are available on the demo webpage https://aeon-tutorials.github.io/ECML-Demo-2025/.

Keywords: Time series · Classification · Regression · aeon

1 Introduction

Time series machine learning (TSML) is an active research field that finds areas of application in all domains of machine learning and data science. The largest and most well-known field of research for time series is forecasting, having an abundance of tutorials and software suites available to prospective users such as `statsmodels`, `statsforecast`, `darts`, `kats`, and `greykite`. This has left the more traditional machine learning tasks such as classification and regression with a comparative lack of resources despite also being a thriving area of research [3, 4, 12, 13].

Time series classification (TSC) [12] involves fitting a model from a continuous, ordered sequence of real valued observations (a time series) to a discrete response variable. Time series extrinsic regression (TSER) [4] uses a continuous response variable. TSC and TSER problems come from various domains, including medical signals such as electrocardiography (ECG) and Electroencephalography (EEG); human activity recognition and other motion data; spectrograms;

audio; electricity usage; and many more with industrial and research applications. For simplicity, we refer to the grouping of these learning tasks as TSML.

In this demonstration, we show simple use case examples of algorithms for each task and demonstrate how aeon is interoperable with scikit-learn. We describe modules from the aeon toolkit that fill the current resource gap and provide easy access to the most recent TSML algorithms and tools.

2 The aeon Toolkit

The aeon [9] toolkit is an open-source framework for all time series learning tasks. aeon estimators extend the scikit-learn BaseEstimator framework, retaining the familiar fit and predict structure. The aeon BaseClassifier and BaseRegressor base classes inherited by TSML algorithms are used to process data and provide common utilities. aeon provides efficient implementations of the latest advances for a broad range of TSML tasks, including modules for classification, regression, clustering, forecasting, anomaly detection, segmentation and similarity search, as well as a variety of utilities, transformations, and distance measures designed for time series data. In this demonstration we will provide an overview of the functionality available for classification and regression. The toolkit supports both univariate and multivariate (if the algorithm allows) time series, with growing support and utilities for unequal length data. Using a system of optional dependencies, aeon integrates a wide variety of packages such as the previously mentioned TSML projects into a single interface while keeping the core framework with minimal dependencies. Our aim is to provide optimised implementations wherever possible using numba.

The toolkit follows the taxonomy presented in a recent comparative study [12] for its design of the classification and regression modules. Algorithms are grouped into packages of the following categories: convolutions, deep learning, dictionaries/bags-of-words, distance functions, feature extraction, random intervals, shapelets and hybrids. Two recent studies showed that HIVE-COTEv2 [11] and MultiROCKET-HYDRA [2,15] were the state-of-the-art for TSC using the UCR archive datasets [1]; and FreshPRINCE [7], DrCIF [10,11] and RIST [8] were the state-of-the-art for TSER on the Monash/UEA regression archive [4,8,14]. aeon contains implementations of all these algorithms, as well as a majority of the approaches they were compared against.

The package is open-source and distributed under the 3-Clause BSD license. The source code is shared on GitHub[1]. New additions to the codebase are thoroughly tested, with code quality standards upheld. The package is distributed through both pip[2] and conda-forge. The project documentation is sphinx based, hosted by Read the Docs and is available at https://aeon-toolkit.org.

---

[1] https://github.com/aeon-toolkit/aeon.
[2] https://pypi.org/project/aeon/.

2.1 Other TSML Packages

Other packages which can be used for TSML in the Python ecosystem include `tslearn` and `pyts`. However, these present a smaller range of simpler algorithms and lack the state-of-the-art and latest advances. Both packages contain under ten algorithms at the time of writing, compared to the 80+ implementations available in the `aeon` classification and regression modules. The `tsai` package includes deep learning models usable for TSML, but is missing more recent approaches [5,6] available in `aeon` and does not use the `scikit-learn` API.

Other packages such as `tsfresh` and `stumpy` focus on a single algorithm or set of features to extract. While effective, they are not toolkits. The framework in such packages has been developed to best fit the algorithm rather than a range of approaches. This can cause friction when including them in evaluations of multiple approaches, introducing issues such as differing input layouts and results formats which can be avoided with the `aeon` framework.

3 Using aeon

We provide some simple usage examples for selected algorithms for each of the `aeon` TSML modules using datasets from the UCR [1] and Monash/UEA [4, 14] archives. A list of available estimators is available on the `aeon` webpage. Further examples pertaining to the modules discussed such as data formatting and loading are available on the repository and the demo webpage. The following code is from version 1.2.0 of `aeon`.

3.1 Classification

The classification module workflow will be familiar to anyone who has worked with `scikit-learn` previously. We use the `load_classification` function to download the ArrowHead UCR archive dataset. We train a `MultiRocketHydraClassifier` on the loaded data using the `fit` method, which requires the training data `X` and the training labels `y`. Following this, the `predict_proba` method is used to predict the class probabilities for each case in `X_test`. To directly predict class labels, the `predict` method can be used.

```
from aeon.datasets import load_classification
from aeon.classification.convolution_based import import
    MultiRocketHydraClassifier
X, y = load_classification("ArrowHead", split="TRAIN")
X_test, _ = load_classification("ArrowHead", split="TEST")
clf = MultiRocketHydraClassifier().fit(X, y)
probabilities = clf.predict_proba(X_test)
```

3.2 Regression

The regression module is similar to classification in its workflow, but numeric labels are required and finding label probabilities with `predict_proba` is not supported. We load the BarCrawl6min dataset from the Monash archive and fit a `DrCIFRegressor` on it. Label predictions are found using the `predict` method.

```
from aeon.datasets import load_regression
from aeon.regression.interval_based import DrCIFRegressor
X, y = load_regression("BarCrawl6min", split="TRAIN")
X_test, _ = load_regression("BarCrawl6min", split="TEST")
reg = DrCIFRegressor(n_estimators=100).fit(X, y)
predictions = reg.predict(X_test)
```

4 Contributing to aeon

The aeon package welcomes code contributions via Pull Requests on GitHub. The community strives to maintain a consistent style and framework throughout the codebase, but can be flexible in accommodating other approaches. The primary requirement for contributing a new algorithm is that it must have been published in a reputable venue. Comprehensive contribution and developer guidelines are available in the documentation[3], and developers are available to guide researchers who want to submit their published algorithms. The aeon framework can be easily extended by inheriting the `BaseClassifier` or `BaseRegressor` abstract classes and implementing the abstract methods within. The core framework manages tasks such as data validation and conversion, metadata tag handling, as well as integration with the `scikit-learn` API. The codebase contains extensive documentation and automatic testing to avoid common implementation errors.

5 Conclusions

We present the classification and regression modules of the aeon toolkit. aeon innovates through its breadth of coverage, its ease of use and inclusion of efficient implementations of the latest state-of-the-art algorithms. Our primary goal with aeon is to reduce the lead time between the publication of a description of an algorithm and its availability to practitioners to use for solving real-world problems. We believe it is a useful tool for researchers wanting to explore new algorithms. We believe aeon has three sets of target users. Firstly, researchers implementing their algorithms within the framework can help extend the impact of their work through reproducible research and easy comparison to the current state of the art. Secondly, scientists and those in industry benefit from a reduced lead time between the proposing of a new technique and its easy integration into existing workflows. Finally, our easy-to-use and familiar `scikit-learn` interface

---
[3] https://www.aeon-toolkit.org/en/stable/developer_guide.html

makes aeon a useful teaching tool for TSML and reduces barriers to entry into the research field. The aeon package is open to all, integrated into the Python ecosystem, and a big step toward reproducible research for TSML.

Acknowledgements. This work is supported by the UK Engineering and Physical Sciences Research Council (EPSRC) grant number EP/W030756/2.

References

1. Dau, H.A., et al.: The UCR time series archive. IEEE/CAA J. Automatica Sin. **6**(6), 1293–1305 (2019)
2. Dempster, A., Schmidt, D.F., Webb, G.I.: Hydra: competing convolutional kernels for fast and accurate time series classification. Data Min. Knowl. Disc. **37**(5), 1779–1805 (2023)
3. Ismail Fawaz, H., Forestier, G., Weber, J., Idoumghar, L., Muller, P.-A.: Deep learning for time series classification: a review. Data Min. Knowl. Disc. **33**(4), 917–963 (2019). https://doi.org/10.1007/s10618-019-00619-1
4. Guijo-Rubio, D., Middlehurst, M., Arcencio, G., Silva, D.F., Bagnall, A.: Unsupervised feature based algorithms for time series extrinsic regression. Data Min. Knowl. Discov. (2024). https://doi.org/10.1007/s10618-024-01027-w
5. Ismail-Fawaz, A., Devanne, M., Berretti, S., Weber, J., Forestier, G.: Look into the lite in deep learning for time series classification. Int. J. Data Science and Analytics, 1–21 (2025). https://doi.org/10.1007/s41060-024-00708-5
6. Ismail-Fawaz, A., Devanne, M., Weber, J., Forestier, G.: Deep learning for time series classification using new hand-crafted convolution filters. In: 2022 IEEE International Conference on Big Data (Big Data), pp. 972–981. IEEE (2022)
7. Middlehurst, M., Bagnall, A.: The FreshPRINCE: a simple transformation based pipeline time series classifier. In: International Conference on Pattern Recognition and Artificial Intelligence, pp. 150–161. Springer (2022). https://doi.org/10.1007/978-3-031-09282-4_13
8. Middlehurst, M., Bagnall, A.: Extracting features from random subseries: a hybrid pipeline for time series classification and extrinsic regression. In: Ifrim, G., et al. (eds.) International Workshop on Advanced Analytics and Learning on Temporal Data, pp. 113–126. Springer (2023). https://doi.org/10.1007/978-3-031-49896-1_8
9. Middlehurst, M., et al.: Aeon: a python toolkit for learning from time series. J. Mach. Learn. Res. **25**(289), 1–10 (2024)
10. Middlehurst, M., Large, J., Bagnall, A.: The canonical interval forest (CIF) classifier for time series classification. In: 2020 IEEE International Conference on Big Data (Big Data), pp. 188–195. IEEE (2020)
11. Middlehurst, M., Large, J., Flynn, M., Lines, J., Bostrom, A., Bagnall, A.: Hivecote 2.0: a new meta ensemble for time series classification. Mach. Learn. **110**(11), 3211–3243 (2021)
12. Middlehurst, M., Schäfer, P., Bagnall, A.: Bake off redux: a review and experimental evaluation of recent time series classification algorithms. Data Min. Knowl. Discov. (2024). https://doi.org/10.1007/s10618-024-01022-1
13. Ruiz, A.P., Flynn, M., Large, J., Middlehurst, M., Bagnall, A.: The great multivariate time series classification bake off: a review and experimental evaluation of recent algorithmic advances. Data Min. Knowl. Disc. **35**(2), 401–449 (2021)

14. Tan, C.W., Bergmeir, C., Petitjean, F., Webb, G.I.: Time series extrinsic regression: predicting numeric values from time series data. Data Min. Knowl. Disc. **35**, 1032–1060 (2021)
15. Tan, C.W., Dempster, A., Bergmeir, C., Webb, G.I.: MultiRocket: multiple pooling operators and transformations for fast and effective time series classification. Data Min. Knowl. Discov., 1–24 (2022). https://doi.org/10.1007/s10618-022-00844-1

Machine Learning for Data Streams with CapyMOA

Yibin Sun[1,2(✉)], Heitor Murilo Gomes[2], Anton Lee[2], Nuwan Gunasekara[3], Guilherme Weigert Cassales[1], Jia Justin Liu[1], Marco Heyden[4], Vitor Cerqueira[5], Maroua Bahri[6], Yun Sing Koh[7], Bernhard Pfahringer[1], and Albert Bifet[1,8]

[1] AI Institute, University of Waikato, Hamilton, New Zealand
yibin.spencer.sun@gmail.com
[2] Victoria University of Wellington, Wellington, New Zealand
[3] Halmstad University, Halmstad, Sweden
[4] Karlsruhe Institute of Technology, Karlsruhe, Germany
[5] University of Porto, Porto, Portugal
[6] Sorbonne Université, CNRS, LIP6, Paris, France
[7] University of Auckland, Auckland, New Zealand
[8] LTCI, Télécom Paris, IP Paris, Paris, France

Abstract. The exponential growth of data in recent decades has underscored the need for high-speed, real-time, and adaptive processing in machine learning. Data stream learning provides an effective framework to address this challenge. This article introduces CapyMOA, an open-source library designed specifically for data stream learning, offering powerful tools for building and deploying adaptive ML models. GitHub: https://github.com/adaptive-machine-learning/CapyMOA. Website: https://capymoa.org.

Keywords: Open-source · Data Streams · Machine Learning · Concept Drift · Online Continual Learning · Semi-supervised Learning

1 Introduction

CapyMOA [2] is a cutting-edge open-source framework for machine learning on data streams, evolving beyond its origins as an extension of MOA [1] to offer a more comprehensive ecosystem for real-time analytics. It supports a diverse range of streaming algorithms while integrating modern machine learning libraries such as PyTorch [3] and Scikit-learn [4]. With optimized performance, scalable processing, and advanced evaluation strategies, CapyMOA enables seamless experimentation with high-velocity data streams. By continuously incorporating novel algorithms and state-of-the-art tools, it provides researchers and practitioners with a powerful platform for developing and benchmarking next-generation stream learning models. In this work, we provide code snippets and screenshots to demonstrate CapyMOA's abilities. A demonstration video is presented at: https://youtu.be/OEYUe6q04u4.

2 CapyMOA Key Features

Integration with Established Tools. CapyMOA provides a straightforward Python interface to the well-established algorithms and functionalities available in MOA by utilizing JPype as a bridging library. Additionally, CapyMOA integrates algorithms, datasets, and utilities from PyTorch and Scikit-learn, further expanding its applicability.

High Level Evaluation Functions. CapyMOA provides standard evaluation loops in stream learning as evaluation functions.

```
from capymoa.evaluation import prequential_evaluation
result = prequential_evaluation(stream, learner, window_size=500)
```

Concept Drift. CapyMOA simulates different types of concept drift using the DriftStream class and stores the drifting information in the stream. The following code defines a stream possessing an abrupt drift after 5,000 instances, and a gradual drift happening between 9,000 and 11,000 instances.

```
from capymoa.stream.generator import SEA
from capymoa.stream.drift import
    (DriftStream, AbruptDrift, GradualDrift)
stream = DriftStream(stream=[SEA(1), AbruptDrift(position=5000),
        SEA(3), GradualDrift(position=10000, width=2000), SEA(1)])
```

Dedicated Visualization Functions. CapyMOA offers a variety of visualization functions that are specifically designed for streaming scenarios. Figure 1 exhibits a plotting example. The stream data used in this plot is the same as in the previous subsection, and the associated drifts are highlighted by a red vertical line (abrupt drift) a shaded area (gradual drift).

```
from capymoa.evaluation.visualization import plot_windowed_results
plot_windowed_results(knn_result, ht_result, arf_result,
                    metric='accuracy')
```

Pipelines. Building a pipeline is challenging in data stream scenarios because it requires continuous updates and synchronization, especially when concept drift occurs. CapyMOA tackles this by introducing the PipelineElement class—a modular component that supports feature selection, normalization, missing-value imputation, parameter searching and tuning, and more.

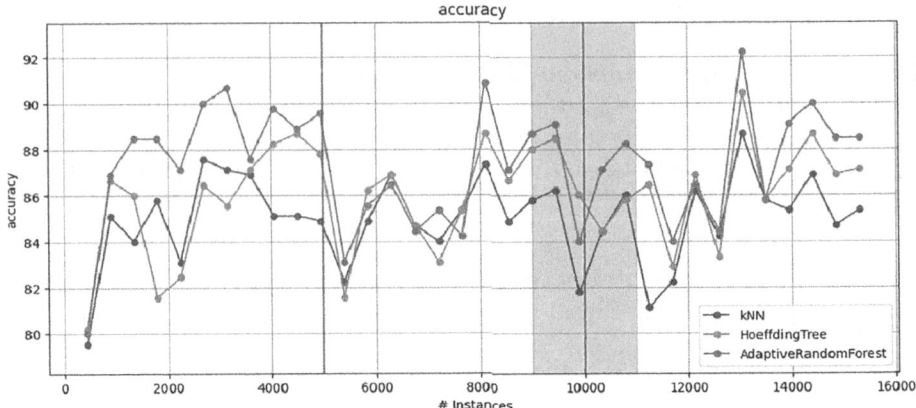

Fig. 1. Prequential Accuracy Over Time Highlighting Two Concept Drifts

```
from capymoa.stream.preprocessing import
    (ClassifierPipeline, MOATransformer)
from moa.streams.filters import NormalisationFilter
from capymoa.drift.detectors import ADWIN
normalisation = MOATransformer(schema=stream.get_schema(),
            moa_filter=NormalisationFilter())
pipeline = ClassifierPipeline().add_transformer(normalisation)
        .add_classifier(learner).add_drift_detector(ADWIN())
```

3 Learning Tasks

Since learning on data streams is the main focus of CapyMOA, plenty of streaming tasks and functionalities are provided.

Supervised Learning. The supervised learning procedures are wrapped into the prequential evaluation function (aforementioned in Sect. 2), including classification, regression, and prediction interval.

Semi-supervised Learning. CapyMOA also supports the under-explored Semi-supervised learning for data streams, including algorithms and evaluation functions.

```
from capymoa.ssl.classifier import OSNN
from capymoa.evaluation import prequential_ssl_evaluation
osnn = OSNN(schema=stream.get_schema(), optim_steps=10)
results_osnn = prequential_ssl_evaluation(stream=stream,
            learner=osnn, label_probability=0.01)
```

Unsupervised Learning.
– Data Stream Clustering. CapyMOA supports most clustering algorithms from MOA while introduces a redesigned evaluation framework for a more streamlined process. It visualizes the evolution of micro- and macro-clusters over time for 2D datasets (as illustrated in Fig. 2) and supports the extraction of clustering metrics based on established methods from the literature.

```
from capymoa.cluster import Clustream_with_kmeans as WithKmeans
from capymoa.cluster.visualization import plot_clustering_evolution
from capymoa.stream.generator import RandomRBFGeneratorDrift
plot_clustering_evolution(RandomRBFGeneratorDrift(), WithKmeans(),
            frame_duration=1000)
```

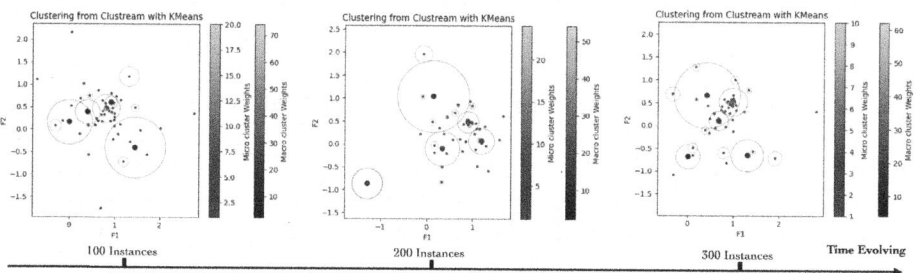

Fig. 2. Clusters Evolving Over Time

– Anomaly Detection. CapyMOA includes a wide range of anomaly detection algorithms from MOA. In addition, it features cutting-edge algorithms and is constantly updated with the latest ones.

```
from capymoa.evaluation import prequential_evaluation_anomaly
from capymoa.anomaly import HalfSpaceTrees
from capymoa.stream import NumpyStream
stream_ad = NumpyStream(X, y, "AD_Dataset", feature_names,
            target_name, "categorical")
hst = HalfSpaceTrees(schema=stream_ad.get_schema())
results_hst = prequential_evaluation_anomaly(stream=stream_ad,
            learner=hst, window_size=1000)
```

AutoML for Data Streams. CapyMOA provides AutoML capabilities for streaming data by the introduction of the `AutoClass` class, which reads a json file containing algorithm configuration options and automatically selects the best-performing one for prediction.

```
from capymoa.automl import AutoClass
autoclass = AutoClass(schema=schema,
            configuration_json="./settings_autoclass.json")
results_autoclass = prequential_evaluation(stream=stream,
                    learner=autoclass)
```

AutoML in CapyMOA can also be applied using Random search to find the best configuration for a combination of a preprocessor and a learner in a **streaming scenario**. This is achieved via the use of pipelines, enabled by the RandomSearchClassifierPE class, which facilitates the composition of preprocessing steps, learning algorithms, and automated hyperparameter optimization.

```
from capymoa.stream.preprocessing import RandomSearchClassifierPE
randomsearch_pe = RandomSearchClassifierPE(HoeffdingTree,
                hparams_ranges, n_combinations, rng)
```

Online Continual Learning. In a recent release, CapyMOA introduced support for Online Continual Learning (OCL), an advanced research area that integrates continual learning with stream learning. Similar to the previously introduced stream learning interface, OCL in CapyMOA also offers high-level evaluation and additional functionalities. An example code snippet is shown below.

```
from capymoa.classifier import HoeffdingTree
from capymoa.datasets.ocl import TinySplitMNIST
from capymoa.evaluation.ocl import ocl_train_eval_loop
scenario = TinySplitMNIST()
model = HoeffdingTree(scenario.schema)
metrics = ocl_train_eval_loop(model, scenario.train_streams,
            scenario.test_streams)
```

4 Conclusions

CapyMOA is an open-source platform for machine learning and continual learning on streaming data, supporting both Java and Python. It offers essential tools for building, training, and evaluating models in real-time environments.

Education. CapyMOA helps students learn stream learning concepts through hands-on experience.

Research. Its transparency and flexibility support reproducible and extensible experimentation.

Development. Developers benefit from easy prototyping and integration into real-world applications.

Overall, CapyMOA serves as a valuable resource across education, research, and development, lowering the barrier to effective streaming data analysis. Please refer to the CapyMOA website for more information and tutorials, and [2] for an empirical comparison of CapyMOA against other frameworks.

References

1. Bifet, A., et al.: MOA: massive online analysis, a framework for stream classification and clustering. In: Proceedings of the First Workshop on Applications of Pattern Analysis, pp. 44–50. PMLR (2010)
2. Gomes, H.M., .: CapyMOA: efficient machine learning for data streams in python (2025). htttps://arxiv.org/abs/2502.07432
3. Paszke, A., et al.: Pytorch: an imperative style, high-performance deep learning library. Adv. Neural Inf. Process. Syst. **32** (2019)
4. Pedregosa, F., et al.: Scikit-learn: machine learning in python. J. Mach. Learn. Res. **12**, 2825–2830 (2011)

ProxyLLM : LLM-Driven Framework for Customer Support Through Text-Style Transfer

Sehyeong Jo[1] and Jungwon Seo[2](✉)

[1] University of Colorado Boulder, Boulder, CO, USA
se.jo@colorado.edu
[2] University of Stavanger, Stavanger, Norway
jungwon.seo@uis.no

Abstract. LLM-based chatbots have improved response quality and reduced costs in customer support, while the experiences of human agents, essential to the service ecosystem, have remained largely overlooked. Stress from harmful texts poses a major challenge for agents, undermining their efficiency, customer satisfaction, and business outcomes. In this work, we propose an LLM-powered system designed to enhance the working conditions of customer service agents by addressing emotionally intensive communications. Our proposed system leverages LLMs to transform the tone of customer messages, preserving actionable content while mitigating the emotional impact on human agents. Furthermore, the application is implemented as a Chrome extension, making it highly adaptable and easy to integrate into existing systems. Our method aims to enhance the overall service experience for businesses, customers, and agents. The code related to this paper is available at: https://github.com/sehyeongjo/Proxy-LLM.

Keywords: Large Language Models · Human-centered Interfaces · Sentiment Analysis

1 Introduction

Advancements in large language models (LLMs) have driven the widespread adoption of chatbot-based customer support services across industries, enabling companies to reduce operational costs and enhance response accuracy and contextual relevance. While these improvements have contributed to higher customer satisfaction, human agents remain indispensable for managing complex interactions. Agents are required to address the actionable aspects of customer interactions while also withstanding emotionally charged or negative responses, all within the constraints of strict organizational protocols. This ongoing burden underscores the need to reevaluate the current customer interaction framework. Therefore, we propose ProxyLLM, a system that functions similarly to a proxy server, positioned between human agents and existing systems to prevent human

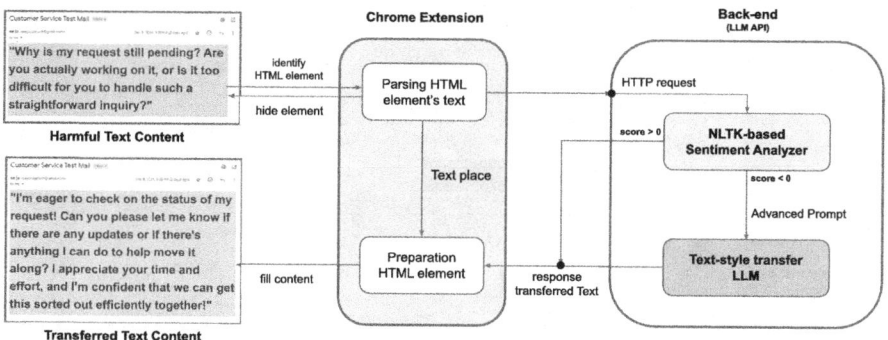

Fig. 1. Overview of the ProxyLLM Application System.

agents from being directly exposed to raw harmful messages. Specifically, we propose using LLMs to adjust the tone of incoming messages using text-style transfer [3] while preserving their core content. This adjustment aims to shield agents from unnecessary emotional distress, enabling them to work more efficiently and with greater composure. Furthermore, to ensure ease of use and seamless integration, ProxyLLM is implemented as a Chrome extension. This implementation enables effortless integration into diverse web-based customer service systems without necessitating modifications to existing system pipelines or the deployment of additional components, such as databases.

Contributions. We propose a novel application that leverages large language models (LLMs) to enhance mental health support for human agents in high-stress environments. By utilizing the style-transfer capabilities of LLMs, the system preserves the critical content of communications while filtering harmful or distressing material before it reaches agents. Implemented as a lightweight Chrome extension, it integrates seamlessly into existing workflows without causing disruptions.

2 ProxyLLM

ProxyLLM is a proposed system that consists of two primary components: (1) a Chrome extension and (2) a back-end machine learning model server, as depicted in Fig. 1. An introductory video can be viewed at https://youtu.be/MTCMmlmOTpQ

2.1 Chrome Extension

A Chrome extension is a third-party application that enhances browser functionality through packaged HTML, JavaScript, and CSS files, operating under user-granted permissions. The ProxyLLM extension automatically identifies and

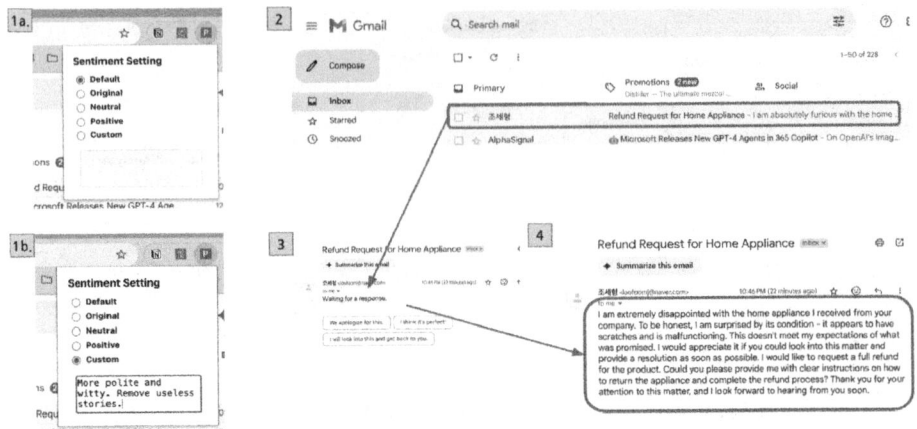

Fig. 2. ProxyLLM UI components and Chrome Extension workflow example. (1a) Users can select a predefined sentiment preset, and (1b) optionally apply a custom prompt. (2) After completing the setup, selecting email content triggers (3) the original text to be hidden and a waiting message to be displayed. Subsequently, (4) the content is replaced with the prompt-applied output.

obscures HTML elements containing harmful text, shielding human agents from exposure, and transmits the content to a back-end API for style transformation. It also provides a graphical user interface (GUI) for customizing prompts, enabling context-sensitive style-transfer responses (Fig. 2).

2.2 Back-End Processing

The back-end component processes incoming requests by first applying sentiment analysis using the Natural Language Toolkit (NLTK) [1] and then refining the sentiment scores through the LLM's self-feedback mechanism, ultimately producing scores ranging from -1 to 1. The lightweight sentiment analyzer reduces computational overhead by bypassing the LLM for scores outside predefined thresholds. Requests requiring style transfer are processed through a text-style transfer module using simple prompting, and the transformed text is seamlessly injected into the agent's interface via the Chrome extension. The overall workflow is illustrated in Fig. 3.

3 Text-Style Transfer and Implementation

ProxyLLM achieves text-style transfer by leveraging fine-tuned LLMs through prompt engineering, appending instructions to rephrase original text with greater politeness while minimizing training costs and supporting customization. The basic prompt structure is :

> This is original text. Change this text style. *[Original Text]*. Change this text content to be more polite.

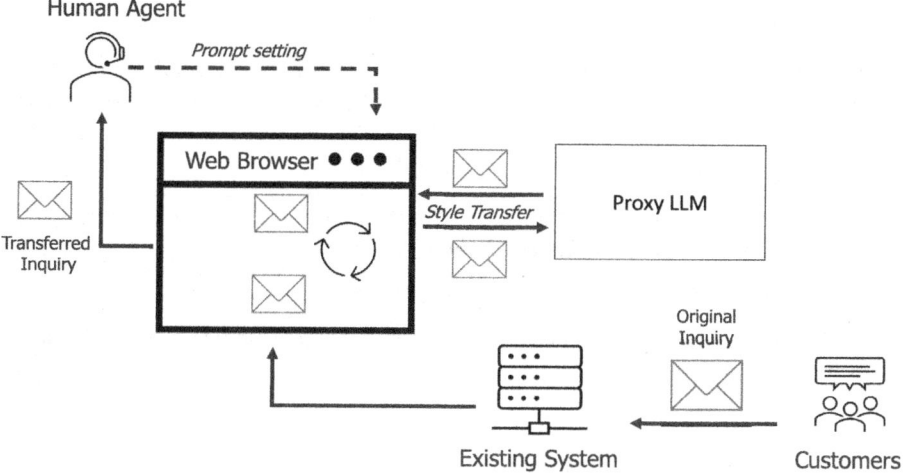

Fig. 3. ProxyLLM Workflow Diagram

While the LLM determines sentiment based on its inherent standards, basic prompting leaves the criteria fully dependent on the model without personalization. ProxyLLM addresses this by embedding personalized configuration parameters into the prompt to tailor outputs for human agents. The advanced prompt structure is:

> *This is original text. Change this text style.* ***[Original Text]****. Change this text content to be more* ***[Custom Parameter]****.*

Text modification is guided by personalized configuration settings. Predefined presets trigger the use of corresponding predesigned prompts, whereas custom configurations employ dynamically constructed prompts to realize the specified transformation. An example of a prompt corresponding to a custom parameter is as follows:

- **Neutral :** *a neutral tone to remove any emotional, biased, or subjective elements while preserving the original meaning.*
- **Positive :** *a positive tone, enhancing the optimism and uplifting language while preserving the original meaning.*

Implementation Details The application's back-end, built with Flask, enables efficient communication with the Chrome extension through a lightweight API. Text-style transfer and sentiment-aware transformations are handled by a Llama 3.1 8B model [2], fine-tuned on sentiment data to optimize performance under limited GPU resource(Test Server : RTX 2060 GPU).

3.1 Evaluation

To evaluate ProxyLLM's style transfer, we employed commercial LLMs (GPT-4o-mini, Claude Sonnet, Gemini) as proxy evaluators. Each was given 10 pairs of negative inquiries and their corresponding positive versions. The structure of the prompt for requesting the score is as follows:

> *Please mark the sentimental score I present from -1.0 (very negative) to 1.0 (very positive).* ***[Original Text]***.

Table 1. The average sentiment score variations original and transferred applying LLMs to sample texts.

LLMs	Original	Transferred
GPT-4o-mini	−0.48	0.28
Claude Sonnet	−0.66	0.24
Gemini	−0.6	0.18
NLTK	−0.48	0.83

Table 1 shows that our fine-tuned LLM consistently achieved positive tone conversion across all LLMs using a simple prompt. The NLTK-based sentiment analysis also aligned closely with LLM scores, confirming its efficiency and reliability for detecting negative tone.

4 Conclusion

In this study, we introduced ProxyLLM, a Chrome extension designed to enhance customer support by leveraging LLM capabilities to improve service quality while safeguarding the mental well-being of human agents. By transforming harmful or emotionally charged customer messages into positive tones, ProxyLLM fosters a more constructive interaction environment without requiring additional infrastructure changes. Its modular and adaptable design also positions it for broader applications across various web services and platforms. Future work could enhance ProxyLLM by advancing personalization, model efficiency, and multilingual capabilities to better support human-centric service delivery.

References

1. Bird, S.: Nltk: the natural language toolkit. In: Proceedings of the COLING/ACL 2006 Interactive Presentation Sessions, pp. 69–72 (2006)
2. Dubey, A., et al.: The llama 3 herd of models. arXiv preprint arXiv:2407.21783 (2024)
3. Toshevska, M., Gievska, S.: A review of text style transfer using deep learning. IEEE Trans. Artifi. Intell. **3**(5), 669–684 (2021)

Introducing PYRA: A High-Level Linter for Data Science Software

Greta Dolcetti[1], Vincenzo Arceri[2(✉)], Antonella Mensi[3], Enea Zaffanella[2], Caterina Urban[4], and Agostino Cortesi[1]

[1] Ca' Foscari University of Venice, Via Torino 155, 30170 Venice, Italy
{greta.dolcetti,cortesi}@unive.it
[2] University of Parma, Parco Area delle Scienze 53/A, 43124 Parma, Italy
{vincenzo.arceri,enea.zaffanella}@unipr.it
[3] University of Verona, Piazzale L. A. Scuro 10, 37134 Verona, Italy
antonella.mensi@univr.it
[4] Inria and École Normale Supérieure, Université PSL, Paris, France
caterina.urban@inria.fr

Abstract. We present PYRA, a static analysis tool that aims at detecting code smells in data science workflows. Our goal is to capture potential issues, focusing on misleading visualizations, challenges for reproducibility, as well as misleading, unreliable or unexpected results.

Link to the demo: https://www.youtube.com/watch?v=D-Asyuhs Tyo

GitHub repository: https://github.com/spangea/Pyra.

Keywords: Static analysis · Code smells · Data science · Jupyter Notebooks · Python

1 Introduction

In this demo, we present PYRA, a high-level linter for data science software. PYRA is a static analysis tool that helps developers identify potential issues in their data science code written in Python. PYRA focuses primarily on code smells, aiming at capturing anti-patterns that, although not raising a warning due to Python's inherent flexibility, can result in potential issues for the data science pipeline being implemented.

PYRA is inspired by the pervasiveness and versatility of data science software, which is often applied in interdisciplinary fields. Due to this nature, many projects [1,3,4] aim at easing and making the development of data science software more reliable: yet, they often require a huge effort by the users (such as manually annotating program variables) or they focus either on the data or general best practices for the code, but not on the combination of both. Conversely, PYRA is designed to be easy to use and integrates seamlessly with Python code, without requiring any additional annotations or modifications of the code. Moreover, our goal is to infer and reason about more abstract datatypes, potentially capturing a broader and less conventional set of code smells. Therefore we propose an easily extensible framework to help developers achieve correct results.

2 PYRA's Architecture

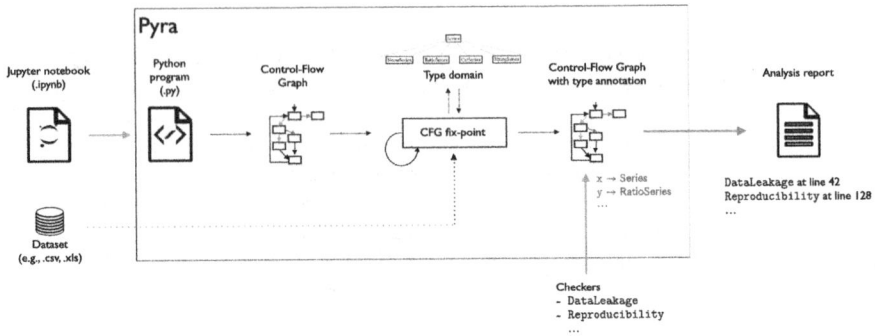

Fig. 1. PYRA high-level execution flow.

The high-level execution flow of PYRA is reported in Fig. 1. PYRA takes as input a Jupyter Notebook and produces a report containing the detected code smells and the results of the analysis. First, the notebook is converted into a Python script; then, PYRA performs static analysis on the Control Flow Graph (CFG) extracted from the script, computing a fixpoint over the CFG to infer abstract type information for each variable at each program point; finally, a set of checkers is applied to the annotated CFG to detect code smells.[1]

The 55 abstract datatypes that PYRA can infer extend those described in [2]: some correspond to concrete datatypes (e.g., List, DataFrame, Series), others are more abstract (e.g., Numeric, which can represent either a float or an int), and some are specific to data science (e.g., encoders, scalers, standardized/normalized Series). Such information is exploited by the checkers to identify code smells in the input Python script. The rationale behind the checkers is intuitive: the static analysis computes and propagates types while maintaining the abstract type environment Γ; whenever a procedure associated with one of the code smells is encountered, the analyzer uses the information in Γ to determine whether it might represent a code smell; if so, it raises a warning and provides the user with a description of the issue, its cause, and a suggestion about how to fix it. We grouped the code smells and their corresponding checkers into four categories:

- **Misleading visualizations**: issues that can compromise data interpretation due to inappropriate visualization choices, such as using line plots for categorical data or applying PCA for visualization when more suitable techniques like t-SNE could reveal clearer patterns.

---

[1] PYRA can optionally use the information about the concrete dataset used in the notebook, if provided, to improve the accuracy of the analysis.

- **Misleading results**: issues that can lead to incorrect/biased outcomes without raising exceptions. Examples include data leakage (e.g., pre-processing before the train-test split), improper PCA usage, failure to remove duplicates, and poor handling of missing values.
- **Challenges for reproducibility**: issues that can hinder the reproducibility of data science pipelines, such as the omission of random seed ('random_state') settings in operations involving randomness (e.g., train-test split).
- **General issues** such as high dimensionality (too many features vs. samples), which may lead to the curse of dimensionality, and assignment of the result of in-place operations that can cause unexpected behavior.

Currently, PYRA includes 16 different checkers for detecting code smells. In this demo, we highlight four of them, one per category, to demonstrate PYRA's core capabilities.

3 Demo

We demonstrate PYRA by analyzing the code shown in Fig. 2. The code represents a simple data science pipeline that reads a CSV file, drops duplicates, plots the data, scales it, splits it into training and testing sets, and fits a logistic regression model. The dataset contains three columns: 'Fruit' (categorical), 'Amount' (integer), and 'Label' (0 or 1). This code, although short, contains several issues that belongs to the four identified categories of code smells, specifically:

- The `drop_duplicates` method is called with `inplace=True`, which modifies the DataFrame in place and returns `None`. This can lead to confusion, as the variable `result` will be assigned `None`.
- The `plot` method is used to create a line plot with a categorical x-axis. This is inappropriate, as line plots are typically used for continuous data. A bar plot would be more suitable in this case.
- The `train_test_split` method is called without setting the `random_state` parameter, meaning the split will differ each time the code is run. This can result in non-reproducible outcomes.
- The data is scaled before the train-test split. This can cause data leakage, as the scaling parameters are computed using the entire dataset, including the test set. The scaling should be performed after the split to avoid this issue.

PYRA detects these issues and raises warnings, including the type of the code smell, its cause, and suggestions for fixing it.

```
In     import pandas as pd
[1]:   import matplotlib.pyplot as plt
       from sklearn import StandardScaler
       from sklearn.model_selection import train_test_split
       from sklearn.linear_model import LogisticRegression

       df = pd.read_csv("data.csv")
       # Columns: ['Fruit', 'Amount', 'Label']
       result = df.drop_duplicates(inplace=True)

       plt.plot(df["Fruit"], df["Amount"])

       scaler = StandardScaler()
       X_scaled = scaler.fit_transform(df[["Amount"]])

       X_train, X_test, y_train, y_test =
           train_test_split(X_scaled, df["Label"])

       model = LogisticRegression()
       model.fit(X_train, y_train)
```

Fig. 2. Example of a pipeline with a plotting issue due to a categorical x-axis and an in-place DataFrame modification that results in a `None` return from `drop_duplicates`.

4 Conclusion

In this demo, we presented PYRA, a high-level linter for data science software. PYRA is designed to help developers identify code smells in the data science software. By analyzing code and issuing warnings, PYRA supports the development of more robust and reliable data science pipelines. The demo showcased how PYRA can analyze a data science pipeline and identify several issues, offering valuable feedback and suggestions for improvement. The presented tool stands out from other static analysis tools or linters by specifically addressing the unique challenges and pitfalls of data science software, making it a valuable addition to the data science ecosystem. Moreover, PYRA can be easily integrated into existing IDEs as a plugin, providing real-time feedback to developers as they write their code. This feature makes the tool especially useful, given that our target audience includes not only experienced data scientists but also beginners and experts from other fields who may not be familiar with the peculiarities, routines and best practices of data science software.

Acknowledgments. Work partially supported by Bando di Ateneo 2024 per la Ricerca, funded by University of Parma (FIL_2024_PROGETTI_B_IOTTI - CUP D93C24001250005) and SERICS (PE00000014 - CUP H73C2200089001) project funded by PNRR NextGeneration EU.

References

1. Bantilan, N.: pandera: Statistical data validation of pandas dataframes. In: Agarwal, M., Calloway, C., Niederhut, D., Shupe, D. (eds.) Proceedings of the 19th Python in Science Conference 2020 (SciPy 2020), Virtual Conference, July 6 - July 12, 2020, pp. 116–124. scipy.org (2020). https://doi.org/10.25080/MAJORA-342D178E-010
2. Dolcetti, G., Cortesi, A., Urban, C., Zaffanella, E.: Towards a high level linter for data science. In: Proceedings of the 10th ACM SIGPLAN International Workshop on Numerical and Symbolic Abstract Domains, NSAD 2024, Co-located with SPLASH 2024, pp. 18 – 25 (2024). https://doi.org/10.1145/3689609.3689996
3. Quaranta, L., Calefato, F., Lanubile, F.: Pynblint: a static analyzer for python Jupyter notebooks. In: Crnkovic, I. (ed.) Proceedings of the 1st International Conference on AI Engineering: Software Engineering for AI, CAIN 2022, Pittsburgh, Pennsylvania, May 16-17, 2022, pp. 48–49. ACM (2022). https://doi.org/10.1145/3522664.3528612
4. Urban, C., Müller, P.: An abstract interpretation framework for input data usage. In: Ahmed, A. (ed.) Programming Languages and Systems - 27th European Symposium on Programming, ESOP 2018, Held as Part of the European Joint Conferences on Theory and Practice of Software, ETAPS 2018, Thessaloniki, Greece, April 14-20, 2018, Proceedings, pp. 683–710. Lecture Notes in Computer Science, Springer (2018). https://doi.org/10.1007/978-3-319-89884-1_24

SustainaML: Enhancing Transparency, Control, and Green Sustainability in AutoML

Mehak Mushtaq Malik and Radwa El Shawi[✉]

University of Tartu, Tartu, Estonia
{mehak.mushtaq.malik,radwa.elshawi}@ut.ee

Abstract. Automated machine learning (AutoML) enhances accessibility but often suffers from a lack of transparency and user control due to its complex and opaque processes. We introduce SustainaML, a lightweight visualization interface built atop FLAML, H2O, and MLJAR, enabling interactive refinement of AutoML search spaces and evaluation based on both performance and sustainability metrics. SustainaML offers flexible configurations and actionable visual feedback. A user study comparing SustainaML with ATMSeer demonstrates superior usability and effectiveness in promoting transparent, resource-efficient AutoML workflows.

1 Introduction

Automated Machine Learning (AutoML) speeds up model development by reducing the need for manual intervention and expert knowledge [1,2,4,9]. Open-source tools like H2O AutoML [7], FLAML [11], and MLJAR [5] enable rapid experimentation and model deployment across diverse domains. Despite these advances, most AutoML systems remain opaque, offering limited insight into decision processes [12]. This lack of transparency hinders trust, and the incorporation of domain knowledge—especially in complex workflows requiring informed or context-sensitive decisions. As a result, the collaborative potential between human experts and AutoML systems remains underexploited.

Recent tools aim to improve transparency and user control [3]. ATMSeer [12] supports visualization and refinement of hyperparameter tuning within the ATM framework. AutoAIViz [13] visualizes full pipeline evolution and comparisons, yet favors observability over steerability [6]. SigOpt [10], a commercial platform for Bayesian optimization, offers multi-metric tracking and convergence visualization but lacks access to internal pipeline processes or interactive configuration. Importantly, none of these tools consider environmental impact, such as energy use or CO_2 emissions [8]. To address this gap, we introduce SustainaML[1], an interactive online tool designed to improve transparency,

---

[1] Source code is available on: https://github.com/DataSystemsGroupUT/SustainaML.

steerability, and sustainability in AutoML workflows. It integrates sustainability metrics (energy consumption and CO_2 emissions) with performance evaluation, enabling users to explore trade-offs between performance and environmental impact. The tool allows real-time refinement of search spaces, comparison across frameworks (FLAML, H2O, MLJAR), and greater control over pipeline configurations.

2 SustainaML Overview

SustainaML is an interactive tool for refining AutoML search spaces and analyzing results. It supports pipeline comparison across metrics and frameworks with configurable search options. In addition to performance metrics, it integrates sustainability indicators, such as energy consumption (μWh) and CO_2 emissions (μg), measured via CodeCarbon's energy usage and carbon emission, enabling environmentally conscious model selection. We demonstrate its functionality on a classification task using the Heart Disease dataset[2].

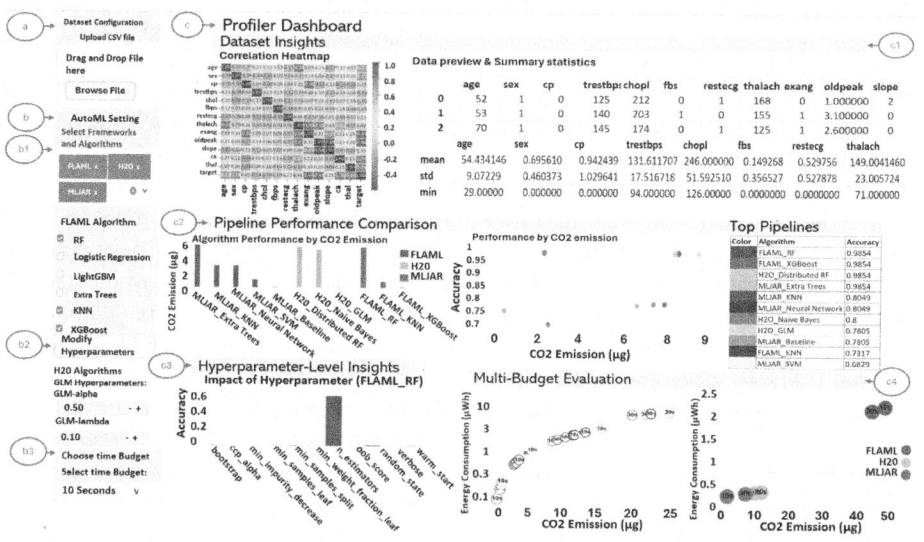

Fig. 1. Interface of SustainaML.

2.1 Interface and Demo Scenario

The interface consists of three panels: (a) dataset configuration, (b) AutoML settings, and (c) profiler dashboard (Fig. 1). Panel (a) enables dataset upload.

[2] https://www.kaggle.com/datasets/johnsmith88/heart-disease-dataset Demo video: https://www.youtube.com/watch?v=I0nxUgzN4dI.

In (b1), users select frameworks (e.g., FLAML, H2O, MLJAR) and define their search spaces by specifying included algorithms (e.g., XGBoost, KNN, Random Forest for FLAML). Hyperparameters can be configured in (b2); otherwise, default search spaces are used. A time budget is set in (b3). After execution, panel (c) visualizes outcomes, providing dataset statistics (c1), pipeline comparisons (c2), hyperparameter analysis (c3), and multi-budget evaluations (c4).

2.2 Profiler Dashboard

The AutoML Profiler includes dataset insights (c1) and provides multi-level analysis of the AutoML process at the algorithm (c2), hyperparameter (c3), and time-budget (c4) levels. These visualizations help users interpret performance and sustainability trade-offs. `Dataset Insights (c1)` presents dataset-level statistics including minimum, mean, and standard deviation values for each feature, along with a feature correlation heatmap (see Fig. 1(c1)). Users can identify strongly correlated features (e.g., slope and oldpeak), which informs feature relevance prior to model fitting. `Pipeline Performance Comparison (c2)` visualizes the performance of top pipelines across selected AutoML frameworks (e.g., FLAML, H2O, MLJAR) based on user-selected metrics. In this demo scenario, accuracy, energy consumption, and CO_2 emissions are selected to evaluate the pipelines of the selected frameworks. As shown in the middle plot of Fig. 1(c2), `MLJAR_Extra Trees` and `H2O_distributed RF` pipelines achieve similar accuracy, but `H2O_distributed RF` incurs lower CO_2 emissions. These insights enable users to identify efficient pipelines that balance between predictive performance and sustainability. `Hyperparameter-Level Analysis (c3)` provides an on-demand breakdown of how hyperparameters affect performance. In this demo, we analyze the `FLAML_RF` pipeline, and as shown in the left plot of Fig. 1(c3), the number of estimators has the greatest impact on accuracy. `Multi-Budget Evaluation (c4)` provides an on-demand breakdown that enables users to assess selected pipelines across varying time budgets based on user-defined metrics. In this demo, 11 pipelines are selected from the table in panel (c2) for comparative visualization of performance and resource consumption. The left plot in Fig. 1(c4) displays CO_2 emissions versus energy consumption across selected time budgets, highlighting MLJAR_baseline as the most efficient pipeline at 10 s and 30 s. The right plot in panel (c4) compares the top-performing pipeline (by accuracy) from each framework—FLAML, H2O, and MLJAR—across time budgets highlighting trade-offs between performance and environmental impact.

3 User Study

User Study Setup: We conducted a user study to evaluate `SustainaML`, focusing on its support for algorithmic analysis, environmental assessment, and decision support. To assess usability, we benchmarked `SustainaML` against `ATMSeer`, comparing shared features and identifying unique capabilities. The

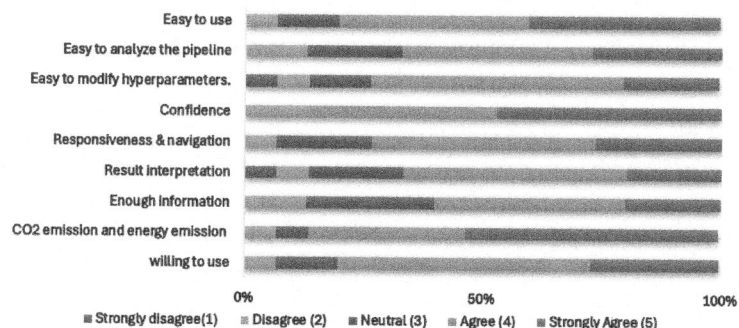

Fig. 2. Usability Results (Q1–Q9)

Table 1. Interpretability and Decision Support Results (Q10-Q16)

QUESTIONS	Algorithm	Environmental Impact	Feature Analysis
	Q10. Find best performing algorithm in terms of accuracy. **(15/15)**	Q13. Find the algorithm that consumes less energy and emits less CO_2. **(15/15)**	Q15. Find the feature that influences the most. **(14/15)**
	Q11. Find the stable algorithm. **(15/15)**	Q14. Find time budget's impact on algorithms' performance. **(15/15)**	Q16. Which feature is more important for the framework? **(12/15)**
	Q12. Which framework is more suitable for the specific dataset? **(15/15)**		

study involved 15 participants with prior machine learning or data science experience, two of whom had used AutoML tools. The Heart Disease dataset[3] was used for evaluation. A 16-item survey captured user experience, including nine Likert-scale questions (Q1–Q9) on usability and seven open-ended questions (Q10–Q16) evaluating interpretability and decision support using SustainaML.

Procedure: Each session began with a brief demonstration of SustainaML and ATMSeer, followed by approximately 30 min of hands-on interaction, task completion, and feedback. For SustainaML, participants used three AutoML frameworks—FLAML, H2O, and MLJAR—across 20 algorithms.

Usability Results. (Q1–Q9; see Fig. 2): Participants rated nine aspects of usability on a five-point Likert scale. Users found SustainaML highly usable and informative: 87% agreed it was easy to use, 79% found it easy to analyze pipelines, and 73% agreed it was easy to modify hyperparameters. Confidence in decision-making was high (87%), and 84% rated the tool as responsive. Clarity in interpreting results was noted by 77%, while 80% felt the tool provided sufficient information and clearly conveyed energy consumption and CO_2 emissions. In comparison, usability ratings for ATMSeer were slightly lower: SustainaML

---

[3] https://www.kaggle.com/datasets/johnsmith88/heart-disease-dataset.

outperformed `ATMSeer` in both confidence (87% vs 84.6%) and willingness to use (93% vs 92.3%).

Interpretability and Decision Support Results. (Q10–Q16; see Table 1): Participants consistently identified the best-performing algorithm in terms of accuracy (15/15), selected the most stable algorithm (15/15), and chose the most suitable framework for the dataset (15/15). They accurately identified the algorithm with the lowest energy and CO_2 emissions (15/15), understood the impact of time budget on performance (15/15), and recognized the most influential feature (14/15). Additionally, 12 out of 15 correctly identified the key feature influencing framework selection.

Acknowledgements. This work was supported by the project "Increasing the knowledge intensity of Ida-Viru entrepreneurship" co-funded by the European Union.

References

1. El Shawi, R., Rozgonjuk, D.: OnlineAutoClust: a framework for online automated clustering. In: Proceedings of the 32nd ACM International Conference on Information and Knowledge Management, pp. 3870–3874 (2023)
2. Eldeeb, H., Maher, M., Elshawi, R., Sakr, S.: AutoMLBench: a comprehensive experimental evaluation of automated machine learning frameworks. Expert Syst. Appl. **243**, 122877 (2024)
3. ElShawi, R., Sakr, S.: cSmartML-Glassbox: increasing transparency and controllability in automated clustering. In: 2022 IEEE International Conference on Data Mining Workshops (ICDMW), pp. 47–54. IEEE (2022)
4. Maher, M., Oun, O.F., Mesmeh, M.S., Shawi, R.E.: FedForecaster: an automated federated learning approach for time-series forecasting. In: Simitsis, A., Kemme, B., Queralt, A., Romero, O., Jovanovic, P. (eds.) Proceedings 28th International Conference on Extending Database Technology, EDBT 2025, Barcelona, Spain, March 25-28, 2025, pp. 867–873. OpenProceedings.org (2025). https://doi.org/10.48786/EDBT.2025.70, https://doi.org/10.48786/edbt.2025.70
5. Mota, B., Faria, P., Ramos, C.: Automated machine learning and explainable artificial intelligence in predictive maintenance: an MLJAR framework review. In: International Symposium on Distributed Computing and Artificial Intelligence. Springer (2024)
6. Olson, R.S., Bartley, N., Urbanowicz, R.J., Moore, J.H.: Evaluation of a tree-based pipeline optimization tool for automating data science. In: Proceedings of the Genetic and Evolutionary Computation Conference 2016, pp. 485–492 (2016)
7. Prusty, S., Patnaik, S., Dash, S.K., Prusty, S.G.P., Rautaray, J., Sahoo, G.: Predicting cervical cancer risk probabilities using advanced H20 AutoML and local interpretable model-agnostic explanation techniques. Peer J. Comput. Sci. **10** (2024)
8. Radersma, R.: Green coding: reduce your carbon footprint. Ethical Softw. Eng. **19** (2022)
9. Sayed, E., et al.: GizaML: a collaborative meta-learning based framework using LLM for automated time-series forecasting. In: EDBT, pp. 830–833 (2024)
10. Sorokin, A., Zhu, X., Lee, E.H., Cheng, B.: SigOpt mulch: an intelligent system for AutoML of gradient boosted trees. Knowl. Based Syst. **273**, 110604 (2023)

11. Wang, C., Wu, Q., Weimer, M., Zhu, E.: FLAML: a fast and lightweight AutoML library. Proc. Mach. Learn. Syst. **3**, 434–447 (2021)
12. Wang, Q., et al.: ATMSeer: increasing transparency and controllability in automated machine learning. In: Proceedings of the 2019 CHI, pp. 1–12 (2019)
13. Weidele, D.K.I., et al.: AutoAIViz: opening the Blackbox of automated artificial intelligence with conditional parallel coordinates. In: Proceedings of the 25th International Conference on Intelligent User Interfaces, pp. 308–312 (2020)

An LLM-Based Decision Support System for Strategic Decision-Making

Majd Alkayyal, Simon Malberg(✉)[iD], and Georg Groh

School of Computation, Information and Technology, Technical University of Munich,
80333 Munich, Germany
{majd.alkayyal,simon.malberg}@tum.de, grohg@in.tum.de

Abstract. We introduce StrategicAI, a decision support system (DSS) for organization leaders and managers responsible for making strategic decisions on the course of their organizations. The main idea behind StrategicAI is to reduce the inherent complexity of strategic decisions using logic trees. These tree structures recursively decompose the involved problem and solution spaces into less-complex parts until these parts become straightforward to answer based on known information. StrategicAI follows a human-AI collaboration philosophy where users are in full control of the tree decompositions applied and can decide flexibly which parts of the trees they create manually and which parts the artificial intelligence (AI) creates. The AI is a multi-agent system based on retrieval-augmented large language models (LLMs). To obtain data-driven insights, StrategicAI actively retrieves facts from user-uploaded files and online sources and incorporates them throughout the created trees. A demo video is available at https://youtu.be/uKx8L4XZI9A. We release our code at https://github.com/PortgasXDXMajd/StrategicAI.

Keywords: Decision Support System · Strategic Decision-Making · Large Language Models · Human-AI Collaboration

1 Introduction

Strategic decision-making is a cornerstone of organizational success, requiring leaders to navigate complex challenges and shape an organization's future. Strategic decisions—spanning market entry, technology adoption, resource allocation, strategic partnerships, and others—are characterized by complexity, ambiguity, and uncertainty while often carrying significant consequences. The stakes are high, as the quality of strategic decisions, or even the failure to make a decision at all, is a key determinant of an organization's performance and survival. For example, Netflix's decision to shift from DVD rentals to streaming in 2007 boosted its market capitalization to over $500 billion by 2025. In contrast, Kodak's failure to embrace digital photography–despite its invention of

---

M. Alkayyal and S. Malberg —These authors contributed equally.

© The Author(s), under exclusive license to Springer Nature Switzerland AG 2026
I. Dutra et al. (Eds.): ECML PKDD 2025, LNAI 16022, pp. 460–464, 2026.
https://doi.org/10.1007/978-3-032-06129-4_31

the technology—caused its market capitalization to plummet from $31 billion in 1997 to under $300 million by 2012, ending in bankruptcy.

Managers often operate under high pressure, expected to deliver maximum results in the shortest possible time. Their work involves making multiple decisions of vastly different kinds and consequences in a rapid succession, demanding speed-accuracy trade-offs [5] due to information overload, and possibly materializing cognitive biases as a consequence of taking mental shortcuts. This calls for *decision support systems* (DSS) for managers to enable faster and more accurate strategic decisions through automated and comprehensive analysis of known information. However, traditional DSS and *business intelligence* (BI) solutions such as Tableau or PowerBI typically require expert-crafted analysis pipelines tailored to the particular type of decision or fail to generalize across the large variety of real-world strategic decisions. This makes existing tools suitable for supporting reoccurring operational decisions or for performing selected analyses that feed into a strategic decision but leaves these tools ineffective as end-to-end DSS for complex and unique strategic decisions. Motivated by the recent success stories surrounding *large language models* (LLMs) [2,3], we present StrategicAI, a novel DSS for strategic decision-making powered by retrieval-augmented LLM-based agents. StrategicAI requires no task-specific fine-tuning of models and is usable even without technical expertise.

StrategicAI is centered around the concept of *logic trees*—often used as *issue trees* or *hypothesis trees* by management consulting firms such as McKinsey or BCG [4,6]—for structuring complex problems and exploring solutions. StrategicAI understands decision-making as a **problem-solving process** that identifies the root cause of a problem, explores possible solutions, and then decides which solution is the best response to the problem.

2 System Description

In StrategicAI, every problem-solving process is a **task**. Users can start a task by describing a business problem, goal, or hypothesis in natural language. StrategicAI then guides users through a three-phase process:

1. **Problem analysis** breaks down a problem into possible causes and estimates the likelihood of each cause, conditional on all known information. This phase ends when one or more causes are selected as root causes.
2. **Solution exploration** identifies possible solutions to the problem by hierarchically structuring the solution space into discrete choices and estimating each solution's likelihood to effectively solve the problem. This phase ends when the user or AI selects one or more solutions for validation.
3. **Solution validation** takes one solution hypothesis and decomposes it into its underlying assumptions, estimating the likelihood that each assumption is true based on all known information (see Fig. 1). This phase ends when the user or AI selects one or more verified solutions as the final solutions.

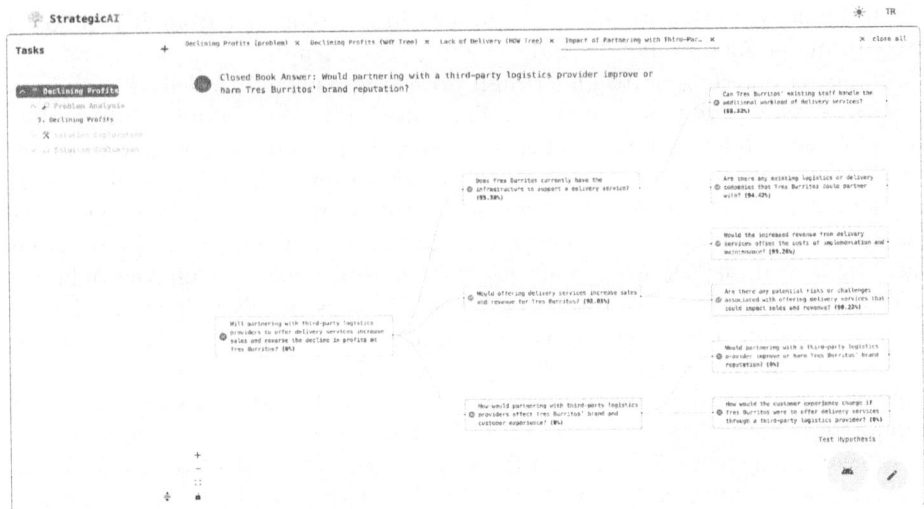

Fig. 1. The screenshot shows a tree built during the solution validation phase. The tree breaks down a solution hypothesis into the sub-hypotheses that need to be true for this solution to effectively solve the problem. StrategyAI is currently performing a hypothesis test by conducting a post-order traversal of the tree from its leaves to the root, estimating the likelihood of each sub-hypothesis based on evidence from the task context, uploaded files, online sources, and the likelihood of the descendant hypotheses.

Users can optionally skip phases 1–2 if they start directly with a task describing a goal or hypothesis rather than a problem.

During all three phases, users build logic trees that structure the underlying problem, solution, or assumption spaces. In every tree, StrategicAI applies an evidence-based search process, estimating the likelihood of different tree nodes based on known facts. StrategicAI maintains an **organization profile** with key facts about the organization and a **fact database** with all known information about a task, which it extracts from the user's task description, the organization profile, files uploaded by the user, and relevant online sources found through search engines. Every tree node comes with a natural-language **explanation**, a **trace to sources** containing facts relevant to that node, and with a **confidence score** from 0 to 100% that indicates the likelihood of that node. Inspired by *Probabilistic Tree-of-Thoughts* [1], confidence scores are derived from the LLM's output logits after including known information as context in the prompts:

$$\text{Confidence} = \exp\left(\frac{1}{n}\sum_{i=1}^{n}\log p_i\right),$$

where p_i is the probability of the i-th output token in the LLM's response and n is the total number of tokens in the response.

Users of StrategicAI can alternate between different execution flows of the problem-solving workflow, including manual human-only, human-AI collaborative, and fully autonomous AI-only execution (which we call **AutoRun**). The AutoRun coordinates several LLM-based agents as illustrated in Fig. 2.

StrategicAI also offers optional AI-based functionalities for reoccuring user needs. These include a **potential candidates** function that uses *self-consistency* [7] to narrow down potential root causes or effective solutions, a **node verification** to verify and enrich individual nodes with information from selected sources, an **integrated chatbot** which has access to everything within the task and can make recommendations or execute certain actions, and a **textual summary** of the entire problem-solving process and results that can be exported as a PDF or Word document and shared with other stakeholders.

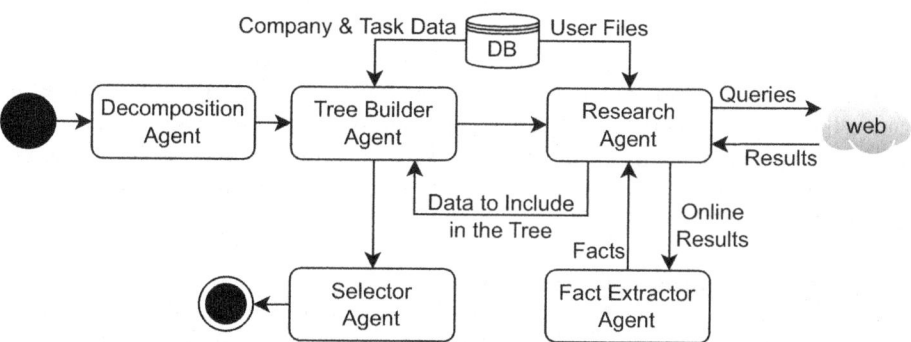

Fig. 2. When the user starts an AutoRun during the problem analysis, StrategyAI coordinates multiple LLM-based agents to decompose the problem into a tree (**Decomposition Agent**), build and refine the tree (**Tree Builder Agent**), find relevant evidence (**Research Agent**), extract facts from found sources (**Fact Extractor Agent**), as well as select the most likely root causes (**Selector Agent**).

3 System Evaluation

To evaluate StrategicAI, we compiled a dataset of six business case studies from well-known business schools[1] and recruited a group of six human testers aged 24–34 with different educational backgrounds and bachelor's degrees or higher. We annotated all case studies with ground-truth root causes and solutions and let each tester solve one case study using StrategicAI. We also let StrategicAI's AutoRun and ChatGPT solve each case study. All tests used a GPT-4o LLM.

Results can be seen in Table 1. In the problem analysis, the human test takers using StrategicAI achieved an average F1 score of 84% (vs. AutoRun's 71% and ChatGPT's 60%). In the solution exploration and validation, the human test takers using StrategicAI achieved 65% (vs. AutoRun's 52% and ChatGPT's

---

[1] Further documentation of the included case studies can be found in our GitHub repository https://github.com/PortgasXDXMajd/StrategicAI.

Table 1. Accuracy results from the problem analysis and solution exploration & validation phases observed for ChatGPT (baseline), StrategicAI's AI-only execution (AutoRun), and human-AI collaborative execution of StrategicAI. Best results in **bold**.

Phase	Method	Mode	Precision	Recall	F1
Problem analysis	ChatGPT	AI-only	43%	**100%**	60%
	StrategicAI	AI-only (AutoRun)	59%	94%	71%
	StrategicAI	Human-AI collaboration	**79%**	92%	**84%**
Solution exploration & validation	ChatGPT	AI-only	40%	76%	50%
	StrategicAI	AI-only (AutoRun)	40%	**83%**	52%
	StrategicAI	Human-AI collaboration	**65%**	69%	**65%**

50%). In a separate anonymous survey, all test takers expressed a high satisfaction with the tool and stated that they find StrategicAI's main features either somewhat useful or very useful. These findings suggest that StrategicAI is effective at supporting its users in strategic problem-solving and decision-making. We plan to further extend the functionality of StrategicAI and evaluate it under additional realistic scenarios.

Ethical Considerations. Recommendations by AI-based tools may be biased and inaccurate. The tools should never be used to make fully automated decisions about humans. Recommendations should always be thoroughly checked by an expert.

Disclosure of Interests. Majd Alkayyal works as a system engineer at an accounting firm. Simon Malberg works as a management consultant at a consulting firm. Both firms were not involved in this research project and had no influence over the outcomes.

References

1. Cao, S., et al.: Probabilistic tree-of-thought reasoning for answering knowledge-intensive complex questions. In: Findings of the Association for Computational Linguistics: EMNLP 2023, pp. 12541–12560. Association for Computational Linguistics, Singapore (2023)
2. Csaszar, F.A., Ketkar, H., Kim, H.: Artificial intelligence and strategic decision-making: evidence from entrepreneurs and investors. Strategy Sci. **9**(4), 322–345 (2024)
3. Doshi, A.R., Bell, J.J., Mirzayev, E., Vanneste, B.S.: Generative artificial intelligence and evaluating strategic decisions. Strateg. Manag. J. **46**(3), 583–610 (2025)
4. Garrette, B., Phelps, C., Sibony, O.: Cracked it!: how to solve big problems and sell solutions like top strategy consultants. Springer (2018)
5. Heitz, R.P.: The speed-accuracy tradeoff: history, physiology, methodology, and behavior. Front. Neurosci. **8**, 150 (2014)
6. Minto, B.: The Pyramid Principle: Logic in Writing and Thinking. Pearson Education (2009)
7. Wang, X., et al.: Self-consistency improves chain of thought reasoning in language models. arXiv preprint arXiv:2203.11171 (2022)

BellatrExplorer: An Interactive Random Forest Local Explainability Dashboard

Robbe D'hondt[1,2] and Celine Vens[1,2]

[1] KU Leuven Campus Kulak, Etienne Sabbelaan 53, 8500 Kortrijk, Belgium
{robbe.dhondt,celine.vens}@kuleuven.be
[2] KU Leuven, imec research group itec, Kortrijk, Belgium

Abstract. This paper presents BellatrExplorer, a dashboard application to interactively explore random forest predictions on the individual instance level. The application is inspired by the recently proposed local interpretability toolbox Bellatrex, that exploits the internal random forest structure to extract 1-3 prototype rules that act as a surrogate model for an instance of interest. BellatrExplorer is aimed at expert users trying to better understand the behavior of their random forest in a specific application, and could allow to uncover potential biases or artifacts arising in model training. Currently, the tool supports random forests for binary classification, regression, and survival analysis tasks. It features (1) intuitive exploration of univariate predictive counterfactuals, (2) analysis of decision tree rules to the individual split level, and (3) a visualisation of the rules extracted by Bellatrex that allow to assess the local interpretation at a glance. The tool is available at https://github.com/robbedhondt/BellatrExplorer/ and a demonstration video can be found at https://itec.kuleuven-kulak.be/bellatrexplorer/

Keywords: random forest · local explainability · interactive dashboard

1 Introduction

Random forests [2] are popular machine learning models at the state-of-the-art for tabular data learning. The learning algorithm is based on building an ensemble of decision trees, which are simple rule-based models that recursively partition the data. Randomization across the trees is achieved by training each tree on an independent bootstrapped sample of the original dataset and by using only a random subset of the available features per split. In theory, this makes the decision process of the random forest fully transparent. However, the inherent explainability is limited due to the typically large number of trees (100 or more) and their depth (typically deeper than a 'normal' decision tree[1]).

---

[1] As the trees in a random forest are built using only a subset of the features per split (weak learners), they can grow deeper to capture more complex patterns in the dataset. Overfitting is mitigated by the ensemble nature of the random forest—averaging multiple trees naturally reduces the variance problems that deep decision trees present.

Several tools have been proposed in the literature to open up the random forest black box, both on a population level (global explainability) as well as on an individual prediction level (local explainability). Here, we focus on the recently proposed model-specific local explainability toolbox Bellatrex [3]. For a given sample, Bellatrex extracts 1 to 3 representative prototype rules from the random forest that, when taken together, closely approximate the prediction of the full ensemble.

Many dashboard applications integrating these model explainability tools already exist. Two notable examples are modelStudio [1] and explainerdashboard[2], that allow the user to select a set of graphs to evaluate any general-purpose model based on a validation of its performance and on model-agnostic explainability toolboxes.

For random forests, two model-specific dashboards are of interest. The first one, RfX [5], focuses on global explainability through icicle plots and two-dimensional embeddings of the decision trees. The second one, by Gurung et al. [6], probably comes the closest to our work. However, it is focused only on binary classification problems, whereas we also tackle regression and survival analysis. Additionally, their choices of visualisations represents a mix of global explainability (statistics like the number of times each feature is used at each split and feature split points) and local explainability (surrogate tree construction and counterfactual generation using the actionable tweaking algorithm). This is very different from our choices of visualizations that focus on local explainability, giving detailed information on the rule level and allowing counterfactual exploration (rather than focusing on generation). Finally, in Gurung et al. the target audience is mostly non-expert, whereas here the proposed dashboard focuses on the machine learning engineer familiar with the random forest algorithm.

2 Dashboard Components

A screenshot of the dashboard is shown in Fig. 1. In this section, we discuss the different components of the dashboard and the possibilities of the application in more detail.

Modeling: In the modeling pane, the random forest is set up. First, a built-in dataset is selected, or the user uploads their own dataset. One of the columns of this dataset is selected as the target variable. This variable represents a binary classification, regression, or survival analysis (through random survival forests [7]) task. The final button starts the training of the random forest.

Instance Selection: Once the random forest finished training, this section is populated with a slider for each feature in the dataset. The slider options are the percentiles of that feature in the training data, but the options are presented and spaced in the scale of the original feature distribution. In the background of each slider, a linear gradient indicates the change in predicted value of the random forest when moving one of the sliders to a certain position.

---

[2] See https://explainerdashboard.readthedocs.io/ (last visited 2025-04-28).

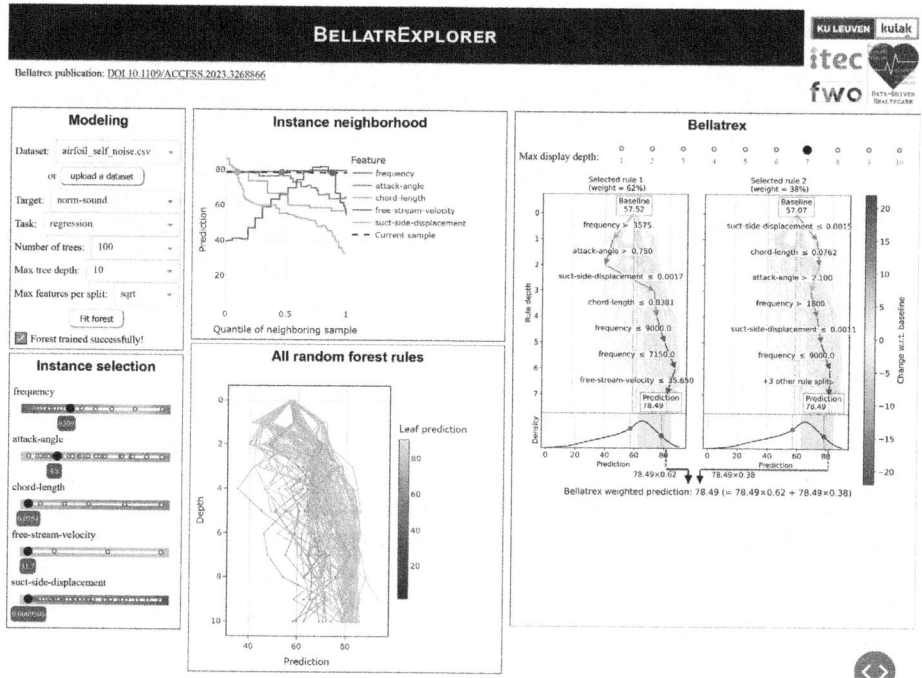

Fig. 1. Screenshot of the dashboard application.

Instance Neighborhood: This panel shows the information from the background gradient of the sliders in a more quantitative way. In essence, this plot shows for each feature the univariate effect of changing that feature from the current sample to any percentile of interest (shown on the x axis). The current sample is indicated by a circle for each feature, at the current prediction and the corresponding currently selected percentile. Double-clicking one of the features in the legend isolates the line for that feature, allowing a better visual inspection. Additionally, hovering over any point in the graph gives extra information about the raw feature value at the quantile of interest.

All Random Forest Rules: This panel shows the decision path for the current sample for each tree in the random forest. The sample starts at the root node for each tree with a baseline prediction based on the bootstrapped sample for that tree. With each split, the sample works its way down each tree, gradually changing its predicted value based on the prototype function[3] that aggregates all the training samples in that node. The decision path of each tree is colored according to the final prediction of that tree (in the leaf node). Hovering over a

---

[3] For regression and binary classification, this is simply the mean of the target. For survival analysis, we compute the mean survival time (by integrating the survival function that is computed at each node with the trapezoidal rule).

node in the plot results in a tooltip giving more information on what split was made in that node and all the nodes before it (partial rule path).

Bellatrex Rules: The final panel displays the rules selected by Bellatrex. The original Bellatrex publication [3] presented the selected prototype rules to the user in a textual format. Here, we display them in a similar way as in the "All random forest rules" panel[4], a visualisation that we have used before in the context of multiple sclerosis progression predictions [4]. A separate graph for this is preferred, as it allows the user to view the selected rules with all their splits at a single glance.

3 Future Work

As Bellatrex can be applied to any random forest ensemble, we aim to also provide an interface in the future allowing users to upload their own random forest model (from any machine learning package). Additionally, the dashboard could also be extended to the multi-target setting (multi-label classification, multi-target regression, and multi-event survival analysis) by showing linked rulepaths for each target. Finally, the dashboard can then be evaluated in a user study for any further refinements.

Acknowledgements. This work was funded by Research Fund Flanders (FWO fellowship 1S38025N and grant G0A2120N) and supported by the Flemish government (through the AI Research Program). We thank Arthur Cremelie for implementing a first version of the dashboard.

Disclosure of Interests. The authors have no competing interests to declare that are relevant to the content of this article.

References

1. Baniecki, H., Biecek, P.: modelStudio: interactive studio with explanations for ML predictive models. J. Open Source Softw. **4**(43), 1798 (2019). https://doi.org/10.21105/joss.01798
2. Breiman, L.: Random forests. Mach. Learn. **45**, 5–32 (2001)
3. Dedja, K., Nakano, F.K., Pliakos, K., Vens, C.: Bellatrex: building explanations through a locally accurate rule extractor. IEEE Access **11**, 41348–41367 (2023). https://doi.org/10.1109/ACCESS.2023.3268866
4. D'hondt, R., et al.: Explainable time-to-progression predictions in multiple sclerosis. Comput. Methods Programs Biomed. 108624 (2025)
5. Eirich, J., Münch, M., Jäckle, D., Sedlmair, M., Bonart, J., Schreck, T.: RFX: a design study for the interactive exploration of a random forest to enhance testing procedures for electrical engines. In: Computer Graphics Forum, vol. 41, pp. 302–315. Wiley Online Library (2022)

---

[4] For more information about how to interpret the plot, see https://itec.kuleuven-kulak.be/a-guide-to-bellatrex/.

6. Gurung, R., Lindgren, T., Boström, H.: An interactive visual tool to enhance understanding of random forest predictions. In: European Conference on Data Analysis (ECDA) (2019)
7. Ishwaran, H., Kogalur, U.B., Blackstone, E.H., Lauer, M.S.: Random survival forests. Ann. Appl. Stat. (2008)

T-REX: Table – Refute or Entail eXplainer

Tim Luka Horstmann(✉), Baptiste Geisenberger, and Mehwish Alam

Institut Polytechnique de Paris, Palaiseau, France
{tim.horstmann,geisenberger}@ip-paris.fr, mehwish.alam@telecom-paris.fr

Abstract. Verifying textual claims against structured tabular data is a critical yet challenging task in Natural Language Processing with broad real-world impact. While recent advances in Large Language Models (LLMs) have enabled significant progress in table fact-checking, current solutions remain inaccessible to non-experts. We introduce T-REX (Table – Refute or Entail eXplainer), the first live, interactive tool for claim verification over multimodal, multilingual tables using state-of-the-art instruction-tuned reasoning LLMs. Designed for accuracy and transparency, T-REX empowers non-experts by providing access to advanced fact-checking technology. The system is openly available online.

Online Demo: https://t-rex.r2.enst.fr
Demo (video): https://www.youtube.com/watch?v=HHIxVCOT8X0
Github: https://github.com/TimLukaHorstmann/T-REX

Keywords: Table Fact-Checking · Large Language Models · Real-Time Fact Verification

1 Introduction

Table fact-checking is the Natural Language Processing task of classifying textual claims as *entailed* or *refuted* based on information contained in a table. Unlike traditional fact-checking, which primarily deals with unstructured text, this task demands a combination of capabilities, including linguistic understanding, symbolic reasoning, and numerical computation. For example, a BBC headline once claimed *"Germany: Migrants 'may have fueled violent crime rise'"*, despite official crime statistics showing no such trend.[1] With the right tools, such discrepancies could be automatically detected by reasoning over the corresponding tabular data. Since tables are a primary format for structured data across domains like journalism, finance, policymaking, and science, robust and accessible table fact-checking systems are increasingly vital to combat misinformation.

Advances in Large Language Models (LLMs) have driven significant progress in table fact-checking. RePanda [1] translates claims into executable queries for explainable verification, while DATER [2] and ARTEMIS-DA [3] decompose tables and claims into structured reasoning steps, surpassing human performance

---

[1] BBC News article; Federal Criminal Police Office – Police Crime Statistics 2020.

on the TabFact dataset [4]. Despite these advances, most LLM-based verification systems remain confined to offline evaluation, lack interactivity, and require technical expertise—ultimately restricting accessibility for non-expert users.

Some tools partially address these limitations. OpenTFV [5] retrieves tables from corpora and verifies claims with table-aware models and textual explanations, while Aletheia [6] maps claims to structured datasets for article fact-checking with visualized evidence presentation. However, both assume predefined datasets, rely on earlier-generation encoder-only or proprietary LLMs, and are not designed to operate with arbitrary, user-provided tables as primary inputs.

To bridge these gaps, we introduce T-REX (Table – Refute or Entail eXplainer), the first tool for real-time table fact-checking using state-of-the-art (SOTA) instruction-tuned reasoning LLMs. T-REX prioritizes accuracy through a robust verification pipeline, accessibility via a multilingual, multimodal, and user-friendly interface, and interpretability through transparent reasoning outputs. T-REX extends table fact-checking beyond expert interactions into real-world applications, where accurate and accessible claim verification is critical.

2 System Architecture and Design

T-REX integrates a modular framework for table processing, LLM inference, Optical Character Recognition (OCR), and a web-based frontend for interactive verification, visualization, and real-time explanations (see Fig. 1).

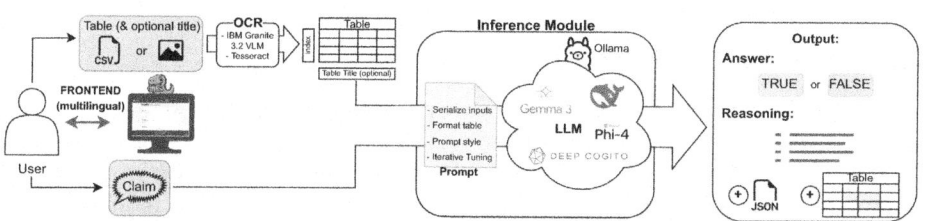

Fig. 1. T-REX system overview. Users provide tables and claims via the frontend, while the backend handles OCR, preprocessing, and LLM-based verification.

2.1 Table Processing and Verification Pipeline

T-REX supports table input via CSV files or OCR-extracted images, using IBM's Granite 3.2 vision model for high accuracy or Tesseract as a faster alternative. Tables are preprocessed for robustness (unifying delimiters, cleaning contents, and standardizing structure) and interpretability (by injecting a synthetic `row_index` column to aid the model's cell referencing). A claim, and optionally a table title for additional context, are then paired with the table and passed to the inference engine for verification.

To guide the design of our inference pipeline, we conducted extensive offline experiments on the TabFact test set [4]. We compared three strategies: (1) direct prompting for claim verification, (2) prompting the model to generate code (Python or SQL) that returns *True* or *False*, and (3) Retrieval-Augmented Generation, embedding the claim and the table (row-, column-, or cell-wise) and selecting relevant table content based on cosine similarity. Each approach was evaluated across five open-source LLMs (Llama 3.2 (3B), Mistral (7B), DeepSeek-R1 (8B and 32B), and Phi-4 (14B)), four formats for representing the table within the prompt (Markdown, HTML, JSON, and naturalized text), and two prompting techniques (zero-shot and chain-of-thought (CoT)). We iteratively refined the prompt design through manual evaluation, drawing on best practices from prior work. We found that concise, directive, and clear prompts consistently led to more reliable outputs. Detailed results for (1) are available in the online demo; final results for (1-3) on our GitHub.

Our best-performing setup, Phi-4 with naturalized table formatting and CoT prompting, achieved 89% accuracy, surpassing prior methods like RePanda on TabFact [1,4]. Beyond accuracy, direct prompting with CoT enhances interpretability (Sect. 2.2) by allowing us to guide the model to output its reasoning, followed by a JSON object containing the final verdict and self-identified relevant table cells. We apply post-processing to the model's output to robustly extract the JSON, using fallback mechanisms to recover the verdict in case the JSON parsing fails. T-REX currently supports four open-source SOTA LLMs, balancing structured reasoning abilities with GPU constraints: Phi-4 (14B), Cogito v1 Preview (8B), DeepSeek-R1-Distill-Qwen-7B (7B), and Gemma 3 (4B).

2.2 Interface Design and User Features

The T-REX interface (Fig. 2) prioritizes accessibility and transparency. Users initiate the verification process by uploading or pasting a table (CSV or image) and a claim (Sect. 2.1), or by selecting a TabFact [4] example, choosing an LLM, and clicking the "Run Live Check" button. For the hybrid reasoning model Cogito, users can enable the "Deep Thinking" mode to allow deeper reasoning. T-REX streams its reasoning in real time, generates a verdict, and highlights relevant table cells within the table preview for improved interpretability.

To further enhance usability, T-REX offers multilingual input and output in eight languages, exportable JSON outputs, Wikipedia previews for the original source pages of TabFact examples [4], intuitive navigation via dropdown selectors, and dark mode. T-REX also automatically renders all table inputs as editable CSV within the interface, synchronized with a live table preview for enhanced visualization. This feature is particularly useful for OCR inputs, where recognition errors can be quickly identified and manually corrected by the user.

2.3 Implementation Details

T-REX is built on a modular FastAPI backend that orchestrates LLM inference, OCR processing, and data management via asynchronous HTTP calls.

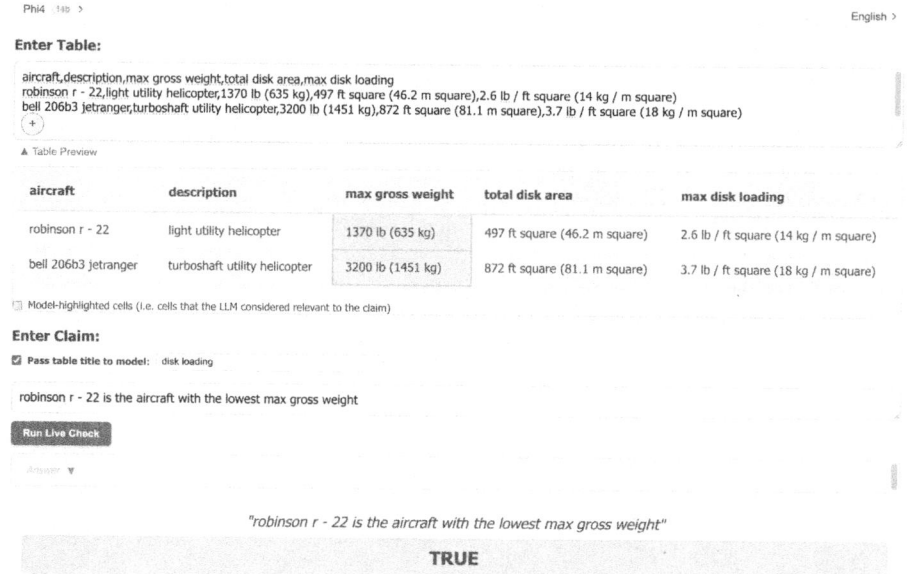

Fig. 2. T-REX interface after claim verification. Relevant cells are highlighted for interpretability and reflect the model's self-identified reasoning steps. The model's reasoning is accessible via dropdown menus.

Ollama serves both LLM inference and OCR tasks, while SlowAPI enforces request rate limiting to maintain robustness under load. T-REX currently runs on two NVIDIA GTX 1080 GPUs, and its modular design makes it easy to scale to larger LLMs as hardware improves. All inference and data handling is performed in memory, ensuring that no user data is stored or transmitted externally.

3 Conclusion

This paper introduced T-REX, the first live, interactive, and domain-agnostic table fact-checking tool powered by SOTA open-source instruction-tuned reasoning LLMs. Designed to facilitate access to advanced claim verification for non-experts, T-REX provides accurate and interpretable verification in real time, without storing or exposing any user data externally. In the future, we plan to extend T-REX to integrate precise numerical computation, structured claim decomposition, and support for additional table-centric tasks such as table completion, semantic table retrieval, and cell-level evidence justification.

Disclosure of Interests. The authors have no competing interests to declare that are relevant to the content of this article.

References

1. Chegini, A.M., Rezaei, K., Eghbalzadeh, H., Feizi, S.: RePanda: pandas-powered tabular verification and reasoning. arXiv:2503.11921 (2025)
2. Ye, Y., Hui, B., Yang, M., Li, B., Huang, F., Li, Y.: Large language models are versatile decomposers: decompose evidence and questions for table-based reasoning. arXiv:2301.13808. arXiv (2023)
3. Hussain, A.S.: ARTEMIS-DA: an advanced reasoning and transformation engine for multi-step insight synthesis in data analytics with large language models. arXiv:2412.14146 (2024)
4. Chen, W., et al.: TabFact: a Large-scale dataset for table-based fact verification. In: International Conference on Learning Representations (2020)
5. Gu, Z., Fan, R., Zhao, X., Zhang, M., Fan, J., Du, X.: OpenTFV: an open domain table-based fact verification system. In: International Conference on Management of Data (2022)
6. Fu, Y., Guo, S., Hoffswell, J., Bursztyn, V.S., Rossi, R., Stasko, J.: "the data says otherwise"-towards automated fact-checking and communication of data claims. In: Annual ACM Symposium on User Interface Software and Technology (2024)

Fairbeat: Assessing and Mitigating Bias with the Composite Balance Score

Pierre-Antoine Lequeu[1], Sofiane Lagraa[2(✉)], Geoffroy Robin[2], and Moussa Ouedraogo[2]

[1] Sorbonne University, Paris, France
pierre-antoine.lequeu@sorbonne-universite.fr
[2] Fujitsu Technology Solutions S.A., Capellen, Luxembourg
{geoffroy.robin,moussa.ouedraogo}@fujitsu.com

Abstract. *Fairbeat*, a novel Fairness Assessment tool for Resampling-based Bias Elimination and Algorithm Training, addresses the critical challenge of fairness in machine learning. Machine learning models often exhibit biases stemming from imbalances in training data concerning protected attributes, leading to discriminatory outcomes. *Fairbeat* leverages the Composite Balance Score (CBS), a comprehensive metric that evaluates the balance of the dataset by integrating the imbalance of attributes, the imbalance of labels and the association of attributes and labels into a single normalized score. This tool facilitates proactive bias assessment prior to model training, supports multi-class attributes, and provides a user-friendly environment for exploring and visualizing the impact of various bias mitigation techniques, including resampling methods, thereby promoting the development of more equitable and ethically sound AI systems. The demonstration video can be found at https://youtu.be/9aHKfZgtXKg.

Keywords: Composite Balance Score · Fairness · Bias Mitigation · Machine Learning

1 Introduction

Ensuring fairness in machine learning models is crucial for ethical compliance and societal impact. Models often exhibit biases due to imbalances in training data, particularly concerning protected attributes like gender, age, and ethnicity. Addressing these biases is essential to prevent discrimination and achieve equitable outcomes.

Problem Statement. Machine learning models are increasingly used in human-centric decision-making areas such as judiciary systems, human resources, credit assessment, and healthcare. However, these models often show unfair behavior towards social groups based on protected attributes, leading to discrimination and ethical concerns. The challenge lies in predicting the fairness of these models by analyzing their training data and implementing bias mitigation strategies without compromising performance.

Existing Works. Previous studies have explored various bias mitigation techniques, including pre-processing [3], in-processing [4], and post-processing [5] methods. These approaches often focus on single, binary protected attributes, neglecting the complexities of multi-class attributes. While some methods have shown promise in improving fairness, they frequently lead to a reduction in utility, known as the fairness-utility trade-off [1]. Moreover, handling missing data and proxy attributes remains a challenge, influencing both fairness and model performance [2]. Moreover, FairnessEval [9] is a Python framework for evaluating and comparing fairness in ML models, streamlining data preparation, evaluation, and result presentation to aid in model selection and validation.

Novelty and Contribution. Our paper introduces *Fairbeat*, a Fairness Assessment Interface for Resampling-based Bias Elimination and Algorithm Training. It is based on the Composite Balance Score (CBS), a novel metric designed to evaluate the balance of datasets with respect to protected attributes and predict model fairness by analyzing the training data. *Fairbeat* informs the decision of whether or not to apply bias mitigation. It offers several key advantages, including a **comprehensive balance measure** that combines attribute imbalance, label imbalance, and attribute-label association into a single, normalized score ranging from 0 to 1. This easy-to-interpret metric assesses overall dataset balance and **predicts model fairness** by focusing on dataset balance as an indicator of potential bias. Furthermore, CBS supports multi-class attributes, extending beyond binary categories, and enables **proactive bias assessment and mitigation**, allowing for bias evaluation before model training begins. Finally, *Fairbeat* has a friendly user interface for bias assessment and mitigation. The video of the demonstration is available at https://youtu.be/9aHKfZgtXKg.

2 *Fairbeat*: Assessing and Mitigating Bias with the Composite Balance Score

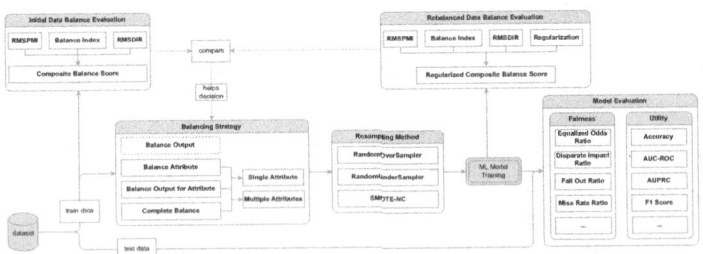

Fig. 1. *Fairbeat*: balancing strategies and resampling methods workflow.

Fairbeat is a tool designed to simplify the evaluation and mitigation of bias in machine learning datasets. It provides an intuitive tool for users to assess dataset fairness, explore bias mitigation techniques, and visualize their impact. The tool democratizes fairness-aware machine learning, enabling practitioners to build equitable AI systems. Figure 1 outlines the workflow for evaluating and mitigating bias using the Composite Balance Score (CBS) and related metrics. If bias mitigation is needed, a balancing strategy and a resampling method are selected. The balance of the rebalanced data is then evaluated, and a machine learning model is trained and tested for fairness and utility. The CBS value helps determine the success of the balancing, comparing results to the initial data balance.

2.1 Assessing Dataset Balance Using the Composite Balance Score (CBS)

We introduce the *Composite Balance Score*, a new metric for evaluating the balance of protected attributes. It uses three measures: the *Balance Index*, *RMSDIR*, and *RMSPMI*.

Balance Index (Bal) is introduced as a novel metric to quantify the balance of classes within a protected attribute, addressing a critical aspect of dataset fairness. $\text{Bal}(A) = 1 - \frac{\text{imb}(A)}{\sqrt{\frac{n-1}{n}}}$, where $\text{imb}(A)$ is the imbalance index, n is the number of classes, and A is the protected attribute. Unlike prior works [6] that often rely on arithmetic means to assess imbalance, the Balance Index employs a quadratic mean of the distribution deviation, providing a more sensitive measure to variations in class representation. Furthermore, it's normalized to a [0, 1] scale, offering intuitive interpretability where 1 signifies perfect balance and 0 indicates extreme imbalance. The Balance Index offers a unique combination of sensitivity and interpretability, making it a valuable tool for evaluating and addressing attribute imbalances in fairness-aware machine learning.

Root Mean Squared Disparate Impact Ratio (RMSDIR): To quantify label imbalance across protected attribute classes, this paper introduces the Root Mean Squared Disparate Impact Ratio (RMSDIR): $\text{RMSDIR}(A) = \sqrt{\frac{\sum_{c \neq c_{\text{priv}}} \text{DIR}_{\text{nor}}(c)^2}{|\{c \neq c_{\text{priv}}\}|}}$, where $\text{DIR}_{\text{nor}}(c)$ is the normalized disparate impact ratio for class c proposed in [7,8]. Building upon the concept of Disparate Impact Ratio (DIR): $DIR(c_i) = \frac{P(Y=1 \mid A=c_i)}{P(Y=1 \mid A=c_{privi})}$ with $c_i \neq c_{privi}$, commonly used to compare favorable outcome rates between groups, RMSDIR offers a crucial normalization step. Unlike traditional DIR, which lacks an upper bound and can be challenging to interpret [7], RMSDIR leverages the normalized disparate impact introduced by Badran et al. to ensure a [0, 1] scale. This normalization allows for a more intuitive understanding of label imbalance, where 1 signifies perfect balance and 0 indicates significant disparity, regardless of whether it favors the privileged or unprivileged class. By aggregating these normalized values using a root mean square, RMSDIR provides a single, robust measure of label imbalance for the entire protected attribute, offering a more comprehensive assessment than individual pairwise comparisons.

Root Mean Squared Pointwise Mutual Information (RMSPMI) is introduced as a novel measure to capture the information shared between classes of a protected attribute and the target variable's labels, offering a unique perspective on dataset bias. $\text{RMSPMI}(A) = \sqrt{\frac{\sum_{i=1}^{n}\sum_{y=0}^{1}\text{PMI}_{\text{nor}}(c_i,y)^2}{2n}}$, where $\text{PMI}_{\text{nor}}(c_i, y)$ is the normalized pointwise mutual information for class c_i and label y. Unlike traditional fairness metrics that focus solely on outcome disparities [7,8], RMSPMI leverages the normalized Pointwise Mutual Information (PMI): $PMI(c_i, y) = \log \frac{P(A=c_i, Y=y)}{P(A=c_i)P(Y=y)}$ to quantify the degree of association between each class and each label. While in [8], the authors used PMI to measure unwarranted associations, RMSPMI aggregates these individual PMI values using a root mean square, providing a single, comprehensive measure of the overall dependency between the protected attribute and the target variable. This approach allows for a more nuanced understanding of how a protected attribute might be influencing predictions beyond simple outcome disparities, capturing subtle biases that could be missed by other metrics. By focusing on information sharing, RMSPMI complements existing fairness measures and provides valuable insights for bias mitigation strategies.

Composite Balance Score (CBS) is a new metric designed to evaluate the balance of a dataset concerning a protected attribute, as shown in Fig. 2a. CBS is calculated as: $\text{CBS}(A) = \frac{\text{Bal}(A)+\text{RMSDIR}(A)+(1-\text{RMSPMI}(A))}{3}$. CBS captures attribute and label imbalances and the statistical dependence between the attribute and the target variable. Normalized to a [0, 1] scale, CBS helps assess dataset fairness, guiding bias mitigation strategies and tracking their effectiveness. By calculating CBS for each protected attribute, users can identify attributes with scores below a threshold (e.g., 0.80) that may need bias mitigation. CBS guides the application of bias mitigation techniques, such as resampling methods, to improve dataset balance and model fairness. Integrating CBS into workflows enables organizations to proactively address biases, resulting in fairer and more equitable machine learning models.

2.2 Resampling Techniques

Resampling techniques are integral tools in data preprocessing after fairness assessment using the CBS score, enabling modification of datasets through the addition or removal of rows for bias mitigation, as shown in Fig. 2b. These techniques are used predominantly to rectify imbalanced labels in classification tasks. In the realm of fairness, prior research has investigated resampling methods to equilibrate protected attributes. The strategies for balancing include: no balance, balancing labels, balancing classes, balancing labels across all classes/attributes, and achieving complete balance. Resampling methods to implement these strategies are classified into over-sampling (Random Over-Sampling (ROS), SMOTE-NC) and under-sampling (Random Under-Sampling (RUS)).

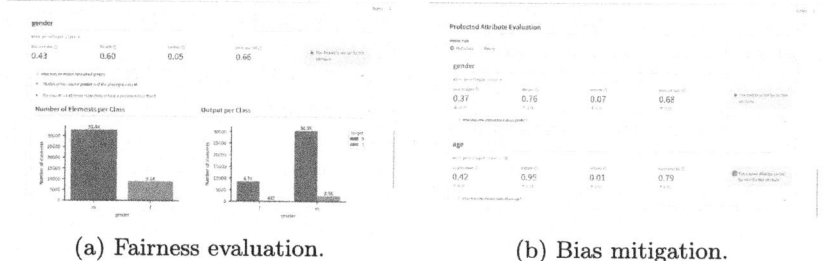

(a) Fairness evaluation.   (b) Bias mitigation.

Fig. 2. *Fairbeat* dashboard.

3 Conclusion

Fairbeat underscores the pivotal importance of dataset balance in reducing bias within machine learning models, particularly in binary classification scenarios involving multi-class protected attributes. The introduced Composite Balance Score (CBS) serves as a robust predictor of model fairness. Implementing balancing strategies, notably the equalization of labels within classes, markedly enhances fairness while incurring minimal utility loss. Although the efficacy of CBS wanes with intersectional attributes, maintaining balanced datasets is essential for fostering fairer and more equitable machine learning outcomes.

Acknowledgments. This work was supported by the European Union's HE RAIDO project under the grant agreement number 101135800.

References

1. Bertsimas, D., Farias, V.F., Trichakis, N.: On the efficiency-fairness trade-off. Manage. Sci. **58**, 2234–2250 (2012)
2. Caton, S., Malisetty, S., Haas, C.: Impact of imputation strategies on fairness in machine learning. J. Artif. Intell. Res. **74**, 1011–1035 (2022)
3. Lahoti, P., et al.: Fairness without demographics through adversarially reweighted learning. In: Advances in Neural Information Processing Systems, vol. 33, pp. 728–740 (2020)
4. Wadsworth, C., Vera, F., and Piech, C. (2018). Achieving fairness through adversarial learning: an application to recidivism prediction. CoRR, abs/1807.00199
5. Mishler, A., Kennedy, E. H., and Chouldechova, A.: Fairness in risk assessment instruments: post-processing to achieve counterfactual equalized odds. In: ACM FAccT, pp. 386–400 (2021)
6. Gong, Y., Liu, G., Xue, Y., Li, R., Meng, L.: A survey on dataset quality in machine learning. Inf. Softw. Technol. **162**, 107268 (2023)

7. Badran, et al.: Can ensembling preprocessing algorithms lead to better machine learning fairness? Computer **56**, 71–79 (2023)
8. Tramèr, F., et al.: Discovering unwarranted associations in data-driven applications with the FairTest testing toolkit. CoRR, abs/1510.02377 (2015)
9. Baraldi, A., Brucato, M., Dudík, M., Guerra, F., Interlandi, M.: FairnessEval: a framework for evaluating fairness of machine learning models. In: EDBT, pp. 123–134. ACM (2025)

PRIMULA-3 for Probabilistic Modeling and Reasoning on Graph Data

Raffaele Pojer[✉] and Manfred Jaeger

Aalborg University, Aalborg, Denmark
{rafpoj,jaeger}@cs.aau.dk

Abstract. The PRIMULA system is a versatile software tool for modeling and reasoning with probabilistic relational structures based on the symbolic Relational Bayesian Networks (RBN) language. The new version 3 of PRIMULA extends previous versions by adding support for categorical variables, and by integrating Graph Neural Networks (GNN) as model components into a full generative RBN model, thus combining the predictive power and scalable learning tools of GNNs with the high expressivity and flexible inference capabilities of RBNs.

1 Introduction

Probabilistic modeling of relational data is a cornerstone of modern artificial intelligence, enabling systems to reason under uncertainty in complex, structured domains, such as social or sensor networks, or biological and environmental systems. Relational Bayesian Networks (RBNs) [1] are a powerful framework for working with probabilistic relational models. The PRIMULA software implements the RBN language and provides support for a wide range of learning and reasoning tasks, including: predictive inference comprising standard supervised tasks such as node, link and graph prediction; general probabilistic reasoning for diagnostic inference and decision support, and unsupervised learning, e.g. for community detection. PRIMULA-3 is a revised and updated version that adds as new functionalities: support for categorical variables, and integration with graph neural networks (GNNs) implemented in PyTorch. This integration connects the predictive capabilities of GNNs with the expressive relational logic of RBNs, enabling neuro-symbolic reasoning on graph-structured data. PRIMULA-3 is a *proof-of-concept* software, providing a uniform framework supporting a wide spectrum of graph analysis tasks. It is intended for research and educational purposes by enabling design and experimentation within a rich and versatile framework for modeling and learning with graph data.

2 The PRIMULA-3 System

PRIMULA takes as input a probabilistic model specification in the RBN language (possibly containing GNN components), and a relational domain specification.

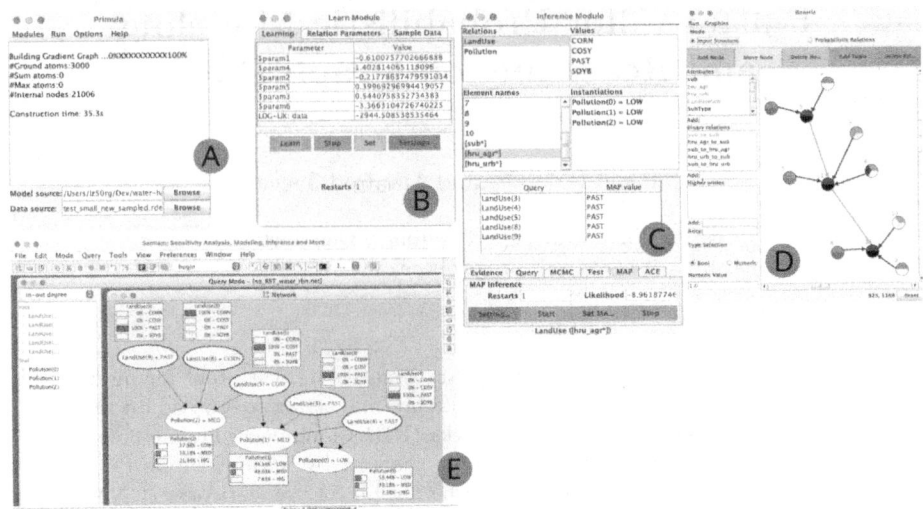

Fig. 1. PRIMULA modules: A: main console, B: learn module for parameter learning, C: inference module for conditional probability and maximum a-posteriori inference, D: module for editing and visualizing relational input domains, E: the external SamIam tool for probabilistic inference by Bayesian networks.

Together, these inputs define a generative model for probabilistic attributes and relations. Several forms of inference for the resulting models are provided: *exact* inference by compiling the model into a Bayesian network or arithmetic circuit representation, and applying the dedicated, external SamIam[1] and ACE[2] tools; *approximate* inference with Gibbs sampling for probability computations, and combinatorial optimization for maximum-a-posteriori queries. All inference techniques are equally applicable for models with or without GNN components.

Model Specification. We illustrate the RBN language and its GNN integration by the example in Listing 1.1 of an environmental domain with *land* and *water* nodes connected by a spatial *adjacent* relation. Figure 1 D. shows a tiny example domain with node colors representing node types and attributes.

An external GNN model has been trained to model the pollution level based on the agricultural land use at adjacent land units. Lines 3.-6. import this GNN into the RBN model by specifying its Python source and logical signature (input attributes, relation used for message passing, output dimension). Lines 8.-10. are a user-defined function for the profit obtained by the agricultural use of a land unit. Lines 12-15 define a logistic regression model for a Boolean variable indicating whether an intervention at (and around) water node w is necessary to mitigate high pollution or low profit in this area. As shown in [4], a large class of GNN models can also directly be encoded in the native RBN language. However,

---

[1] http://reasoning.cs.ucla.edu/samiam/.
[2] http://reasoning.cs.ucla.edu/ace/.

Listing 1.1. Modeling environmental and economic impact of land use

```
 1    LandUse([land]l) = SOFTMAX 1,1,1;
 2
 3    Pollution([water]w) =  COMPUTEWITHTORCH   <path to PyTorch model>
 4                           WITHNUMVALUES 3
 5                           FORFREEVARS (w)
 6                           USINGRELS LandUse(l) WITHEDGE adjacent(l,w);
 7
 8    @profit([land]l) = WIF LandUse(l)=corn THEN (2.4*Area(l))
 9                       ELSE WIF LandUse(l)=pasture THEN (1.0*Area(l))
10                       ELSE WIF LandUse(l)=soy THEN (1.9*Area(l)) ELSE
                              0.0;
11
12    Intervention([water]w) = COMBINE 1.8*(Pollution(w)=high),
13                                     0.7*(Pollution(w)=medium),
14                                     -1.1*@profit([land]l)
15                             WITH log-reg FORALL l WHERE adjacent(l,w);
```

the ability to also connect to external PyTorch models leads to greater flexibility with regard to GNN architectures, and computational benefits arising from the greater efficiency of dedicated GNN learners for GNN models. A detailed RBN language documentation and a tutorial example similar to Listing 1.1 is provided with the PRIMULA distribution.

Inference. Given an RBN model instantiated with an input domain the following inference tasks can be solved:

1. Conditional probability queries: given a partial observation of some attributes and relations, what are the conditional probabilities of a specified list of queries? In our environmental domain example: given observed land use, what are the probabilities for pollution levels? For smaller sized problems, these queries can be solved exactly using SamIam and ACE. For larger problems approximate inference by Gibbs sampling is used.
2. MAP queries: given a partial observation of some attributes/relations, what is the most probable joint configuration of a list of query attributes/relations? An example is shown in Fig. 1 C, where the most probable land use at all land nodes was queried, given an observation of low pollution at all water nodes. MAP queries are solved by a combinatorial optimization process operating on the *likelihood graph* data structure that also plays a key role in learning.

Figure 2 illustrates a probabilistic inference scenario for an information diffusion model (included in the PRIMULA distribution). The underlying RBN model here encodes the standard *independent cascade* model for information diffusion. We apply the model to the famous Zachary's Karate Club network (Fig. 2 A), where node 34 has been labeled as the source node for the diffusion process (indicated by a blue marking in the graph viewer). We can now query for all nodes the probability that they have received the information at time 4, conditioned on the information that node 4 had the information at time 2 (Fig. 2 B).

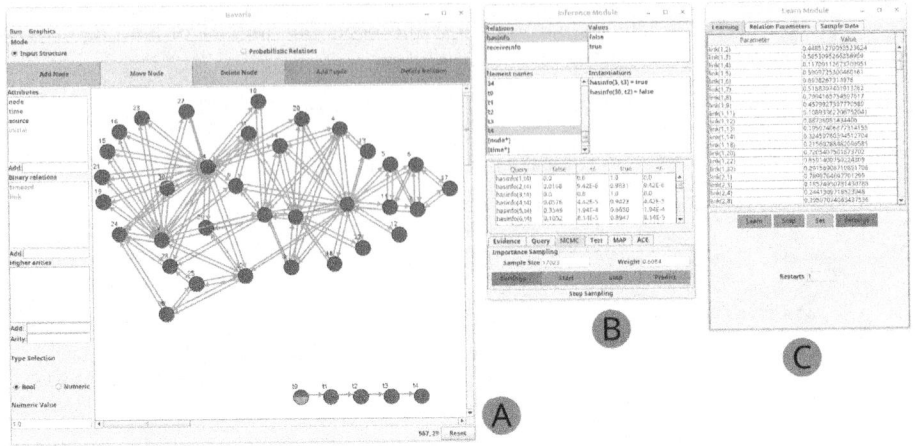

Fig. 2. Information diffusion on the Karate Club network. A: graph viewer/editor, B: inference module, C: learned diffusion probabilities.

Learning. Parameter learning is supported by gradient descent using LBFGS or Adam. The original learning approach of [2] consists of compiling the model into a *likelihood graph* for automatic computation of likelihood values and likelihood gradients. PRIMULA-3 also provides an alternative method that directly computes gradients from the syntactic model representation. The two methods provide different space/time tradeoff characteristics, with the likelihood graph requiring more space, but offering time advantages when the gradient descent requires many iterations, and can benefit from a higher degree of model compilation before learning. With parameter learning, all numerical model parameters can be learned based on a maximum likelihood objective. As a different application of the same underlying optimization routines, one can define numerical node attributes or numerical relations as model parameters. Optimizing the likelihood function for these parameters amounts to learning latent (node/edge) representations. The PRIMULA distribution contains as an application of this approach a multi-factor clustering (or multi-level community detection) of geographic regions in Switzerland based on their plant distribution patterns.

In the information diffusion example of Fig. 2, all edges are associated with a probability of information propagation along that edge. Figure 2 shows the result of learning these parameters from a set of sampled diffusion processes.

The PRIMULA *Distribution.* PRIMULA-3 is implemented in JAVA and available at https://github.com/manfred-jaeger-aalborg/primula3. Both the source code and a platform independent runnable .jar file are provided. The GNN integration is currently only tested on Linux and MacOS platforms. The distribution also contains four tutorial examples demonstrating applications in genetic modeling, information diffusion, community detection, and environmental modeling and decision support. The first three of these examples are pure RBN models, whereas the last includes a GNN component. A video demonstration is available at https://www.youtube.com/watch?v=6DcWcX-_vA0.

3 Related Tools

Other systems that combine neural networks with logic-symbolic knowledge representation are DeepProbLog[3] [3] and NeurASP[4] [5]. However, these systems differ substantially in terms of the underlying logic-symbolic representations and the way neural components are integrated. The logic element of DeepProbLog and NeurASP is based on logic programming, which, on the one hand, limits expressivity to simple rules, but on the other hand enables via the application of least fixed point or stable model semantics, the modeling of transitive closures of relations, which is outside the scope of PRIMULA-3. The logic of PRIMULA-3 is a generalization of full first-order logic, which allows 'deep' nesting of logic constructs, enabling, among other things, the direct encoding of GNNs in the underlying RBN language. Regarding neural integration, the underlying philosophy in the logic programming-oriented tools is that of a division of labor: the neural components handle low-level tasks related to perception, whereas the symbolic parts handle high-level reasoning. PRIMULA-3 is not based on such an a priori distinction between 'neural' and 'logical' reasoning and their associated relations. Compared to the alternatives, PRIMULA-3 supports a richer class of probabilistic queries, including conditioning on arbitrary observations (including negative facts) and MAP inference.

Acknowledgment. This research has been partially funded by the Villum Investigator Grant S4OS (37819) from Villum Foundation.

References

1. Jaeger, M.: Relational Bayesian networks. In: Proceedings of UAI (1997)
2. Jaeger, M.: Parameter learning for relational Bayesian networks. In: Proceedings of the 24th International Conference on Machine Learning (ICML) (2007)
3. Manhaeve, R., Dumancic, S., Kimmig, A., Demeester, T., Raedt, L.: Deepproblog: neural probabilistic logic programming. Adv. Neural. Inf. Process. Syst. **31**, 3749–3759 (2018)
4. Pojer, R., Passerini, A., Jaeger, M.: Generalized reasoning with graph neural networks by relational Bayesian network encodings. In: The Second Learning on Graphs Conference. PMLR, vol. 231 (2023)
5. Yang, Z., Ishay, A., Lee, J.: NeurASP: embracing neural networks into answer set programming. In: IJCAI (2021)

---

[3] https://github.com/ML-KULeuven/deepproblog.
[4] https://github.com/azreasoners/NeurASP.

LLM GameLab: An Interactive Platform for Testing Large Language Models in Board Games

Paulina Morillo[1,2] (✉), Alex Terreros[1], Cèsar Ferri[2], and José Hernández-Orallo[2]

[1] Universidad Politécnica Salesiana, IDEIAGEOCA Research Group, Quito 179381, Ecuador
{pmorillo,aterreros}@ups.edu.ec
[2] Universitat Politècnica de València, Valencian Research Institute for Artificial Intelligence (VRAIN), València 46022, Spain
paumoal@upv.es, {cferri,jorallo}@dsic.upv.es

Abstract. While large language models are constantly evaluated in various skills, such as math, general knowledge, and coding, their ability to understand and follow game rules has not yet been deeply explored. The latter is especially important as it allows testing whether LLMs can operate within predefined limits without deviating or making illogical mistakes. Therefore, this demo paper presents a tool for interacting with LLMs in board games. The tool allows the creation of players with different large language models pitted against each other or to play in human vs. LLM mode. The platform includes rules predefined in prompts for four simple games based on Tic-Tac-Toe and Connect Four. Each player can be evaluated to account for their illegal movements, wins, draws, losses, and response times. The application also allows for the creation of new games, opening up the possibility of examining LLM behavior in situations they have not previously encountered.

Keywords: General Game Playing · decision-making · LLM evaluation

1 Introduction

We make decisions constantly, whether in everyday situations–like choosing a route to work–or in more complex contexts, such as problem-solving or future planning. This process depends on the information available, the time we have to decide, our prior experience, and our ability to assess risks and potential consequences. Moreover, it occurs within a set of rules specific to each situation. Understanding these rules allows us to optimize our decisions, anticipate outcomes, and avoid mistakes. In this way, board games are a tangible example of decision-making since players must understand the rules, develop strategies, adapt to their opponents' decisions, and optimize their moves to achieve victory [17]. These structured environments allow us to analyze the aspects behind decision-making in humans and artificial intelligence [9].

Large Language Models (LLMs) have shown impressive capabilities in natural language processing tasks and decision-making, with emergent abilities increasingly observed as model scale grows [1,3,15], though some of these abilities remain debated [10]. Nevertheless, we acknowledge that LLMs continue to perform well across various domains–such as mathematics [11], programming [18], general knowledge, and language understanding–as demonstrated by multiple benchmarks [4,6,12]. Some works have evaluated the LLMs' abilities to understand rules, strategize, and make decisions using board games. For instance, Liga D. and Pasetto L. [7] evaluated several language models playing Tic-Tac-Toe, analyzing spatial reasoning and internal/external state monitoring but found no correlation between identifying winning sequences and performance, emphasizing the impact of prompt design on response variability. Topsakal et al. [13] examined how board structure and prompt formats influence model performance, highlighting difficulties with illustrated and list prompts, leading to numerous cancel matches. They later proposed a new benchmark [14] using grid-based games and assessed multiple LLMs across games and prompt types, obtaining similar results. Likewise, Hora de Carvalho [5] assessed the generalization ability of GPT models in spatial and strategic reasoning through ASCII-based games, finding that while models gave relevant responses in some tasks, their overall performance was weak, challenging claims of emerging intelligence.

Therefore, to gain new insights into the ability of LLMs to understand, follow, and apply rules not yet deeply explored, we present LLM GameLab. This web application enables LLMs to play against each other and introduces a novel human-LLM interaction mode within a board game setting. We can simulate players using various LLMs, ranging from less robust models like Phi to more advanced ones like O3 mini and Deepseek R1. We established four games–Tic-Tac-Toe, Connect4, Suicide, and Not Connect4–which are generally considered low-difficulty due to their simple rules, easily understood by children [16]. However, the last two games are less common, and feature rules that contradict those of the first two, potentially making them challenging for humans and LLMs. The application also supports the creation of new games to avoid no contamination [2,8]. This platform allows us to capture valuable data to assess LLM decision-making in structured environments with clearly defined rules and visualize the games in real time.

2 Game Setup and Player Interactions

By default, we define four main board games based on Tic-Tac-Toe and Connect Four. They are played on finite grids where players alternate placing their marks to form a specific pattern. We use the game description and the game rules translating to natural language from Human Readable Format file (.hrf), written in the Game Description Language (GDL), available in http://gamemaster.

stanford.edu/homepage/showgames.php. The games Suicide and Not Connect Four share the same rules as their classic versions, but their goals are completely opposite those of Tic-Tac-Toe and Connect Four, respectively.

We have a graphic board for the four games where the pieces are placed as the game progresses (Fig. 2). Additionally, we have implemented a function that validates whether the player's movement is legal, using the rules defined in the .hrf file of each game available on the General Game Playing (Game Master) online competition environment, this file is executed in a Node.js environment, where the "compiler" interprets the rules and verifies whether the player's move is valid under the current game conditions. If the user loads a new game, this validation is not applied automatically, so it is necessary to specify the number of plays to be made manually.

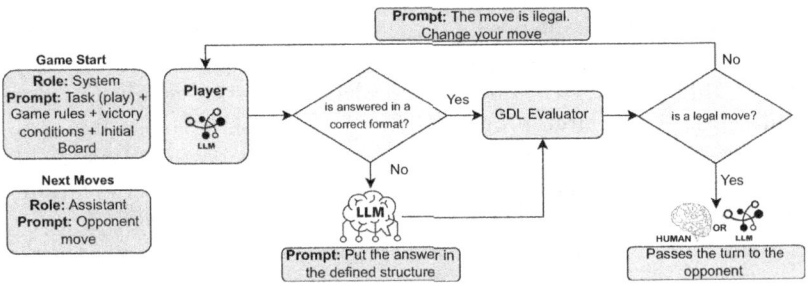

Fig. 1. LLM player mode operation

On the other hand, our application provides two-player modes. The first one is an LLM player. We can choose a free LLM available at https://openrouter.ai/ or connect to paid LLMs by entering the user's API key. Figure 1 describes the operation of the LLM player. To initialize the game for both players, we use the system role to inform the model of the game rules, victory conditions, the structure of the expected LLM response, the initial board state, and the opponent's mark. Starting with the second turn, we use the assistant role and provide only the opponent's last move as context. In cases where the LLM does not return the response in the specified format, we turn to a more robust model (such as DeepSeek R1 or ChatGPT-4o) to process the response and return the move in the required format. This way, we can use it as input to the move validation functions. If the move is valid, we pass the turn to the opposing player; otherwise, we resend a message indicating that the play is invalid. If the LLM does not correct its movement until after ten times, we cancel the game and assign the victory to the opposing player.

The second player mode is a Human Mode. In this case, we do not perform a validation since the user can play directly on the board, making illegal moves impossible. At the end of the matches, we can download the results in a .csv file.

The application and code are available at : http://llm-gamelab.ideiageoca.org/play, https://github.com/paumoal/llm-gamelab. The video of the demonstration can be seen at https://dmip.webs.upv.es/demos/Demo-video.mp4

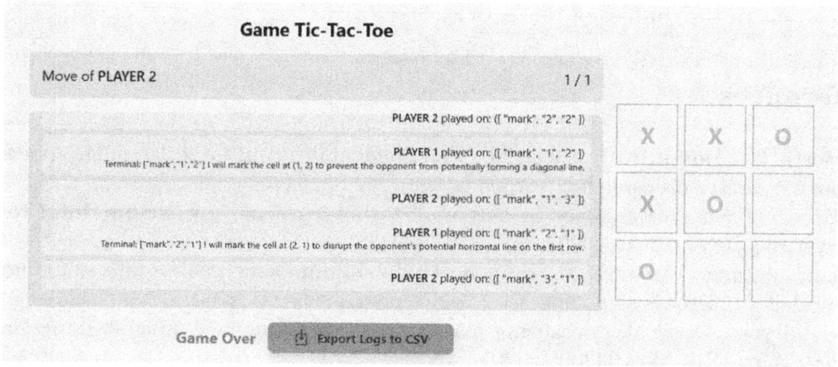

Fig. 2. Tic-Tac-Toe example: the left side shows real time plays between two players; the right side displays a graphical view of the board and moves. Once the game ends–either by a win or a draw–the results can be exported as a .csv file.

3 Conclusion, Limitations, and Future Work

This paper presents LLM GameLab, an interactive platform designed to evaluate the performance of large language models in structured board games. Our proposal seeks to offer an accessible, reproducible, and flexible environment in which models can be evaluated for both their rule-following ability and their strategic skill. The tool allows two models to compete against each other in a game or enables a match between a human and an LLM. It also supports inverted variants and game customization. In addition, based on GDL game descriptions and automatic move validation, its modular design allows for its extension to new domains without requiring a complete re-implementation.

Despite our system's strengths, the experimental analysis is still preliminary: no exhaustive study has been conducted about the performance of LLM or the types of errors the models make, nor has their frequency, nature, or relationship to factors such as model size or architecture been characterized.

To advance this line of work, we aim to conduct a tournament setting to assess model performance more rigorously and expand the platform with more complex game scenarios. Likewise, future work could include a detailed examination of the errors produced by the models, with particular attention to formatting mistakes, rule violations, and weak strategic choices. Furthermore, it would be valuable to investigate how model characteristics–such as size, computational cost, and architecture–correlate with performance across different games and task types.

Acknowledgements. This work was supported by IDEIAGEOCA and VRAIN Research Groups of Universidad Politécnica Salesiana and Universitat Politècnica de València, respectively.

Disclosure of Interests. The authors have no competing interests to declare that are relevant to the content of this article.

References

1. Berti, L., Giorgi, F., Kasneci, G.: Emergent abilities in large language models: a survey. arXiv preprint arXiv:2503.05788 (2025)
2. Brown, T., et al.: Language models are few-shot learners. Adv. Neural. Inf. Process. Syst. **33**, 1877–1901 (2020)
3. Du, Z., Zeng, A., Dong, Y., Tang, J.: Understanding emergent abilities of language models from the loss perspective. arXiv preprint arXiv:2403.15796 (2024)
4. Hendrycks, D., et al.: Measuring massive multitask language understanding. arXiv preprint arXiv:2009.03300 (2020)
5. Hora de Carvalho, G.: Evaluating Large Language Models Beyond Textual Understanding and on Knowledge of Chemistry with CHILDPLAY and CHEMRESQA. Master's Thesis, University of Groningen (2024)
6. Liang, P., et al.: Holistic evaluation of language models. arXiv preprint arXiv:2211.09110 (2022)
7. Liga, D., Pasetto, L.: Testing spatial reasoning of large language models: the case of tic-tac-toe (2023)
8. Mehrbakhsh, B., Garigliotti, D., Martínez-Plumed, F., Hernandez-Orallo, J.: Confounders in instance variation for the analysis of data contamination. In: Proceedings of the 1st Workshop on Data Contamination (CONDA), pp. 13–21 (2024)
9. Samarasinghe, D., et al.: A data driven review of board game design and interactions of their mechanics. IEEE Access **9**, 114051–114069 (2021)
10. Schaeffer, R., Miranda, B., Koyejo, S.: Are emergent abilities of large language models a mirage? Adv. Neural. Inf. Process. Syst. **36**, 55565–55581 (2023)
11. Shao, Z., et al.: Deepseekmath: pushing the limits of mathematical reasoning in open language models. arXiv preprint arXiv:2402.03300 (2024)
12. Srivastava, A., et al.: Beyond the imitation game: quantifying and extrapolating the capabilities of language models. arXiv preprint arXiv:2206.04615 (2022)
13. Topsakal, O., Harper, J.B.: Benchmarking large language model (llm) performance for game playing via tic-tac-toe. Electronics **13**(8), 1532 (2024)
14. Topsakal, O., Edell, C.J., Harper, J.B.: Evaluating large language models with grid-based game competitions: an extensible LLM benchmark and leaderboard. arXiv preprint arXiv:2407.07796 (2024)
15. Wei, J., et al.: Emergent abilities of large language models. arXiv preprint arXiv:2206.07682 (2022)
16. Yong, A., Yong, D.: An estimation method for game complexity. arXiv preprint arXiv:1901.11161 (2019)
17. Zhang, J., Jiang, J., Li, L., Zeng, D.: BG-Planner: a planning-based decision-making model for playing board game. In: 31st International Conference on Neural Information Processing, vol. 1 (2024)
18. Zhang, Y., Pan, Y., Wang, Y., Cai, J.: PYBench: evaluating LLM agent on various real-world coding tasks. arXiv preprint arXiv:2407.16732 (2024)

EXTREMUM: A Web-Based Tool to Generate and Explore Counterfactual Explanations on Tabular and Time-Series Data

Athanasios Lakes[iD], Luis Quintero[iD], and Panagiotis Papapetrou[✉][iD]

Department of Computer and Systems Sciences (DSV), Stockholm University, Stockholm, Sweden
{athanasio.lakes,luis.quintero,panagiotis}@dsv.su.se

Abstract. There is an increasing need to include explainability on the machine learning (ML) models. Among the various approaches, counterfactual (CF) explanations allow the design of what-if scenarios and the interactive exploration of ML model behavior on sensitive decision-making domains. However, the generation of CF for tabular and time-series data requires technical skills that are not always available to the end-users of ML-powered systems. Therefore, we propose a modular web-based tool to easily generate, visualize, and interact with CF on any tabular or time-series dataset. The EXTREMUM platform provides access to state-of-the-art CF algorithms, where users can train ML models and explore CF on their tabular or time-series datasets with an intuitive user interface. The project is instantiated on two tabular datasets within healthcare and five time-series datasets with various domains. The open-source repository lets ML researchers adapt the existing ML tool to new application domains: https://gitea.dsv.su.se/DataScienceGroup/EXTREMUM-demo.

Keywords: Counterfactual · Explainability · Interpretability · Time Series · Machine Learning · Interactive · Dashboard · User Interface

1 Introduction

The increasing use of artificial intelligence (AI) tools and predictive machine learning (ML) models also permeates high-stake application domains, such as healthcare. These decision-support systems must strongly emphasize the interpretability of the ML models to ensure accountability, ethical compliance, and trust among end users [1,9]. Several forms of interpretability have emerged to understand the factors that most significantly influence a model's output. For example, feature importance scores provide intuitive insights into which variables affect a prediction; more sophisticated model-agnostic approaches, like LIME and SHAP, allow users to assess the contribution of individual features at a local or global level; and counterfactual (CF) explanations describe how the features from a given data instance would need to change to alter the model's initial prediction.

CF explanations have emerged as a promising direction for AI-powered tools within sensitive domains, as they offer a trade-off between technical (e.g., model performance, explanation validity) and human perspectives (e.g., task performance, explanation understandability). CF explanations remain in the data domain, whereas other explanation techniques often require users to learn ML-specific metrics and visualizations. Moreover, CF reasoning through what-if scenarios is naturally embedded in prescriptive practices like healthcare and banking. Lastly, CF lets end-users keep control of the decision-making process by iteratively examining the factors that influence the model's prediction.

The interest to design ML algorithms for CF generation is increasing for all data modalities [5,8,10,12]. However, running algorithms for CF generation require technical skills that differ vastly from the domain-specific skills held by the end-users exploring CF explanations. Hence, there is a need to simplify the construction of AI-powered tools including state-of-the-art CF explanations, and thus bridge the gap between designers of AI-powered systems and end-users leveraging interpretability in real-life contexts.

Prior **related work** on user-centered explainable AI has identified that web interactive user interfaces are the primary medium to evaluate AI-powered systems with end users [1]. They also outline methodological aspects to assess human-related factors of AI-powered systems such as trust, understanding, usability, and human-AI collaboration performance [9]. There are several open-source implementations of tools related to explainability in AI. Most toolkits aim to simplify the work of data scientists and ML engineers [3], such as the AI explainability 360 [2] that includes ten techniques for non-interactive explanations, or the WebSHAP [13] library that offers model-agnostic explanations for a single technique but with high interactivity. However, these solutions do not offer CF explanations, and their online implementation is restricted to a predefined dataset. Other approaches aimed at end-users, such as What-If Tool [14] and Outcome-Explorer [4], allow interactive exploration of data, ML classifiers, and interpretability with CF reasoning. However, they are aimed to work with tabular data, images, or text; excluding time-series datasets. Interactive user interfaces focused on time series allow imputation techniques [6], and our closest related work [11] allows interactive CF generation tool for univariate time series. However, it involves interpreting projected activation and attributions in deep learning models, which are too technical to be interpreted by real-life practitioners.

Therefore, the main **contribution** of this work is an open-source web-based tool to visualize datasets, train ML classifiers, and explore CF explanations. It allows post-hoc model-agnostic local explanations through CF reasoning using state-of-the-art algorithms. Tabular datasets generate CF with DiCE [8], whereas Glacier [12] generates locally constrained CF where users can favor or discourage specific changes on parts of the time series. EXTREMUM is designed modular and private so that practitioners can deploy the tool locally, upload their dataset, and explore AI-powered decision-making tools within their expertise domain.

2 EXTREMUM: Web-Based Tool for Counterfactuals

The tool is publicly accessible on the project's website[1]. The open-source repository[2] contains an example video and installation instructions. The system workflow is divided in three parts, as described below:

2.1 Data Selection and Exploratory Data Analysis

The homepage lists available datasets. Users can choose between tabular or time-series data and explore visualizations accordingly. For tabular data, interactive plots are generated asynchronously based on features and classes selected through drop-down menus. For time series, users can browse from predefined generic datasets. Users import and manage their own private data in the locally deployed version. The public version of the tool allows exploration with three example datasets, as shown in Fig. 1.

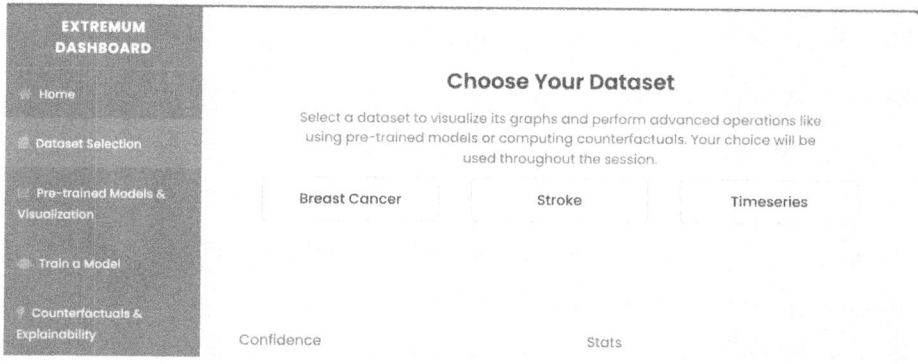

Fig. 1. Example of the EXTREMUM tool allowing interactive exploration of several example datasets, two tabular or five time series.

2.2 Model Training

The local version allows training new ML models; in the online version, users choose pre-trained models and see their performance via classification reports, feature importance, and PCA plots. For tabular data, the available models are

---

[1] Online version: https://extremum.dsv.su.se/app.
[2] Open-source repo: https://gitea.dsv.su.se/DataScienceGroup/EXTREMUM-demo.

Linear Regression, Decision Tree, Random Forest, SVM, and XGBoost. For time series, 1D-CNN is used for Glacier, while K-NN and Random Shapelet Forest are used with Wildboar [10]. Users must also define preprocessing, test set ratio, and (for tabular) the target label. After training, a report is shown to help decide to save the model for future interactive sessions.

2.3 Counterfactual Generation and Exploration

CFs are generated through an interactive workflow, where users pick specific data samples to view the CF list from a pre-trained model. The process varies by dataset type. A t-SNE plot is rendered for tabular data, allowing interactive point selection. These 2D points map back to the original data for CF generation. For time series, if Glacier is chosen, the user selects a constraint (either from a pre-computed experiment or a new one) before generating CF. On top of that, sample selection and target label remain the same for both CF algorithms. The Fig. 2 displays a counterfactual for an example instance in the ECG dataset.

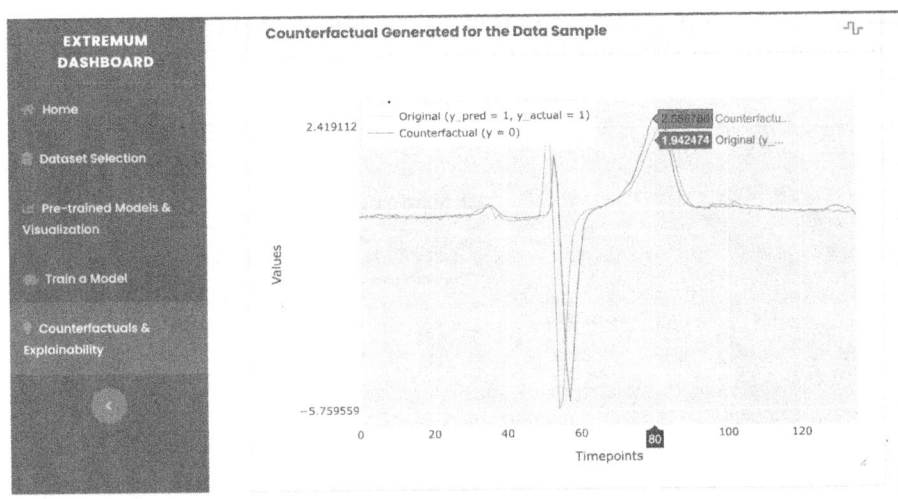

Fig. 2. Example of interactive exploration of counterfactuals for time-series data.

3 Conclusion and Future Work

EXTREMUM is inspired by the possibilities of CF to support human-AI collaborative decision-making within healthcare [7]. It allows the abstraction of advanced ML algorithms, instantiated on two tabular datasets for medical applications (breast cancer, stroke) and two time-series ECG datasets. The intuitive user interface is an end-to-end workflow that enables users to upload private datasets, train and manage ML classifiers, visualize results, and conduct interactive CF reasoning. It may support assistive tools for practitioners assessing patient data and wanting actionable insights for possible treatment plans. The open-source project may also be adapted to other high-stake applications.

Acknowledgments. This study was partly funded by the Digital Futures project titled EXTREMUM, and partly by DSV at Stockholm University.

Disclosure of Interests. The authors have no competing interests to declare that are relevant to the content of this article.

References

1. Al-Ansari, N., Al-Thani, D., Al-Mansoori, R.S.: User-centered evaluation of explainable artificial intelligence (XAI): a systematic literature review. Human Behav. Emerging Technol. **2024**(1), 4628855 (2024). https://doi.org/10.1155/2024/4628855
2. Arya, V., Bellamy, R.K.E., Chen, P.Y.., Zhang, Y.: AI explainability 360: an extensible toolkit for understanding data and machine learning models. J. Mach. Learn. Res. **21**(1), 130:5114–130:5119 (2020)
3. Hohman, F., Park, H., Robinson, C., Polo Chau, D.H.: Summit: scaling deep learning interpretability by visualizing activation and attribution summarizations. IEEE Trans. Visual Comput. Graph. **26**(1), 1096–1106 (2020). https://doi.org/10.1109/TVCG.2019.2934659
4. Hoque, M.N., Mueller, K.: Outcome-explorer: a causality guided interactive visual interface for interpretable algorithmic decision making. IEEE Trans. Visual Comput. Graph. **28**(12), 4728–4740 (2022). https://doi.org/10.1109/TVCG.2021.3102051
5. Karlsson, I., Rebane, J., Papapetrou, P., Gionis, A.: Locally and globally explainable time series tweaking. Knowl. Inf. Syst. **62**(5), 1671–1700 (2019). https://doi.org/10.1007/s10115-019-01389-4
6. Khayati, M., Nater, Q., Pasquier, J.: ImputeVIS: an interactive evaluator to benchmark imputation techniques for time series data. Proc. VLDB Endow. **17**(12), 4329–4332 (2024). https://doi.org/10.14778/3685800.3685867
7. Lee, M.H., Chew, C.J.: Understanding the effect of counterfactual explanations on trust and reliance on AI for human-ai collaborative clinical decision making. Proc. ACM Hum.-Comput. Interact. **7**, 369:1–369:22 (2023). https://doi.org/10.1145/3610218
8. Mothilal, R.K., Sharma, A., Tan, C.: Explaining machine learning classifiers through diverse counterfactual explanations. In: Proceedings of the 2020 Conference on Fairness, Accountability, and Transparency, pp. 607–617 (2020). https://doi.org/10.1145/3351095.3372850
9. Rong, Y., et al.: Towards human-centered explainable AI: a survey of user studies for model explanations. IEEE Trans. Pattern Anal. Mach. Intell. **46**(4), 2104–2122 (2024). https://doi.org/10.1109/TPAMI.2023.3331846
10. Samsten, I.: isaksamsten/wildboar: wildboar (2020). https://doi.org/10.5281/ZENODO.4264062
11. Schlegel, U., Rauscher, J., Keim, D.A.: Interactive Counterfactual Generation for Univariate Time Series (2024). https://doi.org/10.48550/arXiv.2408.10633

12. Wang, Z., Samsten, I., Miliou, I., Mochaourab, R., Papapetrou, P.: Glacier: guided locally constrained counterfactual explanations for time series classification. Mach. Learn. **113**(3) (Mar 2024). https://doi.org/10.1007/s10994-023-06502-x
13. Wang, Z.J., Chau, D.H.: WebSHAP: towards explaining any machine learning models anywhere. In: Companion Proceedings of the ACM Web Conference 2023, pp. 262–266 (2023). https://doi.org/10.1145/3543873.3587362
14. Wexler, J., Pushkarna, M., Bolukbasi, T., Wattenberg, M., Viégas, F., Wilson, J.: The what-if tool: interactive probing of machine learning models. IEEE Trans. Visual Comput. Graphics **26**(1), 56–65 (2020). https://doi.org/10.1109/TVCG.2019.2934619

VisualTreeSearch: Understanding Web Agent Test-Time Scaling

Danqing Zhang[1,2,3,4(✉)], Yaoyao Qian[1,2,3,4], Shiying He[1,2,3,4], Yuanli Wang[1,2,3,4], Jingyi Ni[1,2,3,4], and Junyu Cao[1,2,3,4]

[1] PathOnAI.org, Burlingame, USA
danqing0703@gmail.com
[2] Northeastern University, Boston, USA
[3] Boston University, Boston, USA
[4] The University of Texas at Austin, Austin, USA

Abstract. We present VisualTreeSearch, a fully-deployed system for visualizing and understanding web agent test-time scaling. While test-time search algorithms substantially improve web agent success rates, they remain confined to research contexts with limited practical deployment. Our system bridges this gap with three key contributions: (1) a production-ready solution with cloud-based architecture, (2) an efficient API-based state reset mechanism that reduces state reset time from 50 to 2 s, and (3) an interactive web UI that transparently demonstrates the agent's decision-making process. VisualTreeSearch provides an intuitive framework for both researchers and users to understand tree search execution in web agents.

Keywords: Web Agents · Tree Search · Vision-Language Models · Test-time Scaling · Interactive Visualization

1 Introduction

Recent years have witnessed significant advancements in autonomous web agents powered by LLMs and VLMs for browser automation, enhancing human-computer interaction by executing complex tasks from natural language instructions [10].

VLM-based Web/GUI Agent Architectures. Current VLM-based frameworks typically implement a two-phase sequential approach: action generation followed by action grounding. The action generation phase employs either VLM-based policies with carefully engineered prompts [8] or specialized purpose-built models [1,6]. For action grounding, web agents utilize website structural features [8], whereas GUI agents primarily rely on visual grounding techniques [3,6].

VLM-based Agent Test-time Scaling. Since late 2024, researchers have explored test-time scaling methodologies using search algorithms (BFS, DFS,

---

VisualTreeSearch-Demo: https://github.com/PathOnAI/VisualTreeSearch-Demo, Demonstration Video: https://www.youtube.com/watch?v=FCvxPH21Iwc.

MCTS) [2,7] and reinforcement learning [4,5] to improve web agent performance. Despite promising results, test-time scaling approaches remain confined to research contexts with limited practical deployment.

VisualTreeSearch addresses several critical gaps in existing research by providing an end-to-end solution for understanding web agent test-time scaling:

1. *Fully-deployed web agent tree search system:* Our production-ready solution includes AWS ECS services for backend and browser operations, a Vercel-hosted frontend, and CI/CD pipeline integration. The source code is fully open-sourced.
2. *Fast state reset mechanism:* We solve the critical problem of persistent website states during backtracking through an API-based account reset method that reduces reset time from 50 to 2 s, enabling accurate trajectory evaluation during tree search.
3. *Interactive Visualization Interface:* Our web UI demonstrates agent decision-making through D3.js tree visualizations, live browser interfaces, and execution logs.

This allows non-technical users to understand test-time scaling, while enabling researchers to deploy their web agents for demonstration purposes.

2 Demonstration

2.1 High Level Overview

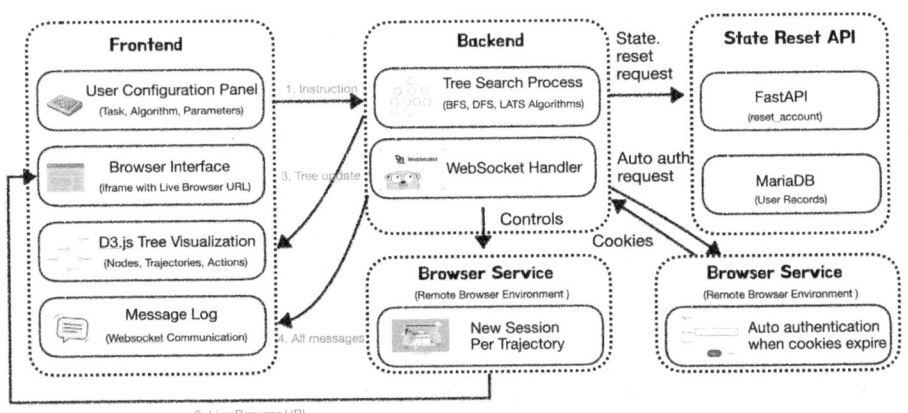

Fig. 1. System Design: High Level Overview.

Figure 1 provides a high-level overview of our implemented system. Our web agent tree search visualization system consists of four main components working together:

- **State Reset API**: A specialized service provides an efficient state reset mechanism. It enables web agents to restore a clean initial state before starting each new trajectory. This prevents evaluation inconsistencies caused by persistent website state changes.
- **Backend**: A backend service that implements various tree search algorithms and manages real-time WebSocket communication with the frontend to transmit agent execution information.
- **Browser Service**: A remote browser service that provides isolated browser sessions where web agents can execute actions, while also managing automatic authentication using Playwright.
- **Frontend**: Provides the user interface for configuring search tasks, visualizing tree search trajectories, and observing agent behavior through embedded browser views and execution logs.

2.2 API-Based State Reset

When web agents interact with UIs, they modify states that persist in the website's database, causing evaluation inconsistencies across trajectories. This state persistence creates scoring inaccuracies, as one trajectory may incorrectly include website state changes from previous trajectories. Our solution implements an API-based state reset mechanism with a FastAPI server hosted on AWS EC2 that manages the website database to control website state (MariaDB for our demo), reducing reset time from **50** s with previous docker container restarts to just **2** s.

2.3 Backend

In our backend, we implement several tree search algorithms like BFS, DFS and MCTS variants like LATS [9] as examples. Unlike previous Vercel-based web agent demo [8], our system implements AWS ECS container-based services to overcome Vercel's serverless execution limitations. This architecture supports persistent WebSocket communication and accommodates extended processing times, both of which are essential for comprehensive tree search operations.

2.4 Browser Service

For browser integration, our primary solution employs BrowserBase for remote browser sessions, utilizing session identifiers to maintain connection continuity and render live browser interactions in the frontend interface. However, we encountered CAPTCHA challenges with our BrowserBase hobby account during automated authentication. To address this limitation, we deployed a custom Docker-based browser service on Amazon ECS running Chromium.

2.5 Frontend

The VisualTreeSearch frontend visualization system enhances web agent research by providing an interpretable monitoring environment. As shown in Fig. 2, the system comprises three main components for observing agent decision-making. The main visualization area features: (1) Browser Interface: Real-time web environment view through BrowserBase integration. (2) Tree Visualization: Hierarchical D3.js visualization highlighting the active trajectory, with interactive nodes providing action descriptions and execution outcomes. (3) Execution Log (Message Log): Chronological communication log documenting action generation requests, grounding processes, execution commands, and status updates, providing comprehensive insight into the agent's operational sequence.

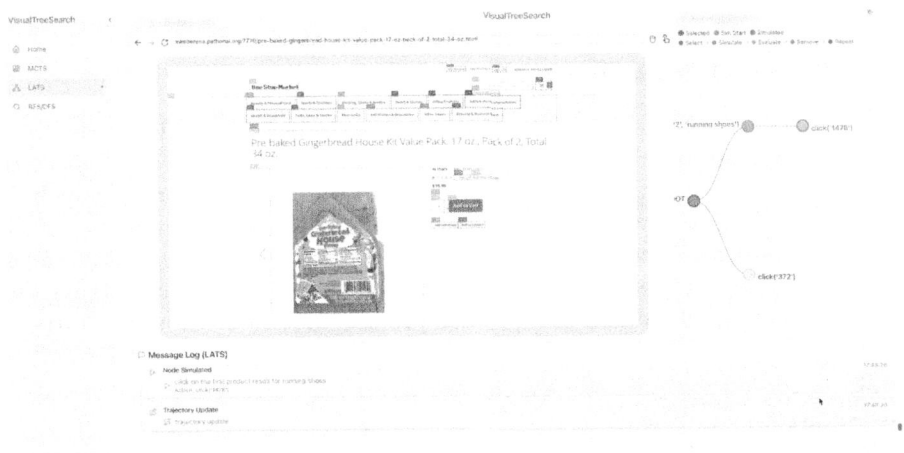

Fig. 2. Screenshot of the frontend UI showing browser interface, tree visualization and execution log.

3 Conclusion

This paper introduces VisualTreeSearch, a system that deploys web agent test-time scaling techniques in a production environment with a transparent, interactive visualization interface. To the best of our knowledge, VisualTreeSearch is the first such framework for web agents. By enabling efficient tree search execution in real-world web environments, VisualTreeSearch helps democratize these advanced techniques for broader use. The open-source implementation serves as both a demonstration tool and a foundation for future research on agent decision-making optimization. As web agents advance, robust visualization frameworks will be essential for developing more reliable autonomous systems.

References

1. Claude computer use model (2024)
2. Koh, J.Y., et al.: Tree search for language model agents. arXiv preprint arXiv:2407.01476 (2024)
3. Lu, Y., et al.: Omniparser for pure vision based gui agent. arXiv preprint arXiv:2408.00203 (2024)
4. Lu, Z., et al.: Ui-r1: enhancing action prediction of gui agents by reinforcement learning. arXiv preprint arXiv:2503.21620 (2025)
5. Putta, P., et al.: Agent q: advanced reasoning and learning for autonomous ai agents. arXiv preprint arXiv:2408.07199 (2024)
6. Qin, Y., et al.: Ui-tars: pioneering automated gui interaction with native agents. arXiv preprint arXiv:2501.12326 (2025)
7. Yu, X., et al.: Exact: teaching ai agents to explore with reflective-mcts and exploratory learning. arXiv preprint arXiv:2410.02052 (2024)
8. Zhang, D., et al.: Litewebagent: the open-source suite for vlm-based web-agent applications. arXiv preprint arXiv:2503.02950 (2025)
9. Zhou, A., et al.: Language agent tree search unifies reasoning, acting, and planning in language models. In: Forty-First International Conference on Machine Learning (2023)
10. Zhou, S., et al. Webarena: a realistic web environment for building autonomous agents. arXiv preprint arXiv:2307.13854 (2023)

DetoxAI: A Python Toolkit for Debiasing Deep Learning Models in Computer Vision

Ignacy Stępka[ID], Lukasz Sztukiewicz[ID], Michał Wiliński[ID], and Jerzy Stefanowski[(✉)][ID]

Institute of Computing Science, Poznan University of Technology, Poznan, Poland
jerzy.stefanowski@cs.put.poznan.pl

Abstract. While machine learning fairness has made significant progress in recent years, most existing solutions focus on tabular data and are poorly suited for vision-based classification tasks, which rely heavily on deep learning. To bridge this gap, we introduce DetoxAI, an open-source Python library for improving fairness in deep learning vision classifiers through post-hoc debiasing. DetoxAI implements state-of-the-art debiasing algorithms, fairness metrics, and visualization tools. It supports debiasing via interventions in internal representations and includes attribution-based visualization tools and quantitative algorithmic fairness metrics to show how bias is mitigated. This paper presents the motivation, design, and use cases of DetoxAI, demonstrating its tangible value to engineers and researchers.

Keywords: Fairness · Deep Learning · Computer Vision · Debiasing

1 Introduction

Ensuring fairness in machine learning models has become critical, particularly in high-stakes fields [5]. While several libraries address fairness, most focus on tabular data and are ill-suited for unstructured, high-dimensional tasks like computer vision. We identify two major gaps in the current landscape.

The first is technical: existing tools such as AIF360 [2] and Fairlearn [4] are built around the scikit-learn API, expecting datasets to fit in memory as Pandas DataFrames or NumPy arrays. This design is incompatible with deep learning workflows, where data must be processed in small batches, forcing practitioners to abandon popular toolkits and manually reimplement fairness methods.

The second issue is methodological: current tools primarily offer quantitative metrics or basic visualization capabilities, which are insufficient for analyzing biases in computer vision models. Furthermore, the post-hoc debiasing techniques they provide typically operate only on the model's outputs - such as by

---

I. Stępka, L. Sztukiewicz and M. Wiliński—Equal contribution.

© The Author(s), under exclusive license to Springer Nature Switzerland AG 2026
I. Dutra et al. (Eds.): ECML PKDD 2025, LNAI 16022, pp. 502–505, 2026.
https://doi.org/10.1007/978-3-032-06129-4_39

adjusting classification thresholds - without addressing or removing bias in the model's underlying reasoning process.

To address these gaps, we introduce DetoxAI, a post-hoc debiasing toolkit for image classification that operates at the representation level. DetoxAI enables desensitization of neural networks to protected attributes (e.g., gender, race) without requiring full retraining. Designed for deep learning and seamlessly integrated with PyTorch, DetoxAI equips AI practitioners and researchers with a practical tool for empirical evaluation, comparative studies, and the deployment of fairness interventions in real-world vision models.

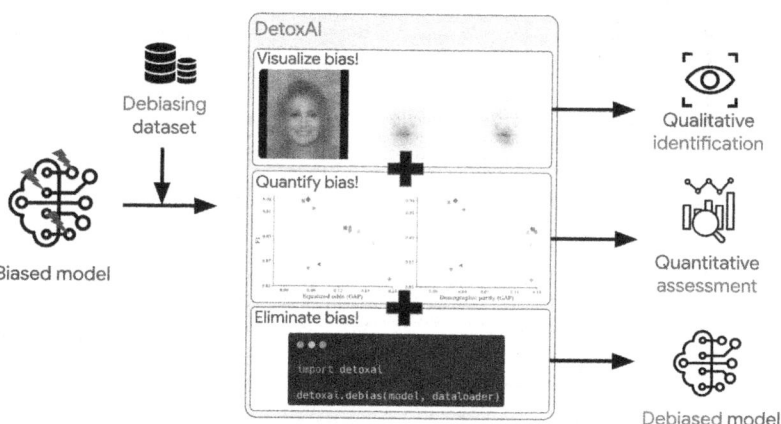

Fig. 1. DetoxAI incorporates multiple tools to mitigate biases in vision models. Biased model with debiasing dataset is passed to our module, where biases can be inspected, measured and finally eliminated.

2 Use Cases

Engineering Use Case: Debiasing a Facial Expression Recognition System. Consider a facial expression recognition system deployed to detect whether customers are smiling. In practice, it is observed that the system consistently misclassifies individuals wearing neckties as not smiling, revealing unintended bias. Using DetoxAI, engineers can address this by treating the necktie as a protected attribute. DetoxAI allows them to load the existing model (e.g., an already trained and deployed ResNet50) and apply targeted debiasing techniques - all without full model retraining. The updated model can then be seamlessly redeployed, mitigating the bias while maintaining overall performance. Engineers can evaluate fairness metrics, visualize attribution shifts, and select the optimized model, enhancing both fairness and system reliability.

Research Use Case: Fairness Studies and Comparative Benchmarking. Researchers studying fairness can leverage DetoxAI as a standardized platform for systematic benchmarking (Fig. 2). DetoxAI enables easy comparison of post-hoc debiasing methods under consistent pipelines, evaluation on common fairness metrics, and qualitative analysis of shifts in feature importance. Its modular design and clear abstractions simplify the integration of novel debiasing methods and benchmarking against established techniques. This flexibility can help accelerate fairness research in image classification and supports rigorous, extensible and reproducible experimentation.

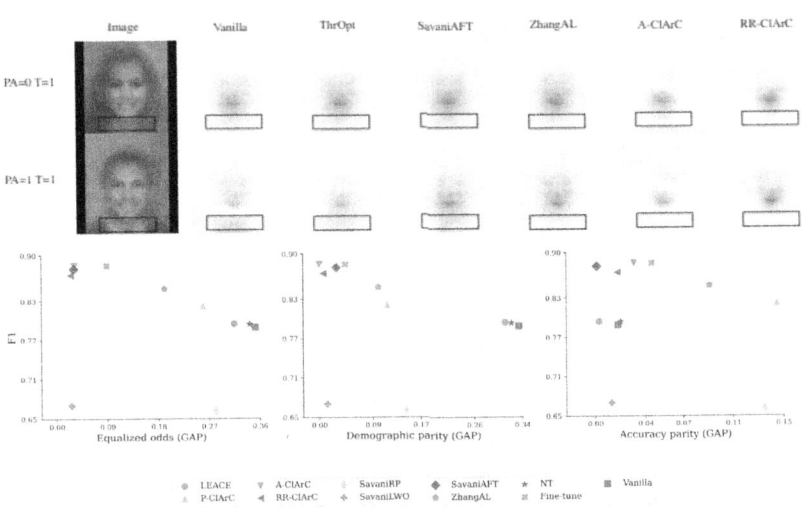

Fig. 2. In the upper image, we visualize saliency maps before (Vanilla) and after bias mitigation using a selection of implemented methods. The image on the bottom is a quantitative evaluation of the debiasing techniques on the predictive performance (F1 Score) - fairness trade-off. Fairness metrics are EqualizedOdds, DemographicParity and AccuracyParity, calculated in a difference between protected groups variation [5].

3 System Overview

DetoxAI implements several post-hoc debiasing methods, including Savani and Zhang based methods [6], LEACE [3], and post-hoc Threshold Optimization [5] It also includes ClArC variants [1] originally used as artifact-removal methods but repurposed for fairness [7]. All methods, except Threshold Optimization, modify internal representations instead of merely calibrating outputs, enabling deeper mitigation of learned biases.

Debiasing techniques are accessed through a unified `detoxai.debias(...)` interface (Fig. 1). The API supports debiasing, performance evaluation (e.g., F1, GMean, Balanced Accuracy), and fairness metric computation (e.g., Equalized Odds, Demographic Parity, Accuracy Parity), offering seamless integration into existing PyTorch workflows.

DetoxAI is model-agnostic and focuses on binary classification tasks with binary protected attributes. Even though certain debiasing methods require internal model interventions (e.g., hooks) and fine-tuning, DetoxAI automatically adapts to a variety of PyTorch models without requiring additional user input. All debiasing methods come with default configurations, empirically tuned for robustness across various model sizes and architectures. Advanced users can override these defaults by passing custom configurations to the API to better meet specific needs, such as computational budget or optimized fairness metrics. All components follow an object-oriented design, making it straightforward to extend DetoxAI with new methods, metrics, or visualization tools (see Sect. 4 for examples and documentation).

4 Conclusions

DetoxAI offers a unified platform for implementing fairness interventions in deep learning systems for image classification tasks. Designed to be production-ready, yet highly extensible, the toolkit supports a wide range of practical applications across both industry and research. Its simple and consistent API lowers the barrier to applying bias mitigation techniques, making fairness interventions accessible to engineers and researchers alike.

Additional Information. Webpage and video: https://detoxai.github.io, GitHub: https://github.com/DetoxAI/detoxai, Documentation: https://detoxai.readthedocs.io.

Acknowledgments. The work was supported by a Ministry of Science and Higher Education grant (No. MNiSW/2025/DPI/56) as part of the FERS programme, co-financed by the European Union. Jerzy Stefanowski was supported by a National Science Centre grant (No. 2022/47/D/ST6/01770).

References

1. Anders, C.J., Weber, L., Neumann, D., Samek, W., Müller, K.R., Lapuschkin, S.: Finding and removing Clever Hans: using explanation methods to debug and improve deep models. Inf. Fusion **77**, 261–295 (2022)
2. Bellamy, R.K., et al.: AI fairness 360: an extensible toolkit for detecting and mitigating algorithmic bias. IBM J. Res. Dev. **63**(4/5), 1–4 (2019)
3. Belrose, N., Schneider-Joseph, D., Ravfogel, S., Cotterell, R., Raff, E., Biderman, S.: LEACE: perfect linear concept erasure in closed form. In: Proceedings of the 37th International Conference on Neural Information Processing Systems, pp. 66044–66063 (2023)
4. Bird, S., et al.: Fairlearn: a toolkit for assessing and improving fairness in AI. Microsoft, Technical Report. MSR-TR-2020-32 (2020)
5. Mehrabi, N., Morstatter, F., Saxena, N., Lerman, K., Galstyan, A.: a survey on bias and fairness in machine learning. ACM Comput. Surv. **54**(6) (2021)
6. Savani, Y., White, C., Govindarajulu, N.S.: Intra-processing methods for debiasing neural networks. In: Larochelle, H., Ranzato, M., Hadsell, R., Balcan, M., Lin, H. (eds.) Advances in Neural Information Processing Systems, vol. 33, pp. 2798–2810. Curran Associates, Inc. (2020)
7. Sztukiewicz, L., Stępka, I., Wiliński, M., Stefanowski, J.: Investigating the relationship between debiasing and artifact removal using saliency maps. arXiv preprint arXiv:2503.00234 (2025)

Obfuscation of Sensitive Text in Audiovisual Content Using AI

Kexin Jiang-Chen(✉) and Cèsar Ferri

VRAIN, Universitat Politècnica de València, València, Spain
kjiache@etsinf.upv.es, cferri@dsic.upv.es

Abstract. The digital revolution has led to an increase in audiovisual content across platforms, creating new challenges for privacy protection. Sensitive information, such as personal identifiers, financial data or contact information, frequently appears in images and videos, often unintentionally. These accidental disclosures can lead to serious privacy breaches or misuse of personal data. To address this issue, we present an automated solution for detecting and obscuring sensitive text in multimedia content, with particular focus on Spanish-language educational materials. Our system combines Microsoft Presidio's advanced Natural Language Processing (NLP) capabilities for Personally Identifiable Information (PII) detection with Tesseract Optical Character Recognition (OCR) text extraction from visual media. Detected sensitive content is then obfuscated using advanced image processing techniques, ensuring privacy protection while maintaining the visual quality of the multimedia. This integrated approach provides an effective, efficient method for protecting personal data in multimedia applications without compromising usability.

Keywords: Computer Vision · Obfuscation · Personally Identifiable Information

1 Introduction

The rapid growth of audiovisual content on digital platforms has transformed information sharing while creating new privacy vulnerabilities. Personal data (names, addresses, phone numbers) frequently appears unintentionally in educational materials, social media, and streaming content, risking exposure under regulations like GDPR [1]. This is especially relevant in contexts such as tutorials and instructional videos created by educators, which may contain sensitive information, requiring careful handling to prevent privacy breaches. Current solutions face some limitations as manual review is inefficient, pure machine learning requires excessive resources, and rule-based systems lack flexibility.

We present a hybrid system combining Microsoft Presidio [7] for PII detection (using both rule-based and Machine Learning (ML) approaches) with Tesseract OCR [4] for text extraction from multimedia. The framework automatically obscures sensitive Spanish-language text via image processing while preserving content quality. The system is customizable based on user-defined criteria and open-source, available on GitHub[1], and a demonstration video at link[2].

2 Related Work

The identification and obfuscation of sensitive information in multimedia is a growing research area [2,6] and approaches generally fall into two categories: machine learning-based and rule-based methods.

Rule-based methods, such as spaCy [3] and Stanford NLP [10] offer transparency but struggle with multimedia variability. Microsoft Presidio bridges this gap through customisable rule patterns, though it remains limited for novel data types. Machine learning models, including CNNs and RNNs, excel in generalising across diverse data types, but can be inaccurate in ambiguous cases and require large datasets and computational resources [9].

For text extraction, Tesseract OCR [4] remains the open-source standard despite challenges with low-quality inputs, while commercial APIs (e.g., Google Vision) offer improved accuracy at higher costs. Complementary work in visual anonymisation (e.g., FaceNet [8]) focuses on anonymising visual content by blurring facial features, but does not address text-based obfuscation. Our system uniquely integrates Presidio's hybrid detection with Tesseract's extraction capabilities, creating a unified solution for multimedia privacy that handles both textual and contextual challenges.

3 Methodology

The proposed methodology is primarily designed to identify and obfuscate sensitive textual content in videos, but it also works effectively for static images.

Video Frame Extraction. The video is first broken down into individual frames at a predetermined frame rate. These frames serve as input for further analysis. Frame extraction ensures that each moment of the video is thoroughly scanned for sensitive content, allowing for a comprehensive detection and obfuscation process.

Text Detection and Preprocessing. We employ the OpenCV library [5], which provides a range of image processing functions to enhance text detection, including grayscale conversion, noise reduction, thresholding, and morphological operations (dilation/erosion) to improve OCR accuracy under challenging conditions such as motion blur or low contrast.

Text Recognition. The preprocessed frames undergo OCR analysis using Tesseract, which detects character patterns and converts them to machine-readable text while recording precise spatial coordinates. This dual output, both

---

[1] https://github.com/Kexinjc/Text-obfuscation-in-videos.
[2] https://drive.google.com/file/d/1ThsYGQc7qCIm7IizW4JTeGm7Jes5Wflt.

textual content and positional data (bounding boxes), serves two key functions: (1) enabling NLP-based sensitivity analysis through Presidio, and (2) guiding targeted obfuscation by identifying exact regions requiring blurring. The bounding boxes maintain visual context during redaction, ensuring only sensitive elements are modified while preserving surrounding content integrity.

Sensitive Information Identification. We used Microsoft Presidio, a service designed to identify PII in text, employing a combination of predefined and custom PII recognisers primarily based on machine learning models. These recognisers detect sensitive information using techniques like Named Entity Recognition (NER) and heuristic methods. Presidio is capable of identifying a wide range of PII, such as names and locations, in multiple languages, including Spanish and English, which are key to this project.

In addition to the built-in recognisers, we extended Presidio with custom rule-based recognisers to detect sensitive information specific to our needs, such as dates of birth, Spanish ID numbers (DNI), phone numbers, addresses, and Spanish postal codes using regex patterns.

Additionally, we integrated contextual rules within the recognisers to improve detection accuracy by analysing the surrounding text to determine the likelihood of a word or phrase being sensitive. For instance, if a potential PII entity appears next to key phrases like "Date of Birth:", "Address:", or "Phone:", its probability of being classified as sensitive increases. This contextual approach reduces false positives and enhances the reliability of the detection process.

Obfuscation. Once sensitive content is identified, the tool applies obfuscation techniques. This process involves drawing bounding boxes around the sensitive text and applying a Gaussian blur filter to that area, effectively masking the text while preserving the overall integrity of the video frame. This approach ensures that the obfuscated content remains natural-looking, minimising distractions for viewers.

Frame Difference Calculation. Processing every frame in a video independently can be computationally expensive. To optimise performance, we implemented a frame differencing technique that calculates the percentage of change between consecutive frames. If the change is below a predefined threshold, the system reuses the bounding boxes from the previous frame, skipping redundant OCR and PII detection steps. This significantly reduces processing time, particularly in videos with minimal motion or static backgrounds, without compromising detection accuracy. The default threshold is 2%, chosen as a good trade-off between speed and precision, but it can be adjusted by the user as needed.

Post-processing and Video Reconstruction. After the obfuscation is applied to all frames, the modified frames are recompiled into a video format. The post-processing step ensures the integrity and quality of the original video are preserved while obfuscating the sensitive content.

4 Application

To make the system user-friendly and accessible, a Command Line Interface (CLI) is provided for managing the anonymisation process. This CLI supports both images and videos, using separate pipelines optimised for each input type. Users can customise the anonymisation process using various flags for flexible detection and obfuscation of sensitive content. The *-i* flag specifies the input video or image, and *-o* sets an optional output name. Use *-r* to select specific recognisers or *-e* to exclude them. The *-f* flag obfuscates specific words, while *-u* unmasks information to remain visible. The *-v* flag enables verbose mode for detailed process output, and *-t* sets the threshold for reusing bounding boxes based on frame-to-frame changes.

Figure 1 shows an example of a university intranet image with sensitive information obfuscated after being processed through the command line.

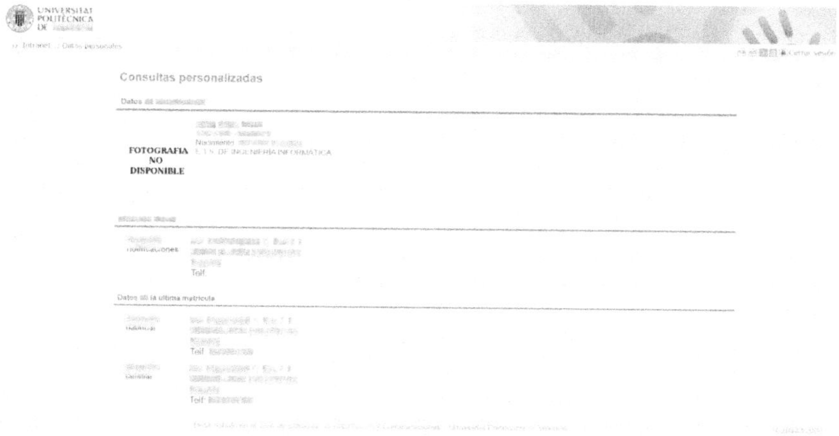

Fig. 1. University intranet image with sensitive information obfuscated after being processed through the command line interface.

5 Conclusions and Future Work

This paper presented a video processing system that detects and obfuscates sensitive text by combining Tesseract OCR and Microsoft Presidio. The system employs a frame differencing technique to optimise efficiency, reducing redundant processing and enhancing its practicality for non-real-time applications. It effectively preserves video integrity while obfuscating sensitive content, making it suitable for privacy and data protection use cases. The system's flexibility allows for extensive customisation, adapting to different content types and specific privacy requirements.

Future development will focus on three key areas:

1. **Detection improvements**: Integrating transformer-based OCR models for better handling of distorted text and extending recognisers to cover financial data, handwritten notes, and graphical PII (logos, signatures).
2. **Performance optimisation**: Implementing GPU acceleration and parallel processing to enable near real-time operation.
3. **Usability enhancements**: Adding multilingual support (starting with EU languages), cloud deployment options, and an interactive web interface to complement the existing CLI.

Acknowledgments. We acknowledge support from: Cátedra de Inteligencia Artificial aplicada a la Administración Pública and grant CIPROM/2022/6 (FASSLOW), both funded by Generalitat Valenciana; and Spanish grant PID2021-122830OB-C42 (SFERA) funded by MCIN/AEI/10.13039/501100011033 and "ERDF A way of making Europe".

References

1. de Carvalho, R., Del Prete, C., Martin, Y.E.A.: Protecting citizens' personal data and privacy: joint effort from GDPR EU cluster research projects. SN Comput. Sci. **1**(217) (2020)
2. Di Cerbo, F., Trabelsi, S.: Towards personal data identification and anonymization using machine learning techniques. In: Benczúr, A., et al. (eds.) ADBIS 2018. CCIS, vol. 909, pp. 118–126. Springer, Cham (2018). https://doi.org/10.1007/978-3-030-00063-9_13
3. Explosion: spaCy: industrial-strength NLP. https://spacy.io (2014), Accessed 1 Oct 2024
4. Google: tesseract OCR. https://github.com/tesseract-ocr/tesseract (2014), Accessed: 1 Oct 2024
5. Itseez: open source computer vision library. https://github.com/itseez/opencv (2015)
6. Marulli, F., Verde, L., Marrone, S., Barone, R., De Biase, M.: Evaluating efficiency and effectiveness of federated learning approaches in knowledge extraction tasks. In: Proceedings of the 2021 International Joint Conference on Neural Networks (IJCNN), pp. 1–6. IEEE (2021)
7. Microsoft: presidio - data protection and de-identification SDK. https://github.com/microsoft/presidio (2018), Accessed 1 Oct 2024
8. Schroff, F., Kalenichenko, D., Philbin, J.: Facenet: a unified embedding for face recognition and clustering. In: 2015 IEEE Conference on Computer Vision and Pattern Recognition (CVPR), IEEE (2015). https://doi.org/10.1109/cvpr.2015.7298682, http://dx.doi.org/10.1109/CVPR.2015.7298682
9. Alzubaidi, L., et al.: Review of deep learning: concepts, CNN architectures, challenges, applications, future directions. J. Big Data **8**(1), 1–74 (2021). https://doi.org/10.1186/s40537-021-00444-8
10. Stanford: stanford CoreNLP: a suite of core NLP tools. https://stanfordnlp.github.io/CoreNLP/ (2013), Accessed 1 Oct 2024

WildInsight: a Chatbot for Wildlife Conservation Research

Anna Sokol[✉], Xiangliang Zhang, and Nitesh V. Chawla

University of Notre Dame, Notre Dame, Indiana 46556, USA
{asokol,xzhang33,nchawla}@nd.edu

Abstract. The exponential growth of machine learning (ML) and artificial intelligence (AI) presents significant benefits for wildlife conservation. However, researchers are still struggling to navigate the vast and cross-disciplinary body of literature. We introduce **WildInsight**, an LLM-powered chatbot that uses retrieval-augmented generation (RAG) to surface relevant ML applications in wildlife management. Drawing on thousands of peer-reviewed studies, WildInsight returns method overviews, species details, and geographic context answers grounded in cited sources. By bridging computational techniques and ecological practice, WildInsight accelerates evidence-based conservation decisions. Live chat is available at: http://wildinsight.lucyapps.net:1337/.

Keywords: Retrieval-Augmented Generation · Wildlife Conservation · Large Language Models · Scientific Discovery

1 Introduction

The rapid growth and complexity of ecological data presents significant challenges for traditional analytical methods. Historically, wildlife researchers relied heavily on classical statistical approaches such as regression, clustering, classification, etc. Although effective for smaller, structured datasets, these methods are increasingly inadequate given today's expansive and heterogeneous data sources, including high-volume camera-trap images, continuous acoustic recordings, satellite imagery, and genomic sequencing. Their high-dimensional, often nonlinear nature makes traditional statistics insufficient. [5].

Advancements in ML, particularly deep neural networks and LLM, offer powerful solutions, significantly enhancing the accuracy and efficiency of data-driven ecological research. State-of-the-art ML techniques, including convolutional neural networks and transformer models, now enable sophisticated tasks such as species recognition from visual and acoustic data, habitat modeling, and rapid synthesis of ecological knowledge. However, the proliferation of these ML approaches has triggered another critical issue: an exponential increase in scientific publications, making it nearly impossible for researchers to remain current. The Web of Science database, for instance, reports over one million wildlife conservation papers published in the last decade.

In response to these dual challenges of complex data analysis and literature overload, we introduce **WildInsight**, a RAG system specifically designed for ecological and wildlife research. WildInsight is built upon a rigorously curated corpus comprising the most cited peer-reviewed articles that apply ML and AI techniques in wildlife conservation research. The system's knowledge base is constructed by embedding concatenated title, abstract, and keyword texts from each publicationand storing data and metadata in a structured format. In addition, we employ query rewriting to ensure high-quality retrieval.

WildInsight's RAG framework retrieves specific, evidence-backed passages relevant to a user's query, from which an LLM generates accurate, contextually grounded responses. This methodology significantly reduces model inaccuracies and hallucinations common in generative systems.

To better understand the limitations of general-purpose research assistants for this domain, we examined prominent tools such as OpenAI's Deep Research and Google's Gemini Advanced. We observed that only a few sources suggested by these systems were peer-reviewed papers (most of the sources are links from the Internet), indicating the need for a domain-specific approach like WildInsight. Continuous input and iterative testing from domain experts, biologists, and conservation practitioners were central to refining WildInsight, ensuring that it meets real-world research and decision-making needs.

WildInsight provides citation-supported, verifiable responses through persistent DOI links, offering scientists reliable, evidence-based insights delivered at conversational speed. By integrating advanced retrieval mechanisms and robust language models, WildInsight provides a scalable and replicable framework applicable to other complex and data-rich scientific domains. Its primary users are wildlife researchers and conservation practitioners, providing rapid, evidence-based insights essential for informed ecological decision-making.

2 Related Work

RAG combines dense retrieval with sequence-to-sequence generation, enabling language models to access external knowledge sources. Lewis et al. introduced this framework, demonstrating its effectiveness in knowledge-intensive NLP tasks [3]. The system's knowledge base is constructed by embedding concatenated title, abstract, and keyword texts from each publication, and storing data and metadata in a structured format. Additionally, we employ query rewriting to ensure high-quality retrieval. Addressing the issue of hallucinations in dialogue systems, Shuster et al. showed that incorporating retrieval mechanisms significantly reduces factual inaccuracies, underscoring the importance of grounding responses in external evidence [4]. In the realm of scientific literature, Lála et al. developed PaperQA, a RAG-based agent designed to answer questions over scientific texts, highlighting the potential of RAG in facilitating scientific research [2]. While WildlifeLookup offers a chatbot for wildlife management, it lacks peer-reviewed evaluation and a comprehensive corpus. In contrast, our system, WildInsight, provides a rigorously evaluated, citation-grounded tool tailored for wildlife conservation research [6].

3 Data Collection

We constructed WildInsight's knowledge base through a disciplined, reproducible pipeline. We queried the Web of Science Core Collection starting from a seed query—"species" OR "wildlife", we expanded it with families of terms drawn from five methodological themes: (i) remote imaging (camera-traps, drones, satellites), (ii) computer vision and pattern recognition, (iii) bio-acoustics and environmental sensing, (iv) telemetry and tracking, and (v) statistical or ML models. We restricted to English-language journal and conference papers published between 1990 and 2024. Citation count ranked results and the 100,000 records were retained to prioritise influential, peer-reviewed work at the intersection of AI/ML and wildlife science. For each record we captured standard metadata (title, abstract, authors, year, DOI, keywords).

3.1 Knowledge Base Development

Our RAG approach tailored for academic paper analysis. During indexing, we merge each paper's title, abstract, and keywords into a single text chunk and create embeddings using OpenAI's text-embedding-3-large model. We selected this embedding model for its strong performance on semantic similarity tasks involving scientific texts. These embeddings are stored in Milvus, an optimized vector database. Additional metadata such as authors, publication year, and journal name are saved in separate database columns for efficient retrieval.

For the chatbot, we employ GPT-4o as the core model. Upon receiving a query, the model assesses if paper retrieval is necessary. If so, it reformulates the query to match database content (e.g., *"How is AI used to study whales?"* becomes *"Applications of AI to whale studies"*). The reformulated query is embedded and used to find the top 5 relevant papers via cosine similarity. This top-5 retrieval strategy was empirically determined to balance accuracy and concise responses during preliminary testing. The chatbot then summarizes key insights and includes DOI links from these papers in its response. If retrieval isn't needed, GPT-4o directly generates an answer without database interaction.

4 Interface and Evaluation

WildInsight features an intuitive chat interface with structured answers and *mandatory inline citations*. Typical queries-such as *"What ML methods work best for identifying birds in camera-trap images?"* *"What threats do Red Wolves face, especially related to sound and coyote hybridisation?,"* or *"What are some recent ML studies on elk migration in Yellowstone?"* receive concise responses that each link to at least one DOI for seamless follow-up reading. This design promotes efficient navigation and deeper research exploration. User interactions remain anonymous, ensuring ethical and responsible use of the system while maintaining research integrity.

To enhance usability and facilitate intuitive interaction, we have incorporated a user-friendly interface. Figure 1 illustrates the key components: a chat history panel to access past interactions, an input area to pose queries, and an output area to display WildInsight responses. This design prioritizes clarity and efficiency. Information is presented in a structured format using bullet points and headings, with source citations and DOIs readily accessible for seamless navigation to relevant publications. The interactive nature of WildInsight allows researchers to engage in a dynamic exchange, posing follow-up questions or refining queries to delve deeper into specific topics.

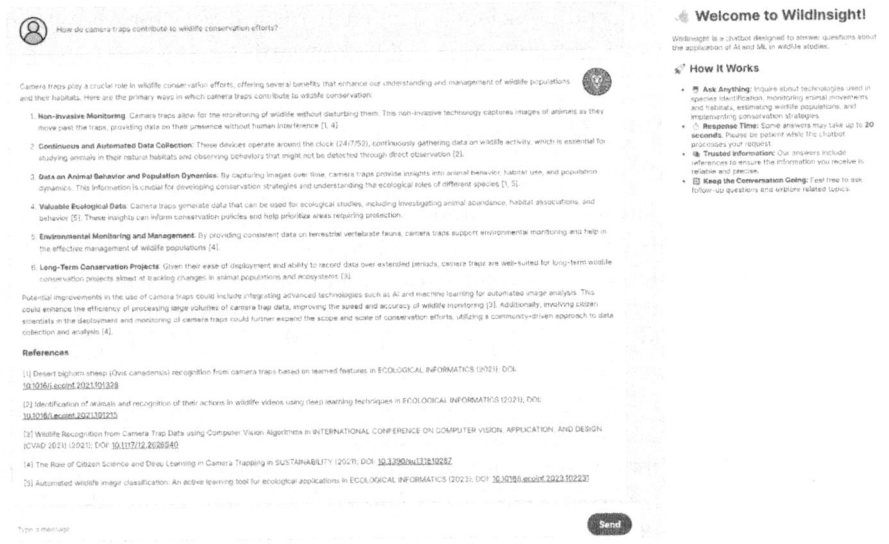

Fig. 1. Example of ChatBot Interface.

We ran 50 expert-written queries three times each; the returned paper lists overlapped with a mean Jaccard score of 0.86, showing stable retrieval on real-world questions. With no formal benchmark for this domain, the result offers a clear quantitative check on WildInsight's reliability.

5 Limitations and Future Work

WildInsight currently relies on titles, abstracts, and keywords, limiting access to full-text details. As a result, some discrepancies may occur when comparing outputs to full articles. Our evaluation reflects abstract-level consistency, with full-text integration and analysis planned in future work. Additionally, the corpus is restricted to English-language publications, potentially excluding valuable regional studies published in other languages. We plan to expand the system's knowledge integration capabilities through: (i) implementation of knowledge graph structures representing taxonomic and ecological relationships, (ii) incorporation of grey literature including technical reports and conservation assessments, and (iii) integration with biodiversity databases such as GBIF [1] and national species inventories. Also, future evaluation frameworks will incorporate comprehensive user studies with practitioners across multiple sub-disciplines, measuring both quantitative performance metrics and qualitative assessments.

6 Conclusion

WildInsight helps researchers manage information overload in wildlife conservation by quickly finding relevant scientific literature. Our specialized RAG system connects computational methods with ecological applications through citation-based responses. This approach can be adapted to other scientific fields where researchers struggle to keep up with rapidly growing literature. We believe WildInsight provides a robust foundation for developing scalable, domain-specific research assistants that bridge computational techniques and applied ecological practices.

Acknowledgement. This work is supported by the National Science Foundation (No: 2333795).

References

1. GBIF.Org user: occurrence download (2025). https://doi.org/10.15468/DL.MVSESC, https://www.gbif.org/occurrence/download/0003372-250214102907787
2. Lála, J., O'Donoghue, O., Shtedritski, A., Cox, S., Rodriques, S.G., White, A.D.: Paperqa: retrieval-augmented generative agent for scientific research. arXiv preprint arXiv:2312.07559 (2023)
3. Retrieval-augmented generation for knowledge-intensive NLP tasks: Lewis, P., et al. Adv. Neural. Inf. Process. Syst. **33**, 9459–9474 (2020)
4. Shuster, K., Poff, S., Chen, M., Kiela, D., Weston, J.: Retrieval augmentation reduces hallucination in conversation. arXiv preprint arXiv:2104.07567 (2021)
5. Tuia, D., et al.: Perspectives in machine learning for wildlife conservation. Nature commun. **13**(1), 1–15 (2022). https://www.nature.com/articles/s41467-022-27980-y/1000, publisher: Nature Publishing Group
6. Wang, X., Yang, T., Rohr, J., Scheffers, B., Chawla, N., Zhang, X.: Wildlifelookup: a chatbot facilitating wildlife management with accessible data and insights. In: Proceedings of the Eighteenth ACM International Conference on Web Search and Data Mining, pp. 1064–1067 (2025)

Future Designer - Generative AI Meets Interior Design

Filip Nowicki[(✉)], Arkadiusz Charliński, and Andrzej Wójtowicz

Faculty of Mathematics and Computer Science, Adam Mickiewicz University, Poznań, Poland
filnow3@st.amu.edu.pl

Abstract. Interior design visualization plays a crucial role in property evaluation, yet traditional methods, such as professional consultations and 3D modeling, are often time-consuming and costly. This paper introduces an AI-driven system that enables room customization in real time through automated image generation and intelligent furniture search. Our solution democratizes design visualization by reducing dependence on professional services, empowering users to instantly tailor spaces to their preferences during property comparisons. This approach enhances decision-making efficiency while offering scalable personalization, redefining how individuals engage with potential living environments. Importantly, the implementation relies entirely on open-source models and is optimized for consumer-class GPU execution. The system architecture also supports facile scaling, making it suitable for companies seeking to integrate a customizable interior design feature, potentially linked to their specific furniture catalogues.

Keywords: Diffusion · Interior design · Vision language model

1 Introduction

Visualizing potential living spaces is crucial when choosing or redesigning a home. AI-powered commercial tools like Interior AI[1], Collov[2], and ApplyDesign[3] simplify this with virtual staging and style application. However, these often proprietary, subscription-based services can limit accessibility, customization, and integration with specific furniture catalogues. To address these gaps, we introduce a novel AI system built on open-source foundations. Our solution offers near real-time room customization, integrating automated image generation with furniture search. The key contribution is an accessible, flexible alternative; by using open-source models optimized for consumer GPUs[4], we lower the entry barrier compared to traditional methods and commercial AI platforms.

---

[1] https://interiorai.com/.
[2] https://collov.ai/.
[3] https://www.applydesign.io/.
[4] Refers to GPUs with at least 24GB of Video RAM (VRAM), e.g., NVIDIA GeForce RTX 4090 or RTX 3090.

2 Furniture Search

A critical limitation of many AI interior design tools is the gap between visualizations and tangible products, hindering practical implementation. Our system's core innovation bridges this by enabling users to search for similar, potentially purchasable furniture based on items selected within the visualization.

2.1 Furniture Localization and Isolation

The initial stage of the furniture search pipeline involves accurately identifying and isolating target furniture items within the input image. This is accomplished through a two-step process:

Object Detection: We employ Grounding-DINO [6] to object detection, specifically localizing instances belonging to predefined furniture categories relevant to interior design (e.g., bed, table, sofa, chair). This step yields bounding boxes around detected furniture items.

Semantic Segmentation: For each detected bounding box, we utilize the Segment Anything Model 2 [7] to generate a precise instance segmentation mask of furniture. The generated segmentation mask is inverted to make background white and isolate only the furniture.

2.2 Structured Attribute Extraction via Vision-Language Model

Following isolation, the system derives a structured semantic description of the furniture item. For this task, we use the Qwen-2-VL 2B model [8], fine-tuned with a custom LoRA [9]. This fine-tuning was performed on our synthetically generated dataset[5] comprising diverse furniture images paired with structured descriptions.

The fine-tuned model is prompted to generate a caption for the isolated furniture image, constrained to a specific JSON format. This format enforces the extraction of key descriptive attributes: type, style, color, material, details, and room type. Our selection of the Qwen-VL model and the LoRA fine-tuning approach was based on comparative experiments involving several VLMs in the 2B parameter range. The fine-tuned Qwen model demonstrated superior performance in consistently generating valid JSON outputs and achieved higher CLIP-Score metrics [10].

Notably, the LoRA fine-tuning proved essential for constraining the verbosity of the details field, which was challenging to control via prompt engineering alone in baseline models. Furthermore, this approach facilitated the normalization of attribute values, such as mapping diverse color descriptions (e.g., "jet black," "charcoal," "ebony") to a standardized term (e.g., "black"), thereby improving consistency for user interaction.

---

[5] https://huggingface.co/datasets/filnow/furniture-synthetic-dataset.

2.3 Attribute-Driven Search and Integration

Once generated, the structured JSON caption enables the following interactive functionalities:

- **Attribute Refinement**: The UI allows for direct refinement of attributes (e.g., changing color). These modifications then guide a diffusion model-based inpainting pipeline to regenerate the furniture item accordingly.
- **Similarity Search**: Based on the current attributes, a similarity search can be initiated. This triggers a semantic query within a vector database populated with text embeddings derived from the JSON captions to retrieve comparable items.

Retrieved items can be swapped in to replace the original furniture, or added to empty space.

This closed-loop system, connecting visual identification, structured semantic description, attribute-based refinement, and text-based vector search, forms the foundation for practical application. For enterprise use, the vector database can be populated with embeddings corresponding to a real-world furniture catalogue. Each entry can link its JSON description to actual product images, details, and purchasing URLs. This transforms the system from a purely visualization tool into an interactive visual search engine, enabling users to discover and potentially purchase real items that closely match their visualized preferences directly from the interface.

3 Image Generation

Our system at its core is using the Stable Diffusion XL [1] model, fine-tuned for realistic images called RealVisXL V5.0[6], renowned for producing photorealistic interior scenes efficiently, even on standard consumer hardware. To maintain structural integrity and spatial coherence during image manipulation, we integrate a unified ControlNet [2]. This ensures that the fundamental layout of a room remains intact while allowing for stylistic and content modifications. For near real-time user interaction, we employ Trajectory Consistency Distillation [3], which accelerates the diffusion sampling process.

The system supports a versatile suite of distinct image generation pipelines tailored to specific user interactions:

1. **Furniture Modification:** Utilizes inpainting guided by ControlNet to alter attributes (e.g., color, material) of existing furniture items.
2. **Furniture Addition:** Employs outpainting techniques to seamlessly introduce new furniture elements into designated empty spaces.
3. **Style-Consistent Furniture Replacement:** Leverages an Image Prompt Adapter [4] to replace selected furniture with similar one.

---

[6] https://huggingface.co/SG161222/RealVisXL-V5.0.

4. **Object Removal:** Implements a tile-based ControlNet strategy for cleanly removing unwanted furniture or objects from the scene.
5. **Global Style Transformation:** Enables comprehensive changes to the room's overall aesthetic (e.g., transforming to 'Scandinavian' or 'Modern' style) using a depth-conditioned ControlNet. The requisite depth map is made using DepthAnything V2 model [5].

4 Conclusion

In conclusion, we presented an open-source AI system that leverages deep learning on consumer GPUs for real-time interior design visualization and customization. **For individuals** Like homebuyers and tenants, it democratizes design by providing an accessible, cost-effective tool for instant personalization that connects virtual ideas to tangible item characteristics. **For businesses** Such as retailers or real estate platforms, its open architecture allows flexible integration and customization, enabling engaging visual experiences potentially linked directly to their product catalogs. Project source code and documentation are available on GitHub[7] and an introductory video can be viewed at https://youtu.be/NOlGHFNzzrM.

5 Appendix

To extract furniture attributes, the vision-language model is prompted using a multi-turn conversational format that ensures structured and consistent outputs in JSON. Firstly, the system prompt sets a clear expectation by emphasizing the following schema:

```
You are a furniture expert. Analyze images and provide
descriptions in this exact JSON format:
{"type": "<must be one of: bed, chair, table, sofa>",
"style": "<describe overall style>", "color": "<describe main
color>", "material": "<describe primary material>", "shape":
"<describe general shape>", "details": "<describe one
decorative feature>", "room_type": "<specify room type>",
"price_range": "<specify price range>"}
Focus on maintaining this exact structure while providing
relevant descriptions.
```

To confirm comprehension, we used the assistant prompt:

```
I will analyze the image and respond with a valid JSON object
following the exact schema.
```

After that, a multi-modal input, combining the image with a textual prompt, is added:

---
[7] https://github.com/future-d3signer/future-designer-api.

```
Describe this furniture piece in JSON format.
```

This carefully designed prompt sequence guides the model to generate consistent, high-quality attribute descriptions in JSON (see Sect. 2.2).

The generation prompts for tasks such as furniture modification or addition (see Sect. 3) are systematically constructed. Initially, a descriptive prompt is formed based on the structured attributes extracted by the VLM. For instance, this might take the form:

```
A ${color} ${type}, made of ${material}, with a ${style}style,
featuring ${details},suitable for a ${room_type}.
```
[8]

This base prompt is then augmented with an enhancement string, *"masterpiece, professional lighting, realistic materials, highly detailed"*, to improve image quality. Concurrently, a negative prompt, *"deformed, low quality, blurry, noise, grainy, duplicate, watermark, text, out of frame"*, is employed to mitigate common generation artifacts.

References

1. Podell et al.: Sdxl: improving latent diffusion models for high-resolution image synthesis. In: The Twelfth International Conference on Learning Representations (2023)
2. Zhao et al.: Uni-controlnet: all-in-one control to text-to-image diffusion models. Adv. Neural Inf. Process. Syst. **36**, 11127–11150..0 (2023)
3. Zheng et al.: Trajectory consistency distillation: improved latent consistency distillation by semi-linear consistency function with trajectory mapping. arXiv preprint arXiv:2402.19159 (2024)
4. Ye et al.: Ip-adapter: text compatible image prompt adapter for text-to-image diffusion models. arXiv preprint arXiv:2308.06721 (2023)
5. Yang, L., et al.: Depth anything v2. Adv. Neural Inf. Process. Syst. **37**, 21875–21911 (2024)
6. Liu et al.: Grounding dino: marrying dino with grounded pre-training for open-set object detection. In: European Conference on Computer Vision. Springer, Cham (2024)
7. Ravi et al.: Sam 2: segment anything in images and videos. In: The Thirteenth International Conference on Learning Representations (2024)
8. Wang et al.: Qwen2-vl: enhancing vision-language model's perception of the world at any resolution. arXiv preprint arXiv:2409.12191 (2024)
9. Hu et al.: Lora: low-rank adaptation of large language models. In: International Conference on Learning Representations (2022)
10. Hessel et al.: Clipscore: a reference-free evaluation metric for image captioning. In: Proceedings of the 2021 Conference on Empirical Methods in Natural Language Processing, pp. 7514–7528 (2021)

---

[8] Placeholders like ${color} are dynamically replaced with the actual attribute values (e.g., "blue," "red") from the JSON caption.

Author Index

A
Alam, Mehwish 470
Alkayyal, Majd 460
Anand Gopalakrishnan, Atul 283
Arceri, Vincenzo 449
Ashraf, Inaam 41

B
Bagnall, Anthony 432
Bahri, Maroua 438
Barandas, Marília 427
Beigl, Michael 164
Ben Taieb, Souhaib 111
Bender, Andreas 180
Bernier, Fabien 60
Bifet, Albert 438
Boracchi, Giacomo 3
Boussaid, Taha 76
Brinker, Klaus 319

C
Calikus, Ece 375
Cao, Junyu 497
Cerqueira, Vítor 427
Cerqueira, Vitor 438
Charliński, Arkadiusz 516
Choi, Han-Jun 336
Claeys, Emmanuelle 299
Clausse, Marc 76
Cordy, Maxime 60, 95
Cortesi, Agostino 449

D
D'hondt, Robbe 465
De Francisci Morales, Gianmarco 375
de Jong, Matthijs 129
Dogoulis, Pantelis 95
Dolcetti, Greta 449
Dong, Hongbin 147

E
Elmas, Tuğrulcan 283
Erdem Sarıyüce, Ahmet 283
Estievenart, Yorick 111

F
Ferri, Cèsar 486, 506
Filimon, Sascha 180
Forestier, Germain 432

G
Geisenberger, Baptiste 470
Gionis, Aristides 375
Glasmachers, Tobias 213
Gomes, Heitor Murilo 438
Groh, Georg 460
Guillaume, Antoine 432
Gunasekara, Nuwan 438

H
Hammer, Barbara 41
Hassouna, Mohamed 129
He, Shiying 497
Hermes, Luca 41
Hernández-Orallo, José 486
Heyden, Marco 438
Hiratsuka Rezende, Arthur 229
Holzhüter, Clara 129
Horstmann, Tim Luka 470
Hossain, Jakir 283

I
Inácio, Ricardo 427
Ismail-Fawaz, Ali 432

J
Jaeger, Manfred 481
Jeong, Minchul 336
Ji, Jianuo 147
Jiang-Chen, Kexin 506

Jin, Beihong 410
Jo, Sehyeong 444

K
Ke, Xiaopeng 246
Kim, Changjo 336
Kim, Hyunsung 336
Ko, Sang-Ki 336
Koh, Yun Sing 438

L
Lafargue, Valentin 299
Lagraa, Sofiane 475
Lakes, Athanasios 491
Le Traon, Yves 60
Lee, Anton 438
Lee, Minho 336
Lehna, Malte 129
Lequeu, Pierre-Antoine 475
Li, Beibei 410
Li, Chaofan 164
Li, Wei 263
Liu, Jia Justin 438
Liu, Xin 393
Loubes, Jean-Michel 299
Lu, Xuesong 393

M
Malberg, Simon 460
Malik, Mehak Mushtaq 454
Margheritti, Riccardo 3
Meireles, Luís 354
Men, Chang 246
Mendes-Moreira, João 354
Mendes-Neves, Tiago 354
Meng, Kexin 246
Mensi, Antonella 449
Middlehurst, Matthew 432
Morillo, Paulina 486

N
Neubauer, Melanie 21
Ni, Jingyi 497
Nishino, Kaneharu 196
Nowicki, Filip 516

O
Ouedraogo, Moussa 475
Özdenizci, Ozan 21

Özeren, Enes 180

P
P. de L. F. de Carvalho, André 229
Papapetrou, Panagiotis 491
Patra, Sukanya 111
Paul, Topon 196
Pendyala, Abhijeet 213
Pfahringer, Bernhard 438
Piater, Justus 21
Pojer, Raffaele 481
Prem Kumar Ayyagari, Sai 196

Q
Qian, Yaoyao 497
Quadrio, Maurizio 3
Quintero, Luis 491

R
Reddy, Vidhisha 196
Riedel, Till 164
Robin, Geoffroy 475
Rousset, François 76
Rueckert, Elmar 21
Rügamer, David 180

S
Scholz, Christoph 129
Scuturici, Vasile-Marian 76
Semeraro, Onofrio 3
Seo, Jungwon 444
Shawi, Radwa El 454
Shi, Fangzhou 246
Shi, Yunchuan 263
Shiga, Yoshiaki 196
Shingaki, Ryusei 196
Sick, Bernhard 129
Soares, Carlos 427
Sokol, Anna 511
Stefanowski, Jerzy 502
Stępka, Ignacy 502
Strotherm, Janine 41
Su, Hang 393
Sun, Yibin 438
Sztukiewicz, Lukasz 502

T
Terreros, Alex 486
Tit, Karim 95

Author Index

U
Ulbrich, Alexander 180
Urban, Caterina 449

V
V.Chawla, Nitesh 511
Vens, Celine 465
Viebahn, Jan 129

W
Wang, Yuanli 497
Weigert Cassales, Guilherme 438
Wiliński, Michał 502
Wójtowicz, Andrzej 516

X
Xiong, Xinye 246

Y
Y. Zomaya, Albert 263
Yoon, Jinsung 336

Z
Zaffanella, Enea 449
Zhang, Danqing 497
Zhang, Xiangliang 511
Zhang, Xiaoping 147
Zhao, Rui 410
Zheng, Yiyuan 410
Zhu, Zhengdan 246

Made in the USA
Monee, IL
03 May 2026